Financial Markets and Institutions

Abridged 8th Edition

W9-AZR-976

Jeff Madura
Florida Atlantic University

SOUTH-WESTERN
CENGAGE Learning

Australia • Brazil • Japan • Korea • Mexico • Singapore • Spain • United Kingdom • United States

SOUTH-WESTERN
CENGAGE Learning

Financial Markets and Institutions, Abridged 8th Edition

Jeff Madura

VP of Editorial, Business: Jack W. Calhoun

VP/Editor-in-Chief: Alex von Rosenberg

Executive Editor: Michael R. Reynolds

Developmental Editor: Michael Guendelsberger

Sr. Marketing Comm. Manager: Jim Overly

Marketing Coordinator: Suellen Ruttkay

Executive Marketing Manager: Brian Joyner

Content Project Manager: Scott Dillon

Manager of Technology, Editorial: Matt McKinney

Manager of Media, Editorial: John Barans

Media Editor: Scott Fidler

Frontlist Buyer, Manufacturing: Kevin Kluck

Sr. Editorial Assistant: Adele Scholtz

Marketing Manager: Nathan Anderson

Production Service: Newgen–Austin

Copyeditor: Pat Lewis

Compositor: Newgen–Chennai

Art Director: Bethany Casey

Internal Design: Craig Ramsdell, Ramsdell Design

Cover Design: Craig Ramsdell, Ramsdell Design

Cover Image: © Getty Images, Inc. / Stockbyte

For product information and technology assistance, contact us at **Cengage Learning Customer & Sales Support, 1-800-354-9706**

For permission to use material from this text or product, submit all requests online at **www.cengage.com/permissions**
Further permissions questions can be emailed to **permissionrequest@cengage.com**

Library of Congress Control Number: 2008932600
PKG ISBN-13: 978-0-324-59364-8
PKG ISBN-10: 0-324-59364-3
Student Edition ISBN 13: 978-0-324-59359-4
Student Edition ISBN 10: 0-324-59359-7

South-Western/Cengage Learning
5191 Natorp Boulevard
Mason, OH 45040
USA

Cengage Learning products are represented in Canada by Nelson Education, Ltd.

For your course and learning solutions, visit **academic.cengage.com**

Purchase any of our products at your local college store or at our preferred online store **www.ichapters.com**

Printed in Canada
1 2 3 4 5 6 7 12 11 10 09 08

Dedication

This text is dedicated to Best Friends Animal Sanctuary in Kanab, Utah, for its commitment to, compassion for, and care of more than 1,500 animals, many of which were previously homeless. Most of the royalties the author receives from this text will be invested in an estate that will ultimately be donated to Best Friends.

Brief Contents

Part 1: Overview of the Financial Environment   1

1   Role of Financial Markets and Institutions   2
2   Determination of Interest Rates   24
3   Structure of Interest Rates   43

Part 2: The Fed and Monetary Policy   73

4   Functions of the Fed   74
5   Monetary Policy   90

Part 3: Debt Security Markets   115

6   Money Markets   116
7   Bond Markets   141
8   Bond Valuation and Risk   167
9   Mortgage Markets   199

Part 4: Equity Markets   227

10   Stock Offerings and Investor Monitoring   228
11   Stock Valuation and Risk
     This chapter is made available to you at
     http://academic.cengage.com/finance/madura.
12   Market Microstructure and Strategies
     This chapter is made available to you at
     http://academic.cengage.com/finance/madura.

Part 5: Derivative Security Markets   333

13   Financial Futures Markets   334
14   Options Markets
     This chapter is made available to you at
     http://academic.cengage.com/finance/madura.
15   Interest Rate Derivative Markets
     This chapter is made available to you at
     http://academic.cengage.com/finance/madura.
16   Foreign Exchange Derivative Markets
     This chapter is made available to you at
     http://academic.cengage.com/finance/madura.

Part 6: Commercial Banking   475

17   Commercial Bank Operations   476
18   Bank Regulation   498
19   Bank Management   520
20   Bank Performance   553

Part 7: Nonbank Operations   **573**

21 Thrift Operations
    This chapter is made available to you at
    http://academic.cengage.com/finance/madura.
22 Finance Operations
    This chapter is made available to you at
    http://academic.cengage.com/finance/madura.
23 Mutual Fund Operations   613
24 Securities Operations
    This chapter is made available to you at
    http://academic.cengage.com/finance/madura.
25 Insurance and Pension Fund Operations
    This chapter is made available to you at
    http://academic.cengage.com/finance/madura.

Appendix A Comprehensive Project   707
Appendix B Using Excel to Conduct Analyses   719
Glossary   723
Index   733

Contents

From the Publisher, xv
Preface, xvi

Part 1: Overview of the Financial Environment — 1

Chapter 1: Role of Financial Markets and Institutions — 2

Overview of Financial Markets, 2
  Types of Financial Markets, 3
  How Financial Markets Facilitate Corporate Finance and Investment Management, 4
Securities Traded in Financial Markets, 5
  Money Market Securities, 5
  Capital Market Securities, 5
  Derivative Securities, 6
Valuation of Securities in Financial Markets, 6
  Market Pricing of Securities, 6
Market Efficiency, 8
Financial Market Regulation, 9
  Disclosure, 9
  Regulatory Response to Financial Scandals, 9
Global Financial Markets, 10
  International Corporate Governance, 10
  Global Integration, 11
  Role of the Foreign Exchange Market, 11
Role of Financial Institutions in Financial Markets, 12
  Role of Depository Institutions, 12
  Role of Nondepository Financial Institutions, 13
  Comparison of Roles among Financial Institutions, 15
Overview of Financial Institutions, 16
  Competition between Financial Institutions, 17
  Consolidation of Financial Institutions, 18
Global Expansion by Financial Institutions, 19

Summary, 20

Point Counter-Point: Will Computer Technology Cause Financial Intermediaries to Become Extinct? 20

Questions and Applications, 21
  Advanced Questions, 21
  Interpreting Financial News, 22
  Managing in Financial Markets, 22
Flow of Funds Exercise: Roles of Financial Markets and Institutions, 22
Internet/Excel Exercises, 23
WSJ Exercise: Differentiating between Primary and Secondary Markets, 23

Chapter 2: Determination of Interest Rates — 24

Loanable Funds Theory, 24
  Household Demand for Loanable Funds, 24
  Business Demand for Loanable Funds, 25
  Government Demand for Loanable Funds, 26
  Foreign Demand for Loanable Funds, 27
  Aggregate Demand for Loanable Funds, 28
  Supply of Loanable Funds, 28
  Equilibrium Interest Rate, 29
Economic Forces That Affect Interest Rates, 31
  Impact of Economic Growth on Interest Rates, 31
  Impact of Inflation on Interest Rates, 32
  Impact of Monetary Policy on Interest Rates, 34
  Impact of the Budget Deficit on Interest Rates, 34
  Impact of Foreign Flows of Funds on Interest Rates, 35
  Summary of Forces That Affect Interest Rates, 36
Forecasting Interest Rates, 37

Summary, 39
Point Counter-Point: Does a Large Fiscal Budget Deficit Result in Higher Interest Rates? 39
Questions and Applications, 39
  Advanced Questions, 40

Interpreting Financial News, 40

Managing in Financial Markets, 41

Problems, 41

Flow of Funds Exercise: How the Flow of Funds Affects Interest Rates, 41

Internet/Excel Exercises, 42

WSJ Exercise: Forecasting Interest Rates, 42

Chapter 3: Structure of Interest Rates   43

Characteristics of Debt Securities That Cause Their Yields to Vary, 43

Credit (Default) Risk, 43

Using the Wall Street Journal: Yield Differentials across Securities, 45

Liquidity, 45

Tax Status, 45

Term to Maturity, 46

Explaining Actual Yield Differentials, 47

Yield Differentials of Money Market Securities, 48

Yield Differentials of Capital Market Securities, 49

Estimating the Appropriate Yield, 49

Using the Wall Street Journal: Assessing the Yield Curve, 51

A Closer Look at the Term Structure, 51

Pure Expectations Theory, 51

Liquidity Premium Theory, 56

Segmented Markets Theory, 58

Research on Term Structure Theories, 60

Integrating the Theories of the Term Structure, 60

Uses of the Term Structure, 61

Why the Slope of the Yield Curve Changes over Time, 62

How the Yield Curve Has Changed over Time, 62

International Structure of Interest Rates, 63

Summary, 65

Point Counter-Point: Should a Yield Curve Influence a Borrower's Preferred Maturity of a Loan? 66

Questions and Applications, 66

Advanced Questions, 67

Interpreting Financial News, 67

Managing in Financial Markets, 67

Problems, 68

Flow of Funds Exercise: Influence of the Structure of Interest Rates, 69

Internet/Excel Exercises, 69

WSJ Exercise: Interpreting the Structure of Interest Rates, 69

Part 1 Integrative Problem: Interest Rate Forecasts and Investment Decisions is made available to you at http://academic.cengage.com/finance/madura.

Part 2: The Fed and Monetary Policy   73

Chapter 4: Functions of the Fed   74

Organization of the Fed, 74

Federal Reserve District Banks, 75

Member Banks, 76

Board of Governors, 76

Federal Open Market Committee (FOMC), 76

Advisory Committees, 76

Integration of Federal Reserve Components, 77

How the Fed Controls Money Supply, 77

Open Market Operations, 77

Role of the Fed's Trading Desk, 79

How Open Market Operations Affect All Interest Rates, 80

Adjusting the Reserve Requirement Ratio, 81

Adjusting the Fed's Loan Rate, 83

Factors Considered When the Fed Controls the Money Supply, 83

Technical Factors, 83

Which Form of Money to Control?, 84

Global Monetary Policy, 84

A Single Eurozone Monetary Policy, 85

Global Central Bank Coordination, 86

Summary, 87

Point Counter-Point: Should There Be a Global Central Bank? 87

Questions and Applications, 87

Interpreting Financial News, 88

Managing in Financial Markets, 88

Flow of Funds Exercise: Monitoring the Fed, 88

Internet/Excel Exercises, 89

WSJ Exercise: Reviewing Fed Policies, 89

Chapter 5: Monetary Policy   90

Mechanics of Monetary Policy, 90

Correcting a Weak Economy, 91

Correcting High Inflation, 91

Limitations of Monetary Policy, 92

Tradeoff in Monetary Policy, 95

Impact of Other Forces on the Tradeoff, 96

How the Fed's Emphasis Shifted during 2001–2007, 97

Proposals to Focus on Inflation, 98

Economic Indicators Monitored by the Fed, 99
   Indicators of Economic Growth, 99
   Indicators of Inflation, 100
How Monetary Policy Affects All Sectors, 101
   Impact on Financial Markets, 101
   Impact on Financial Institutions, 104
Integrating Monetary and Fiscal Policies, 105
   Monetizing the Debt, 106
Monetary Policy in a Global Environment, 107
   Impact of the Dollar, 107
   Impact of Global Economic Conditions, 107
   Transmission of Interest Rates, 107

Summary, 108
Point Counter-Point: Can the Fed Prevent U.S. Recessions? 108
Questions and Applications, 109
   Advanced Questions, 109
   Interpreting Financial News, 110
   Managing in Financial Markets, 110
Flow of Funds Exercise: Anticipating Fed Actions, 110
Internet/Excel Exercises, 111
WSJ Exercise: Market Assessment of Fed Policy, 111

Part 2 Integrative Problem: Fed Watching is made available to you at http://academic.cengage.com/finance/madura.

Part 3: Debt Security Markets   115

Chapter 6: Money Markets   116

Money Market Securities, 116
   Treasury Bills, 117
   Commercial Paper, 120
   Negotiable Certificates of Deposit (NCDs), 122
   Repurchase Agreements, 123
   Federal Funds, 124
   Banker's Acceptances, 125
Institutional Use of Money Markets, 126
Valuation of Money Market Securities, 128
   Explaining Money Market Price Movements, 128
   Efficiency of Money Market Securities, 129
   Indicators of Future Money Market Security Prices, 130
Risk of Money Market Securities, 130
   Credit Risk, 130
   Measuring Risk, 131
Interaction among Money Market Yields, 131
Globalization of Money Markets, 132
   Eurodollar Securities, 133

Using the Wall Street Journal: Money Rate Quotations, 134
   International Money Markets, 135
   Performance of Foreign Money Market Securities, 135
Summary, 137
Point Counter-Point: Should Firms Invest in Money Market Securities? 137
Questions and Applications, 137
   Advanced Questions, 138
   Interpreting Financial News, 138
   Managing in Financial Markets, 138
Problems, 139
Flow of Funds Exercise: Financing in the Money Markets, 139
Internet/Excel Exercises, 140
WSJ Exercise: Assessing Yield Differentials of Money Market Securities, 140

Chapter 7: Bond Markets   141

Background on Bonds, 141
   Bond Yields, 142
Treasury and Federal Agency Bonds, 143
   Treasury Bond Auction, 143
   Trading Treasury Bonds, 144
   Treasury Bond Quotations, 145
   Stripped Treasury Bonds, 145
   Inflation-Indexed Treasury Bonds, 146
   Savings Bonds, 146
   Federal Agency Bonds, 147
Municipal Bonds, 147
   Credit Risk, 147
   Characteristics of Municipal Bonds, 147
   Trading and Quotations, 148
   Yields Offered on Municipal Bonds, 148
Corporate Bonds, 150
   Corporate Bond Offerings, 150
   Characteristics of Corporate Bonds, 151
   Corporate Bond Yields and Risk, 153
   Secondary Market for Corporate Bonds, 155
   Corporate Bond Quotations, 156
   Junk Bonds, 156
Using the Wall Street Journal: Bond Index Yield Quotations, 157
   How Corporate Bonds Facilitate Restructuring, 160
   Structured Notes, 161
Institutional Use of Bond Markets, 162
Globalization of Bond Markets, 162
   Eurobond Market, 163

Summary, 163

Point Counter-Point: Should Financial Institutions Invest in Junk Bonds? 164

Questions and Applications, 164

Advanced Questions, 164

Interpreting Financial News, 165

Managing in Financial Markets, 165

Problems, 165

Flow of Funds Exercise: Financing in Bond Markets, 165

Internet/Excel Exercise, 166

WSJ Exercise: Impact of Treasury Financing on Bond Prices, 166

Chapter 8: Bond Valuation and Risk   167

Bond Valuation Process, 167

Impact of the Discount Rate on Bond Valuation, 168

Impact of the Timing of Payments on Bond Valuation, 169

Valuation of Bonds with Semiannual Payments, 169

Relationships between Coupon Rate, Required Return, and Bond Price, 170

Implications for Financial Institutions, 171

Explaining Bond Price Movements, 172

Factors That Affect the Risk-Free Rate, 173

Factors That Affect the Credit (Default) Risk Premium, 175

Summary of Factors Affecting Bond Prices, 177

Bond Market Efficiency, 177

Sensitivity of Bond Prices to Interest Rate Movements, 179

Bond Price Elasticity, 180

Duration, 181

Bond Investment Strategies Used by Investors, 185

Matching Strategy, 185

Laddered Strategy, 185

Barbell Strategy, 185

Interest Rate Strategy, 185

Return and Risk of International Bonds, 186

Influence of Foreign Interest Rate Movements, 186

Influence of Credit Risk, 186

Influence of Exchange Rate Fluctuations, 187

International Bond Diversification, 187

Summary, 188

Point Counter-Point: Does Governance of Firms Affect the Prices of Their Bonds? 188

Questions and Applications, 189

Advanced Questions, 189

Interpreting Financial News, 190

Managing in Financial Markets, 190

Problems, 191

Flow of Funds Exercise: Interest Rate Expectations, Economic Growth, and Bond Financing, 193

Internet/Excel Exercises, 193

Appendix 8: Forecasting Bond Prices and Yields is made available to you at **http://academic.cengage.com/ finance/madura.**

Chapter 9: Mortgage Markets   199

Background on Mortgages, 199

Types of Property Financed with Mortgages, 200

Residential Mortgage Characteristics, 200

Insured versus Conventional Mortgages, 200

Types of Residential Mortgages, 202

Using the Wall Street Journal: Mortgage Rate Quotations, 204

Institutional Use of Mortgage Markets, 206

Financial Institutions That Originate Mortgages, 207

Participation in the Secondary Market, 207

The Freddie Mac Accounting Scandal, 208

The Fannie Mae Accounting Scandal, 209

Unbundling of Mortgage Activities, 209

Using the Wall Street Journal: Mortgage Market Information, 210

Valuation of Mortgages, 210

Factors That Affect the Risk-Free Interest Rate, 211

Factors That Affect the Risk Premium, 212

Summary of Factors Affecting Mortgage Prices, 212

Indicators of Changes in Mortgage Prices, 212

Risk from Investing in Mortgages, 213

Interest Rate Risk, 213

Prepayment Risk, 214

Credit Risk, 214

Measuring Risk, 216

Mortgage-Backed Securities, 217

Mortgage Pass-Through Securities, 217

Types of Mortgage Pass-Through Securities, 219

Mortgage-Backed Securities for Small Investors, 221

Globalization of Mortgage Markets, 221

Summary, 222

Point Counter-Point: Is the Trading of Mortgages Similar to the Trading of Corporate Bonds? 222

Questions and Applications, 222

Advanced Questions, 223

Interpreting Financial News, 223

Managing in Financial Markets, 223

Problem, 223

Flow of Funds Exercise: Mortgage Financing, 223

Internet/Excel Exercises, 224
WSJ Exercise: Explaining Mortgage Rate Premiums, 224

Part 3 Integrative Problem: Asset Allocation is made available to you at http://academic.cengage.com/finance/madura.

Part 4: Equity Markets   227

Chapter 10: Stock Offerings and Investor Monitoring   228

Private Equity, 228
   Financing by Venture Capital Funds, 228
   Financing by Private Equity Funds, 229
Public Equity, 229
   Ownership and Voting Rights, 231
   Preferred Stock, 231
   Participation in Stock Markets, 231
Initial Public Offerings, 233
   Process of Going Public, 233
   Underwriter Efforts to Ensure Price Stability, 235
   Timing of IPOs, 236
   Initial Returns of IPOs, 236
Using the Wall Street Journal: Recent IPO Performance, 237
   Google's IPO, 238
   Abuses in the IPO Market, 239
   Long-Term Performance Following IPOs, 240
   Impact of the Sarbanes-Oxley Act on IPOs, 240
Secondary Stock Offerings, 240
   Shelf-Registration, 241
Stock Exchanges, 241
   Organized Exchanges, 241
   Over-the-Counter Market, 243
   Electronic Stock Exchanges, 244
   Extended Trading Sessions, 244
   Stock Quotations Provided by Exchanges, 245
   Stock Index Quotations, 246
Using the Wall Street Journal: Stock Index Yield Quotations, 247
Using the Wall Street Journal: Stock Market Review, 248
Monitoring by Investors, 248
   Accounting Irregularities, 249
   Sarbanes-Oxley Act, 249
   Shareholder Activism, 250
   Shareholder Lawsuits, 252
Monitoring by Financial Managers, 252
   Stock Repurchases, 253
   Market for Corporate Control, 253
   Barriers to the Market for Corporate Control, 254

Globalization of Stock Markets, 255
   Foreign Stock Offerings in the United States, 255
   International Placement Process, 255
   Global Stock Exchanges, 256
   Emerging Stock Markets, 257
Using the Wall Street Journal: Biggest Movers, 258
   Methods Used to Invest in Foreign Stocks, 258
Summary, 259
Point Counter-Point: Should a Stock Exchange Enforce Some Governance Standards on the Firms Listed on the Exchange? 260
Questions and Applications, 260
   Advanced Questions, 261
   Interpreting Financial News, 261
   Managing in Financial Markets, 261
Problem, 261
Flow of Funds Exercise: Contemplating an Initial Public Offering (IPO), 261
Internet/Excel Exercises, 262
WSJ Exercise: Assessing Stock Market Movements, 262

Chapter 11: Stock Valuation and Risk

This chapter is made available to you at http://academic.cengage.com/finance/madura.

Appendix 11: The Link between Accounting and Stock Valuation is made available to you at **http://academic.cengage.com/finance/madura.**

Chapter 12: Market Microstructure and Strategies

This chapter is made available to you at http://academic.cengage.com/finance/madura.

Part 4 Integrative Problem: Stock Market Analysis is made available to you at http://academic.cengage.com/finance/madura.

Part 5: Derivative Security Markets   333

Chapter 13: Financial Futures Markets   334

Background on Financial Futures, 334
   Purpose of Trading Financial Futures, 334
   Structure of the Futures Market, 335
   Trading Futures, 336

Interpreting Financial Futures Tables, 336

Valuation of Financial Futures, 337

Impact of the Opportunity Cost, 338

Explaining Price Movements of Bond Futures Contracts, 338

Speculating with Interest Rate Futures, 339

Impact of Leverage, 341

Closing Out the Futures Position, 341

Hedging with Interest Rate Futures, 342

Using Interest Rate Futures to Create a Short Hedge, 342

Using Interest Rate Futures to Create a Long Hedge, 344

Using the Wall Street Journal: Interest Rate Futures Quotations, 345

Hedging Net Exposure, 345

Bond Index Futures, 346

Stock Index Futures, 346

Valuing Stock Index Futures Contracts, 347

Using the Wall Street Journal: Stock Index Futures Quotations, 348

Speculating with Stock Index Futures, 349

Hedging with Stock Index Futures, 349

Dynamic Asset Allocation with Stock Index Futures, 351

Prices of Stock Index Futures versus Stocks, 351

Arbitrage with Stock Index Futures, 352

Circuit Breakers on Stock Index Futures, 352

Single Stock Futures, 354

Risk of Trading Futures Contracts, 354

Market Risk, 355

Basis Risk, 355

Liquidity Risk, 355

Credit Risk, 355

Prepayment Risk, 355

Operational Risk, 356

Regulation in the Futures Markets, 356

Institutional Use of Futures Markets, 357

Globalization of Futures Markets, 357

Non-U.S. Participation in U.S. Futures Contracts, 358

Foreign Stock Index Futures, 358

Currency Futures Contracts, 358

Summary, 359

Point Counter-Point: Has the Futures Market Created More Uncertainty for Stocks? 359

Questions and Applications, 360

Advanced Questions, 360

Interpreting Financial News, 361

Managing in Financial Markets, 361

Problems, 361

Flow of Funds Exercise: Hedging with Futures Contracts, 362

Internet/Excel Exercises, 362

Chapter 14: Options Markets

This chapter is made available to you at http://academic.cengage .com/finance/madura.

Appendix 14: Option Valuation is made available to you at **http://academic.cengage.com/finance/madura.**

Chapter 15: Interest Rate Derivative Markets

This chapter is made available to you at http://academic.cengage .com/finance/madura.

Chapter 16: Foreign Exchange Derivative Markets

This chapter is made available to you at http://academic.cengage .com/finance/madura.

Appendix 16A: Impact of the Asian Crisis on Foreign Exchange Markets and Other Financial Markets is made available to you at **http://academic.cengage .com/finance/madura.**

Appendix 16B: Currency Option Pricing is made available to you at **http://academic.cengage.com/finance/ madura.**

Part 5 Integrative Problem: Choosing among Derivative Securities is made available to you at http://academic .cengage.com/finance/madura.

Midterm Self-Exam, 469

Midterm Review, 469

Midterm Self-Exam, 470

Answers to Midterm Self-Exam, 471

Part 6: Commercial Banking 475

Chapter 17: Commercial Bank Operations 476

Background on Commercial Banks, 476

Bank Market Structure, 476

Bank Sources of Funds, 477

  Transaction Deposits, 478

  Savings Deposits, 478

  Time Deposits, 479

  Money Market Deposit Accounts, 480

  Federal Funds Purchased, 480

  Borrowing from the Federal Reserve Banks, 480

  Repurchase Agreements, 481

  Eurodollar Borrowings, 481

  Bonds Issued by the Bank, 481

  Bank Capital, 482

  Summary of Bank Sources of Funds, 482

Uses of Funds by Banks, 483

  Cash, 483

  Bank Loans, 484

  Investment in Securities, 488

  Federal Funds Sold, 489

  Repurchase Agreements, 490

  Eurodollar Loans, 490

  Fixed Assets, 490

  Summary of Bank Uses of Funds, 490

Off-Balance Sheet Activities, 491

  Loan Commitments, 493

  Standby Letters of Credit, 493

  Forward Contracts on Currencies, 493

  Interest Rate Swap Contracts, 493

International Banking, 494

  Global Competition in Foreign Countries, 494

  Expansion by Foreign Banks in the United States, 494

  Impact of the Euro on Global Competition, 495

Summary, 495

Point Counter-Point: Should Banks Engage in Other Financial Services Besides Banking? 495

Questions and Applications, 496

  Interpreting Financial News, 496

  Managing in Financial Markets, 496

Flow of Funds Exercise: Services Provided by Financial Conglomerates, 497

Internet/Excel Exercises, 497

Chapter 18: Bank Regulation   498

Background, 498

Regulatory Structure, 498

  Regulators, 499

  Regulation of Bank Ownership, 499

Regulation of Bank Deposits, 499

  Deregulation Act of 1980, 500

  Garn-St Germain Act, 501

Regulation of Operations, 502

  Regulation of Bank Assets, 502

  Regulation of Securities Services, 502

  Regulation of Insurance Services, 504

  Regulation of Off-Balance Sheet Transactions, 504

  Regulation of the Accounting Process, 504

Regulation of Interstate Expansion, 505

  Interstate Banking Act, 505

Regulation of Capital, 506

  Basel Accord, 506

  Basel II Accord, 507

  Use of the Value-at-Risk Method to Determine Capital Requirements, 509

How Regulators Monitor Banks, 510

  Capital Adequacy, 510

  Asset Quality, 511

  Management, 511

  Earnings, 511

  Liquidity, 512

  Sensitivity, 512

  Limitations of the CAMELS Rating System, 512

  Corrective Action by Regulators, 512

  Funding the Closure of Failing Banks, 513

  Preferential Regulatory Treatment, 514

Global Bank Regulations, 516

  Uniform Global Regulations, 516

Summary, 517

Point Counter-Point: Should Regulators Intervene to Take Over Weak Banks? 518

Questions and Applications, 518

  Interpreting Financial News, 519

  Managing in Financial Markets, 519

Flow of Funds Exercise: Impact of Regulation and Deregulation on Financial Services, 519

Internet/Excel Exercise, 519

WSJ Exercise: Impact of Bank Regulations, 519

Chapter 19: Bank Management   520

Bank Management, 520

  Board of Directors, 520

Managing Liquidity, 521

  Use of Securitization to Boost Liquidity, 521

Managing Interest Rate Risk, 522

  Methods Used to Assess Interest Rate Risk, 523

  Determining Whether to Hedge Interest Rate Risk, 527

  Methods Used to Reduce Interest Rate Risk, 529

  International Interest Rate Risk, 532

Managing Credit Risk, 532

  Tradeoff between Credit Risk and Expected Return, 533

Measuring Credit Risk, 534
Reducing Credit Risk, 535
Managing Market Risk, 536
Measuring Market Risk, 537
Methods Used to Reduce Market Risk, 538
Operating Risk, 538
Managing Risk of International Operations, 538
Exchange Rate Risk, 538
Settlement Risk, 539
Bank Capital Management, 539
Management Based on Forecasts, 540
Bank Restructuring, 542
Bank Acquisitions, 542
Integrated Bank Management, 543
Example, 543
Participation in Financial Markets, 546

Summary, 546
Point Counter-Point: Can Bank Failures Be Avoided? 547
Questions and Applications, 547
Advanced Questions, 548
Interpreting Financial News, 548
Managing in Financial Markets, 548
Problems, 549
Flow of Funds Exercise: Managing Credit Risk, 551
Internet/Excel Exercises, 551
WSJ Exercise: Bank Management Strategies, 552

Chapter 20: Bank Performance   553

Valuation of a Commercial Bank, 553
Factors That Affect Cash Flows, 554
*Factors That Affect the Required Rate of
Return by Investors, 555*
Performance of Banks, 556
Interest Income and Expenses, 557
Noninterest Income and Expenses, 559
Net Income, 560
How to Evaluate a Bank's Performance, 562
Examination of Return on Assets (ROA), 563
Example, 564

Summary, 566
Point Counter-Point: Does a Bank's Income Statement
Clearly Indicate the Bank's Performance? 566
Questions and Applications, 566
Interpreting Financial News, 567
Managing in Financial Markets, 567
Problem, 567
Flow of Funds Exercise: How the Flow of Funds Affects
Bank Performance, 568
Internet/Excel Exercises, 568
WSJ Exercise: Assessing Bank Performance, 568

Part 6 Integrative Problem: Forecasting
Bank Performance is made available to you
at http://academic.cengage.com/finance/
madura.

Part 7: Nonbank Operations   573

Chapter 21: Thrift Operations

This chapter is made available to
you at http://academic.cengage
.com/finance/madura.

Chapter 22: Finance Operations

This chapter is made available to
you at http://academic.cengage
.com/finance/madura.

Chapter 23: Mutual Fund Operations   613

Background on Mutual Funds, 613
Types of Funds, 614
Using the Wall Street Journal: Exchange-
Traded Funds, 615
Comparison to Depository Institutions, 617
Regulation, 617
Information Contained in a Prospectus, 617
Estimating the Net Asset Value, 617
Distributions to Shareholders, 618
Mutual Fund Classifications, 618
Management of Mutual Funds, 619
Expenses Incurred by Shareholders, 619
Sales Load, 620
12b-1 Fees, 621
Governance of Mutual Funds, 622
Mutual Fund Scandals, 622
Corporate Control by Mutual Funds, 623
Stock Mutual Fund Categories, 623
Growth Funds, 624
Capital Appreciation Funds, 624
Growth and Income Funds, 624
International and Global Funds, 624
Using the Wall Street Journal: Mutual Fund
Prices and Performance, 625
Specialty Funds, 625
Index Funds, 625
Multifund Funds, 626
Bond Mutual Fund Categories, 626
Income Funds, 626

Tax-Free Funds, 626
High-Yield (Junk) Bond Funds, 626
International and Global Bond Funds, 626
Maturity Classifications, 627
Asset Allocation Funds, 627
Growth and Size of Mutual Funds, 627
Performance of Mutual Funds, 628
Performance of Stock Mutual Funds, 628
Using the Wall Street Journal: Mutual Fund
    Performance, 631
Performance of Closed-End Stock Funds, 631
Performance of Bond Mutual Funds, 632
Performance of Closed-End Bond Funds, 633
*Performance from Diversifying among Mutual
    Funds, 633*
Research on Stock Mutual Fund Performance, 633
Research on Bond Mutual Fund Performance, 634
Money Market Funds, 634
Asset Composition of Money Market Funds, 636
Maturity of Money Market Funds, 636
Risk of Money Market Funds, 636
Management of Money Market Funds, 637
*Regulation and Taxation of Money Market
    Funds, 638*
Venture Capital and Private Equity Funds, 638
Venture Capital Funds, 638
Private Equity Funds, 639
Views of Private Equity Funds, 640
Hedge Funds, 641
Hedge Fund Fees, 641
Regulation, 641
*Financial Problems Experienced by Long-Term
    Capital Management, 641*
Short Selling by Hedge Funds, 642
Hedge Funds of Funds, 643
Real Estate Investment Trusts, 643
Interaction with Other Financial Institutions, 644
Use of Financial Markets, 645
Globalization through Mutual Funds, 646

Summary, 646

Point Counter-Point: Should Mutual Funds Be Subject to
    More Regulation? 646
Questions and Applications, 647
Advanced Questions, 647
Interpreting Financial News, 648
Managing in Financial Markets, 648
Flow of Funds Exercise: How Mutual Funds Facilitate the
    Flow of Funds, 648
Internet/Excel Exercises, 648
WSJ Exercise: Performance of Mutual Funds, 649

Chapter 24: Securities Operations

This chapter is made available to you at http://academic.cengage .com/finance/madura.

Chapter 25: Insurance and Pension Fund Operations

This chapter is made available to you at http://academic.cengage .com/finance/madura.

Part 7 Integrative Problem: Assessing the Influence of Economic Conditions across a Financial Conglomerate's Units is made available to you at http:// academic.cengage.com/finance/madura.

Final Self-Exam, 702

Final Review, 702

Final Self-Exam, 703

Answers to Final Self-Exam, 704

Appendix A: Comprehensive Project, 707
Appendix B: Using Excel to Conduct Analyses, 719
Glossary, 723
Index, 733

From the Publisher

Financial Markets and Institutions: Abridged 8th Edition is our offering of a more course-specific, lower cost alternative to *Financial Markets and Institutions: 8th Edition*. Based on market research with faculty using *Financial Markets and Institutions: 8th Edition*, we found that many instructors covered less than the 25 chapters contained in that textbook. That same research showed that the chapters contained in this abridged version are those that most professors cover in a one-term course. For those instructors that subscribe to this coverage trend, this abridged version is a more efficient and economical alternative to use with students taking this course.

The approach we have taken with *Financial Markets and Institutions: Abridged 8th Edition* is to remove whole specific chapters in their entirety, all the end-of-chapter appendixes, and end-of-part integrative problems. Pagination of this abridged version is consistent with *Financial Markets and Institutions: 8th Edition* so that all student-oriented supplements as well as instructor supplements will work with either version of the book. A classroom of students using either version of the book will be able to follow along on the same page without need for "translating" page numbers. For those instructors who feel that one or more of the eliminated chapters, chapter appendices, or integrated problems are needed in their course, both instructors and students can freely access PDFs of these chapters or appendices at the textbook's website at **http://academic.cengage.com/finance/madura.**

Preface

Financial markets facilitate the flow of funds in order to finance investments by corporations, governments, and individuals. Financial institutions are the key players in financial markets because they serve as intermediaries that determine the flow of funds. *Financial Markets and Institutions,* Abridged Eighth Edition, describes financial markets and the financial institutions that serve those markets. It provides a conceptual framework that can be used to understand why markets exist. Each type of financial market is described, with a focus on the securities that are traded in that market and the participation by financial institutions.

Today, many financial institutions offer all types of financial services, such as banking, securities services, mutual fund services, and insurance services. Although financial institutions overlap in the services they offer, the services that can be offered are distinctly different. Therefore, the discussion of financial services in this book is organized by type of service.

Intended Market

This text is suitable for both undergraduate and master's level courses in financial markets, financial institutions, or both. To maximize students' comprehension level, the more difficult questions and problems should be assigned, along with the special applications at the end of each chapter and the Comprehensive Project.

Organization of the Text

Part 1 (Chapters 1 through 3) introduces the key financial markets and financial institutions, explains interest rate movements in the financial markets, and explains why yields vary among securities. Part 2 (Chapters 4 and 5) describes the functions of the Federal Reserve System (the Fed) and explains how its monetary policy influences interest rates and other economic conditions. Part 3 (Chapters 6 through 9) covers the major debt security markets, Part 4 (Chapter 10) describes equity securities markets, and Part 5 (Chapter 13) covers the derivative security markets. Each chapter in Parts 3 through 5 focuses on a particular market. The integration of each market with other markets is stressed throughout these chapters. Part 6 (Chapters 17 through 20) concentrates on commercial banking, and Part 7 (Chapter 23) covers mutual fund operations.

Courses that emphasize financial markets should focus on the first five parts (Chapters 1 through 16); however, some chapters in the section on commercial banking are also relevant. Courses that emphasize financial institutions and financial services should focus on Parts 1, 2, 6, and 7, although some background on securities markets (Parts 3, 4, and 5) may be helpful.

Finally, the instructors of courses that emphasize financial markets and institutions may wish to focus on certain chapters of this book and skip others, depending on other courses available to their students. For example, if a course on derivative securities is commonly offered, Part 5 of this text may be ignored. Alternatively, if an investments course provides a thorough background on types of securities, Parts 3 and 4 can be given limited attention.

Chapters can be rearranged without a loss in continuity. Regardless of the order in which chapters are studied, it is highly recommended that the special exercises and selected questions in each chapter be assigned. These exercises may serve as a focal point for class discussion.

Coverage of Major Concepts and Events

Numerous concepts relating to recent events and current trends in financial markets are discussed throughout the chapters, including the following:

- Behavioral finance
- Private equity funding
- Venture capitalists
- Backdating of options
- Governance in financial markets
- Impact of the Sarbanes-Oxley Act on financial markets
- Role of specialists
- The Fed's impact on financial markets
- Subprime loan problems
- Role of analysts
- Value-at-risk measurements
- Asymmetric information
- Emerging stock markets
- Option pricing
- Valuation of financial institutions
- Regulatory reform in financial services
- Mutual fund trading scandals
- Modified duration
- Interest rate swaps and currency swaps
- Collateralized mortgage obligations (CMOs)
- Portfolio insurance strategies

Each chapter is self-contained, so professors can use classroom time to focus on the more complex concepts and rely on the text to cover the other concepts.

Major Content Changes

Behavioral finance applications have been infused throughout the text. More attention is given to private equity and venture capital financing, innovations in financial markets, the consolidation of stock exchanges, the Fed's recent dilemmas and tradeoffs, exchange-traded funds, the backdating in the stock option market, and restructuring by financial institutions.

Features of the Text

The features of the text are as follows:

- *Part-Opening Diagram.* A diagram is provided at the beginning of each part to illustrate generally how the key concepts in that part are related. This offers information about the organization of chapters in that part.
- *Objectives.* A bulleted list at the beginning of each chapter identifies the key concepts in that chapter.
- *Illustrations.* Illustrations are provided to reinforce key concepts.
- *Behavioral Finance.* Applications of behavioral finance to financial markets and financial institutions are offered throughout the text and are indicated with icons in the margins.

- *Global Aspects.* Global Aspects icons in the margins throughout the text indicate international coverage of the chapter topics being discussed.
- *Summary.* A bulleted list at the end of each chapter summarizes the key concepts. This list corresponds to the list of objectives at the beginning of the chapter.
- *Point Counter-Point.* A controversial issue is introduced, along with opposing arguments, and students are asked to determine which argument is correct and explain why.

Point Counter-Point

- *Questions and Applications.* The Questions and Applications section at the end of each chapter tests students' understanding of the key concepts and may serve as homework assignments or study aids in preparation for exams.
- *Flow of Funds Exercise.* A running exercise is provided at the end of each chapter to illustrate how a manufacturing company relies on all types of financial markets and financial services provided by financial institutions.
- *Interpreting Financial News.* At the end of each chapter, students are challenged to interpret comments made in the media about the chapter's key concepts. This gives students practice in interpreting announcements by the financial media.

Interpreting Financial News

- *Internet/Excel Exercises.* At the end of each chapter, there are exercises that expose students to applicable website information, enable the application of Excel to related topics, or a combination of these. For example, the exercises allow students to assess yield curves, risk premiums, and stock volatility.

Internet/Excel Exercises

- *Managing in Financial Markets.* At the end of each chapter, students are placed in the position of financial managers and must make decisions about specific situations related to the key concepts in that chapter.

- *Problems.* Selected chapters include problems to test students' computational skills.

- *WSJ Exercise.* At the end of selected chapters, this exercise allows students to apply information provided in *The Wall Street Journal* to specific concepts explained in that chapter.

- *Integrative Problem.* The integrative problem found on the book's website (http:// academic.cengage.com/finance/madura) integrates the key concepts of chapters within that part.

- *Comprehensive Project.* This project, found in Appendix A, requires students to apply real data to several key concepts described throughout the book.

- *Midterm and Final Self-Examinations.* At the end of Part 5, a midterm self-exam is offered to test students' knowledge of financial markets. At the end of Part 7, a final self-exam is offered to test students' knowledge of financial institutions. An answer key is provided so that students can evaluate their answers after they take the exam.

The concepts in each chapter can be reinforced by using one or more of the above features. Each professor will have his or her own method for helping students get the most out of the text. Professors' use of the features will vary depending on the level of their students and the focus of the course. A course that focuses mostly on financial markets may emphasize tools such as the WSJ Exercises and Part 1 of the Comprehensive Project (on taking positions in securities and derivative instruments). Conversely, a course that focuses on financial institutions may assign an exercise in which students have to review recent annual reports (see Part 2 of the Comprehensive Project) to fully understand how a particular financial institution's performance is affected by its policies, industry regulations, and economic conditions. In addition, the Internet/Excel Exercises on financial institutions allow students to assess the operations and performance of financial institutions.

Supplements to the Text

The following supplements are available:

- The **website** for *Financial Markets and Institutions,* Abridged Eighth Edition, can be found at http://academic.cengage.com/finance/madura. This robust site contains the Data Bank, Internet exercises, updated URLs, downloadable PowerPoint slides, links to finance sites, additional text chapters, chapter appendices, and end-of-part integrative problems.

- A **PowerPoint** presentation package of lecture slides is available on the text website and the Instructor's Resource CD (IRCD) as a lecture aid for instructors and a study aid for students. In addition, key figures from the text are also provided in a separate PowerPoint package, also included on the website and IRCD.

- The **South-Western Finance Resource Center,** found at http://academic.cengage .com/cengage/finance, provides unique features, customer service information, and links to book-related websites. It also has resources such as Finance in the News, FinanceLinks Online, Wall Street Analyst Reports from the Gale Group, and more. Learn about valuable products and services to help with your finance studies, or contact the finance editors at South-Western.

- An **Instructor's Manual** contains the chapter outline and a summary of key concepts for discussion as well as answers to the end-of-chapter Questions, Problems, Managing in Financial Markets, and Interpreting Financial News. The Instructor's Manual is also available to instructors on the text website and the Instructor's Resource CD.

- The **Test Bank,** available on the text website and IRCD, has been revised and expanded with new multiple-choice questions.

- The **ExamView**™ computerized testing program contains all of the questions in the Test Bank. It is an easy-to-use test creation software package compatible with Microsoft Windows. Instructors can add or edit questions, instructions, and answers, and select questions at random or by number after previewing them on the screen. Instructors can also create and administer quizzes online, whether over a LAN, a WAN, or the Internet. ExamView is available on the Instructor's Resource CD.

- **CaseNet**® brings the practical lessons of real business to your classroom with premier teaching cases, all based on data from business and industry. Cases help students make the connection between theory and practice, build analytical skills, and solve realistic problems. For more information, contact your South-Western/Cengage Learning sales representative or visit CaseNet at www.text choice.com/casenet.

- The **WSJ Subscription** is a special, 15-week subscription offer to *The Wall Street Journal* that is available to students of instructors adopting this text. *The Wall Street Journal* is the unprecedented resource for financial information in the marketplace, which the text integrates throughout. Contact your South-Western/Cengage Learning sales representative for package pricing and ordering information.

Acknowledgments

The motivation to write this textbook came primarily from the encouragement of E. Joe Nosari (Florida State University). Several professors helped develop the text outline and offered suggestions on which of the concepts from earlier editions of this book should be covered in this edition. They are acknowledged in alphabetical order:

Ibrihim Affaneh, Indiana University of Pennsylvania
Henry C. F. Arnold, Seton Hall University
James C. Baker, Kent State University
Gerald Bierwag, Florida International University
Carol Billingham, Central Michigan University
Randy Billingsley, Virginia Tech University
Rita M. Biswas, State University of New York at Albany
Howard W. Bohnen, St. Cloud State University
Paul J. Bolster, Northeastern University
M. E. Bond, University of Memphis
Carol Marie Boyer, Long Island University, C.W. Post
Alka Bramhandkar, Ithaca College
Emile J. Brinkman, University of Houston–University Park

Christopher L. Brown, Western Kentucky University
Sarah Bryant, George Washington University
James B. Burnham, Duquesne University
Deanne Butchey, Florida International University
William Carner, University of Missouri–Columbia
Joseph Cheng, Ithaca College
William T. Chittenden, Northern Illinois University
C. Steven Cole, University of North Texas
M. Cary Collins, University of Tennessee
Mark Correll, University of Colorado
Wayne C. Curtis, Troy State University
Steven Dobson, California Polytechnic State University
Robert M. Donchez, University of Colorado–Boulder
Richard J. Dowen, Northern Illinois University
Imad Elhaj, University of Louisville
James Felton, Central Michigan University
Stuart Fletcher, Appalachian State University
Clifford L. Fry, University of Houston
Edward K. Gill, California State University–Chico
Claire G. Gilmore, St. Joseph's University
Owen Gregory, University of Illinois–Chicago
Paul Grier, SUNY–Binghamton
Ann Hackert, Idaho State University
John Halloran, University of Notre Dame
Gerald A. Hanweck, George Mason University
Hildegard R. Hendrickson, Seattle University
Bradley K. Hobbs, Ph.D., Florida Gulf Coast University
Jerry M. Hood, Loyola University–New Orleans
Ronald M. Horowitz, Oakland University
Paul Hsueh, University of Central Florida
Carl D. Hudson, Auburn University
John S. Jahera, Jr., Auburn University
Robert James, Babson College
Mel Jameson, University of Nevada
Shane Johnson, Bowling Green State University
Richard H. Keehn, University of Wisconsin–Parkside
James B. Kehr, Miami University of Ohio
David F. Kern, Arkansas State University
James W. Kolari, Texas A&M University
Vladimir Kotomin, University of Wisconsin–Eau Claire
Robert A. Kunkel, University of Wisconsin–Oshkosh
George Kutner, Marquette University
Robert Lamy, Wake Forest University
David J. Leahigh, King's College
David N. Leggett, Bentley College
William Lepley, University of Wisconsin–Green Bay
Morgan Lynge, Jr., University of Illinois
Judy E. Maese, New Mexico State University
Timothy A. Manuel, University of Montana
L. R. Martindale, Texas A&M University
Joseph S. Mascia, Adelphi University
Robert W. McLeod, University of Alabama
Kathleen S. McNichol, LaSalle University

James McNulty, Florida Atlantic University
Charles Meiburg, University of Virginia
Jose Mercado-Mendez, Central Missouri State University
Kenneth O. Moran, Freed Hardeman University
Neil Murphy, Virginia Commonwealth University
Hossein Noorain, Boston University & Wentworth Institute of Technology
Dale Osborne, University of Texas–Dallas
Coleen Pantalone, Northeastern University
Thomas H. Payne, University of Tennessee–Chattanooga
Sarah Peck, University of Iowa
D. Anthony Plath, University of North Carolina–Charlotte
Barbara Poole, Roger Williams University
Rose Prasad, Central Michigan University
Mitchell Ratner, Rider University
David Rayome, Northern Michigan University
Alan Reichert, Cleveland State University
Kenneth L. Rhoda, LaSalle University
Lawrence C. Rose, Massey University
Jack Rubens, Bryant College
Robert Schweitzer, University of Delaware
Mehmet Sencicek, University of New Haven
Kilman Shin, Ferris State University
Ahmad Sorhabian, California State Polytechnic University–Pomona
Andrew Spieler, Hofstra University
S. R. Stansell, East Carolina University
Richard W. Stolz, University of South Carolina Upstate
Richard S. Swasey, Northeastern University
John Thornton, Kent State University
Olaf J. Thorp, Babson College
James D. Tripp, University of Tennessee–Martin
K. C. Tseng, California State University–Fresno
Harry J. Turtle, University of Manitoba
Cevdet Uruk, University of Memphis
Geraldo M. Vasconcellos, Lehigh University
Michael C. Walker, University of Cincinnati
Fang Wang, West Virginia University
Bruce Watson, Wellesley College
David A. Whidbee, Washington State University
Colin Young, Bentley College
Stephen Zera, California State University–San Marcos
Mei "Miranda" Zhang, Mercer University

Other colleagues who offered suggestions for clarification include Jarrod Johnston (Appalachian State University), Victor Kalafa (Cross Country Staffing), Stephen Larson (Minnesota State University), Thanh Ngo (Florida Atlantic University), Oliver Schnusenberg (University of North Florida), Alan Tucker (Pace University), and John Walker (Kutztown University).

This text also benefited from the research departments of several Federal Reserve district banks, the Federal National Mortgage Association, the National Credit Union Administration, the American Council of Life Insurance, the Investment Company Institute, and the Chicago Mercantile Exchange.

I acknowledge the help and support from the people at South-Western, including Mike Reynolds (Executive Editor), Jason Krall (Marketing Manager), Mike

Guendelsberger (Developmental Editor), Adele Scholtz (Senior Editorial Assistant), and Angela Glassmeyer (Senior Marketing Coordinator). A special thanks is due to the production editors, Amy Hackett and Scott Dillon, the project manager, Jamie Armstrong, and Pat Lewis (copy editor) for their efforts to ensure a quality final product.

Finally, I wish to thank my parents, Arthur and Irene Madura, and my wife, Mary, for their moral support.

About the Author

Jeff Madura is the SunTrust Bank Professor of Finance at Florida Atlantic University. He has written several textbooks, including *International Financial Management*. His research on banking and financial markets has been published in numerous journals, including *Journal of Financial and Quantitative Analysis, Journal of Money, Credit and Banking, Journal of Banking and Finance, Financial Review, Financial Management, Journal of Risk and Insurance, Journal of Financial Research,* and *Journal of Financial Services Research*. He has received awards for excellence in teaching and research and has served as a consultant for commercial banks, securities firms, and other corporations. He has served as a director for the Southern Finance Association and Eastern Finance Association and has been president of the Southern Finance Association.

Part 1: Overview of the Financial Environment

Part 1 focuses on the flow of funds across financial markets, interest rates, and security prices. Chapter 1 introduces the key financial markets and the financial institutions that participate in those markets. Chapter 2 explains how various factors influence interest rates and how interest rate movements in turn affect the values of securities purchased by financial institutions. Chapter 3 identifies factors other than interest rates that influence security prices. Participants in financial markets use this information to value securities and make investment decisions within financial markets.

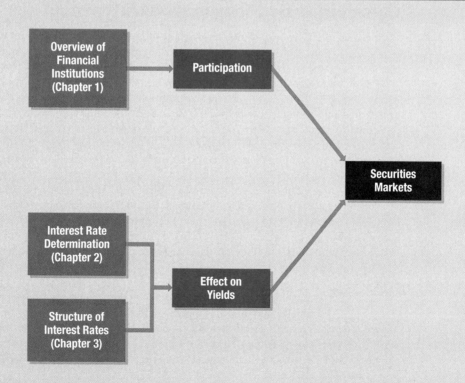

Chapter 1: Role of Financial Markets and Institutions

A financial market is a market in which financial assets (securities) such as stocks and bonds can be purchased or sold. Funds are transferred in financial markets when one party purchases financial assets previously held by another party. Financial markets facilitate the flow of funds and thereby allow financing and investing by households, firms, and government agencies. This chapter provides a background on financial markets and the financial institutions that participate in them.

The specific objectives of this chapter are to:

■ describe the types of financial markets that facilitate the flow of funds,

■ introduce the concept of security valuation within financial markets,

■ describe the role of financial institutions within financial markets, and

■ identify the types of financial institutions that facilitate transactions in financial markets.

Overview of Financial Markets

Financial markets transfer funds from those who have excess funds to those who need funds. They enable college students to obtain student loans, families to obtain mortgages, businesses to finance their growth, and governments to finance their expenditures. Without financial markets, many students could not go to college, many families could not purchase a home, corporations could not grow, and the government could not provide as many public services. Households and businesses that supply funds to financial markets earn a return on their investment; the return is necessary to ensure that funds are supplied to the financial markets. If funds were not supplied, the financial markets would not be able to transfer funds to those who need them.

Those participants who receive more money than they spend are referred to as **surplus units.** They provide their net savings to the financial markets. Those participants who spend more money than they receive are referred to as **deficit units.** They access funds from financial markets so that they can spend more money than they receive. Many individuals provide funds to financial markets in some periods and access funds in other periods.

ILLUSTRATION College students are typically deficit units, as they often borrow from financial markets to support their education. After they obtain their degree, they earn more income than they spend and thus become surplus units. A few years later, they may become deficit units again by purchasing a home. At this stage, they may provide funds to and access funds from financial markets simultaneously.

That is, they may periodically deposit savings in a financial institution, but also borrow money from a financial institution to buy a home. ■

Many deficit units such as firms and government agencies access funds from financial markets by issuing securities. **Securities** are certificates that represent a claim on the issuer. **Debt securities** are certificates that represent debt (borrowed funds) incurred by the issuer. Deficit units issue the securities to surplus units and pay interest to the surplus units on a periodic basis (such as every six months). Debt securities have a maturity date, when the surplus units (net savers) can redeem them, receiving the principal (face value) from the issuer. **Equity securities** (also called stocks) are certificates that represent equity or ownership in the issuer. Some businesses issue equity securities as an alternative way of raising funds.

Issuing securities enables corporations and government agencies to obtain money from surplus units and thus to spend more money than they receive from normal operations.

ILLUSTRATION If the U.S. government wants to spend $10 billion more than it receives in taxes this month, it can issue U.S. Treasury securities to net savers. The U.S. government is a major deficit unit and therefore frequently relies on financial markets. The Treasury securities that it issues are a form of debt owed by the Treasury to the net savers who purchased the securities. Other government agencies also commonly issue debt securities to obtain funds.

Similarly, if Google wants to spend $40 million more than it receives in revenue this month, it can issue corporate debt securities to net savers. Alternatively, it can issue equity securities to raise funds. Each method of raising funds has distinct advantages and disadvantages, as will be discussed in later chapters. ■

Types of Financial Markets

Each financial market is created to satisfy particular preferences of market participants. For example, some participants may want to invest funds for a short-term period, whereas others want to invest for a long-term period. Some participants are willing to tolerate a high level of risk when investing, whereas others need to avoid risk. Some participants that need funds prefer to borrow, whereas others prefer to issue stock. There are many different types of financial markets, and each market can be distinguished by the maturity structure and trading structure of its securities.

Money versus Capital Markets The financial markets that facilitate the transfer of debt securities are commonly classified by the maturity of the securities. Those financial markets that facilitate the flow of short-term funds (with maturities of one year or less) are known as **money markets,** while those that facilitate the flow of long-term funds are known as **capital markets.**

http://

http://www.nyse.com
New York Stock Exchange market summary, quotes, financial statistics, and more.

http://www.nasdaq.com
Comprehensive historic and current data on all Nasdaq transactions.

Primary versus Secondary Markets Whether referring to money market securities or capital market securities, it is necessary to distinguish between transactions in the primary market and transactions in the secondary market. **Primary markets** facilitate the issuance of new securities. **Secondary markets** facilitate the trading of existing securities, which allows for a change in the ownership of the securities. Primary market transactions provide funds to the initial issuer of securities; secondary market transactions do not. The issuance of new corporate stock or new Treasury securities is a primary market transaction, while the sale of existing corporate stock or Treasury security holdings by one investor to another is a secondary market transaction.

An important characteristic of securities that are traded in secondary markets is **liquidity,** which is the degree to which securities can easily be liquidated (sold) without a loss of value. Some securities have an active secondary market, meaning that there are many willing buyers and sellers of the security at a given point in time. Investors prefer liquid securities so that they can easily sell the securities whenever they want (without a loss in value). If a security is illiquid, investors may not be able to find a willing buyer for it in the secondary market and may have to sell the security at a large discount just to attract a buyer.

How Financial Markets Facilitate Corporate Finance and Investment Management

Finance is commonly partitioned into three segments as shown in Exhibit 1.1: (1) corporate finance, (2) investment management, (3) financial markets and institutions. Corporate finance involves decisions such as how much funding to obtain and how to invest the proceeds to expand operations.

The financial markets attract funds from investors and channel the funds to corporations. Thus, they serve as the means by which corporations finance their existing operations and their growth. The money markets enable corporations to borrow funds on a short-term basis so that they can support their existing operations. The capital markets enable corporations to obtain long-term funds to support corporate expansion. The decisions by the managers of publicly traded firms affect a firm's performance and stock price, which affects the returns to the investors who provided funding in the capital markets by purchasing the stock.

Investment management involves decisions by investors regarding how to invest their funds. The financial markets offer investors a wide variety of investment opportunities, including securities issued by the U.S. Treasury and government agencies as well as corporate securities. A major part of investment management is deciding which securities to purchase. When investing in stock, investors assess the financial management of various firms. They look for firms that are currently undervalued and have the potential to improve. They monitor and may even attempt to influence the financial management of the firms in which they invest to ensure that the financial managers make decisions that maximize the stock price. The market price of the stock serves as a measure of how well each publicly traded firm is being managed by its managers.

Financial institutions (discussed later in this chapter) are shown in Exhibit 1.1. They serve as intermediaries that execute the transactions within the financial markets so that funds from investors are channeled to corporations. They also commonly serve as investors and channel their own funds to corporations.

Exhibit 1.1   How Financial Markets Facilitate Corporate Finance and Investment Management

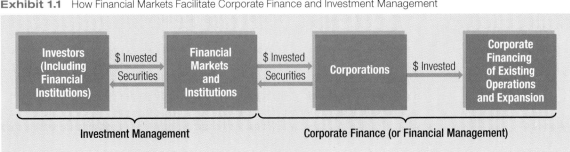

Securities Traded in Financial Markets

Each type of security tends to have specific return and risk characteristics, as described in detail in the chapters covering financial markets. The term *risk* is used here to represent the uncertainty surrounding the expected return. The more uncertain the expected return, the greater the risk is. When surplus units have funds available for one year, for example, they can purchase one-year Treasury securities and know exactly what return they will receive on their investment. In contrast, the return from investing in debt securities issued by firms is not guaranteed because the firms could go bankrupt and never repay the surplus units. Equity securities are also risky because their values depend on the future performance of the firms that issued them. Surplus units will consider investing in a risky security only if it has the potential to offer a higher return than what they can earn on a risk-free investment such as a Treasury security. In other words, the issuer of a security has to price the security such that the expected return is sufficient to compensate for the risk. Thus, there is a positive relationship between the risk of a security and the expected return to be earned from investing in that security.

Securities can be classified as money market securities, capital market securities, or derivative securities.

Money Market Securities

Money market securities are debt securities that have a maturity of one year or less. They generally have a relatively high degree of liquidity. Money market securities tend to have a low expected return but also a low degree of risk. Common types of money market securities include Treasury bills (issued by the Treasury), commercial paper (issued by corporations), and negotiable certificates of deposit (issued by depository institutions).

Capital Market Securities

Securities with a maturity of more than one year are called **capital market securities.** Capital market securities are commonly issued to finance the purchase of capital assets, such as buildings, equipment, or machinery. Three common types of capital market securities are bonds, mortgages, and stocks.

http://

http://www.bondmarkets
.com/ Data and other information about bonds.

Bonds and Mortgages Bonds are long-term debt securities issued by corporations and government agencies to support their operations. Mortgages are long-term debt obligations created to finance the purchase of real estate.

Bonds provide a return to investors in the form of interest income (coupon payments) every six months. Since bonds and mortgages represent debt, they specify the amount and timing of interest and principal payments to investors who purchase them. At maturity, investors holding the debt securities are paid the principal. Debt securities can be sold in the secondary market if investors do not want to hold them until maturity. Since the prices of debt securities can change over time, investors may be able to enhance their return by selling the securities for a higher price than they paid for them.

Some debt securities are risky because the issuer could default on its obligation to repay the debt. Under these circumstances, the debt security will not provide the entire amount of coupon payments and principal that was promised. Long-term debt securities tend to have a higher expected return than money market securities, but they have more risk as well.

Stocks Stocks (also referred to as equity securities) are certificates representing partial ownership in the corporations that issued them. They are classified as capital market securities because they have no maturity and therefore serve as a long-term source of funds. Some corporations provide income to their stockholders by distributing a portion of their quarterly earnings in the form of dividends. Other corporations retain and reinvest all of their earnings, which allows them more potential for growth.

Equity securities differ from debt securities in that they represent partial ownership. As corporations grow and increase in value, the value of the stock increases, and investors can earn a capital gain from selling the stock for a higher price than they paid for it. Thus, investors can earn a return from stocks in the form of periodic dividends (if there are any) and a capital gain when they sell the stock. Investors can experience a negative return, however, if the corporation performs poorly and its stock price declines over time as a result. Equity securities have a higher expected return than most long-term debt securities, but they also exhibit a higher degree of risk.

Derivative Securities

http://www.cboe.com
Information about derivative securities.

In addition to money market and capital market securities, derivative securities are also traded in financial markets. **Derivative securities** are financial contracts whose values are derived from the values of underlying assets (such as debt securities or equity securities). Many derivative securities enable investors to engage in speculation and risk management.

Speculation Derivative securities allow an investor to speculate on movements in the value of the underlying assets without having to purchase those assets. Some derivative securities allow investors to benefit from an increase in the value of the underlying assets, whereas others allow investors to benefit from a decrease in the assets' value. Investors who speculate in derivative contracts can achieve higher returns than if they had speculated in the underlying assets, but they are also exposed to higher risk.

Risk Management Derivative securities can be used in a manner that will generate gains if the value of the underlying assets declines. Consequently, financial institutions and other firms can use derivative securities to adjust the risk of their existing investments in securities. If a firm maintains investments in bonds, for example, it can take specific positions in derivative securities that will generate gains if bond values decline. In this way, derivative securities can be used to reduce a firm's risk. The loss on the bonds is offset by the gains on these derivative securities.

Valuation of Securities in Financial Markets

Each type of security generates a unique stream of expected cash flows to investors. As mentioned earlier, investors holding securities may receive periodic (coupon or dividend) payments and also receive a payment when they sell the securities. In addition, each security has a unique level of uncertainty surrounding the expected cash flows that it will provide to investors and therefore surrounding its return. The valuation of a security is measured as the present value of its expected cash flows, discounted at a rate that reflects the uncertainty. Since the cash flows and the uncertainty surrounding the cash flows for each security are unique, the value of each security is unique.

Market Pricing of Securities

Securities are priced in the market according to how they are valued by market participants. Each security has an equilibrium market price at which the demand for that security is equal to the supply of that security for sale.

 Nike stock provides cash flows to investors in the form of quarterly dividends and its stock price at the time investors sell the stock. Both the future dividends and the future stock price are uncertain. Thus, the cash flows that Nike stock will provide to investors in the future are also uncertain. Investors can attempt to estimate the future cash flows that they will receive by obtaining information that may indicate Nike's future performance, such as reports about the athletic shoe industry, announcements by Nike about its recent sales, and published opinions about Nike's management ability. The valuation process is illustrated in Exhibit 1.2. ■

Impact of Information on Valuations Although all investors rely on valuation to make investment decisions, different investors may interpret and use information in different ways. Thus, they may derive different valuations of a security based on the available information. Some investors rely mostly on economic or industry information to value a security, while others rely more on published opinions about the firm's management.

Impact of Valuations on Pricing When investors receive new information about a security that clearly indicates the likelihood of higher cash flows or less uncertainty, they revise their valuations of that security upward. Consequently, the prevailing price is no longer in equilibrium, as most investors now view the security as undervalued at that price. The demand for the security increases at that price, and the supply of that security for sale decreases. As a result, the market price rises to a new equilibrium level.

Conversely, when investors receive unfavorable information, they reduce the expected cash flows or increase the discount rate used in valuation. All of the valuations of the security are revised downward, which results in shifts in the demand and supply conditions and a decline in the equilibrium price.

Announcements that do not contain any valuable new information will not elicit a market response. Sometimes, market participants take a position in anticipation of a particular announcement. If an announcement is fully anticipated, there will be no market response when the announcement occurs.

Exhibit 1.2
Use of Information
to Make Investment
Decisions

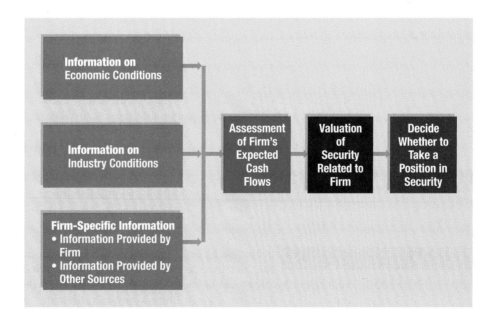

Impact of the Internet on the Valuation Process The Internet has improved the valuation of securities in several ways. Prices of securities are quoted online and can be obtained at any given moment by investors. For some securities, investors can track the actual sequence of transactions. Because much more information about the firms that issue securities is available online, securities can be priced more accurately. Furthermore, orders to buy or sell many types of securities can be submitted online, which expedites the adjustment in security prices to new information.

Market Efficiency

http://

http://finance.yahoo.com
Market quotations and overview of financial market activity.

Investors differ with respect to the risk they are willing to incur, the desired liquidity of securities, and their tax status, making some types of securities more desirable to some investors than to others. Normally, investors attempt to balance the objective of high return with their particular preference for low risk and adequate liquidity. Investors may still consider purchasing some securities that are not as safe and liquid as desired if the potential return is sufficiently high.

Because securities have market-determined prices, their favorable or unfavorable characteristics as perceived by the market are reflected in their prices. When security prices fully reflect all available information, the markets for these securities are referred to as efficient.

In an efficient market, securities are rationally priced. If a security is clearly undervalued based on public information, some investors will capitalize on the discrepancy by purchasing that security. This strong demand for the security will push the security's price higher until the discrepancy no longer exists. The investors who recognized the discrepancy will be rewarded with higher returns on their investment. Thus, investors are naturally motivated to monitor market prices of securities. Their actions to capitalize on discrepancies typically ensure that securities are properly priced, based on the information that is available.

Even if markets are efficient, a firm's security's price is subject to much uncertainty because investors have limited information available to value the security. The price of the security may change substantially over time as investors obtain more information about the firm's management, or its industry, or the economy.

ILLUSTRATION When Google first issued stock on August 18, 2004, there was much uncertainty as to its value. Investors knew that Google's stock would be affected by factors such as its management, industry conditions (such as competition), and economic conditions, but there was much uncertainty surrounding these factors. Some investors thought that Google's initial price of $85 per share was excessive, while others purchased as many shares as they could at that price. Within the first year, more information became available about Google's business plans and performance, and its stock price more than tripled. Thus, for every $1,000 invested in Google, investors earned more than $3,000 within one year. ■

BEHAVIORAL FINANCE In some cases, a security is mispriced because of the psychology involved in the decision making. **Behavioral finance** is the application of psychology to make financial decisions. It explains why markets are not always efficient.

ILLUSTRATION A positive report about Nadal Company's earnings caused the demand for Nadal stock to increase. The stock's price rose by 2 percent, an adjustment in the stock's price that was justified by the new information. As other media reported the same positive news, however, investors' demand for Nadal stock increased again, causing the stock price to rise an additional 4 percent. The next day there was more media buzz about how well Nadal's stock was performing, and this caused a further increase in demand, and the share price increased another 3 percent. Thus, the stock's price increased much more than was justified because some investors based their investment decisions on the degree of media exposure that the stock received rather than on the actual information. The stock's price declined once the media hype subsided, but the point is that the stock was temporarily priced improperly as a result of the psychology used by investors to make their decisions. ■

Various conditions can affect the psychology used by investors or corporate managers to make decisions. Consequently, behavioral finance can sometimes explain the movements of a security's price or even the entire stock market. Behavioral finance topics covered in this text are designated with the label shown in the margin. ■

Much of the information that investors use to value securities issued by firms is provided by the managers of those firms. As part of the valuation process, investors also rely on accounting reports of a firm's revenue and expenses as a base for estimating its future cash flows. Although firms with publicly traded stock are required to disclose financial information and accounting statements, a firm's managers still possess information about its financial condition that is not necessarily available to investors. This situation is referred to as asymmetric information. Even when information is disclosed, an asymmetric information problem may still exist if some of the information provided by the firm's managers is misleading.

Financial Market Regulation

In general, securities markets are regulated to ensure that the participants are treated fairly. Many regulations were enacted in response to fraudulent practices before the Great Depression.

Disclosure

Since the use of incorrect information can result in poor investment decisions, many regulations attempt to ensure that businesses disclose accurate information. Similarly, when information is disclosed to only a small set of investors, those investors have a major advantage over other investors. Thus, another regulatory goal is to provide all investors with equal access to disclosures by firms. The Securities Act of 1933 was intended to ensure complete disclosure of relevant financial information on publicly offered securities and to prevent fraudulent practices in selling these securities. The Securities Exchange Act of 1934 extended the disclosure requirements to secondary market issues. It also declared illegal a variety of deceptive practices, such as misleading financial statements and trading strategies designed to manipulate the market price. In addition, it established the Securities and Exchange Commission (SEC) to oversee the securities markets, and the SEC has implemented additional laws over time. Securities laws do not prevent investors from making poor investment decisions but only attempt to ensure full disclosure of information and thus protect against fraud.

Regulatory Response to Financial Scandals

BEHAVIORAL FINANCE   The Enron, WorldCom, and other financial scandals in the 2001–2002 period proved that the existing regulations were not sufficient to prevent fraud. Enron misled investors by exaggerating its earnings. It also failed to disclose relevant information that would have adversely affected its stock price. By the time the information became public, many of Enron's executives had sold off their holdings of Enron stock. They were able to sell the stock at a relatively high price because the negative information was withheld from the public. WorldCom also misled its investors by exaggerating its earnings. Participants in the financial markets were shocked by the degree to which these firms were able to distort their financial statements before the adverse information became public.

Many financial market participants had assumed that financial statements were accurate. In some cases, the auditors who were hired to ensure that a firm's financial statements were accurate were not meeting their responsibility. As a result, executives were able to sell their stock before most financial market participants were aware of the firm's real financial condition.

In response to the financial scandals, the Sarbanes-Oxley Act (discussed throughout this text) was passed to require firms to provide more complete and accurate financial information. It also imposed more restrictions to ensure proper auditing by auditors and proper oversight by the firm's board of directors. These rules were intended to regain the trust of investors who supply the funds to the financial markets. Through these measures, regulators tried to eliminate or reduce the asymmetric information problem.

Given the potential wealth that may be earned in financial markets when the regulations are circumvented, it is safe to say that unethical behavior of some sort will occur in the future. New financial scandals will result in new regulations, which will be followed by new types of scandals that circumvent the latest regulations. Often the most naïve (least informed) investors are those most adversely affected by financial scandals.

Global Financial Markets

GL🌐BALASPECTS Financial markets are continuously being developed throughout the world to improve the transfer of funds from surplus units to deficit units. The financial markets are much more developed in some countries than in others, however, and vary in terms of the volumes of funds that are transferred from surplus units to deficit units and the types of funding that are available. Some countries have had financial markets for a long time, but other countries have converted to market-oriented economies and established financial markets relatively recently.

ILLUSTRATION Before 1990, many countries in Eastern Europe had very limited opportunities for surplus units and deficit units. Consequently, private businesses did not have access to funds and could not expand. In addition, households did not have access to funds and could not purchase homes. Businesses were mostly owned by the government and had to rely on government funding. Since 1990, the governments of these countries have allowed for **privatization,** or the sale of government-owned firms to individuals. In addition, some businesses have issued stock, which allows many other investors who do not work in the business to participate in the ownership. Financial markets have been established in these countries to ensure that these businesses can obtain funding from surplus units. With these changes, private businesses are now able to obtain funds by borrowing or by issuing stock to investors. Surplus units have the opportunity to provide credit (loans) to some businesses or become stockholders of other businesses. ∎

International Corporate Governance

Since financial markets channel funds from surplus units to deficit units, they can function only if surplus units are willing to provide funds to the markets. If there is a lack of information about the securities traded in the market, or a lack of safeguards to ensure that investors are treated fairly, surplus units will not participate. Consequently, the financial markets will not be liquid.

Financial markets have developed slowly in some less developed countries for several reasons. First, the issuers of debt securities do not provide much financial information to indicate how they intend to repay the surplus units who would buy the securities. Second, regulatory agencies provide very little enforcement to ensure that the financial information provided by the issuers is correct. Third, businesses that do not repay the surplus units are rarely prosecuted. Fourth, courts in these countries do not provide an efficient system that surplus units can use to obtain the funds they believe they are owed.

Global Integration

http://www.bloomberg.com
World market coverage, various financial instruments, financial analysis, charts, quotes, news.

Many financial markets are globally integrated, allowing participants to move funds out of one country's markets and into another's. Foreign investors serve as key surplus units in the United States by purchasing U.S. Treasury securities and other types of securities issued by businesses. Conversely, some investors based in the United States serve as key surplus units for foreign countries by purchasing securities issued by foreign corporations and government agencies. In addition, investors assess the potential return and the risk of securities in financial markets across countries and invest in the market that satisfies their return and risk preferences.

With these more integrated financial markets, U.S. market movements may have a greater impact on foreign market movements, and vice versa. Because interest rates are influenced by the supply of and demand for available funds, they are now more susceptible to foreign lending or borrowing activities.

Financial Market Integration within Europe The most pronounced progress in global financial market integration has occurred in Europe. Numerous regulations were eliminated so that surplus and deficit units in one European country could use financial markets throughout Europe. Some stock exchanges in different European countries merged, making it easier for investors to conduct all of their stock transactions on one exchange. Since 1999, the adoption of the euro as the currency by 12 European countries (the so-called eurozone) has encouraged more financial market integration within Europe because securities issued within these countries are now denominated in the euro. Thus, investors in any of these countries do not have to convert their currency.

Role of the Foreign Exchange Market

International financial transactions (except for those within the eurozone) normally require the exchange of currencies. The **foreign exchange market** facilitates the exchange of currencies. Many commercial banks and other financial institutions serve as intermediaries in the foreign exchange market by matching up participants who want to exchange one currency for another. Some of these financial institutions also serve as dealers by taking positions in currencies to accommodate foreign exchange requests.

Foreign Exchange Rates Like securities, most currencies have a market-determined price (exchange rate) that changes in response to supply and demand conditions. If there is a sudden shift in the aggregate demand by corporations, government agencies, and individuals for a given currency, or a shift in the aggregate supply of that currency for sale (to be exchanged), the price will change.

Role of Financial Institutions in Financial Markets

If financial markets were **perfect,** all information about any securities for sale in primary and secondary markets (including the creditworthiness of the security issuer) would be continuously and freely available to investors. In addition, all information identifying investors interested in purchasing securities as well as investors planning to sell securities would be freely available. Furthermore, all securities for sale could be broken down (or unbundled) into any size desired by investors, and security transaction costs would be nonexistent. Under these conditions, financial intermediaries would not be necessary.

Because markets are **imperfect,** securities buyers and sellers do not have full access to information and cannot always break down securities to the precise size they desire. Financial institutions are needed to resolve the problems caused by market imperfections. They receive requests from surplus and deficit units on what securities are to be purchased or sold, and they use this information to match up buyers and sellers of securities. Because the amount of a specific security to be sold does not always equal the amount desired by investors, financial institutions sometimes unbundle the securities by spreading them across several investors until the entire amount is sold. Without financial institutions, the information and transaction costs of financial market transactions would be excessive.

Role of Depository Institutions

Depository institutions accept deposits from surplus units and provide credit to deficit units through loans and purchases of securities. They are popular financial institutions for the following reasons:

- They offer deposit accounts that can accommodate the amount and liquidity characteristics desired by most surplus units.
- They repackage funds received from deposits to provide loans of the size and maturity desired by deficit units.
- They accept the risk on loans provided.
- They have more expertise than individual surplus units in evaluating the creditworthiness of deficit units.
- They diversify their loans among numerous deficit units and therefore can absorb defaulted loans better than individual surplus units could.

To appreciate these advantages, consider the flow of funds from surplus units to deficit units if depository institutions did not exist. Each surplus unit would have to identify a deficit unit desiring to borrow the precise amount of funds available for the precise time period in which funds would be available. Furthermore, each surplus unit would have to perform the credit evaluation and incur the risk of default. Under these conditions, many surplus units would likely hold their funds rather than channel them to deficit units. Thus, the flow of funds from surplus units to deficit units would be disrupted.

When a depository institution offers a loan, it is acting as a creditor, just as if it had purchased a debt security. Yet, the more personalized loan agreement is less marketable in the secondary market than a debt security, because detailed provisions on a loan can differ significantly among loans. Any potential investors would need to review all provisions before purchasing loans in the secondary market.

A more specific description of each depository institution's role in the financial markets follows.

Commercial Banks In aggregate, commercial banks are the most dominant depository institution. They serve surplus units by offering a wide variety of deposit accounts, and they transfer deposited funds to deficit units by providing direct loans or purchasing debt securities. Commercial banks serve both the private and public sectors, as their deposit and lending services are utilized by households, businesses, and government agencies. Some commercial banks, such as Bank of America, J.P. Morgan Chase & Co., Citigroup, Wachovia Corporation, and SunTrust Banks, have more than $100 billion in assets.

Savings Institutions Savings institutions, which are sometimes referred to as thrift institutions, are another type of depository institution. Savings institutions include savings and loan associations (S&Ls) and savings banks. Like commercial banks, S&Ls offer deposit accounts to surplus units and then channel these deposits to deficit units. Whereas commercial banks have concentrated on commercial loans, however, S&Ls have concentrated on residential mortgage loans. This difference in the allocation of funds has caused the performance of commercial banks and S&Ls to differ significantly over time. In recent decades, however, deregulation has permitted S&Ls more flexibility in allocating their funds, causing their functions to become more similar to those of commercial banks. Although S&Ls can be owned by shareholders, most are mutual (depositor owned).

Savings banks are similar to S&Ls, except that they have more diversified uses of funds. However, this difference has narrowed over time. Like S&Ls, most savings banks are mutual.

Credit Unions Credit unions differ from commercial banks and savings institutions in that they (1) are nonprofit and (2) restrict their business to the credit union members, who share a common bond (such as a common employer or union). Because of the common bond characteristic, credit unions tend to be much smaller than other depository institutions. They use most of their funds to provide loans to their members. Some of the largest credit unions, such as the Navy Credit Union, State Employees Credit Union of North Carolina, and the Pentagon Credit Union, have assets of more than $5 billion.

Role of Nondepository Financial Institutions

Nondepository institutions generate funds from sources other than deposits but also play a major role in financial intermediation. These institutions are briefly described here and are covered in more detail in Part 7.

Finance Companies Most finance companies obtain funds by issuing securities, then lend the funds to individuals and small businesses. The functions of finance companies overlap the functions of depository institutions, yet each type of institution concentrates on a particular segment of the financial markets (explained in the chapters devoted to these institutions). Many large finance companies are owned by large multinational corporations, including American Express, Ford Motor Company, General Motors, and General Electric.

Mutual Funds Mutual funds sell shares to surplus units and use the funds received to purchase a portfolio of securities. They are the dominant nondepository financial institution when measured in total assets. Some mutual funds concentrate their investment in capital market securities, such as stocks or bonds. Others, known as **money market mutual funds,** concentrate in money market securities. The minimum denomination of the types of securities purchased by mutual funds is typically greater than the savings of an individual surplus unit. By purchasing shares of mutual funds and money market mutual funds, small savers are able to invest in a diversified portfolio of securities with a relatively small amount of funds.

Securities Firms Securities firms provide a wide variety of functions in financial markets. Some securities firms use their information resources to act as a **broker,** executing securities transactions between two parties. Many financial transactions are standardized to a degree. For example, stock transactions are normally in multiples of 100 shares. To expedite the securities trading process, the delivery procedure for each security transaction is also somewhat standard.

Brokers charge a fee for executing transactions. The fee is reflected in the difference (or **spread**) between their **bid** and **ask** quotes. The markup as a percentage of the transaction amount will likely be greater for less common transactions, as more time is needed to match up buyers and sellers. It will also likely be greater for transactions of relatively small amounts in order to provide adequate compensation for the time involved in executing the transaction.

In addition to brokerage services, securities firms also provide investment banking services. Some securities firms place newly issued securities for corporations and government agencies; this task differs from traditional brokerage activities because it involves the primary market. When securities firms **underwrite** newly issued securities, they may sell the securities for a client at a guaranteed price, or they may simply sell the securities at the best price they can get for their client.

Furthermore, securities firms often act as **dealers,** making a market in specific securities by adjusting their inventory of securities. Although a broker's income is mostly based on the markup, the dealer's income is influenced by the performance of the security portfolio maintained. Some dealers also provide brokerage services and therefore earn income from both types of activities.

Another investment banking activity offered by securities firms is advisory services on mergers and other forms of corporate restructuring. Securities firms may not only help a firm plan its restructuring but also execute the change in the firm's capital structure by placing the securities issued by the firm. Some securities firms, such as Merrill Lynch, Morgan Stanley, and Goldman Sachs, play a major role in brokerage, underwriting, and advisory services.

Insurance Companies Insurance companies provide insurance policies to individuals and firms that reduce the financial burden associated with death, illness, and damage to property. They charge premiums in exchange for the insurance that they provide. They invest the funds that they receive in the form of premiums until the funds are needed to cover insurance claims. Insurance companies commonly invest the funds in stocks or bonds issued by corporations or in bonds issued by the government. In this way, they finance the needs of deficit units and thus serve as important financial intermediaries. Their overall performance is linked to the performance of the stocks and bonds in which they invest. Large insurance companies include State Farm Group, Allstate Insurance, Travelers PC Group, CNA Insurance, and Liberty Mutual.

Pension Funds Many corporations and government agencies offer pension plans to their employees. The employees, their employers, or both periodically contribute funds to the plan. Pension funds provide an efficient way for individuals to save for their retirement. The pension funds manage the money until the individuals withdraw the funds from their retirement accounts. The money that is contributed to individual retirement accounts is commonly invested by the pension funds in stocks or bonds issued by corporations or in bonds issued by the government. In this way, pension funds finance the needs of deficit units and thus serve as important financial intermediaries.

Comparison of Roles among Financial Institutions

The role of financial institutions in facilitating the flow of funds from individual surplus units to deficit units is illustrated in Exhibit 1.3. Surplus units are shown on the left side of the exhibit, and deficit units are shown on the right side. Three different flows of funds from surplus units to deficit units are shown in the exhibit. One set of flows represents deposits from surplus units that are transformed by depository institutions into loans for deficit units. A second set of flows represents purchases of securities (commercial paper) issued by finance companies that are transformed into finance company loans for deficit units. A third set of flows reflects the purchases of shares issued by mutual funds, which are used by the mutual funds to purchase debt and equity securities of deficit units.

The deficit units also receive funding from insurance companies and pension funds. Because insurance companies and pension funds purchase massive amounts of stocks and bonds, they finance much of the expenditures made by large deficit units, such as corporations and government agencies.

Securities firms are not shown in Exhibit 1.3, but they play a very important role in facilitating the flow of funds. Many of the transactions between the financial institutions and deficit units are executed by securities firms. Furthermore, some funds flow directly from surplus units to deficit units as a result of security transactions, with securities firms serving as brokers.

Exhibit 1.3   Comparison of Roles among Financial Institutions

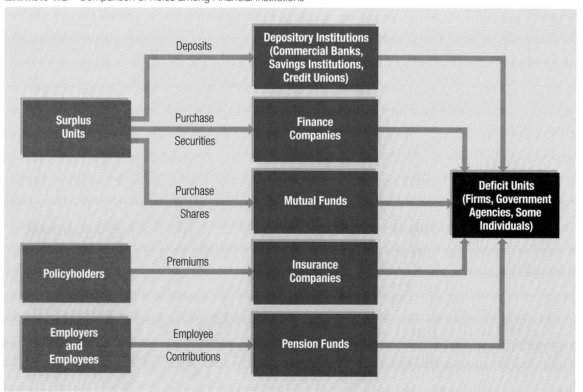

Role as a Monitor of Publicly Traded Firms In addition to the roles just described, financial institutions also serve as monitors of publicly traded firms. Because insurance companies, pension funds, and some mutual funds are major investors in stocks, they can have some influence over the management of publicly traded firms. In recent years, many large institutional investors have publicly criticized the management of specific firms, which has resulted in corporate restructuring or even the firing of executives in some cases. Thus, institutional investors not only provide financial support to companies but exercise some degree of corporate control over them. By serving as activist shareholders, they can help ensure that managers of publicly held corporations are making decisions that are in the best interests of the shareholders.

Overview of Financial Institutions

Exhibit 1.4 illustrates the relative sizes of the different types of financial institutions, based on assets. The percentage next to the dollar amount for each type of financial institution represents its proportion of the total dollars in assets held by all financial institutions. Together, all of these financial institutions hold assets equal to about $38 trillion. Commercial banks have $9.2 trillion in assets, which represents 25 percent of the total assets held by all financial institutions. In aggregate, commercial banks have more assets than the combined assets of savings institutions, credit unions, finance companies, and securities firms. Pension funds and mutual funds have more than $8 trillion in assets, while all types of insurance companies hold more than $5 trillion in assets.

Exhibit 1.5 summarizes the main sources and uses of funds for each type of financial institution. Households with savings are served by depository institutions.

Exhibit 1.4
Asset Sizes of Financial Institutions (in Billions of Dollars)

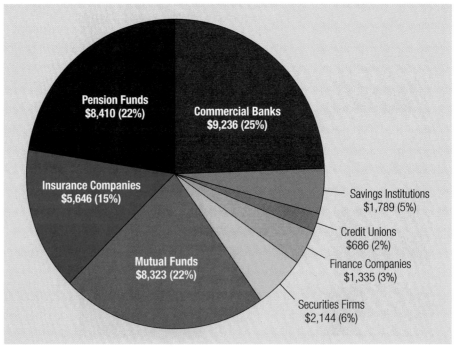

Source: Board of Governors, Federal Reserve System, 2007.

Exhibit 1.5
Summary of Institutional Sources and Uses of Funds

Financial Institutions	Main Sources of Funds	Main Uses of Funds
Commercial banks	Deposits from households, businesses, and government agencies	Purchases of government and corporate securities; loans to businesses and households
Savings institutions	Deposits from households, businesses, and government agencies	Purchases of government and corporate securities; mortgages and other loans to households; some loans to businesses
Credit unions	Deposits from credit union members	Loans to credit union members
Finance companies	Securities sold to households and businesses	Loans to households and businesses
Mutual funds	Shares sold to households, businesses, and government agencies	Purchases of long-term government and corporate securities
Money market funds	Shares sold to households, businesses, and government agencies	Purchases of short-term government and corporate securities
Insurance companies	Insurance premiums and earnings from investments	Purchases of long-term government and corporate securities
Pension funds	Employer/employee contributions	Purchases of long-term government and corporate securities

Households with deficient funds are served by depository institutions and finance companies. Large corporations and governments that issue securities obtain financing from all types of financial institutions.

Competition between Financial Institutions

Until the 1970s, deposits provided by surplus units to commercial banks and savings institutions were heavily regulated to prevent competition. Then, in the 1970s, the development of mutual funds created competition for funds held by surplus units. Deregulation of deposit rates in the early 1980s provided additional competition for these funds. Furthermore, in the 1980s, regulators allowed savings institutions, insurance companies, and other financial institutions to be more flexible in their use of funds. The momentum for additional flexibility continued in the 1990s. Today, many financial institutions are offering a greater variety of products and services to diversify their business. As a consequence, their services overlap more and competition has increased. Several different regulatory agencies regulate the various types of financial institutions, and these differential regulations can cause some financial institutions to have a comparative advantage over others.

Impact of the Internet on Competition The Internet has created more intense competition among financial institutions. Some commercial banks have been created solely as online entities. Because they have lower costs, they can offer higher interest rates on deposits and lower rates on loans. Other banks also offer online services, which can reduce costs, increase efficiency, and intensify banking competition. Some insurance companies conduct much of their business online, which reduces their operating costs and forces other insurance companies to price their services competitively. Some brokerage firms conduct much of their business online, which reduces their operating costs; because these firms can lower the fees they charge, they force other brokerage firms to price their services competitively. The

Internet has also made it possible for corporations and municipal governments to circumvent securities firms by conducting security offerings online and selling directly to investors. This capability forces securities firms to be more competitive in the services they offer to issuers of securities.

Consolidation of Financial Institutions

As regulations have been reduced, managers of financial institutions have more flexibility to offer services that could increase their cash flows and value. The reduction in regulations has allowed financial institutions more opportunities to capitalize on economies of scale. Commercial banks have acquired other commercial banks so that they can generate a higher volume of business supported by a given infrastructure. By increasing the volume of services produced, the average cost of providing the services (such as loans) can be reduced. Savings institutions have consolidated to achieve economies of scale for their mortgage lending business. Insurance companies have consolidated so that they can reduce the average cost of providing insurance services.

The reduction in regulations has also allowed different types of financial institutions to expand the types of services they offer and capitalize on economies of scope. Commercial banks have merged with savings institutions, securities firms, finance companies, mutual funds, and insurance companies. Although the operations of each type of financial institution are commonly managed separately, a financial conglomerate offers advantages to customers who prefer to obtain all of their financial services from a single financial institution.

ILLUSTRATION Wells Fargo is a classic example of the evolution in financial services. It originally focused on commercial banking, but has expanded its nonbank services to include mortgages, small business loans, consumer loans, real estate, brokerage, investment banking, online financial services, and insurance. In a recent annual report, Wells Fargo stated:

> *Our diversity in businesses makes us much more than a bank. We're a diversified financial services company. We're competing in a highly fragmented and fast growing industry: Financial Services. This helps us weather downturns that inevitably affect any one segment of our industry.* ∎

Typical Structure of a Financial Conglomerate A typical organizational structure of a financial conglomerate is shown in Exhibit 1.6. Historically, each of the financial services (such as banking, mortgages, brokerage, and insurance) had significant barriers to entry, so only a limited number of firms competed in that industry. The barriers prevented most firms from offering a wide variety of these services. In recent years, the barriers to entry have been reduced, allowing firms that had specialized in one service to more easily expand into other financial services. Many firms expanded by acquiring other financial service firms. Thus, many financial conglomerates are composed of various financial institutions that were originally independent, but are now units (or subsidiaries) of the conglomerate.

Impact of Consolidation on Valuation When managers of financial institutions pursue consolidation to achieve economies of scale or scope, they may be able to increase their firm's value by increasing cash flows (increasing revenue or reducing expenses). Alternatively, consolidation may be intended to diversify the institution's services and reduce risk. A lower level of risk allows for a reduction in the required rate of return by investors and can increase value.

Exhibit 1.6   Organizational Structure of a Financial Conglomerate

```
                    Holding Company of a Financial Conglomerate
```

Commercial Bank Operations	Thrift Operations	Consumer Finance Operations	Mutual Fund Operations	Securities Operations	Insurance Operations
• Commercial Loans • Other Corporate Services	• Mortgages	• Consumer Loans • Small Business Loans	• Stock Funds • Bond Funds • Money Market Funds	• Brokerage • Investment Banking	• Insurance for Individuals • Insurance for Firms

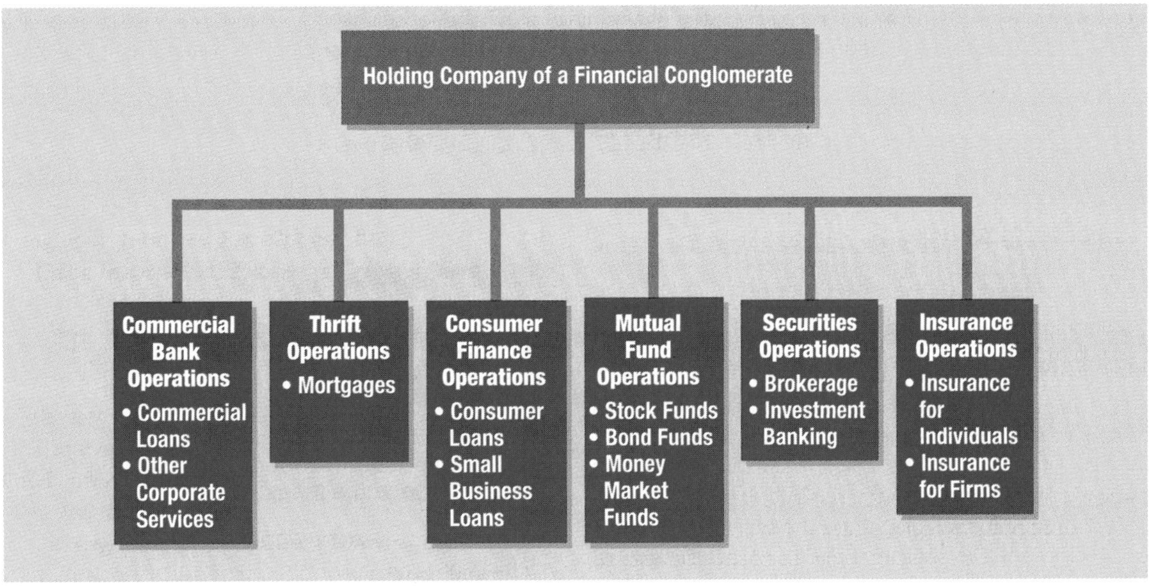

Impact of Consolidation on Customers An individual customer can rely on the financial conglomerate for convenient access to life and health insurance, brokerage, mutual funds, investment advice and financial planning, bank deposits, and personal loans. A corporate customer can turn to the financial conglomerate for property and casualty insurance, health insurance plans for employees, business loans, advice on restructuring its businesses, issuing new debt or equity securities, and management of its pension plan. Many financial conglomerates expect to grow by providing additional financial services to their existing customers.

Global Expansion by Financial Institutions

GL**⊕**BALASPECTS Many financial institutions have expanded internationally to capitalize on their expertise. Commercial banks, insurance companies, and securities firms have expanded through international mergers. An international merger between financial institutions enables the merged company to offer the services of both entities to its entire customer base. For example, a U.S. commercial bank may have specialized in lending while a European securities firm specialized in services such as underwriting securities. A merger between the two entities allows the U.S. bank to provide its services to the European customer base (clients of the European securities firm), while the European securities firm can offer its services to the U.S. customer base. By combining specialized skills and customer bases, the merged financial institutions can offer more services to clients and have an international customer base.

The adoption of the euro by 12 European countries has increased business between European countries and created a more competitive environment in Europe. European financial institutions, which had primarily competed with other financial institutions based in their own country, recognized that they would now face more competition from financial institutions in other countries.

Many financial institutions have attempted to benefit from opportunities in emerging markets. For example, Merrill Lynch and other large securities firms have expanded into many countries to offer underwriting services for firms and government agencies. The need for this service has increased most dramatically in countries where businesses have been privatized. In addition, commercial banks have expanded into emerging markets to provide loans.

Summary

■ Financial markets facilitate the transfer of funds from surplus units to deficit units. Because funding needs vary among deficit units, various financial markets have been established. The primary market allows for the issuance of new securities, while the secondary market allows for the sale of existing securities. Money markets facilitate the sale of short-term securities, while capital markets facilitate the sale of long-term securities.

■ The valuation of a security represents the present value of future cash flows that it is expected to generate. New information that indicates a change in expected cash flows or degree of uncertainty affects prices of securities in financial markets. Investors monitor economic conditions and firm-specific conditions that may have an impact on expected cash flows or the degree of uncertainty surrounding securities issued by that firm.

■ Depository and nondepository institutions help to finance the needs of deficit units. Depository institutions can serve as effective intermediaries within financial markets because they have greater information on possible sources and uses of funds, they are capable of assessing the creditworthiness of borrowers, and they can repackage deposited funds in sizes and maturities desired by borrowers.

Nondepository institutions are major purchasers of securities and therefore provide funding to deficit units.

■ The main depository institutions are commercial banks, savings institutions, and credit unions. The main nondepository institutions are finance companies, mutual funds, pension funds, and insurance companies. Many financial institutions have been consolidated (due to mergers) into financial conglomerates, where they serve as subsidiaries of the conglomerate while conducting their specialized services. Thus, some financial conglomerates are able to provide all types of financial services. Consolidation allows for economies of scale and scope, which can enhance cash flows and increase the financial institution's value. In addition, consolidation can diversify the institution's services and increase value through the reduction in risk.

Point Counter-Point

Will Computer Technology Cause Financial Intermediaries to Become Extinct?

Point Yes. Financial intermediaries benefit from access to information. As information becomes more accessible, individuals will have the information they need before investing or borrowing funds. They will not need financial intermediaries to make their decisions.

Counter-Point No. Individuals rely not only on information, but also on expertise. Some financial intermediaries specialize in credit analysis so that they can make loans. Surplus units will continue to provide funds to financial intermediaries rather than make direct loans, because they are not capable of credit analysis, even if more information about prospective borrowers is available. Some financial intermediaries no longer have physical buildings for customer service, but they still require people who have the expertise to assess the creditworthiness of prospective borrowers.

Who Is Correct? Use the Internet to learn more about this issue. Offer your own opinion on this issue.

Questions and Applications

1. **Surplus and Deficit Units** Explain the meaning of surplus units and deficit units. Provide an example of each. Which types of financial institutions do you deal with? Explain whether you are acting as a surplus unit or a deficit unit in your relationship with each financial institution.

2. **Types of Markets** Distinguish between primary and secondary markets. Distinguish between money and capital markets.

3. **Imperfect Markets** Distinguish between perfect and imperfect security markets. Explain why the existence of imperfect markets creates a need for financial intermediaries.

4. **Efficient Markets** Explain the meaning of efficient markets. Why might we expect markets to be efficient most of the time? In recent years, several securities firms have been guilty of using inside information when purchasing securities, thereby achieving returns well above the norm (even when accounting for risk). Does this suggest that the security markets are not efficient? Explain.

5. **Securities Laws** What was the purpose of the Securities Act of 1933? What was the purpose of the Securities Exchange Act of 1934? Do these laws prevent investors from making poor investment decisions? Explain.

6. **International Barriers** If barriers to international securities markets are reduced, will a country's interest rate be more or less susceptible to foreign lending or borrowing activities? Explain.

7. **International Flow of Funds** In what way could the international flow of funds cause a decline in interest rates?

8. **Securities Firms** What are the functions of securities firms? Many securities firms employ brokers and dealers. Distinguish between the functions of a broker and those of a dealer, and explain how each is compensated.

9. **Standardized Securities** Why is it necessary for securities to be somewhat standardized? Explain why some financial flows of funds cannot occur through the sale of standardized securities. If securities were not standardized, how would this affect the volume of financial transactions conducted by brokers?

10. **Marketability** Commercial banks use some funds to purchase securities and other funds to make loans. Why are the securities more marketable than loans in the secondary market?

11. **Depository Institutions** How have the asset compositions of savings and loan associations differed from those of commercial banks? Explain why and how this distinction may change over time.

12. **Credit Unions** With regard to the profit motive, how are credit unions different from other financial institutions?

13. **Nondepository Institutions** Compare the main sources and uses of funds for finance companies, insurance companies, and pension funds.

14. **Mutual Funds** What is the function of a mutual fund? Why are mutual funds popular among investors? How does a money market mutual fund differ from a stock or bond mutual fund?

15. **Impact of Privatization on Financial Markets** Explain how the privatization of companies in Europe can lead to the development of new securities markets.

Advanced Questions

16. **Comparing Financial Institutions** Classify the types of financial institutions mentioned in this chapter as either depository or nondepository. Explain the general difference between depository and nondepository institution sources of funds. It is often said that all types of financial institutions have begun to offer services that were previously offered only by certain types. Consequently, the operations of many financial institutions are becoming more similar. Nevertheless, performance levels still differ significantly among types of financial institutions. Why?

17. **Financial Intermediation** Look in a recent business periodical for news about a recent financial transaction that involves two financial institutions. For this transaction, determine the following:
    a. How will each institution's balance sheet be affected?
    b. Will either institution receive immediate income from the transaction?
    c. Who is the ultimate user of funds?
    d. Who is the ultimate source of funds?

18. **Role of Accounting in Financial Markets** Integrate the roles of accounting, regulations, and financial market participation. That is, explain how financial market participants rely on accounting, and why regulatory oversight of the accounting process is necessary.

Interpreting Financial News

"Interpreting Financial News" tests your ability to comprehend common statements made by Wall Street analysts and portfolio managers who participate in the financial markets. Interpret the following statements made by Wall Street analysts and portfolio managers:

a. "The price of IBM stock will not be affected by the announcement that its earnings have increased as expected."

b. "The lending operations at Bank of America should benefit from strong economic growth."

c. "The brokerage and underwriting performance at Merrill Lynch should benefit from strong economic growth."

Managing in Financial Markets

Utilizing Financial Markets As a financial manager of a large firm, you plan to borrow $70 million over the next year.

a. What are the more likely ways in which you can borrow $70 million?

b. Assuming that you decide to issue debt securities, describe the types of financial institutions that may purchase these securities.

c. How do individuals indirectly provide the financing for your firm when they maintain deposits at depository institutions, invest in mutual funds, purchase insurance policies, or invest in pensions?

Flow of Funds Exercise

Roles of Financial Markets and Institutions

This continuing exercise focuses on the interactions of a single manufacturing firm (Carson Company) in the financial markets. It illustrates how financial markets and institutions are integrated and facilitate the flow of funds in the business and financial environment. At the end of every chapter, this exercise provides a list of questions about Carson Company that require the application of concepts presented in the chapter, as they relate to the flow of funds.

Carson Company is a large manufacturing firm in California that was created 20 years ago by the Carson family. It was initially financed with an equity investment by the Carson family and 10 other individuals. Over time, Carson Company has obtained substantial loans from finance companies and commercial banks. The interest rate on the loans is tied to market interest rates and is adjusted every six months. Thus, Carson's cost of obtaining funds is sensitive to interest rate movements. It has a credit line with a bank in case it suddenly needs additional funds for a temporary period. It has purchased Treasury securities that it could sell if it experiences any liquidity problems.

Carson Company has assets valued at about $50 million and generates sales of about $100 million per year. Some of its growth is attributed to its acquisitions of other firms. Because of its expectations of a strong U.S. economy, Carson plans to grow in the future by expanding its business and through acquisitions. It

expects that it will need substantial long-term financing and plans to borrow additional funds either through loans or by issuing bonds. It is also considering issuing stock to raise funds in the next year. Carson closely monitors conditions in financial markets that could affect its cash inflows and cash outflows and therefore affect its value.

a. In what way is Carson a surplus unit?

b. In what way is Carson a deficit unit?

c. How might finance companies facilitate Carson's expansion?

d. How might commercial banks facilitate Carson's expansion?

e. Why might Carson have limited access to additional debt financing during its growth phase?

f. How might investment banks facilitate Carson's expansion?

g. How might Carson use the primary market to facilitate its expansion?

h. How might it use the secondary market?

i. If financial markets were perfect, how might this have allowed Carson to avoid financial institutions?

j. The loans provided by commercial banks to Carson require that Carson receive the banks' approval before pursuing any large projects. What is the purpose of this condition? Does this condition benefit the owners of the company?

Internet/Excel Exercises

1. Review the information for the common stock of IBM, using the website http://finance.yahoo.com. Insert the ticker symbol "IBM" in the box labeled "Enter Symbol(s)" and click on "Get Quotes." The main goal at this point is to become familiar with the information that you can obtain at this website. Review the data that are shown for IBM stock. Compare the price of IBM based on its last trade with the price range for the year. Is the price near its high or low price? What is the total value of IBM stock (market capitalization)? What is the average daily trading volume (Avg Vol) of IBM stock? Click on "5y" just below the stock price chart to see IBM's stock price movements over the last five years. Describe the trend in IBM's stock over this period. At what point was the stock price the highest and lowest?

2. Repeat the questions in exercise 1 for the Children's Place Retail Stores (symbol is PLCE). Explain how the market capitalization and trading volume for PLCE differ from IBM.

WSJ Exercise

Differentiating between Primary and Secondary Markets

Review the different tables relating to stock markets and bond markets that appear in Section C of *The Wall Street Journal*. Explain whether each of these tables is focused on the primary or secondary markets.

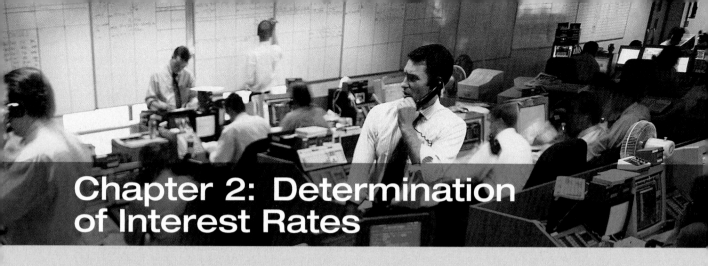

Chapter 2: Determination of Interest Rates

Interest rate movements have a direct influence on the market values of debt securities, such as money market securities, bonds, and mortgages, and have an indirect influence on equity security values. Thus, participants in financial markets attempt to anticipate interest rate movements when restructuring their positions. Interest rate movements also affect the value of most financial institutions. The cost of funds to depository institutions and the interest received on some loans by financial institutions are affected by interest rate movements. In addition, the market values of securities (such as bonds) held by depository institutions or nondepository institutions are affected as well. Thus, managers of financial institutions attempt to anticipate interest rate movements so that they can capitalize on favorable movements or reduce their institution's exposure to unfavorable movements.

The specific objectives of this chapter are to:

- apply the loanable funds theory to explain why interest rates change,
- identify the most relevant factors that affect interest rate movements, and
- explain how to forecast interest rates.

Loanable Funds Theory

http://
http://www.bloomberg.com
Information on interest rates in recent months.

The **loanable funds theory,** commonly used to explain interest rate movements, suggests that the market interest rate is determined by the factors that control the supply of and demand for loanable funds. The theory is especially useful for explaining movements in the general level of interest rates for a particular country. Furthermore, it can be used along with other concepts to explain why interest rates among some debt securities of a given country vary, which is the focus of the next chapter. The phrase "demand for loanable funds" is widely used in financial markets to refer to the borrowing activities of households, businesses, and governments. This chapter looks first at the sectors that commonly affect the demand for loanable funds and then describes the sectors that supply loanable funds to the markets. Finally, the demand and supply concepts are integrated to explain interest rate movements.

Household Demand for Loanable Funds

Households commonly demand loanable funds to finance housing expenditures. In addition, they finance the purchases of automobiles and household items, which results in installment debt. As the aggregate level of household income rises over time, so does installment debt. The level of installment debt as a percentage of disposable income has been increasing since 1983. It is generally lower in recessionary periods.

If households could be surveyed at any given point in time to indicate the quantity of loanable funds they would demand at various interest rate levels, there would be an inverse relationship between the interest rate and the quantity of loanable funds demanded. This simply means that at any point in time, households would demand a greater quantity of loanable funds at lower rates of interest.

Exhibit 2.1

Relationship between
Interest Rates and
Household Demand
(D_h) for Loanable Funds
at a Given Point in Time

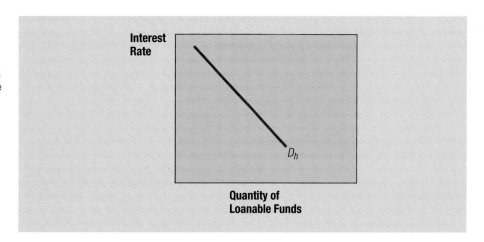

ILLUSTRATION Consider the household demand-for-loanable-funds schedule shown in Exhibit 2.1. This schedule depicts the amount of funds that would be demanded at various possible interest rates at a given point in time. Various events can cause household borrowing preferences to change and thereby shift the demand schedule. For example, if tax rates on household income are expected to significantly decrease in the future, households might believe that they can more easily afford future loan repayments and thus be willing to borrow more funds. For any interest rate, the quantity of loanable funds demanded by households would be greater as a result of the tax law adjustment. This represents an outward shift (to the right) in the demand schedule. ■

Business Demand for Loanable Funds

Businesses demand loanable funds to invest in long-term (fixed) and short-term assets. The quantity of funds demanded by businesses depends on the number of business projects to be implemented. Businesses evaluate a project by comparing the present value of its cash flows to its initial investment, as follows:

$$NPV = -INV + \sum_{t=1}^{n} \frac{CF_t}{(1 + k)^t}$$

where

NPV = net present value of project

INV = initial investment

CF_t = flow in period t

k = required rate of return on project

Projects with a positive net present value (NPV) are accepted because the present value of their benefits outweighs the costs. The required return to implement a given project will be lower if interest rates are lower because the cost of borrowing funds to support the project will be lower. Consequently, more projects will have positive NPVs, and businesses will need a greater amount of financing. This implies that businesses will demand a greater quantity of loanable funds when interest rates are lower, as illustrated in Exhibit 2.2.

In addition to long-term assets, businesses also invest in short-term assets (such as accounts receivable and inventory) in order to support ongoing operations. Any demand for funds resulting from this type of investment is positively related to the number of projects implemented and thus is inversely related to the interest rate. The

Exhibit 2.2

Relationship between Interest Rates and Business Demand (D_b) for Loanable Funds at a Given Point in Time

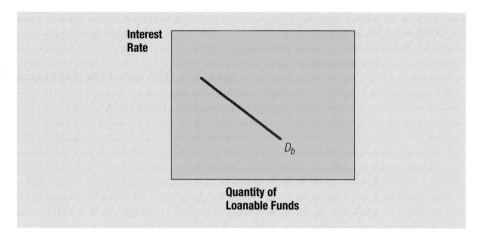

opportunity cost of investing in short-term assets is higher when interest rates are higher. Therefore, firms generally attempt to support ongoing operations with fewer funds during periods of high interest rates. This is another reason that a firm's total demand for loanable funds is inversely related to interest rates at any point in time. Although the demand for loanable funds by some businesses may be more sensitive to interest rates than others, all businesses are likely to demand more funds if interest rates are lower at a given point in time.

Shifts in the Demand for Loanable Funds The business demand-for-loanable-funds schedule can shift in reaction to any events that affect business borrowing preferences. If economic conditions become more favorable, the expected cash flows on various proposed projects will increase. More proposed projects will have expected returns that exceed a particular required rate of return (sometimes called the hurdle rate). Additional projects will be acceptable as a result of more favorable economic forecasts, causing an increased demand for loanable funds. The increase in demand will result in an outward shift in the demand curve (to the right).

Government Demand for Loanable Funds

http://
.gov Information on the U.S. government budget deficit.

http://www.treasurydirect

Whenever a government's planned expenditures cannot be completely covered by its incoming revenues from taxes and other sources, it demands loanable funds. Municipal (state and local) governments issue municipal bonds to obtain funds, while the federal government and its agencies issue Treasury securities and federal agency securities. These securities represent government debt.

The federal government's expenditure and tax policies are generally thought to be independent of interest rates. Thus, the federal government's demand for funds is said to be **interest-inelastic,** or insensitive to interest rates. In contrast, municipal governments sometimes postpone proposed expenditures if the cost of financing is too high, implying that their demand for loanable funds is somewhat sensitive to interest rates.

Like household and business demand, government demand for loanable funds can shift in response to various events.

ILLUSTRATION   The federal government's demand-for-loanable-funds schedule is D_{g1} in Exhibit 2.3. If new bills are passed that cause a net increase of $20 billion in the deficit, the federal government's demand for loanable funds will increase by that amount. The new demand schedule is D_{g2} in the exhibit. ■

Exhibit 2.3

Impact of Increased Government Budget Deficit on the Government Demand for Loanable Funds

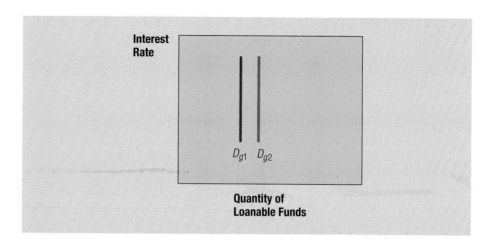

Foreign Demand for Loanable Funds

GL🌐BALASPECTS The demand for loanable funds in a given market also includes foreign demand by foreign governments or corporations. For example, the British government may obtain financing by issuing British Treasury securities to U.S. investors, representing a British demand for U.S. funds. Because foreign financial transactions are becoming so common, they can have a significant impact on the demand for loanable funds in any given country. A foreign country's demand for U.S. funds is influenced by the differential between its interest rates and U.S. rates (along with other factors). Other things being equal, a larger quantity of U.S. funds will be demanded by foreign governments and corporations if their domestic interest rates are high relative to U.S. rates. Therefore, for a given set of foreign interest rates, the quantity of U.S. loanable funds demanded by foreign governments or firms will be inversely related to U.S. interest rates.

The foreign demand schedule can shift in response to economic conditions. For example, assume the original foreign demand schedule is D_{f1} in Exhibit 2.4. If foreign interest rates rise, foreign firms and governments will likely increase their demand for U.S. funds, as represented by the shift from D_{f1} to D_{f2}.

http://
http://www.bloomberg.com/ markets Interest rate information.

Exhibit 2.4

Impact of Increased Foreign Interest Rates on the Foreign Demand for U.S. Loanable Funds

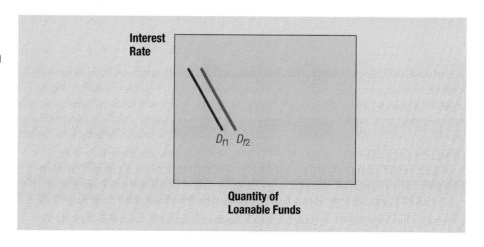

Aggregate Demand for Loanable Funds

The aggregate demand for loanable funds is the sum of the quantities demanded by the separate sectors at any given interest rate, as shown in Exhibit 2.5. Because most of these sectors are likely to demand a larger quantity of funds at lower interest rates (other things being equal), the aggregate demand for loanable funds is inversely related to interest rates at any point in time. If the demand schedule of any sector changes, the aggregate demand schedule will be affected as well.

Supply of Loanable Funds

The term "supply of loanable funds" is commonly used to refer to funds provided to financial markets by savers. The household sector is the largest supplier, but loanable funds are also supplied by some government units that temporarily generate more tax revenues than they spend or by some businesses whose cash inflows exceed outflows. Households as a group, however, represent a net supplier of loanable funds, whereas governments and businesses are net demanders of loanable funds.

Suppliers of loanable funds are willing to supply more funds if the interest rate (reward for supplying funds) is higher, other things being equal (Exhibit 2.6). A supply of loanable funds exists at even a very low interest rate because some households choose to postpone consumption until later years, even when the reward (interest rate) for saving is low.

Exhibit 2.5   Determination of the Aggregate Demand Schedule for Loanable Funds

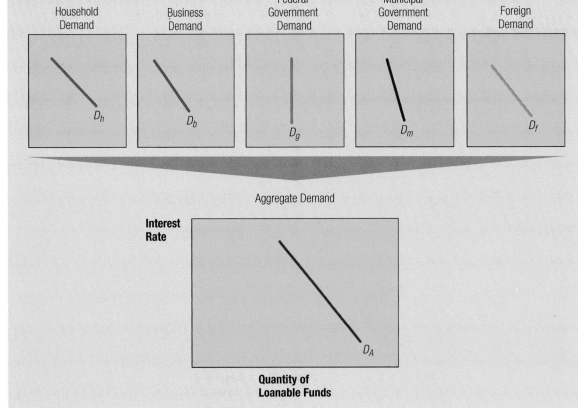

Exhibit 2.6
Aggregate Supply
Schedule for Loanable
Funds

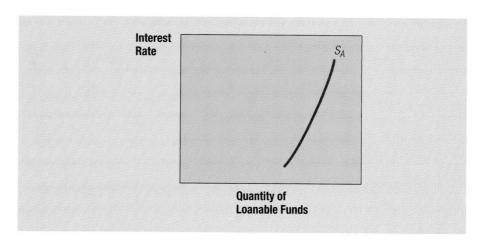

Foreign households, governments, and corporations commonly supply funds to their domestic markets by purchasing domestic securities. In addition, they have been a major creditor to the U.S. government by purchasing large amounts of Treasury securities. The large foreign supply of funds to the U.S. market is partially attributed to the high saving rates of foreign households.

Effects of the Fed The supply of loanable funds in the United States is also influenced by the monetary policy implemented by the Federal Reserve System. The Fed conducts monetary policy in an effort to control U.S. economic conditions. By affecting the supply of loanable funds, the Fed's monetary policy affects interest rates as will be described shortly. By influencing interest rates, the Fed is able to influence the amount of money that corporations and households are willing to borrow and spend.

Aggregate Supply of Funds The aggregate supply schedule of loanable funds represents the combination of all sector supply schedules along with the supply of funds provided by the Fed's monetary policy. The steep slope of the aggregate supply schedule in Exhibit 2.6 indicates that it is interest-inelastic, or somewhat insensitive to interest rates. The quantity of loanable funds demanded is normally expected to be more elastic, meaning more sensitive to interest rates, than the quantity of loanable funds supplied.

The supply curve can shift in or out in response to various conditions. For example, if the tax rate on interest income is reduced, the supply curve will shift outward, as households save more funds at each possible interest rate level. Conversely, if the tax rate on interest income is increased, the supply curve will shift inward, as households save fewer funds at each possible interest rate level.

Note that minimal attention has been given to financial institutions in this section. Although financial institutions play a critical intermediary role in channeling funds, they are not the ultimate suppliers of funds. Any change in a financial institution's supply of funds results only from a change in habits by the households, businesses, or governments that supply the funds.

Equilibrium Interest Rate

An understanding of equilibrium interest rates is necessary to assess how various events can affect interest rates. In reality, there are several different interest rates because some borrowers pay a higher rate than others. At this point, however, the focus is on the forces that cause the general level of interest rates to change, as interest rates across borrowers tend to change in the same direction. The determination of an equilibrium interest rate is presented first from an algebraic perspective and then from a graphic perspective. Following this presentation, several examples are offered to reinforce the concept.

Algebraic Presentation   The equilibrium interest rate is the rate that equates the aggregate demand for funds with the aggregate supply of loanable funds. The aggregate demand for funds (D_A) can be written as

$$D_A = D_h + D_b + D_g + D_m + D_f$$

where D_h = household demand for loanable funds
D_b = business demand for loanable funds
D_g = federal government demand for loanable funds
D_m = municipal government demand for loanable funds
D_f = foreign demand for loanable funds

The aggregate supply of funds (S_A) can be written as

$$S_A = S_h + S_b + S_g + S_m + S_f$$

where S_h = household supply of loanable funds
S_b = business supply of loanable funds
S_g = federal government supply of loanable funds
S_m = municipal government supply of loanable funds
S_f = foreign supply of loanable funds

In equilibrium, $D_A = S_A$. If the aggregate demand for loanable funds increases without a corresponding increase in aggregate supply, there will be a shortage of loanable funds. Interest rates will rise until an additional supply of loanable funds is available to accommodate the excess demand. If the aggregate supply of loanable funds increases without a corresponding increase in aggregate demand, there will be a surplus of loanable funds. Interest rates will fall until the quantity of funds supplied no longer exceeds the quantity of funds demanded.

In many cases, both supply and demand for loanable funds are changing. Given an initial equilibrium situation, the equilibrium interest rate should rise when $D_A > S_A$ and fall when $D_A < S_A$.

Graphic Presentation   By combining the aggregate demand and aggregate supply schedules of loanable funds (refer to Exhibits 2.5 and 2.6), it is possible to compare the total amount of funds that would be demanded to the total amount of funds that would be supplied at any particular interest rate. Exhibit 2.7 illustrates the combined demand and supply schedules. At the equilibrium interest rate of i, the supply of loanable funds is equal to the demand for loanable funds.

At any interest rate above i, there is a surplus of loanable funds. Some potential suppliers of funds would be unable to successfully supply their funds at the prevailing interest rate. Once the market interest rate decreases to i, the quantity of funds supplied is sufficiently reduced and the quantity of funds demanded is sufficiently increased such that there is no longer a surplus of funds. When a disequilibrium situation exists, market forces should cause an adjustment in interest rates until equilibrium is achieved.

If the prevailing interest rate is below i, there will be a shortage of loanable funds. Borrowers will not be able to obtain all the funds that they desire at that rate. Because of the shortage of funds, the interest rate will increase, causing two reactions. First,

Exhibit 2.7
Interest Rate
Equilibrium

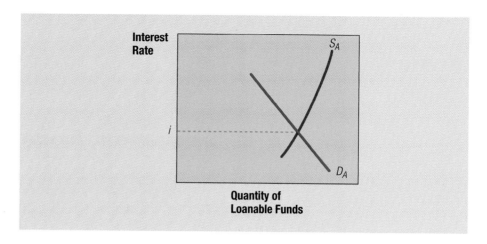

more savers will enter the market to supply loanable funds now that the reward (interest rate) is higher. Second, some potential borrowers will decide not to demand loanable funds at the higher interest rate. Once the interest rate rises to i, the quantity of loanable funds supplied has increased and the quantity of loanable funds demanded has decreased to the extent that a shortage no longer exists. An equilibrium position is achieved once again.

Economic Forces That Affect Interest Rates

Although it is useful to identify those who supply or demand loanable funds, it is also necessary to recognize the underlying economic forces that cause a change in the supply of or the demand for loanable funds. The following economic factors influence the demand for or supply of loanable funds and therefore influence interest rates.

Impact of Economic Growth on Interest Rates

Changes in economic conditions cause a shift in the demand schedule for loanable funds, which affects the equilibrium interest rate.

ILLUSTRATION When businesses anticipate that economic conditions will improve, they revise upward the cash flows expected for various projects under consideration. Consequently, businesses identify more projects that are worth pursuing, and they are willing to borrow more funds. Their willingness to borrow more funds at any given interest rate reflects an outward shift in the demand schedule (to the right).

The supply-of-loanable-funds schedule may also shift in response to economic growth, but it is more difficult to know how it will shift. It is possible that the increased expansion by businesses will lead to more income for construction crews and others who service the expansion. In this case, the quantity of savings, and therefore of loanable funds supplied at any possible interest rate, could increase, causing an outward shift in the supply schedule. There is no assurance that the volume of savings will actually increase, however. Even if a shift occurs, it will likely be of a smaller magnitude than the shift in the demand schedule.

Overall, the expected impact of the increased expansion by businesses is an outward shift in the demand schedule and no obvious change in the supply schedule (Exhibit 2.8). The shift in the aggregate demand schedule to D_{A2} in the exhibit causes an increase in the equilibrium interest rate to i_2. ■

Exhibit 2.8
Impact of Increased
Expansion by Firms

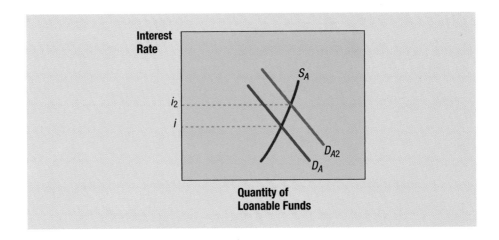

Just as economic growth puts upward pressure on interest rates, an economic slowdown puts downward pressure on the equilibrium interest rate.

ILLUSTRATION   A slowdown in the economy will cause the demand schedule to shift inward (to the left), reflecting less demand for loanable funds at any possible interest rate. The supply schedule may possibly shift a little, but the direction of its shift is uncertain. One could argue that a slowdown should cause increased saving at any possible interest rate as households prepare for the possibility of being laid off. At the same time, the gradual reduction in labor income that occurs during an economic slowdown could reduce households' ability to save. Historical data support this latter expectation. Any shift that does occur will likely be minor relative to the shift in the demand schedule. Therefore, the equilibrium interest rate is expected to decrease, as illustrated in Exhibit 2.9. ■

Impact of Inflation on Interest Rates

Changes in inflationary expectations can affect interest rates by affecting the amount of spending by households or businesses. Decisions to spend affect the amount saved (supply of funds) and the amount borrowed (demand for funds).

Exhibit 2.9
Impact of an Economic
Slowdown

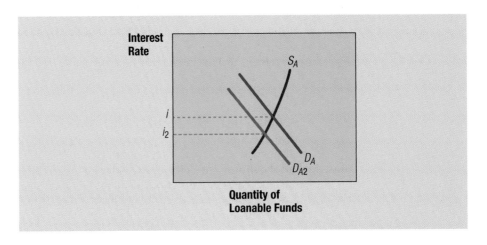

ILLUSTRATION   Assume the U.S. inflation rate is expected to increase. Households that supply funds may reduce their savings at any interest rate level so that they can make more purchases now before prices rise. This shift in behavior is reflected by an inward shift (to the left) in the supply curve of loanable funds. In addition, households and businesses may be willing to borrow more funds at any interest rate level so that they can purchase products now before prices increase. This is reflected by an outward shift (to the right) in the demand curve for loanable funds. These shifts are illustrated in Exhibit 2.10. The new equilibrium interest rate is higher because of the shifts in saving and borrowing behavior. ∎

Fisher Effect   More than 50 years ago, Irving Fisher proposed a theory of interest rate determination that is still widely used today. It does not contradict the loanable funds theory but simply offers an additional explanation for interest rate movements. Fisher proposed that nominal interest payments compensate savers in two ways. First, they compensate for a saver's reduced purchasing power. Second, they provide an additional premium to savers for forgoing present consumption. Savers are willing to forgo consumption only if they receive a premium on their savings above the anticipated rate of inflation, as shown in the following equation:

$$i = E(\text{INF}) + i_R$$

where
$$i = \text{nominal or quoted rate of interest}$$
$$E(\text{INF}) = \text{expected inflation rate}$$
$$i_R = \text{real interest rate}$$

This relationship between interest rates and expected inflation is often referred to as the **Fisher effect.** The difference between the nominal interest rate and the expected inflation rate is the real return to a saver after adjusting for the reduced purchasing power over the time period of concern. It is referred to as the **real interest rate** because, unlike the nominal rate of interest, it adjusts for the expected rate of inflation. The preceding equation can be rearranged to express the real interest rate as

$$i_R = i - E(\text{INF})$$

When the inflation rate is higher than anticipated, the real interest rate is relatively low. Borrowers benefit because they were able to borrow at a lower nominal interest rate than would have been offered if inflation had been accurately forecasted. When the inflation rate is lower than anticipated, the real interest rate is relatively high and borrowers are adversely affected.

Exhibit 2.10
Impact of an Increase in Inflationary Expectations on Interest Rates

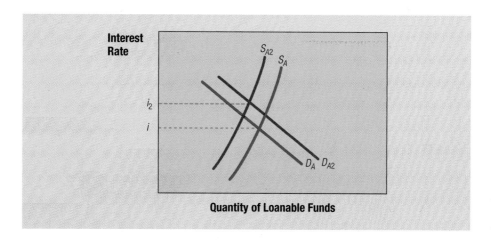

Throughout the text, the term *interest rate* will be used to represent the nominal, or quoted, rate of interest. Keep in mind, however, that because of inflation, purchasing power is not necessarily increasing during periods of rising interest rates.

Impact of Monetary Policy on Interest Rates

The Federal Reserve can affect the supply of loanable funds by increasing or reducing the total amount of deposits held at commercial banks or other depository institutions. The process by which the Fed adjusts the money supply is described in Chapter 4. When the Fed increases the money supply, it increases the supply of loanable funds, which places downward pressure on interest rates.

If the Fed reduces the money supply, it reduces the supply of loanable funds. Assuming no change in demand, this action places upward pressure on interest rates.

Impact of the Budget Deficit on Interest Rates

http://www.federalreserve
.gov/FOMC How the Fed
controls the money supply.

When the federal government enacts fiscal policies that result in more expenditures than tax revenue, the budget deficit is increased. Consider how an increase in the federal government deficit would affect interest rates, assuming no other changes in habits by consumers and firms occur. A higher federal government deficit increases the quantity of loanable funds demanded at any prevailing interest rate, causing an outward shift in the demand schedule. Assuming no offsetting increase in the supply schedule, interest rates will rise. Given a certain amount of loanable funds supplied to the market (through savings), excessive government demand for these funds tends to "crowd out" the private demand (by consumers and corporations) for funds. The federal government may be willing to pay whatever is necessary to borrow these funds, but the private sector may not. This impact is known as the **crowding-out effect.** Exhibit 2.11 illustrates the flow of funds between the federal government and the private sector.

There is a counterargument that the supply schedule might shift outward if the government creates more jobs by spending more funds than it collects from the public (this is what causes the deficit in the first place). If this were to occur, the deficit might not necessarily place upward pressure on interest rates. Much research has investigated this issue and, in general, has shown that higher deficits place upward pressure on interest rates.

The U.S. government is a major participant in the demand for loanable funds due to large budget deficits in recent years. Since a large budget deficit results in a large

Exhibit 2.11
Flow of Funds
between the Federal
Government and the
Private Sector

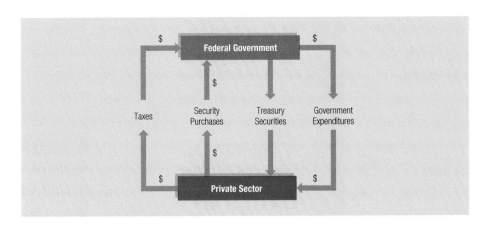

demand for borrowed funds, it may be surprising that U.S. interest rates have been low. The large government demand for funds was offset by a weak demand for funds by firms and individuals, a large supply of savings provided by individuals, and an increase in the money supply provided by the Fed.

Impact of Foreign Flows of Funds on Interest Rates

GL🌐BALASPECTS The interest rate for a specific currency is determined by the demand for funds denominated in that currency and the supply of funds available in that currency.

ILLUSTRATION The supply and demand schedules for the U.S. dollar and for Brazil's currency (the real) are compared for a given point in time in Exhibit 2.12. Although the demand schedule for loanable funds should be downward sloping for every currency and the supply schedule should be upward sloping, the actual positions of these schedules vary among currencies. First, notice that the demand and supply curves are farther to the right for the dollar than for the Brazilian real. The amount of dollar-denominated loanable funds supplied and demanded is much greater than the amount of Brazilian real-denominated loanable funds because the U.S. economy is much larger than Brazil's economy.

Also notice that the positions of the demand and supply schedules for loanable funds are much higher for the Brazilian real than for the dollar. The supply schedule for loanable funds denominated in the Brazilian real shows that hardly any amount of savings would be supplied at low interest rate levels because the high inflation in Brazil encourages households to spend all of their disposable income before prices increase more. It discourages households from saving unless the interest rate is sufficiently high. In addition, the demand for loanable funds in the Brazilian real shows that borrowers are willing to borrow even at very high rates of interest because they want to make purchases now before prices increase. Firms are willing to pay 20 percent interest on a loan to purchase machines whose prices will have increased by 30 percent by next year.

Because of the different positions of the demand and supply schedules for the two currencies shown in Exhibit 2.12, the equilibrium interest rate is much higher for the Brazilian real than for the dollar. As the demand and supply schedules change

Exhibit 2.12
Demand and Supply Schedules for Loanable Funds Denominated in U.S. Dollars and Brazilian Real

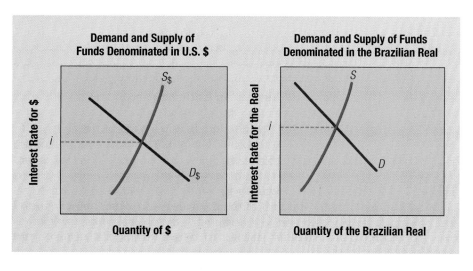

over time for a specific currency, so will the equilibrium interest rate. For example, if Brazil's government could substantially reduce the local inflation, the supply schedule of loanable funds denominated in real would shift out (to the right) while the demand schedule of loanable funds would shift in (to the left), which would result in a lower equilibrium interest rate. Investors from other countries commonly invest in savings accounts in countries such as Brazil where the interest rates are high. However, the currencies of these countries usually weaken over time, which may more than offset the interest rate advantage. ■

In recent years, massive flows of funds have shifted between countries, causing abrupt adjustments in the supply of funds available in each country and therefore affecting interest rates. In general, the shifts are driven by large institutional investors seeking a high return on their investments. These investors commonly attempt to invest funds in debt securities in countries where interest rates are high and where the currency is not expected to weaken.

Summary of Forces That Affect Interest Rates

In general, economic conditions are the primary forces behind a change in the supply of savings provided by households or a change in the demand for funds by households, businesses, or the government. The saving behavior of the households that supply funds in the United States is partially influenced by U.S. fiscal policy, which determines the taxes paid by U.S. households and thus determines the level of disposable income. The Federal Reserve's monetary policy also affects the supply of funds in the United States because it determines the U.S. money supply. The supply of funds provided to the United States by foreign investors is influenced by foreign economic conditions, including foreign interest rates.

The demand for funds in the United States is indirectly affected by U.S. monetary and fiscal policies because these policies influence economic conditions such as economic growth and inflation, which affect business demand for funds. Fiscal policy determines the budget deficit and therefore determines the federal government demand for funds.

ILLUSTRATION   A brief survey of U.S. interest rates over recent decades illustrates how these forces can interact to affect interest rates. In the late 1970s, interest rates were high as a result of a strong economy and inflationary expectations. A recession in the early 1980s caused a weak economy, which led to a decline in interest rates. In the late 1980s, interest rates drifted upward in response to a strong economy but then declined in the early 1990s as the economy weakened. In 1994, when economic growth resumed, interest rates increased. For the next several years, however, they drifted lower. Even though economic growth was strong in the late 1990s, the government demand for funds was unusually low as the U.S. fiscal budget had a surplus at that time. From 2000 to the beginning of 2003, the U.S. economy was very weak, which reduced the demand for loanable funds and caused interest rates to reach their lowest level in more than 30 years. In the 2005–2007 period, U.S. economic growth increased, and interest rates rose. Exhibit 2.13 shows nominal interest rates since 1980. ■

This summary does not cover every possible interaction among the forces that can affect interest rate movements, but it is sufficient for understanding why interest rates change over time. In fact, it will be used as the base to explain why prices of various securities change over time in other chapters, because many security prices are affected by interest rate movements.

Exhibit 2.13   Interest Rates over Time (One-Year Treasury Bill Rate Used as a Proxy)

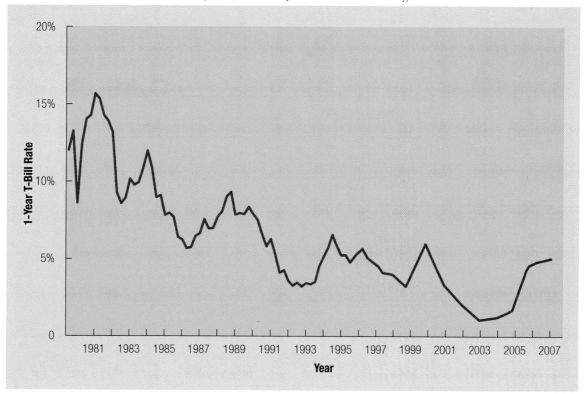

Forecasting Interest Rates

Exhibit 2.14 summarizes the key factors that are evaluated when forecasting interest rates. With an understanding of how each factor affects interest rates, it is possible to forecast how interest rates may change in the future. When forecasting household demand for loanable funds, it may be necessary to assess consumer credit data to determine the borrowing capacity of households. The potential supply of loanable funds provided by households may be determined in a similar manner by assessing factors that affect the earning power of households.

Business demand for loanable funds can be forecasted by assessing future plans for corporate expansion and the future state of the economy. Federal government demand for loanable funds could be influenced by the future state of the economy because it affects tax revenues to be received and the amount of unemployment compensation to be paid out, factors that affect the size of the government deficit. The Federal Reserve System's money supply targets may be assessed by reviewing public statements about the Fed's future objectives, although those statements are somewhat vague.

To forecast future interest rates, the net demand for funds (ND) should be forecast:

$$ND = D_A - S_A$$
$$= (D_h + D_b + D_g + D_m + D_f) - (S_h + S_b + S_g + S_m + S_f)$$

Exhibit 2.14   Framework for Forecasting Interest Rates

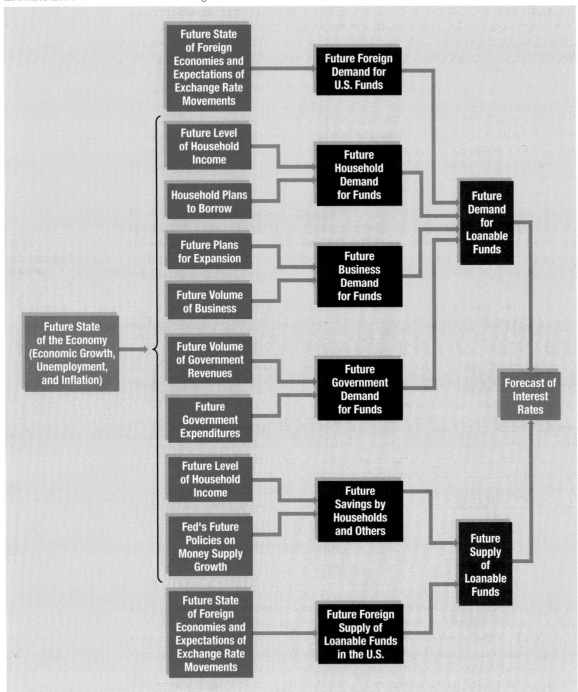

If the forecasted level of *ND* is positive or negative, a disequilibrium will exist temporarily. If positive, it will be corrected by an upward adjustment in interest rates. If negative, it will be corrected by a downward adjustment. The larger the forecasted magnitude of *ND*, the larger the adjustment in interest rates.

Some analysts focus more on changes in D_A and S_A than on estimating the aggregate level of D_A and S_A. For example, assume that today the equilibrium interest rate is 7 percent. This interest rate will change only if D_A and S_A change to create a temporary disequilibrium. If the government demand for funds (D_g) is expected to increase substantially, and no other components are expected to change, D_A will exceed S_A, placing upward pressure on interest rates. Thus, the forecast of future interest rates can be derived without estimating every component comprising D_A and S_A.

Summary

■ The loanable funds framework shows how the equilibrium interest rate is dependent on the aggregate supply of available funds and the aggregate demand for funds. As conditions cause the aggregate supply or demand schedules to change, interest rates gravitate toward a new equilibrium.

■ The relevant factors that affect interest rate movements include changes in economic growth, inflation, the budget deficit, foreign interest rates, and the money supply. These factors can have a strong impact on the aggregate supply of funds or on the aggregate demand for funds and therefore can affect the equilibrium interest rate. In particular, economic growth has a strong influence on the demand for loanable funds, and changes in the money supply have a strong impact on the supply of loanable funds.

■ Given that the equilibrium interest rate is determined by supply and demand conditions, changes in the interest rate can be forecasted by forecasting changes in the supply of or the demand for loanable funds. Thus, the factors that influence the supply of and the demand for funds must be forecasted in order to forecast interest rates.

Point Counter-Point

Does a Large Fiscal Budget Deficit Result in Higher Interest Rates?

Point No. In some years (such as 2003), the fiscal budget deficit was large and interest rates were very low.

Counter-Point Yes. When the federal government borrows large amounts of funds, it can crowd out other potential borrowers, and the interest rates are bid up by the deficit units.

Who Is Correct? Use the Internet to learn more about this issue. Offer your own opinion on this issue.

Questions and Applications

1. **Interest Rate Movements** Explain why interest rates changed as they did over the past year.

2. **Interest Elasticity** Explain what is meant by interest elasticity. Would you expect the federal government's demand for loanable funds to be more or less interest-elastic than household demand for loanable funds? Why?

3. **Impact of Government Spending** If the federal government planned to expand the space program, how might this affect interest rates?

4. **Impact of a Recession** Explain why interest rates tend to decrease during recessionary periods. Review historical interest rates to determine how they reacted to recessionary periods. Explain this reaction.

5. **Impact of the Economy** Explain how the expected interest rate in one year is dependent on your expectation of economic growth and inflation.

6. **Impact of the Money Supply** Should increasing money supply growth place upward or downward pressure on interest rates?

7. **Impact of Exchange Rates on Interest Rates** Assume that if the U.S. dollar strengthens, it can place downward pressure on U.S. inflation. Based on this information, how might expectations of a strong dollar affect the demand for loanable funds in the United States and U.S. interest rates? Is there any reason to think that expectations of a strong dollar could also affect the supply of loanable funds? Explain.

8. **Nominal versus Real Interest Rate** What is the difference between the nominal interest rate and the real interest rate? What is the logic behind the Fisher effect's implied positive relationship between expected inflation and nominal interest rates?

9. **Real Interest Rate** Estimate the real interest rate over the last year. If financial market participants overestimate inflation in a particular period, will real interest rates be relatively high or low? Explain.

10. **Forecasting Interest Rates** Why do forecasts of interest rates differ among experts?

Advanced Questions

11. **Impact of Stock Market Crises** During periods in which investors suddenly become fearful that stocks are overvalued, they dump their stocks, and the stock market experiences a major decline. During these periods, interest rates tend to decline. Use the loanable funds framework discussed in this chapter to explain how the massive selling of stocks leads to lower interest rates.

12. **Impact of Expected Inflation** How might expectations of higher oil prices affect the demand for loanable funds, the supply of loanable funds, and interest rates in the United States? Will the interest rates of other countries be affected in the same way? Explain.

13. **Global Interaction of Interest Rates** Why might you expect interest rate movements of various industrialized countries to be more highly correlated in recent years than in earlier years?

14. **Impact of War** A war tends to cause significant reactions in financial markets. Why would a war in Iraq place upward pressure on U.S. interest rates? Why might some investors expect a war like this to place downward pressure on U.S. interest rates?

15. **Impact of September 11** Offer an argument for why the terrorist attack on the United States on September 11, 2001, could have placed downward pressure on U.S. interest rates. Offer an argument for why the terrorist attack could have placed upward pressure on U.S. interest rates.

16. **Impact of Government Spending** Jayhawk Forecasting Services analyzed several factors that could affect interest rates in the future. Most factors were expected to place downward pressure on interest rates. Jayhawk also felt that although the annual budget deficit was to be cut by 40 percent from the previous year, it would still be very large. Thus, Jayhawk believed that the deficit's impact would more than offset the other effects and therefore forecast interest rates to increase by 2 percent. Comment on Jayhawk's logic.

17. **Decomposing Interest Rate Movements** The interest rate on a one-year loan can be decomposed into a one-year risk-free (free from default risk) component and a risk premium that reflects the potential for default on the loan in that year. A change in economic conditions can affect the risk-free rate and the risk premium. The risk-free rate is normally affected by changing economic conditions to a greater degree than the risk premium. Explain how a weaker economy will likely affect the risk-free component, the risk premium, and the overall cost of a one-year loan obtained by (a) the Treasury, and (b) a corporation. Will the change in the cost of borrowing be more pronounced for the Treasury or for the corporation? Why?

18. **Forecasting Interest Rates Based on Prevailing Conditions** Consider the prevailing conditions for inflation (including oil prices), the economy, the budget deficit, and the Fed's monetary policy that could affect interest rates. Based on prevailing conditions, do you think interest rates will likely increase or decrease during this semester? Offer some logic to support your answer. Which factor do you think will have the biggest impact on interest rates?

Interpreting Financial News

Interpret the following comments made by Wall Street analysts and portfolio managers:

a. "The flight of funds from bank deposits to U.S. stocks will pressure interest rates."

b. "Since Japanese interest rates have recently declined to very low levels, expect a reduction in U.S. interest rates."

c. "The cost of borrowing by U.S. firms is dictated by the degree to which the federal government spends more than it taxes."

Managing in Financial Markets

Forecasting Interest Rates As the treasurer of a manufacturing company, your task is to forecast the direction of interest rates. You plan to borrow funds and may use the forecast of interest rates to determine whether you should obtain a loan with a fixed interest rate or a floating interest rate. The following information can be considered when assessing the future direction of interest rates:

■ Economic growth has been high over the last two years, but you expect that it will be stagnant over the next year.

■ Inflation has been 3 percent over each of the last few years, and you expect that it will be about the same over the next year.

■ The federal government has announced major cuts in its spending, which should have a major impact on the budget deficit.

■ The Federal Reserve is not expected to affect the existing supply of loanable funds over the next year.

■ The overall level of savings by households is not expected to change.

a. Given the preceding information, determine how the demand for and the supply of loanable funds would be affected (if at all), and determine the future direction of interest rates.

b. You can obtain a one-year loan at a fixed rate of 8 percent or a floating-rate loan that is currently at 8 percent but would be revised every month in accordance with general interest rate movements. Which type of loan is more appropriate based on the information provided?

c. Assume that Canadian interest rates have abruptly risen just as you have completed your forecast of future U.S. interest rates. Consequently, Canadian interest rates are now 2 percentage points above U.S. interest rates. How might this specific situation place pressure on U.S. interest rates? Considering this situation along with the other information provided, would you change your forecast of the future direction of U.S. interest rates?

Problems

1. **Nominal Rate of Interest** Suppose the real interest rate is 6 percent and the expected inflation is 2 percent. What would you expect the nominal rate of interest to be?

2. **Real Interest Rate** Suppose that Treasury bills are currently paying 9 percent and the expected inflation is 3 percent. What is the real interest rate?

Flow of Funds Exercise

How the Flow of Funds Affects Interest Rates

Recall that Carson Company has obtained substantial loans from finance companies and commercial banks. The interest rate on the loans is tied to market interest rates and is adjusted every six months. Thus, its cost of obtaining funds is sensitive to interest rate movements. Because of its expectations that the U.S. economy will strengthen, Carson plans to grow in the future by expanding its business and through acquisitions. Carson expects that it will need substantial long-term financing to finance its growth and plans to borrow additional funds either through loans or by issuing bonds. It is also considering issuing stock to raise funds in the next year.

a. Explain why Carson should be very interested in future interest rate movements.

b. Given Carson's expectations, do you think that Carson expects interest rates to increase or decrease in the future? Explain.

c. If Carson's expectations of future interest rates are correct, how would this affect its cost of borrowing on its existing loans and on future loans?

d. Explain why Carson's expectations about future interest rates may affect its decision about when to borrow funds and whether to obtain floating-rate or fixed-rate loans.

Internet/Excel Exercises

1. Go to http://research.stlouisfed.org/fred2. Under "Categories," select "Interest rates" and then select the three-month Treasury bill series (secondary market). Describe how this rate has changed in recent months. Using the information in this chapter, explain why the interest rate changed as it did.

2. Using the same website, retrieve data at the beginning of the last 20 quarters for interest rates (based on the three-month Treasury bill rate) and the producer price index for all commodities and place the data in two columns of an Excel spreadsheet. Derive the change in interest rates on a quarterly basis. Then derive the percentage change in the producer price index on a quarterly basis, which serves as a measure of inflation. Apply regression analysis in which the change in interest rates is the dependent variable and inflation is the independent variable (see Appendix B for information about applying regression analysis). Explain the relationship that you find. Does it appear that inflation and interest rate movements are positively related?

WSJ Exercise

Forecasting Interest Rates

Review the "Credit Markets" section in a recent issue of *The Wall Street Journal* (listed in the index on the first page of Section C). Use this section to determine the factors likely to have the largest impact on future interest rate movements. Then create your own forecasts as to whether interest rates will increase or decrease from now until the end of this school term, based on your assessment of any factors that affect interest rates. Explain your forecast.

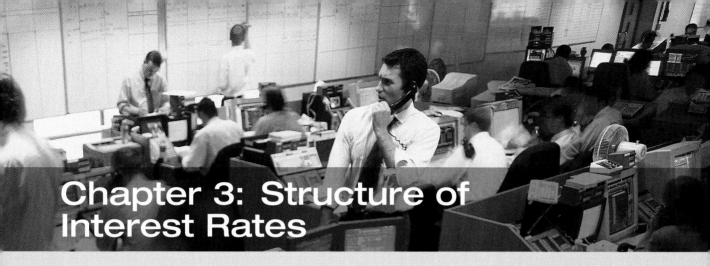

Chapter 3: Structure of Interest Rates

The annual interest rate offered by debt securities at a given point in time varies among debt securities. Consequently, the yields offered by debt securities at a given point in time have a particular structure. Some types of debt securities always offer a higher yield than others. Individual and institutional investors must understand why quoted yields vary so that they can determine whether the extra yield on a given security outweighs any unfavorable characteristics. Financial managers of corporations or government agencies in need of funds must understand why quoted yields of debt securities vary so that they can estimate the yield they would have to offer in order to sell new debt securities.

The specific objectives of this chapter are to:

■ describe how characteristics of debt securities cause their yields to vary,

■ demonstrate how to estimate the appropriate yield for any particular debt security, and

■ explain the theories behind the term structure of interest rates (relationship between the term to maturity and the yield of securities).

Characteristics of Debt Securities That Cause Their Yields to Vary

Debt securities offer different yields because they exhibit different characteristics that influence the yield to be offered. In general, securities with unfavorable characteristics will offer higher yields to entice investors. Some debt securities, however, have favorable features as well. The yields on debt securities are affected by the following characteristics:

- Credit (default) risk
- Liquidity
- Tax status
- Term to maturity

The yields on bonds may also be affected by special provisions, as described in Chapter 7.

Credit (Default) Risk

Because most securities are subject to the risk of default, investors must consider the creditworthiness of the security issuer. Although investors always have the option of purchasing risk-free Treasury securities, they may prefer some other securities if the yield compensates them for the risk. Thus, if all other characteristics besides credit (default) risk are equal, securities with a higher degree of risk would have to offer higher yields to be chosen. Credit risk is especially relevant for longer-term securities that expose creditors to the possibility of default for a longer time.

Credit risk premiums of 1 percent, 2 percent, or more may not seem significant. But for a corporation borrowing $30 million through the issuance of bonds, an extra percentage point as a premium reflects $300,000 in additional interest expenses per year.

Investors may personally assess the creditworthiness of corporations that issue bonds, or they may use bond ratings provided by rating agencies. These ratings are based on a financial assessment of the issuing corporation. The higher the rating, the lower the perceived credit risk. As time passes, economic conditions can change, and the perceived credit risk of a corporation can change as well. Thus, bonds previously issued by a firm may be rated at one level, while a subsequent issue from the same firm is rated at a different level. The ratings can also differ if the collateral provisions differ among the bonds.

Rating Agencies Rating agencies charge the issuers of debt securities a fee for assessing the default risk of their securities. The ratings are then provided through various financial media outlets at no cost to investors who wish to use the ratings. The most popular rating agencies are Moody's Investor Service and Standard & Poor's Corporation. A summary of their rating classification schedules is provided in Exhibit 3.1. Moody's ratings range from Aaa for highest quality to C for lowest quality, and Standard & Poor's range from AAA to D. Because these rating agencies use different methods to assess the creditworthiness of firms and state governments, a particular bond could be assigned a different rating by each agency; nevertheless, differences are usually small.

Some financial institutions such as commercial banks are required by law to invest only in **investment-grade bonds,** that is, bonds that are rated as Baa or better by Moody's and BBB or better by Standard & Poor's. This requirement is intended to limit the portfolio risk of the financial institutions.

Accuracy of Credit Ratings The ratings issued by the agencies are opinions, not guarantees. In general, credit ratings have served as reasonable indicators of the likelihood of default. Bonds assigned a low credit rating experience default more frequently than bonds assigned a high credit rating. Nevertheless, credit rating agencies do not always detect firms' financial problems. For example, they did not recognize Enron's financial problems until shortly before Enron filed for bankruptcy.

Exhibit 3.1
Rating Classification by
Rating Agencies

Description of Security	Ratings Assigned by:	
	Moody's	Standard & Poor's
Highest quality	Aaa	AAA
High quality	Aa	AA
High-medium quality	A	A
Medium quality	Baa	BBB
Medium-low quality	Ba	BB
Low quality (speculative)	B	B
Poor quality	Caa	CCC
Very poor quality	Ca	CC
Lowest quality (in default)	C	DDD, D

Yields on Treasury bonds and other types of securities like those shown here are provided by *The Wall Street Journal*. This information can be used to determine the yield differential between bonds. The differential is commonly due to credit risk but may also reflect a difference in liquidity or taxes. Notice from the table that the Dow Jones (DJ) corporate yield (on bonds issued by highly rated corporations) is higher than the Treasury bond yield. Also notice that the yield on high-yield bonds (corporate bonds that have a higher level of credit risk) is higher than the DJ corporate yield. The muni-master yield reflects municipal bonds. Notice that their yields are even lower than the Treasury bond yield. This occurs because the income from municipal bonds is not subject to federal income tax. The table also shows the range of yields offered on the various types of securities in the last

Corporate Borrowing Rates and Yields

Bond total return index	Close	YIELD (%) Last	YIELD (%) Week ago	52-WEEK High	52-WEEK Low	TOTAL RETURN (%) 52-wk	TOTAL RETURN (%) 3-yr
Treasury, Ryan ALM	904.20	**4.636**	4.592	5.257	4.460	**5.38**	1.98
10-yr Treasury, Ryan ALM	1018.38	**4.652**	4.620	5.247	4.427	**5.74**	2.75
DJ Corporate	198.76	**5.667**	5.627	6.308	5.442	**6.61**	3.77
Aggregate, Lehman Bros.	1211.79	**5.280**	5.250	5.900	5.080	**6.65**	11.63
High Yield 100, Merrill Lynch	1586.12	**7.105**	7.039	8.250	6.866	**10.48**	n.a.
Fixed-Rate MBS, Lehman	1259.43	**5.560**	5.550	6.230	5.400	**7.06**	13.65
Muni Master, Merrill	335.54	**3.920**	3.890	6.305	3.730	**5.03**	4.29
EMBI Global, J.P. Morgan	n.a.	**n.a.**	6.414	7.565	6.391	**n.a.**	n.a.

Sources: J.P. Morgan; Ryan ALM; Ryan Labs; Lehman Brothers; Merrill Lynch

year, as well as the return from holding these types of securities over the last year and over the last three years.

Their inability to detect Enron's problems may be partially attributed to Enron's fraudulent financial statements that the credit agencies presumed were accurate.

Liquidity

Investors prefer securities that are *liquid*, meaning that they could be easily converted to cash without a loss in value. Thus, if all other characteristics are equal, securities with less liquidity will have to offer a higher yield to be preferred. Securities with a short-term maturity or an active secondary market have greater liquidity. For investors who will not need their funds until the securities mature, less liquidity is tolerable. Other investors, however, are willing to accept a lower return in exchange for a high degree of liquidity.

Tax Status

Investors are more concerned with after-tax income than before-tax income earned on securities. If all other characteristics are similar, taxable securities will have to offer a higher before-tax yield to investors than tax-exempt securities to be preferred. The extra compensation required on such taxable securities depends on the tax rates of individual and institutional investors. Investors in high tax brackets benefit most from tax-exempt securities.

When assessing the expected yields of various securities with similar risk and maturity, it is common to convert them into an after-tax form, as follows:

$$Y_{at} = Y_{bt}(1 - T)$$

where

Y_{at} = after-tax yield

Y_{bt} = before-tax yield

T = investor's marginal tax rate

Investors retain only a percentage $(1 - T)$ of the before-tax yield once taxes are paid.

45

ILLUSTRATION Consider a taxable security that offers a before-tax yield of 14 percent. When converted into after-tax terms, the yield will be reduced by the tax percentage. The precise after-tax yield is dependent on the tax rate (T). If the tax rate of the investor is 20 percent, the after-tax yield will be

$$Y_{at} = Y_{bt}(1 - T)$$
$$Y_{at} = 14\%(1 - .2)$$
$$= 11.2\%$$

Exhibit 3.2 presents after-tax yields based on a variety of tax rates and before-tax yields. For example, a taxable security with a before-tax yield of 6 percent will generate an after-tax yield of 5.4 percent to an investor in the 10 percent tax bracket, 4.8 percent to an investor in the 20 percent tax bracket, and so on. This exhibit shows why investors in high tax brackets are attracted to tax-exempt securities. ■

Computing the Equivalent Before-Tax Yield In some cases, investors wish to determine the before-tax yield necessary to match the after-tax yield of a tax-exempt security that has a similar risk and maturity. This can be done by rearranging the terms of the previous equation:

$$Y_{bt} = \frac{Y_{at}}{(1 - T)}$$

Suppose that a firm in the 20 percent tax bracket is aware of a tax-exempt security that is paying a yield of 8 percent. To match this after-tax yield, taxable securities must offer a before-tax yield of

$$Y_{bt} = \frac{Y_{at}}{(1 - T)} = \frac{8\%}{(1 - .2)} = 10\%$$

State taxes should be considered along with federal taxes in determining the after-tax yield. Treasury securities are exempt from state income tax, and municipal securities are sometimes exempt as well. Because states impose different income tax rates, a particular security's after-tax yield may vary with the location of the investor.

Term to Maturity

Maturity differs among debt securities and is another reason that debt security yields differ. The **term structure of interest rates** defines the relationship between the term to maturity and the annualized yield of debt securities at a specific point in time, holding other factors such as risk constant.

Exhibit 3.2 After-Tax Yields Based on Various Tax Rates and Before-Tax Yields

Tax Rate	\multicolumn{8}{c}{Before-Tax Yield}
	6%	8%	10%	12%	14%	16%	18%	20%
10%	5.40%	7.20%	9.00%	10.80%	12.60%	14.40%	16.20%	18.00%
15	5.10	6.80	8.50	10.20	11.90	13.60	15.30	17.00
20	4.80	6.40	8.00	9.60	11.20	12.80	14.40	16.00
28	4.32	5.76	7.20	8.64	10.08	11.52	12.96	14.40
34	3.96	5.28	6.60	7.92	9.24	10.56	11.88	13.20

Exhibit 3.3   Example of Relationship between Maturity and Yield of Treasury Securities (as of March 21, 2007)

Time to Maturity	Annualized Yield
1 month	5.1%
6 months	5.0
1 year	4.9
2 years	4.8
3 years	4.7
4 years	4.7
5 years	4.7
6 years	4.6
7 years	4.6
8 years	4.6
9 years	4.6
10 years	4.6
20 years	4.6
30 years	4.6

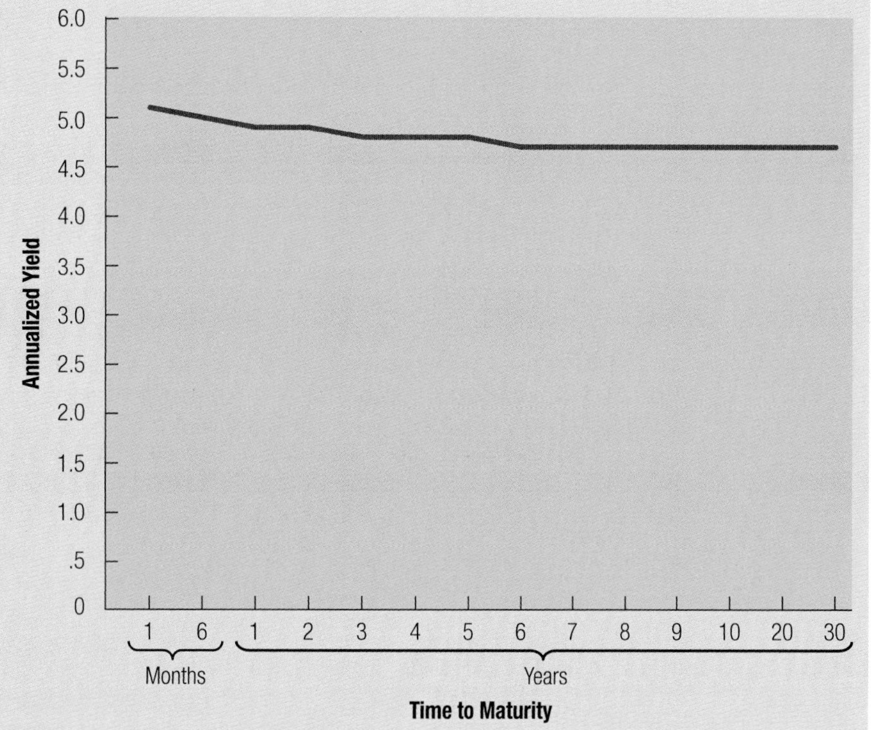

ILLUSTRATION Assume that as of today, the annualized yields for federal government securities (free from default risk) of varied maturities are as shown in Exhibit 3.3. The curve created by connecting the points plotted in the exhibit is commonly referred to as a yield curve. Notice that this yield curve exhibits a slight downward slope for relatively short terms to maturity. For maturities of 6 years or longer, the slope is horizontal, which implies a similar annualized yield among those maturities.

The term structure of interest rates in Exhibit 3.3 shows that securities that are similar in all ways except their term to maturity may offer different yields. Because the demand and supply conditions for securities may vary among maturities, so may the price (and therefore the yield) of securities. A comprehensive explanation of the term structure of interest rates is provided later in this chapter. ∎

Since the yield curve in Exhibit 3.3 is based on Treasury securities, the curve is not influenced by default risk. A yield curve for AA-rated corporate bonds would typically have a slope similar to that of the Treasury yield curve, but the yield at any term to maturity would be higher to reflect the risk premium.

http://

http://www.bloomberg.com
Assess the most recent yield curve.

Explaining Actual Yield Differentials

Even small differentials in yield can be relevant to financial institutions that are borrowing or investing millions of dollars. Yield differentials are sometimes measured in basis points; a basis point equals .01 percent, and 100 basis points equals 1 percent. If security Q offers a yield of 5.4 percent while security R offers a yield of 5.1 percent, the yield differential is .30 percent or 30 basis points. Yield differentials are measured for money market securities next, followed by capital market securities.

Yield Differentials of Money Market Securities

The yields offered on commercial paper (short-term securities offered by creditworthy firms) are typically just slightly higher than T-bill (Treasury bill) rates, as investors require a slightly higher return to compensate for default risk and less liquidity. Negotiable certificates of deposit rates are higher than yields on Treasury bills with the same maturity because of their lower degree of liquidity and higher degree of default risk during that period.

Exhibit 3.4 illustrates the annualized yields of T-bills and commercial paper (with a three-month maturity). Although these yields are quite volatile from year to year, their respective differences normally do not change much over time. The difference between yields on T-bills and other commercial paper is higher during recessionary periods because the default risk is higher then.

Market forces cause the yields of all securities to move in the same direction. To illustrate, assume the budget deficit increases substantially and the Treasury issues a large number of T-bills to finance the increased deficit. This action creates a large supply of T-bills in the market, placing downward pressure on the price and upward pressure on the T-bill yield. As the yield begins to rise, it approaches the yield of other short-

Exhibit 3.4   Yield Comparison of Securities with Identical (Three-Month) Maturities over Time

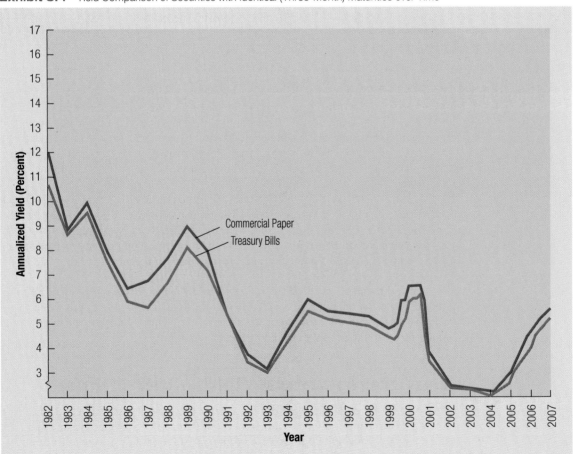

term securities. Businesses and individual investors are now encouraged to purchase T-bills rather than these risky securities because they can achieve about the same yield while avoiding default risk. The switch to T-bills lowers the demand for risky securities, thereby placing downward pressure on their price and upward pressure on their yields. Thus, the risk premium on risky securities would not disappear completely.

Yield Differentials of Capital Market Securities

With regard to capital market securities, municipal bonds have the lowest before-tax yield, yet their after-tax yield is typically above that of Treasury bonds from the perspective of investors in high tax brackets. Treasury bonds are expected to offer the lowest yield because they are free from default risk and can easily be liquidated in the secondary market. Investors prefer municipal or corporate bonds over Treasury bonds only if the after-tax yield is sufficiently higher to compensate for default risk and a lower degree of liquidity.

To illustrate how capital market security yields can vary because of default risk, Exhibit 3.5 shows yields of corporate bonds in two different risk classes. The yield differentials among capital market securities can change over time as perceptions of risk change.

Estimating the Appropriate Yield

The discussion up to this point suggests that the appropriate yield to be offered on a debt security is based on the risk-free rate for the corresponding maturity, with adjustments to capture various characteristics. This model is specified below:

$$\Upsilon_n = R_{f,n} + DP + LP + TA$$

where

Υ_n = yield of an n-day debt security

$R_{f,n}$ = yield of an n-day Treasury (risk-free) security

DP = default premium to compensate for credit risk

LP = liquidity premium to compensate for less liquidity

TA = adjustment due to the difference in tax status

Exhibit 3.5 Yield Differentials of Corporate Bonds

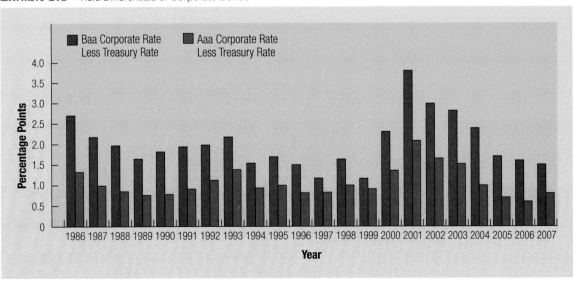

Note: Chart shows yield to maturity on seasoned corporate and Treasury debt with 10 years to maturity.

These are the characteristics identified earlier that explain yield differentials among securities (special provisions applicable to bonds may also be included, as described in Chapter 7). Although maturity is another characteristic that can affect the yield, it is not included here because it is controlled for by matching the maturity of the risk-free security to that of the security of concern.

ILLUSTRATION   Suppose that the three-month T-bill's annualized rate is 8 percent and Elizabeth Company plans to issue 90-day commercial paper. Elizabeth will need to determine the default premium (DP) and liquidity premium (LP) to offer on its commercial paper to make it as attractive to investors as a three-month (13-week) T-bill. The federal tax status of commercial paper is the same as for T-bills. Income earned from investing in commercial paper is subject to state taxes, however, whereas income earned from investing in T-bills is not. Investors may require a premium for this reason alone if they reside in a location where state and local income taxes apply.

Assume that Elizabeth Company believes that a 0.7 percent default risk premium, a 0.2 percent liquidity premium, and a 0.3 percent tax adjustment are necessary to sell its commercial paper to investors. The appropriate yield to be offered on the commercial paper (called Y_{cp}) is

$$Y_{cp,n} = R_{f,n} + DP + LP + TA$$
$$= 8\% + .7\% + .2\% + .3\%$$
$$= 9.2\% \blacksquare$$

As time passes, the appropriate commercial paper rate will change, perhaps because of changes in the risk-free rate, default premium, liquidity premium, and tax adjustment.

Some corporations may postpone plans to issue commercial paper until the economy improves and the required premium for credit risk is reduced. Yet even then, the market rate of commercial paper may increase if interest rates increase.

ILLUSTRATION   If the default risk premium decreases from 0.7 percent to 0.5 percent but $R_{f,n}$ increases from 8 percent to 8.7 percent, the appropriate yield to be offered on commercial paper (assuming no change in the previously assumed liquidity and tax adjustment premiums) would be

$$Y_{cp} = R_{f,n} + DP + LP + TA$$
$$= 8.7\% + .5\% + .2\% + .3\%$$
$$= 9.7\%$$

The strategy to postpone issuing commercial paper would backfire in this example. Even though the default premium decreased by 0.2 percent, the general level of interest rates rose by 0.7 percent, so the net change in the commercial paper rate is +0.5 percent. $\blacksquare$

As this example shows, the increase in a security's yield over time does not necessarily mean that the default premium has increased.

The assessment of yields as described here could also be applied to long-term securities. If, for example, a firm desires to issue a 20-year corporate bond, it will use the yield of a new 20-year Treasury bond as the 20-year risk-free rate and add on the premiums for credit risk, liquidity risk, and so on, to determine the yield at which it can sell corporate bonds.

A simpler and more general relationship is that the yield offered on a debt security is positively related to the prevailing risk-free rate and the security's risk premium

A graph of the prevailing yield curve like that shown here is provided by *The Wall Street Journal*. Notice that the prevailing yield curve shown here has a slight downward slope. According to the expectations theory, this yield curve signals the market's expectation of a reduction in interest rates. The yield curve that existed one year before this time is also provided in the graph. Notice that the yield curve one year earlier reflected slightly lower short-term rates and higher long-term rates. Thus, its slope was flat. Investors may use the yield curve to compare the yield they could earn on securities with various maturities. The Treasury may use the yield curve when deciding what maturity to select when issuing new securities to raise additional funds. Even corporations that want to borrow funds assess the yield curve, because their cost of borrowing is partially influenced by the prevailing Treasury yield for whatever maturity they select when borrowing funds.

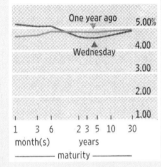

Treasury yield curve
Yield to maturity of current bills, notes and bonds

(RP). This risk premium captures any risk characteristics of the security, including credit risk and liquidity risk.

A Closer Look at the Term Structure

Of all the factors that affect the yields offered on debt securities, the factor that is most difficult to understand is the term to maturity. For this reason, a more comprehensive explanation of the relationship between term to maturity and annualized yield (referred to as the term structure of interest rates) is necessary.

Various theories have been used to explain the relationship between maturity and annualized yield of securities, including the pure expectations theory, liquidity premium theory, and segmented markets theory. Each of these theories is explained here.

Pure Expectations Theory

According to the **pure expectations theory,** the term structure of interest rates (as reflected in the shape of the yield curve) is determined solely by expectations of future interest rates.

Impact of an Expected Increase in Interest Rates
To understand how interest rate expectations may influence the yield curve, assume that the annualized yields of short-term and long-term risk-free securities are similar; that is, the yield curve is flat. Then assume that investors begin to believe that interest rates will rise. They will respond by investing their funds mostly in the short term so that they can soon reinvest their funds at higher yields after interest rates increase. When investors flood the short-term market and avoid the long-term market, they may cause

Exhibit 3.6   How Interest Rate Expectations Affect the Yield Curve

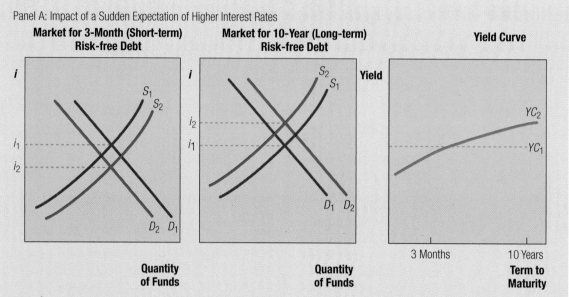

Panel A: Impact of a Sudden Expectation of Higher Interest Rates

$E(\uparrow i) \rightarrow$ Supply of funds provided by investors ↑ in short-term (such as 3-month) markets, and ↓ in long-term (such as 10-year) markets. Demand for funds by borrowers ↑ in long-term markets and ↓ in short-term markets. Therefore, the yield curve becomes upward sloping as shown here.

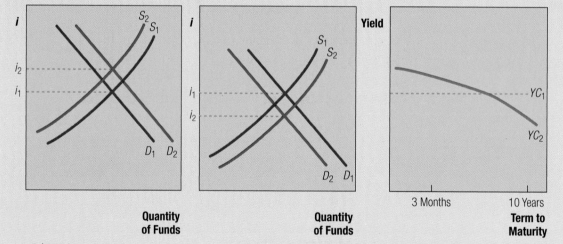

Panel B: Impact of a Sudden Expectation of Lower Interest Rates

$E(\downarrow i) \rightarrow$ Supply of funds provided by investors ↑ in long-term (such as 10-year) markets, and ↓ in short-term (such as 3-month) markets. Demand for funds by borrowers ↑ in short-term markets and ↓ in long-term markets. Therefore, the yield curve becomes downward sloping as shown here.

the yield curve to adjust as shown in Panel A of Exhibit 3.6. The large supply of funds in the short-term markets will force annualized yields down. Meanwhile, the reduced supply of long-term funds forces long-term yields up.

Even though the annualized short-term yields become lower than annualized long-term yields, investors in short-term funds are satisfied because they expect interest rates to rise. They will make up for the lower short-term yield when the short-term securities mature, and they reinvest at a higher rate (if interest rates rise) at maturity.

Assuming that the borrowers who plan to issue securities also expect interest rates to increase, they will prefer to lock in the present interest rate over a long period of time. Thus, borrowers will generally prefer to issue long-term securities rather than short-term securities. This results in a relatively small demand for short-term funds. Consequently, there is downward pressure on the yield of short-term funds. There is also an increase in the demand for long-term funds by borrowers, which places upward pressure on long-term funds. Overall, the expectation of higher interest rates changes the demand for funds and the supply of funds in different maturity markets, which forces the original flat yield curve (labeled YC_1) to pivot upward (counterclockwise) and become upward sloping (YC_2).

Impact of an Expected Decline in Interest Rates If investors expect interest rates to decrease in the future, they will prefer to invest in long-term funds rather than short-term funds, because they could lock in today's interest rate before interest rates fall. Borrowers will prefer to borrow short-term funds so that they can reborrow at a lower interest rate once interest rates decline.

Based on the expectation of lower interest rates in the future, the supply of funds provided by investors will be low for short-term funds and high for long-term funds. This will place upward pressure on short-term yields and downward pressure on long-term yields as shown in Panel B of Exhibit 3.6. Overall, the expectation of lower interest rates causes the shape of the yield curve to pivot downward (clockwise).

Algebraic Presentation Investors monitor the yield curve to determine the rates that exist for securities with various maturities. They can purchase either a security with a maturity that matches their investment horizon or a security with a shorter term and reinvest the proceeds at maturity. If a particular investment strategy is expected to generate a higher return over the investment horizon, investors may use that strategy. This could affect the prices and yields of securities with different maturities, realigning the rates so that the expected return over the entire investment horizon would be similar, regardless of the strategy used. If investors were indifferent to security maturities, they would want the return of any security to equal the compounded yield of consecutive investments in shorter-term securities. That is, a two-year security should offer a return that is similar to the anticipated return from investing in two consecutive one-year securities. A four-year security should offer a return that is competitive with the expected return from investing in two consecutive two-year securities or four consecutive one-year securities, and so on.

ILLUSTRATION To illustrate these equalities, consider the relationship between interest rates on a two-year security and a one-year security as follows:

$$(1 + {}_ti_2)^2 = (1 + {}_ti_1)(1 + {}_{t+1}r_1)$$

where ${}_ti_2$ = known annualized interest rate of a two-year security as of time t

${}_ti_1$ = known annualized interest rate of a one-year security as of time t

${}_{t+1}r_1$ = one-year interest rate that is anticipated as of time $t + 1$ (one year ahead)

The term i represents a quoted rate, which is therefore known, whereas r represents a rate to be quoted at some point in the future, which is therefore uncertain. The left side of the equation represents the compounded yield to investors who purchase a two-year security, while the right side of the equation represents the anticipated compounded yield from purchasing a one-year security and reinvesting the proceeds in a new one-year security at the end of one year. If time t is today, $_{t+1}r_1$ can be estimated by rearranging terms:

$$1 + {}_{t+1}r_1 = \frac{(1 + {}_t i_2)^2}{(1 + {}_t i_1)}$$

$${}_{t+1}r_1 = \frac{(1 + {}_t i_2)^2}{(1 + {}_t i_1)} - 1$$

The term $_{t+1}r_1$, referred to as the **forward rate,** is commonly estimated in order to represent the market's forecast of the future interest rate. As a numerical example, assume that as of today (time t) the annualized two-year interest rate is 10 percent, while the one-year interest rate is 8 percent. The forward rate is estimated as follows:

$$_{t+1}r_1 = \frac{(1 + .10)^2}{(1 + .08)} - 1$$

$$= .1203704$$

Conceptually, this rate implies that one year from now, a one-year interest rate must equal about 12.037 percent in order for consecutive investments in two one-year securities to generate a return similar to that of a two-year investment. If the actual one-year rate beginning one year from now (at period $t + 1$) is above (below) 12.037 percent, the return from two consecutive one-year investments will exceed (be less than) the return on a two-year investment. ∎

The forward rate is sometimes used as an approximation of the market's consensus interest rate forecast, because if the market had a different perception, demand and supply of today's existing two-year and one-year securities would adjust to capitalize on this information. Of course, there is no guarantee that the forward rate will forecast the future interest rate with perfect accuracy.

The greater the difference between the implied one-year forward rate and today's one-year interest rate, the greater the expected change in the one-year interest rate. If the term structure of interest rates is solely influenced by expectations of future interest rates, the following relationships hold:

Scenario	Structure of Yield Curve	Expectations about the Future Interest Rate
1. $_{t+1}r_1 > {}_t i_1$	Upward slope	Higher than today's rate
2. $_{t+1}r_1 = {}_t i_1$	Flat	Same as today's rate
3. $_{t+1}r_1 < {}_t i_1$	Downward slope	Lower than today's rate

Forward rates can be determined for various maturities. The relationships described here can be applied when assessing the change in the interest rate of a security with any particular maturity.

The previous example can be expanded to solve for other forward rates. The equality specified by the pure expectations theory for a three-year horizon is

$$(1 + {}_t i_3)^3 = (1 + {}_t i_1)(1 + {}_{t+1}r_1)(1 + {}_{t+2}r_1)$$

where $\quad {}_t i_3 =$ annualized rate on a three-year security as of time t

$\quad\quad {}_{t+2}r_1 =$ one-year interest rate that is anticipated as of time $t + 2$ (two years)

All other terms were already defined. By rearranging terms, we can isolate the forward rate of a one-year security beginning two years from now:

$$1 + {}_{t+2}r_1 = \frac{(1 + {}_t i_3)^3}{(1 + {}_t i_1)(1 + {}_{t+1}r_1)}$$

$$_{t+2}r_1 = \frac{(1 + {}_t i_3)^3}{(1 + {}_t i_1)(1 + {}_{t+1}r_1)} - 1$$

If the one-year forward rate beginning one year from now $({}_{t+1}r_1)$ has already been estimated, this estimate along with actual one-year and three-year interest rates can be used to estimate the one-year forward rate two years from now. Recall that our previous example assumed ${}_t i_1 = 8$ percent and estimated ${}_{t+1}r_1$ to be about 12.037 percent.

ILLUSTRATION Assume that a three-year security has an annualized interest rate of 11 percent $({}_t i_3 = 11$ percent). Given this information, the one-year forward rate two years from now is

$$_{t+2}r_1 = \frac{(1 + {}_t i_3)^3}{(1 + {}_t i_1)(1 + {}_{t+1}r_1)} - 1$$

$$= \frac{(1 + .11)^3}{(1 + .08)(1 + .12037)} - 1$$

$$= \frac{1.367631}{1.21} - 1$$

$$= 13.02736\%$$

Thus, the market anticipates a one-year interest rate of 13.02736 percent as of two years from now. ∎

The yield curve can also be used to forecast annualized interest rates for periods other than one year. For example, the information provided in the last example could be used to determine the two-year forward rate beginning one year from now.

According to the pure expectations theory, a one-year investment followed by a two-year investment should offer the same annualized yield over the three-year horizon as a three-year security that could be purchased today. This equality is shown as follows:

$$(1 + {}_{t+1}i_3)^3 = (1 + {}_t i_1)(1 + {}_{t+1}r_2)^2$$

where $\quad {}_{t+1}r_2 =$ annual interest rate of a two-year security anticipated as of time $t + 1$

By rearranging terms, ${}_{t+1}r_2$ can be isolated:

$$(1 + {}_{t+1}r_2)^2 = \frac{(1 + {}_t i_3)^3}{(1 + {}_t i_1)}$$

ILLUSTRATION Recall that today's annualized yields for one-year and three-year securities are 8 percent and 11 percent, respectively. With this information, $_{t+1}r_2$ is estimated as follows:

$$(1 + {}_{t+1}r_2)^2 = \frac{(1 + {}_ti_3)^3}{(1 + {}_ti_1)}$$
$$= \frac{(1 + .11)^3}{(1 + .08)}$$
$$= 1.266325$$
$$(1 + {}_{t+1}r_2) = \sqrt{1.266325}$$
$$= 1.1253$$
$$_{t+1}r_2 = .1253$$

Thus, the market anticipates an annualized interest rate of about 12.53 percent for two-year securities beginning one year from now. ∎

Pure expectations theory is based on the premise that the forward rates are unbiased estimators of future interest rates. If forward rates are biased, investors could attempt to capitalize on the bias.

ILLUSTRATION In the previous numerical example, the one-year forward rate beginning one year ahead was estimated to be about 12.037 percent. If the forward rate was thought to contain an upward bias, the expected one-year interest rate beginning one year ahead would be less than 12.037 percent. Therefore, investors with funds available for two years would earn a higher yield by purchasing two-year securities rather than purchasing one-year securities for two consecutive years. Their actions would cause an increase in the price of two-year securities and a decrease in that of one-year securities. The yields of the securities would move inversely with the price movements. The attempt by investors to capitalize on the forward rate bias would essentially eliminate the bias. ∎

If forward rates are unbiased estimators of future interest rates, financial market efficiency is supported, and the information implied by market rates about the forward rate cannot be used to generate abnormal returns. As new information develops, investor preferences would change, yields would adjust, and the implied forward rate would adjust as well.

If a long-term rate is expected to equal a geometric average of consecutive short-term rates covering the same time horizon (as is suggested by pure expectations theory), long-term rates would likely be more stable than short-term rates. As expectations about consecutive short-term rates change over time, the average of these rates is less volatile than the individual short-term rates. Thus, long-term rates are much more stable than short-term rates.

Liquidity Premium Theory

Some investors may prefer to own short-term rather than long-term securities because a shorter maturity represents greater liquidity. In this case, they may be willing to hold long-term securities only if compensated with a premium for the lower degree of liquidity. Although long-term securities can be liquidated prior to maturity, their prices are more sensitive to interest rate movements. Short-term securities are normally considered to be more liquid because they are more likely to be converted to cash without a loss in value.

The preference for the more liquid short-term securities places upward pressure on the slope of a yield curve. Liquidity may be a more critical factor to investors at particular points in time, and the liquidity premium will change over time accordingly. As it does, so will the yield curve. This is the **liquidity premium theory** (also sometimes referred to as the liquidity preference theory).

Exhibit 3.7 combines the simultaneous existence of expectations theory and a liquidity premium. Each graph shows different interest rate expectations by the market. Regardless of the interest rate forecast, the yield curve is affected in a somewhat similar manner by the liquidity premium.

Estimation of the Forward Rate Based on a Liquidity Premium

When expectations theory is combined with the liquidity theory, the yield on a security will not necessarily be equal to the yield from consecutive investments in shorter-term securities over the same investment horizon. For example, the yield on a two-year security can be determined as

$$(1 + {}_ti_2)^2 = (1 + {}_ti_1)(1 + {}_{t+1}r_1) + LP_2$$

where LP_2 represents the liquidity premium on a two-year security. The yield generated from the two-year security should exceed the yield from consecutive investments in one-year securities by a premium that compensates the investor for less liquidity. The relationship between the liquidity premium and term to maturity can be expressed as follows:

$$0 < LP_1 < LP_2 < LP_3 < \cdots < LP_{20}$$

where the subscripts represent years to maturity. This implies that the liquidity premium would be more influential on the difference between annualized interest rates on one-year and 20-year securities than on the difference between one-year and two-year securities.

Exhibit 3.7   Impact of Liquidity Premium on the Yield Curve under Three Different Scenarios

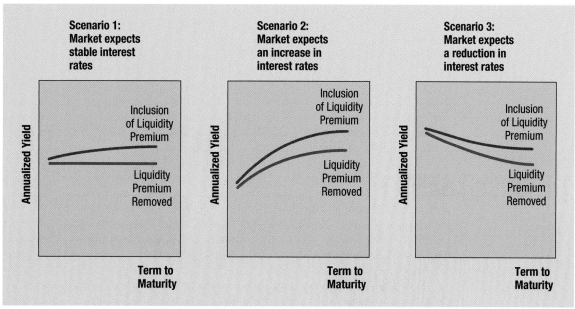

If liquidity influences the yield curve, the forward rate overestimates the market's expectation of the future interest rate. A more appropriate formula for the forward rate would account for the liquidity premium. By rearranging the terms of the previous equation, the one-year forward rate can be derived as follows:

$$_{t+1}r_1 = \frac{(1 + {}_ti_2)^2}{(1 + {}_ti_1)} - 1 - [LP_2/(1 + {}_ti_1)]$$

ILLUSTRATION Reconsider the example where $i_1 = 8$ percent and $i_2 = 10$ percent. Assume that the liquidity premium on a two-year security is 0.5 percent. The one-year forward rate can be derived from this information:

$$_{t+1}r_1 = \frac{(1 + {}_ti_2)^2}{(1 + {}_ti_1)} - 1 - [LP_2/(1 + {}_ti_1)]$$

$$_{t+1}r_1 = \frac{(1.10)^2}{1.08} - 1 - [.005/(1 + .08)]$$

$$= .11574$$

This estimate of the one-year forward rate is below the estimate derived in the previous related example in which the liquidity premium was not considered. The previous estimate (12.037 percent) of the forward rate should overstate the market's expected interest rate, because it did not account for a liquidity premium. Forecasts of future interest rates implied by a yield curve are reduced slightly when accounting for the liquidity premium. ∎

Even with the existence of a liquidity premium, yield curves could still be used to interpret interest rate expectations. A flat yield curve would be interpreted to mean that the market is expecting a slight decrease in interest rates (without the effect of the liquidity premium, the yield curve would have had a slight downward slope). A slight upward slope would be interpreted as no expected change in interest rates because if the liquidity premium were removed, this yield curve would be flat.

Segmented Markets Theory

According to the **segmented markets theory,** investors and borrowers choose securities with maturities that satisfy their forecasted cash needs. Pension funds and life insurance companies may generally prefer long-term investments that coincide with their long-term liabilities. Commercial banks may prefer more short-term investments to coincide with their short-term liabilities. If investors and borrowers participate only in the maturity market that satisfies their particular needs, markets are segmented. That is, investors (or borrowers) will shift from the long-term market to the short-term market or vice versa only if the timing of their cash needs changes. According to the segmented markets theory, the choice of long-term versus short-term maturities is predetermined according to need rather than expectations of future interest rates.

ILLUSTRATION Assume that most investors have funds available to invest for only a short period of time and therefore desire to invest primarily in short-term securities. Also assume that most borrowers need funds for a long period of time and therefore desire to issue mostly long-term securities. The result will be downward pressure on the yield of short-term securities and upward pressure on the yield of long-term securities. Overall, the scenario described would create an upward-sloping yield curve.

Now consider the opposite scenario in which most investors wish to invest their funds for a long period of time, while most borrowers need funds for only a short period of time. According to the segmented markets theory, there will be upward pressure on the yield of short-term securities and downward pressure on the yield of long-term securities. If the supply of funds provided by investors and the demand for funds by borrowers were better balanced between the short-term and long-term markets, the yields of short- and long-term securities would be more similar. ■

The example separated the maturity markets into just short term and long term. In reality, several maturity markets may exist. Within the short-term market, some investors may prefer maturities of one month or less, while others prefer maturities of one to three months. Regardless of how many maturity markets exist, the yields of securities with various maturities should be somewhat influenced by the desires of investors and borrowers to participate in the maturity market that best satisfies their needs. A corporation that needs additional funds for 30 days would not consider issuing long-term bonds for such a purpose. Savers with short-term funds would avoid some long-term investments, such as 10-year certificates of deposit, that cannot be easily liquidated.

Limitation of the Theory A limitation of the segmented markets theory is that some borrowers and savers have the flexibility to choose among various maturity markets. Corporations that need long-term funds may initially obtain short-term financing if they expect interest rates to decline. Investors with long-term funds may make short-term investments if they expect interest rates to rise. Some investors with short-term funds available may be willing to purchase long-term securities that have an active secondary market.

Some financial institutions focus on a particular maturity market, but others are more flexible. Commercial banks obtain most of their funds in short-term markets but spread their investments into short-, medium-, and long-term markets. Savings institutions have historically focused on attracting short-term funds and lending funds for long-term periods. If maturity markets were completely segmented, an adjustment in the interest rate in one market would have no impact on other markets. Yet, there is clear evidence that interest rates among maturity markets move closely in tandem over time, proving there is some interaction among markets, which implies that funds are being transferred across markets. Note that this theory of segmented markets conflicts with the general presumption of the pure expectations theory that maturity markets are perfect substitutes for one another.

Implications Although markets are not completely segmented, the preference for particular maturities can affect the prices and yields of securities with different maturities and therefore affect the yield curve's shape. Therefore, the segmented markets theory appears to be a partial explanation for the yield curve's shape, but not the sole explanation.

A more flexible perspective of the segmented markets theory, called the **preferred habitat theory,** offers a compromise explanation for the term structure of interest rates. This theory suggests that although investors and borrowers may normally concentrate on a particular natural maturity market, certain events may cause them to wander from it. For example, commercial banks that obtain mostly short-term funds may select investments with short-term maturities as a natural habitat. However, if they wish to benefit from an anticipated decline in interest rates, they may select medium- and long-term maturities instead. Preferred habitat theory acknowledges that natural maturity markets may influence the yield curve but recognizes that interest rate expectations could entice market participants to stray from preferred maturities.

Research on Term Structure Theories

An abundance of research has been conducted on the term structure of interest rates, offering insight into the various theories. Researchers have found that interest rate expectations have a strong influence on the term structure of interest rates. However, the forward rate derived from a yield curve does not accurately predict future interest rates. This may suggest that other factors are relevant. The liquidity premium, for example, could cause consistent positive forecasting errors, meaning that forward rates tend to overestimate future interest rates. Studies have documented variation in the yield-maturity relationship that cannot be explained by interest rate expectations or liquidity. Thus, the variation could be attributed to different supply and demand conditions for particular maturity segments.

General Research Implications Although the results of research differ, there is some evidence that expectations theory, liquidity premium theory, and segmented markets theory all have some validity. Thus, if the term structure is used to assess the market's expectations of future interest rates, investors should first net out the liquidity premium and any unique market conditions for various maturity segments.

Integrating the Theories of the Term Structure

To illustrate how all three theories can simultaneously affect the yield curve, assume the following conditions:

1. Investors and borrowers who select security maturities based on anticipated interest rate movements currently expect interest rates to rise.
2. Most borrowers are in need of long-term funds, while most investors have only short-term funds to invest.
3. Investors prefer more liquidity to less.

The first condition, related to expectations theory, suggests the existence of an upward-sloping yield curve, other things being equal. This is shown in Exhibit 3.8 as Curve E. The segmented markets information (condition 2) also favors the upward-

Exhibit 3.8
Effect of Conditions in
Example of Yield Curve

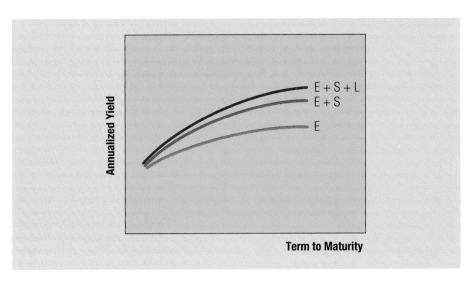

sloping yield curve. When conditions 1 and 2 are considered simultaneously, the appropriate yield curve may look like Curve E + S. The third condition relating to liquidity would then place a higher premium on the longer-term securities because of their lower degree of liquidity. When this condition is included with the first two, the yield curve may look like Curve E + S + L.

In this example, all conditions placed upward pressure on long-term yields relative to short-term yields. In reality, there will sometimes be offsetting conditions, as one condition places downward pressure on the slope of the yield curve while the others place upward pressure on the slope. If condition 1 were revised to suggest the expectation of lower interest rates in the future, this condition by itself would result in a downward-sloping yield curve. When combined with the other conditions that favor an upward-sloping curve, it would create a partial offsetting effect. This yield curve would exhibit a downward slope if the effect of the interest rate expectations dominated the combined liquidity premium and segmented markets effects. Conversely, an upward slope would exist if the liquidity premium and segmented markets effects dominated the effects of interest rate expectations.

Uses of the Term Structure

The term structure of interest rates is used to forecast interest rates, forecast recessions, and make investment and financing decisions, as explained next.

Forecast Interest Rates At any point in time, the shape of the yield curve can be used to assess the general expectations of investors and borrowers about future interest rates. Recall from expectations theory that an upward-sloping yield curve generally results from the expectation of higher interest rates, while a downward-sloping yield curve generally results from the expectation of lower interest rates. The expectations about future interest rates must be interpreted cautiously, however, because liquidity and specific maturity preferences could influence the yield curve's shape. It is generally believed, though, that interest rate expectations are a major contributing factor to the yield curve's shape, and the curve's shape should provide a reasonable indication (especially if the liquidity premium effect is accounted for) of the market's expectations about future interest rates.

Although investors can use the yield curve to interpret the market's consensus expectation of future interest rates, they may have their own interest rate projections. By comparing their projections to those implied by the yield curve, they can attempt to capitalize on the difference. For example, if an upward-sloping yield curve exists, suggesting a market expectation of increasing rates, investors expecting stable interest rates could benefit from investing in long-term securities. From their perspective, long-term securities are undervalued because they reflect the market's expectation of higher interest rates. Strategies such as this are effective only if the investor can consistently forecast better than the market.

Forecast Recessions Some analysts believe that flat or inverted yield curves indicate a recession in the near future. The rationale is that given a positive liquidity premium, such yield curves reflect the expectation of lower interest rates. This is commonly associated with expectations of a reduced demand for loanable funds, which could be attributed to expectations of a weak economy.

The yield curve became flat or slightly inverted in 2000. At that time, the shape of the curve indicated expectations of a slower economy, which would result in lower interest rates. In 2001, the economy weakened substantially. In March 2007, the yield curve exhibited a slight negative slope, which caused some market participants to forecast a recession.

Investment Decisions If the yield curve is upward sloping, some investors may attempt to benefit from the higher yields on longer-term securities, even though they have funds to invest for only a short period of time. The secondary market allows investors to attempt this strategy, referred to as *riding the yield curve*. Consider an upward-sloping yield curve such that some one-year securities offer an annualized yield of 7 percent while 10-year bonds can be purchased at par value and offer a coupon rate of 10 percent. An investor with funds available for one year may decide to purchase the bonds and sell them in the secondary market after one year. The investor earns 3 percent more than was possible on the one-year securities, if the bonds can be sold after one year at the price at which they were purchased. The risk of this strategy is the uncertainty of the price at which the security can be sold in the near future. If the upward-sloping yield is interpreted as the market's consensus of higher interest rates in the future, the price of a security would be expected to decrease in the future.

The yield curve is commonly monitored by financial institutions whose liability maturities are distinctly different from their asset maturities. Consider a bank that obtains much of its funds through short-term deposits and uses the funds to provide long-term loans or purchase long-term securities. An upward-sloping yield curve is favorable to the bank because annualized short-term deposit rates are significantly lower than annualized long-term investment rates. The bank's spread is higher than it would be if the yield curve were flat. Yet, if the bank believes that the upward slope of the yield curve indicates higher interest rates in the future (as reflected in the expectations theory), it will expect its cost of liabilities to increase over time, as future deposits would be obtained at higher interest rates.

Financing Decisions The yield curve is also useful for firms that plan to issue bonds. By assessing the prevailing rates on securities for various maturities, firms can estimate the rates to be paid on bonds with different maturities. This may enable them to decide the maturity for the bonds they issue.

Why the Slope of the Yield Curve Changes over Time

If interest rates at all maturities are affected in the same manner by existing conditions, the slope of the yield curve would remain the same. However, conditions may cause short-term yields to change in a manner that differs from the change in long-term yields.

ILLUSTRATION Assume that last July the yield curve had a large upward slope as shown by yield curve YC_1 in Exhibit 3.9. Since then, the Treasury decided to restructure its debt by retiring $100 billion of long-term Treasury securities and increasing its offering of short-term Treasury securities. This caused a large increase in the demand for short-term funds and a large decrease in the demand for long-term funds. The increase in the demand for short-term funds caused an increase in short-term interest rates and therefore increased yields offered on newly issued short-term securities. Conversely, the decline in the demand for long-term funds caused a decrease in long-term interest rates and therefore reduced yields offered on newly issued long-term securities. Today, the yield curve is YC_2 and is much flatter than it was last July. ∎

How the Yield Curve Has Changed over Time

Changes in the shape of the yield curve over time are illustrated in Exhibit 3.10. Notice that the slope of each yield curve is more pronounced for maturities up to five years and then levels off somewhat for longer maturities. Yield curves are not

Exhibit 3.9 Potential Impact of Treasury Shift from Long-Term to Short-Term Financing

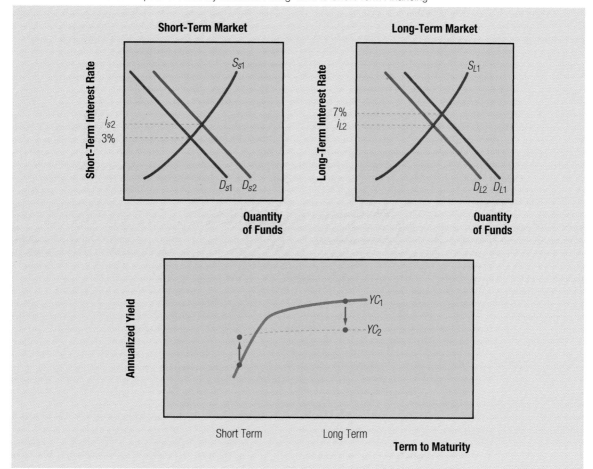

always upward sloping. In the early 1980s, securities with shorter maturities commonly offered higher annualized yields because of the very high interest rates of that period combined with the expectation that rates would decrease. Although the upward slope has generally persisted since 1982, the degree of slope has changed.

International Structure of Interest Rates

GL🌐BALASPECTS Since the factors that affect the shape of the yield curve can vary among countries, the shape of the yield curve at any given point in time varies among countries. Exhibit 3.11 shows the yield curve for six different countries at a given point in time. Each country with a different currency has its own interest rate levels for various maturities. Each country's interest rates are based on supply and demand conditions.

Interest rate movements across countries tend to be positively correlated as a result of internationally integrated financial markets. Nevertheless, the actual interest rates may vary significantly across countries at a given point in time. This implies that the differential in interest rates is primarily attributed to general supply and demand

Exhibit 3.10

Yield Curves at Various Points in Time

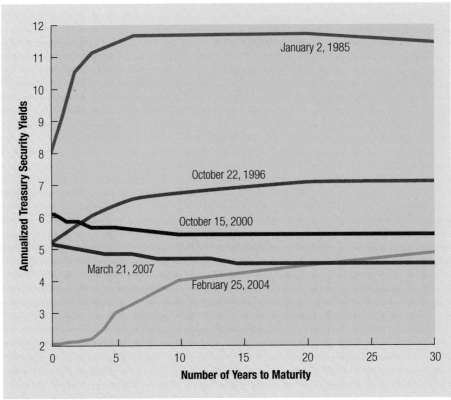

Source: *FRBNY Quarterly Review,* various issues.

conditions across countries rather than differences in default premiums, liquidity premiums, or other factors unique to the individual securities.

Because forward rates (as defined in this chapter) reflect the market's expectations of future interest rates, the term structure of interest rates for various countries should be monitored for the following reasons. First, with the integration of financial markets, movements in one country's interest rate can affect interest rates in other countries. Thus, some investors may estimate the forward rate in a foreign country to predict the foreign interest rate, which in turn may affect domestic interest rates. Second, foreign securities and some domestic securities are influenced by foreign economies, which are dependent on foreign interest rates. If the foreign forward rates can be used to forecast foreign interest rates, they can enhance forecasts of foreign economies. Because exchange rates are also influenced by foreign interest rates, exchange rate projections may be more accurate when using foreign forward rates to forecast foreign interest rates.

If the real interest rate was fixed, inflation rates for future periods could be predicted for any country in which the forward rate could be estimated. Recall that the nominal interest rate consists of an expected inflation rate plus a real interest rate. Because the forward rate represents an expected nominal interest rate for a future period, it also represents an expected inflation rate plus a real interest rate in that period. The expected inflation in that period is estimated as the difference between the forward rate and the real interest rate.

Exhibit 3.11   Yield Curves among Foreign Countries (as of March 2007)

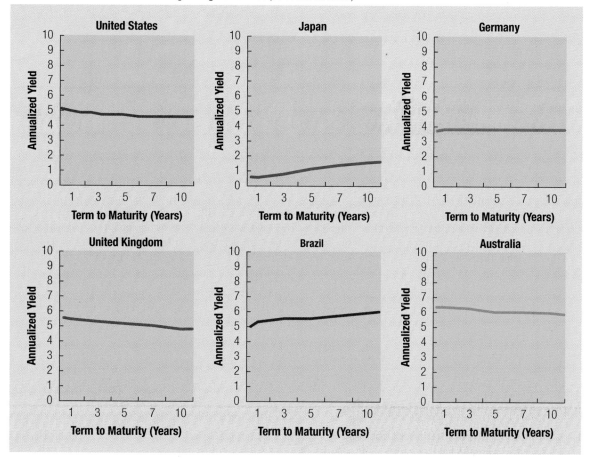

Summary

■ Quoted yields of debt securities at a given point vary for the following reasons. First, securities with higher credit (default) risk must offer a higher yield. Second, securities that are less liquid must offer a higher yield. Third, taxable securities must offer a higher before-tax yield than tax-exempt securities. Fourth, securities with longer maturities offer a different yield (not consistently higher or lower) than securities with shorter maturities.

■ The appropriate yield for any particular debt security can be estimated by first determining the risk-free yield that is presently offered by a Treasury security with a similar maturity. Then, adjustments can be made according to the credit risk, liquidity, tax status, and other provisions.

■ The term structure of interest rates can be explained by three theories. The pure expectations theory suggests that the shape of the yield curve is dictated by interest rate expectations. The liquidity premium theory suggests that securities with shorter maturities have greater liquidity and therefore should not have to offer as high a yield as securities with longer terms to maturity. The segmented markets theory suggests that investors and borrowers have different needs, which cause the demand and supply conditions to vary across different maturities; that is, there is a segmented market for each term to maturity, which causes yields to vary among these maturity markets. When consolidating the theories, the term structure of interest rates is dependent on interest rate expectations, investor preferences for liquidity, and unique needs of investors and borrowers in each maturity market.

Point Counter-Point

Should a Yield Curve Influence a Borrower's Preferred Maturity of a Loan?

Point Yes. If there is an upward-sloping yield curve, a borrower should pursue a short-term loan to capitalize on the lower annualized rate charged for a short-term period. The borrower can obtain a series of short-term loans rather than one loan to match the desired maturity.

Counter-Point No. The borrower will face uncertainty regarding the interest rate charged on subsequent loans that are needed. An upward-sloping yield

curve suggests that interest rates may rise in the future, which will cause the cost of borrowing to increase. Overall, the cost of borrowing may be higher when using a series of loans than when matching the debt maturity to the time period in which funds are needed.

Who Is Correct? Use the Internet to learn more about this issue. Offer your own opinion on this issue.

Questions and Applications

1. **Characteristics That Affect Security Yields** Identify the relevant characteristics of any security that can affect the security's yield.

2. **Impact of Credit Risk on Yield** What effect does a high credit risk have on securities?

3. **Impact of Liquidity on Yield** Discuss the relationship between the yield and liquidity of securities.

4. **Tax Effects on Yields** Do investors in high tax brackets or those in low tax brackets benefit more from tax-exempt securities? Why? Do municipal bonds or corporate bonds offer a higher before-tax yield at a given point in time? Why? Which has the higher after-tax yield? If taxes did not exist, would Treasury bonds offer a higher or lower yield than municipal bonds with the same maturity? Why?

5. **Pure Expectations Theory** Explain how a yield curve would shift in response to a sudden expectation of rising interest rates, according to the pure expectations theory.

6. **Forward Rate** What is the meaning of the forward rate in the context of the term structure of inter-

est rates? Why might forward rates consistently overestimate future interest rates? How could such a bias be avoided?

7. **Pure Expectations Theory** Assume there is a sudden expectation of lower interest rates in the future. What would be the effect on the shape of the yield curve? Explain.

8. **Liquidity Premium Theory** Explain the liquidity premium theory.

9. **Impact of Liquidity Premium on Forward Rate** Explain how consideration of a liquidity premium affects the estimate of a forward interest rate.

10. **Segmented Markets Theory** If a downward-sloping yield curve is mainly attributed to segmented markets theory, what does that suggest about the demand for and supply of funds in the short-term and long-term maturity markets?

11. **Segmented Markets Theory** If the segmented markets theory causes an upward-sloping yield curve, what does this imply? If markets are not completely segmented, should we dismiss the

segmented markets theory as even a partial explanation for the term structure of interest rates? Explain.

12. **Preferred Habitat Theory** Explain the preferred habitat theory.

13. **Yield Curve** What factors influence the shape of the yield curve? Describe how financial market participants use the yield curve.

Advanced Questions

14. **Segmented Markets Theory** Suppose that the Treasury decides to finance its deficit with mostly long-term funds. How could this decision affect the term structure of interest rates? If short-term and long-term markets are segmented, would the Treasury's decision have a more or less pronounced impact on the term structure? Explain.

15. **Yield Curve** If liquidity and interest rate expectations are both important for explaining the shape of a yield curve, what does a flat yield curve indicate about the market's perception of future interest rates?

16. **Global Interaction among Yield Curves** Assume that the yield curves in the United States, France, and Japan are flat. If the U.S. yield curve then suddenly becomes positively sloped, do you think the yield curves in France and Japan would be affected? If so, how?

17. **Multiple Effects on the Yield Curve** Assume that (1) investors and borrowers expect that the economy will weaken and that inflation will decline, (2) investors require a small liquidity premium, and (3) markets are partially segmented and the Treasury currently has a preference for borrowing in short-term markets. Explain how each of these forces would affect the term structure, holding other factors constant. Then explain the effect on the term structure overall.

18. **Effect of Crises on the Yield Curve** During some crises, investors shift their funds out of the stock market and into money market securities for safety, even if they do not fear rising interest rates. Explain how and why these actions by investors affect the yield curve. Is the shift due to the expectations theory, liquidity premium theory, or segmented markets theory?

19. **How the Yield Curve May Respond to Prevailing Conditions** Consider how economic conditions affect the default risk premium. Do you think the default risk premium will likely increase or decrease during this semester? How do you think the yield curve will change during this semester? Offer some logic to support your answers.

20. **Assessing Interest Rate Differentials among Countries** In some countries where there is high inflation, the annual interest rate is more than 50 percent, while in other countries, such as the United States and many European countries, the annual interest rates are typically less than 10 percent. Do you think such a large interest rate differential is primarily attributed to the difference in the risk-free rates or to the difference in the credit risk premiums between countries? Explain.

21. **Applying the Yield Curve to Risky Debt Securities** Assume that the yield curve for Treasury bonds has a slight upward slope, starting at 6 percent for a 10-year maturity and slowly rising to 8 percent for a 30-year maturity. Create a yield curve that you believe would exist for A-rated bonds. Create a yield curve that you believe would exist for B-rated bonds.

Interpreting Financial News

Interpret the following comments made by Wall Street analysts and portfolio managers:

a. "An upward-sloping yield curve persists because many investors stand ready to jump into the stock market."

b. "Low-rated bond yields rose as recession fears caused a flight to quality."

c. "The shift from an upward-sloping yield curve to a downward-sloping yield curve is sending a warning about a possible recession."

Managing in Financial Markets

Monitoring Yield Curve Adjustments As an analyst of a bond rating agency, you have been asked to interpret the implications of the recent shift in the yield curve. Six months ago, the yield curve exhibited a slight downward slope. Over the last six months, long-term yields declined, while short-term yields remained the same. Analysts said that the shift was due to revised expectations of interest rates.

a. Given the shift in the yield curve, does it appear that firms increased or decreased their demand for long-term funds over the last six months?

b. Interpret what the shift in the yield curve suggests about the market's changing expectations of future interest rates.

c. Recently, an analyst argued that the underlying reason for the yield curve shift is that many large U.S. firms anticipate a recession. Explain why an anticipated recession could force the yield curve to shift as it has.

d. What could the specific shift in the yield curve signal about the ratings of existing corporate bonds? What types of corporations would be most likely to experience a change in their bond ratings as a result of the specific shift in the yield curve?

Problems

1. **Forward Rate**
   a. Assume that as of today, the annualized two-year interest rate is 13 percent, while the one-year interest rate is 12 percent. Use only this information to estimate the one-year forward rate.
   b. Assume that the liquidity premium on a two-year security is 0.3 percent. Use this information to reestimate the one-year forward rate.

2. **Forward Rate** Assume that as of today, the annualized interest rate on a three-year security is 10 percent, while the annualized interest rate on a two-year security is 7 percent. Use only this information to estimate the one-year forward rate two years from now.

3. **Forward Rate** If $_ti_1 > _ti_2$, what is the market consensus forecast about the one-year forward rate one year from now? Is this rate above or below today's one-year interest rate? Explain.

4. **After-Tax Yield** You need to choose between investing in a one-year municipal bond with a 7 percent yield and a one-year corporate bond with an 11 percent yield. If your marginal federal income tax rate is 30 percent and no other differences exist between these two securities, which one would you invest in?

5. **Deriving Current Interest Rates** Assume that interest rates for one-year securities are expected to be 2 percent today, 4 percent one year from now, and 6 percent two years from now. Using only the pure expectations theory, what are the current interest rates on two-year and three-year securities?

6. **Commercial Paper Yield**
   a. A corporation is planning to sell its 90-day commercial paper to investors offering an 8.4 percent yield. If the three-month T-bill's annualized rate is 7 percent, the default risk premium is estimated to be 0.6 percent, and there is a 0.4 percent tax adjustment, what is the appropriate liquidity premium?
   b. If due to unexpected changes in the economy the default risk premium increases to 0.8 percent, what is the appropriate yield to be offered on the commercial paper (assuming no other changes occur)?

7. **Forward Rate**
   a. Determine the forward rate for various one-year interest rate scenarios if the two-year interest rate is 8 percent, assuming no liquidity premium. Explain the relationship between the one-year interest rate and the one-year forward rate, holding the two-year interest rate constant.
   b. Determine the one-year forward rate for the same one-year interest rate scenarios as in question (a), assuming a liquidity premium of .4 percent. Does the relationship between the one-year interest rate and the forward rate change when considering a liquidity premium?
   c. Determine how the one-year forward rate would be affected if the quoted two-year interest rate rises, holding the quoted one-year interest rate constant. Also hold the liquidity premium constant. Explain the logic of this relationship.
   d. Determine how the one-year forward rate would be affected if the liquidity premium rises, holding the quoted one-year interest rates constant. Also, hold the two-year interest rates constant. Explain the logic of this relationship.

8. **After-Tax Yield** Determine how the after-tax yield from investing in a corporate bond is affected by higher tax rates, holding the before-tax yield constant. Explain the logic of this relationship.

9. **Debt Security Yield**
   a. Determine how the appropriate yield to be offered on a security is affected by a higher risk-free rate. Explain the logic of this relationship.
   b. Determine how the appropriate yield to be offered on a security is affected by a higher default risk premium. Explain the logic of this relationship.

Flow of Funds Exercise

Influence of the Structure of Interest Rates

Recall that Carson Company has obtained substantial loans from finance companies and commercial banks. The interest rate on the loans is tied to the six-month Treasury bill rate (and includes a risk premium) and is adjusted every six months. Thus, Carson's cost of obtaining funds is sensitive to interest rate movements. Because of its expectations that the U.S. economy will strengthen, Carson plans to grow in the future by expanding its business and through acquisitions. Carson expects that it will need substantial long-term financing to finance its growth and plans to borrow additional funds either through loans or by issuing bonds. It is also considering issuing stock to raise funds in the next year.

a. Assume that the market's expectations of the economy are similar to those of Carson. Also assume that the yield curve is primarily influenced by interest rate expectations. Would the yield curve be upward sloping or downward sloping? Why?

b. If Carson could obtain more debt financing for 10-year projects, would it prefer to obtain credit at a long-term fixed interest rate or at a floating rate? Why?

c. If Carson attempts to obtain funds by issuing 10-year bonds, explain what information would help to estimate the yield it would have to pay on 10-year bonds. That is, what are the key factors that would influence the rate it would pay on the 10-year bonds?

d. If Carson attempts to obtain funds by issuing loans with floating interest rates every six months, explain what information would help to estimate the yield it would have to pay over the next 10 years. That is, what are the key factors that would influence the rate it would pay over the 10-year period?

e. An upward-sloping yield curve suggests that the initial rate that financial institutions could charge on a long-term loan to Carson would be higher than the initial rate that they could charge on a loan that floats in accordance with short-term interest rates. Does this imply that creditors should prefer to provide a fixed-rate loan rather than a floating-rate loan to Carson? Explain why Carson's expectations of future interest rates are not necessarily the same as those of some financial institutions.

Internet/Excel Exercises

1. Assess the shape of the yield curve, using the website http://www.bloomberg.com. Click on "Market data" and then on "Rates and bonds." Is the Treasury yield curve upward or downward sloping? What is the yield of a 90-day Treasury bill? What is the yield of a 30-year Treasury bond?

2. Based on the various theories attempting to explain the shape of the yield curve, what could explain the difference between the yields of the 90-day Treasury bill and the 30-year Treasury bond? Which theory, in your opinion, is the most reasonable? Why?

WSJ Exercise

Interpreting the Structure of Interest Rates

a. **Explaining Yield Differentials** Using the most recent issue of *The Wall Street Journal,* review the yields for the following securities:

Type	Maturity	Yield
Treasury	10-year	_____
Corporate: high-quality	10-year	_____
Corporate: medium-quality	10-year	_____
Municipal: (tax-exempt)	10-year	_____

If credit (default) risk is the only reason for the yield differentials, what is the default risk premium on the corporate high-quality bonds? On the medium-quality bonds?

During a recent recession, high-quality corporate bonds offered a yield of 0.8 percent above Treasury bonds, and medium-quality bonds offered a yield of about 3.1 percent above Treasury bonds. How do these yield differentials compare to the differentials today? Explain the reason for the change in yield differentials.

Using the information in the previous table, complete the table below.

Marginal tax bracket of investors	Before-tax yield necessary to achieve existing after-tax yield of tax-exempt bonds	If the tax-exempt bonds have the same risk and other features as high-quality corporate bonds, which type of bond is preferable for investors in each tax bracket?
10%		
15%		
20%		
28%		
34%		

b. **Examining Recent Adjustments in Credit Risk** Using the most recent issue of *The Wall Street Journal,* review the corporate debt section showing the high-yield issue with the biggest price decrease.

- ■ Why do you think there was such a large decrease in price?

- ■ How does this decrease in price affect the expected yield for any investors who buy bonds now?

c. **Determining and Interpreting Today's Term Structure** Using the most recent issue of *The Wall Street Journal,* review the yield curve to determine the approximate yields for the following maturities:

Term to Maturity	Annualized Yield
1 year	
2 years	
3 years	

Assuming that the differences in these yields are solely because of interest rate expectations, determine the one-year forward rate as of one year from now and the one-year forward rate as of two years from now.

d. *The Wall Street Journal* provides a "Treasury Yield Curve." Use this curve to describe the market's expectations about future interest rates. If a liquidity premium exists, how would this affect your perception of the market's expectations?

Part 2: The Fed and Monetary Policy

The chapters in Part 2 explain how the Federal Reserve System (the Fed) affects economic conditions. Because the policies implemented by the Fed can influence securities prices, they are closely monitored by financial market participants. By assessing the Fed's policies, market participants can more accurately value securities and make more effective investment and financing decisions.

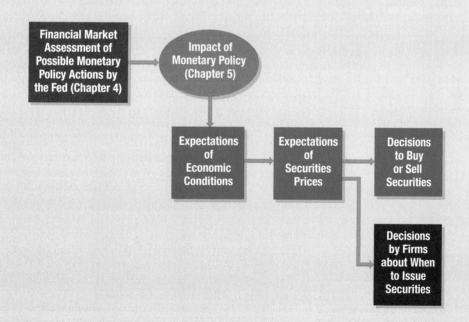

Chapter 4: Functions of the Fed

The Federal Reserve System (the Fed), as the central bank of the United States, has the responsibility for conducting national monetary policy. This policy influences interest rates and other economic variables that determine the prices of securities. Hence, participants in the financial markets closely monitor the Fed's monetary policy. It is important for them to understand how the Fed's actions may influence security prices so that they can manage their security portfolios in response to the Fed's policies.

The specific objectives of this chapter are to:

■ identify the key components of the Fed,

■ describe how the Fed influences monetary policy, and

■ explain how monetary policy is used in other countries.

Organization of the Fed

During the late 1800s and early 1900s, the United States experienced several banking panics, culminating with a major crisis in 1907. This motivated Congress to establish a central bank. Accordingly, in 1913 the Federal Reserve Act was passed, establishing reserve requirements for those commercial banks that chose to become members. It also specified 12 districts across the United States as well as a city in each district where a Federal Reserve district bank was to be established. Initially, each district bank had the ability to affect the money supply (as will be explained later in this chapter). Each district bank focused on its particular district, without much concern for other districts. Over time, the system became more centralized, and money supply decisions were assigned to a particular group of individuals rather than across 12 district banks.

http://www.clevelandfed.org
Features economic and banking topics.

The Fed earns most of its income in the form of interest on its holdings of U.S. government securities (to be discussed shortly). It also earns some income from providing services to financial institutions. Most of its income is transferred to the Treasury.

The Fed is involved (along with other agencies) in regulating commercial banks. It also conducts monetary policy, adjusting the money supply in an attempt to achieve full employment and price stability (low or zero inflation) in the United States.

The Fed as it exists today has five major components:

- Federal Reserve district banks
- Member banks
- Board of Governors
- Federal Open Market Committee (FOMC)
- Advisory committees

Federal Reserve District Banks

The 12 Federal Reserve districts are identified in Exhibit 4.1, along with the city where each district bank is located. The New York district bank is considered the most important because many large banks are located in this district. Commercial banks that become members of the Fed are required to purchase stock in their **Federal Reserve district bank.** This stock, which is not traded in a secondary market, pays a maximum dividend of 6 percent annually.

Each Fed district bank has nine directors. Six are elected by member banks in that district. Of these six directors, three are professional bankers and three have careers in business. The other three directors are appointed by the Board of Governors (to be discussed shortly). The nine directors appoint the president of their Fed district bank.

Fed district banks facilitate operations within the banking system by clearing checks, replacing old currency, and providing loans (through the discount window) to depository institutions in need of funds. They also collect economic data and conduct research projects on commercial banking and economic trends.

Exhibit 4.1   Locations of Federal Reserve District Banks

LEGEND

———— Boundaries of Federal Reserve Districts

———— Boundaries of Federal Reserve Branch Territories

⊙ Board of Governors of the Federal Reserve System

⊚ Federal Reserve Bank Cities

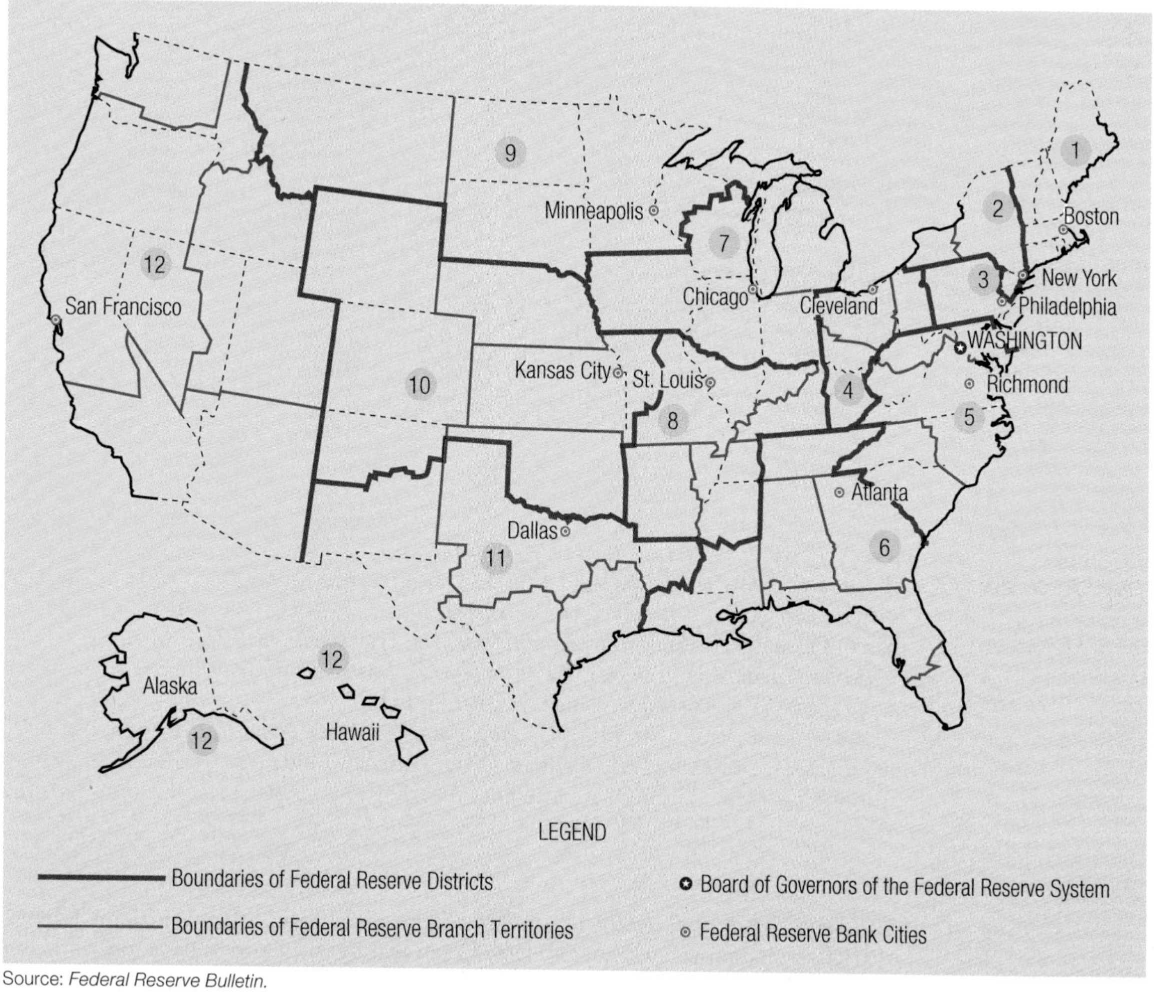

Source: *Federal Reserve Bulletin.*

Member Banks

Commercial banks can elect to become member banks if they meet specific requirements of the Board of Governors. All national banks (chartered by the Comptroller of the Currency) are required to be members of the Fed, but other banks (chartered by their respective states) are not. Currently, about 35 percent of all banks are members; these banks account for about 70 percent of all bank deposits.

Board of Governors

http://www.federalreserve
.gov Background on the
Board of Governors, board
meetings, board members,
and the structure of the Fed.

The **Board of Governors** (sometimes called the Federal Reserve Board) is made up of seven individual members with offices in Washington, D.C. Each member is appointed by the President of the United States and serves a nonrenewable 14-year term. This long term is thought to reduce political pressure on the governors and thus encourage the development of policies that will benefit the U.S. economy over the long run. The terms are staggered so that one term expires in every even-numbered year.

One of the seven board members is selected by the President to be Federal Reserve chairman for a four-year term, which may be renewed. The chairman has no more voting power than any other member, but may have more influence. Paul Volcker (chairman from 1979 to 1987), Alan Greenspan (chairman from 1987 to 2006), and Ben Bernanke (whose term began in 2006) were regarded as very persuasive.

The board has two main roles: (1) regulating commercial banks and (2) controlling monetary policy. It supervises and regulates commercial banks that are members of the Fed and bank holding companies. It oversees the operation of the 12 Federal Reserve district banks as they provide services to depository institutions and supervise specific commercial banks. It also establishes regulations on consumer finance. Previously, the board was responsible for determining ceiling interest rates on bank deposits, but those ceilings were completely phased out by 1986 as a result of the Depository Institutions Deregulation and Monetary Control Act of 1980. The board continues to participate in the supervision of member banks and in setting credit controls, such as margin requirements (percentage of a purchase of securities that must be paid with nonborrowed funds).

With regard to monetary policy, the board has the power to revise reserve requirements imposed on depository institutions. The board can also control the money supply by participating in the decisions of the Federal Open Market Committee, discussed next.

Federal Open Market Committee (FOMC)

http://www.federalreserve
.gov Obtain the minutes
of the most recent Federal
Open Market Committee
(FOMC).

The **Federal Open Market Committee (FOMC)** is made up of the seven members of the Board of Governors plus the presidents of five Fed district banks (the New York district bank plus 4 of the other 11 Fed district banks as determined on a rotating basis). Presidents of the seven remaining Fed district banks typically participate in the FOMC meetings but are not allowed to vote on policy decisions. The chairman of the Board of Governors serves as chairman of the FOMC.

The main goals of the FOMC are to achieve stable economic growth and price stability (low inflation). Achievement of these goals would stabilize financial markets and interest rates. The FOMC attempts to achieve its goals through control of the money supply, as described shortly.

Advisory Committees

The Federal Advisory Council consists of one member from each Federal Reserve district. Each district's member is elected each year by the board of directors of the respective district bank. The council meets with the Board of Governors in Washington,

Exhibit 4.2
Integration of Federal
Reserve Components

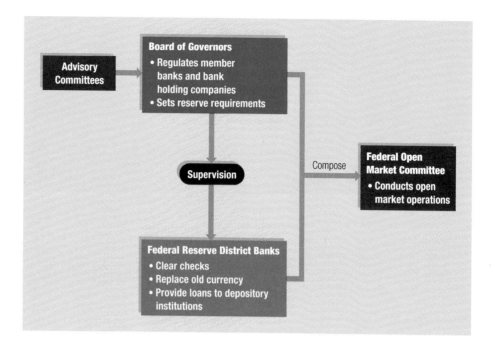

D.C., at least four times a year and makes recommendations about economic and banking issues.

The Consumer Advisory Council is made up of 30 members, representing the financial institutions industry and its consumers. This committee normally meets with the Board of Governors four times a year to discuss consumer issues.

The Thrift Institutions Advisory Council is made up of 12 members, representing savings banks, savings and loan associations, and credit unions. Its purpose is to offer views on issues specifically related to these institutions. It meets with the Board of Governors three times a year.

Integration of Federal Reserve Components

Exhibit 4.2 shows the relationships among the various components of the Federal Reserve System. The advisory committees advise the board, while the board oversees operations of the district banks. The board and representatives of the district banks make up the FOMC.

How the Fed Controls Money Supply

http://www.federalreserve
.gov/policy.htm Provides
minutes of FOMC meetings.
Notice from the minutes how
much attention is given to
any economic indicators that
can be used to anticipate
future economic growth or
inflation.

Changes in the money supply can have a major impact on economic conditions. Financial market participants closely monitor the Fed's actions so that they can anticipate how the money supply will be affected. They then use this information to forecast economic conditions and securities prices. The relationship between the money supply and economic conditions is discussed in detail in the following chapter. First, it is important to understand *how* the Fed controls the money supply.

Open Market Operations

The FOMC meets eight times a year. At each meeting, the target money supply growth level and interest rate level are determined, and actions are taken to implement the monetary policy dictated by the FOMC. If the Fed wants to consider changing its money growth or interest rate targets before its next scheduled meeting because of unusual circumstances, it may engage in a conference call meeting.

Pre-Meeting Economic Report About two weeks before the FOMC meeting, FOMC members are sent the **Beige Book,** which is a consolidated report of regional economic conditions in each of the 12 districts. Each Federal Reserve district bank is responsible for reporting its regional conditions, and all of these reports are consolidated to compose the Beige Book.

Economic Presentations The FOMC meeting is conducted in the board room of the building where the Board of Governors is located in Washington, D.C. The meeting is attended by the seven members of the Board of Governors, the 12 presidents of the Fed district banks, and staff members (typically economists) of the Board of Governors. The meeting begins with presentations by the staff members about current economic conditions and recent economic trends. They provide data and trends for wages, consumer prices, unemployment, gross domestic product, business inventories, foreign exchange rates, interest rates, and financial market conditions.

The staff members also assess production levels, business investment, residential construction, international trade, and international economic growth. This assessment is conducted to predict economic growth and inflation in the United States, assuming that the Fed does not adjust its monetary policy. For example, a decline in business inventories may lead to an expectation of stronger economic growth, as firms will need to boost production in order to replenish inventories. Conversely, an increase in inventories may indicate that firms will reduce their production and possibly their workforce as well. An increase in business investment indicates that businesses are expanding their production capacity and are likely to increase production in the future. An increase in economic growth in foreign countries is important because a portion of the rising incomes in those countries will be spent on U.S. products or services. The Fed uses this information to determine whether U.S. economic growth is adequate.

Much attention is also given to any factors that can affect inflation. For example, oil prices are closely monitored because they affect the cost of producing and transporting many products. A decline in business inventories when production is near full capacity may indicate an excessive demand for products that will pull prices up. This condition indicates higher inflation because firms may raise the prices of their products when they are producing near full capacity and experience shortages. If firms attempt to expand capacity under these conditions, they will have to raise wages to obtain additional qualified employees. They will incur higher costs from raising wages and therefore raise the prices of their products. The Fed becomes concerned when several indicators suggest that higher inflation is likely.

The staff members typically base their forecasts for economic conditions on the assumption that the prevailing monetary growth level will still be applied in the future. When it is highly likely that the monetary growth level will be changed, they provide forecasts for economic conditions under different monetary growth scenarios. Their goal is to provide facts and economic forecasts, but not to make judgments about the appropriate monetary policy. The members normally receive some economic information a few days before the meeting so that they are prepared when listening to the presentations by staff members.

FOMC Decisions Once the presentations are completed, each FOMC member has a chance to offer recommendations as to whether the prevailing monetary growth and interest rate target levels should be changed and, if so, how they should be changed. Even the nonvoting members may offer recommendations. The chairman of the Fed may also offer a recommendation and usually has some influence over the other members. After each member of the FOMC has provided his or her recommendation, the voting members of the FOMC vote on whether the prevailing money supply and interest rate target levels should be revised. Most FOMC decisions on monetary policy are unanimous, although it is not unusual for some decisions to have one or two dissenting votes.

Role of the Fed's Trading Desk

If the Fed determines that a change in its monetary policy is appropriate, its decision is forwarded to the **Trading Desk** (or the **Open Market Desk**) at the New York Fed district bank. It is here that open market operations, or the Fed's trading of government securities, are carried out. The FOMC's decision on the target money supply level is forwarded to the Trading Desk at the New York Federal Reserve district bank through a statement called the **policy directive.** The FOMC objectives are specified in the form of a target range, such as an annualized growth rate of 3 to 5 percent in the money supply over the next few months, rather than one specific money supply level.

The FOMC also specifies a desired target range for the federal funds rate, the rate charged by banks on short-term loans to each other. Even though this rate is determined by the banks that participate in the federal funds market, it is subject to the supply and demand for funds in the banking system. Thus, the Fed can influence the federal funds rate by revising the amount of funds in the banking system. In recent years, the Fed has specified a single federal funds target rate when it has engaged in open market operations. Since all short-term interest rates are affected by the supply of and demand for funds, they tend to move together. Thus, the Fed's actions affect all short-term interest rates that are market determined and may even affect long-term interest rates as well.

http://www.treasurydirect .gov Treasury note and bond auction results.

After receiving the policy directive from the FOMC, the manager of the Trading Desk instructs traders who work at that desk on the amount of Treasury securities to buy or sell in the secondary market based on the directive. The buying and selling of government securities (through the Trading Desk) is referred to as **open market operations.** Even though the Trading Desk at the Federal Reserve Bank of New York receives a policy directive from the FOMC only eight times a year, it continuously conducts open market operations to control the money supply in response to ongoing changes in bank deposit levels.

Fed Purchase of Securities When traders at the Trading Desk at the Federal Reserve Bank of New York are instructed to purchase a specified dollar amount of securities, they call government securities dealers. The dealers provide a list of securities for sale that gives the denomination and maturity of each security as well as the dealer's ask quote (the price at which the dealer is willing to sell the security). From this list, the traders attempt to purchase those that are most attractive (lowest prices for whatever maturities are desired) until they have purchased the amount requested by the manager of the Trading Desk. The accounting department of the New York district bank then notifies the government bond department to receive and pay for those securities.

When the Fed purchases securities through the government securities dealers, the account balances of the dealers are credited with the dollar amount of their sales. Thus, the total amount of funds at the dealers' banks increases. The total funds of commercial banks increase by the dollar amount of securities purchased by the Fed. This activity initiated by the Fed's policy directive represents a loosening of money supply growth.

The Trading Desk is sometimes directed to buy a sufficient amount of Treasury securities to force a decline in the federal funds rate to a new targeted level set by the FOMC. The Trading Desk then buys Treasury securities until it has reduced the federal funds rate to the new targeted level. As the supply of funds in the banking system increases, the federal funds rate declines along with other interest rates.

The Fed's purchase of government securities has a different impact than a purchase by another investor would have because the Fed's purchase results in additional bank funds and increases the ability of banks to make loans and create new deposits. An increase in funds can allow for a net increase in deposit balances and therefore an increase in the money supply. Conversely, the purchase of government securities by someone other than the Fed (such as an investor) results in offsetting account balance positions at commercial banks.

Fed Sale of Securities If the Trading Desk at the Federal Reserve Bank of New York is instructed to decrease the money supply, its traders sell government securities (obtained from previous purchases) to government securities dealers. The securities are sold to the dealers that submit the highest bids. As the dealers pay for the securities, their account balances are reduced. Thus, the total amount of funds at commercial banks is reduced by the market value of the securities sold by the Fed. This activity initiated by the FOMC's policy directive is referred to as a tightening of money supply growth.

The Trading Desk is sometimes directed to sell a sufficient amount of Treasury securities to increase the federal funds rate to a new targeted level set by the FOMC. When the Trading Desk sells a sufficient amount of Treasury securities, it creates a shortage of funds in the banking system. Consequently, the federal funds rate increases along with other interest rates.

Fed Use of Repurchase Agreements In some cases, the Fed may desire to increase the aggregate level of bank funds for only a few days to ensure adequate liquidity in the banking system on those days. Under these conditions, the Trading Desk may trade **repurchase agreements** rather than government securities. It purchases Treasury securities from government securities dealers with an agreement to sell back the securities at a specified date in the near future. Initially, the level of funds rises as the securities are sold; it is then reduced when the dealers repurchase the securities. The Trading Desk uses repurchase agreements during holidays and other such periods to correct temporary imbalances in the level of bank funds. To correct a temporary excess of funds, the Trading Desk sells some of its Treasury securities holdings to securities dealers and agrees to repurchase them at a specified future date.

How Open Market Operations Affect All Interest Rates

Even though most interest rates are market determined, the Fed can have a strong influence on these rates by controlling the supply of loanable funds. The use of open market operations to increase bank funds can affect various market-determined interest rates. First, the federal funds rate may decline because some banks have a larger supply of excess funds to lend out in the federal funds market. Second, banks with excess funds may offer new loans at a lower interest rate in order to make use of these funds. Third, these banks may also lower interest rates offered on deposits because they have more than adequate funds to conduct existing operations.

Since open market operations commonly involve the buying or selling of Treasury bills, the yields on Treasury securities are influenced along with the yields (interest rates) offered on bank deposits. For example, when the Fed buys Treasury bills as a means of increasing the money supply, it places upward pressure on their prices. Since these securities offer a fixed value to investors at maturity, a higher price translates into a lower yield for investors who buy them and hold them until maturity. While Treasury yields are affected directly by open market operations, bank rates are also affected because of the change in the money supply that open market operations bring about.

As the yields on Treasury bills and bank deposits decline, investors search for alternative investments such as other debt securities. As more funds are invested in these securities, the yields will decline. Thus, open market operations used to increase bank funds influence not only bank deposit and loan rates but also the yields on other debt securities. The reduction in yields on debt securities lowers the cost of borrowing for the issuers of new debt securities. This can encourage potential borrowers (including corporations and individuals) to borrow and make expenditures that they might not have made if interest rates were higher.

If open market operations are used to reduce bank funds, the opposite effects occur. More banks have deficient funds, and fewer banks have any excess funds. Thus, there is upward pressure on the federal funds rate, on the loan rates charged to individuals and firms, and on the rates offered to bank depositors. As bank deposit rates rise, some investors may be encouraged to create bank deposits rather than invest in other debt securities. This activity reduces the amount of funds available for these debt instruments, thereby increasing the yield offered on the instruments. More specific details about how money supply adjustments can affect interest rates and economic conditions are provided in the following chapter.

Dynamic versus Defensive Open Market Operations

Depending on the intent, open market operations can be classified as either **dynamic** or **defensive.** Dynamic operations are implemented to increase or decrease the level of funds; defensive operations offset the impact of other conditions that affect the level of funds. For example, if the Fed expects a large inflow of cash into commercial banks, it could offset this inflow by selling some of its Treasury security holdings.

Open Market Operations in Response to Economic Conditions

During the 2001–2003 period, when economic conditions were weak, the Fed frequently used open market operations to reduce interest rates. In the 2004–2007 period, the economy improved, and the Fed's concern shifted from a weak economy to high inflation. The Fed frequently used open market operations to raise interest rates over this period.

Adjusting the Reserve Requirement Ratio

Depository institutions are subject to a **reserve requirement ratio,** which is the proportion of their deposit accounts that must be held as reserves. This ratio is set by the Board of Governors. Depository institutions have historically been forced to maintain between 8 and 12 percent of their transactions accounts (such as checking accounts) and a smaller proportion of their other savings accounts as required reserves, which cannot be used to earn interest. In 1980 Congress passed the **Depository Institutions Deregulation and Monetary Control Act (DIDMCA),** which mandated that all depository institutions be subject to the reserve requirements imposed by the Fed. The reserve requirements were reduced relative to what the Fed previously required, but all required reserves were still to be held in a non-interest-bearing form.

Because the reserve requirement ratio affects the degree to which the money supply can change, it is sometimes modified by the Board of Governors to adjust the money supply. When the board reduces the reserve requirement ratio, it increases the proportion of a bank's deposits that can be lent out by depository institutions. As the funds loaned out are spent, a portion of them will return to the depository institutions in the form of new deposits. The lower the reserve requirement ratio, the greater the lending capacity of depository institutions, so any initial change in bank reserves can cause a larger change in the money supply. In 1992, the reserve requirement ratio on transactions accounts was reduced from 12 percent to 10 percent, where it has remained.

How Reserve Requirement Adjustments Affect Money Growth
An adjustment in the reserve requirement ratio changes the proportion of financial institution funds that can be lent out, which, in turn, affects the degree to which the money supply can grow.

ILLUSTRATION Assume the following conditions in the banking system:

Assumption 1. Banks obtain all their funds from demand deposits and use all funds except required reserves to make loans.

Assumption 2. The public does not store any cash; any funds withdrawn from banks are spent; and any funds received are deposited in banks.

Assumption 3. The reserve requirement ratio on demand deposits is 10 percent.

Based on these assumptions, 10 percent of all bank deposits are maintained as required reserves, and the other 90 percent are loaned out (zero excess reserves). Now assume that the Fed initially uses open market operations by purchasing $100 million worth of Treasury securities.

As the Treasury securities dealers sell securities to the Fed, their deposit balances at commercial banks increase by $100 million. Banks maintain 10 percent of the $100 million, or $10 million, as required reserves and lend out the rest. As the $90 million lent out is spent, it returns to banks as new demand deposit accounts (by whoever receives the funds that were spent). Banks maintain 10 percent, or $9 million, of these new deposits as required reserves and lend out the remainder ($81 million). The initial increase in demand deposits (money) multiplies into a much larger amount. This process, illustrated in Exhibit 4.3, will not continue forever. Every time the funds lent out return to a bank, a portion (10 percent) is retained as required reserves. Thus, the amount of new deposits created is less for each round. Under the previous assump-

Exhibit 4.3
Illustration of Multiplier Effect

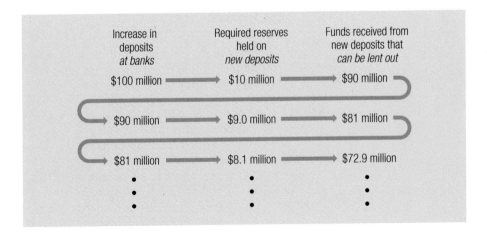

tions, the initial money supply injection of $100 million would multiply by 1/(reserve requirement ratio), or 1/.10, to equal 10, so the total change in the money supply once the cycle is complete is $100 million × 10 = $1 billion. ■

As this simplified example demonstrates, an initial injection of funds will multiply into a larger amount. The reserve requirement controls the amount of loanable funds that can be created from new deposits. A higher reserve requirement ratio causes an initial injection of funds to multiply by a smaller amount. Conversely, a lower reserve requirement ratio causes it to multiply by a greater amount. In this way, the Fed can adjust money supply growth by adjusting the reserve requirement ratio.

In reality, households sometimes hold cash, and banks sometimes hold excess reserves, contradicting the assumptions of banks holding only demand deposits and zero excess reserves. Consequently, major leakages occur, and money does not multiply to the extent shown in the example. The money multiplier can change over time because of changes in the excess reserve level and in household preferences for demand deposits versus time deposits (which are not included in the most narrow definition of money). This complicates the task of forecasting how an initial adjustment in bank reserves will ultimately affect the money supply level. Another disadvantage of using the reserve requirement as a monetary policy tool is that an adjustment in the reserve requirement ratio can cause erratic shifts in the money supply. Thus, the probability of missing the target money supply level is higher when using the reserve requirement ratio.

Adjusting the Fed's Loan Rate

Before 2003, the Fed set its loan rate (which was called the "discount rate") at low levels when it wanted to encourage banks to borrow, as this activity increased the amount of funds injected into the financial system. The discount rate was viewed as a monetary policy tool, because it could have been used to affect the money supply (although it was not an effective tool).

Since 2003, the Fed's rate on short-term loans to depository institutions is referred to as the primary credit lending rate and is set slightly above the federal funds rate (the rate charged on short-term loans between depository institutions). Thus, depository institutions rely on the Fed only as a backup for loans, because they should be able to obtain short-term loans from other institutions at a lower interest rate.

As of 2003, the Fed classified the loans that it provides into primary credit and secondary credit. Primary credit may be used for any purpose and is available only to depository institutions that satisfy specific criteria reflecting financial soundness. Secondary credit is provided to depository institutions that do not satisfy those criteria, and they must pay a premium above the loan rate charged on primary credit. The Fed's lending facility can be an important source of liquidity for some depository institutions, but it is no longer used to control the money supply.

Factors Considered When the Fed Controls the Money Supply

When the Fed attempts to control the money supply, it must consider the following factors.

Technical Factors

The money supply can shift abruptly as a result of so-called technical factors, such as currency in circulation and Federal Reserve float. When the amount of currency in circulation increases (such as during the holiday season), the corresponding increase in net deposit withdrawals reduces funds. When it decreases, the net addition to deposits increases funds. Federal Reserve float is the amount of checks credited to bank funds that have not yet been collected. A rise in float causes an increase in bank funds, and a decrease in float causes a reduction in bank funds.

Staff at the Federal Reserve Bank of New York along with those at the Board of Governors in Washington, D.C., provide daily forecasts of how technical factors such as these will affect the level of funds. The Fed must account for such influences when implementing monetary policy. The manager of the Trading Desk incorporates the expected impact of technical factors on funds into the instructions to traders. If the policy directive calls for growth in funds but technical factors are expected to increase funds, the instructions will call for a smaller injection of funds than if the technical factors did not exist. Conversely, if technical factors are expected to reduce funds, the instructions will call for a larger injection of funds to offset the impact of the technical factors.

Which Form of Money to Control?

http://www.federalreserve.gov/releases Features various Federal Reserve statistical releases.

When the Fed attempts to control the money supply, it must decide which form of money to control. The optimal form of money should (1) be controllable by the Fed and (2) have a predictable impact on economic variables when adjusted by the Fed. The most narrow form of money, known as **M1,** includes currency held by the public and checking deposits (such as demand deposits, NOW accounts, and automatic transfer balances) at depository institutions. M1 does not include all funds that can be used for transactions purposes. For example, checks can be written against a **money market deposit account (MMDA)** offered by depository institutions or against a money market mutual fund. In addition, funds can easily be withdrawn from savings accounts to make transactions. For this reason, a broader measure of money, called **M2,** also deserves consideration. It includes everything in M1 as well as savings accounts and small time deposits, MMDAs, and some other items. Another measure of money, called **M3,** includes everything in M2 as well as large time deposits and other items. Although there are even a few broader measures of money, M1, M2, and M3 receive the most attention. A comparison of M1, M2, and M3 is provided in Exhibit 4.4.

The M1 money measure is more volatile than M2 or M3. Since M1 can change simply because of changes in the types of deposits maintained by households, M2 and M3 are more reliable measures for monitoring and controlling the money supply.

Global Monetary Policy

GL🌐BALASPECTS Each country has its own central bank that conducts monetary policy. The central banks of industrialized countries tend to have somewhat similar goals, which

Exhibit 4.4
Comparison of Money Supply Measures

Money Supply Measures
M1 = currency + checking deposits
M2 = M1 + savings deposits, MMDAs, overnight repurchase agreements, Eurodollars, noninstitutional money market mutual funds, and small time deposits
M3 = M2 + institutional money market mutual funds, large time deposits, and repurchase agreements and Eurodollars lasting more than one day

essentially reflect price stability (low inflation) and economic growth (low unemployment). Resouces and conditions vary among countries, however, so a given central bank may focus more on a particular economic goal.

Like the Fed, central banks of other industrialized countries use open market operations and reserve requirement adjustments as monetary tools. They also make adjustments in the interest rate they charge on loans to banks as a monetary policy tool. The monetary policy tools are generally used as a means of affecting local market interest rates in order to influence economic conditions.

Because country economies are integrated, the Fed must consider economic conditions in other major countries when assessing the U.S. economy. The Fed may be most effective when it coordinates its activities with those of central banks of other countries. Central banks commonly work together when they intervene in the foreign exchange market, but coordinating monetary policies can be difficult because of conflicts of interest.

A Single Eurozone Monetary Policy

http://www.federalreserve.gov Provides links on the European Central Bank and other foreign central banks.

The national currencies of the following 12 European countries were recently withdrawn from the financial system and replaced by the euro: Austria, Belgium, Finland, France, Germany, Greece, Ireland, Italy, Luxembourg, the Netherlands, Portugal, and Spain. The three other members of the European Union (Denmark, Sweden, United Kingdom) at that time decided not to participate in the euro initially but may join later. Since the euro was introduced in 1999, 12 emerging countries in Europe have joined the European Union (10 countries, including the Czech Republic and Hungary, joined in 2004, and Bulgaria and Romania joined in 2007). These new members may participate in the euro later if they satisfy the limitations imposed on government deficits.

The European Central Bank (ECB), based in Frankfurt, is responsible for setting monetary policy for all participating European countries. Its objective is to control inflation in the participating countries and to stabilize (within reasonable boundaries) the value of the euro with respect to other major currencies. Thus, the ECB's monetary goals of price stability and currency stability are somewhat similar to those of individual countries around the world, but differ in that they are focused on a group of countries rather than a single country. Because participating countries are subject to the monetary policy imposed by the ECB, a given country no longer has full control over the monetary policy implemented within its borders at any given time. The implementation of a common monetary policy may lead to more political unification among participating countries and encourage them to develop similar national defense and foreign policies.

Impact of the Euro on Monetary Policy As just described, the use of a common currency forces countries to abide by a common monetary policy. Any changes in the money supply affect all European countries using the euro as their form of money. Having a single currency also means that the interest rate offered on government securities must be similar across the participating European countries. Any discrepancy in rates would encourage investors within these countries to invest in the country with the highest rate, which would realign the interest rates among the countries.

Although having a single monetary policy may allow for more consistent economic conditions across the eurozone countries, it prevents any participating country from solving local economic problems with its own unique monetary policy. Eurozone governments may disagree on the ideal monetary policy for their local economies, but they must nevertheless agree on a single monetary policy. Yet any given policy used in a particular period may enhance economic conditions in some countries and adversely affect others. Each participating country is still able to apply its own fiscal policy (tax and government expenditure decisions), however.

One concern about the euro is that each of the participating countries has its own agenda, which may prevent unified decisions about the future direction of the euro-zone economies. Each country was supposed to show restraint on fiscal policy spending so that it could improve its budget deficit situation. Nevertheless, some countries have ignored restraint in favor of resolving domestic unemployment problems. The euro's initial instability was partially attributed to political maneuvering as individual countries tried to serve their own interests at the expense of the other participating countries. This lack of solidarity is exactly the reason why there was some concern about using a single currency (and therefore monetary policy) among several European countries.

Variations in the Value of the Euro Since the euro was introduced in 1999, it has experienced a bumpy ride. Its value initially declined substantially against the British pound, the dollar, and many other currencies. By October 2001, its value was $.90, or about 25 percent less than its value when it was introduced. The weakness was partially attributed to capital outflows from Europe. More money was flowing out of Europe and into U.S. and other financial markets than was flowing from these countries to Europe. The net outflows from Europe were partially caused by lack of confidence in the euro. Investors preferred to hold assets denominated in dollars than in euros.

During the 2002–2007 period, however, the euro appreciated substantially. One reason for its strength in this period was that the interest rate on the euro was higher than that of the dollar. Thus, capital flowed to the eurozone to take advantage of the higher interest rate on euro-denominated debt securities.

Global Central Bank Coordination

In some cases, the central banks of various countries coordinate their efforts for a common cause. Shortly after the terrorist attack on the United States on September 11, 2001, central banks of several countries injected money denominated in their respective currencies into the banking system to provide more liquidity. This strategy was intended to ensure that sufficient money would be available in case customers began to withdraw funds from banks or cash machines. On September 17, 2001, the Fed's move to reduce interest rates before the U.S. stock market reopened was immediately followed by similar decisions by the Bank of Canada (Canada's central bank) and the European Central Bank.

Sometimes, however, central banks have conflicting objectives. For example, it is not unusual for two countries to simultaneously experience weak economies. In this situation, each central bank may consider intervening to weaken its home currency, which could increase foreign demand for exports denominated in that currency. If both central banks attempt this type of intervention simultaneously, however, the exchange rate between the two currencies will be subject to conflicting forces.

ILLUSTRATION Today, the Fed plans to intervene directly in the foreign exchange market by selling dollars for yen in an attempt to weaken the dollar. Meanwhile, the Bank of Japan plans to sell yen for dollars in the foreign exchange market in an attempt to weaken the yen. The effects are offsetting. One central bank can attempt to have a more powerful impact by selling more of its home currency in the foreign exchange market, but the other central bank may respond to offset that force. ∎

Summary

■ The key components of the Federal Reserve System are the Board of Governors and the Federal Open Market Committee. The Board of Governors determines the reserve requirements on account balances at depository institutions. It also represents an important subset of the Federal Open Market Committee (FOMC), which determines U.S. monetary policy. The FOMC's monetary policy has a major influence on interest rates and other economic conditions.

■ The Fed uses open market operations (the buying and selling of securities) as a means of adjusting the money supply. The Fed purchases securities as a means of increasing the money supply, whereas it sells them as a means of reducing the money supply.

■ Each country has its own central bank, which is responsible for conducting monetary policy to achieve economic goals such as low inflation and low unemployment. Twelve countries in Europe recently adopted a single currency, which causes all of these countries to be subject to the same monetary policy.

Point Counter-Point

Should There Be a Global Central Bank?

Point Yes. A global central bank could serve all countries in the manner that the European Central Bank now serves several European countries. With a single central bank, there could be a single monetary policy across all countries.

Counter-Point No. A global central bank could create a global monetary policy only if a single currency was used throughout the world. Moreover, all countries would not agree on the monetary policy that would be appropriate.

Who Is Correct? Use the Internet to learn more about this issue. Offer your own opinion on this issue.

Questions and Applications

1. **The Fed** Briefly describe the origin of the Federal Reserve System. Describe the functions of the Fed district banks.

2. **FOMC** What are the main goals of the Federal Open Market Committee (FOMC)? How does it attempt to achieve these goals?

3. **Open Market Operations** Explain how the Fed increases the money supply through open market operations.

4. **Policy Directive** What is the policy directive, and who carries it out?

5. **Beige Book** What is the Beige Book, and why is it important to the FOMC?

6. **Reserve Requirements** How is money supply growth affected by an increase in the reserve requirement ratio?

7. **Control of Money Supply** Describe the characteristics that would be desirable for a measure of money to be manipulated by the Fed.

8. **FOMC Economic Presentations** What is the purpose of economic presentations during an FOMC meeting?

9. **Open Market Operations** Explain how the Fed can use open market operations to reduce the money supply.

10. **Effect on Money Supply** Why do the Fed's open market operations have a different effect on the money supply than transactions between two depository institutions?

Interpreting Financial News

Interpret the following statements made by Wall Street analysts and portfolio managers:

a. "The Fed's future monetary policy will be dependent on the economic indicators to be reported this week."

b. "The Fed's role is to take the punch bowl away just as the party is coming alive."

c. "Inflation will likely increase because real short-term interest rates currently are negative."

Managing in Financial Markets

Anticipating the Fed's Actions As a manager of a large U.S. firm, one of your assignments is to monitor U.S. economic conditions so that you can forecast the demand for products sold by your firm. You recognize that the Federal Reserve attempts to implement monetary policy to affect economic growth and inflation. In addition, you recognize that the federal government implements spending and tax policies (fiscal policy) to affect economic growth and inflation. It is difficult to achieve high economic growth without igniting inflation, however. Although the Federal Reserve is often said to be independent of the administration in Washington, D.C., there is much interaction between monetary and fiscal policies.

Assume that the economy is currently stagnant, and some economists are concerned about the possibility of a recession. Some industries, however, are experiencing high growth, and inflation is higher this year than in the previous five years. Assume that the Federal Reserve chairman's term will expire in four months and that the President of the United States will have to appoint a new chairman (or reappoint the existing chairman). It is widely known that the existing chairman would like to be reappointed. Also assume that next year is an election year for the administration.

a. Given the circumstances, do you expect that the administration will be more concerned about increasing economic growth or reducing inflation?

b. Given the circumstances, do you expect that the Fed will be more concerned about increasing economic growth or reducing inflation?

c. Your firm is relying on you for some insight on how the government will influence economic conditions and therefore the demand for your firm's products. Given the circumstances, what is your forecast of how the government will affect economic conditions?

Flow of Funds Exercise

Monitoring the Fed

Recall that Carson Company has obtained substantial loans from finance companies and commercial banks. The interest rate on the loans is tied to market interest rates and is adjusted every six months. Because of its expectations of a strong U.S. economy, Carson plans to grow in the future by expanding its business and through acquisitions. It expects that it will need substantial long-term financing and plans to borrow additional funds either through loans or by issuing bonds. It is also considering issuing stock to raise funds in the next year.

Given its large exposure to interest rates charged on its debt, Carson closely monitors Fed actions. It subscribes to a special service that attempts to monitor the Fed's actions in the Treasury security markets. It re-

cently received an alert from the service that suggested the Fed has been selling large holdings of its Treasury securities in the secondary Treasury securities market.

a. How should Carson interpret the actions by the Fed? That is, will these actions place upward or downward pressure on Treasury securities prices? Explain.

b. Will these actions place upward or downward pressure on Treasury yields? Explain.

c. Will these actions place upward or downward pressure on interest rates? Explain.

Internet/Excel Exercises

Assess the current structure of the Federal Reserve System, using the website http://www.federalreserve.gov.fomc.

Go to the minutes of the most recent meeting. Who is the current chairman? Who is the current vice chairman? How many people attended the meeting? Describe the main issues discussed at the meeting.

WSJ Exercise

Reviewing Fed Policies

Review the "Credit Markets" section in recent issues of *The Wall Street Journal* and search for any comments that relate to the Fed's money supply targets or the federal funds target rate. Does it appear that the Fed may attempt to revise its money supply growth target or its federal funds target rate? If so, why?

Chapter 5: Monetary Policy

The previous chapter discussed the Federal Reserve System and how it controls the money supply, information essential to financial market participants. It is just as important for participants to know how changes in the money supply affect the economy, which is the subject of this chapter.

The specific objectives of this chapter are to:

- describe monetary policy,
- explain the tradeoffs involved in monetary policy,
- describe how financial market participants monitor and forecast the Fed's policies, and
- explain how monetary and fiscal policies are related.

Mechanics of Monetary Policy

The monetary policy goals of most central banks are focused on stabilizing the economy. Recall that the Fed's goals are to achieve a low level of inflation and a low level of unemployment. The Fed periodically adjusts its interest rate targets in order to achieve its monetary policy goals.

Money supply adjustments by a nation's central bank (such as the Fed in the United States) affect interest rates, which affect the level of aggregate borrowing and spending by households and firms. The level of aggregate spending affects demand for products and services, and therefore affects price levels (inflation) and the unemployment level. This can be illustrated using the loanable funds framework described in Chapter 2. Recall that the interaction of the supply of loanable funds available and the demand for loanable funds determines the interest rate charged on loanable funds. Much of the demand for loanable funds is by households, corporations, and government agencies that need to borrow money. Recall that the demand schedule indicates the quantity of funds that would be demanded (at that time) at various possible interest rates. This schedule is downward sloping because many potential borrowers would borrow a larger quantity of funds at lower interest rates.

The supply schedule of loanable funds indicates the quantity of funds that would be supplied (at that time) at various possible interest rates. This schedule is upward sloping because suppliers of funds tend to supply a larger amount of funds when the interest rate is higher. Assume that as of today, the demand and supply schedules for loanable funds are represented by D_1 and S_1 in the left graph of Exhibit 5.1. Based on these schedules, the equilibrium interest rate would be i_1. The right graph of Exhibit 5.1 represents the typical relationship between the interest rate on loanable funds and the level of business investment as of today. The relation is inverse because corporations are more willing to expand when interest rates are relatively low. Given today's equilibrium interest rate of i_1, the level of business investment is B_1.

Exhibit 5.1
Effects of an Increased
Money Supply

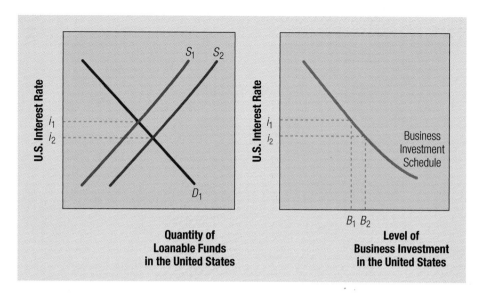

Correcting a Weak Economy

If the economy is weak, the Fed can increase the level of spending as a means of stimulating the economy. It uses open market operations to increase the money supply, a move that is intended to reduce interest rates and encourage more borrowing and spending.

ILLUSTRATION The Fed can attempt to stimulate the economy by purchasing Treasury securities in the secondary market. As the investors who sell their Treasury securities receive payment from the Fed, their account balances at financial institutions increase, without any offsetting decrease in the account balances of any other financial institutions. Thus, there is a net increase in the supply of loanable funds. If the Fed's action results in an increase of $5 billion in loanable funds, the quantity of loanable funds supplied will now be $5 billion higher at any possible interest rate level. This means that the supply schedule for loanable funds shifts outward to S_2 in Exhibit 5.1. The difference between S_2 and S_1 is that S_2 incorporates the $5 billion of loanable funds added as a result of the Fed's actions.

Given the shift in the supply schedule for loanable funds, the quantity of loanable funds supplied exceeds the quantity of loanable funds demanded at the interest rate level i_1. Thus, the interest rate will decline to i_2, the level at which the quantities of loanable funds supplied and demanded are equal.

The lower interest rate level causes an increase in the level of business investment from B_1 to B_2. The increase in business investment represents new business spending that was triggered by lower interest rates, which reduced the corporate cost of financing new projects. ∎

Correcting High Inflation

If excessive inflation is the main concern, monetary policy would still focus on aggregate spending as the variable that must be adjusted. The Fed can use open market operations to reduce money supply growth, a move that can reduce the level of spending, thereby slowing economic growth and reducing inflationary pressure. A portion of the high inflation is possibly due to excessive spending that is pulling up prices, commonly referred to as **demand-pull inflation.**

ILLUSTRATION The Fed can slow economic growth by selling some of its holdings of Treasury securities in the secondary market. As investors make payments to purchase these Treasury securities, their account balances decrease, without any offsetting increase in the account balances of any other financial institutions. Thus, there is a net decrease in deposit accounts (money), which results in a net decrease in the quantity of loanable funds. Assume that the Fed's action causes a decrease of $5 billion in loanable funds. The quantity of loanable funds supplied will now be $5 billion lower at any possible interest rate level. This reflects an inward shift in the supply schedule from S_1 to S_2, as shown in Exhibit 5.2.

Given the inward shift in the supply schedule for loanable funds, the quantity of loanable funds demanded exceeds the quantity of loanable funds supplied at the original interest rate level (i_1). Thus, the interest rate will increase to i_2, the level at which the quantities of loanable funds supplied and demanded are equal.

The higher interest rate level increases the corporate cost of financing new projects and therefore causes a decrease in the level of business investment from B_1 to B_2. As economic growth is slowed by the reduction in business investment, inflationary pressure may be reduced. Thus, reducing the money supply is an indirect means by which the Fed may reduce inflation. ■

Exhibit 5.3 summarizes how the Fed (as the central bank of the United States) can affect economic conditions through its influence on the supply of loanable funds. The top part of the exhibit illustrates a stimulative monetary policy intended to boost economic growth, and the bottom part illustrates a restrictive monetary policy intended to reduce inflation.

Limitations of Monetary Policy

Monetary policy has limitations, which may prevent the Fed from achieving its goals. Some of the more important limitations are mentioned here.

Impact of a Credit Crunch The effects of monetary policy on the economy are dependent on the willingness of depository institutions to lend funds. Even if the Fed increases the level of bank funds during a weak economy, banks may be

Exhibit 5.2
Effects of a Reduced
Money Supply

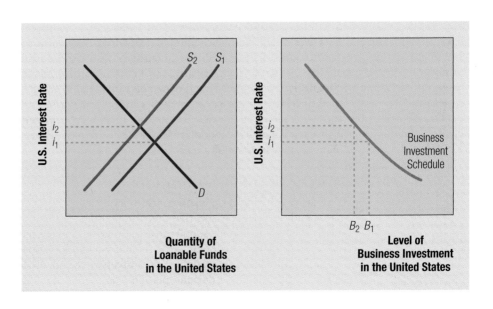

Quantity of
Loanable Funds
in the United States

Level of
Business Investment
in the United States

Exhibit 5.3
How Monetary Policy
Can Affect Economic
Conditions

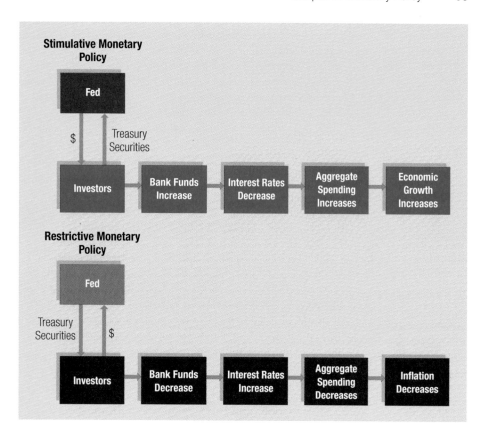

unwilling to extend credit to some potential borrowers, and the result is a *credit crunch*. If banks do not lend out the newly created funds, the economy will not be stimulated. The banks are reluctant to lend out sufficient funds because they are concerned about the effects of a weak economy on loan repayment probability. Banks provide loans only after confirming that the borrower's future cash flows will be adequate to make loan repayments. In a weak economy, the future cash flows of many potential borrowers are more uncertain, causing a reduction in loan applications (demand for loans) and in the number of qualified loan applicants.

Banks and other lending institutions have a responsibility to their depositors, shareholders, and regulators to avoid loans that are likely to default. Because default risk rises during a weak economy, some potential borrowers will be unable to obtain loans. Others may qualify only if they pay high-risk premiums to cover their default risk. Thus, the effects of the Fed's monetary policy may be limited if potential borrowers do not qualify or are unwilling to incur the high-risk premiums. Nevertheless, the credit crunch should not affect borrowers with very low risk. A stimulative monetary policy is more effective when there are sufficient qualified borrowers that will borrow more funds once interest rates are reduced.

A credit crunch could occur even during a period when a restrictive monetary policy is implemented. As the money supply is reduced, and interest rates rise, some potential borrowers may be unable to obtain loans because the interest payments would be too high. Thus, the effects of the restrictive monetary policy are magnified because the higher interest rates not only discourage some potential borrowers but also prevent others from obtaining loans.

Overall, a credit crunch may partially offset the desired effects of a stimulative monetary policy and magnify the effects of a restrictive monetary policy.

Lagged Effects of Monetary Policy Another reason that monetary policy may not achieve the desired results is that there are lags between the time that an economic problem occurs and the time that the monetary policy is implemented and has an effect. Three specific lags are involved. First, there is a **recognition lag,** or the lag between the time a problem arises and the time it is recognized. Most economic problems are initially revealed by statistics, not actual observation. Because economic statistics are reported only periodically, they will not immediately signal a problem. For example, the unemployment rate is reported monthly. A sudden increase in unemployment may not be detected until the end of the month when statistics reveal the problem. If unemployment increases slightly each month for two straight months, the Fed may not necessarily act on this information, because the information may not appear to be significant. Only after a few more months of steadily increasing unemployment might the Fed recognize that a serious problem exists. In such a case, the recognition lag may be four months or longer.

The lag from the time a serious problem is recognized until the time the Fed implements a policy to resolve it is known as the **implementation lag.** Then, even after the Fed implements a policy, there will be an **impact lag** until the policy has its full impact on the economy. For example, an adjustment in money supply growth may have an immediate impact on the economy to some degree, but its full impact may not be manifested until a year or so after the adjustment.

These lags hinder the Fed's control of the economy. Suppose the Fed uses a loose-money policy to stimulate the economy and reduce unemployment. By the time the implemented monetary policy begins to take effect, the unemployment rate may have already reversed itself as a result of some other outside factors (such as a weakened dollar that increased foreign demand for U.S. goods and created U.S. jobs). Thus, the more serious problem may now be inflation (because the economy is heating up again), which may be further ignited by the loose-money policy. Without monetary policy lags, implemented policies would have a higher rate of success.

Impact of a Stimulative Policy on Expected Inflation When a stimulative monetary policy is used, the effect of an increase in money supply growth may be disrupted due to an increase in inflationary expectations.

ILLUSTRATION Assume that the U.S. economy is very weak, and the Fed responds by using open market operations (purchasing Treasury securities) in order to increase the supply of loanable funds. This action is supposed to reduce interest rates and increase the level of borrowing and spending. However, there is some evidence that high money growth may also lead to higher inflation over time. To the extent that businesses and households recognize that an increase in money growth will cause higher inflation, they will revise their inflationary expectations upward as a result. This effect is often referred to as the **theory of rational expectations.** Higher inflationary expectations encourage businesses and households to increase their demand for loanable funds (as explained in Chapter 2), in order to borrow and make planned expenditures before price levels increase. This increase in demand reflects a rush to make planned purchases now.

These effects of the Fed's monetary policy are shown in Exhibit 5.4. The result is an increase in both the supply of loanable funds and the demand for loanable funds. The effects are offsetting, so the Fed may not necessarily be capable of reducing interest rates for a sustained period of time. If the Fed cannot force interest rates lower with an active monetary policy, it is unable to stimulate an increase in the level of business investment. Business investment will increase only if the cost of financing some business projects is lower so that some proposed business ventures become feasible. If the increase in business investment does not occur, economic conditions will not improve. ∎

Exhibit 5.4
Effects of an Increased
Money Supply Accord-
ing to the Rational
Expectations Theory

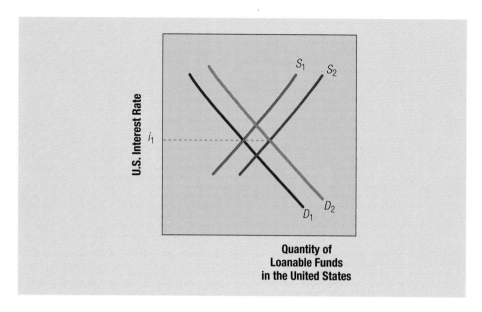

Given the limitations of an active monetary policy illustrated here, an alternative approach is a passive monetary policy that allows the economy to correct itself rather than rely on the Fed's intervention. Even if the Fed is passive, interest rates should ultimately decline in a weak economy because the demand for loanable funds should decline as economic growth weakens. In this case, interest rates would have declined without a corresponding increase in inflationary expectations, so the rates may stay lower for a sustained period of time. Consequently, the level of business investment should ultimately increase, which should lead to a stronger economy and more jobs. The major criticism of a passive monetary policy is that the weak economy could take years to correct itself. Many people would prefer that the Fed take an active role in improving economic conditions rather than hope that the economy will correct itself.

How the Fed Deals with the Limitations The economists who work at the Fed tend to believe that monetary policy can be an effective tool for controlling economic growth, inflation, and the unemployment level. Therefore, they periodically revise money supply growth in order to fine-tune the economy. Nevertheless, they are aware of the potential limitations. In particular, they recognize that a stimulative monetary policy will not always cure a high unemployment rate and could even ignite inflation. They also recognize that a restrictive monetary policy will not always reduce inflation. The effects of monetary policy are dependent on other existing conditions that also affect the economy. These conditions are discussed in more detail in the following section.

Tradeoff in Monetary Policy

Ideally, the Fed would like to achieve both a very low level of unemployment and a very low level of inflation in the United States. The U.S. unemployment rate should be low in a period when U.S. economic conditions are strong. Inflation will likely be relatively high at this time, however, because wages and price levels tend to increase when economic conditions are strong. Conversely, inflation may be lower when economic conditions are weak, but unemployment will be relatively high. There is an inverse relationship between the inflation rate and the unemployment rate, as shown in Exhibit 5.5. Therefore, it is difficult, if not impossible, for the Fed to cure both problems simultaneously.

When inflation is higher than the Fed deems acceptable, the Fed may consider implementing a tight-money policy to reduce economic growth. As economic growth slows, producers cannot as easily raise their prices and still maintain sales volume. Similarly, workers are not in demand and do not have much bargaining power on wages. Thus, the use of tight money to slow economic growth can reduce the inflation rate. A possible cost of the lower inflation rate is higher unemployment. If the economy becomes stagnant because of the tight-money policy, sales decrease, inventories accumulate, and firms may reduce their workforce to reduce production.

Given that a loose-money policy can reduce unemployment whereas a tight-money policy can reduce inflation, the Fed must determine whether unemployment or inflation is the more serious problem. It may not be able to solve both problems simultaneously. In fact, it may not be able to fully eliminate either problem. Although a loose-money policy can stimulate the economy, it does not guarantee that unskilled workers will be hired. Although a tight-money policy can reduce inflation caused by excessive spending, it cannot reduce inflation caused by such factors as an agreement by the members of the oil cartel to keep oil prices high.

Impact of Other Forces on the Tradeoff

Other forces may also affect the tradeoff faced by the Fed. Consider a situation where because of specific cost factors (higher energy and insurance costs, etc.), inflation will be at least 3 percent. This amount of inflation will exist no matter what type of monetary policy the Fed implements. Also assume that because of the number of unskilled workers and people between jobs, the unemployment rate will be at least 4 percent. A loose-money policy will sufficiently stimulate the economy to maintain unemployment at that minimum level of 4 percent. However, such a stimulative policy may also cause additional inflation beyond the 3 percent level. A tight-money policy could maintain inflation at the 3 percent minimum, but unemployment would likely rise above the 4 percent minimum.

This tradeoff is illustrated in Exhibit 5.5. Here the Fed can use a very stimulative (loose-money) policy that is expected to result in Point A (9 percent inflation and 4 percent unemployment). Alternatively, it can use a very restrictive (tight-money) policy that is expected to result in Point B (3 percent inflation and 8 percent unemployment).

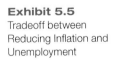

Exhibit 5.5
Tradeoff between Reducing Inflation and Unemployment

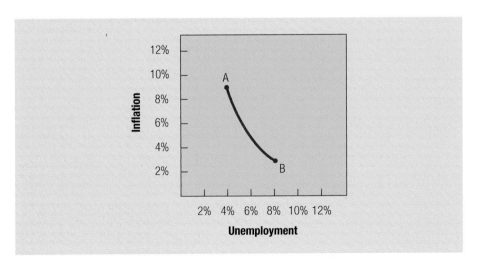

Or it can implement a compromise policy that will result in some point along the curve between A and B.

Historical data on annual inflation and unemployment rates show that when one of these problems worsens, the other does not automatically improve. Both variables can rise or fall over time. Yet this does not refute the tradeoff faced by the Fed. It simply means that some outside factors have affected inflation or unemployment or both.

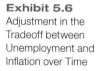 Recall that the Fed could have achieved Point A, Point B, or somewhere along the curve connecting these points during a particular time period. Now assume that oil prices have substantially increased and several product liability lawsuits have occurred. These events will affect consumer prices such that the minimum inflation rate will be, say, 6 percent. In addition, assume that various training centers for unskilled workers have been closed, leaving a higher number of unskilled workers. This forces the minimum unemployment rate to 6 percent. Now the Fed's tradeoff position has changed. The Fed's new set of possibilities is shown as Curve CD in Exhibit 5.6. Note that the points reflected on Curve CD are not as desirable as the points along Curve AB that were previously attainable. No matter what type of monetary policy the Fed uses, both the inflation rate and the unemployment rate will be higher than in the previous time period. This is not the Fed's fault. In fact, the Fed is still faced with a tradeoff between Point C (11 percent inflation, 6 percent unemployment), Point D (6 percent inflation, 10 percent unemployment), or somewhere within those points along Curve CD. ■

When FOMC members are primarily concerned with either inflation or unemployment, they tend to agree on the type of monetary policy that should be implemented. When both inflation and unemployment are relatively high, however, there is more disagreement among the members about the proper monetary policy to implement. Some members would likely argue for a tight-money policy to prevent inflation from rising, while other members would suggest that a loose-money policy should be implemented to reduce unemployment even if it results in higher inflation.

How the Fed's Emphasis Shifted during 2001–2007

The tradeoffs involved in monetary policy can be understood by considering the Fed's decisions during the 2001–2007 period. In 2001 when economic conditions were

Exhibit 5.6
Adjustment in the Tradeoff between Unemployment and Inflation over Time

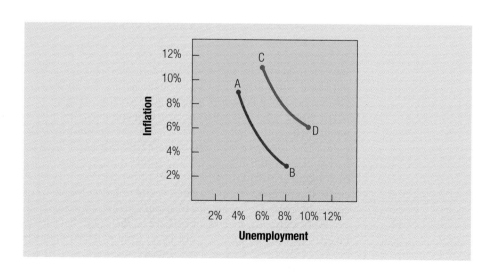

http://www.federalreserve.gov Click on "federal funds rate." Shows recent changes in the federal funds target rate.

weak, the Fed reduced the targeted federal funds rate 10 times, resulting in a cumulative decline of 4.25 percent in the targeted federal funds rate. As the federal funds rate was reduced, other market interest rates declined as well.

Despite these interest rate reductions, the economy did not respond during this period. One reason for the limited effect on the economy may be that the Fed was focusing on influencing short-term interest rates rather than long-term interest rates. To the extent that corporations rely on long-term funding to support most of their projects, their cost of borrowing was not significantly reduced over this period. The Fed's effects on the economy might have been stronger had it been able to reduce long-term interest rates.

After the economy failed to respond as hoped in 2001, the Fed reduced the federal funds target rate twice more in 2002 and 2003. Finally, in 2004 the economy began to show some signs of improvement. The Fed's focus then began to shift from concern about the economy to concern about the potential for higher inflation. It raised the federal funds target rate 17 times over the period from mid-2004 to the summer of 2006. The typical adjustment in the target rate was 0.25 percent. By adjusting in small increments, as it did during this period, the Fed is unlikely to overadjust. After making each small adjustment, it monitors the economic effects and decides whether additional adjustments are needed at the next meeting. During the 2004–2006 period, there were periodic indications of rising prices, mostly due to high oil prices. While the Fed's monetary policy could not control oil prices, it wanted to prevent any inflation that could be triggered if the economy was very strong and there was excessive demand for products or labor shortages. Thus, the Fed tried to maintain economic growth, without letting the growth become so high that it could cause higher inflation.

Proposals to Focus on Inflation

Recently, the proposal has been made that the Fed should focus more on controlling the inflation rate than on unemployment. Ben Bernanke, the current chairman of the Fed, has made some arguments in favor of inflation targeting. If this proposal was adopted in its strictest form, the Fed would no longer face a tradeoff between controlling inflation and controlling unemployment. Presumably, it would be able to control inflation better if it could concentrate on that problem without having to worry about the unemployment rate. In addition, the Fed's role would be more transparent, and there would be less uncertainty in the financial markets about how the Fed would respond to specific economic conditions.

Nevertheless, inflation targeting also has some disadvantages. First, if the U.S. inflation rate deviated substantially from the Fed's target inflation rate, the Fed could lose credibility. Factors such as oil prices could cause high inflation regardless of the Fed's targeted inflation rate. Second, a complete focus on inflation could result in a much higher unemployment level. Bernanke has argued, however, that inflation targeting could be flexible enough that the employment level would still be given consideration. He believes that inflation targeting may not only satisfy the inflation goal, but could also achieve the employment stabilization goal in the long run. For example, if unemployment was slightly higher than normal, while inflation was at the peak of the target range, an inflation targeting approach might be to leave monetary policy unchanged. In this situation, stimulating the economy with lower interest rates might reduce the unemployment rate temporarily, but could ultimately lead to excessive inflation. This would require the Fed to use a tight-money policy (higher interest rates) to correct the inflation, which could ultimately lead to a slower economy and an increase in unemployment. In general, the inflation targeting approach would discourage such "quick fix" strategies to stimulate the economy.

Although some Fed members have publicly said that they do not believe in inflation targeting, their opinions are not necessarily much different from those of Bernanke.

Flexible inflation targeting would allow changes in monetary policy to increase employment. The differences in opinion among Fed members are about how bad unemployment would have to be before monetary policy would be used to stimulate the economy, at the risk of raising inflation.

Economic Indicators Monitored by the Fed

Given the Fed's goals of controlling economic growth and inflation, it needs reliable indicators of these economic variables so that it can monitor changes over time. The Fed relies on various indicators described here.

Indicators of Economic Growth

The Fed monitors various indicators of economic growth because high economic growth creates a more prosperous economy and can result in lower unemployment. Gross domestic product (GDP), which measures the total value of goods and services produced during a specific period, is measured each month. It serves as the most direct indicator of economic growth in the United States. The level of production adjusts in response to changes in consumers' demand for goods and services. A high production level indicates strong economic growth and can result in an increased demand for labor (lower unemployment).

The Fed also monitors national income, which is the total income earned by firms and individual employees during a specific period. A strong demand for U.S. goods and services results in a large amount of income to firms and employees.

The unemployment rate is monitored as well, because one of the Fed's primary goals is to maintain a low rate of unemployment in the United States. The unemployment rate does not necessarily indicate the degree of economic growth, however, because it measures only the number and not the types of jobs that are being filled. It is possible to have a substantial reduction in unemployment during a period of weak economic growth if new low-paying jobs are created during that period.

Several other indexes serve as indicators of growth in specific sectors of the U.S. economy, including an industrial production index, a retail sales index, and a home sales index. A composite index combines various indexes to indicate economic growth across sectors. In addition to the many indicators reflecting recent conditions, the Fed may also desire to use forward-looking indicators, such as consumer confidence surveys, to forecast future economic growth.

Index of Leading Economic Indicators Among the economic indicators widely followed by market participants are the indexes of leading, coincident, and lagging economic indicators, which are published by the Conference Board. **Leading economic indicators** are used to predict future economic activity. Usually, three consecutive monthly changes in the same direction in these indicators suggest a turning point in the economy. **Coincident economic indicators** tend to reach their peaks and troughs at the same time as business cycles. **Lagging economic indicators** tend to rise or fall a few months after business-cycle expansions and contractions.

The Conference Board is an independent, not-for-profit membership organization whose stated goal is to create and disseminate knowledge about management and the marketplace to help businesses strengthen their performance and better serve society. The Conference Board conducts research, convenes conferences, makes forecasts, assesses trends, and publishes information and analyses. A summary of the Conference Board's leading, coincident, and lagging indexes is provided in Exhibit 5.7.

Leading Index
1. Average weekly hours, manufacturing
2. Average weekly initial claims for unemployment insurance
3. Manufacturers' new orders, consumer goods and materials
4. Vendor performance, slower deliveries diffusion index
5. Manufacturers' new orders, nondefense capital goods
6. Building permits, new private housing units
7. Stock prices, 500 common stocks
8. Money supply, M2
9. Interest rate spread, 10-year Treasury bonds less federal funds
10. Index of consumer expectations

Coincident Index
1. Employees on nonagricultural payrolls
2. Personal income less transfer payments
3. Industrial production
4. Manufacturing and trade sales

Lagging Index
1. Average duration of unemployment
2. Inventories to sales ratio, manufacturing and trade
3. Labor cost per unit of output, manufacturing
4. Average prime rate
5. Commercial and industrial loans
6. Consumer installment credit to personal income ratio
7. Consumer price index for services

Indicators of Inflation

The Fed closely monitors price indexes and other indicators to assess the U.S. inflation rate.

Producer and Consumer Price Indexes The producer price index represents prices at the wholesale level, and the consumer price index represents prices paid by consumers (retail level). There is a lag time of about one month after the period being measured due to the time required to compile price information for the indexes. Nevertheless, financial markets closely monitor the price indexes because they may be used to forecast inflation, which affects nominal interest rates and the prices of some securities. Agricultural price indexes reflect recent price movements in grains, fruits, and vegetables. Housing price indexes reflect recent price movements in homes and rental properties.

Other Indicators In addition to price indexes, there are several other indicators of inflation. Wage rates are periodically reported in various regions of the United States. Because wages and prices are highly correlated over the long run, wages can indicate price movements. Oil prices can signal future inflation because they affect the costs of some forms of production, as well as transportation costs and the prices paid by consumers for gasoline.

The price of gold is closely monitored because gold prices tend to move in tandem with inflation. Some investors buy gold as a hedge against future inflation. Therefore, a rise in gold prices may signal the market's expectation that inflation will increase.

In some cases, indicators of economic growth are also used to indicate inflation. For example, the release of several favorable employment reports may arouse concern that the economy will overheat and cause demand-pull inflation. Although these reports offer favorable information about economic growth, their information about inflation is unfavorable. The financial markets can be adversely affected by such reports, as investors anticipate that the Fed will have to increase interest rates to reduce the inflationary momentum.

How Monetary Policy Affects All Sectors

The Fed's monetary policy affects many parts of the economy as shown in Exhibit 5.8. Households monitor the Fed because their loan rates on cars and mortgages will be affected. Corporations monitor the Fed because their cost of borrowing from loans and from issuing new bonds will be affected. The Treasury monitors the Fed because its cost of financing the budget deficit will be affected.

Impact on Financial Markets

Because monetary policy can have a strong influence on interest rates and economic growth, it affects the valuation of most securities traded in financial markets. The values of existing bonds are inversely related to interest rate movements. Thus, investors who own Treasury, corporate, or municipal bonds are adversely affected when the Fed raises interest rates, and are favorably affected when the Fed reduces interest rates (as explained in Chapter 8).

The values of stocks (discussed in Chapter 11) also are commonly affected by interest rate movements, but the effects are not as consistent as they are for bonds.

ILLUSTRATION   If the Fed lowers interest rates because the economy is weak, and investors anticipate that this action will enhance economic growth, they may expect that corporations will generate higher sales and earnings in the future. Thus, the values of stocks would increase due to this favorable information. However, the Fed's decision to reduce interest rates could make investors realize that economic conditions are worse than they thought. In this case, the Fed's actions could signal that corporate sales and earnings may weaken, and the values of stocks will decline due to this negative information. ■

To appreciate the potential impact of the Fed's actions on financial markets, go to any financial news website during the week in which the Fed holds its open market meeting, and you will see predictions of whether the Fed will change the target federal funds rate, by how much, and how that change will affect the financial markets. Sometimes the markets fully anticipate the Fed's actions. In this case, prices of securities should adjust to the anticipated news before the meeting, and they will not adjust further when the Fed's decision is announced.

http://

http://www.federalreserve
.gov Schedule of FOMC
meetings and minutes of
previous FOMC meetings.

Fed's Communication to the Markets When the Fed holds a meeting, it announces its monetary policy through a press release. The press releases issued

Exhibit 5.8
How Monetary Policy
Affects Financial
Conditions

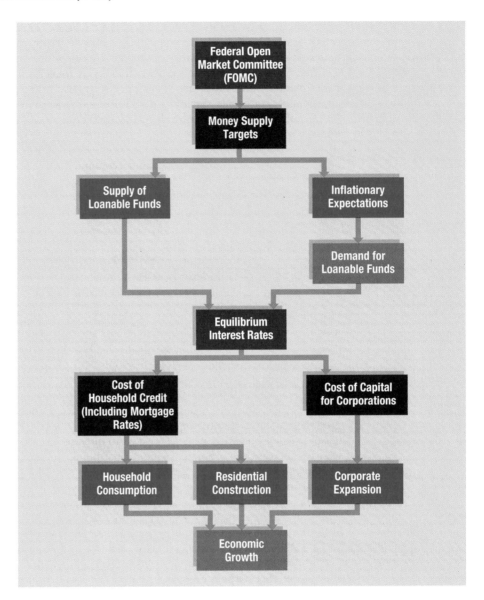

after previous meetings are available at http://www.federalreserve.gov/FOMC. The following is an example of a typical press release.

The Federal Open Market Committee decided to raise its target for the federal funds rate by .25% to 5.00%.

Economic growth has been strong so far this year. The Committee expects that growth will continue at a more sustainable pace, partly reflecting a cooling of the housing market.

Energy prices have had a modest impact on inflation. Unit labor costs have been stable. Energy prices have the potential to add to inflation.

The Committee judges that some further policy firming may be needed to address inflation risks, but emphasizes that the extent and timing of any firming will depend on the evolution of the economic outlook as implied by future information. The Committee will respond to changes in economic prospects as needed to support the attainment of its objectives.

Voting for the FOMC monetary policy action were [list of voting members provided here].

Financial market participants closely review the press release to interpret the Fed's future plans. Some institutions hire economists to focus on assessing monetary policy so that they can determine how their various securities portfolios will be affected.

ILLUSTRATION In the press release above, the key phrase is "further policy firming may be needed" because this implies that the Fed stands ready to tighten monetary policy further in the future if it senses more upward pressure on inflation.

The Fed is saying that it wants to achieve stable economic growth and price stability (low inflation), but based on existing conditions, it is more worried about price stability. Therefore, it is biased toward tightening monetary policy (raising interest rates) in the future. Sometimes the Fed will explicitly state that it is biased toward tightening. If the financial markets did not anticipate the news of this bias, it will probably cause concerns that higher interest rates will occur in the future.

Now assume that the Fed's press release used this phrase instead: "The reduced growth in aggregate demand should help to limit the inflation pressure over time. However, if the economy shows further signs of weakening, the Committee anticipates that some stimulus may be needed." In this case, the Fed is suggesting that inflation is not such a threat and that it is more concerned about stimulating the economy. Thus, it has a bias toward loosening the money supply. ∎

The type of influence monetary policy can have on each financial market is summarized in Exhibit 5.9.

How Oil Price Shocks and the Fed's Reaction Affect Financial Markets

Given the Fed's continual efforts to maintain a low rate of inflation, news that causes concerns about an abrupt increase in inflation typically creates a major negative response in financial markets. A month rarely goes by without the financial press reporting a potential inflation crisis, such as a hurricane that could affect oil production and refining in Louisiana or Texas, or friction in the Middle East or Russia that could disrupt oil production there. Most of the concerns ultimately turn out to be false alarms, but they strike fear in financial markets at the time.

Whenever an event occurs that could affect the world's production of oil, people presume that there will be an oil shortage. If their expectations are correct, inflation will be higher, because oil prices affect gasoline prices and airline fuel, which affect the costs of transporting many products and supplies. Oil is also used in the production of some products. Firms that experience higher costs due to higher oil expenses may raise their prices. An increase in inflation puts pressure on the Fed to tighten monetary policy. The Fed does not have control over oil prices, but it reasons that it can at least dampen any inflationary pressure on prices if it slows economic growth. That is, firms are less likely to increase the prices of their products if the economy is weak, because they may not be able to sell their products if they raise prices.

BEHAVIORAL FINANCE The concerns that an oil price shock will occur and that the Fed will raise interest rates to offset the high oil prices tend to have the following effects. First, bond markets react strongly because bond prices are inversely re-

Exhibit 5.9
Impact of Monetary
Policy across
Financial Markets

Type of Financial Market	Relevant Factors Influenced by Monetary Policy	Key Institutional Participants
Money market	• Secondary market values of existing money market securities • Yields on newly issued money market securities	Commercial banks, savings institutions, credit unions, money market funds, insurance companies, finance companies, pension funds
Bond market	• Secondary market values of existing bonds • Yields offered on newly issued bonds	Commercial banks, savings institutions, bond mutual funds, insurance companies, finance companies, pension funds
Mortgage market	• Demand for housing and therefore the demand for mortgages • Secondary market values of existing mortgages • Interest rates on new mortgages • Risk premium on mortgages	Commercial banks, savings institutions, credit unions, insurance companies, pension funds
Stock market	• Required return on stocks and therefore the market values of stocks • Projections for corporate earnings and therefore stock values	Stock mutual funds, insurance companies, pension funds
Foreign exchange	• Demand for currencies and therefore the values of currencies, which in turn affect currency option prices	Institutions that are exposed to exchange rate risk

lated to interest rates. The fear of rising interest rates is enough to cause a major sell-off of bonds, which reduces bond prices. Stock prices are affected by expectations of corporate earnings. If corporations will incur higher costs of production and transportation due to higher oil prices, their earnings could decrease. In addition, if the Fed increases interest rates in order to slow economic growth (to reduce inflationary pressure), corporations will experience an increase in the cost of financing. This also would reduce their earnings. Consequently, investors who expect a reduction in earnings may sell their holdings of stock, and stock prices will decline.

In some cases, the fears of higher oil prices turn out to be correct, and the Fed decides that it has no choice but to slow economic growth. The prices of bonds and stocks tend to suffer as a result. In many other cases, the fears of an oil price shock subside, the Fed does not need to adjust its monetary policy, and the prices of bonds and stocks rise back toward their previous levels. Nevertheless, some investors will have incurred losses because they sold their bonds and stocks after prices declined in financial markets due to the possible effects of an oil price shock. By the time the fears have subsided and they invest in bonds and stocks again, bond and stock prices may have increased. ■

Impact on Financial Institutions

Many depository institutions obtain most of their funds in the form of short-term loans and then use their funds to provide long-term fixed-rate loans. When interest rates rise, their cost of funds rises faster than the return they receive on their loans. Thus, they are adversely affected when the Fed increases interest rates.

Financial institutions such as commercial banks, bond mutual funds, insurance companies, and pension funds maintain large portfolios of bonds, so their portfolios are adversely affected when the Fed raises interest rates. Financial institutions such as stock mutual funds, insurance companies, and pension funds maintain large portfolios of stocks, and their stock portfolios are also susceptible to changes in the Fed's monetary policy.

Integrating Monetary and Fiscal Policies

Although the Fed has the power to make decisions without the approval of the presidential administration, the Fed's monetary policy is commonly influenced by the administration's fiscal policies. In some situations, the Fed and the administration have used complementary policies to resolve economic problems. In other situations, they have used conflicting policies. A framework for explaining how monetary policy and fiscal policy affect interest rates is shown in Exhibit 5.10. As this framework shows, monetary policy not only has a direct effect on the supply of funds, but can have an indirect effect on the supply of funds and on the demand for funds. Although fiscal

Exhibit 5.10
Framework for Explaining How Monetary Policy and Fiscal Policy Affect Interest Rates over Time

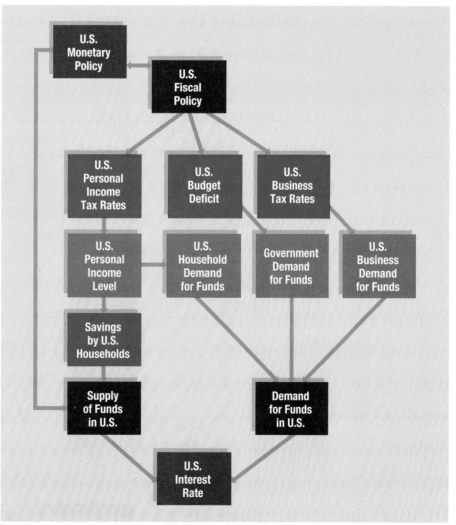

Note: Diagram does not account for possible international effects

policy typically influences the demand for loanable funds, monetary policy normally has a larger impact on the supply of loanable funds.

Monetizing the Debt

An ongoing dilemma faced by the Fed is whether to help finance the federal budget deficit that has been created by fiscal policy.

ILLUSTRATION Consider a situation in which the presidential administration decides to implement a new fiscal policy that will result in a larger federal deficit than was originally expected. The Fed must first assess the potential impact that this new fiscal policy will have on the economy. A likely concern of the Fed is the possibility of a crowding-out effect, in which excessive borrowing by the Treasury crowds out other potential borrowers (such as households or corporations) in competing for whatever loanable funds are available. This can cause higher interest rates and therefore may restrict economic growth. The Fed may counter by loosening the money supply, which might offset the increased demand for loanable funds by the federal government. This action is known as **monetizing the debt,** as the Fed is partially financing the federal deficit. Exhibit 5.11 illustrates how this works. As the Treasury issues new securities in the primary market to finance the deficit, there may be upward pressure on interest rates. The Fed could offset this pressure by using open market operations to purchase Treasury securities (from government securities dealers) in the secondary market. Before the Fed monetizes the debt, it may first monitor how the additional borrowing by the Treasury is affecting interest rates. If there is no significant change in interest rates, the Fed may decide not to intervene.

When the Fed purchases Treasury securities, the Treasury must repurchase the securities at maturity just as if an individual or a firm owned them. Thus, Treasury securities held by the Fed still reflect debt from the Treasury's perspective. The Treasury

Exhibit 5.11
Fed's Process of
Monetizing the Debt

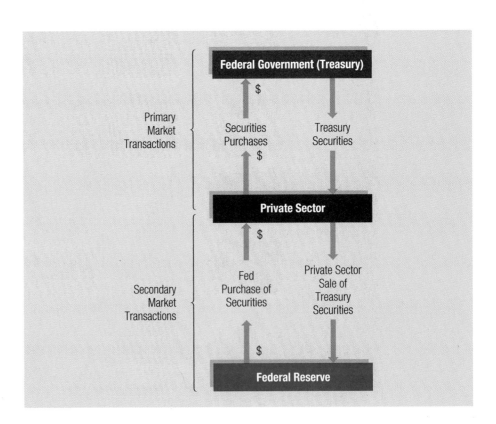

may sometimes prefer that the Fed monetize the debt, however, because if it does not, interest rates could rise and slow economic growth. ■

The Fed may prefer not to monetize the debt because this strategy requires higher money supply growth, which could ignite inflation. If the Fed does not monetize the debt, however, a weak economy may be more likely.

Monetary Policy in a Global Environment

GL🌐BALASPECTS Financial market participants must recognize that the type of monetary policy implemented by the Fed is somewhat dependent on various international factors, as explained next.

Impact of the Dollar

A weak dollar can stimulate U.S. exports, discourage U.S. imports, and therefore stimulate the U.S. economy. In addition, it tends to exert inflationary pressure in the United States. Thus, the Fed is less likely to use a stimulative monetary policy when the dollar is weak. A strong dollar tends to reduce inflationary pressure but also dampens the U.S. economy. Therefore, the Fed is more likely to use a stimulative policy during a strong-dollar period.

Impact of Global Economic Conditions

The Fed recognizes that economic conditions are integrated across countries, so it considers prevailing global economic conditions when conducting monetary policy. When global economic conditions are strong, foreign countries purchase more U.S. products and can stimulate the U.S. economy. When global economic conditions are weak, the foreign demand for U.S. products weakens.

In 2001, when the United States experienced a very weak economy, the economies of many other countries were also weak. The Fed's decision to lower U.S. interest rates and stimulate the U.S. economy was partially driven by these weak global economic conditions. The Fed recognized that the United States would not receive any stimulus from other countries (such as a strong demand for U.S. products) where income and aggregate spending levels were also relatively low.

Transmission of Interest Rates

Each country has its own currency (with the exception of countries in the Eurozone), and its own interest rate, which is based on the supply of and demand for loanable funds in that currency. Investors residing in one country may attempt to capitalize on high interest rates in another country. If there is upward pressure on U.S. interest rates that can be offset by foreign inflows of funds, the Fed may not feel compelled to use a loose-money policy. However, if foreign investors reduce their investment in U.S. securities, the Fed may be forced to intervene to prevent interest rates from rising.

Given the international integration in money and capital markets, a government's budget deficit can affect interest rates of various countries. This concept, referred to as **global crowding out,** is illustrated in Exhibit 5.12. An increase in the U.S. budget deficit causes an outward shift in the federal government demand for U.S. funds and therefore in the aggregate demand for U.S. funds (from D_1 to D_2). This crowding-out effect forces the U.S. interest rate to increase from i_1 to i_2 if the supply curve (S) is unchanged. As U.S. rates rise, they attract funds from investors in other countries, such as Germany and Japan. As foreign investors use more of their funds to invest in U.S. securities, the supply of available funds in their respective countries declines.

Exhibit 5.12
Illustration of Global
Crowding Out

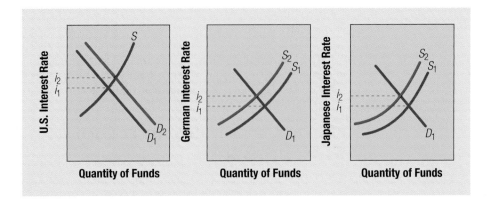

Consequently, there is upward pressure on non-U.S. interest rates as well. The impact will be most pronounced in those countries whose investors are most likely to be attracted to the higher U.S. interest rates. The possibility of global crowding out has caused national governments to criticize one another for large budget deficits.

Summary

■ By using monetary policy, the Fed can affect the interaction between the demand for money and the supply of money, which affects interest rates, aggregate spending, and economic growth. As the Fed increases the money supply, interest rates should decline, which results in more aggregate spending (because of cheaper financing rates) and higher economic growth. As the Fed decreases the money supply, interest rates should increase, which results in less aggregate spending (because of higher financing rates), lower economic growth, and lower inflation.

■ A stimulative monetary policy by the Fed may have limited effects because increasing the money supply may also result in higher inflationary expectations. Thus, interest rates may not necessarily be controlled by the Fed's adjustment in the money supply.

■ A restrictive monetary policy is likely to reduce inflation, but may also reduce economic growth. Thus, the Fed faces a tradeoff when implementing monetary policy. Given a possible tradeoff, the Fed tends to assess whether the potential benefits of any proposed monetary policy outweigh the potential adverse effects.

■ Financial market participants attempt to forecast the Fed's future monetary policies and the effects of these policies on economic conditions. Using this information, they can determine how their security holdings would be affected and can adjust their security portfolios accordingly.

■ The proper monetary policy may be dependent on the prevailing fiscal policy. If the fiscal policy involves excessive government borrowing, there is upward pressure on interest rates, and a loose monetary policy may be necessary to offset that pressure on interest rates. However, such a strategy could cause higher inflation in the long run.

Point Counter-Point

Can the Fed Prevent U.S. Recessions?

Point   Yes. The Fed has the power to reduce market interest rates and can therefore encourage more borrowing and spending. In this way, it stimulates the economy.

Counter-Point   No. When the economy is weak, individuals and firms are unwilling to borrow regardless of the interest rate. Thus, the borrowing (by those who are qualified) and spending will not be influenced by the Fed's actions. The Fed should not intervene, but should let the economy work itself out of a recession.

Who Is Correct? Use the Internet to learn more about this issue. Offer your own opinion on this issue.

Questions and Applications

1. **Impact of Monetary Policy** How does the Fed's monetary policy affect economic conditions?

2. **Tradeoffs of Monetary Policy** Describe the economic tradeoff faced by the Fed in achieving its economic goals.

3. **Choice of Monetary Policy** When does the Fed use a loose-money policy, and when does it use a tight-money policy? What is a criticism of a loose-money policy? What is the risk of using a monetary policy that is too tight?

4. **Active Monetary Policy** Describe an active monetary policy.

5. **Passive Monetary Policy** Describe a passive monetary policy.

6. **Fed Control** Why may the Fed have difficulty in controlling the economy in the manner desired? Be specific.

7. **Lagged Effects of Monetary Policy** Compare the recognition lag and the implementation lag.

8. **Fed's Control of Inflation** Assume that the Fed's primary goal is to cure inflation. How can it use open market operations to achieve its goal? What is a possible adverse effect of this action by the Fed (even if it achieves its goal)?

9. **Monitoring Money Supply** Why do financial market participants closely monitor money supply movements?

10. **Fed's Monetary Policy** Why would the Fed try to avoid frequent changes in the money supply?

11. **Impact of Money Supply Growth** Explain why an increase in the money supply can affect interest rates in different ways. Include the potential impact of the money supply on the supply of and the demand for loanable funds when answering this question.

12. **Confounding Effects** What factors might be considered by financial market participants who are assessing whether an increase in money supply growth will affect inflation?

13. **Monetizing the Debt** Explain what monetizing the debt means. How can this action improve economic conditions? What is the risk involved?

Advanced Questions

14. **Interpreting the Fed's Monetary Policy** When the Fed increases the money supply to lower the federal funds rate, will the cost of capital to U.S. companies be reduced? Explain how the segmented markets theory regarding the term structure of interest rates could influence the degree to which the Fed's monetary policy affects long-term interest rates.

15. **Monetary Policy Today** Assess the economic situation today. Is the administration more concerned with reducing unemployment or inflation? Does the Fed have a similar opinion? If not, is the administration publicly criticizing the Fed? Is the Fed publicly criticizing the administration? Explain.

16. **Impact of Foreign Policies** Why might a foreign government's policies be closely monitored by investors in other countries, even if the investors plan no investments in that country? Explain how monetary policy in one country can affect interest rates in other countries.

17. **Monetary Policy during the War in Iraq** Consider the likely discussion that was occurring in the FOMC meetings when the war in Iraq began in 2003. The U.S. economy was weak at that time. Do you think the FOMC should have proposed a loose-money policy or a tight-money policy once the war began? This war could have resulted in major damage to oil wells. Explain why this possible effect would have received much attention at the FOMC meetings. If this possibility was perceived to be highly likely at the time of the meetings, explain how it may have complicated the decision about monetary policy at that time. Given the conditions stated in this question, would you have suggested that the Fed use a tight-money policy, a loose-money policy, or a stable-money policy? Support your decision with logic, and acknowledge any adverse effects of your decision.

18. **Economic Indicators** Stock market conditions serve as a leading economic indicator. Assuming the U.S. economy is currently in a recession, discuss the implications of this indicator. Why might this indicator possibly be inaccurate?

19. **How the Fed Should Respond to Prevailing Conditions** Consider the current economic conditions,

including inflation and economic growth. Do you think the Fed should increase interest rates, reduce interest rates, or leave interest rates at their present levels? Offer some logic to support your answer.

20. **Impact of Inflation Targeting by the Fed** Assume the Fed adopts an inflation-targeting strategy. Describe how the Fed's monetary policy would be affected by an abrupt 15 percent rise in oil prices in response to an oil shortage. Do you think the Fed's inflation-targeting strategy would be more or less effective in this situation than a strategy of balancing inflation concerns with unemployment concerns? Explain.

21. **Predicting the Fed's Actions** Assume these existing conditions. The last time the FOMC met, it decided to raise interest rates. At that time economic growth was very strong, and as a result of the strong economy, inflation was relatively high. Since the last meeting, economic growth has weakened, and the unemployment rate will likely rise by .5 percentage point over the quarter. The FOMC's next meeting is tomorrow. Do you think the FOMC will revise its targeted federal funds rate, and if so, how?

22. **The Fed's Impact on the Housing Market** In some periods when home prices declined substantially, some homeowners blamed the Fed. In other periods when home prices increased, homeowners gave credit to the Fed. How can the Fed have such a large impact on home prices? Why would news that the general inflation level has increased substantially possibly affect the Fed's monetary policy and therefore affect home prices?

Interpreting Financial News

Interpret the following statements made by Wall Street analysts and portfolio managers:

a. "Lately, the Fed's policies are driven by gold prices and other indicators of the future rather than by recent economic data."

b. "The Fed cannot boost money growth at this time because of the weak dollar."

c. "The Fed's fine-tuning may distort the economic picture."

Managing in Financial Markets

Forecasting Monetary Policy As a manager of a firm, you are concerned about a potential increase in interest rates, which would reduce the demand for your firm's products. The Fed is scheduled to meet in one week to assess economic conditions and set monetary policy. Economic growth has been high, but inflation has also increased from 3 percent to 5 percent (annualized) over the last four months. The level of unemployment is very low and cannot possibly go much lower.

a. Given the situation, is the Fed likely to adjust monetary policy? If so, how?

b. Recently, the Fed has allowed the money supply to expand beyond its long-term target range. Does this affect your expectation of what the Fed will decide at its upcoming meeting?

c. Assume that the Fed has just learned that the Treasury will need to borrow a larger amount of funds than originally expected. Explain how this information may affect the degree to which the Fed changes the monetary policy.

Flow of Funds Exercise

Anticipating Fed Actions

Recall that Carson Company has obtained substantial loans from finance companies and commercial banks. The interest rate on the loans is tied to market interest rates and is adjusted every six months. Because of its expectations of a strong U.S. economy, Carson plans to grow in the future by expanding its business and through acquisitions. It expects that it will need substantial long-term financing and plans to borrow additional funds either through loans or by issuing bonds. It also considers issuing stock to raise funds in the next year.

An economic report just noted the strong growth in the economy, which has caused the economy to be close to full employment. In addition, the report estimated that the annualized inflation rate increased to

5 percent, up from 2 percent last month. The factors that caused the higher inflation (shortages of products and shortages of labor) are expected to continue.

a. How will the Fed's monetary policy change based on the report?

b. How will the likely change in the Fed's monetary policy affect Carson's future performance? Could it affect Carson's plans for future expansion?

c. Explain how a tight monetary policy could affect the amount of funds borrowed at financial institutions by deficit units such as Carson Company. How might it affect the credit risk of deficit units such as Carson Company? How might it affect the performance of financial institutions that provide credit to deficit units such as Carson Company?

Internet/Excel Exercises

1. Review the website http://www.federalreserve .gov/fomc with a focus on the activities of the FOMC. Succinctly summarize the minutes of the last FOMC meeting. What did the FOMC discuss at the last meeting? Did the FOMC make any changes in the current monetary policy? What is the FOMC's current monetary policy?

2. Is the Fed's present policy focused more on stimulating the economy or on reducing inflation? Or is the present policy evenly balanced? Explain.

3. Using the website http://www.research .stlouisfed.org/fred2/, retrieve interest rate data at the beginning of the last 20 quarters for the federal funds rate and the three-month Treasury bill (T-bill) rate, and place the data in two columns of an Excel spreadsheet. Derive the change in interest rates on a quarterly basis. Apply regression analysis in which the quarterly change in the T-bill rate is the dependent variable and the quarterly change in the federal funds rate is the independent variable (see Appendix B for more information about using regression analysis). If the Fed's effect on the federal funds rate influences other interest rates (such as the T-bill rate), there should be a positive and significant relationship between the interest rates. Is there a positive relationship? Explain.

WSJ Exercise

Market Assessment of Fed Policy

Review the "Credit Markets" section in a recent issue of *The Wall Street Journal* (listed in the index on the first page of Section C). Summarize the market assessments of the Fed. Also summarize the market's expectations about future interest rates. Are these expectations based primarily on the Fed's monetary policy or on other factors?

Part 3: Debt Security Markets

Part 3 focuses on how debt security markets facilitate the flow of funds from surplus units to deficit units. Chapter 6 focuses on money markets for investors and borrowers trading short-term securities. Chapters 7 and 8 focus on the bond markets, and Chapter 9 focuses on the mortgage markets. Because some financial market participants trade securities in all of these markets, there is much interaction among these markets, as emphasized throughout the chapters.

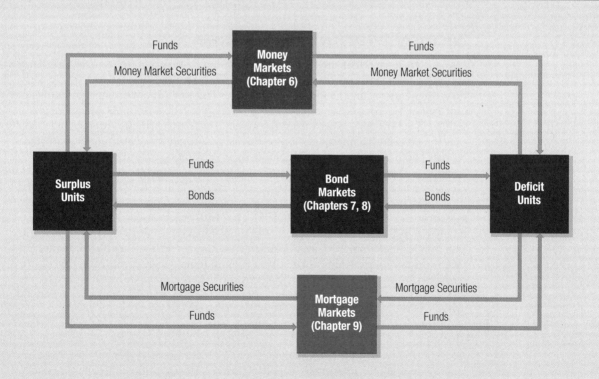

Chapter 6: Money Markets

Money markets are used to facilitate the transfer of short-term funds from individuals, corporations, or governments with excess funds to those with deficient funds. Even investors who focus on long-term securities tend to hold some money market securities. Money markets enable financial market participants to maintain liquidity.

The specific objectives of this chapter are to:

- provide a background on the most popular money market securities,
- explain how money markets are used by institutional investors,
- explain the valuation and risk of money market securities, and
- explain how money markets have become globally integrated.

Money Market Securities

Money market securities are debt securities with a maturity of one year or less. They are issued in the primary market through a telecommunications network by the Treasury, corporations, and financial intermediaries that wish to obtain short-term financing. The means by which money markets facilitate the flow of funds are illustrated in Exhibit 6.1. The U.S. Treasury issues money market securities (Treasury bills) and uses the proceeds to finance the budget deficit. Corporations issue money market securities and use the proceeds to support their existing operations or to expand their operations. Financial institutions issue money market securities and bundle the proceeds to make loans to households or corporations. Thus, the funds are channeled to support household purchases, such as cars and homes, and to support corporate investment in buildings and machinery. The Treasury and some corporations commonly pay off their debt from maturing money market securities with the proceeds from issuing new money market securities. In this way, they are able to finance expenditures for long periods of time even though money market securities have short-term maturities. Overall, money markets allow households, corporations, and the U.S. government to increase their expenditures, and therefore finance economic growth.

Money market securities are commonly purchased by households, corporations (including financial institutions), and government agencies that have funds available for a short-term period. Because money market securities have a short-term maturity and can typically be sold in the secondary market, they provide liquidity to investors. Most firms and financial institutions maintain some holdings of money market securities for this reason.

Exhibit 6.1 How Money Markets Facilitate the Flow of Funds

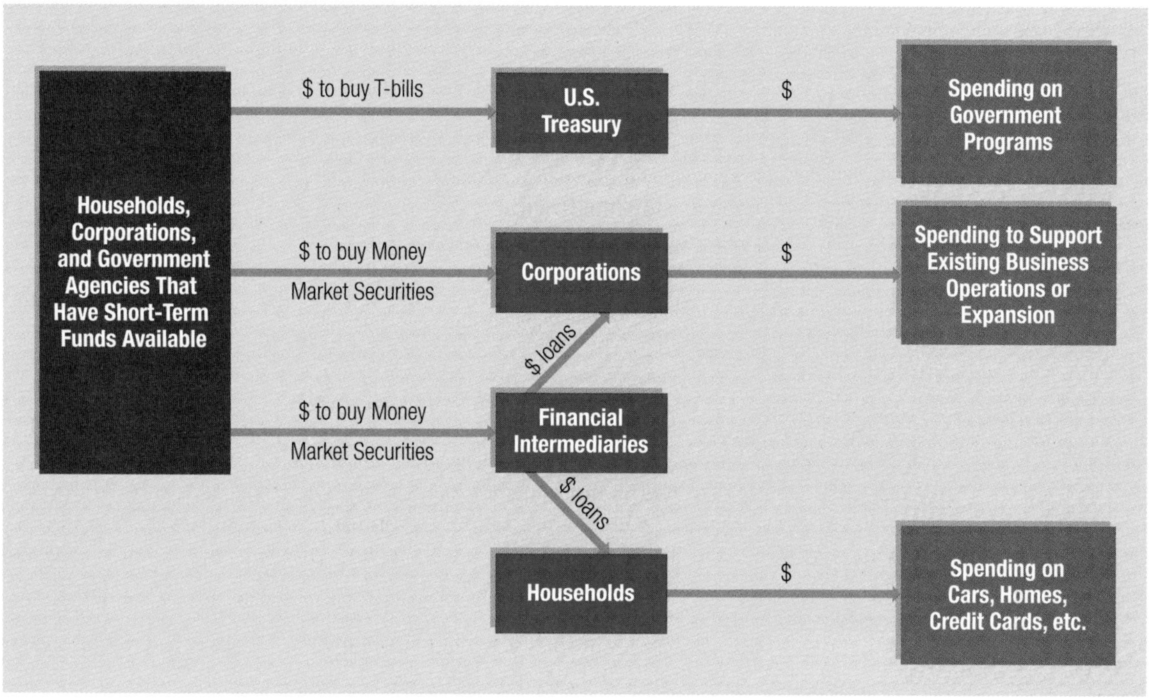

The more popular money market securities are

- Treasury bills
- Commercial paper
- Negotiable certificates of deposit
- Repurchase agreements
- Federal funds
- Banker's acceptances

Each of these instruments is described in turn.

Treasury Bills

When the U.S. government needs to borrow funds, the U.S. Treasury frequently issues short-term securities known as Treasury bills (or T-bills). The Treasury issues T-bills on a weekly basis with 4-week, 13-week, and 26-week maturities. It periodically issues T-bills called cash management bills that have shorter-term maturities. It also issues T-bills on a monthly basis with a one-year maturity. T-bills used to be issued in paper form but are now maintained electronically. The par value (amount received by investors at maturity) of T-bills was historically a minimum of $10,000, but is now $1,000 and in multiples of $1,000 thereafter. Since T-bills do not pay interest, they are sold at a discount from par value, and the gain to an investor holding a T-bill until maturity is the difference between par value and the price paid.

T-bills are attractive to investors because they are backed by the federal government and therefore are virtually free of credit (default) risk. Another attractive feature of T-bills is their liquidity, which is due to their short maturity and strong secondary market. Existing T-bills can be sold in the secondary market through government securities dealers, who profit by purchasing the bills at a slightly lower price than the price at which they sell them.

Investors in Treasury Bills Depository institutions commonly invest in T-bills so that they can retain a portion of their funds in assets that can easily be liquidated if they suddenly need to accommodate deposit withdrawals. Other financial institutions also invest in T-bills in the event that they need cash because cash outflows exceed cash inflows. Individuals with substantial savings invest in T-bills for liquidity purposes. Many individuals invest in T-bills indirectly by investing in money market funds, which in turn purchase large amounts of T-bills. Corporations invest in T-bills so that they have easy access to funding if they incur sudden unanticipated expenses.

Pricing Treasury Bills The price that an investor will pay for a T-bill with a particular maturity is dependent on the investor's required rate of return on that T-bill. That price is determined as the present value of the future cash flows to be received. Since the T-bill does not generate interest payments, the value of a T-bill is the present value of the par value. Thus, because T-bills do not pay interest, investors are willing to pay a price for a one-year T-bill that ensures that the amount they receive a year later will generate their desired return.

ILLUSTRATION If investors require a 7 percent annualized return on a one-year T-bill with a $10,000 par value, the price that they are willing to pay is

$$P = \$10,000/1.07$$
$$= \$9,345.79$$

If the investors require a higher return, they will discount the $10,000 at that higher rate of return, which will result in a lower price that they are willing to pay today. You can verify this by estimating the price based on a required return of 8 percent and then on a required return of 9 percent. ■

To price a T-bill with a maturity shorter than one year, the annualized return can be reduced by the fraction of the year in which funds will be invested.

ILLUSTRATION If investors require a 6 percent annualized return on a six-month T-bill, this reflects a 3 percent unannualized return over six months. The price that they will be willing to pay for a T-bill with a par value of $10,000 is:

$$P = \$10,000/1.03$$
$$= \$9,708.74 ■$$

Treasury Bill Auction The primary T-bill market is an auction. Individual investors can submit bids online for newly issued T-bills at http://www.treasurydirect.gov.

Financial institutions can submit their bids for T-bills (and other Treasury securities) online using the Treasury Automated Auction Processing System (TAAPS-*Link*). Individuals and financial institutions can set up an account with the Treasury. Then they can select the specific maturity and face value that they desire and submit their bids electronically. Payments to the Treasury are withdrawn electronically from the account, and payments received from the Treasury when the securities mature are deposited electronically into the account.

At the auctions, investors have the option of bidding competitively or noncompetitively. The Treasury has a specified amount of funds that it plans to borrow, which dictates the amount of T-bill bids that it will accept for that maturity. Investors who wish to ensure that their bids will be accepted can use noncompetitive bids. Noncompetitive bidders are limited to purchasing T-bills with a maximum par value of $5 million per auction, however. Consequently, large corporations typically make competitive bids so they can purchase larger amounts.

After accounting for noncompetitive bids, the Treasury accepts the highest competitive bids first and works it way down until it has generated the amount of funds from competitive bids that it needs. Any bids below that cutoff point are not accepted. The Treasury applies the lowest accepted bid price to all competitive bids that are accepted and to all noncompetitive bids. Thus, the price paid by competitive and noncompetitive bidders reflects the lowest price of the competitive bids. Competitive bids are still submitted because, as noted above, many bidders want to purchase more T-bills than the maximum that can be purchased on a noncompetitive basis.

http://www.treasurydirect .gov Results of recent Treasury bill auctions.

The results of the weekly auction of 13-week and 26-week T-bills are summarized in major daily newspapers each Tuesday and are also provided online at the Treasury's Public Debt website. Some of the more commonly reported statistics are the dollar amount of applications and Treasury securities sold, the average price of the accepted competitive bids, and the coupon equivalent (annualized yield) for investors who paid the average price.

An example of results from a recent T-bill auction are shown in Exhibit 6.2. At each auction, the prices paid for six-month T-bills are significantly lower than the prices paid for three-month T-bills because the investment term is longer. The lower price results in a higher unannualized yield that compensates investors for their longer-term investment.

http://www.federalreserve .gov/releases Links to a database of Treasury bill rates over time.

Estimating the Yield As explained earlier, T-bills do not offer coupon payments but are sold at a discount from par value. Their yield is influenced by the difference between the selling price and the purchase price. If an investor purchases a newly issued T-bill and holds it until maturity, the return is based on the difference between the par value and the purchase price. If the T-bill is sold prior to maturity, the return is based on the difference between the price for which the bill was sold in the secondary market and the purchase price.

http://research.stlouisfed .org Obtain yields offered on T-bills and various other money market securities.

The annualized yield from investing in a T-bill (Y_T) can be determined as

$$Y_T = \frac{SP - PP}{PP} \times \frac{365}{n}$$

where SP = selling price

PP = purchase price

n = number of days of the investment (holding period)

Exhibit 6.2
Example of Treasury Bill Auction Results

	13-Week Treasury Bill Auction	26-Week Treasury Bill Auction
Applications	$44,685,977,000	$45,991,246,000
Accepted bids	$19,022,977,000	$18,005,496,000
Average price of accepted bids (per $100 par value)	$98.792	$97.508
Coupon equivalent (yield)	4.918%	5.139%

Source: *The Wall Street Journal.* See *The Wall Street Journal* on any Tuesday for the information pertaining to Monday's Treasury bill auction.

An investor purchases a T-bill with a six-month (182-day) maturity and $10,000 par value for $9,600. If this T-bill is held to maturity, its yield is

$$\Upsilon_T = \frac{\$10,000 - \$9,600}{\$9,600} \times \frac{365}{182} = 8.36\%$$

If the T-bill is sold prior to maturity, the selling price and therefore the yield are dependent on market conditions at the time of the sale.

Suppose the investor plans to sell the T-bill after 120 days and forecasts a selling price of $9,820 at that time. The expected annualized yield based on this forecast is

$$\Upsilon_T = \frac{\$9,820 - \$9,600}{\$9,600} \times \frac{365}{120} = 6.97\%$$

The higher the forecasted selling price, the higher the expected annualized yield. ■

Estimating the Treasury Bill Discount Business periodicals frequently quote the T-bill discount (or T-bill rate) along with the T-bill yield. The T-bill discount represents the percent discount of the purchase price from par value (Par) for newly issued T-bills and is computed as

$$\text{T-bill discount} = \frac{\text{Par} - PP}{\text{Par}} \times \frac{360}{n}$$

A 360-day year is used to compute the T-bill discount.

Using the information from the previous example, the T-bill discount is

$$\text{T-bill discount} = \frac{\$10,000 - \$9,600}{\$10,000} \times \frac{360}{182} = 7.91\% \ ■$$

For a newly issued T-bill that is held to maturity, the T-bill yield will always be higher than the discount. The difference occurs because the purchase price is the denominator of the yield equation, while the par value is the denominator of the T-bill discount equation, and the par value will always exceed the purchase price of a newly issued T-bill. In addition, the yield formula uses a 365-day year versus a 360-day year for the discount computation.

Commercial Paper

http://

http://beginnersinvest.about
.com/od/commercialpaper
Provides valuable information and related articles about commercial paper.

Commercial paper is a short-term debt instrument issued only by well-known, creditworthy firms and is typically unsecured. It is normally issued to provide liquidity or finance a firm's investment in inventory and accounts receivable. The issuance of commercial paper is an alternative to short-term bank loans. Financial institutions such as finance companies and bank holding companies are major issuers of commercial paper.

The minimum denomination of commercial paper is usually $100,000. The typical denominations are in multiples of $1 million. Maturities are normally between 20 and 45 days but can be as short as one day or as long as 270 days. The 270-day maximum is due to a Securities and Exchange Commission (SEC) ruling that paper with a maturity exceeding 270 days must be registered.

Because of the high minimum denomination, individual investors rarely purchase commercial paper directly although they may invest in it indirectly by investing in money market funds that have pooled the funds of many individuals. Money market funds are major investors in commercial paper. An active secondary market for commercial paper does not exist. However, it is sometimes possible to sell the paper back to the dealer who initially helped to place it. In most cases, investors hold commercial paper until maturity.

Ratings Since commercial paper is issued by corporations that are susceptible to business failure, the commercial paper could possibly default. The risk of default is influenced by the issuer's financial condition and cash flow. Investors can attempt to assess the probability that commercial paper will default by monitoring the issuer's financial condition. The focus is on the issuer's ability to repay its debt over the short term because the payments will be completed within a short-term period. The rating serves as an indicator of the potential risk of default. Money market funds can invest only in commercial paper that has a top-tier or second-tier rating, and second-tier paper cannot represent more than 5 percent of their assets. Thus, corporations can more easily place commercial paper that is assigned a top-tier rating. The ratings are assigned by rating agencies such as Moody's Investor Service, Standard & Poor's Corporation, and Fitch Investor Service.

A higher-risk classification can increase a corporation's commercial paper rate by as much as 150 basis points (1.5 percent). The difference has reached 150 basis points during some recessions but has been less than 50 basis points over other periods.

In 1989, several major issuers of commercial paper defaulted, including Wang Labs, Lomas Financial, and Drexel Burnham Lambert. All of these issues were rated highly until the default. These defaults led to a growing number of commercial paper issues (called **junk commercial paper**) that were rated low or not rated at all. In the last decade, the number of defaults on commercial paper has been very low.

Placement Some firms place commercial paper directly with investors. Ford Motor Credit and other firms have recently sold their commercial paper online to investors. Other firms rely on commercial paper dealers to sell their commercial paper, at a cost of usually one-eighth of 1 percent of the face value. This transaction cost is generally less than it would cost to establish a department within the firm to place commercial paper directly. Companies that frequently issue commercial paper may reduce expenses by creating an in-house department, however. Most nonfinancial companies use commercial paper dealers rather than in-house resources to place their commercial paper. Their liquidity needs, and therefore their commercial paper issues, are cyclical, so they would use an in-house direct-placement department only a few times during the year. Finance companies typically maintain an in-house department because they frequently borrow in this manner.

Backing Commercial Paper Issuers of commercial paper typically maintain backup lines of credit in case they cannot roll over (reissue) commercial paper at a reasonable rate because, for example, their assigned rating was lowered. A backup line of credit provided by a commercial bank gives the company the right (but not the obligation) to borrow a specified maximum amount of funds over a specified period of time. The fee for the line can either be a direct percentage of the total accessible credit (such as 0.5 percent) or be in the form of required compensating balances (such as 10 percent of the line).

Estimating the Yield At a given point in time, the yield on commercial paper is slightly higher than the yield on a T-bill with the same maturity because commercial paper carries some credit risk and is less liquid. Like T-bills, commercial paper is sold at a discount from par value. The nominal return to investors who retain the paper until maturity is the difference between the price paid for the paper and the par value. Thus, the yield received by a commercial paper investor can be determined in a manner similar to the T-bill yield, although a 360-day year is usually used.

ILLUSTRATION   If an investor purchases 30-day commercial paper with a par value of $1,000,000 for a price of $990,000, the yield ($Y_{cp}$) is

$$Y_{cp} = \frac{\$1,000,000 - \$990,000}{\$990,000} \times \frac{360}{30}$$

$$= 12.12\%$$

When a firm plans to issue commercial paper, the price (and therefore yield) to investors is uncertain. Thus, the cost of borrowing funds is uncertain until the paper is issued. Consider the case of a firm that plans to issue 90-day commercial paper with a par value of $5,000,000. It expects to sell the commercial paper for $4,850,000. The yield it expects to pay investors (its cost of borrowing) is estimated to be

$$Y_{cp} = \frac{Par - PP}{PP} \times \frac{360}{n}$$

$$= \frac{\$5,000,000 - \$4,850,000}{\$4,850,000} \times \frac{360}{90}$$

$$= 12.37\% \blacksquare$$

http://www.federalreserve
.gov/releases Links to a
database of commercial
paper rates over time.

When firms sell their commercial paper at a lower (higher) price than projected, their cost of raising funds will be higher (lower) than they initially anticipated. For example, if the firm initially sold the commercial paper for $4,865,000, the cost of borrowing would have been about 11.1 percent. (Check the math as an exercise.)

Ignoring transaction costs, the cost of borrowing with commercial paper is equal to the yield earned by investors holding the paper until maturity. The cost of borrowing can be adjusted for transaction costs (charged by the commercial paper dealers) by subtracting the nominal transaction fees from the price received.

Some corporations prefer to issue commercial paper rather than borrow from a bank because it is usually a cheaper source of funds. Nevertheless, even the large creditworthy corporations that are able to issue commercial paper normally obtain some short-term loans from commercial banks in order to maintain a business relationship with them.

Commercial Paper Yield Curve The commercial paper yield curve represents the yield offered on commercial paper at various maturities. The curve is typically established for a maturity range from 0 to 90 days because most commercial paper has a maturity within that range. This yield curve is important because it may influence the maturity that is used by firms that issue commercial paper and by the institutional investors that purchase commercial paper. The shape of this yield curve could be roughly drawn from the short-term range of the traditional Treasury yield curve. However, that curve is graphed over a long time period, so it is difficult to derive the precise shape of a yield curve over a three-month range from that graph.

The same factors that affect the Treasury yield curve from 0 to 10 years affect the commercial paper yield curve, but are applied to very short-term horizons. In particular, expectations of interest over the next few months can influence the commercial paper yield curve.

Negotiable Certificates of Deposit (NCDs)

Negotiable certificates of deposit (NCDs) are certificates that are issued by large commercial banks and other depository institutions as a short-term source of funds. The minimum denomination is $100,000, although a $1 million denomination is more common. Nonfinancial corporations often purchase NCDs. Although NCD denominations are typically too large for individual investors, they are sometimes purchased by money market funds that have pooled individual investors' funds. Thus, money market funds allow individuals to be indirect investors in NCDs, creating a more active NCD market.

Maturities on NCDs normally range from two weeks to one year. A secondary market for NCDs exists, providing investors with some liquidity. However, institutions prefer not to have their newly issued NCDs compete with their previously issued NCDs that are being resold in the secondary market. An oversupply of NCDs for sale can force them to sell their newly issued NCDs at a lower price.

Placement Some issuers place their NCDs directly; others use a correspondent institution that specializes in placing NCDs. Another alternative is to sell NCDs to securities dealers, who in turn resell them. A portion of unusually large issues is commonly sold to NCD dealers. Normally, however, NCDs can be sold to investors directly at a higher price.

Premium NCDs must offer a premium above the T-bill yield to compensate for less liquidity and safety. The premiums are generally higher during recessionary periods. The premiums also reflect the market's perception about the safety of the financial system.

Yield NCDs provide a return in the form of interest along with the difference between the price at which the NCD is redeemed (or sold in the secondary market) and the purchase price. Given that an institution issues an NCD at par value, the annualized yield that it will pay is the annualized interest rate on the NCD. If investors purchase this NCD and hold it until maturity, their annualized yield is the interest rate. However, the annualized yield can differ from the annualized interest rate for investors who either purchase or sell the NCD in the secondary market instead of holding it from inception until maturity.

ILLUSTRATION An investor purchased an NCD a year ago in the secondary market for $970,000. He redeems it today upon maturity and receives $1,000,000. He also receives interest of $40,000. His annualized yield (Y_{NCD}) on this investment is

$$Y_{NCD} = \frac{SP - PP + \text{interest}}{PP}$$

$$= \frac{\$1,000,000 - \$970,000 + \$40,000}{\$970,000}$$

$$= 7.22\% \ \blacksquare$$

Repurchase Agreements

With a repurchase agreement (or repo), one party sells securities to another with an agreement to repurchase the securities at a specified date and price. In essence, the repo transaction represents a loan backed by the securities. If the borrower defaults on the loan, the lender has claim to the securities. Most repo transactions use government securities, although some involve other securities such as commercial paper or NCDs. A **reverse repo** refers to the purchase of securities by one party from another with an agreement to sell them. Thus, a repo and a reverse repo can refer to the same transaction but from different perspectives. These two terms are sometimes used interchangeably, so a transaction described as a repo may actually be a reverse repo.

Financial institutions such as banks, savings and loan associations, and money market funds often participate in repurchase agreements. Many nonfinancial institutions are active participants as well. Transaction amounts are usually for $10 million or more. The most common maturities are from one day to 15 days and for one, three, and six months. A secondary market for repos does not exist. Some firms in need of funds will set the maturity on a repo to be the minimum time period for which they need temporary financing. If they still need funds when the repo is about to mature, they will borrow additional funds through new repos and use these funds to fulfill their obligation on maturing repos.

Placement Repo transactions are negotiated through a telecommunications network. Dealers and repo brokers act as financial intermediaries to create repos for firms with deficient and excess funds, receiving a commission for their services.

When the borrowing firm can find a counterparty to the repo transaction, it avoids the transaction fee involved in having a government securities dealer find the counterparty. Some companies that commonly engage in repo transactions have an in-house department for finding counterparties and executing the transactions. These same companies that borrow through repos may, from time to time, serve as the lender. That is, they purchase the government securities and agree to sell them back in the near future. Because the cash flow of any large company changes on a daily basis, it is not unusual for a firm to act as an investor one day (when it has excess funds) and a borrower the next (when it has a cash shortage).

Estimating the Yield The repo rate is determined by the difference between the initial selling price of the securities and the agreed-upon repurchase price, annualized with a 360-day year.

ILLUSTRATION An investor initially purchased securities at a price (*PP*) of $9,852,217, with an agreement to sell them back at a price (*SP*) of $10,000,000 at the end of a 60-day period. The yield (or repo rate) on this repurchase agreement is

$$\text{Repo rate} = \frac{SP - PP}{PP} \times \frac{360}{n}$$

$$= \frac{\$10,000,000 - \$9,852,217}{\$9,852,217} \times \frac{360}{60}$$

$$= 9\% \ \blacksquare$$

Federal Funds

http://www.federalreserve.gov/fomc Provides an excellent summary of the Fed's adjustment in the federal funds rate over time.

The federal funds market allows depository institutions to effectively lend or borrow short-term funds from each other at the so-called **federal funds rate.** The federal funds rate is the rate charged on federal funds transactions. It is influenced by the supply and demand for funds in the federal funds market. The Federal Reserve adjusts the amount of funds in depository institutions in order to influence the federal funds rate (as explained in Chapter 4) and several other short-term interest rates. All types of firms closely monitor the federal funds rate because the Federal Reserve manipulates it to affect general economic conditions. Many market participants view changes in the federal funds rate as an indicator of potential changes in other money market rates.

The federal funds rate is normally slightly higher than the T-bill rate at any point in time. A lender in the federal funds market is subject to credit risk, since it is possible that the financial institution borrowing the funds could default on the loan. Once a loan transaction is agreed upon, the lending institution can instruct its Federal Reserve district bank to debit its reserve account and to credit the borrowing institution's reserve account by the amount of the loan. If the loan is for just one day, it will likely be based on an oral agreement between the parties, especially if the institutions commonly do business with each other.

Commercial banks are the most active participants in the federal funds market. Federal funds brokers serve as financial intermediaries in the market, matching up institutions that wish to sell (lend) funds with those that wish to purchase (borrow) them. The brokers receive a commission for their service. The transactions are negotiated through a telecommunications network that links federal funds brokers with the participating institutions. Most loan transactions are for $5 million or more and usually have a one- to seven-day maturity (although the loans may often be extended by the lender if the borrower desires more time).

The volume of interbank loans on commercial bank balance sheets over time is an indication of the importance of lending between depository institutions. The interbank loan volume outstanding now exceeds $200 billion.

Banker's Acceptances

A **banker's acceptance** indicates that a bank accepts responsibility for a future payment. Banker's acceptances are commonly used for international trade transactions. An exporter that is sending goods to an importer whose credit rating is not known will often prefer that a bank act as a guarantor. The bank therefore facilitates the transaction by stamping ACCEPTED on a draft, which obligates payment at a specified point in time. In turn, the importer will pay the bank what is owed to the exporter along with a fee to the bank for guaranteeing the payment.

Exporters can hold a banker's acceptance until the date at which payment is to be made, but they frequently sell the acceptance before then at a discount to obtain cash immediately. The investor who purchases the acceptance then receives the payment guaranteed by the bank in the future. The investor's return on a banker's acceptance, like that on commercial paper, is derived from the difference between the discounted price paid for the acceptance and the amount to be received in the future. Maturities on banker's acceptances often range from 30 to 270 days. Because there is a possibility that a bank will default on payment, investors are exposed to a slight degree of credit risk. Thus, they deserve a return above the T-bill yield as compensation.

Because acceptances are often discounted and sold by the exporting firm prior to maturity, an active secondary market exists. Dealers match up companies that wish to sell acceptances with other companies that wish to purchase them. A dealer's bid price is less than its ask price, which creates the spread, or the dealer's reward for doing business. The spread is normally between one-eighth and seven-eighths of 1 percent.

Steps Involved in Banker's Acceptances
The sequence of steps involved in a banker's acceptance is illustrated in Exhibit 6.3. To understand these steps, consider the example of a U.S. importer of Japanese goods. First, the importer places a purchase order for the goods (Step 1). If the Japanese exporter is unfamiliar with the U.S. importer, it may demand payment before delivery of goods, which the U.S. importer may be unwilling to make. A compromise may be reached through the creation of a banker's acceptance. The importer asks its bank to issue a **letter of credit (L/C)** on its behalf (Step 2). The L/C represents a commitment by that bank to back the payment owed to the Japanese exporter. Then the L/C is presented to the exporter's bank (Step 3), which informs the exporter that the L/C has been received (Step 4). The exporter then sends the goods to the importer (Step 5) and sends the shipping documents to its bank (Step 6), which passes them along to the importer's bank (Step 7). At this point, the banker's acceptance is created, which obligates the importer's bank to make payment to the holder of the banker's acceptance at a specified future date. The banker's acceptance may be sold to a money market investor at a discount. Potential purchasers of acceptances are short-term investors. When the acceptance matures, the importer pays its bank, which in turn pays the money market investor who presents the acceptance.

Exhibit 6.3
Sequence of Steps
in the Creation of a
Banker's Acceptance

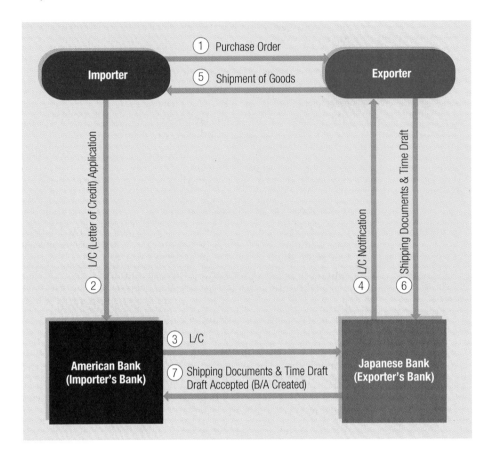

Exhibit 6.3 Sequence of Steps in the Creation of a Banker's Acceptance

The creation of a banker's acceptance allows the importer to receive goods from an exporter without sending immediate payment. The selling of the acceptance creates financing for the exporter. Even though banker's acceptances are often created to facilitate international transactions, they are not limited to money market investors with international experience. Investors who purchase acceptances are more concerned with the credit of the bank that guarantees payment than with the credit of the exporter or importer. For this reason, the credit risk on a banker's acceptance is somewhat similar to that of NCDs issued by commercial banks. Because acceptances have the backing of the bank as well as the importing firm, however, they may be perceived as having slightly less credit risk than NCDs.

The money market securities are summarized in Exhibit 6.4. When money market securities are issued to obtain funds, the type of securities issued depends on whether the issuer is the Treasury, a depository institution, or a corporation. When investors decide which type of money market securities to invest in, their choice is dependent on the desired return and liquidity characteristics.

Institutional Use of Money Markets

The institutional use of money market securities is summarized in Exhibit 6.5. Financial institutions purchase money market securities in order to simultaneously earn a return and maintain adequate liquidity. They issue money market securities when experiencing a temporary shortage of cash. Because money markets serve businesses, the

Exhibit 6.4　Summary of Commonly Issued Money Market Securities

Securities	Issued by	Common Investors	Common Maturities	Secondary Market Activity
Treasury bills	Federal government	Households, firms, and financial institutions	13 weeks, 26 weeks, 1 year	High
Negotiable certificates of deposit (NCDs)	Large banks and savings institutions	Firms	2 weeks to 1 year	Moderate
Commercial paper	Bank holding companies, finance companies, and other companies	Firms	1 day to 270 days	Low
Banker's acceptances	Banks (exporting firms can sell the acceptances at a discount to obtain funds)	Firms	30 days to 270 days	High
Federal funds	Depository institutions	Depository institutions	1 day to 7 days	Nonexistent
Repurchase agreements	Firms and financial institutions	Firms and financial institutions	1 day to 15 days	Nonexistent

Exhibit 6.5　Institutional Use of Money Markets

Type of Financial Institution	Participation in the Money Markets
Commercial banks and savings institutions	• Bank holding companies issue commercial paper. • Some banks and savings institutions issue NCDs, borrow or lend funds in the federal funds market, engage in repurchase agreements, and purchase T-bills. • Commercial banks create banker's acceptances. • Commercial banks provide backup lines of credit to corporations that issue commercial paper.
Finance companies	• Issue large amounts of commercial paper.
Money market mutual funds	• Use proceeds from shares sold to invest in T-bills, commercial paper, NCDs, repurchase agreements, and banker's acceptances.
Insurance companies	• May maintain a portion of their investment portfolio as money market securities for liquidity.
Pension funds	• May maintain a portion of their investment portfolio as money market securities that may be liquidated when portfolio managers desire to increase their investment in bonds or stocks.

average transaction size is very large and is typically executed through a telecommunications network.

Money market securities can be used to enhance liquidity in two ways. First, newly issued securities generate cash. The institutions that issue new securities have created a short-term liability in order to boost their cash balance. Second, institutions that previously purchased money market securities will generate cash upon liquidation of the securities. In this case, one type of asset (the security) is replaced by another (cash).

Most financial institutions maintain sufficient liquidity by holding either securities that have very active secondary markets or securities with short-term maturities. T-bills are the most popular money market instrument because of their marketability, safety, and short-term maturity. Although T-bills are purchased through an auction, other money market instruments are commonly purchased through dealers or specialized brokers. For example, commercial paper is purchased through commercial paper dealers or directly from the issuer, NCDs are usually purchased through brokers specializing in NCDs, federal funds are purchased (borrowed) through federal funds brokers, and repurchase agreements are purchased through repo dealers.

Financial institutions whose future cash inflows and outflows are more uncertain will generally maintain additional money market instruments for liquidity. For this reason, depository institutions such as commercial banks allocate a greater portion of their asset portfolio to money market instruments than pension funds usually do.

Financial institutions that purchase money market securities are acting as a creditor to the initial issuer of the securities. For example, when they hold T-bills, they are creditors to the Treasury. The T-bill transactions in the secondary market commonly reflect a flow of funds between two nongovernment institutions. T-bills represent a source of funds for those financial institutions that liquidate some of their T-bill holdings. In fact, this is the main reason that financial institutions hold T-bills. Liquidity is also the reason financial institutions purchase other money market instruments, including federal funds (purchased by depository institutions), repurchase agreements (purchased by depository institutions and money market funds), banker's acceptances, and NCDs (purchased by money market funds).

Some financial institutions issue their own money market instruments to obtain cash. For example, depository institutions issue NCDs, and bank holding companies and finance companies issue commercial paper. Depository institutions also obtain funds through the use of repurchase agreements or in the federal funds market.

Many money market transactions involve two financial institutions. For example, a federal funds transaction involves two depository institutions. Money market funds commonly purchase NCDs from banks and savings institutions. Repurchase agreements are frequently negotiated between two commercial banks.

Valuation of Money Market Securities

Many types of money market securities make no interest payments but do provide principal at maturity. The value of these money market securities is measured as the present value of the principal payment to be paid at maturity. The discount rate used to discount the money market security is the required rate of return by investors, which includes a risk premium if the security is risky.

If short-term interest rates decline, the required rate of return on money market securities will decline, and the values of money market securities will increase. Although money market security values are sensitive to interest rate movements in the same direction as bonds, they are not as sensitive as bond values to interest rate movements. The lower degree of sensitivity is primarily attributed to the shorter term to maturity. With money market securities, the principal payment will occur in the next year, whereas the principal payment on bonds may be 10 or 20 years away. In other words, an increase in interest rates is not as harmful to a money market security because it will mature soon anyway, and the investor can reinvest the proceeds at the prevailing rate at that time. An increase in interest rates is more harmful to a bond with 20 years until maturity because the investor will be earning a low rate on the bond for the next 20 years.

Explaining Money Market Price Movements

The market price of money market securities (P_m) should equal the present value of their future cash flows. Since money market securities normally do not make periodic interest payments, their cash flows are in the form of one lump-sum payment of principal. Therefore, the market price of a money market security can be determined as

$$P_m = \text{Par}/(1 + k)^n$$

where   **Par = par value or principal amount to be provided at maturity**

   k = required rate of return by investors

   n = time to maturity

Exhibit 6.6   Framework for Pricing Money Market Securities

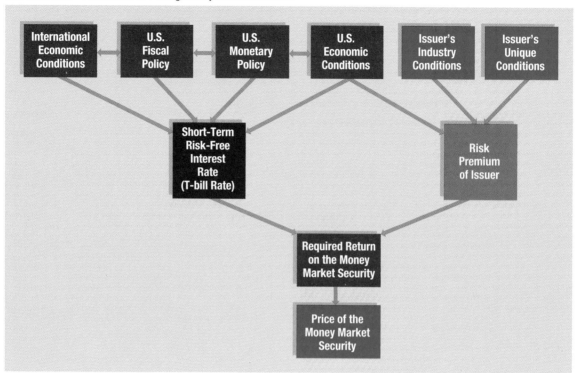

Since money market securities have maturities of one year or less, n is measured as a fraction of one year.

A change in P_m can be modeled as

$$\Delta P_m = f(\Delta k) \text{ and } \Delta k = f(\Delta R_f, \Delta RP)$$

where
$$R_f = \text{risk-free interest rate}$$
$$RP = \text{risk premium}$$

Therefore,

$$\Delta P_m = f(\Delta R_f, \Delta RP)$$

Exhibit 6.6 identifies the underlying forces that can affect the short-term risk-free interest rate (the T-bill rate) and the risk premium and can therefore cause the price of a money market security to change over time. When pricing T-bills, the focus is on the factors that affect the risk-free interest rate, as the risk premium is not needed. Thus, the difference in the required return of a risky money market security (such as commercial paper) versus the T-bill (for a given maturity) is the risk premium, which is influenced by economic, industry, and firm-specific conditions.

Efficiency of Money Market Securities

The money markets are referred to as efficient if the prices of the securities reflect all available information. In general, the money markets are widely perceived to be efficient, in that the prices reflect all available public information. Most money market securities are subject to large trading volume and therefore are monitored by many investors. The price of a money market security such as commercial paper can decline quickly if the issuer suddenly announces financial problems. However, this type of adjustment in price does not reflect a violation of market efficiency. In fact, it is because of market efficiency that the price adjusts so quickly to new information. Most investors buy money market securities because they need liquidity, not because they think they can capitalize on mispricing of the securities. They are more likely to think that they could earn larger gains in other financial markets, but rely on the money markets for liquidity.

Indicators of Future Money Market Security Prices

Money market participants closely monitor economic indicators that may signal future changes in the strength of the economy, which can signal changes in short-term interest rates and in the required return from investing in money market securities. Some of the more closely monitored indicators of economic growth include employment, gross domestic product, retail sales, industrial production, and consumer confidence. An unexpected favorable movement in these indicators tends to create expectations of increased economic growth and higher interest rates, which place downward pressure on prices of money market securities.

Money market participants also closely monitor indicators of inflation, such as the consumer price index and the producer price index. In general, an unexpected increase in these indexes tends to create expectations of higher interest rates and places downward pressure on money market prices. Whenever indicators signal a potential increase in interest rates, money market participants tend to shift their investments into securities with relatively short terms to maturity so that they can receive a higher yield by reinvesting in newly issued securities once interest rates rise.

Risk of Money Market Securities

When corporate treasurers, institutional investors, and individual investors invest in money market securities, they are subject to the risk that the return on their investment will be less than anticipated. The forces that influence price movements of money market securities cannot be perfectly anticipated, so future money market prices (and therefore yields) cannot be perfectly anticipated either. If the money market securities will not be held until maturity, the prices at which they can be sold in the future (and therefore the return on the investment) will depend primarily on the risk-free interest rate and the perceived credit risk at the time the securities are sold. Because the investment horizon for money market securities is short term, the investment is not subject to a major loss in value as a result of an increase in interest rates, but it can be subject to a major loss of value if the issuer of the money market security defaults.

Credit Risk

If investors want to avoid risk, they can purchase T-bills and hold them to maturity. They must weigh the higher potential return of investing in other money market securities against the exposure to risk (that the actual return could be lower than the expected return). Since the risk of a large loss is primarily attributed to the possibility of default, investors commonly invest in money market securities (such as commercial paper) that offer a slightly higher yield than T-bills and are very unlikely to default. Although investors can assess economic and firm-specific conditions to determine the credit risk of an issuer of a money market security, information about the issuer's financial condition is limited.

Investors who plan to reinvest their funds in another money market investment at maturity are exposed to rollover risk, which is the potential decline in the yield offered when the proceeds from a maturing money market security are rolled over into a subsequent investment. Since this risk results from a change in market interest rates, it is also referred to as interest rate risk.

ILLUSTRATION Covington Company has $7 million that it will not need to spend until 12 months from now. It purchases commercial paper with a nine-month maturity date. After nine months, the commercial paper will mature, and Covington will roll the proceeds into another money market investment. If interest rates decline over the next nine months, the annualized yield offered on money market securities at that time will likely be lower than the annualized yields offered today. ■

Measuring Risk

Participants in the money markets can use sensitivity analysis to determine how the value of money market securities may change in response to a change in interest rates.

ILLUSTRATION Assume that Long Island Bank has money market securities with a par value of $100 million that will mature in nine months. Since the bank will need a substantial amount of funds in three months, it wants to know how much cash it will receive from selling these securities three months from now. Assume that it expects the unannualized required rate of return on those securities for the remaining six months to be 3 percent, or 3.5 percent, or 3.8 percent with a 33.3 percent chance for each of these three scenarios.

Exhibit 6.7 shows the probability distribution of the proceeds that Long Island Bank will receive from selling the money market securities in three months, based on the possible scenarios for the required rate of return at that time. Based on this exhibit, the bank expects that it will receive at least $96,339,113, but it could receive more if interest rates (and therefore the required rate of return) are relatively low in three months. By deriving a probability distribution of outcomes, the bank can anticipate whether the proceeds to be received will be sufficient to cover the amount of funds that it needs in three months. ■

Interaction among Money Market Yields

Companies investing in money markets closely monitor the yields on the various instruments. Because the instruments serve as reasonable substitutes for each other,

Exhibit 6.7
Probability Distribution of Proceeds from Selling Money Market Securities

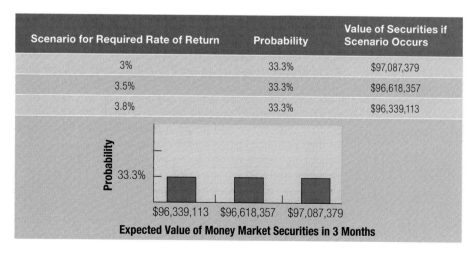

Scenario for Required Rate of Return	Probability	Value of Securities if Scenario Occurs
3%	33.3%	$97,087,379
3.5%	33.3%	$96,618,357
3.8%	33.3%	$96,339,113

Exhibit 6.8 Money Market Yields (3-Month Maturity)

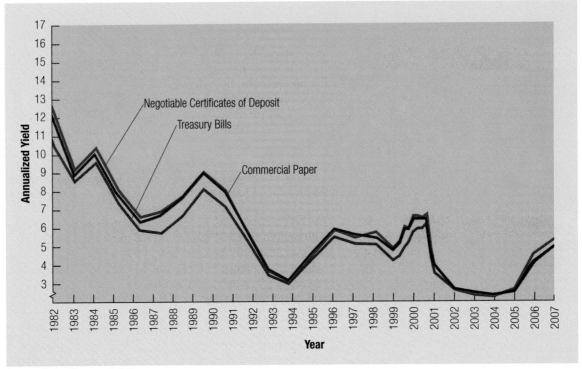

Source: *Federal Reserve Bulletin.*

the investing companies may exchange instruments to achieve a more attractive yield. This causes yields among these instruments to be somewhat similar. If a disparity in yields arises, companies will avoid the low-yield instruments in favor of the high-yield instruments. This places upward pressure on the yields of the low-yield securities and downward pressure on the high-yield securities, causing realignment.

During periods of heightened uncertainty about the economy, investors tend to shift from risky money market securities to Treasury securities. This so-called flight to quality creates a greater differential between yields, as risky money market securities must provide a larger premium to attract investors.

Exhibit 6.8 shows the yields of money market securities over time. The high degree of correlation among security yields is obvious. T-bills consistently offer slightly lower yields than the other securities because they are very liquid and free from credit risk.

Globalization of Money Markets

GL🌐BALASPECTS Market interest rates vary among countries, as shown in Exhibit 6.9. The interest rate differentials occur because geographic markets are somewhat segmented. The interest rates of several European countries are the same as a result of the conversion of their currencies to the euro in January 1999. In addition, the interest rates of some other countries have become more highly correlated over time, as the flow of funds between countries has increased. The increase in the flow of funds is attributed to tax differences among countries, speculation on exchange rate movements, and a reduction in government barriers that were previously imposed on foreign investment in securities. U.S. T-bills and commercial paper are very accessible to foreign investors. In addition, securities such as Eurodollar deposits, Euronotes, and Euro-commercial

Exhibit 6.9 International Money Market Rates over Time

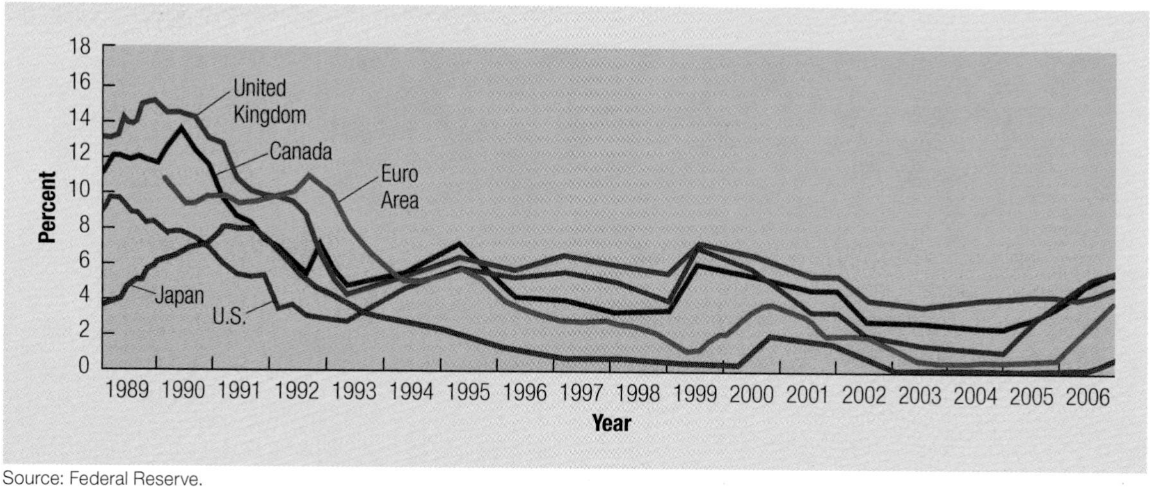

Source: Federal Reserve.

paper are widely traded throughout the international money markets, as discussed in the following subsections.

Eurodollar Securities

As corporations outside the United States (especially in Europe) increasingly engaged in international trade transactions in U.S. dollars, U.S. dollar deposits in non-U.S. banks grew. Furthermore, because interest rate ceilings were historically imposed on dollar deposits in U.S. banks, corporations with large dollar balances often deposited their funds overseas to receive a higher yield. These dollar deposits in overseas banks came to be referred to as Eurodollars. Several types of money market securities utilize Eurodollars.

Eurodollar CDs **Eurodollar certificates of deposit** are large dollar-denominated deposits (such as $1 million) accepted by banks in Europe. Eurodollar CD volume has grown substantially over time, as the U.S. dollar is used as a medium of exchange in a significant portion of international trade and investment transactions. Some firms overseas receive U.S. dollars as payment for exports and invest in Eurodollar CDs. Because these firms may need dollars to pay for future imports, they retain dollar-denominated deposits rather than convert dollars to their home currency.

In the so-called **Eurodollar market,** banks channel the deposited funds to other firms that need to borrow them in the form of Eurodollar loans. The deposit and loan transactions in Eurodollars are typically $1 million or more per transaction, so only governments and large corporations participate in this market. Because transaction amounts are large, investors in the market avoid some costs associated with the continuous small transactions that occur in retail-oriented markets. In addition, Eurodollar CDs are not subject to reserve requirements, which means that banks can lend out 100 percent of the deposits that arrive. For these reasons, the spread between the rate banks pay on large Eurodollar deposits and what they charge on Eurodollar loans is relatively small. Consequently, interest rates in the Eurodollar market are attractive for both depositors and borrowers. The rates offered on Eurodollar deposits are slightly higher than the rates offered on NCDs.

A secondary market for Eurodollar CDs exists, allowing the initial investors to liquidate their investment if necessary. The growth in Eurodollar volume has made the secondary market more active.

The Wall Street Journal provides a "Money Rates" table that contains quotations for the prime rates (on bank loans to their most credit-worthy customers), federal funds rate, T-bill rates, banker's acceptance rates, and commercial paper rates. It also contains quotations for foreign prime rates and other foreign interest rates. Using this table, market participants can compare yields to decide whether to invest in any particular type of money market security. For some money market securities, the rates are also shown for various maturities, so market participants can decide which maturity is most attractive. Borrowers such as corporations and the Treasury can also use this table to assess prevailing interest rates when deciding whether to borrow funds.

Source: Reprinted with permission of Dow Jones & Company, Inc., from The Wall Street Journal, April 4, 2007; permission conveyed through the Copyright Clearance Center, Inc.

Money Rates

April 4, 2007

Key annual interest rates paid to borrow or lend money in U.S. and international markets. Rates below are a guide to general levels but don't always represent actual transactions.

Inflation

	Feb. index level	CHG FROM (%) Jan. '07	Feb. '06
U.S. consumer price index			
All items	**203.5**	0.5	2.4
Core	**209.1**	0.5	2.7

International rates

	Latest	Week ago	—52-WEEK— High	Low
Prime rates				
U.S.	**8.25**	8.25	8.25	7.75
Canada	**6.00**	6.00	6.00	5.50
Euro zone	**3.75**	3.75	3.75	2.50
Japan	**1.875**	1.875	1.875	1.375
Switzerland	**4.02**	3.80	4.14	2.57
Britain	**5.25**	5.25	5.25	4.50
Australia	**6.25**	6.25	6.25	5.50
Hong Kong	**8.00**	8.00	8.25	8.00
Overnight repurchase				
U.S.	**5.25**	5.24	5.28	4.62
U.K. (BBA)	**5.263**	5.288	5.312	4.342
Euro zone	**3.87**	3.81	3.87	2.43

U.S. government rates

Discount				
	6.25	6.25	6.25	5.75
Federal funds				
Effective rate	**5.21**	5.27	5.42	4.71
High	**5.3750**	5.3750	7.0000	4.8750
Low	**5.0000**	4.7500	5.2500	3.0000
Bid	**5.1250**	3.0000	6.7500	3.0000
Offer	**5.2500**	4.7500	7.0000	3.7500
Treasury bill auction				
4 weeks	**5.060**	5.130	5.175	4.460
13 weeks	**4.910**	4.925	5.035	4.535
26 weeks	**4.870**	4.875	5.110	4.670

Other short-term rates

	Latest	Week ago	—52-WEEK— High	Low
Call money	**7.00**	7.00	7.00	6.50
Commercial paper				
30 to 44 days	**5.24**	...	...	...
45 to 61 days	**5.23**	...	...	...
62 to 93 days	**5.21**	...	...	...
94 to 120 days	**5.18**	...	...	...
121 to 153 days	**5.16**	...	...	...
154 to 180 days	**5.14**	...	...	...
181 to 210 days	**5.10**	...	...	...
211 to 240 days	**5.07**	...	...	...
241 to 270 days	**5.03**	...	...	...
Dealer commercial paper				
30 days	**5.26**	5.26	5.36	4.77
60 days	**5.28**	5.27	5.41	4.86
90 days	**5.29**	5.27	5.46	4.91
Euro commercial paper				
30 day	**3.80**	3.80	3.81	2.00
Two month	**3.81**	3.81	3.82	2.63
Three month	**3.88**	3.85	3.88	2.71
Four month	**3.93**	3.89	3.93	2.77
Five month	**3.97**	3.93	3.97	2.81
Six month	**4.00**	3.96	4.00	2.87
London interbank offered rate, or Libor				
One month	**5.32000**	5.32000	5.42000	4.84000
Three month	**5.35000**	5.35000	5.52000	5.01375
Six month	**5.33563**	5.32375	5.64000	5.16000
One year	**5.23656**	5.20563	5.76625	5.11000
Euro Libor				
One month	**3.865**	3.867	3.867	2.635
Three month	**3.943**	3.917	3.943	2.760
Six month	**4.069**	4.031	4.069	2.912
One year	**4.204**	4.160	4.207	3.163
Euro interbank offered rate (Euribor)				
One month	**3.863**	3.865	3.865	2.635
Three month	**3.944**	3.914	3.944	2.762

Investors in fixed-rate Eurodollar CDs are adversely affected by rising market interest rates, while issuers of these CDs are adversely affected by declining rates. To deal with this interest rate risk, **Eurodollar floating-rate CDs** (called **FRCDs**) have been used in recent years. The rate adjusts periodically to the London Interbank Offer Rate (LIBOR), which is the interest rate charged on international interbank loans. As with other floating-rate instruments, the rate on FRCDs ensures that the borrower's cost and the investor's return reflect prevailing market interest rates.

Euronotes Short-term **Euronotes** are short-term securities issued in bearer form, with common maturities of one, three, and six months. Typical investors in Euronotes often include the Eurobanks (banks that accept large deposits and make large loans in foreign currencies) that are hired to place the paper. These Euronotes are sometimes underwritten in a manner that guarantees the issuer a specific price.

Euro-Commercial Paper **Euro-commercial paper (Euro-CP)** is issued without the backing of a banking syndicate. Maturities can be tailored to satisfy investors. Dealers that place commercial paper have created a secondary market by being willing to purchase existing Euro-CP before maturity.

The Euro-CP rate is typically between 50 and 100 basis points above LIBOR. Euro-CP is sold by dealers, at a transaction cost ranging between 5 and 10 basis points of the face value. This market is tiny compared to the U.S. commercial paper market. Nevertheless, some non-U.S. companies can more easily place their paper here, where they have a household name.

International Money Markets

As international trade and financing have grown in Asia and South America, money markets have developed in those areas. Corporations commonly accept foreign currencies as revenue if they will need those currencies to pay for imports in the future. Since a corporation may not need to use funds at the time it receives them, it deposits the funds to earn interest until they are needed. Meanwhile, other corporations may need funds denominated in foreign currencies and therefore may wish to borrow those funds from a bank. International banks facilitate the international money markets by accepting deposits and providing loans in a wide variety of currencies.

International Interbank Market Some international banks periodically have an excess of funds beyond the amount that other corporations want to borrow. Other international banks may be short of funds because their client corporations want to borrow more funds than the banks have available. An international interbank market facilitates the transfer of funds from banks with excess funds to those with deficient funds. This market is similar to the federal funds market in the United States, but it is worldwide and conducts transactions in a wide variety of currencies. Some of the transactions are direct from one bank to another, while others are channeled through large banks that serve as intermediaries between the lending bank and the borrowing bank. Historically, international banks in London carried out many of these transactions.

The rate charged for a loan from one bank to another in the international interbank market is the LIBOR, which is similar to the federal funds rate in the United States. The LIBOR varies among currencies and is usually in line with the prevailing money market rates in the currency. It varies over time in response to changes in money market rates in a particular currency, which are driven by changes in the demand and supply conditions for short-term money in that currency. The term LIBOR is still frequently used, even though many international interbank transactions do not pass through London.

Performance of Foreign Money Market Securities

The performance of an investment in a foreign money market security is measured by the **effective yield** (yield adjusted for the exchange rate), which is dependent on the

(1) yield earned on the money market security in the foreign currency and (2) the exchange rate effect. The yield earned on the money market security (Y_f) is

$$Y_f = \frac{SP_f - PP_f}{PP_f}$$

where SP_f = selling price of the foreign money market security in the foreign currency

PP_f = purchase price of the foreign money market security in the foreign currency

The exchange rate effect (denoted as %ΔS) measures the percentage change in the spot exchange rate (in dollars) from the time the foreign currency was obtained to invest in the foreign money market security until the time the security was sold and the foreign currency was converted into the investor's home currency. Thus, the effective yield is

$$Y_e = (1 + Y_f) \times (1 + \%\Delta S) - 1$$

ILLUSTRATION   A U.S. investor obtains Mexican pesos when the peso is worth $.12 and invests in a one-year money market security that provides a yield (in pesos) of 22 percent. At the end of one year, the investor converts the proceeds from the investment back to dollars at the prevailing spot rate of $.13 per peso. In this example, the peso increased in value by 8.33 percent, or .0833. The effective yield earned by the investor is

$$
\begin{aligned}
Y_e &= (1 + Y_f) \times (1 + \%\Delta S) - 1 \\
&= (1.22) \times (1.0833) - 1 \\
&= 32.16\% \ \blacksquare
\end{aligned}
$$

The effective yield exceeds the yield quoted on the foreign currency whenever the currency denominating the foreign investment increases in value over the investment horizon.

To illustrate the potential effects of exchange rate movements, the effective yield for a U.S. investor that invests in British money market securities is shown in Exhibit 6.10. The effective yield was higher than the alternative domestic yields during

Exhibit 6.10   Comparison of Effective Yields between U.S. and British Money Market Yields for a U.S. Investor

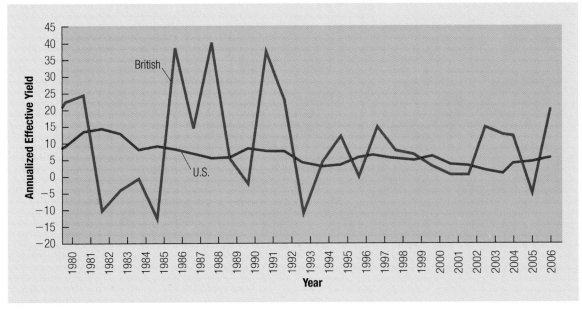

certain periods as a result of the strengthened pound. Conversely, the effective yield on British money market securities was negative in periods when the pound depreciated. Most investors would not invest in foreign money market securities in every period but would do so only when the foreign currency is expected to appreciate. The results displayed in Exhibit 6.10 show both the high potential yields and the risk from investing in foreign money market securities. The risk could be reduced somewhat by spreading the investment across securities denominated in several currencies.

Summary

■ The main money market securities are Treasury bills, commercial paper, NCDs, repurchase agreements, federal funds, and banker's acceptances. These securities vary according to the issuer. Consequently, their perceived degree of credit risk can vary. They also have different degrees of liquidity. Therefore, the quoted yields at any given point in time vary among money market securities.

■ Financial institutions manage their liquidity by participating in money markets. They may issue money market securities when they experience cash shortages and need to boost liquidity. They can also sell holdings of money market securities to obtain cash.

■ The value of a money market security represents the present value of future cash flows generated by that security. Since money market securities represent debt, their expected cash flows are typically known. However, the pricing of money market securities changes in response to a shift in the required rate of return by investors. The required rate of return changes in response to interest rate movements or to a shift in the security's credit risk.

■ Interest rates vary among countries. Some investors are attracted to high interest rates in foreign countries, which cause funds to flow to those countries. Consequently, money markets have become globally integrated. Investments in foreign money market securities are subject to exchange rate risk because the foreign currency denominating the securities could depreciate over time.

Point Counter-Point

Should Firms Invest in Money Market Securities?

Point No. Firms are supposed to use money in a manner that generates an adequate return to shareholders. Money market securities provide a return that is less than that required by shareholders. Thus, firms should not be using shareholder funds to invest in money market securities. If firms need liquidity, they can rely on the money markets for short-term borrowing.

Counter-Point Yes. Firms need money markets for liquidity. If they do not hold any money market securities, they will frequently be forced to borrow to cover unanticipated cash needs. The lenders may charge higher risk premiums when lending so frequently to these firms.

Who Is Correct? Use the Internet to learn more about this issue. Offer your own opinion on this issue.

Questions and Applications

1. **Primary Market** Explain how the Treasury uses the primary market to obtain adequate funding.

2. **T-bill Auction** How can investors using the primary T-bill market be assured that their bid will be accepted? Why do large corporations typically make competitive bids rather than noncompetitive bids for T-bills?

3. **Secondary Market for T-bills** Describe the activity in the secondary T-bill market. How can this degree of activity benefit investors in T-bills? Why

might a financial institution sometimes consider T-bills as a potential source of funds?

4. **Commercial Paper** Who issues commercial paper? What types of financial institutions issue commercial paper? Why do some firms create a department that can directly place commercial paper? What criteria affect the decision to create such a department?

5. **Commercial Paper Ratings** Why do ratings agencies assign ratings to commercial paper?

6. **Commercial Paper Rates** Explain how investors' preferences for commercial paper change during a recession. How should this reaction affect the difference between commercial paper rates and T-bill rates during recessionary periods?

7. **Negotiable CDs** How can small investors participate in investments in negotiable certificates of deposits (NCDs)?

8. **Repurchase Agreements** Based on what you know about repurchase agreements, would you expect them to have a lower or higher annualized yield than commercial paper? Why?

9. **Banker's Acceptances** Explain how each of the following would use banker's acceptances: (a) exporting firms, (b) importing firms, (c) commercial banks, and (d) investors.

10. **Foreign Money Market Yield** Explain how the yield on a foreign money market security would be affected if the foreign currency denominating that security declines to a greater degree.

11. **Motive to Issue Commercial Paper** The maximum maturity of commercial paper is 270 days. Why would a firm issue commercial paper instead of longer-term securities, even if it needs funds for a long period of time?

12. **Risk and Return of Commercial Paper** You have the choice of investing in top-rated commercial paper or commercial paper that has a lower risk rating. How do you think the risk and return performances of the two investments differ?

13. **Commercial Paper Yield Curve** How do you think the shape of the yield curve for commercial paper and other money market instruments compares to the yield curve for Treasury securities? Explain your logic.

Advanced Questions

14. **Influence of Money Market Activity on Working Capital** Assume that interest rates for most maturities are unusually high. Also, assume that the net working capital (defined as current assets minus current liabilities) levels of many corporations are relatively low in this period. Explain how the

money markets play a role in the relationship between the interest rates and the level of net working capital.

15. **Applying Term Structure Theories to Commercial Paper** Apply the term structure of interest rate theories that were discussed in Chapter 3 to explain the shape of the existing commercial paper yield curve.

16. **How Money Market Rates May Respond to Prevailing Conditions** How have money market rates changed since the beginning of the semester? Consider the current economic conditions. Do you think money market rates will increase or decrease during the semester? Offer some logic to support your answer.

Interpreting Financial News

Interpret the following statements made by Wall Street analysts and portfolio managers.

a. "Money markets are not used to get rich, but to avoid being poor."

b. "Until conditions are more favorable, investors are staying on the sidelines."

c. "My portfolio is overinvested in stocks because of the low money market rates."

Managing in Financial Markets

Money Market Portfolio Dilemma As the treasurer of a corporation, one of your jobs is to maintain investments in liquid securities such as Treasury securities and commercial paper. Your goal is to earn as high a return as possible but without taking much of a risk.

a. The yield curve is currently upward sloping, such that 10-year Treasury bonds have an annualized yield 3 percentage points above the annualized yield of three-month T-bills. Should you consider using some of your funds to invest in 10-year Treasury securities?

b. Assume that you have substantially more cash than you would possibly need for any liquidity problems. Your boss suggests that you consider investing the excess funds in some money market securities that have a higher return than short-term Treasury securities, such as negotiable certificates of deposit (NCDs). Even though NCDs are less liquid, this would not cause a problem if you have more funds than you need. Given the situation, what use of the excess funds would benefit the firm the most?

c. Assume that commercial paper is currently offering an annualized yield of 7.5 percent, while Treasury securities are offering an annualized yield of 7 percent. Economic conditions have been stable, and you expect conditions to be very favorable over the next six months. Given this situation, would you prefer to hold a diversified portfolio of commercial paper issued by various corporations or T-bills?

d. Assume that commercial paper typically offers a premium of 0.5 percent above the T-bill rate.

Given that your firm typically maintains about $10 million in liquid funds, how much extra will you generate per year by investing in commercial paper versus T-bills? Is this extra return worth the risk that the commercial paper could default?

Problems

1. **T-bill Yield** Assume an investor purchased a six-month T-bill with a $10,000 par value for $9,000 and sold it 90 days later for $9,100. What is the yield?

2. **T-bill Discount** Newly issued three-month T-bills with a par value of $10,000 sold for $9,700. Compute the T-bill discount.

3. **Commercial Paper Yield** Assume an investor purchased six-month commercial paper with a face value of $1 million for $940,000. What is the yield?

4. **Repurchase Agreement** Stanford Corporation arranged a repurchase agreement in which it purchased securities for $4.9 million and will sell the securities back for $5 million in 40 days. What is the yield (or repo rate) to Stanford Corporation?

5. **T-bill Yield** You paid $98,000 for a $100,000 T-bill maturing in 120 days. If you hold it until maturity, what is the T-bill yield? What is the T-bill discount?

6. **T-bill Yield** The Treasury is selling 91-day T-bills with a face value of $10,000 for $8,800. If the investor holds them until maturity, calculate the yield.

7. **Required Rate of Return** A money market security that has a par value of $10,000 sells for $8,816.60. Given that the security has a maturity of two years, what is the investor's required rate of return?

8. **Effective Yield** A U.S. investor obtains British pounds when the pound is worth $1.50 and invests in a one-year money market security that provides a yield of 5 percent (in pounds). At the end of one year, the investor converts the proceeds from the investment back to dollars at the prevailing spot rate of $1.52 per pound. Calculate the effective yield.

9. **T-bill Yield**
a. Determine how the annualized yield of a T-bill would be affected if the purchase price is lower. Explain the logic of this relationship.
b. Determine how the annualized yield of a T-bill would be affected if the selling price is lower. Explain the logic of this relationship.
c. Determine how the annualized yield of a T-bill would be affected if the number of days is shorter, holding the purchase price and selling price constant. Explain the logic of this relationship.

10. **Return on NCDs** Phil purchased an NCD a year ago in the secondary market for $980,000. The NCD matures today at a price of $1 million, and Phil received $45,000 in interest. What is Phil's return on the NCD?

11. **Return on T-bills** Current T-bill yields are approximately 2 percent. Assume an investor considering the purchase of a newly issued three-month T-bill expects interest rates to increase within the next three months and has a required rate of return of 2.5 percent. Based on this information, how much is this investor willing to pay for a three-month T-bill?

Flow of Funds Exercise

Financing in the Money Markets

Recall that Carson Company has obtained substantial loans from finance companies and commercial banks. The interest rate on the loans is tied to market interest rates and is adjusted every six months. It has a credit line with a bank in case it suddenly needs to obtain funds for a temporary period. It previously purchased Treasury securities that it could sell if it experiences any liquidity problems.

If the economy continues to be strong, Carson may need to increase its production capacity by about 50 percent over the next few years to satisfy demand. It is concerned about a possible slowing of the economy because of potential Fed actions to reduce inflation. It needs funding to cover payments for supplies. It is also considering issuing stock or bonds to raise funds in the next year.

a. The prevailing commercial paper rate on paper issued by large publicly traded firms is lower than the rate Carson would pay when using a line of credit.

Do you think that Carson could issue commercial paper at this prevailing market rate?

b. Should Carson obtain funds to cover payments for supplies by selling its holdings of Treasury securities or by using its credit line? Which alternative has a lower cost? Explain.

Internet/Excel Exercises

1. Go to http://research.stlouisfed.org/fred2. Under "Categories," select "Interest rates." Compare the yield offered on a T-bill to the yield offered by another money market security with a similar maturity. What is the difference in yields? Why do you think the yields differ?

2. How has the risk premium on a specific risky money market security (versus the T-bill) changed since one year ago? Is the change due to a change in economic conditions? Explain.

3. Using the same website, retrieve interest rate data at the beginning of the last 20 quarters for the three-month T-bill and another money market security and place the data in two columns of an Excel spreadsheet. Derive the change in interest rates for both money market securities on a quarterly basis. Apply regression analysis in which the quarterly change in the interest rate of the risky money market security is the dependent variable and the quarterly change in the T-bill rate is the independent variable (see Appendix B for more information about using regression analysis). Is there a positive and significant relationship between the interest rate movements? Explain.

WSJ Exercise

Assessing Yield Differentials of Money Market Securities

Use the "Money Rates" section of *The Wall Street Journal* to determine the 30-day yield (annualized) of commercial paper, certificates of deposit, banker's acceptances, and T-bills. Which of these securities has the highest yield? Why? Which of these securities has the lowest yield? Why?

Chapter 7: Bond Markets

From this chapter through Chapter 12, the focus is on capital market securities. These chapters are distinctly different from the previous chapter on money market securities in that they focus on a long-term rather than a short-term perspective. This chapter and the following chapter focus on bond markets, which facilitate the flow of long-term debt from surplus units to deficit units.

The specific objectives of this chapter are to:

- provide a background on bonds,
- explain how bond markets are used by institutional investors, and
- explain how bond markets have become globally integrated.

Background on Bonds

Bonds are long-term debt securities that are issued by government agencies or corporations. The issuer of a bond is obligated to pay interest (or coupon) payments periodically (such as annually or semiannually) and the par value (principal) at maturity. An issuer must be able to show that its future cash flows will be sufficient to enable it to make its coupon and principal payments to bondholders. Investors will consider buying bonds for which the repayment is questionable only if the expected return from investing in the bonds is sufficient to compensate for the risk.

Bonds are often classified according to the type of issuer. Treasury bonds are issued by the Treasury, federal agency bonds are issued by federal agencies, municipal bonds are issued by state and local governments, and corporate bonds are issued by corporations.

Bonds are issued in the primary market through a telecommunications network. The means by which bond markets facilitate the flow of funds are illustrated in Exhibit 7.1. The U.S. Treasury issues bonds and uses the proceeds to support deficit spending on government programs. Federal agencies issue bonds and use the proceeds to buy mortgages that are originated by financial institutions. Thus, they indirectly finance purchases of homes. Corporations issue bonds and use the proceeds to expand their operations. Overall, by allowing households, corporations, and the U.S. government to increase their expenditures, bond markets finance economic growth.

The primary investors in bond markets are institutional investors such as commercial banks, bond mutual funds, pension funds, and insurance companies. Since most bonds have a secondary market, investors can sell the bonds prior to maturity.

Most bonds have maturities of between 10 and 30 years. Bonds are classified by the ownership structure as either bearer bonds or registered bonds. **Bearer bonds** require the owner to clip coupons attached to the bonds and send them to the issuer to receive coupon payments. **Registered bonds** require the issuer to maintain records of who owns the bond and automatically send coupon payments to the owners.

Exhibit 7.1 How Bond Markets Facilitate the Flow of Funds

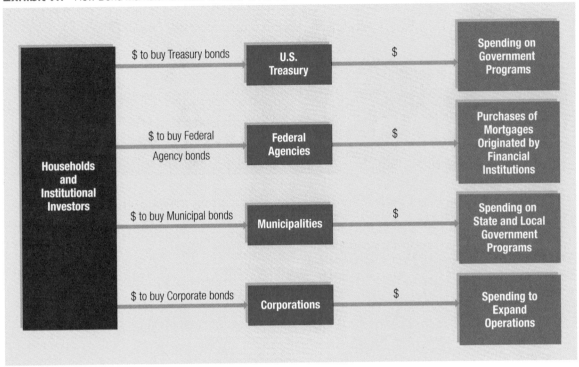

Bond Yields

The yield on a bond may depend on whether it is viewed from the perspective of the issuer of the bond who is obligated to make payments on the bond until maturity or from the perspective of the investors who purchase the bond.

Yield from the Issuer's Perspective The issuer's cost of financing with bonds is commonly measured by the so-called **yield to maturity,** which reflects the annualized yield that is paid by the issuer over the life of the bond. The yield to maturity is the annualized discount rate that equates the future coupon and principal payments to the initial proceeds received from the bond offering. It is based on the assumption that coupon payments received can be reinvested at the same yield.

ILLUSTRATION Consider an investor who can purchase bonds with 10 years until maturity, a par value of $1,000, and an 8 percent annualized coupon rate for $936. The yield to maturity on this bond can be determined by using a financial calculator as follows:

Input	10	936	80	1000		
Function Key	N	PV	PMT	FV	CPT	I
Answer						9%

Notice that the yield paid to investors is composed of two components: (1) a set of coupon payments and (2) the difference between the par value that the issuer must pay to investors at maturity versus the price it received when selling the bonds. In this example and in most cases, the biggest component of the yield to maturity is the set of coupon payments. The yield to maturity does not include the transaction costs associated with issuing the bonds. When those transaction costs are considered, the issuer's actual cost of borrowing is higher than the yield to maturity. ∎

http://money.cnn.com/markets/bondcenter Yields and information on all types of bonds for various maturities.

Yield from the Investor's Perspective An investor who invests in a bond when it is issued and holds it until maturity will earn the yield to maturity. Many investors, however, do not hold a bond to maturity and therefore focus on their holding period return, or the return from their investment over a particular holding period. If they hold the bond for a very short time period (such as less than one year), they may estimate their holding period return as the sum of the coupon payments plus the difference between the selling price and the purchase price of the bond, as a percentage of the purchase price. For relatively long holding periods, a better approximation of the holding period yield is the annualized discount rate that equates the payments received to the initial investment. Since the selling price to be received by investors is uncertain if they do not hold the bond to maturity, their holding period yield is uncertain at the time they purchase the bond. Consequently, an investment in bonds is subject to the risk that the holding period return will be less than expected. The valuation and return of bonds from the investor's perspective are discussed more thoroughly in the following chapter.

Treasury and Federal Agency Bonds

The U.S. Treasury commonly issues Treasury notes or Treasury bonds to finance federal government expenditures. The minimum denomination for Treasury notes or bonds is $1,000. The key difference between a note and a bond is that note maturities are usually less than 10 years, whereas bond maturities are 10 years or more. An active over-the-counter secondary market allows investors to sell Treasury notes or bonds prior to maturity.

The yield from holding a Treasury bond, as with other bonds, depends on the coupon rate and on the difference between the purchase price and the selling price. Investors in Treasury notes and bonds receive semiannual interest payments from the Treasury. Although the interest is taxed by the federal government as ordinary income, it is exempt from state and local taxes, if any exist. Domestic and foreign firms and individuals are common investors in Treasury notes and bonds.

http://www.treas.gov Details about Treasury bonds.

Since October 2001, the Treasury has relied on 10-year Treasury bonds to finance the U.S. budget deficit instead of also issuing 30-year Treasury bonds, as it had done previously. Consequently, the Treasury's influence on yields offered on other types of bonds with maturities of 30 years has been reduced.

Treasury Bond Auction

The Treasury obtains long-term funding through Treasury bond offerings, which are conducted through periodic auctions. Treasury bond auctions are normally held in the middle of each quarter. The Treasury announces its plans for an auction, including the date, the amount of funding that it needs, and the maturity of the bonds to be issued. At the time of the auction, financial institutions submit bids for their own accounts or for their clients.

Bids can be submitted on a competitive or a noncompetitive basis. Competitive bids specify a price that the bidder is willing to pay and a dollar amount of securities to be purchased. Noncompetitive bids specify only a dollar amount of securities to be purchased (subject to a maximum limit). The Treasury ranks the competitive bids in descending order according to the price bid per $100 of par value. All competitive bids are accepted until the point at which the desired amount of funding is achieved. Since November 1998, the Treasury has used the lowest accepted bid price as the price applied to all accepted competitive bids and all noncompetitive bids. Competitive bids are commonly used because many bidders want to purchase more Treasury bonds than the maximum that can be purchased on a noncompetitive basis.

BEHAVIORAL FINANCE During each Treasury bond offering, bond dealers purchase Treasury bonds and then redistribute them to clients (other financial institutions) that wish to purchase them. During a 1990 Treasury bond auction, Salomon Brothers (now part of Smith Barney, a division of Citigroup) purchased 65 percent of the bonds issued, exceeding the 35 percent maximum allowed for any single bond dealer. Some other bond dealers had made commitments to sell Treasury bonds to their clients (financial institutions), but were unable to obtain a sufficient amount because Salomon Brothers had dominated the auction. The other dealers had to obtain the Treasury bonds from Salomon in order to fulfill their commitments. Because Salomon controlled most of the auction, it was able to charge high prices for the bonds desired by the other dealers.

The episode aroused concern that investors might lose faith in the auction process and be discouraged from obtaining Treasury bonds. If the market came to perceive that bond prices were being manipulated, the demand for Treasury bonds would decline, raising the yields that the Treasury would have to offer to sell the bonds and ultimately increasing the cost to taxpayers.

In the summer of 1991, the Securities and Exchange Commission (SEC) and the Justice Department reviewed Salomon Brothers' involvement in the Treasury auction process. On August 18, 1991, the Treasury Department temporarily barred Salomon Brothers from bidding on Treasury securities for clients. In May 1992, Salomon paid fines of $190 million to the SEC and Justice Department. It also created a reserve fund of $100 million to cover claims from civil lawsuits. ■

Trading Treasury Bonds

Bond dealers serve as intermediaries in the secondary market by matching up buyers and sellers of Treasury bonds, and they also take positions in these bonds. About 2,000 brokers and dealers are registered to trade Treasury securities, but about 22 so-called primary dealers dominate the trading. These dealers make the secondary market for the Treasury bonds. They quote a bid price for customers who want to sell existing Treasury bonds to the dealers and an ask price for customers who want to buy existing Treasury bonds from them. The dealers profit from the spread between the bid and ask prices. Because of the large volume of secondary market transactions and intense competition among bond dealers, the spread is very narrow. When the Federal Reserve engages in open market operations, it normally conducts trading with the primary dealers of government securities. The primary dealers also trade Treasury bonds among themselves.

Treasury bonds are registered at the New York Stock Exchange, but the secondary market trading occurs over-the-counter (through a telecommunications network). The typical daily transaction volume in government securities (including money market securities) for the primary dealers is about $550 billion. Most of this trading volume occurs in the United States, but Treasury bonds are traded worldwide. They are traded in Tokyo from 7:30 P.M. to 3:00 A.M. New York time. The Tokyo and London markets overlap for part of the time, and the London market remains open until 7:30 A.M., when trading begins in New York.

Investors can contact their broker to buy or sell Treasury bonds. The brokerage firms serve as an intermediary between the investors and the bond dealers. Discount brokers usually charge a fee between $40 and $70 for Treasury bond transactions valued at $10,000. Institutional investors tend to contact the bond dealers directly.

Online Trading Investors can also buy bonds through the TreasuryDirect program (http://www.treasurydirect.gov). They can have the Treasury deduct their purchase from their bank account. They can also reinvest proceeds received when Treasury bonds mature into newly issued Treasury bonds.

Treasury Bond Quotations

Quotations for Treasury bond prices are published in financial newspapers such as *The Wall Street Journal, Barron's,* and *Investor's Business Daily.* They are also provided in *USA Today* and local newspapers. A typical format for Treasury bond quotations is shown in Exhibit 7.2. Each row represents a specific bond. The coupon rate, shown in the first column, will vary substantially among bonds because bonds issued when interest rates were high will have higher coupon rates than those issued when interest rates were low.

The Treasury bonds are organized in the table according to their maturity (shown in the second column), with those closest to maturity listed first. This allows investors to easily find Treasury bonds that have a specific maturity. If the bond contains a call feature allowing the issuer to repurchase the bonds prior to maturity, it is specified beside the maturity date in the second column. For example, the second and third bonds in Exhibit 7.2 mature in the year 2018 but can be called from the year 2013 on.

The bid price (what a bond dealer is willing to pay) and the ask price (what a bond dealer is willing to sell the bond for) are quoted per hundreds of dollars of par value, with fractions (to the right of the colon) expressed as thirty-seconds of a dollar. For example, the top listed bond has a face value of $100,000, so its ask price will be $120,719. This bond has a much higher price than the other two bonds shown, primarily because it offers a higher coupon rate. However, its yield to maturity is similar to the other yields (see the last column in Exhibit 7.2). From an investor's point of view, the coupon rate advantage over the other two bonds is essentially offset by the high price to be paid for that bond.

Online Quotations Treasury bond prices are accessible online at http://www .investinginbonds.com. This website provides the spread between the bid and the ask (offer) prices for various maturities. Treasury bond yields are accessible online at http:// www.federalreserve.gov/releases/H15/. The yields are updated on a daily basis and are disclosed for several different maturities.

Stripped Treasury Bonds

The cash flows of bonds are commonly transformed (stripped) by securities firms so that one security represents the principal payment only while a second security represents the interest payments. For example, consider a 10-year Treasury bond with a par value of $100,000 that has a 12 percent coupon rate and semiannual coupon payments. This bond could be stripped into a principal-only (PO) security that will provide $100,000 upon maturity and an interest-only (IO) security that will provide 20 semiannual payments of $6,000 each.

Exhibit 7.2
Example of Bond Price Quotations

Rate	Maturity Date	Bid	Ask	Yield
10.75	Aug. 2011	120:17	120:23	8.37%
8.38	Aug. 2013–18	100:09	100:15	8.32%
8.75	Nov. 2013–18	103:05	103:11	8.34%

Investors who desire a lump-sum payment in the distant future can choose the PO part, and investors desiring periodic cash inflows can select the IO part. Because the cash flows of the underlying securities are different, so are the degrees of interest rate sensitivity. The 10-year Treasury bond could even be stripped to create a PO security and 20 different IO securities, with each IO security representing one of the semiannual coupon payments.

A market for Treasury strips was originally created by securities firms in the early 1980s. Merrill Lynch created the Treasury Investment Growth Receipts (TIGRs) by purchasing Treasury securities and then stripping them to create PO and IO securities. Other firms also began to create their own versions of these **stripped securities.** In 1985, the Treasury created the STRIPS program, which exchanges stripped securities for underlying Treasury securities. STRIPS are not issued by the Treasury, but are created and sold by various financial institutions. They can be created for any Treasury security. Since they are components of Treasury securities, they are backed by the U.S. government. They do not have to be held until maturity, as there is an active secondary market. STRIPS have become very popular. More than $11 billion of securites are being stripped every month.

Inflation-Indexed Treasury Bonds

In 1996, the Treasury announced that it would periodically issue inflation-indexed bonds that provide returns tied to the inflation rate. These bonds, commonly referred to as TIPS (Treasury inflation-protected securities), are intended for investors who wish to ensure that the returns on their investments keep up with the increase in prices over time. The coupon rate offered on TIPS is lower than the rate on typical Treasury bonds, but the principal value is increased by the amount of the U.S. inflation rate (as measured by the percentage increase in the consumer price index) every six months.

ILLUSTRATION Consider a 10-year inflation-indexed bond that has a par value of $10,000 and a coupon rate of 4 percent. Assume that during the first six months since the bond was issued, the inflation rate (as measured by the consumer price index) was 1 percent. The principal of the bond is increased by $100 (1% × $10,000). Thus, the coupon payment after six months will be 2 percent (half of the yearly coupon rate) of the new par value, or 2% × $10,100 = $202. Assume that the inflation rate over the next six months is 3 percent. The principal of the bond is increased by $303 (3% × $10,100), which results in a new par value of $10,403. The coupon payment at the end of the year is based on the coupon rate and the new par value, or 2% × $10,403 = $208.06. This process is applied every six months over the life of the bond. If prices double over the 10-year period in which the bond exists, the par value of the bond will also double and thus will be equal to $20,000 at maturity. ■

Inflation-indexed government bonds have become very popular in some other countries where inflation tends to be high, including Australia, Turkey, Brazil, and the United Kingdom. They are also becoming popular in the United States.

Savings Bonds

Savings bonds are issued by the Treasury, but can be purchased from many financial institutions. They are attractive to small investors because they can be purchased with as little as $25. Larger denominations are available as well. The Series EE savings bond provides a market-based rate of interest, while the I savings bond provides a rate of interest that is tied to inflation. The interest accumulates monthly and adds value to the amount received at the time of redemption.

Savings bonds have a 30-year maturity and do not have a secondary market. The Treasury does allow savings bonds issued after February 2003 to be redeemed anytime after a 12-month period, but there is a penalty equal to the last three months of interest.

The interest income on savings bonds is not subject to state and local taxes, but is subject to federal taxes. For federal tax purposes, investors holding savings bonds can report the accumulated interest on an annual basis or only at the time they redeem the bonds or at maturity.

Federal Agency Bonds

Federal agency bonds are issued by federal agencies. The **Government National Mortgage Association (Ginnie Mae)** issues bonds and uses the proceeds to purchase mortgages that are insured by the Federal Housing Administration (FHA) and by the Veterans Administration (VA). The bonds are backed both by the mortgages that are purchased with the proceeds and by the federal government.

The Federal Home Loan Mortgage Association (called Freddie Mac) issues bonds and uses the proceeds to purchase conventional mortgages. These bonds are not backed by the federal government, but have a very low degree of credit risk.

The **Federal National Mortgage Association (Fannie Mae)** is a federally chartered corporation owned by individual investors. It issues bonds and uses the proceeds to purchase residential mortgages. These bonds are not backed by the federal government, but have a very low degree of credit risk.

Municipal Bonds

Like the federal government, state and local governments frequently spend more than the revenues they receive. To finance the difference, they issue **municipal bonds,** most of which can be classified as either **general obligation bonds** or **revenue bonds.** Payments on general obligation bonds are supported by the municipal government's ability to tax, whereas payments on revenue bonds must be generated by revenues of the project (tollway, toll bridge, state college dormitory, etc.) for which the bonds were issued. Revenue bonds have generally dominated since 1975. The total amount of bond financing by state and local governments has generally increased over time.

Credit Risk

Both types of municipal bonds are subject to some degree of credit (default) risk. If a municipality is unable to increase taxes, it could default on general obligation bonds. If it issues revenue bonds and does not generate sufficient revenue, it could default on these bonds.

Nevertheless, in general the risk of default on municipal bonds is low. Less than .5 percent of all municipal bonds issued since 1940 have defaulted. Because there is some concern about the risk of default, investors commonly monitor the ratings of municipal bonds. Moody's, Standard & Poor's, and Fitch Investor Service assign ratings to municipal bonds based on the ability of the issuer to repay the debt. The ratings are important to the issuer because a better rating will cause investors to require a smaller risk premium, and the municipal bonds can be issued at a higher price (lower yield).

Some municipal bonds are insured to protect against default. The issuer pays for this protection, so that it can issue the bond at a higher price, which translates into a higher price paid by the investor. Thus, investors indirectly bear the cost of the insurance.

Characteristics of Municipal Bonds

Revenue bonds and general obligation bonds typically promise semiannual interest payments. Common purchasers of these bonds include financial and nonfinancial institutions as well as individuals. The minimum denomination of municipal bonds is typically $5,000. A secondary market exists for them, although it is less active than the one for Treasury bonds.

Most municipal bonds contain a call provision, which allows the issuer to repurchase the bonds at a specified price before the bonds mature. A municipality may exercise its option to repurchase the bonds if interest rates decline substantially because it can reissue bonds at the lower interest rate and reduce its cost of financing.

Variable-Rate Municipal Bonds Variable-rate municipal bonds have a floating interest rate based on a benchmark interest rate. The coupon payment adjusts to movements in the benchmark interest rate. Some variable-rate municipal bonds are convertible to a fixed rate until maturity under specified conditions. In general, variable-rate municipal bonds are desirable to investors who expect that interest rates will rise. However, there is the risk that interest rates may decline over time, which would cause the coupon payments to decline as well.

Tax Advantages One of the most attractive features of municipal bonds is that the interest income is normally exempt from federal taxes. Second, the interest income earned on bonds that are issued by a municipality within a particular state is normally exempt from state income taxes (if any). Thus, investors who reside in states that impose income taxes can reduce their taxes further.

Trading and Quotations

Today, there are more than 1 million different bonds outstanding, and more than 50,000 different issuers of municipal bonds. There are hundreds of bond dealers that can accommodate investor requests to buy or sell municipal bonds in the secondary market, but only five dealers account for more than half of all the trading volume. Bond dealers can also take positions in municipal bonds.

Investors who expect that they will not hold a municipal bond until maturity should ensure that the bonds they consider have active secondary market trading. Many of the municipal bonds have an inactive secondary market. Therefore, it is difficult to know the prevailing market values of these bonds. Although investors do not pay a direct commission on trades, they incur transaction costs in the form of a bid-ask spread on the bonds. This spread can be large, especially for the municipal bonds that are rarely traded in the secondary market.

The electronic trading of municipal bonds is becoming very popular, in part because it enables investors to circumvent the more expensive route of calling brokers. A popular electronic bond website is http://www.eBondTrade.com. Such websites provide access to information on municipal bonds and allow online buying and selling of municipal bonds.

Yields Offered on Municipal Bonds

The yield offered by a municipal bond differs from the yield on a Treasury bond with the same maturity for three reasons. First, the municipal bond must pay a risk premium to compensate for the possibility of default risk. Second, the municipal bond must pay a slight premium to compensate for being less liquid than Treasury bonds with the same maturity. Third, as explained earlier, the income earned from a municipal bond is exempt from federal taxes. This tax advantage of municipal bonds more than offsets their two disadvantages and allows municipal bonds to offer a lower yield than Treasury bonds. The yield offered on municipal bonds over time is displayed in Exhibit 7.3.

Yield Curve on Municipal Bonds At any given time, there are municipal bonds in the secondary market that have only a short time to maturity and others that have longer terms to maturity. A municipal bond yield curve can be constructed

Exhibit 7.3   Yield Offered on General Obligation Municipal Bonds over Time

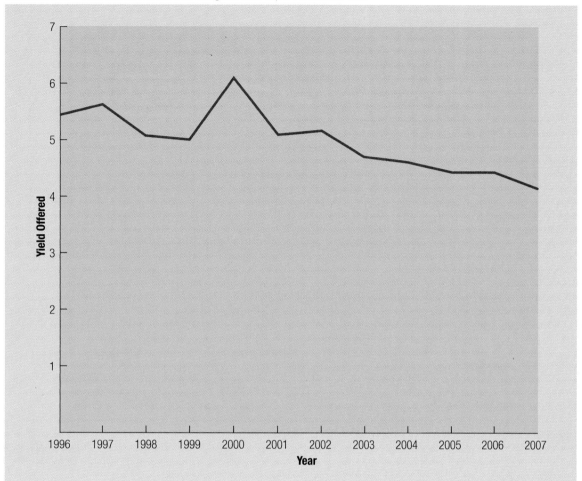

from the municipal bonds that are available. An example of a municipal bond yield curve is shown in Exhibit 7.4, which also includes a Treasury yield curve for comparison. Notice that the municipal security yield curve is lower than the Treasury yield curve, which is primarily attributed to the tax differential between the two types of securities. The gap due to the tax differential is offset slightly by the default risk and liquidity differential. The yield on municipal securities is commonly 20 to 30 percent less than the yield offered on Treasury securities with similar maturities.

The shape of a municipal security yield curve tends to be similar to the shape of a Treasury security yield curve for two reasons. First, like the Treasury yield curve, the municipal yield curve is influenced by interest rate expectations. If investors expect interest rates to rise, they tend to favor shorter-term securities, which results in high short-term security prices and low short-term yields in both the municipal and Treasury markets. Second, investors require a premium for longer-term securities with lower liquidity in both the municipal and Treasury markets. If supply conditions differ, the shapes could differ.

ILLUSTRATION   At a particular point in time, assume that the economy is strong and municipalities experience budget surpluses. Many of them will not have to issue new bonds, so those municipalities that do need long-term funds can

Exhibit 7.4
Annualized Yield
Offered on Securities

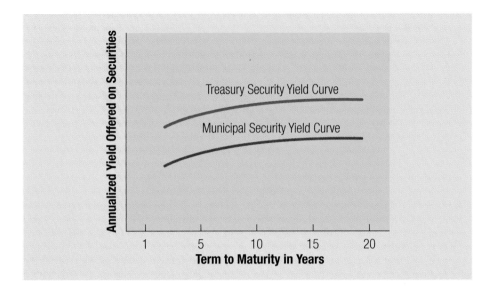

more easily find buyers. Meanwhile, the Treasury may still issue new long-term securities to finance the existing federal deficit. In this case, the gap between the Treasury and municipal yields may be larger for new long-term securities than for the securities that were issued in the past and now have a shorter term to maturity. ∎

Corporate Bonds

Corporate bonds are long-term debt securities issued by corporations. They promise the owner coupon payments (interest) on a semiannual basis. The minimum denomination is $1,000. Their maturity is typically between 10 and 30 years, although Boeing, ChevronTexaco, and other corporations have issued 50-year bonds, and Disney, BellSouth, and the Coca-Cola Company issued 100-year bonds. The interest paid by the corporation to investors is tax-deductible to the corporation, which reduces the cost of financing with bonds. Since equity financing does not involve interest payments, it does not offer the same tax advantage. This is a major reason why many corporations rely heavily on bonds to finance their operations. Nevertheless, there is a limit to the amount of funds a corporation can obtain by issuing bonds, because it must be capable of making the coupon payments.

Corporate Bond Offerings

Corporate bonds can be placed with investors through a public offering or a private placement.

Public Offering Corporations commonly issue bonds through a public offering. A corporation that plans to issue bonds hires an investment bank to underwrite the bonds. The underwriter assesses market conditions and attempts to determine the price at which the corporation's bonds can be sold and the appropriate size (dollar amount) of the offering. The goal is to price the bonds high enough to satisfy the issuer, but also low enough so that the entire bond offering can be placed. If the offering is too large or the price is too high, there may not be enough investors who are willing to purchase the bonds. In this case, the underwriter will have to lower the price in order to sell all the bonds. The issuer registers with the SEC and submits a prospectus that explains the planned size of the offering, its updated financial condition (supported by financial statements), and its planned use of funds. Meanwhile, the underwriter distributes the prospectus to other investment banks that it invites to join a syndicate to help place the bonds in the market. Once the SEC approves the issue, the underwriting syndicate attempts to place the bonds. A portion of the bonds that are registered can be shelved for up to two years if the issuer wants to defer placing the entire offering at once.

Underwriters typically try to place newly issued corporate bonds with institutional investors, such as pension funds, bond mutual funds, and insurance companies, because these investors are more likely to purchase large pieces of the offering. Many of these institutional investors may plan to hold the bonds for a long-term period, but if they decide to sell the bonds, they can sell them to other investors.

Private Placement Some corporate bonds are privately placed rather than sold in a public offering. A private placement does not have to be registered with the SEC. Small firms that borrow relatively small amounts of funds (such as $30 million) may consider private placements rather than public offerings, since they may be able to find an institutional investor that will purchase the entire offering. Although the issuer does not need to register with the SEC, it still needs to disclose financial data to convince any prospective purchasers that the bonds will be repaid in a timely manner. The issuer may hire a securities firm to place the bonds because such firms are normally better able to identify institutional investors that may be interested in purchasing privately placed debt.

The institutional investors that commonly purchase a private placement include insurance companies, pension funds, and bond mutual funds. Since privately placed bonds do not have an active secondary market, they are more desirable to institutional investors that are willing to invest for long periods of time. The SEC's Rule 144A creates liquidity for privately placed securities by allowing large institutional investors to trade privately placed bonds (and some other securities) with each other even though the securities are not required to be registered with the SEC.

Characteristics of Corporate Bonds

Corporate bonds can be described according to a variety of characteristics. The bond **indenture** is a legal document specifying the rights and obligations of both the issuing firm and the bondholders. It is very comprehensive (normally several hundred pages) and is designed to address all matters related to the bond issue (collateral, payment dates, default provisions, call provisions, etc.).

Federal law requires that for each bond issue of significant size a **trustee** be appointed to represent the bondholders in all matters concerning the bond issue. The trustee's duties include monitoring the issuing firm's activities to ensure compliance with the terms of the indenture. If the terms are violated, the trustee initiates legal action against the issuing firm and represents the bondholders in that action. Bank trust departments are frequently hired to perform the duties of trustee.

Bonds are not as standardized as stocks. A single corporation may issue more than 50 different bonds with different maturities and payment terms. Some of the characteristics that differentiate one bond from another are identified here.

Sinking-Fund Provision Bond indentures frequently include a **sinking-fund provision,** or a requirement that the firm retire a certain amount of the bond issue each year. This provision is considered to be an advantage to the remaining bondholders because it reduces the payments necessary at maturity.

Specific sinking-fund provisions can vary significantly among bond issues. For example, a bond with 20 years until maturity could have a provision to retire 5 percent of the bond issue each year. Or it could have a requirement to retire 5 percent each year beginning in the fifth year, with the remaining amount to be retired at maturity. The actual mechanics of bond retirement are carried out by the trustee.

Protective Covenants Bond indentures normally place restrictions on the issuing firm that are designed to protect the bondholders from being exposed to increasing risk during the investment period. These so-called protective covenants frequently limit the amount of dividends and corporate officers' salaries the firm can pay and also restrict the amount of additional debt the firm can issue. Other financial policies may be restricted as well.

Protective covenants are needed because shareholders and bondholders have different expectations of a firm's management. Shareholders may prefer that managers use a relatively large amount of debt because they can benefit directly from risky managerial decisions that will generate higher returns on investment. In contrast, bondholders simply hope to receive their principal back, with interest. Since they do not share in the excess returns generated by a firm, they would prefer that managerial decisions be conservative. Protective covenants can prevent managers from taking excessive risk and therefore satisfy the preferences of bondholders. If managers are unwilling to accept some protective covenants, they may not be able to obtain debt financing.

Call Provisions Most bonds include a provision allowing the firm to call the bonds. A **call provision** normally requires the firm to pay a price above par value when it calls its bonds. The difference between the bond's call price and par value is the **call premium.** Call provisions have two principal uses. First, if market interest rates decline after a bond issue has been sold, the firm might end up paying a higher rate of interest than the prevailing rate for a long period of time. Under these circumstances, the firm may consider selling a new issue of bonds with a lower interest rate and using the proceeds to retire the previous issue by calling the old bonds.

ILLUSTRATION Four years ago, Mirossa Company issued 10-year bonds that offered a yield of 11 percent. Since then, interest rates have declined, and Mirossa's credit rating has improved. It could issue 10-year bonds today for a yield of 7 percent. The company is sure that it will need funding for the next 10 years. It issues new 10-year bonds at a yield of 7 percent and uses some of the proceeds to call (buy back) the bonds issued four years ago. It reduces its cost of financing as a result of calling these bonds. Ten years from today, Mirossa Company will repay the principal on the newly issued bonds. ∎

Second, a call provision may be used to retire bonds as required by a sinking-fund provision. Many bonds have two different call prices: a lower price for calling the bonds to meet sinking-fund requirements and a higher price if the bonds are called for any other reason.

Bondholders normally view a call provision as a disadvantage because it can disrupt their investment plans and reduce their investment returns. As a result, firms must pay slightly higher rates of interest on bonds that are callable, other things being equal.

Bond Collateral Bonds can be classified according to whether they are secured by collateral and by the nature of that collateral. Usually, the collateral is a mortgage on real property (land and buildings). A **first mortgage bond** has first claim on the specified assets. A **chattel mortgage bond** is secured by personal property.

Bonds unsecured by specific property are called **debentures** (backed only by the general credit of the issuing firm). These bonds are normally issued by large, financially sound firms whose ability to service the debt is not in question. **Subordi-**

nated **debentures** have claims against the firm's assets that are junior to the claims of both mortgage bonds and regular debentures. Owners of subordinated debentures receive nothing until the claims of mortgage bondholders, regular debenture owners, and secured short-term creditors have been satisfied. The main purchasers of subordinated debt are pension funds and insurance companies.

Low- and Zero-Coupon Bonds   In the early 1980s, firms began issuing bonds with coupons roughly half the size of the prevailing rate and later issued bonds with zero coupons. These **low-coupon** or **zero-coupon bonds** are therefore issued at a deep discount from par value. Investors are taxed annually on the amount of interest earned, even though much or all of the interest will not be received until maturity. The amount of interest taxed is the amortized discount. (The gain at maturity is prorated over the life of the bond.) Low- and zero-coupon corporate bonds are purchased mainly for tax-exempt investment accounts (pension funds, individual retirement accounts, etc.).

To the issuing firm, these bonds have the advantage of requiring low or no cash outflow during their life. Additionally, the firm is permitted to deduct the amortized discount as interest expense for federal income tax purposes, even though it does not pay interest. This adds to the firm's cash flow. Finally, the demand for low- and zero-coupon bonds has been great enough that firms can, in most cases, issue them at a lower cost than regular bonds.

Variable-Rate Bonds   The highly volatile interest rates experienced during the 1970s inspired the development of **variable-rate bonds** (also called floating-rate bonds), which affect the investor and borrower as follows: (1) they allow investors to benefit from rising market interest rates over time, and (2) they allow issuers of bonds to benefit from declining rates over time.

Most issues tie their coupon rate to the London Interbank Offer Rate (LIBOR), the rate at which banks lend funds to each other on an international basis. The rate is typically adjusted every three months.

Variable-rate bonds became very popular in 2004, when interest rates were at low levels. Since most investors presumed that interest rates were likely to rise, they were more willing to purchase variable-rate than fixed-rate bonds. In fact, the volume of variable-rate bonds exceeded that of fixed-rate bonds during this time.

Convertibility   Another type of bond, known as a **convertible bond,** allows investors to exchange the bond for a stated number of shares of the firm's common stock. This conversion feature offers investors the potential for high returns if the price of the firm's common stock rises. Investors are therefore willing to accept a lower rate of interest on these bonds, which allows the firm to obtain financing at a lower cost.

Corporate Bond Yields and Risk

Institutional and individual investors who want an investment that provides stable income may consider purchasing corporate bonds. The interest income earned on corporate bonds represents ordinary income to the bondholders and is therefore subject to federal and state (if any) taxes. Thus, corporate bonds do not provide the same tax benefits to bondholders as municipal bonds.

Yield Curve   At a given point in time, the yield curve for corporate bonds will be affected by interest rate expectations, a liquidity premium, and the specific maturity preferences of corporations issuing bonds. Since these are the same factors that affect the yield curve of Treasury bonds, the shape of the yield curve for corporate bonds

Exhibit 7.5
Default Rate on
Corporate Bonds over
Time

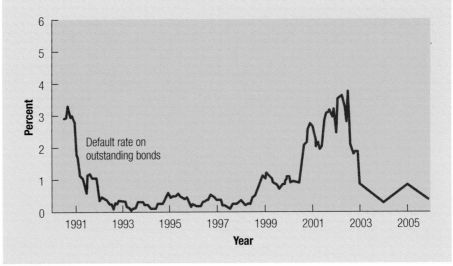

Source: Federal Reserve.

will also normally be similar to the yield curve for Treasury bonds, except that the curve will be higher to reflect credit risk and less liquidity.

Default Rate The general level of defaults on corporate bonds is dependent on economic conditions. When the economy is strong, firms generate higher revenue and are better able to cover their debt payments. When the economy is weak, some firms may not generate sufficient revenue to cover their operating and debt expenses and therefore default on their bonds. Exhibit 7.5 shows the default rate on corporate bonds over time. Notice that the default rate was less than 1 percent in the late 1990s when U.S. economic conditions were strong, but it exceeded 3 percent in 2002 when economic conditions were weak.

Investor Assessment of Risk Since credit risk is associated with corporate bonds, investors may consider purchasing corporate bonds only after assessing the issuing financial condition and ability to cover its debt payments. Thus, investors may rely heavily on financial statements created by the issuing firm. This presents an asymmetric information problem in that the firm knows its true condition, but investors do not. Thus, it can be a challenge for investors to properly assess a firm's ability to cover its debt payments.

ILLUSTRATION Last year, Spectral Insurance Company considered purchasing bonds that were recently issued by Ladron Company. Spectral assessed Ladron's financial statements to determine whether it would have sufficient cash flows in the future to cover its debt payments. In reviewing the revenue and expenses that Ladron reported for the last year, Spectral noticed that Ladron had a large expense categorized as "nonrecurring," which indicates a onetime expense that should not occur again. Spectral ignored those expenses because it wanted to focus only on the typical operating expenses that will occur every year. After estimating Ladron's future cash flows in this manner, Spectral decided that Ladron would be capable of covering its debt payments and purchased bonds issued by Ladron for $20 million.

Last week, Ladron announced that it must file for bankruptcy because it incurred another huge nonrecurring expense this year. Spectral's mistake was that it fully trusted the financial statements reported by Ladron. Like many companies, Ladron classified some operating expenses as "nonrecurring expenses" so that it could reduce its reported operating expenses and increase its reported operating earnings. This is misleading, but may be within accounting guidelines. Nevertheless, Spectral incurred major losses on its investments because of the asymmetric information problem. ■

Bond Ratings Corporate bonds are rated by rating agencies. Corporate bonds that receive higher ratings can be placed at higher prices (lower yields). Therefore, corporations can achieve a lower cost of financing when their bonds are rated highly. Corporations are especially interested in achieving an investment-grade status on their bonds (medium quality or above) because commercial banks will only invest in bonds that have investment-grade status. A corporate bond's rating may change over time if the issuer's ability to repay the debt changes.

Although bond rating agencies are skilled at assessing ability to repay debt, they are also subject to the asymmetric information problem. They commonly consider the financial statements provided by the issuer of bonds when making their assessment and will not necessarily detect any misleading information contained in the financial statements.

Secondary Market for Corporate Bonds

http://bonds.yahoo.com/ rates.html Yields on all types of bonds for various maturities.

Corporate bonds have a secondary market, so investors who purchase them can sell them to other investors if they prefer not to hold them until maturity. The value of all corporate bonds in the secondary market exceeds $5 trillion. Bonds issued by large well-known corporations in large volume are liquid because they attract a large number of buyers and sellers in the secondary market. Bonds issued by small corporations in small volume are less liquid because there may not be any buyers for those bonds in some periods. Thus, investors who wish to sell these bonds in the secondary market may have to accept a discounted price in order to attract buyers. About 95 percent of the trading volume of corporate bonds is attributed to institutional investors.

Often, a particular company issues many different bonds with variations in maturity, price, and credit rating. Having many different bonds allows investors to find a bond issued by a particular company that fits their desired maturity and other preferences. However, it also creates higher transaction costs because brokers require more time to execute transactions for investors. In addition, some bonds issued by a particular firm may have limited liquidity, because their features are less attractive to investors.

Corporate Bond Listing Corporate bonds are listed on an over-the-counter market or on an exchange. The over-the-counter bond market is served by bond dealers, who can play a broker role by matching up buyers and sellers. In addition, bond dealers have an inventory of bonds, so they may serve as the counter-party in a bond transaction desired by an investor. For example, if an investor wants to sell bonds that were previously issued by the Coca Cola company, bond dealers may execute the deal by matching the sellers with investors who want to buy the bonds, or by purchasing the bonds for their own inventories. Dealers commonly handle large transactions, such as those valued at more than $1 million. Information about the trades in the over-the-counter market is provided by the National Association of Securities Dealers' Trade Reporting and Compliance Engine, which is referred to as "TRACE." Some bonds also trade on the American Stock Exchange.

More than 1,000 bonds are listed on the New York Stock Exchange (NYSE). Corporations whose stocks are listed on the exchange can list their bonds for free. In 2007, the NYSE developed an electronic bond trading as part of its strategy to increase its presence in the corporate bond market. Electronic trading will allow more transparency. Investors will have access to real-time data and can more easily monitor the bid and ask prices and trading volume of corporate bonds. This market should appeal to investors who want to execute relatively small bond transactions (such as $10,000 or $20,000). The bonds listed on the NYSE are traded through its Automated Bond System (ABS), which is an electronic system used by investment firms that are members of the NYSE. The ABS displays prices and matches buy and sell orders.

Types of Orders Various bond dealers take positions in corporate bonds and accommodate orders. Individual investors buy or sell corporate bonds through brokers, who communicate the orders to bond dealers. Investors who wish to buy or sell bonds can normally place a **market order;** in this case, the desired transaction will occur at the prevailing market price. Alternatively, they can place a **limit order;** in this case, the transaction will occur only if the price reaches the specified limit. When purchasing bonds, investors use a limit order to specify the maximum limit price they are willing to pay for a bond. When selling bonds, investors use a limit order to specify a minimum limit price at which they are willing to sell their bonds.

Trading Online Orders to buy and sell corporate bonds are increasingly being placed online. One of the most popular online bond brokerage websites is http://www .tradebonds.com, which provides bond prices for a large sample of brokers. This site is targeted toward investors who buy in large quantities, but other popular online bond brokerage websites, such as http://www.schwab.com and http://www.etrade.com/global .html, are aimed toward small investors. The pricing of bonds is more transparent online because investors can easily compare the bid and ask spreads among brokers. This transparency has encouraged some brokers to narrow their spreads so that they do not lose business to competitors.

Some online bond brokerage services such as Fidelity and Vanguard now charge a commission instead of posting a bid and ask spread. This is a more transparent method of charging investors for their service than using bid and ask prices. In addition, there is a standard fee for every trade, whereas bid and ask spreads may vary among bonds. For example, the fee may be $2 per bond, with a $25 minimum. Thus, an investor who purchases 30 bonds, with a $1,000 par value, would pay a total fee of $60 (computed as 30 × $2). Online bond brokerage services can execute transactions in Treasury and municipal bonds as well. Their fees are generally lower for Treasury bond than corporate bond transactions, but higher for municipal bond transactions.

Corporate Bond Quotations

http://averages.dowjones .com Links to corporate bond indexes so that you can monitor the general performance of corporate bonds.

The financial press publishes quotations for corporate bonds, just as it does for Treasury bonds, although in a slightly different format (look back at Exhibit 7.2 to review the format for Treasury bonds). Corporate bond quotations also typically include the volume of trading, which is normally measured as the number of bonds traded for that day. As in Treasury bond quotations, the yield to maturity is included. A review of bond quotations on any given day will reveal significant differences among the yields of some bonds. These differences may be due to different risk levels, different provisions (such as call features), or different maturities.

Corporate bond price quotations are accessible online at http://www.investingin bonds.com. The quotations can be sorted by maturity, credit rating, coupon rate, or other characteristics.

Junk Bonds

Credit rating agencies assign quality ratings to corporate bonds based on their perceived degree of credit risk. Those bonds that are perceived to have high risk are referred to as **junk bonds.** Junk bonds became popular during the 1980s when firms

Bond Index Yield Quotations

The Wall Street Journal provides quotations on yields of various bond indexes, representing high-quality corporate bonds, high-yield corporate bonds, U.S. agency bonds, municipal bonds, and bonds issued by governments of non-U.S. countries. For some types of bonds, the table provides quotations for different maturity ranges. The yield offered on each type of bond is under the heading "Latest." This table also shows the range of yields offered by each type of bond during the last year.

In addition, the table provides the year-to-date (YTD) returns (from the beginning of the year) for investors who held each type of bond over this period. Using this table, market participants can compare the past performance of various types of bonds. They can also decide whether to purchase any particular type of bonds based on the prevailing yields offered on various types of bonds.

Source: Reprinted with permission of Dow Jones & Company, Inc., from *The Wall Street Journal*, April 6, 2007; permission conveyed through the Copyright Clearance Center, Inc.

Tracking Bond Benchmarks

Return on investment and spreads over Treasurys and/or yields paid to investors compared with 52-week highs and lows for different types of bonds

Total return close	YTD total return (%)	Index	Latest	Low	High
1210.94	1.5%	**Broad market** Lehman Aggregate	5.300	5.080	5.900
1523.95	1.4	**U.S. Corporate** Lehman Brothers	5.640	5.390	6.270
1543.22	1.6	Intermediate	5.430	5.210	6.110
1761.28	0.8	Long term	6.230	5.290	6.786
320.01	1.2	Double-A-rated	5.370	5.071	5.966
326.63	1.7	Tripe-B-rated	5.910	5.700	6.570
n.a.	n.a.	**High Yield Constrained** Merrill Lynch	n.a.	7.380	8.610
n.a.	n.a.	Triple-C-rated	n.a.	9.248	11.330
n.a.	n.a.	High Yield 100	n.a.	6.866	8.250
n.a.	n.a.	Global High Yield Constrained	n.a.	7.239	8.380
n.a.	n.a.	Europe High Yield Constrained	n.a.	6.036	7.040
1134.07	1.4	**U.S Agency** Lehman	5.070	4.825	5.663
1048.00	1.4	10-20 years	5.040	4.805	5.646
1672.08	0.8	20-plus years	5.370	5.021	5.862
1258.68	1.6	**Mortgage-Backed** Lehman	5.570	5.400	6.230
1237.45	1.5	Ginnie Mae (GNMA)	5.630	5.433	6.204
722.83	1.6	Fannie mae (FNMA)	5.580	5.385	6.218
1131.71	1.6	Freddie Mae (FHLMC)	5.610	5.406	6.245
n.a.	n.a.	**Muni Master** Merrill Lynch	n.a.	3.730	4.292
n.a.	n.a.	7-12 year	n.a.	3.669	4.285
n.a.	n.a.	12-22 year	n.a.	3.940	4.591
n.a.	n.a.	22-plus year	n.a.	4.119	4.849
1453.81	1.7	**Yankee** Lehman	5.370	5.200	6.070
363.16	0.4	**Global Government** J.P. Morgan	3.610	3.343	3.791
501.27	0.6	Canada	4.170	3.901	4.646
227.19	unch	EMU	4.250	3.780	4.250
426.86	−0.1%	France	4.190	3.705	4.190
320.22	unch	Germany	4.170	3.699	4.170
224.79	0.5	Japan	1.570	1.488	1.833
342.55	unch	Netherlands	4.180	3.694	4.180
485.02	−0.9	U.K.	4.710	4.208	4.710
n.a.	n.a.	Emerging Markets **	n.a.	6.391	7.565

YIELD (%), 52-WEEK RANGE ○ Latest — scale: 0 3 6 9 12 15

* Constrained indexes limit individual issuer concentrations to 2%; the High Yield 100 are the 100 largest bonds   In U.S. - dollar terms Euro-zone bonds

** EMBI Global Index   Sources: Dow Jones Indexes; Merrill Lynch; Lehman Brothers; J.P.Morgan

desired debt financing to finance acquisitions. These firms were attempting to expand without issuing new stock so that profits could ultimately be distributed to existing shareholders. Some of the firms planning to use debt financing were perceived to have high risk, especially given the high proportion of debt in their capital structure. About two-thirds of all junk bond issues are used to finance takeovers (including leveraged buyouts, or LBOs). Some junk bond issues are used by firms to revise their capital structure. The proceeds from issuing bonds are used to repurchase stock, thereby increasing the proportion of debt in the capital structure. Although the newly issued bonds are assigned a low-grade ("junk") quality rating, numerous financial institutions are willing to purchase them because of the relatively high yield offered.

Size of the Junk Bond Market There are currently more than 4,000 junk bond offerings in the United States, with a total market value of more than $600 billion. Junk bonds represent about 25 percent of the value of all corporate bonds and about 5 percent of the value of all bonds (including Treasury and municipal bonds). About one-third of all junk bonds were once rated higher but have been downgraded to below investment grade. The remaining two-thirds were considered to be below investment-grade quality when they were initially issued.

Participation in the Junk Bond Market There are numerous issuers of junk bonds with more than $1 billion in debt outstanding. The primary investors in junk bonds are mutual funds, life insurance companies, and pension funds. Some bond mutual funds only invest in bonds with high ratings, but there are more than 100 so-called high-yield mutual funds that commonly invest in junk bonds. Individuals account for about one-tenth of all investors in the junk bond market. Recently, some issuers of junk bonds have attempted to attract more individual investors by lowering the minimum denomination to $1,000. High-yield mutual funds allow individual investors to invest in a diversified portfolio of junk bonds with a small investment.

The secondary market for junk bonds in the United States is facilitated by about 20 bond traders (or market makers) that make a market for junk bonds. That is, they execute secondary market transactions for customers and also invest in junk bonds for their own account.

Risk Premium of Junk Bonds Junk bonds offer high yields that contain a risk premium (spread) to compensate investors for the high risk. Typically, the premium is between 3 percent and 7 percent above Treasury bonds with the same maturity. Exhibit 7.6 shows the premium offered by junk bonds over time. Notice that the premium offered by junk bonds changes over time. During periods of weak economies, such as 2002, the difference is larger. Although investors always require a higher yield on junk bonds than other bonds, they require a higher premium during weak economies when there is a greater likelihood that the issuer will not generate sufficient cash to cover the debt payments.

Performance of Junk Bonds Junk bonds are generally perceived to offer high returns with high risk. During the mid-1980s, junk bond defaults were relatively infrequent, which may have renewed public interest in them and encouraged corporations to issue more.

After the stock market crash of October 1987, the market became more concerned about the risk of junk bonds. Issuers had to lower the price to compensate for the higher perceived risk. The junk bond market received another blow in the late 1980s, when insider trading charges were filed against Drexel Burnham Lambert, Inc., the main dealer in the market, for violating various regulations.

Exhibit 7.6
Premium (Spread)
Offered on Junk Bonds

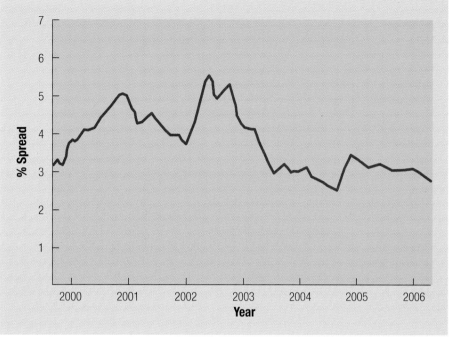

Source: Federal Reserve.

In the early 1990s, the popularity of junk bonds declined as a result of three key factors. First, there were allegations of insider trading against some participants in the junk bond market. Second, the financial problems of a few major issuers of junk bonds scared some investors away. Third, the financial problems in the thrift industry caused regulators to regulate investments by thrifts more closely. The Financial Institutions Reform, Recovery, and Enforcement Act (FIRREA) mandated that savings institutions liquidate their investments in junk bonds. Because savings institutions controlled about 7 percent of the junk bond market, there was additional downward pressure on prices. Although these institutions were given five years to liquidate their junk bonds to alleviate this pressure on prices, many thrifts liquidated their bonds within a few months after the FIRREA was enacted.

During the late-1990s, junk bonds performed very well, and there were few defaults. Consequently, junk bonds became popular once again. However, the defaults increased during the 2001–2002 period when economic conditions were weak. Yet, they were commonly used in the 2005–2007 period to finance leveraged buyouts.

BEHAVIORAL FINANCE   Investors may be systematically discouraged from investment in junk bonds by specific adverse information, which means that the junk bond market is susceptible to **contagion effects.** Many firms that issue junk bonds have excessive debt service payments and may possibly experience cash flow deficiencies if sales are less than anticipated. Thus, they are all susceptible to a single underlying event, such as an economic downturn. Furthermore, media reports about a single well-known firm that may be unable to service its junk bond payments can cause increased concern (whether justified or not) about other highly leveraged firms. Such concern can encourage investors to sell holdings of junk bonds or discourage other investors from purchasing junk bonds. ∎

How Corporate Bonds Facilitate Restructuring

http://

http://bonds.yahoo.com/
glossary1.html Provides a
glossary of common terms
used in the bond market.

Firms can issue corporate bonds to finance the restructuring of their assets and to revise their capital structure. Such restructuring can have a major impact on the firm's degree of financial leverage, the potential return to shareholders, the risk to shareholders, and the risk to bondholders.

Using Bonds to Finance a Leveraged Buyout A leveraged buyout (LBO) is typically financed with senior debt (such as debentures and collateralized loans) and subordinated debt. The senior debt accounts for 50 to 60 percent of LBO financing on average.

LBO activity increased dramatically in the late 1980s, when it was more than double the level in the early 1960s. In 1988, there were more than 100 LBOs in which a publicly held firm was taken private. The premium paid when repurchasing shares to execute an LBO typically ranged between 30 percent and 40 percent above the prevailing market price. This suggests that the investors conducting the LBO believed that the firm was substantially undervalued when it was publicly held. Their expectation was that by reducing the equity interest of the firm down to a small group of people (possibly management and other employees), managerial efficiency of the firm would increase. The costs of monitoring to ensure that management's decisions are in the best interests of the shareholders are negligible when management owns all of the stock.

Although LBOs may possibly enhance managerial efficiency, they raised concerns about corporate debt levels. During the 1980s, corporate debt of U.S. firms increased substantially. The impact of the recession in the early 1990s on corporate performance may have been more pronounced because of the high degree of financial leverage.

The best-known LBO was the $24.7 billion buyout of RJR Nabisco, Inc. by Kohlberg Kravis Roberts, Inc. (KKR) in 1988. KKR's equity investment was only about $1.4 billion, less than 6 percent of the purchase price. The debt financing was primarily composed of long-term bonds and bank loans. Before the acquisition, RJR's long-term debt was less than its shareholders' equity. After the acquisition, RJR's long-term debt was more than 12 times its shareholders' equity. Annual interest expenses were expected to be more than five times what they were before the acquisition. In 1988, RJR's cash flows totaled $1.8 billion, which was not expected to be sufficient to meet interest payments on the debt. Thus, the company needed additional cash flow to accommodate the substantial increase in financial leverage. As a result of the increase in financial leverage, prices of RJR bonds declined by 20 percent when the LBO was announced. After the LBO, RJR attempted to sell various businesses to improve its cash position.

It is of interest to note that RJR issued stock to reduce its degree of financial leverage in 1990 and again in 1991. Nabisco has since been sold by RJR. Many other firms with excessive financial leverage resulting from a previous LBO also reissued stock in the 1990s. They typically used some of the proceeds from the stock issuance to retire some outstanding debt, thereby reducing their periodic interest payments on debt. This process was more feasible for firms that could issue shares of stock for high prices because the proceeds would retire a larger amount of outstanding debt. In 2005, LBOs became popular again, and many of them relied on junk bond financing. Fifteen of the 20 largest LBOs occurred in the 2005–2007 period.

Using Bonds to Revise the Capital Structure Corporations commonly issue bonds in order to revise their capital structure. If they believe that they will have sufficient cash flows to cover their debt payments, they may consider using more debt and less equity, which implies a higher degree of financial leverage. Debt is normally perceived to be a cheaper source of capital than equity, as long as the corporation has the ability to meet its debt payments. Furthermore, a high degree of financial leverage allows the earnings of the firm to be distributed to a smaller group of shareholders. In some cases, corporations issue bonds and use the proceeds to repurchase some of their existing stock. This strategy is referred to as a debt-for-equity swap.

When corporations use an excessive amount of debt, they may be unable to make their debt payments. Consequently, they may revise their capital structure by reducing their level of debt. In an equity-for-debt swap, corporations issue stock and use the proceeds to retire existing debt.

Structured Notes

Firms may also borrow funds by issuing structured notes. For these notes, the amount of interest and principal to be paid is based on specified market conditions. The amount of the repayment may be tied to a Treasury bond price index or even to a stock index or a currency. Sometimes issuers use structured notes to reduce their risk. For example, a structured product may specify that the principal payment will decline if bond prices decline. A bond portfolio manager that needs to borrow funds could partially insulate the portfolio risk by using structured notes, because the required repayments on the notes would decline if the bond market (and therefore the manager's bond portfolio) performed poorly.

BEHAVIORAL FINANCE Structured notes became very popular in the 1990s when many participants took positions in the notes in their quest for a high return. One of the reasons for the popularity of structured notes is that some investors may be able to use them to bet indirectly on or against a specific market that they cannot bet on directly because of restrictions.

ILLUSTRATION The pension fund manager at Cicero Company wants to invest in Brazilian bonds, but the fund has specific restrictions against investing in emerging markets. The restrictions are intended to prevent the manager from taking excessive risk, because he is investing the money that will provide pensions for Cicero's employees when they retire. However, the manager's annual bonus is directly tied to how well the portfolio performs, so he wants to pursue strategies that might generate very large returns. He can invest in a structured note issued by a highly rated investment bank that provides high payments when Brazilian bonds perform well. The pension fund's investment holdings will show that it owns a structured product issued by a highly rated investment bank. In this way, the manager circumvents the restrictions, and his portfolio has a chance to generate a higher return, but it is also exposed to substantial risk. ∎

In the early 1990s, the portfolio manager responsible for managing more than $7 billion for Orange County, California, invested in structured notes that would earn high returns if interest rates declined. The rating agencies rated these notes AAA. Apparently, the portfolio manager and the rating agencies did not understand the risk of the structured notes. The portfolio manager guessed wrong, and interest rates increased, which caused the values of the notes to decline substantially. The portfolio manager attempted to make up for the losses by borrowing funds and investing more money in structured notes, but these investments also performed poorly. In 1994, Orange County filed for bankruptcy. Many other state and local governments also suffered losses because their portfolio managers had invested in structured notes. The portfolio managers took excessive risks with the state and local government money. These managers benefited directly by receiving substantial bonuses or raises when their investments generated high returns. Their investments were questioned only after they suffered losses. ∎

Exhibit 7.7 Participation of Financial Institutions in Bond Markets

Financial Institution	Participation in Bond Markets
Commercial banks and savings and loan associations (S&Ls)	• Purchase bonds for their asset portfolio. • Sometimes place municipal bonds for municipalities. • Sometimes issue bonds as a source of secondary capital.
Finance companies	• Commonly issue bonds as a source of long-term funds.
Mutual funds	• Use funds received from the sale of shares to purchase bonds. Some bond mutual funds specialize in particular types of bonds, while others invest in all types.
Brokerage firms	• Facilitate bond trading by matching up buyers and sellers of bonds in the secondary market.
Investment banking firms	• Place newly issued bonds for governments and corporations. They may place the bonds and assume the risk of market price uncertainty or place the bonds on a best-efforts basis in which they do not guarantee a price for the issuer.
Insurance companies	• Purchase bonds for their asset portfolio.
Pension funds	• Purchase bonds for their asset portfolio.

Institutional Use of Bond Markets

http://www.bloomberg.com
Yield curves of major countries' government securities.

All financial institutions participate in the bond markets, as summarized in Exhibit 7.7. Commercial banks, bond mutual funds, insurance companies, and pension funds are dominant investors in the bond market activity on any given day. A financial institution's investment decisions will often simultaneously affect bond market and other financial market activity. For example, an institution that anticipates higher interest rates may sell its bond holdings and purchase either money market securities or stocks. Conversely, financial institutions that expect lower interest rates may shift investments from their money market securities and/or stock portfolios to their bond portfolio.

Globalization of Bond Markets

GL🌐BALASPECTS In recent years, financial institutions such as pension funds, insurance companies, and commercial banks have commonly purchased foreign bonds. For example, pension funds of General Electric, United Technologies Corporation, and IBM frequently invest in foreign bonds with the intention of achieving higher returns for their employees. Many public pension funds also invest in foreign bonds for the same reason. Because of the frequent cross-border investments in bonds, the bond markets have become increasingly integrated among countries. In addition, mutual funds containing U.S. securities are accessible to foreign investors.

http://bonds.yahoo.com
Summary of bond market activity and analysis of bond market conditions.

Primary dealers of U.S. Treasury notes and bonds have opened offices in London, Tokyo, and other foreign cities to accommodate the foreign demand for these securities. When the U.S. markets close, markets in Hong Kong and Tokyo are opening. As these markets close, European markets are opening. The U.S. market opens as markets in London and other European cities are closing. Thus, the prices of U.S. Treasury bonds at the time the U.S. market opens may differ substantially from the previous day's closing price.

In recent years, low-quality bonds have been issued globally by governments and large corporations. These bonds are referred to as **global junk bonds.** The demand for these bonds has been high as some institutional investors are attracted to their high yields. For example, corporate bonds have been issued by Klabin (Brazil) and Cementos Mexicanos (Mexico), while government bonds have been issued by Brazil, Mexico, Venezuela, the Czech Republic, and Spain.

The global development of the bond market is primarily attributed to the bond offerings by country governments. In general, bonds issued by foreign governments (referred to as sovereign bonds) are attractive to investors because of the government's ability to meet debt obligations. Nevertheless, some country governments have defaulted on their bonds, including Argentina (1982, 1989, 1990, 2001), Brazil (1986, 1989, 1991), Costa Rica (1989), Russia and other former Soviet republics (1993, 1998), and the former Yugoslavia (1992). Given that sovereign bonds are exposed to credit risk, credit ratings are assigned to them by Moody's and Standard & Poor's. Rating agencies tend to disagree more about the credit risk of sovereign bonds than about bonds issued by U.S. corporations. Perhaps this is due to a lack of consistent information available for country governments, which results in more arbitrary ratings. Also, the process of rating specific countries is still relatively new.

Eurobond Market

In 1963, U.S.-based corporations were limited to the amount of funds they could borrow in the United States for overseas operations. Consequently, these corporations began to issue bonds in the so-called Eurobond market, where bonds denominated in various currencies were placed. The U.S. dollar is used the most, denominating 70 to 75 percent of the Eurobonds.

Non-U.S. investors who desire dollar-denominated bonds may use the Eurobond market if they prefer bearer bonds to the registered corporate bonds issued in the United States. Alternatively, they may use the Eurobond market because they are more familiar with bond placements within their own country.

An underwriting syndicate of investment banks participates in the Eurobond market by placing the bonds issued. It normally underwrites the bonds, guaranteeing a particular value to be received by the issuer. Thus, the syndicate is exposed to underwriting risk, or the risk that it will be unable to sell the bonds above the price that it guaranteed the issuer.

The issuer of Eurobonds can choose the currency in which the bonds are denominated. The issuer's periodic coupon payments and repayment of principal will normally be in this currency. Moreover, the financing cost from issuing bonds depends on the currency chosen. In some cases, a firm may denominate the bonds in a currency with a low interest rate and use earnings generated by one of its subsidiaries to cover the payments. For example, the coupon rate on a Eurobond denominated in Swiss francs may be 5 percentage points lower than a dollar-denominated bond. A U.S. firm may consider issuing Swiss franc–denominated bonds and converting the francs to dollars for use in the United States. Then it could instruct a subsidiary in Switzerland to cover the periodic coupon payments with earnings that the subsidiary generates. In this way, a lower financing rate would be achieved without exposure to exchange rate risk.

Summary

■ Bonds can be classified in four categories according to the type of issuer: Treasury bonds, federal agency bonds, municipal bonds, and corporate bonds. The issuers are perceived to have different levels of credit risk. In addition, the bonds have different degrees of liquidity and different provisions. Thus, quoted yields at a given point in time vary across bonds.

■ Many institutional investors, such as commercial banks, insurance companies, pension funds, and bond mutual funds, are major investors in bonds. These institutional investors adjust their holdings of bonds in response to expectations of future interest rates.

■ Bond yields vary among countries. Investors are attracted to high bond yields in foreign countries, causing funds to flow to those countries. Consequently, bond markets have become globally integrated.

Point Counter-Point

Should Financial Institutions Invest in Junk Bonds?

Point Yes. Financial institutions have managers who are capable of weighing the risk against the potential return. They can earn a significantly higher return when investing in junk bonds than the return on Treasury bonds. Their shareholders benefit when they increase the return on the portfolio.

Counter-Point No. The financial system is based on trust in financial institutions and confidence that the financial institutions will survive. If financial institutions take excessive risk, the entire financial system is at risk.

Who Is Correct? Use the Internet to learn more about this issue. Offer your own opinion on this issue.

Questions and Applications

1. **Bond Indenture** What is a bond indenture? What is the function of a trustee, as related to the bond indenture?

2. **Sinking-Fund Provision** Explain the use of a sinking-fund provision. How can it reduce the investor's risk?

3. **Protective Covenants** What are protective covenants? Why are they needed?

4. **Call Provisions** Explain the call provision of bonds. How can it affect the price of a bond?

5. **Bond Collateral** Explain the use of bond collateral, and identify the common types of collateral for bonds.

6. **Debentures** What are debentures? How do they differ from subordinated debentures?

7. **Zero-Coupon Bonds** What are the advantages and disadvantages to a firm that issues low- or zero-coupon bonds?

8. **Variable-Rate Bonds** Are variable-rate bonds attractive to investors who expect interest rates to decrease? Explain. Would a firm consider variable-rate bonds if it expected that interest rates will decrease? Explain.

9. **Convertible Bonds** Why can convertible bonds be issued by firms at a higher price than other bonds?

10. **Global Interaction of Bond Yields** Assume that bond yields in Japan rise. How might U.S. bond yields be affected? Why?

11. **Impact of FIRREA on the Junk Bond Market** Explain how the Financial Institutions Reform, Recovery and Enforcement Act (FIRREA) could have affected the market value of junk bonds.

12. **Calling Bonds** As a result of September 11, 2001, economic conditions were expected to decline. How do you think this would have affected the tendency of firms to call bonds?

13. **Yield Curve for Municipal Securities** Explain how the shape of the yield curve for municipal securities compares to the Treasury yield curve. Under what conditions do you think the two yield curves could be different?

14. **Bond Downgrade** Explain how the downgrading of bonds for a particular corporation affects the corporation, the investors that currently hold these bonds, and other investors who may invest in the bonds in the near future.

Advanced Questions

15. **Junk Bonds** Merrito, Inc. is a large U.S. firm that issued bonds several years ago. Its bond ratings declined over time, and about a year ago, the bonds were rated in the junk bond classification. Nevertheless, investors were buying the bonds in the secondary market because of the attractive yield they offered. Last week, Merrito defaulted on its bonds, and the prices of most other junk bonds declined abruptly on the same day. Explain why news of the financial problems of Merrito, Inc. could cause the prices of junk bonds issued by other firms to decrease, even when those firms had no business relationships with Merrito. Explain why the prices of those junk bonds with less liquidity declined more than those with a high degree of liquidity.

16. **Event Risk** An insurance company purchased bonds issued by Hartnett Company two years ago.

Today, Hartnett Company has begun to issue junk bonds and is using the funds to repurchase most of its existing stock. Why might the market value of those bonds held by the insurance company be affected by this action?

Interpreting Financial News

Interpret the following statements made by Wall Street analysts and portfolio managers:

a. "The values of some stocks are dependent on the bond market. When investors are not interested in junk bonds, the values of stocks ripe for leveraged buyouts decline."

b. "The recent trend in which many firms are using debt to repurchase some of their stock is a good strategy as long as they can withstand the stagnant economy."

c. "Although yields among bonds are related, today's rumors of a tax cut caused an increase in the yield on municipal bonds, while the yield on corporate bonds declined."

Managing in Financial Markets

Forecasting Bond Returns As a portfolio manager for an insurance company, you are about to invest funds in one of three possible investments: (1) 10-year coupon bonds issued by the U.S. Treasury, (2) 20-year zero-coupon bonds issued by the Treasury, or (3) one-year Treasury securities. Each possible investment is perceived to have no risk of default. You plan to maintain this investment for a one-year period. The return of each investment over a one-year horizon will be about the same if interest rates do not change over the next year. However, you anticipate that the U.S. inflation rate will decline substantially over the next year, while most of the other portfolio managers in the United States expect inflation to increase slightly.

a. If your expectations are correct, how will the return of each investment be affected over the one-year horizon?

b. If your expectations are correct, which of the three investments should have the highest return over the one-year horizon? Why?

c. Offer one reason why you might not select the investment that would have the highest expected return over the one-year investment horizon.

Problems

1. **Inflation-Indexed Treasury Bond** An inflation-indexed Treasury bond has a par value of $1,000 and a coupon rate of 6 percent. An investor purchases this bond and holds it for one year. During the year, the consumer price index increases by 1 percent every six months, for a total increase in inflation of 2 percent. What are the total interest payments the investor will receive during the year?

2. **Inflation-Indexed Treasury Bond** Assume that the U.S. economy experienced deflation during the year and that the consumer price index decreased by 1 percent in the first six months of the year and by 2 percent during the second six months of the year. If an investor had purchased inflation-indexed Treasury bonds with a par value of $10,000 and a coupon rate of 5 percent, how much would she have received in interest during the year?

Flow of Funds Exercise

Financing in the Bond Markets

If the economy continues to be strong, Carson may need to increase its production capacity by about 50 percent over the next few years to satisfy demand. It would need financing to expand and accommodate the increase in production. Recall that the yield curve is currently upward sloping. Also recall that Carson is concerned about a possible slowing of the economy because of potential Fed actions to reduce inflation. It needs funding to cover payments for supplies. It is also considering issuing stock or bonds to raise funds in the next year.

a. Assume that Carson has two choices to satisfy the increased demand for its products. It could increase production by 10 percent with its existing facilities. In this case, it could obtain short-term financing to cover the extra production expense and then use a portion of the revenue received to finance this level of production in the future. Alternatively, it could issue bonds and use the proceeds to buy a larger facility that would allow for 50 percent more capacity.

b. Carson currently has a large amount of debt, and its assets have already been pledged to back up its existing debt. It does not have additional collateral. At this point in time, the credit risk premium it would pay is similar in the short-term and long-term debt markets. Does this imply that the cost of financing is the same in both markets?

c. Should Carson consider using a call provision if it issues bonds? Why? Why might Carson decide not to include a call provision on the bonds?

d. If Carson issues bonds, it would be a relatively small bond offering. Should Carson consider a private placement of bonds? What type of investor might be interested in participating in a private placement? Do you think Carson could offer the same yield on a private placement as it could on a public placement? Explain.

e. Financial institutions such as insurance companies and pension funds commonly purchase bonds. Explain the flow of funds that runs through these financial institutions and ultimately reaches corporations such as Carson Company that issue bonds.

Internet/Excel Exercise

1. Go to http://finance.yahoo.com/bonds. Click on "Composite Bond Rates." Compare the rate of a 10-year Treasury bond versus a 10-year municipal bond. Which type of bond would offer you a higher annual yield based on your tax bracket, given that the municipal bond is not subject to federal income taxes? Determine the premium contained in the yield of a 10-year corporate A-rated bond as compared to the 10-year Treasury bonds. Compare that premium to the premium that existed one month ago. Did the premium increase or decrease? Offer an explanation for the change. Is the change attributed to economic conditions?

WSJ Exercise

Impact of Treasury Financing on Bond Prices

The Treasury periodically issues new bonds to finance the deficit. Review recent issues of *The Wall Street Journal* or check related online news to find a recent article on such financing. Does the article suggest that financial markets are expecting upward pressure on interest rates as a result of the Treasury financing? What happened to prices of existing bonds when the Treasury announced its intentions to issue new bonds?

Chapter 8: Bond Valuation and Risk

The values of bonds can change substantially over time. Hence, financial institutions that consider buying or selling bonds closely monitor their values.

The specific objectives of this chapter are to:

■ explain how bonds are priced,

■ identify the factors that affect bond prices,

■ explain how the sensitivity of bond prices to interest rates is dependent on particular bond characteristics, and

■ explain the benefits of diversifying bonds internationally.

Bond Valuation Process

http://

http://www.finpipe.com/ valuebnd.htm More information on the process of valuing bonds.

Bonds are debt obligations with long-term maturities commonly issued by governments or corporations to obtain long-term funds. They are commonly purchased by financial institutions that wish to invest funds for long-term periods.

Bond valuation is conceptually similar to the valuation of capital budgeting projects, businesses, or even real estate. The appropriate price reflects the present value of the cash flows to be generated by the bond in the form of periodic interest (or coupon) payments and the principal payment to be provided at maturity. The coupon payment is based on the coupon rate multiplied by the par value of the bond. Thus, a bond with a 9 percent coupon rate and $1,000 par value pays $90 in coupon payments per year. Because these expected cash flows are known, the valuation of bonds is generally perceived to be easier than the valuation of equity securities.

The current price of a bond should be the present value (PV) of its remaining cash flows:

$$PV \text{ of bond} = \frac{C}{(1 + k)^1} + \frac{C}{(1 + k)^2} + \cdots + \frac{C + \text{Par}}{(1 + k)^n}$$

where
C = coupon payment provided in each period

Par = par value

k = required rate of return per period used to discount the bond

n = number of periods to maturity

ILLUSTRATION Consider a bond that has a par value of $1,000, pays $100 at the end of each year in coupon payments, and has three years remaining until maturity. Assume that the prevailing annualized yield on other bonds with similar characteristics is 12 percent. In this case, the appropriate price of the bond can be determined as follows. The future cash flows to investors who would purchase this bond are $100 in Year 1, $100 in Year 2, and $1,100 (computed as $100 in coupon payments plus $1,000 par value) in Year 3. The appropriate market price of the bond is its present value:

$$PV \text{ of bond} = \$100/(1 + .12)^1 + \$100/(1 + .12)^2 + \$1,100/(1 + .12)^3$$
$$= \$89.29 + \$79.72 + \$782.96$$
$$= \$951.97$$

This valuation procedure is illustrated in Exhibit 8.1. Because this example assumes that investors require a 12 percent return, k equals 12 percent. At the price of $951.97, the bondholders purchasing this bond will receive a 12 percent annualized return. ∎

When using a financial calculator, the present value of the bond in the previous example can be determined as follows:

Input	3	12	100	1000		
Function Key	N	I	PMT	FV	CPT	PV
Answer						951.97

Impact of the Discount Rate on Bond Valuation

The discount rate selected to compute the present value is critical to accurate valuation. Exhibit 8.2 shows the wide range of present value results at different discount rates, for a $10,000 payment in 10 years. The appropriate discount rate for valuing

Exhibit 8.1
Valuation of a Three-Year Bond

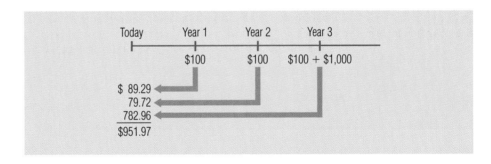

Exhibit 8.2
Relationship between Discount Rate and Present Value of $10,000 Payment to Be Received in 10 Years

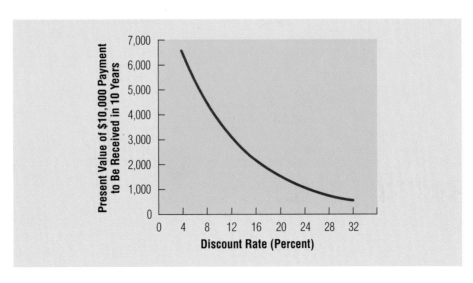

any asset is the yield that could be earned on alternative investments with similar risk and maturity.

Since investors require higher returns on riskier securities, they use higher discount rates to discount the future cash flows of these securities. Consequently, the value of a high-risk security will be lower than the value of a low-risk security when both securities have the same expected cash flows.

Impact of the Timing of Payments on Bond Valuation

The market price of a bond is also affected by the timing of the payments made to bondholders. Funds received sooner can be reinvested to earn additional returns. Thus, a dollar to be received soon has a higher present value than one to be received later. The impact of maturity on the present value of a $10,000 payment is shown in Exhibit 8.3, assuming that a return of 10 percent could be earned on available funds. The $10,000 payment has a present value of $8,264 if it is to be paid in two years. This implies that if $8,264 were invested today and earned 10 percent annually, it would be worth $10,000 in two years. Exhibit 8.3 also shows that a $10,000 payment made 20 years from now has a present value of only $1,486, and a $10,000 payment made 50 years from now has a present value of only $85 (based on the 10 percent discount rate).

Valuation of Bonds with Semiannual Payments

In reality, most bonds have semiannual payments. The present value of such bonds can be computed as follows. First, the annualized coupon should be split in half because two payments are made per year. Second, the annual discount rate should be divided by 2 to reflect two six-month periods per year. Third, the number of periods should be doubled to reflect two times the number of annual periods. Incorporating these adjustments, the present value is determined as follows:

$$\begin{array}{c} PV \text{ of bond with} \\ \text{semiannual payments} \end{array} = \frac{C/2}{[1+(k/2)]^1} + \frac{C/2}{[1+(k/2)]^2} + \cdots + \frac{C/2 + \text{Par}}{[1+(k/2)]^{2n}}$$

where $C/2$ is the semiannual coupon payment (half of what the annual coupon payment would have been) and $k/2$ is the periodic discount rate used to discount the bond. The last part of the equation shows $2n$ in the denominator exponent to reflect the doubling of periods.

Exhibit 8.3
Relationship between Time of Payment and Present Value of Payment

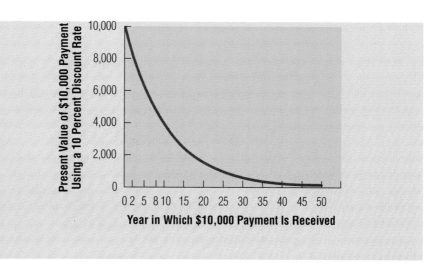

ILLUSTRATION As an example of the valuation of a bond with semiannual payments, consider a bond with $1,000 par value, a 10 percent coupon rate paid semiannually, and three years to maturity. Assuming a 12 percent required return, the present value is computed as follows:

$$PV \text{ of bond} = \frac{\$50}{(1.06)^1} + \frac{\$50}{(1.06)^2} + \frac{\$50}{(1.06)^3} + \frac{\$50}{(1.06)^4} + \frac{\$50}{(1.06)^5} + \frac{\$50 + \$1,000}{(1.06)^6}$$

$$= \$47.17 + \$44.50 + \$41.98 + \$39.60 + \$37.36 + \$740.21$$

$$= \$950.82 \blacksquare$$

When using a financial calculator, the present value of the bond in the previous example can be determined as follows:[1]

Input	6	6	50	1000		
Function Key	N	I	PMT	FV	CPT	PV
Answer						950.82

The remaining examples assume annual coupon payments so that we can focus on the concepts presented without concern about adjusting annual payments.

Relationships between Coupon Rate, Required Return, and Bond Price

Bonds that sell at a price below their par value are called **discount bonds.** The larger the investor's required rate of return relative to the coupon rate, the larger the discount of a bond with a particular par value.

ILLUSTRATION Consider a zero-coupon bond (which has no coupon payments) with three years remaining to maturity and $1,000 par value. Assume the investor's required rate of return on the bond is 13 percent. The appropriate price of this bond can be determined by the present value of its future cash flows:

$$PV \text{ of bond} = \$0/(1 + .13)^1 + \$0/(1 + .13)^2 + \$1,000/(1 + .13)^3$$

$$= \$0 + \$0 + \$693.05$$

$$= \$693.05$$

The very low price of this bond is necessary to generate a 13 percent annualized return to investors. If the bond offered coupon payments, the price would have been higher because those coupon payments would provide part of the return required by investors.

Consider another bond with a similar par value and maturity that offers a 13 percent coupon rate. The appropriate price of the bond would now be

$$PV \text{ of bond} = \$130/(1 + .13)^1 + \$130/(1 + .13)^2 + \$1,130/(1 + .13)^3$$

$$= \$115.04 + \$101.81 + \$783.15$$

$$= \$1,000$$

---

[1]Technically, the semiannual rate of 6 percent is overstated. For a required rate of 12 percent per year, the precise six-month rate would be 5.83 percent. With the compounding effect, which would generate interest on interest, this semiannual rate over two periods would achieve a 12 percent return. Because the approximate semiannual rate of 6 percent is higher than the precise rate, the present value of the bonds is slightly understated.

Notice that the price of this bond is exactly equal to its par value. This is because the entire compensation required by investors is provided by the coupon payments.

Finally, consider a bond with a similar par value and term to maturity and coupon rate that offers a coupon rate of 15 percent, which is above the investor's required rate of return. The appropriate price of this bond as determined by its present value is

$$PV \text{ of bond} = \$150/(1 + .13)^1 + \$150/(1 + .13)^2 + \$1{,}150/(1 + .13)^3$$
$$= \$132.74 + \$117.47 + \$797.01$$
$$= \$1{,}047.22$$

The price of this bond exceeds its par value because the coupon payments are large enough to offset the high price paid for the bond and still provide a 13 percent annualized return. ∎

http://bonds.yahoo.com
Calculates bond returns and yields.

From the examples provided, the following relationships should now be clear. First, if the coupon rate of a bond is below the investor's required rate of return, the present value of the bond (and therefore the price of the bond) should be below the par value. Second, if the coupon rate equals the investor's required rate of return, the price of the bond should be the same as the par value. Finally, if the coupon rate of a bond is above the investor's required rate of return, the price of the bond should be above the par value. These relationships are shown in Exhibit 8.4 for a bond with a 10 percent coupon and a par value of $1,000. If investors require a return of 5 percent and desire a 10-year maturity, they will be willing to pay $1,390 for this bond. If they require a return of 10 percent on this same bond, they will be willing to pay $1,000. If they require a 15 percent return, they will be willing to pay only $745. The relationships described here hold for any bond, regardless of its maturity.

Implications for Financial Institutions

The impact of interest rate movements on a financial institution depends on how the institution's asset and liability portfolios are structured, as illustrated in Exhibit 8.5. Financial institutions with interest rate–sensitive liabilities that invest heavily in bonds are exposed to interest rate risk. Many financial institutions attempt to adjust the size of their bond portfolio according to their expectations about future interest rates. The expected return is higher when unevenly matched rate sensitivities are used because

Exhibit 8.4
Relationship between Required Return and Present Value for a 10 Percent Coupon Bond with Various Maturities

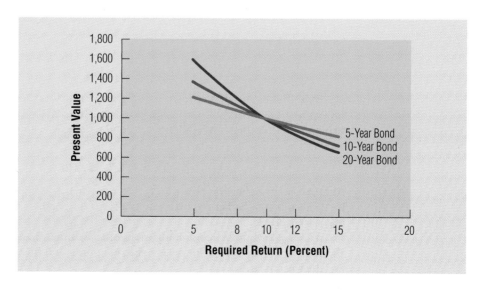

Exhibit 8.5
Potential Returns to
Financial Institutions
with Different Invest-
ment Strategies

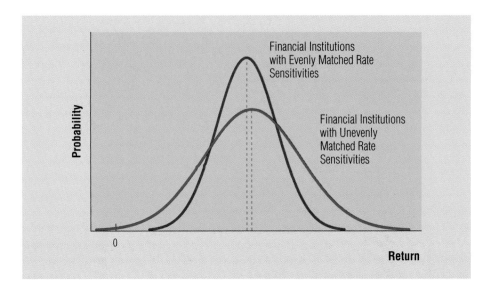

the mismatch allows an institution to take advantage of the effects of interest rate expectations. When rates are expected to rise, bonds can be sold and the proceeds used
to purchase short-term securities, whose market values are less influenced by interest
rate movements. When rates are expected to fall, the bond portfolio can be expanded
in order to capitalize on the expectations. An aggressive approach offers greater potential for high return but also exposes investors to more risk when their expectations
are wrong.

Like bonds, fixed-rate mortgages generate periodic fixed payments. Thus, the preceding comments apply to financial institutions such as savings institutions that hold
mortgage portfolios. A primary reason for the financial problems of savings institutions in the late 1980s was the rise in interest rates, which reduced the market value of
their mortgage portfolios. This is a classic example of **interest rate risk,** or the risk that
the market value of assets will decline in response to interest rate movements.

Explaining Bond Price Movements

As explained earlier, the price of a bond should reflect the present value of future cash
flows (coupon payments and the par value), based on a required rate of return (k), so
that

$$\Delta P_b = f(\Delta k)$$

Since the required rate of return on a bond is primarily determined by the prevailing risk-free rate (R_f), which is the yield on a Treasury bond with the same maturity, and the risk premium (RP) on the bond, the general price movements of bonds
can be modeled as

$$\Delta P_b = f(\Delta R_f, \Delta RP)$$

An increase in either the risk-free rate or the general level of the risk premium on
bonds results in a higher required rate of return on bonds and therefore causes bond
prices to decrease.

The factors that are commonly monitored by bond market participants because
they affect the risk-free rate or default risk premiums, and therefore affect bond prices,
are identified next.

Factors That Affect the Risk-Free Rate

http://research.stlouisfed
.org/ fred2 Assesses
economic conditions that
affect bond prices.

The long-term risk-free rate is driven by inflationary expectations (INF), economic growth (ECON), the money supply (MS), and the budget deficit (DEF):

$$\Delta R_f = f(\Delta INF, \Delta ECON, \Delta MS, \Delta DEF)$$
$$\qquad\quad +\qquad +\qquad ?\qquad +$$

The general relationships are summarized next.

Impact of Inflationary Expectations

If the level of inflation is expected to increase, there will be upward pressure on interest rates (as explained in Chapter 2) and, therefore, on the required rate of return on bonds. Conversely, a reduction in the expected level of inflation results in downward pressure on interest rates and, therefore, on the required rate of return on bonds. Bond market participants closely monitor indicators of inflation, such as the consumer price index and the producer price index.

Inflationary expectations are partially dependent on oil prices, which affect the cost of energy and transportation. Bond portfolio managers therefore forecast oil prices and their potential impact on inflation in order to forecast interest rates. A forecast of lower oil prices results in expectations of lower interest rates, causing bond portfolio managers to purchase more bonds. A forecast of higher oil prices results in expectations of higher interest rates, causing bond portfolio managers to sell some of their holdings.

Inflationary expectations are also partially dependent on exchange rate movements. Holding other things equal, inflationary expectations are likely to rise when a weaker dollar is expected, because that will increase the prices of imported supplies. A weaker dollar also prices foreign competitors out of the market, allowing U.S. firms to increase their prices. Thus, U.S. interest rates are expected to rise and bond prices are expected to decrease when the dollar is expected to weaken. Foreign investors anticipating dollar depreciation are less willing to hold U.S. bonds because the coupon payments will convert to less of their home currency in that event. This could cause an immediate net sale of bonds, placing further downward pressure on bond prices.

Expectations of a strong dollar should have the opposite results. A stronger dollar reduces the prices paid for foreign supplies, thus lowering retail prices. In addition, because a stronger dollar makes the prices of foreign products more attractive, domestic firms must maintain low prices in order to compete. Consequently, low inflation and therefore low interest rates are expected, and bond portfolio managers are likely to purchase more bonds.

http://research.stlouisfed.org
Assess the yield of 30-year
Treasury bonds over the last
24 months.

Impact of Economic Growth

Strong economic growth tends to place upward pressure on interest rates (as explained in Chapter 2), while weak economic conditions place downward pressure on rates. Any signals about future economic conditions will affect expectations about future interest rate movements and cause bond markets to react immediately. For example, any economic announcements (such as measurements of economic growth or unemployment) that signal stronger than expected economic growth tend to reduce bond prices. Investors anticipate that interest rates will rise, causing a decline in bond prices. Therefore, they sell bonds, which places immediate downward pressure on bond prices. Conversely, any economic announcements that signal a weaker than expected economy tend to increase bond prices, because investors anticipate that interest rates will decrease, causing bond prices to rise. Therefore, investors buy bonds, which places immediate upward pressure on bond prices. This explains why sudden news of a possible economic recession can cause the bond market to rally.

Bond market participants closely monitor economic indicators that may signal future changes in the strength of the economy, which signal changes in the risk-free interest rate and in the required return from investing in bonds. Some of the more closely monitored indicators of economic growth include employment, gross domestic product, retail sales, industrial production, and consumer confidence. An unexpected favorable movement in these indicators tends to arouse expectations of an increase in economic growth and an increase in interest rates, thereby placing downward pressure on bond prices.

Conversely, an unexpected unfavorable movement in these indicators tends to signal a weaker economy, which arouses expectations of lower interest rates and places upward pressure on bond prices. However, a weaker economy can also increase the default risk premium on some risky bonds because the issuers may have more difficulty meeting their payment obligations under weaker economic conditions. The upward pressure on the required return on these bonds due to the higher default risk premium may partially offset the downward pressure due to the expected reduction in the risk-free rate.

Impact of Money Supply Growth When the Federal Reserve increases money supply growth, two reactions are possible (as explained in Chapter 5). First, the increased money supply may result in an increased supply of loanable funds. If demand for loanable funds is not affected, the increased money supply should place downward pressure on interest rates, causing bond portfolio managers to expect an increase in bond prices and thus to purchase bonds based on such expectations.

In a high-inflation environment, however, bond portfolio managers may expect a large increase in the demand for loanable funds (as a result of inflationary expectations), which would cause an increase in interest rates and lower bond prices. Such forecasts would encourage immediate sales of long-term bonds.

Impact of Budget Deficit As the annual budget deficit changes, so does the federal government's demand for loanable funds (as explained in Chapter 2). An increase in the annual budget deficit over the previous year results in a higher level of borrowing by the federal government, which can place upward pressure on the risk-free interest rate. In other words, excessive borrowing by the Treasury can result in a higher required return on Treasury bonds. An excessive amount of borrowing by the federal government can indirectly affect the required rate of return and therefore the yield on all types of bonds.

ILLUSTRATION If the Treasury issues an unusually large number of Treasury bonds in the primary market, the result is downward pressure on the market price and upward pressure on the market yield of these bonds. Consequently, holders of corporate bonds with credit risk may then switch to Treasury bonds because by holding such bonds, they can achieve almost the same yield without exposure to credit risk. This tendency places downward pressure on corporate bond prices and upward pressure on corporate bond yields, restoring the yield differential between corporate bonds and Treasury bonds. Since some investors perceive various bonds as substitutes, their buy and sell decisions will stabilize yield differentials among the bonds. ■

Just as an increased budget deficit can increase the yields offered on all bonds, a reduced budget deficit can reduce the yields offered on all bonds. In the late 1990s, the U.S. government had a budget surplus, which resulted in a lower risk-free interest rate, a lower required rate of return on bonds, and higher bond prices.

Factors That Affect the Credit (Default) Risk Premium

The credit risk premium tends to be larger for corporate or municipal bonds than for money market securities issued by a given corporation because the probability of a corporation experiencing financial distress is higher for a bond with a longer term to maturity. The general level of credit risk on corporate or municipal bonds can change in response to a change in economic growth (ECON):

$$\Delta RP = f(\Delta \text{ECON})$$

Strong economic growth tends to improve a firm's cash flows and reduce the probability that the firm will default on its debt payments. Conversely, weak economic growth may increase the probability of default, especially for firms that are very sensitive to economic conditions.

A firm's managers may make decisions that affect its risk and therefore affect the risk of the bonds that it issues. If the managers invest very conservatively, risk may be reduced. Alternatively, risk may increase if they attempt to expand by acquiring businesses that they are not capable of managing effectively. If they increase their reliance on equity financing, they can more easily cover their existing debt payments. Conversely, if they rely more on borrowed funds, they may have more difficulty covering their debt payments.

ILLUSTRATION Last year Breckenridge Company issued bonds that received a BBB rating, while Vail Company issued bonds that received a BB rating. Last week, the bonds of both firms were downgraded. Breckenridge's bonds were downgraded because it recently borrowed additional funds from banks, which raised concerns about its high debt level. Vail's bonds were downgraded because conditions in its industry have weakened. Thus, for different reasons, the rating agency perceived that both companies' bonds have a higher likelihood of default than before. Since these firms already obtained their money from issuing the bonds, they are not directly affected by the downgraded rating (although it may restrict their ability to borrow additional funds). In contrast, the investors who are holding those bonds at the time of the downgrade are directly affected because the market value of bonds normally declines in response to a downgrade. If the investors holding the bonds want to sell them in the secondary market, they will have to sell them at a lower price to compensate potential buyers for the higher level of credit risk. ■

Although the risk of a specific corporate bond can change due to actions of the firm's managers, such as increasing its use of debt, such actions are firm-specific and do not affect the general risk level of all bonds. Conversely, changes in economic conditions can have a systematic effect on the risk of many firms and therefore can affect the valuations of many bonds at the same time.

Changes in the Credit Risk Premium over Time Exhibit 8.6 compares yields on various types of bonds over time. The yields among securities are highly correlated. Notice that the difference between the corporate Baa and corporate Aaa bond yields widened during the weak economic periods of the early 1990s and the 2001–2002 period when investors required a higher credit risk premium.

Exhibit 8.7 illustrates more clearly how the credit risk premium changes over time. Notice how the premium begins to widen in 2000. In the 2001–2002 period, economic conditions were weak. Thus, corporations paid a higher premium for financing in that period because of a heightened risk perception in the bond markets resulting from a weak economy. The premium declined in the 2004–2007 period when the economy improved.

Exhibit 8.6   Comparison of Bond Yields

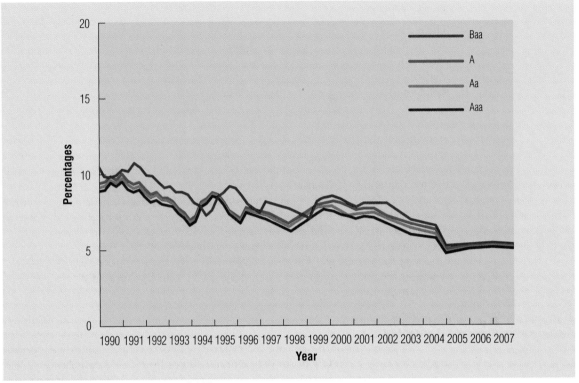

Note: Trends depict quarterly averages of bond yields.
Source: *Federal Reserve Bulletin.*

Exhibit 8.7   Comparison of Baa and Treasury Bond Yields over Time

Source: Federal Reserve.

Changes in Bond Ratings over Time Recall that bond rating agencies periodically assign a rating to bonds, which is supposed to reflect the likelihood that the issuer will satisfy its bond obligations in a timely manner and in full. A corporate bond's rating can change over time in response to changes in its financial condition. Exhibit 8.8 shows the number of bonds that were upgraded and downgraded by Standard & Poor's Corporation in years. The United States experienced a minor recession in 2001–2002. Many corporations experienced downgrades, even as the economy improved in 2004 and 2005. Corporate high-yield bonds were especially susceptible to downgrades during that period. In 2006, high-yield bonds were subjected to more downgrades than upgrades. Investment-grade bonds had a more even balance of downgrades and upgrades in 2006. It is possible that credit-rating agencies maintained higher standards after the Enron scandal in 2001, since they were criticized for not detecting the financial problems of Enron before the problems were publicized in the media.

Summary of Factors Affecting Bond Prices

When considering the factors that affect the risk-free rate and the risk premium, the general price movements in bonds can be modeled as

$$\Delta P_b = f(\Delta R_f, \Delta RP)$$
$$= f(\Delta INF, \Delta ECON, \Delta MS, \Delta DEF)$$
$$\quad\quad - \quad\quad ? \quad\quad + \quad\quad -$$

The relationships suggested here assume that other factors are held constant. In reality, other factors are changing as well, which makes it difficult to disentangle the precise impact of each factor on bond prices. The effect of economic growth is uncertain because a high level of economic growth can adversely affect bond prices by causing a higher risk-free rate, but can favorably affect bond prices by lowering the default risk premium. To the extent that international conditions affect each of the factors, they also influence bond prices.

Exhibit 8.9 summarizes the underlying forces that can affect the long-term risk-free interest rate and the default risk premium and therefore cause the general level of bond prices to change over time. When pricing Treasury bonds, investors focus on the factors that affect the long-term risk-free interest rate, as the default risk premium is not needed. Thus, the primary difference in the required return of a risky bond (such as a corporate bond) versus a Treasury bond for a given maturity is the default risk premium, which is influenced by economic and industry conditions.

http://www.treasurydirect .gov Treasury note and bond auction results.

Impact of Bond-Specific Characteristics The preceding discussion is intended simply to identify factors that affect general price movements of bonds. It is important to note that a bond's price can also be affected by factors specific to the bond, such as a change in the capital structure of the firm that issued the bond. Yield differentials among bonds can also change when investors perceive a characteristic of a particular type of bond to be more or less favorable than before. For example, if interest rates suddenly decline, existing bonds that have a call feature are more likely to be called. Thus, bonds containing a call feature will sell only if the price is lowered. This implies that the yield differential adjusts to the changing perception of the factor that caused the differential.

Bond Market Efficiency

If the bond market is efficient, this would suggest that bond prices fully reflect all available information. In general, bond prices should reflect information that is publicly

Exhibit 8.8 Changes in Corporate Bond Ratings over Time

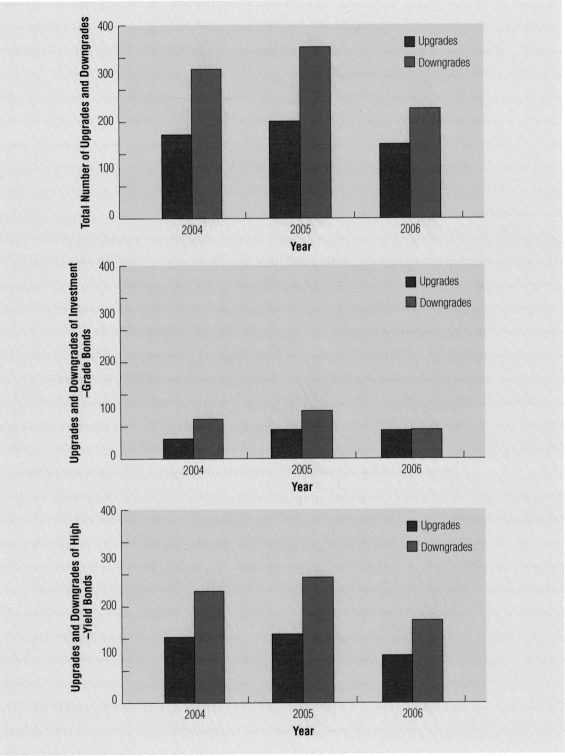

Source: Standard & Poor's.

Exhibit 8.9
Framework for Explaining Changes in Bond Prices over Time

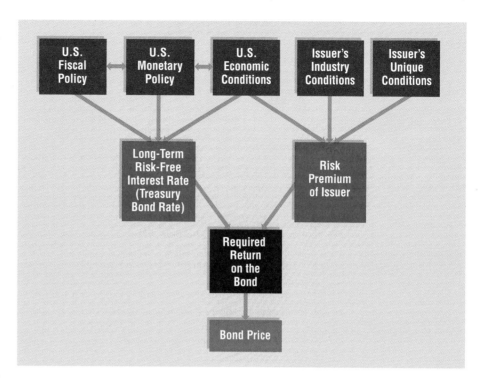

available. However, bond prices may not necessarily reflect information about firms that is known only by the managers of the firms.

ILLUSTRATION Davenport, Inc. is experiencing very weak sales this quarter, but those results are not obvious to bondholders. Thus, the prices of Davenport's bonds remain unchanged. One month later, Davenport discloses to the public that its sales were very weak and it will incur a large loss this quarter. This announcement causes bond market participants to be more concerned about the possibility that Davenport could default on its bonds. Consequently, many bondholders attempt to sell their Davenport bonds, and the prices of the bonds decline as a result. The price adjusted quickly once the information was public. ∎

Sensitivity of Bond Prices to Interest Rate Movements

When institutional and individual investors invest in bonds, they are subject to the risk that the return on their bonds will be less than anticipated. The forces that influence bond price movements cannot be perfectly anticipated, so future bond prices (and therefore returns) cannot be perfectly anticipated. If the bonds are not held until maturity, the prices at which they can be sold in the future (and therefore the return on the investment) are normally most sensitive to changes in the risk-free interest rate.

Investors can at least attempt to determine how sensitive the prices of their bond holdings are to possible changes in any conditions that affect the required rate of return on bonds. Such a measurement of bond price sensitivity can indicate the degree to which the market value of their bond holdings may decline in response to an increase in interest rates (and therefore in the required rate of return).

Bond Price Elasticity

The sensitivity of bond prices (P) to changes in the required rate of return (k) is commonly measured by the **bond price elasticity** (P^e), which is estimated as

$$P^e = \frac{\text{percent change in } P}{\text{percent change in } k}$$

Exhibit 8.10 compares the price sensitivity of 10-year bonds with $1,000 par value and four different coupon rates: 0 percent, 5 percent, 10 percent, and 15 percent. Initially, the required rate of return (k) on the bonds is assumed to be 10 percent. The price of each bond is therefore the present value of its future cash flows, discounted at 10 percent. The initial price of each bond is shown in Column 2. The top panel shows the effect of a decline in interest rates that reduces the investor's required return to 8 percent. The prices of the bonds based on an 8 percent required return are shown in Column 3. The percentage change in the price of each bond resulting from the interest rate movements is shown in Column 4. The bottom panel shows the effect of an increase in interest rates that increases the investor's required return to 12 percent.

The price elasticity for each bond is estimated in Exhibit 8.10 according to the assumed change in the required rate of return. Notice in the exhibit that the price sensitivity of any particular bond is greater for declining interest rates than rising interest rates. The bond price elasticity is negative in all cases, reflecting the inverse relationship between interest rate movements and bond price movements.

Influence of Coupon Rate on Bond Price Sensitivity A zero-coupon bond, which pays all of its proceeds to the investor at maturity, is most sensitive to changes in the required rate of return because the adjusted discount rate is applied to one lump sum in the distant future. Conversely, the price of a bond that pays

Exhibit 8.10 Sensitivity of 10-Year Bonds with Different Coupon Rates to Interest Rate Changes

Effects of a Decline in the Required Rate of Return:					
(1) Bonds with a Coupon Rate of:	(2) Initial Price of Bonds When $k = 10\%$	(3) Price of Bonds When $k = 8\%$	(4) = [(3) − (2)]/(2) Percentage Change in Bond Price	(5) Percentage Change in k	(6) = (4)/(5) Bond Price Elasticity (P^e)
0%	$ 386	$ 463	+19.9%	−20.0%	−.995
5	693	799	+15.3	−20.0	−.765
10	1,000	1,134	+13.4	−20.0	−.670
15	1,307	1,470	+12.5	−20.0	−.625
Effects of an Increase in the Required Rate of Return:					
(1) Bonds with a Coupon Rate of:	(2) Initial Price of Bonds When $k = 10\%$	(3) Price of Bonds When $k = 12\%$	(4) = [(3) − (2)]/(2) Percentage Change in Bond Price	(5) Percentage Change in k	(6) = (4)/(5) Bond Price Elasticity (P^e)
0%	$ 386	$ 322	−16.6%	+20.0%	−.830
5	693	605	−12.7	+20.0	−.635
10	1,000	887	−11.3	+20.0	−.565
15	1,307	1,170	−10.5	+20.0	−.525

all of its yield in the form of coupon payments is less sensitive to changes in the required rate of return because the adjusted discount rate is applied to some payments that occur in the near future. The adjustment in the present value of such payments in the near future due to a change in the required rate of return is not as pronounced as an adjustment in the present value of payments in the distant future.

Exhibit 8.10 confirms that the prices of zero- or low-coupon bonds are more sensitive to changes in the required rate of return than prices of bonds with relatively high coupon rates. Notice in the exhibit that when the required rate of return declines from 10 percent to 8 percent, the price of the zero-coupon bonds rises from $386 to $463. Thus, the bond price elasticity (P^e) is

$$P^e = \frac{\frac{\$463 - \$386}{\$386}}{\frac{8\% - 10\%}{10\%}}$$

$$= \frac{+19.9\%}{-20\%}$$

$$= -.995$$

This implies that for each 1 percent change in interest rates, zero-coupon bonds change by 0.995 percent in the opposite direction. Column 6 in Exhibit 8.10 shows that the price elasticities of the higher-coupon bonds are considerably lower than the price elasticity of the zero-coupon bond.

Financial institutions commonly restructure their bond portfolios to contain higher-coupon bonds when they are more concerned about a possible increase in interest rates (and therefore an increase in the required rate of return). Conversely, they restructure their portfolios to contain low- or zero-coupon bonds when they expect a decline in interest rates and wish to capitalize on their expectations by holding bonds that will be very price-sensitive.

Influence of Maturity on Bond Price Sensitivity As interest rates (and therefore required rates of return) decrease, long-term bond prices (as measured by their present value) increase by a greater degree than short-term bond prices because the long-term bonds will continue to offer the same coupon rate over a longer period of time than the short-term bonds. Of course, if interest rates increase, prices of the long-term bonds will decline by a greater degree.

Duration

http://
http://invest-faq.com Contains links to many different concepts about bonds, including duration.

An alternative measure of bond price sensitivity is the bond's **duration,** which is a measurement of the life of the bond on a present value basis. The longer a bond's duration, the greater its sensitivity to interest rate changes. A commonly used measure of a bond's duration (DUR) is

$$DUR = \frac{\sum_{t=1}^{n} \frac{C_t(t)}{(1+k)^t}}{\sum_{t=1}^{n} \frac{C_t}{(1+k)^t}}$$

where C_t = coupon or principal payment generated by the bond

   t = time at which the payments are provided

   k = bonds yield to maturity, which reflects the required rate of return by investors

The numerator of the duration formula represents the present value of future payments, weighted by the time interval until the payments occur. The longer the intervals until payments are made, the larger the numerator, and the larger the duration. The denominator of the duration formula represents the discounted future cash flows resulting from the bond, which is the present value of the bond.

ILLUSTRATION The duration of a bond with $1,000 par value and a 7 percent coupon rate, three years remaining to maturity, and a 9 percent yield to maturity is

$$DUR = \frac{\dfrac{\$70}{(1.09)^1} + \dfrac{\$70(2)}{(1.09)^2} + \dfrac{\$1,070(3)}{(1.09)^3}}{\dfrac{\$70}{(1.09)^1} + \dfrac{\$70}{(1.09)^2} + \dfrac{\$1,070}{(1.09)^3}}$$

$$= 2.80 \text{ years}$$

By comparison, the duration of a zero-coupon bond with a similar par value and yield to maturity is

$$DUR = \frac{\dfrac{\$1,000(3)}{(1.09)^3}}{\dfrac{\$1,000}{(1.09)^3}}$$

$$= 3 \text{ years}$$

The duration of a zero-coupon bond is always equal to the bond's term to maturity. The duration of any coupon bond is always less than the bond's term to maturity because some of the payments occur at intervals prior to maturity. ∎

Duration of a Portfolio Bond portfolio managers commonly attempt to immunize their portfolio, that is, insulate it from the effects of interest rate movements. A first step in this process is to determine the sensitivity of their portfolio to interest rate movements. Once the duration of each individual bond is measured, the bond portfolio's duration (DUR_p) can be estimated as

$$DUR_p = \sum_{j=1}^{m} w_j DUR_j$$

where m = number of bonds in the portfolio

w_j = bond j's market value as a percentage of the portfolio market value

DUR_j = bond j's duration

In other words, the duration of a bond portfolio is the weighted average of bond durations, weighted according to relative market value. Financial institutions concerned with interest rate risk may compare their asset duration to their liability duration. A positive difference means that the market value of the institution's assets is more rate sensitive than the market value of its liabilities. Thus, during a period of rising interest rates, the market value of the assets would be reduced by a greater degree than that of the liabilities. The institution's real net worth (market value of net worth) would therefore decrease.

Modified Duration The duration measurement of a bond or a bond portfolio can be modified to estimate the impact of a change in the prevailing bond yields on bond prices. The modified duration (denoted as DUR*) is estimated as

$$\text{DUR}^* = \frac{\text{DUR}}{(1 + k)}$$

where k represents the prevailing yield on bonds.

The modified duration can be used to estimate the percentage change in the bond's price in response to a 1 percentage point change in bond yields. For example, assume that Bond X has a duration of 8 while Bond Y has a duration of 12. Assuming that the prevailing bond yield is 10 percent, the modified duration is estimated for each bond:

Bond X	Bond Y
$\text{DUR}^* = \dfrac{8}{(1 + .10)}$	$\text{DUR}^* = \dfrac{12}{(1 + .10)}$
$= 7.27$	$= 10.9$

Given the inverse relationship between the change in bond yields and the response in bond prices, the estimate of modified duration should be applied such that the bond price moves in the opposite direction from the change in bond yields. According to the modified duration estimates, a 1 percentage point increase in bond yields (from 10 percent to 11 percent) would lead to a 7.27 percent decline in the price of Bond X and a 10.9 percent decline in the price of Bond Y. A 0.5 percentage point increase in yields (from 10 percent to 10.5 percent) would lead to a 3.635 percent decline in the price of Bond X (computed as 7.27×0.5) and a 5.45 percent decline in the price of Bond Y (computed as 10.9×0.5). The percentage increase in bond prices in response to a decrease in bond yields is estimated in the same manner.

The percentage change in a bond's price in response to a change in yield can be expressed more directly with a simple equation:

$$\%\Delta P = -\text{DUR}^* \times \Delta y$$

where

$$\%\Delta P = \textbf{percentage change in the bond's price}$$
$$\Delta y = \textbf{change in yield}$$

The equation above simply expresses the relationship discussed in the preceding paragraphs mathematically. For example, the percentage change in price for Bond X for an increase in yield of 0.2 percentage point would be:

$$\%\Delta P = -7.27 \times 0.002$$
$$= -1.45\%$$

Thus, if interest rates rise by 0.2 percentage point, the price of Bond X will drop 1.45 percent. Similarly, if interest rates decrease by 0.2 percentage point, the price of Bond X will increase by 1.45 percent according to the modified duration estimate.

Estimation Errors from Using Modified Duration If investors
rely strictly on modified duration to estimate the percentage change in the price of a bond, they will tend to overestimate the price decline associated with an increase in rates and underestimate the price increase associated with a decrease in rates.

 Consider a bond with a 10 percent coupon that pays interest annually and has 20 years to maturity. Assuming a required rate of return of 10 percent (the same as the coupon rate), the value of the bond is $1,000. Based on the formula provided earlier, this bond's modified duration is 8.514. If investors anticipate that bond yields will increase by 1 percentage point (to 11 percent), then they can estimate the percentage change in the bond's price to be

$$\%\Delta P = -8.514 \times 0.01$$
$$= -0.08514 \text{ or } -8.514\%$$

If bond yields rise by 1 percentage point as expected, the price (present value) of the bond would now be $920.37. (Verify this new price by using the time value function on your financial calculator.) The new price reflects a decline of 7.96 percent [calculated as ($920.37 − $1,000)/$1,000]. The decline in price is less pronounced than was estimated in the previous equation. The difference between the estimated percentage change in price (8.514 percent) and the actual percentage change in price (7.96 percent) is due to convexity. ■

Bond Convexity A more complete formula to estimate the percentage change in price in response to a change in yield will incorporate the property of convexity as well as modified duration.

The estimated modified duration suggests a linear relationship in the response of the bond price to a change in bond yields. This is shown by the straight line in Exhibit 8.11. For a given 1 percentage point change in bond yields from our initially assumed bond yield of 10 percent, the modified duration predicts a specific change in bond price. However, the actual response of the bond's price to a change in bond yields is convex and is represented by the curve in Exhibit 8.11. Notice that if the bond yield (horizontal axis) changes slightly from the initial level of 10 percent, the difference between the expected bond price adjustment according to the modified duration estimate (the line on Exhibit 8.11) and the bond's actual price adjustment (the convex curve on Exhibit 8.11) is small. For relatively large changes in the bond yield, however, the bond price adjustment as estimated by modified duration is less

Exhibit 8.11
Relationship between
Bond Yields and Prices

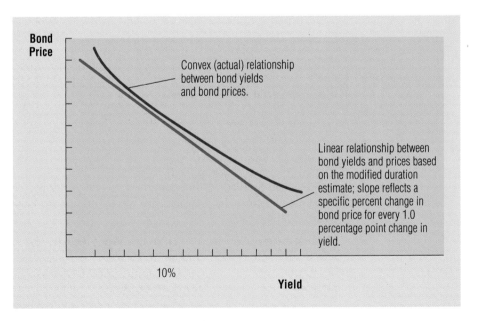

accurate. The larger the change in the bond yield, the larger the error from estimating the change in bond price in response to the change in yield.

Since a bond's price change in response to a change in yields is positively related to the maturity of the bond, convexity is also more pronounced for bonds with a long maturity. The prices of low- or zero-coupon bonds are more sensitive to changes in yields. Similarly, bond convexity is more pronounced for bonds with low (or no) coupon rates.

Bond Investment Strategies Used by Investors

Many investors value bonds and assess their risk when managing investments. Some investors such as bond portfolio managers of financial institutions commonly follow a specific strategy for investing in bonds. Some of the more common strategies are described here.

Matching Strategy

Some investors create a bond portfolio that will generate periodic income that can match their expected periodic expenses. For example, an individual investor may invest in a bond portfolio that will provide sufficient income to cover periodic expenses after retirement. Alternatively, a pension fund may invest in a bond portfolio that will provide employees with a fixed periodic income after retirement. The matching strategy involves estimating future cash outflows and then developing a bond portfolio that can generate sufficient coupon or principal payments to cover those cash outflows.

Laddered Strategy

With a laddered strategy, funds are evenly allocated to bonds in each of several different maturity classes. For example, an institutional investor might create a bond portfolio with one-fourth of the funds invested in bonds with five years until maturity, one-fourth invested in 10-year bonds, one-fourth in 15-year bonds, and one-fourth in 20-year bonds. In five years, when the bonds that had five years until maturity are redeemed, the proceeds can be used to buy 20-year bonds. Since all the other bonds in the portfolio will have five years less until maturity than they had when the portfolio was created, a new investment in 20-year bonds achieves the same maturity structure that existed when the portfolio was created.

The laddered strategy has many variations, but in general, this strategy achieves diversified maturities and therefore different sensitivities to interest rate risk. Nevertheless, because most bonds are adversely affected by rising interest rates, diversification of maturities in the bond portfolio does not eliminate interest rate risk.

Barbell Strategy

http://biz.yahoo.com/c/e
.html Calendar of upcoming announcements of economic conditions that may affect bond prices.

With the barbell strategy, funds are allocated to bonds with a short term to maturity and bonds with a long term to maturity. The bonds with the short term to maturity provide liquidity if the investor needs to sell bonds in order to obtain cash. The bonds with the long term to maturity tend to have a higher yield to maturity than the bonds with shorter terms to maturity. Thus, this strategy allocates some funds to achieving a relatively high return and other funds to covering liquidity needs.

Interest Rate Strategy

With the interest rate strategy, funds are allocated in a manner that capitalizes on interest rate forecasts. This strategy is very active because it requires frequent adjustments in the bond portfolio to reflect the prevailing interest rate forecast.

ILLUSTRATION Consider a bond portfolio with funds initially allocated equally across various bond maturities. If recent economic events result in an expectation of higher interest rates, the bond portfolio will be revised to concentrate on bonds with short terms to maturity. Because these bonds are the least sensitive to interest rate movements, they will limit the potential adverse effects on the bond portfolio's value. The sales of all the intermediate-term and long-term bonds will result in significant commissions paid to brokers.

Now assume that after a few weeks, new economic conditions result in an expectation that interest rates will decline in the future. Again the bond portfolio will be restructured, but now it will concentrate on long-term bonds. If interest rates decline as expected, this type of bond portfolio will be most sensitive to the interest rate movements and will experience the largest increase in value. ■

Although this type of strategy is rational for investors who believe that they can accurately forecast interest rate movements, it is very difficult for even the most sophisticated investors to consistently forecast future interest rate movements. If investors guess wrong, their portfolio will likely perform worse than if they had used a passive strategy of investing in bonds with a wide variety of maturities.

Return and Risk of International Bonds

GL🌐BALASPECTS The value of an international bond represents the present value of future cash flows to be received by the bonds' local investors. Thus, the bond's value changes over time in response to changes in the risk-free interest rate of the currency denominating the bond and in response to changes in the perceived credit risk of the bond. Since these two factors affect the market price of the bond, they also affect the return on the bond to investors over a particular holding period. An additional factor that affects the return to investors from another country is exchange rate risk. The influence of each of these factors is described next.

Influence of Foreign Interest Rate Movements

http://www.bloomberg.com/markets Yields of government securities from major countries.

As the risk-free interest rate of a currency changes, the required rate of return by investors in that country changes as well. Thus, the present value of a bond denominated in that currency changes. A reduction in the risk-free interest rate of the foreign currency will result in a lower required rate of return by investors who use that currency to invest, which results in a higher value for bonds denominated in that currency. Conversely, an increase in the risk-free rate of that currency results in a lower value for bonds denominated in that currency. In general, the return on a bond denominated in a specific currency over a particular holding period is enhanced if the corresponding interest rate declines over that period; the return is reduced if the corresponding interest rate increases over that period. U.S. bond prices may be rising (due to a reduction in U.S. interest rates), while the prices of bonds denominated in other currencies are decreasing (due to an increase in the interest rates of these currencies).

Influence of Credit Risk

As the perceived credit (default) risk of an international bond changes, the risk premium within the required rate of return by investors is affected. Consequently, the present value of the bond changes. An increase in risk causes a higher required rate of return on the bond and therefore lowers the present value of the bond. A reduction in risk causes a lower required rate of return on the bond and increases the present value of the bond. Thus, investors who are concerned about a possible increase in the credit risk of an international bond monitor economic and political conditions in the relevant country that could affect the credit risk.

Influence of Exchange Rate Fluctuations

Changes in the value of the foreign currency denominating a bond affect the U.S. dollar cash flows generated from the bond and thereby affect the return to U.S. investors who invested in the bond. Consider a U.S. financial institution's purchase of bonds with a par value of £2 million, a 10 percent coupon rate (payable at the end of each year), currently priced at par value, and with six years remaining until maturity. Exhibit 8.12 shows how the dollar cash flows to be generated from this investment will differ under three scenarios. The cash flows in the last year also account for the principal payment. The sensitivity of dollar cash flows to the pound's value is obvious.

From the perspective of the investing institution, the most attractive foreign bonds offer a high coupon rate and are denominated in a currency that strengthens over the investment horizon. Although the coupon rates of some bonds are fixed, the future value of any foreign currency is uncertain. Thus, there is a risk that the currency will depreciate and more than offset any coupon rate advantage.

International Bond Diversification

When investors attempt to capitalize on investments in foreign bonds that have higher interest rates than they can obtain locally, they may diversify their foreign bond holdings among countries to reduce their exposure to different types of risk, as explained next.

Reduction of Interest Rate Risk Institutional investors diversify their bond portfolios internationally to reduce exposure to interest rate risk. If all bonds in a portfolio are from a single country, their values will all be systematically affected by interest rate movements in that country. International diversification of bonds reduces the sensitivity of the overall bond portfolio to any single country's interest rate movements.

Reduction of Credit Risk Another key reason for international diversification is the reduction of credit (default) risk. Investment in bonds issued by corporations from a single country can expose investors to a relatively high degree of credit risk. The credit risk of corporations is highly dependent on economic conditions. Shifts in credit risk will likely be systematically related to the country's economic conditions. Because economic cycles differ across countries, there is less chance of a systematic increase in the credit risk of internationally diversified bonds.

Exhibit 8.12   Dollar Cash Flows Generated from a Foreign Bond under Three Scenarios

	Year					
Scenario I (Stable Pound)	1	2	3	4	5	6
Forecasted value of pound	$1.50	$1.50	$1.50	$1.50	$1.50	$1.50
Forecasted dollar cash flows	$300,000	$300,000	$300,000	$300,000	$300,000	$3,300,000
Scenario II (Weak Pound)						
Forecasted value of pound	$1.48	$1.46	$1.44	$1.40	$1.36	$1.30
Forecasted dollar cash flows	$296,000	$292,000	$288,000	$280,000	$272,000	$2,860,000
Scenario III (Strong Pound)						
Forecasted value of pound	$1.53	$1.56	$1.60	$1.63	$1.66	$1.70
Forecasted dollar cash flows	$306,000	$312,000	$320,000	$326,000	$332,000	$3,740,000

Reduction of Exchange Rate Risk Financial institutions may attempt to reduce their exchange rate risk by diversifying among foreign securities denominated in various foreign currencies. In this way, a smaller proportion of their foreign security holdings will be exposed to the depreciation of any particular foreign currency. Because the movements of many foreign currency values within one continent are highly correlated, U.S. investors may reduce exchange rate risk only slightly when diversifying among securities. For this reason, U.S. financial institutions commonly attempt to purchase securities across continents rather than within a single continent, as a review of the foreign securities purchased by pension funds, life insurance companies, or most international mutual funds will reveal.

The conversion of many European countries to a single currency (the euro) in 1999 has resulted in more bond offerings in Europe by European-based firms. Before 1999, a European firm needed a different currency in every European country in which it conducted business and therefore borrowed currency from local banks in each country. Now, a firm can use the euro to finance its operations across several European countries and may be able to obtain all the financing it needs with one bond offering in which the bond is denominated in euros. The firm can then use a portion of the revenue (in euros) to pay coupon payments to bondholders who have purchased the bonds. In addition, European investors based in countries where the euro serves as the local currency can now invest in bonds in other European countries that are denominated in euros without being exposed to exchange rate risk.

Summary

■ The value of a debt security (such as bonds) is the present value of future cash flows generated by that security, using a discount rate that reflects the investor's required rate of return. As market interest rates rise, the investor's required rate of return increases. The discounted value of bond payments declines when the higher discount rate is applied. Thus, the present value of a bond declines, which forces the bond price to decline.

■ Bond prices are affected by the factors that influence interest rate movements, including economic growth, the money supply, oil prices, and the dollar.

Bond prices are also affected by a change in credit risk.

■ Other things being equal, the longer a bond's time to maturity, the more sensitive its price is to interest rate movements. Prices of bonds with relatively low coupon payments are also more sensitive to interest rate movements.

■ Foreign bonds may possibly offer higher returns, but are exposed to exchange rate risk. Investors can reduce their exposure to exchange rate risk by diversifying among various currency denominations.

Point Counter-Point

Does Governance of Firms Affect the Prices of Their Bonds?

Point No. Bond prices are primarily determined by interest rate movements and therefore are not affected by the governance of the firms that issued bonds.

Counter-Point Yes. Bond prices reflect the risk of default. Firms that impose more effective governance

may be able to reduce their default risk and therefore increase the price of the bond.

Who Is Correct? Use the Internet to learn more about this issue. Offer your own opinion on this issue.

Questions and Applications

1. **Bond Investment Decision** Based on your forecast of interest rates, would you recommend that investors purchase bonds today? Explain.

2. **How Interest Rates Affect Bond Prices** Explain the impact of a decline in interest rates on:
   a. An investor's required rate of return.
   b. The present value of existing bonds.
   c. The prices of existing bonds.

3. **Relevance of Bond Price Movements** Why is the relationship between interest rates and bond prices important to financial institutions?

4. **Source of Bond Price Movements** Determine the direction of bond prices over the last year and explain the reason for it.

5. **Exposure to Bond Price Movements** How would a financial institution with a large bond portfolio be affected by falling interest rates? Would it be affected more than a financial institution with a greater concentration of bonds (and fewer short-term securities)? Explain.

6. **Comparison of Bonds to Mortgages** Since fixed-rate mortgages and bonds have similar payment flows, how is a financial institution with a large portfolio of fixed-rate mortgages affected by rising interest rates? Explain.

7. **Coupon Rates** If a bond's coupon rate is above its required rate of return, would its price be above or below its par value? Explain.

8. **Bond Price Sensitivity** Is the price of a long-term bond more or less sensitive to a change in interest rates than the price of a short-term security? Why?

9. **Required Return on Bonds** Why does the required rate of return for a particular bond change over time?

10. **Inflation Effects** Assume that inflation is expected to decline in the near future. How could this affect future bond prices? Would you recommend that financial institutions increase or decrease their concentration in long-term bonds based on this expectation? Explain.

11. **Bond Price Elasticity** Explain the concept of bond price elasticity. Would bond price elasticity suggest a higher price sensitivity for zero-coupon bonds or high-coupon bonds that are offering the same yield to maturity? Why? What does this suggest about the market value volatility of mutual funds containing zero-coupon Treasury bonds versus high-coupon Treasury bonds?

12. **Economic Effects on Bond Prices** An analyst recently suggested that there will be a major economic expansion, which will favorably affect the prices of high-rated fixed-rate bonds, because the credit risk of bonds will decline as corporations experience better performance. Do you agree with the conclusion of the analyst if the economic expansion occurs? Explain.

13. **Impact of War** When tensions rise or a war erupts in the Middle East, bond prices in many countries tend to decline. What is the link between problems in the Middle East and bond prices? Would you expect bond prices to decline more in Japan or in the United Kingdom as a result of the crisis? [The answer is tied to how interest rates may change in those countries.] Explain.

14. **Bond Price Sensitivity** Explain how bond prices may be affected by money supply growth, oil prices, and economic growth.

15. **Impact of Oil Prices** Assume that oil-producing countries have agreed to reduce their oil production by 30 percent. How would bond prices be affected by this announcement? Explain.

16. **Impact of Economic Conditions** Assume that breaking news causes bond portfolio managers to suddenly expect much higher economic growth. How might bond prices be affected by this expectation? Explain. Now assume that breaking news causes bond portfolio managers to suddenly anticipate a recession. How might bond prices be affected? Explain.

Advanced Questions

17. **Impact of the Fed** Assume that bond market participants suddenly expect the Fed to substantially increase the money supply.
    a. Assuming no threat of inflation, how would bond prices be affected by this expectation?
    b. Assuming that inflation may result, how would bond prices be affected?
    c. Given your answers to (a) and (b), explain why expectations of the Fed's increase in the money supply may sometimes cause bond market participants to disagree about how bond prices will be affected.

18. **Impact of the Trade Deficit** Bond portfolio managers closely monitor the trade deficit figures, because the trade deficit can affect exchange rates, which can affect inflationary expectations and therefore interest rates.

    a. When the trade deficit figure is higher than anticipated, bond prices typically decline. Explain why this reaction may occur.

    b. On some occasions, the trade deficit figure has been very large, but the bond markets did not respond to the announcement. Assuming that no other information offset its impact, explain why the bond markets may not have responded to the announcement.

19. **International Bonds** A U.S. insurance company purchased British 20-year Treasury bonds instead of U.S. 20-year Treasury bonds because the coupon rate was 2 percent higher on the British bonds. Assume that the insurance company sold the bonds after five years. Its yield over the five-year period was substantially less than the yield it would have received on the U.S. bonds over the same five-year period. Assume that the U.S. insurance company had hedged its exchange rate exposure. Given that the lower yield was not because of default risk or exchange rate risk, explain how the British bonds could possibly generate a lower yield than the U.S. bonds. (Assume that either type of bond could have been purchased at the par value.)

20. **International Bonds** The pension fund manager of Utterback (a U.S. firm) purchased German 20-year Treasury bonds instead of U.S. 20-year Treasury bonds. The coupon rate was 2 percent lower on the German bonds. Assume that the manager sold the bonds after five years. The yield over the five-year period was substantially more than the yield the manager would have received on the U.S. bonds over the same five-year period. Explain how the German bonds could possibly generate a higher yield than the U.S. bonds for the manager, even if the exchange rate was stable over this five-year period. (Assume that the price of either bond was initially equal to its respective par value.) Be specific.

21. **Implications of a Shift in the Yield Curve** Assume that there is a sudden shift in the yield curve, such that the new yield curve is higher and more steeply sloped today than it was yesterday. If a firm issues new bonds today, would its bonds sell for higher or lower prices than if it had issued the bonds yesterday? Explain.

22. **How Bond Prices May Respond to Prevailing Conditions** Consider the prevailing conditions for inflation (including oil prices), the economy, the budget deficit, and the Fed's monetary policy that could affect interest rates. Based on prevailing conditions, do you think bond prices will increase or decrease during this semester? Offer some logic to support your answer. Which factor do you think will have the biggest impact on bond prices?

23. **Interaction between Bond and Money Markets** Assume that you maintain bonds and money market securities in your portfolio, and you suddenly believe that long-term interest rates will rise substantially tomorrow (even though the market does not share your view), while short-term interest rates will remain the same.

    a. How would you rebalance your portfolio between bonds and money market securities?

    b. If other market participants suddenly recognize that long-term interest rates will rise tomorrow, and they respond in the same manner as you do, explain how the demand for these securities (bonds and money market securities), supply of these securities for sale, and prices and yields of these securities will be affected.

    c. Assume that the yield curve is flat today. Explain how the slope of the yield curve will change tomorrow in response to the market activity.

Interpreting Financial News

Interpret the following statements made by Wall Street analysts and portfolio managers:

a. "Given the recent uncertainty about future interest rates, investors are fleeing from zero-coupon bonds."

b. "Citigroup's stock price increased as a result of the abrupt decline in interest rates, which caused investors to revalue Citigroup's assets."

c. "Bond markets declined when the Treasury flooded the market with its new bond offering."

Managing in Financial Markets

Bond Investment Dilemma As an investor, you plan to invest your funds in long-term bonds. You have $100,000 to invest. You may purchase highly rated municipal bonds at par with a coupon rate of 6 percent; you have a choice of a maturity of 10 years or 20 years. Alternatively, you could purchase highly rated corporate bonds at par with a coupon rate of 8 percent; these bonds also are offered with maturities of 10 years or 20 years. You do not expect to need the funds for five years. At the end of the fifth year, you will definitely sell the bonds because you will need to make a large purchase at that time.

a. What is the annual interest you would earn (before taxes) on the municipal bond? On the corporate bond?

b. Assume that you are in the 20 percent tax bracket. If the level of credit risk and the liquidity for the municipal and corporate bonds are the same, would you invest in the municipal bonds or the corporate bonds? Why?

c. Assume that you expect all yields paid on newly issued notes and bonds (regardless of maturity) to decrease by a total of 4 percentage points over the next two years and to increase by a total of 2 percentage points over the following three years. Would you select the 10-year maturity or the 20-year maturity for the type of bond you plan to purchase? Why?

Problems

1. **Bond Valuation** Assume the following information for an existing bond that provides annual coupon payments:

   Par value = $1,000
   Coupon rate = 11%
   Maturity = 4 years
   Required rate of return by investors = 11%

   a. What is the present value of the bond?
   b. If the required rate of return by investors were 14 percent instead of 11 percent, what would be the present value of the bond?
   c. If the required rate of return by investors were 9 percent, what would be the present value of the bond?

2. **Valuing a Zero-Coupon Bond** Assume the following information for existing zero-coupon bonds:

   Par value = $100,000
   Maturity = 3 years
   Required rate of return by investors = 12%

   How much should investors be willing to pay for these bonds?

3. **Valuing a Zero-Coupon Bond** Assume that you require a 14 percent return on a zero-coupon bond with a par value of $1,000 and six years to maturity. What is the price you should be willing to pay for this bond?

4. **Bond Value Sensitivity to Exchange Rates and Interest Rates** Cardinal Company, a U.S.-based insurance company, considers purchasing bonds denominated in Canadian dollars, with a maturity of six years, a par value of C$50 million, and a coupon rate of 12 percent. Cardinal can purchase the bonds at par. The current exchange rate of the Canadian dollar is $0.80. Cardinal expects that the required return by Canadian investors on these bonds four years from now will be 9 percent. If Cardinal purchases the bonds, it will sell them in the Canadian secondary market four years from now. It forecasts the exchange rates as follows:

Year	Exchange Rate of C$	Year	Exchange Rate of C$
1	$0.80	4	0.72
2	0.77	5	0.68
3	0.74	6	0.66

   a. Refer to earlier examples in this chapter to determine the expected U.S. dollar cash flows to Cardinal over the next four years. Determine the present value of a bond.
   b. Does Cardinal expect to be favorably or adversely affected by the interest rate risk? Explain.
   c. Does Cardinal expect to be favorably or adversely affected by exchange rate risk? Explain.

5. **Predicting Bond Values** (Use the chapter appendix to answer this problem.) Bulldog Bank has just purchased bonds for $106 million that have a par value of $100 million, three years remaining to maturity, and an annual coupon rate of 14 percent. It expects the required rate of return on these bonds to be 12 percent one year from now.

   a. At what price could Bulldog Bank sell these bonds one year from now?
   b. What is the expected annualized yield on the bonds over the next year, assuming they are to be sold in one year?

6. **Predicting Bond Values** (Use the chapter appendix to answer this problem.) Sun Devil Savings has just purchased bonds for $38 million that have a par value of $40 million, five years remaining to maturity, and a coupon rate of 12 percent. It expects the required rate of return on these bonds to be 10 percent two years from now.

a. At what price could Sun Devil Savings sell these bonds two years from now?

b. What is the expected annualized yield on the bonds over the next two years, assuming they are to be sold in two years?

c. If the anticipated required rate of return of 10 percent in two years is overestimated, how would the actual selling price differ from the forecasted price? How would the actual annualized yield over the next two years differ from the forecasted yield?

7. **Predicting Bond Values** (Use the chapter appendix to answer this problem.) Spartan Insurance Company plans to purchase bonds today that have four years remaining to maturity, a par value of $60 million, and a coupon rate of 10 percent. Spartan expects that in three years, the required rate of return on these bonds by investors in the market will be 9 percent. It plans to sell the bonds at that time. What is the expected price it will sell the bonds for in three years?

8. **Bond Yields** (Use the chapter appendix to answer this problem.) Hankla Company plans to purchase either (1) zero-coupon bonds that have 10 years to maturity, a par value of $100 million, and a purchase price of $40 million, or (2) bonds with similar default risk that have five years to maturity, a 9 percent coupon rate, a par value of $40 million, and a purchase price of $40 million.

Hankla can invest $40 million for five years. Assume that the market's required return in five years is forecasted to be 11 percent. Which alternative would offer Hankla a higher expected return (or yield) over the five-year investment horizon?

9. **Predicting Bond Values** (Use the chapter appendix to answer this problem.) The portfolio manager of Ludwig Company has excess cash that is to be invested for four years. He can purchase four-year Treasury notes that offer a 9 percent yield. Alternatively, he can purchase new 20-year Treasury bonds for $2.9 million that offer a par value of $3 million and an 11 percent coupon rate with annual payments. The manager expects that the required return on these same 20-year bonds will be 12 percent four years from now.

a. What is the forecasted market value of the 20-year bonds in four years?

b. Which investment is expected to provide a higher yield over the four-year period?

10. **Predicting Bond Portfolio Value** (Use the chapter appendix to answer this problem). Ash Investment Company manages a broad portfolio with this composition:

	Par Value	Present Market Value	Years Remaining to Maturity
Zero-coupon bonds	$200,000,000	$ 63,720,000	12
8% Treasury bonds	300,000,000	290,000,000	8
11% corporate bonds	400,000,000	380,000,000	10
		$733,720,000	

Ash expects that in four years, investors in the market will require an 8 percent return on the zero-coupon bonds, a 7 percent return on the Treasury bonds, and a 9 percent return on corporate bonds. Estimate the market value of the bond portfolio four years from now.

11. **Valuing a Zero-Coupon Bond**

a. A zero-coupon bond with a par value of $1,000 matures in 10 years. At what price would this bond provide a yield to maturity that matches the current market rate of 8 percent?

b. What happens to the price of this bond if interest rates fall to 6 percent?

c. Given the above changes in the price of the bond and the interest rate, calculate the bond price elasticity.

12. **Bond Valuation** You are interested in buying a $1,000 par value bond with 10 years to maturity and an 8 percent coupon rate that is paid semiannually. How much should you be willing to pay for the bond if the investor's required rate of return is 10 percent?

13. **Predicting Bond Values** A bond you are interested in pays an annual coupon of 4 percent, has a yield to maturity of 6 percent and has 13 years to maturity. If interest rates remain unchanged, at what price would you expect this bond to be selling 8 years from now? Ten years from now?

14. **Sensitivity of Bond Values**

a. How would the present value (and therefore the market value) of a bond be affected if the coupon payments are smaller and other factors remain constant?

b. How would the present value (and therefore the market value) of a bond be affected if the required rate of return is smaller and other factors remain constant?

15. **Bond Elasticity** Determine how the bond elasticity would be affected if the bond price changed

by a larger amount, holding the change in the required rate of return constant.

16. **Bond Duration** Determine how the duration of a bond would be affected if the coupons are extended over additional time periods.

17. **Bond Duration** A bond has a duration of five years and a yield to maturity of 9 percent. If the yield to maturity changes to 10 percent, what should be the percentage price change of the bond?

18. **Bond Convexity** Describe how bond convexity affects the theoretical linear price-yield relationship of bonds. What are the implications of bond convexity for estimating changes in bond prices?

Flow of Funds Exercise

Interest Rate Expectations, Economic Growth, and Bond Financing

Recall that if the economy continues to be strong, Carson Company may need to increase its production capacity by about 50 percent over the next few years to satisfy demand. It would need financing to expand and accommodate the increase in production. Recall that the yield curve is currently upward sloping. Also recall that Carson is concerned about a possible slowing of the economy because of potential Fed actions to reduce inflation. It needs funding to cover payments for supplies. It is also considering issuing stock or bonds to raise funds in the next year.

a. At a recent meeting, the Chief Executive Officer (CEO) stated his view that the economy will remain strong, as the Fed's monetary policy is not likely to have a major impact on interest rates. So he wants to expand the business to benefit from the expected increase in demand for Carson's products. The next step would be to determine how to finance the expansion. The Chief Financial Officer (CFO) stated that if Carson Company needs to obtain long-term funds, the issuance of fixed-rate bonds would be ideal at this point in time because she expects that the Fed's monetary policy to reduce inflation will cause long-term interest rates to rise. If the CFO is correct about future interest rates, what does this suggest about future economic growth, the future demand for Carson's products, and the need to issue bonds?

b. If you were involved in the meeting described here, what do you think needs to be resolved before deciding to expand the business?

c. At the meeting described here, the CEO stated: "The decision to expand should not be dictated by whether interest rates are going to increase or not. Bonds should be issued only if the potential increase in interest rates is attributed to a strong demand for loanable funds rather than the Fed's reduction in the supply of loanable funds." What does this statement mean?

Internet/Excel Exercises

Go to http://www.giddy.org/db/corpspreads.htm. The spreads are listed in the form of basis points (100 basis points = 1 percent) above the Treasury security with the same maturity.

1. First determine the difference between the AAA and CCC spreads. This indicates how much more of a yield is required on CCC-rated bonds versus AAA-rated bonds. Next, determine the difference between AAA and BBB spreads. Then determine the difference between BBB and CCC spreads. Is the difference larger between the AAA and BBB or the BBB and CCC spreads? What does this tell you about the perceived risk of the bonds in these rating categories?

2. Compare the AAA spread for a short-term maturity (such as 2 years) versus a long-term maturity (such as 10 years). Is the spread larger for the short-term or the long-term maturity? Offer an explanation for this.

3. Next, compare the CCC spread for a short-term maturity (such as 2 years) versus a long-term maturity (such as 10 years). Is the spread larger for the short-term or the long-term maturity? Offer an explanation for this. Notice that the difference in spreads for a given rating level among maturities varies with the rating level that you assess. Offer an explanation for this.

Chapter 9: Mortgage Markets

Mortgages are securities used to finance real estate purchases; they are originated by various financial institutions, such as savings institutions and mortgage companies. A secondary mortgage market accommodates originators of mortgages that desire to sell their mortgages prior to maturity. Both the origination process and the secondary market activities for mortgages have become much more complex in recent years. The mortgage markets serve individuals or firms that need long-term funds to purchase real estate. They also serve financial institutions that wish to serve as creditors by lending long-term funds for real estate purchases.

The specific objectives of this chapter are to:

- describe the characteristics of residential mortgages,
- describe the common types of residential mortgages, and
- explain how mortgage-backed securities are used.

Background on Mortgages

A mortgage is a form of debt created to finance investment in property. The debt is secured by the property, so if the property owner does not meet payment obligations, the creditor can seize the property. Financial institutions such as savings institutions and mortgage companies serve as intermediaries by originating mortgages. They accept mortgage applications and assess the creditworthiness of the applicants. They focus on an applicant's monthly income relative to the mortgage payment, but also consider the potential down payment on the property, as well as the applicant's prevailing assets and liabilities. The mortgage represents the difference between the down payment and the value to be paid for the property. The mortgage contract specifies the mortgage rate, the maturity, and the collateral that is backing the loan. The originator charges an origination fee for this process. In addition, if it uses its own funds to finance the property, it will earn profit from the difference between the mortgage rate that it charges and the rate that it paid to obtain the funds.

The means by which mortgage markets facilitate the flow of funds are illustrated in Exhibit 9.1. Financial intermediaries such as savings institutions originate mortgages and finance purchases of homes. Commercial banks originate mortgages for corporations to invest in commercial property. The financial intermediaries that originate mortgages obtain their funding from household deposits. They also obtain funds by selling some of the mortgages that they originate directly to institutional investors. These funds are then used to finance more purchases of homes, condominiums, and commercial property. Overall, mortgage markets allow households and corporations to increase their purchases of homes, condominiums, and commercial property and thereby finance economic growth.

Exhibit 9.1   How Mortgage Markets Facilitate the Flow of Funds

Types of Property Financed with Mortgages

Mortgages are distinguished by type of property. Exhibit 9.2 shows the mortgage debt outstanding over time by type of property. The majority of mortgage debt outstanding is on one- to four-family properties, with nonfarm and nonresidential properties (which includes commercial properties) a distant second. The level of mortgage debt has generally risen over time, although not at a constant rate. During recessions, mortgage debt rises at a slower rate because families tend to avoid housing purchases that would increase their debt. Because residential mortgages (one- to four-family and multifamily) dominate the mortgage market, they receive the most attention in this chapter.

http://www.mbaa.org/
News regarding the mortgage market.

Residential Mortgage Characteristics

When financial institutions originate residential mortgages, the mortgage contract created should specify whether the mortgage is federally insured, the amount of the loan, whether the interest rate is fixed or adjustable, the interest rate to be charged, the maturity, and other special provisions that may vary among contracts. Over time, financial institutions have become more aware of the specific borrowing preferences of those who purchase residential housing. Each family requesting a mortgage may have a different preference for the loan structure.

Insured versus Conventional Mortgages

Mortgages are often classified as federally insured or conventional. Federally insured mortgages guarantee loan repayment to the lending financial institution, thereby protecting it against the possibility of default by the borrower. An insurance fee of 0.5 percent of the loan amount is applied to cover the cost of insuring the mortgage. The guarantor can be either the Federal Housing Administration (FHA) or the Veterans Administration (VA). To qualify for FHA and VA mortgage loans from a financial institution, borrowers must meet various requirements specified by those government agencies. In addition, the maximum mortgage amount is limited by law (although the limit varies among states to account for differences in the cost of housing). The volume of FHA loans has consistently exceeded that of VA loans since 1960. Both types of mortgages have become increasingly popular over the past 30 years.

Exhibit 9.2 Volume of Mortgage Debt by Type of Property

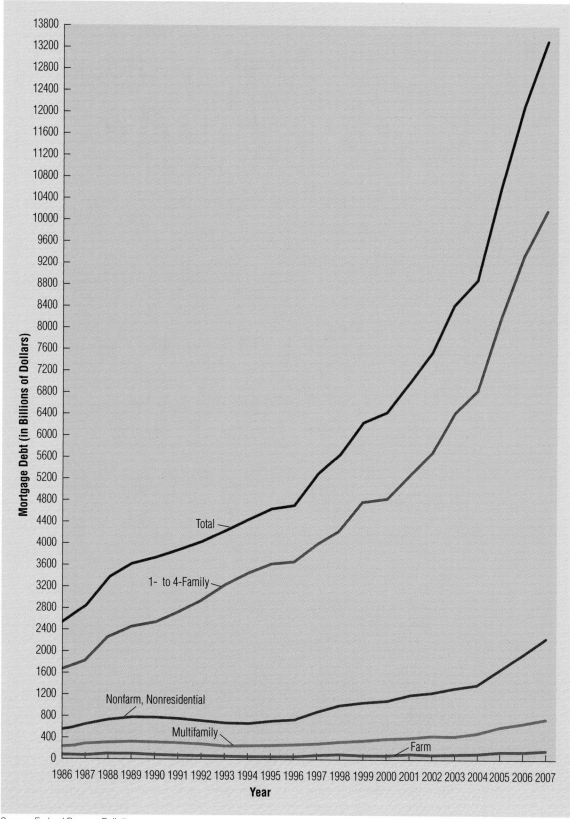

Source: *Federal Reserve Bulletin.*

Financial institutions also provide conventional mortgages. Although not federally insured, they can be privately insured so that the lending financial institutions can still avoid exposure to credit risk. The insurance premium paid for such private insurance will likely be passed on to the borrowers. Lenders can choose to incur the credit risk themselves and avoid the insurance fee. Most participants in the secondary mortgage market will purchase only those conventional mortgages that are privately insured (unless the mortgage's loan-to-value ratio is less than 80 percent).

Types of Residential Mortgages

Various types of residential mortgages are available to homeowners, including the following:

- Fixed-rate mortgages
- Adjustable-rate mortgages
- Graduated-payment mortgages
- Growing-equity mortgages
- Second mortgages
- Shared-appreciation mortgages

Fixed-Rate Mortgages One of the most important provisions in the mortgage contract is the interest rate. It can be specified as a fixed rate or can allow for periodic rate adjustments over time. A **fixed-rate mortgage** locks in the borrower's interest rate over the life of the mortgage. Thus, the periodic interest payment received by the lending financial institution is constant, regardless of how market interest rates change over time. A financial institution that holds fixed-rate mortgages in its asset portfolio is exposed to interest rate risk because it commonly uses funds obtained from short-term customer deposits to make long-term mortgage loans. If interest rates increase over time, the financial institution's cost of obtaining funds (from deposits) will increase. The return on its fixed-rate mortgage loans will be unaffected, however, causing its profit margin to decrease.

Borrowers with fixed-rate mortgages do not suffer from the effects of rising interest rates, but they also fail to benefit from declining rates. Although they can attempt to refinance (obtain a new mortgage to replace the existing mortgage) at the lower prevailing market interest rate, they will incur transaction costs such as closing costs and an origination fee.

Adjustable-Rate Mortgage (ARM) An **adjustable-rate mortgage (ARM)** allows the mortgage interest rate to adjust to market conditions. Its contract will specify a precise formula for this adjustment. The formula and the frequency of adjustment can vary among mortgage contracts. A common ARM uses a one-year adjustment, with the interest rate tied to the average Treasury bill rate over the previous year (for example, the average T-bill rate plus 2 percent may be specified).

Some ARMs now contain an option clause that allows mortgage holders to switch to a fixed rate within a specified period, such as one to five years after the mortgage is originated (the specific provisions vary).

A comparison of fixed and adjustable mortgage rates on new 30-year mortgages is provided in Exhibit 9.3. The fixed rate is typically higher than the adjustable rate at any given point in time when a mortgage is originated. Home buyers attempt to assess future interest rate movements at the time a mortgage is originated. If they expect that interest rates will remain somewhat stable or decline during the period they will own the property, they will prefer an ARM. Conversely, if they expect that interest rates will increase substantially over time, they will prefer a fixed-rate mortgage.

Exhibit 9.3 Comparison of Fixed and Adjustable Mortgage Rates over Time

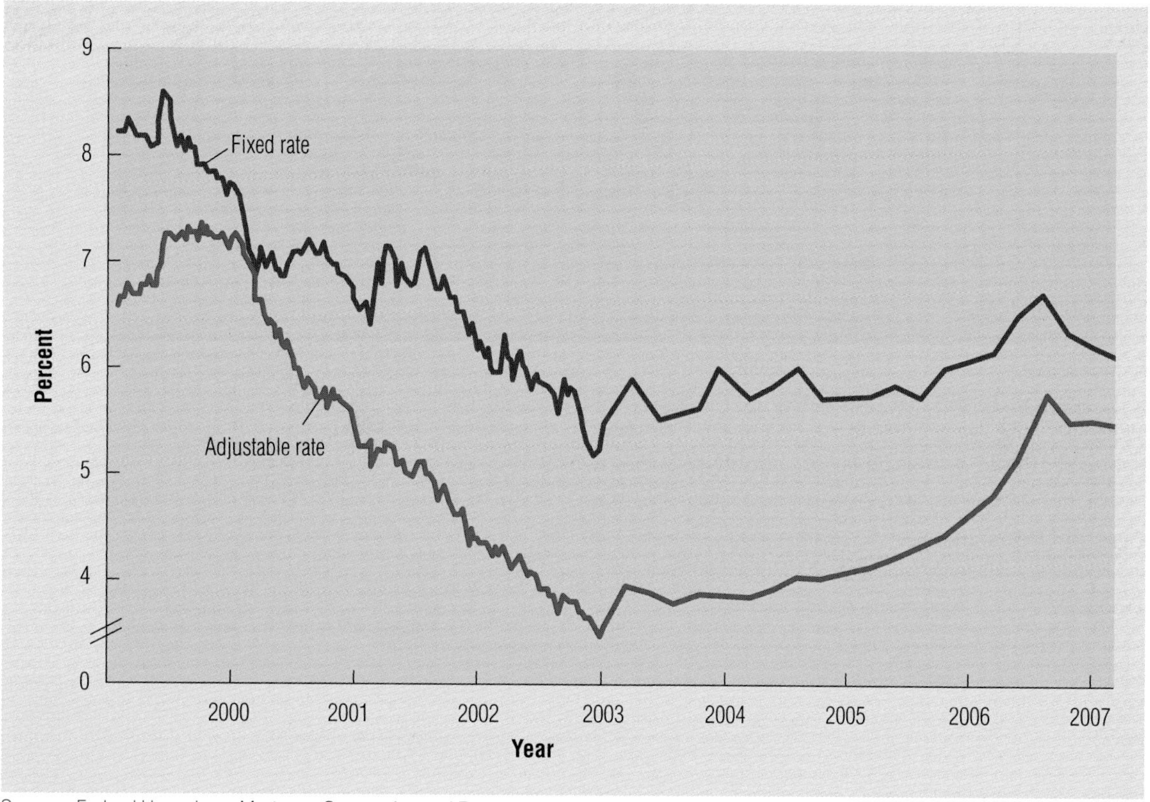

Sources: Federal Home Loan Mortgage Corporation and Federal Reserve.

ARMs from the Financial Institution's Perspective Because the interest rate of an ARM moves with prevailing interest rates, financial institutions can stabilize their profit margin. If their cost of funds rises, so does their return on mortgage loans. For this reason, ARMs have become very popular over time.

Most ARMs specify a maximum allowable fluctuation in the mortgage rate per year and over the mortgage life, regardless of what happens to market interest rates. These so-called caps are commonly 2 percent per year and 5 percent for the mortgage lifetime. To the extent that market interest rates move outside these boundaries, the financial institution's profit margin on ARMs could be affected by interest rate fluctuations. Nevertheless, this interest rate risk is significantly less than that of fixed-rate mortgages.

Although an ARM reduces the uncertainty about the financial institution's profit margin, it creates uncertainty for the borrower, whose future mortgage payments will depend on future interest rates. Because some home purchasers prefer fixed-rate mortgages, lending institutions continue to offer them but, as mentioned, tend to charge a higher rate (at the time of origination) than the initial rate charged on ARMs.

Graduated-Payment Mortgage (GPM) A **graduated-payment mortgage (GPM)** allows the borrower to initially make small payments on the mortgage; the payments increase on a graduated basis over the first 5 to 10 years and then level off. GPMs are tailored for families who anticipate higher income and thus the ability to make larger monthly mortgage payments as time passes. In a sense, they are delaying part of their mortgage payment.

Mortgage quotations like those shown here are provided by *The Wall Street Journal*. The table discloses mortgage rates on a 30-year mortgage quoted by various financial institutions. In addition, it discloses quotes on a 15-year fixed-rate mortgage and a 5-year adjustable-rate mortgage (ARM). Consumers use this information when considering whether to purchase a home or whether to refinance their existing mortgage. *The Wall Street Journal* also provides the home equity loan rate for consumers who want to borrow funds and use their home equity as collateral.

Source: Reprinted with permission of Dow Jones & Company, Inc., from *The Wall Street Journal*, April 4, 2007; permission conveyed through the Copyright Clearance Center, Inc.

Consumer Rates and Returns to Investor

U.S. consumer rates

A consumer rate against its benchmark over the past year

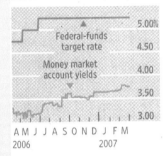

Federal-funds target rate

Money market account yields

5.00%
4.50
4.00
3.50
3.00

A M J J A S O N D J F M
2006   2007

Selected rates

Money market accounts

Bankrate.com avg:		**3.75%**
Geauga Savings Bank		**5.45%**
Newbury, OH		800-472-6250
AmTrust Direct		**5.36%**
Cleveland, OH		888-228-8146
BankUnited		**5.35%**
Miami Lakes, FL		877-779-2265
UFBDirect.com		**5.31%**
Irvine, CA		888-580-0049
iGObanking.com		**5.30%**
Lake Success, NY		888-432-5890

Interest rate	YIELD/RATE (%) Last (●)	Week ago	52-WEEK RANGE (%) Low 0 3 6 9 12 High		3-yr chg (pct pts)
Federal-funds rate target	**5.25**	5.25	4.75	5.25	**4.25**
Prime rate＊	**8.25**	8.25	7.75	8.25	**4.25**
Libor, 3-month	**5.35**	5.35	5.02	5.52	**4.21**
Money market, annual yield	**3.75**	3.76	3.09	3.78	**2.36**
Five-year CD, annual yield	**4.88**	4.87	4.73	5.17	**1.40**
30-year mortgage, fixed†	**5.86**	5.81	5.67	6.51	**0.38**
15-year mortgage, fixed†	**5.60**	5.55	5.46	6.22	**0.82**
Jumbo mortgages, $417,000-plus†	**6.18**	6.13	6.01	6.67	**0.52**
Five-year adj mortgage (ARM)†	**5.63**	5.56	5.53	6.19	**1.48**
New-car loan, 48-month	**6.98**	6.99	6.66	7.08	**1.92**
Home-equity loan, $30,000	**7.44**	7.60	6.31	7.93	**n.a.**

Bankrate.com rates based on survey of over 4,800 online banks. ＊Base rate posted by 75% of the nation's largest banks. † Excludes closing costs.

Sources: Reuters; WSJ Market Data Group; Bankrate.com

Growing-Equity Mortgage A **growing-equity mortgage** is similar to a GPM in that the monthly payments are initially low and increase over time. Unlike the GPM, however, the payments never level off but continue to increase (typically by about 4 percent per +year) throughout the life of the loan. With such an accelerated payment schedule, the entire mortgage may be paid off in 15 years or less.

Second Mortgage A second mortgage can be used in conjunction with the primary or first mortgage. Some financial institutions may limit the amount of the first mortgage based on the borrower's income. Other financial institutions may then offer a second mortgage, with a maturity shorter than on the first mortgage. In addition, the interest rate on the second mortgage is higher because its priority claim against the property in the event of default is behind that of the first mortgage. The higher interest rate reflects greater compensation as a result of the higher risk incurred by the provider of the second mortgage.

Sellers of homes sometimes offer buyers a second mortgage. This is especially common if the old mortgage is assumable and the selling price of the home is much higher than the remaining balance on the first mortgage. By offering a second mortgage, the seller can make the house more affordable and therefore more marketable. The seller and the buyer negotiate specific interest rate and maturity terms.

Shared-Appreciation Mortgage

A **shared-appreciation mortgage** allows a home purchaser to obtain a mortgage at a below-market interest rate. In return, the lender providing the attractive loan rate will share in the price appreciation of the home. The precise percentage of appreciation allocated to the lender is negotiated at the origination of the mortgage.

Mortgage Maturities

During the 1970s, mortgages typically were originated with a 30-year maturity. Recently, however, the 15-year mortgage has become very popular because of the potential savings in total interest expenses. Exhibit 9.4 compares the payments for 15- and 30-year mortgages based on various mortgage loan amounts and an 8 percent rate.

ILLUSTRATION A 30-year $100,000 mortgage at 8 percent requires monthly payments (excluding taxes and insurance) of $733.76. The same mortgage for 15 years would require monthly payments of $955.65, for an approximate total of $172,017 versus $264,155 for the 30-year mortgage. Total payments are lower on mortgages with shorter lives due to the more rapid amortization and consequent lower cumulative interest. Nevertheless, the higher monthly payments on shorter mortgages represent an opportunity cost, as the additional funds could have been put to some other use. Many borrowers, however, believe that this disadvantage is outweighed by the favorable features. ■

From the perspective of the lending financial institution, interest rate risk is lower on a 15-year fixed-rate mortgage than on a 30-year fixed-rate mortgage because the former exists for only half the period of the latter. Accordingly, financial institutions generally charge a lower interest rate on 15-year loans than on 30-year loans, other provisions being equal.

As an alternative to a mortgage with a 15- or 30-year maturity, some borrowers choose a **balloon-payment mortgage,** which requires interest payments for a three- to five-year period. At the end of this period, the borrower must pay the full amount of the principal (the balloon payment). Because no principal payments are made until maturity, the monthly payments are lower. Realistically, most borrowers have not saved enough funds to pay off the mortgage in three to five years, so the balloon payment in effect forces them to request a new mortgage. Therefore, they are subject to the risk that mortgage rates will be higher at the time they refinance the mortgage.

Exhibit 9.4 Comparison of Payments Necessary for 15- and 30-Year Mortgages (Based on an Interest Rate of 8 Percent)

| Amount of Mortgage | Approximate Monthly Payment for a: | | Approximate Total Payments for a: | |
	15-Year Mortgage	30-Year Mortgage	15-Year Mortgage	30-Year Mortgage
$ 75,000	$ 717	$ 550	$129,013	$ 198,116
100,000	956	734	172,017	264,155
200,000	1,911	1,467	344,035	528,310
300,000	2,867	2,201	516,060	792,360
400,000	3,822	2,935	687,960	1,056,600

http://www.bloomberg.com
Click on "Mortgage Calculator." Calculates monthly mortgage payments based on the loan amount, the maturity, and the interest rate.

Amortizing Mortgages Given the maturity and interest rate on a mortgage, an **amortization schedule** can be developed to show the monthly payments broken down into principal and interest. During the early years of a mortgage, most of the payment reflects interest. Over time, as some of the principal is paid off, the interest proportion decreases.

The lending institution that holds a fixed-rate mortgage will receive equal periodic payments over a specified period of time. The amount depends on the principal amount of the mortgage, the interest rate, and the maturity. If insurance and taxes are included in the mortgage payment, then they, too, influence the amount.

ILLUSTRATION   Consider a 30-year (360-month) $100,000 mortgage at an annual interest rate of 8 percent. To focus on the mortgage principal and interest payments, insurance and taxes are not included in this example. A breakdown of the monthly payments into principal versus interest is shown in Exhibit 9.5. In the first month, the interest payment is $666.66, while the principal payment is only $67.10. Note that a larger proportion of interest is paid in the earlier years and a larger portion of principal in the later years. Website calculators are widely available to determine the amortization schedule for any type of mortgage. ■

Institutional Use of Mortgage Markets

Most institutional participation can be broadly classified as either originating and servicing a mortgage (accepting and processing payments) or financing a mortgage. Historically, financial institutions would originate a mortgage, service it, and finance it until it was paid off. The development of an active secondary market has changed the mortgage business in three ways. First, it allows financial institutions that originate mortgages to sell them. Second, the secondary market allows some institutional

Exhibit 9.5
Example of Amortization Schedule for Selected Years (Based on a 30-Year $100,000 Mortgage at 8 Percent)

Payment Number	Payment of Interest	Payment of Principal	Total Payment	Remaining Loan Balance
1	$666.66	$ 67.10	$733.76	$99,932.90
2	666.21	67.55	733.76	99,865.35
100	604.22	129.54	733.76	90,504.68
101	603.36	130.40	733.76	90,374.28
200	482.01	251.75	733.76	72,051.18
201	480.34	253.42	733.76	71,797.76
300	244.52	489.24	733.76	36,188.12
301	241.25	492.51	733.76	35,695.61
359	9.68	724.08	733.76	728.91
360	4.85	728.91	733.76	0

investors to invest in mortgages even if they have no desire to originate or service them. Third, it allows institutional investors in mortgages to sell them whenever they wish to use their funds for other purposes.

Financial Institutions That Originate Mortgages

Mortgage companies originate mortgages and then quickly sell them. The companies do not maintain large mortgage portfolios. The majority of their earnings are generated from origination and servicing fees. Because mortgage companies typically do not finance mortgages themselves, they are not as exposed to interest rate risk as other financial institutions.

Commercial banks and savings institutions are the primary originators of mortgages. Credit unions also originate mortgages for their members and may finance the mortgages they originate.

Participation in the Secondary Market

When financial institutions cannot provide the financing for all the mortgages that they originate, they sell the mortgages in the secondary market. The buyers of mortgages in the secondary mortgage market include various savings institutions, pension funds, life insurance companies, and mutual funds that want to invest in mortgages. If these financial institutions decide to sell the mortgages they invested in prior to maturity, they can sell them in the same secondary market.

ILLUSTRATION USA Savings and Loan originates mortgages and then sells them in the secondary market to Safety Insurance Company. The borrowers continue to send their monthly mortgage payments to USA Savings and Loan, even though USA no longer holds claim to the mortgages. USA processes the payments and charges the new holder of the mortgages (Safety Insurance Company) a fee for the processing. It deducts this fee from the mortgage payments received and sends the remainder to the holder of the mortgages. Two years later, Safety Insurance Company sells the mortgages it is holding in the secondary market. ■

Exhibit 9.6 classifies the mortgages of financial institutions into four borrower categories. Savings institutions are very active in the one- to four-family and multi-family markets. They also participate in commercial mortgages but to a lesser degree. They have continually increased their participation in commercial mortgages in recent years, however. Commercial banks dominate the commercial mortgage market, with life insurance companies behind them. Commercial banks also heavily participate in residential mortgages.

Exhibit 9.6   Mortgage Holdings among Financial Institutions (in Billions of Dollars)

	Mortgages Allocated to:				
	One- to Four-Family	Multi-Family	Commercial	Farm	Total
Savings institutions	$ 870	$ 95	$ 108	$ 1	$ 1,074
Commercial banks	2,052	160	1,137	52	3,402
Life insurance companies	5	45	238	15	304

Source: Federal Reserve, 2007.

Securitization The secondary market for mortgages has been enhanced as a result of **securitization,** or the pooling and repackaging of loans into securities. The securities are then sold to investors, who become the owners of the loans represented by those securities. This process allows for the sale of smaller mortgage loans that could not easily be sold in the secondary market on an individual basis. When several small mortgage loans are packaged together, they become more attractive to the large institutional investors that focus on large transactions. Securitization removes the loans from the balance sheet of the financial institution that provided them. Consequently, securitization can reduce a financial institution's exposure to credit (default) risk or interest rate risk.

Roles of Fannie Mae, Ginnie Mae, and Freddie Mac The Federal National Mortgage Association (Fannie Mae), the Government National Mortgage Association (Ginnie Mae), and the Federal Home Loan Mortgage Association (Freddie Mac) have contributed substantially to the growth of the secondary market for mortgages. Fannie Mae was created by the government in 1938 to develop a more liquid secondary market for mortgages. It issues debt securities and uses the proceeds to purchase mortgages in the secondary mortgage market. It has more than $800 billion of securities outstanding.

Since 1968 Fannie Mae has been a private company. Although it receives no government funding, it is exempt from state income tax and has credit lines from the U.S. Treasury. Thus, it is commonly perceived to be backed by the government, and this enables Fannie Mae to obtain funds by issuing securities at a low cost (at close to the risk-free rate).

Ginnie Mae was created in 1968 as a corporation that is wholly owned by the federal government. It supplies funds to low- and moderate-income homeowners indirectly by facilitating the flow of funds into the secondary mortgage market. It has more than $600 billion of securities outstanding that it has issued to obtain the funds that it invests in mortgages. Freddie Mac was chartered as a corporation by the federal government in 1970 to ensure that sufficient funds flow into the mortgage market. It went public in 1989. Like Fannie Mae, Freddie Mac is exempt from state income tax and has lines of credit with the Treasury. It now has more than $600 billion in debt securities outstanding, which were issued primarily so that it could invest the proceeds in mortgages.

As a result of Fannie Mae, Ginnie Mae, and Freddie Mac, the secondary mortgage market is very liquid. In addition, there is more funding in the mortgage market than there would be without them. Consequently, mortgage rates are more competitive, and housing is more affordable for some homeowners.

The Freddie Mac Accounting Scandal

BEHAVIORAL FINANCE After 2000, Freddie Mac expanded its role by investing not only in mortgages, but also in corporate bonds, strip malls, and hotels. As a result, its overall business became more risky than the type of business for which it was chartered. It then began to use irregular accounting techniques to stabilize its earnings and hide its risk over time. In 2003, the accounting irregularities were publicized, and Freddie Mac's risk became more transparent. This scandal shook the mortgage markets, as market participants were shocked by the lack of oversight over such a large corporation that enjoyed special benefits from the federal government. Freddie Mac was required to restate its earnings over the 2000–2002 period, and its CEO and other senior managers were replaced. ∎

The Fannie Mae Accounting Scandal

BEHAVIORAL FINANCE Fannie Mae also became involved in a scandal involving the manipulating of earnings. During the 1998–2004 period, Fannie Mae commonly shifted its earnings between years to create the illusion of more stable performance and growth in earnings over time, and this led to higher compensation for some of its executives. In May 2006, Fannie Mae agreed to pay $400 million in response to federal allegations of accounting fraud. ■

Unbundling of Mortgage Activities

Given the distinct activities by mortgage market participants, financial institutions must select among them. First, an institution can simply play the role of a mortgage originator, originating mortgages for a fee and then selling them in the secondary market and also selling the servicing rights. Second, it can sell the mortgages but maintain the servicing. Third, it can focus on servicing mortgages originated by other financial institutions. Fourth, it can simply focus on investing in mortgages. Fifth, it can invest in mortgages that it is allowed to service.

A financial institution's choice of mortgage activities depends on whether it prefers to invest funds in mortgages for long periods of time or to generate fee income without tying up funds. The origination role and the servicing role can generate fee income and do not tie up funds. Conversely, investing in mortgages requires a large investment, which is subject to risk, but can also provide a reasonable return.

Many financial institutions prefer to participate in all three activities but to different degrees. For example, an institution may have a fixed amount of funds that it plans to invest in mortgages. When it originates a larger amount of mortgages than it wishes to finance, it sells off the residual. It may also relinquish the servicing of the mortgages that are sold.

The institutional use of mortgage markets is summarized in Exhibit 9.7. Some institutional participation involves neither origination nor financing of mortgages. Brokerage firms participate by matching up sellers and buyers of mortgages in the secondary market. Investment banking firms participate by helping institutional investors hedge their mortgage holdings against interest rate risk by using interest rate swaps, which provide a stream of variable-rate payments in exchange for fixed-rate payments.

Exhibit 9.7 Institutional Use of Mortgage Markets

Type of Financial Institution	Participation in Mortgage Markets
Commercial banks and savings institutions	• Originate and service commercial and residential mortgages and maintain mortgages within their investment portfolios. • Issue mortgage-backed securities to finance some of their mortgage holdings. • Purchase mortgage-based securities.
Credit unions and finance companies	• Originate mortgages and maintain mortgages within their investment portfolios.
Mortgage companies	• Originate mortgages and sell them in the secondary market.
Mutual funds	• May sell shares and use the proceeds to construct portfolios of mortgage pass-through securities.
Brokerage firms	• Serve as financial intermediaries between sellers and buyers of mortgages in the secondary market.
Investment banking firms	• Offer instruments to help institutional investors in mortgages hedge against interest rate risk.
Insurance companies	• Commonly purchase mortgages in the secondary market.

The Wall Street Journal provides the following information related to this chapter on a daily basis:

- Price quotations on mortgage-based securities and on collateralized mortgage obligations.

- Reports on recent performance and new issuances of mortgage-backed securities contained in the "Credit Markets" section.

Valuation of Mortgages

Since mortgages are commonly sold in the secondary market, they are continually valued by institutional investors. The market price (P_M) of mortgages should equal the present value of their future cash flows:

$$P_M = \sum_{t=1}^{n} \frac{C + \text{Prin}}{(1 + k)^t}$$

where C represents the interest payment (similar to a coupon payment on bonds), Prin represents the principal payment made each period, and k represents the required rate of return by investors. Similar to bonds, the market value of a mortgage is the present value of the future cash flows to be received by the investor. Unlike bonds, the periodic cash flows commonly include a payment of principal along with an interest payment.

The required rate of return on a mortgage is primarily determined by the existing risk-free rate for the same maturity. However, other factors such as credit risk and the lack of liquidity will cause the required return on many mortgages to exceed the risk-free rate.

ILLUSTRATION Consider the pricing of a mortgage with 20 years remaining until maturity. Assume that the 20-year risk-free rate is currently 9 percent, which is determined by assessing the yield offered to investors who purchase 20-year Treasury bonds. The required return on 20-year mortgages must be higher than the 20-year risk-free rate to compensate investors for credit risk and the lack of liquidity. Mortgages that have very low credit risk and a high degree of liquidity may require a premium of about 1 or 2 percentage points above the risk-free rate. Thus, they would have a required return of 10 or 11 percent. Mortgages that have more credit risk or less liquidity will require a higher premium beyond the prevailing risk-free rate. ∎

The difference between the 30-year mortgage rate and the 30-year Treasury bond rate is primarily attributed to credit risk and therefore tends to increase during periods when the economy is weak (such as the 2002 recession). The trend in the required rate of return on 30-year fixed-rate mortgages is shown in Exhibit 9.8. The 30-year Treasury bond rate is also shown to illustrate that the mortgage rate is primarily driven by movements in the long-term risk-free rate.

Since the required rate of return on a fixed-rate mortgage is primarily driven by the prevailing risk-free rate (R_f) and the risk premium (RP), the change in the value (and therefore in the market price) of a mortgage (P_M) can be modeled as

$$\Delta P_M = f(\underset{-}{\Delta R_f}, \underset{-}{\Delta RP})$$

Exhibit 9.8
Comparison of 30-Year
Mortgage Rate to
10-Year Treasury
Bond Yield

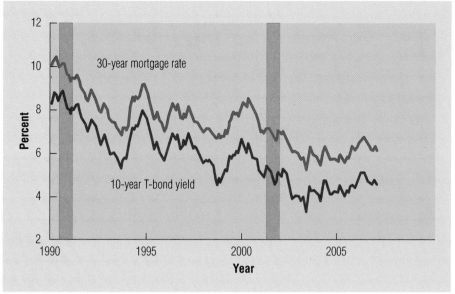

Note: Shaded areas indicate recessions as determined by the NBER.
Source: Federal Reserve.

An increase in either the risk-free rate or the risk premium on a fixed-rate mortgage results in a higher required rate of return when investing in the mortgage and therefore causes the mortgage price to decrease.

The factors that are commonly monitored by mortgage market participants because they affect the risk-free rate or risk premium, and therefore affect mortgage prices, are identified next.

Factors That Affect the Risk-Free Interest Rate

The risk-free rate of interest is driven by inflationary expectations (INF), economic growth (ECON), the money supply (MS), and the budget deficit (DEF):

$$\Delta k = f(\Delta INF, \Delta ECON, \Delta MS, \Delta DEF)$$
$$+ \qquad + \qquad - \qquad +$$

Inflationary Expectations An expectation of higher inflation puts upward pressure on interest rates and therefore on the required return on mortgages. Conversely, an expectation of lower inflation puts downward pressure on interest rates and therefore on the required rate of return on mortgages.

Economic Growth An increase in economic growth can cause an increase in the risk-free interest rate and therefore an increase in the required rate of return on mortgages and a decline in mortgage prices. Conversely, a decrease in economic growth can cause a decrease in the risk-free interest rate and therefore a decrease in the required rate of return on mortgages and an increase in mortgage prices.

Money Supply Growth A relatively high level of money supply growth tends to place downward pressure on the risk-free interest rate (assuming that it does not increase inflation expectations) and therefore places downward pressure on the required rate of return on mortgages and upward pressure on mortgage prices. A relatively low level of money supply growth tends to place upward pressure on the risk-free interest rate and therefore puts upward pressure on the required rate of return on mortgages; the result is lower mortgage prices.

Budget Deficit An increase or decrease in the annual budget deficit changes the federal government's demand for funds and can affect the risk-free interest rate. In 1998, 1999, and 2000, the U.S. government had a budget surplus, which reduced the government's overall demand for loanable funds. This placed downward pressure on the risk-free rate and on the required rate of return on mortgages and increased the price of mortgages.

Factors That Affect the Risk Premium

The average risk premium on all mortgages can change in response to a change in economic growth (ECON):

$$\Delta RP = f(\underset{-}{\Delta \text{ECON}})$$

Strong economic growth tends to improve income or cash flows and reduce the probability that the issuer of a mortgage will default on its debt payments. Conversely, weak economic growth may reduce income or cash flows and therefore increase the probability of default, especially for issuers that are very sensitive to economic conditions.

Summary of Factors Affecting Mortgage Prices

When considering the factors that affect the risk-free rate and the default risk premium, the price movements in a mortgage can be modeled as

$$\Delta P_M = f(\underset{-}{\Delta R_f}, \underset{-}{\Delta RP})$$

or

$$\Delta P_M = f(\underset{-}{\Delta \text{INF}}, \underset{?}{\Delta \text{ECON}}, \underset{+}{\Delta \text{MS}}, \underset{-}{\Delta \text{DEF}})$$

The relationships suggested here assume that other factors are held constant. In reality, other factors are changing as well, which makes it difficult to disentangle the precise impact of each factor on mortgage prices. The effect of economic growth is uncertain because a high level of economic growth can adversely affect mortgage prices by increasing the risk-free rate, but can also favorably affect mortgage prices by lowering the default risk premium.

Exhibit 9.9 summarizes the underlying forces that can affect the long-term risk-free interest rate and the default risk premium and therefore cause the price of a fixed-rate mortgage to change over time. This exhibit provides a broad overview of the factors that must be monitored by mortgage market participants who are attempting to anticipate mortgage prices. International economic conditions can indirectly affect mortgage prices through their effect on the long-term risk-free interest rate.

Indicators of Changes in Mortgage Prices

Mortgage market participants closely monitor economic indicators that may signal future changes in the strength of the economy, which signal changes in the risk-free interest rate and in the required return from investing in mortgages. For example, they monitor indicators of inflation, such as the consumer price index and the producer price index. In general, an unexpected increase in these indexes tends to create expectations of higher interest rates and places downward pressure on fixed-rate mortgage prices. In addition, announcements about the government deficit or the amount

Exhibit 9.9
Framework for Explaining Changes in Mortgage Prices over Time

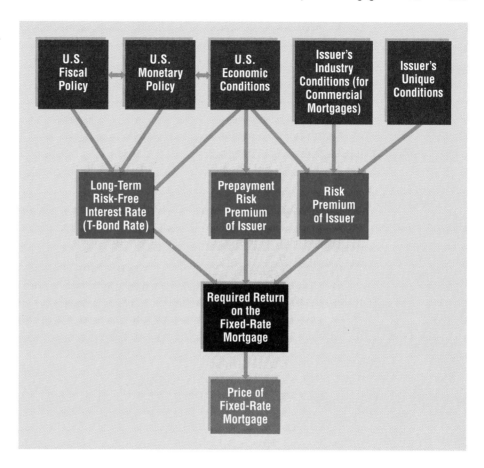

of money that the Treasury hopes to borrow in a Treasury bond auction are closely monitored.

Mortgage market participants also closely monitor indicators of economic growth in the real estate sector, including new sales of single-family homes, construction spending, and office space. An expected increase in housing activity, and therefore in the issuance of mortgages, places downward pressure on mortgage prices.

A decline in indicators such as housing starts can signal a reduction in the issuance of mortgages, which places downward pressure on mortgage rates and upward pressure on mortgage prices. However, such signals reflect a weaker economy, which can increase the default risk premium on some mortgages because the issuers may have more difficulty meeting their payment obligations. The prices of these mortgages are being pressured by opposing forces.

Risk from Investing in Mortgages

Given the uncertainty of the factors that influence mortgage prices, future mortgage prices (and therefore returns) are uncertain. The uncertainty financial institutions face from investing in mortgages is due to three types of risk, as explained next.

Interest Rate Risk

Financial institutions that hold mortgages are subject to interest rate risk because the values of mortgages tend to decline in response to an increase in interest rates. Mortgages are long term but are commonly financed by some financial institutions with short-term deposits, so the investment in mortgages may create high exposure to interest rate risk. Such mortgages can also generate high returns when interest rates fall, but the potential gains are limited because borrowers tend to refinance (obtain new mortgages at the lower interest rate and prepay their mortgages) when interest rates decline.

When investors hold fixed-rate mortgages until maturity, they do not experience a loss due to a change in interest rates. However, holding fixed-rate mortgages to maturity can create an opportunity cost of what the investors might have earned if they had invested in other securities. For example, if interest rates rise consistently from the time fixed-rate mortgages are purchased until they mature, investors who hold the mortgages to maturity gave up the potential higher return that they would have earned if they had simply invested in money market securities over the same period.

Limiting Exposure to Interest Rate Risk Financial institutions can limit their exposure to interest rate risk by selling mortgages shortly after originating them. However, even institutions that use this strategy are partially exposed to interest rate risk. As a financial institution originates a pool of mortgages, it may commit to a specific fixed rate on some of the mortgages. The mortgages are stored in what is referred to as a mortgage pipeline, until there is a sufficient pool of mortgages to sell. By the time the complete pool of mortgages is originated and sold, interest rates may have risen. In this case, the value of the mortgages in the pool may have declined by the time the pool is sold.

Another way financial institutions can limit interest rate risk is by maintaining adjustable-rate residential mortgages. Alternatively, they could invest in fixed-rate mortgages that have a short time remaining until maturity. However, this conservative strategy may reduce the potential gains that could have been earned.

Prepayment Risk

Prepayment risk is the risk that a borrower may prepay the mortgage in response to a decline in interest rates. This type of risk is distinguished from interest rate risk to emphasize that even if investors in mortgages do not need to liquidate the mortgages, they are still susceptible to the risk that the mortgages they hold will be paid off. In this case, the investor receives payment to retire the mortgage and has to reinvest at the prevailing (lower) interest rates. Thus, the interest rate on the new investment will not be as high as the rate that would have been received on the retired mortgages.

Exhibit 9.10 shows mortgage refinancing activity over time. During the 1990s, mortgage refinancing activity was low. When economic growth slowed in the 2001–2002 period, however, interest rates declined, and mortgage refinancing increased substantially. As this exhibit illustrates, financial institutions that invest in fixed-rate mortgages may experience only limited benefits in periods when interest rates decline. Although these mortgages offer attractive yields compared to the prevailing low interest rates, they are commonly retired as a result of refinancing.

Limiting Exposure to Prepayment Risk Financial institutions can insulate against prepayment risk in the same manner that they limit exposure to interest rate risk. They can sell loans shortly after originating them or invest in adjustable-rate mortgages.

Credit Risk

The third type of risk is credit (or default) risk, which is the possibility that borrowers will make late payments or even default. Whether investors sell their mortgages prior to maturity or hold them until maturity, they are subject to credit risk. At one extreme, institutional investors and individual investors who want to avoid credit risk can purchase Treasury bonds as a long-term investment instead of mortgages and

Exhibit 9.10
Mortgage Refinancing
Activity over Time

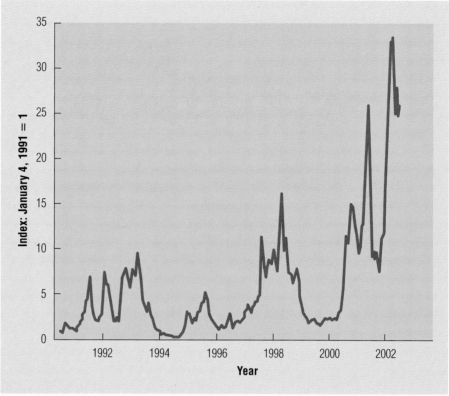

Sources: Mortgage Bankers Association and Federal Reserve.

hold them to maturity. Yet, by doing so, investors would forgo a higher expected return because Treasury bonds do not need to offer a risk premium. Consequently, investors must weigh the higher potential return from investing in mortgages against the exposure to risk (that the actual return could be lower than the expected return).

The probability that a borrower will default is influenced both by economic conditions and by the following characteristics specific to the borrower:

- *Level of equity invested by borrower.* The lower the level of equity invested by the borrower, the higher the probability that the borrower will default. One proxy for this factor is the loan-to-value ratio, which indicates the proportion of the property's value that is financed with debt. When borrowers invest a relatively small amount of equity, the loan-to-value ratio is higher, and borrowers have less to lose in the event that they stop making their mortgage payments. For example, mortgages with a loan-to-value ratio of 90 to 95 percent when they originate default much more frequently than mortgages with a loan-to-value ratio of 80 percent. The loan-to-value ratio is an important factor not only at the time of origination but also throughout the life of the mortgage. If the market value of the property suddenly declines, both the loan-to-value ratio and the probability of default will increase.

- *Borrower's income level.* Borrowers who have a lower level of income relative to the periodic loan payments are more likely to default on their mortgages. Income determines the amount of funds that borrowers have available per month to make mortgage payments. Income levels change over time, however, so it is difficult for mortgage lenders to anticipate whether prospective borrowers will continue to earn their monthly income over the life of the mortgage, especially given the high frequency of layoffs.

- *Borrower's credit history.* Other conditions being similar, borrowers with a history of credit problems are more likely to default on their loans than those without credit problems.

Subprime Mortgages Subprime mortgage loans are granted to borrowers who do not qualify for conventional mortgages. The subprime loans became very popular in the 2003–2004 period when interest rates were very low. Lenders charge a premium of 3 percentage points or more on subprime mortgage loans than on conventional mortgage loans. Many of the subprime loans are initially fixed at a low rate for the first two years and then adjusted in line with market interest rates after that. Market interest rates increased in the 2005–2007 period, which resulted in higher mortgage rates and made it more difficult for subprime borrowers to meet their monthly payments. Consequently, many borrowers defaulted on their subprime mortgage loans in 2007 and several subprime mortgage lenders went bankrupt.

http://loan.yahoo.com/m/
Information about home
values, mortgage rates,
home equity loans, and
credit reports.

Limiting Exposure to Credit Risk Financial institutions can purchase insurance to protect against the possibility of default on mortgages. However, the insurance premium paid may possibly reduce the potential return on the mortgages to the return that could be earned on Treasury bonds with the same maturity. Alternatively, a financial institution can limit its exposure to credit risk by maintaining the mortgages it originates. To the extent that its borrowers are local, the financial institution may have better insight into how they may be affected by economic conditions than if it purchased pools of mortgages from other regions of the country. It may also have more confidence in the creditworthiness of the borrowers it approved for mortgages than it would have buying a pool of mortgages originated by someone else.

Measuring Risk

Financial institutions attempt to estimate the future cash flows to be generated from their mortgage portfolios in various future periods so that they can anticipate how much cash will be available to pay off debt or depositors or to invest in other securities. This task may appear easy for a financial institution whose portfolio is composed of fixed-rate mortgages because the interest payments to be received are known. Prepayment risk and credit risk, however, create uncertainty about the future payments. Sensitivity analysis can be used to forecast the cash flows for different scenarios, such as weak economic conditions and therefore a relatively high default rate on mortgage payments. It can also be used to forecast the mortgage payments for a scenario of low interest rates (and therefore a high amount of mortgage prepayments).

ILLUSTRATION Exhibit 9.11 provides three scenarios for the mortgage prepayment level and a probability of each scenario. The results from assessing all scenarios can be consolidated to develop a probability distribution of expected cash flows one year from now. Assume that the fixed-rate mortgage portfolio has a par value of $100 million with interest payments of $9 million per year, and that none of the mortgages will mature this year. The financial institution can assess the historical relationship between interest rates and the level of prepayments to estimate the percentage of the mortgage portfolio that will be prepaid for a given interest rate scenario.

Notice from the exhibit that the estimate of prepaid principal is very sensitive to the amount of prepayments. If interest rates rise, the level of prepaid principal is low, and the cash flows to be received are relatively low. If interest rates decline, however,

Exhibit 9.11 Prepayment Risk Assessment of Mortgages

Scenario	Probability	Fixed Payments	% of Mortgage Portfolio Prepaid	Prepaid Mortgages	Total Payments Received
Rising interest rates	20%	$9,000,000	3%	$ 3,000,000	$12,000,000
Stable interest rates	50%	9,000,000	7%	7,000,000	16,000,000
Declining interest rates	30%	9,000,000	20%	20,000,000	29,000,000

the level of prepayments is high, and the estimate of the cash flows to be received is very high. In this scenario, the financial institution has to reinvest a large amount of funds (assuming that it does not need to pay off debt or other obligations) at a time when interest rates are low. A financial institution can benefit from anticipating how much cash flow it may receive under various scenarios so that it can prepare to use the cash flows efficiently, regardless of which scenario occurs. ■

The illustration implicitly assumed that the cash flows are solely influenced by the level of mortgage prepayment. In reality, other variables may be influential and could also be included. For example, the sensitivity analysis could incorporate possible scenarios for default rates on the mortgage payments, since a fraction of the expected payments will not be received due to default.

Sensitivity analysis could also be used to estimate the market value of the mortgage portfolio in response to various interest rate conditions because market values of fixed-rate mortgages can easily be estimated for a given estimate of the required rate of return. This would require some assumptions about how the fixed payments and prepaid mortgages received by the institution would be reinvested. Nevertheless, the analysis provides the financial institution with a probability distribution for the market value of its portfolio at a specific point in the future. If the risk of the portfolio is too high (the probability distribution of market values of the portfolio for the specific future time is too wide), the financial institution can restructure its portfolio by including mortgages that are less sensitive to interest rate movements.

Limited Disclosure about Mortgage Valuations Financial institutions that hold mortgages report the value of their mortgage holdings in their financial statements. When interest rates rise, however, the institutions do not revise the reported values of their various mortgage holdings because not all of the market values are known. A financial institution recognizes a loss in the value of the mortgages it holds only when it sells them at a loss. Thus, a financial institution may be highly exposed to rising interest rates, but the values of its mortgage holdings remain unchanged until it sells the mortgages. Although some analysts and sophisticated investors are experienced at assessing the risk of a financial institution's assets, they do not necessarily have enough information to assess the risk.

Mortgage-Backed Securities

As an alternative to selling their mortgages outright in the secondary market, financial institutions can issue **mortgage-backed securities,** which are securities backed by mortgage loans.

Mortgage Pass-Through Securities

Mortgage-backed securities come in various forms; the most common are **mortgage pass-through securities.** A group of mortgages held by a trustee of the issuing institution serves as collateral for these securities. The interest and principal payments on the mortgages are sent to the financial institution, which then transfers (passes through) the payments to the owners of the mortgage-backed securities after deducting fees for servicing and for guaranteeing payments to the owners. This process allows the savings institutions and banks that originate mortgages to adjust their balance sheets. Thus, they can earn fees from servicing the mortgages while avoiding exposure to interest rate risk and credit risk.

Pass-through securities are attractive because they can be purchased in the secondary market without purchasing the servicing of the mortgages that back them. In addition, the holders of pass-throughs are insured in the event of default. Furthermore, pass-throughs are very liquid and can be used as collateral for repurchase agreements.

Interest Rate Risk on Mortgage-Backed Securities A financial institution can reduce its exposure to interest rate risk by issuing pass-through securities because the payments received from mortgages are tied to the payments sent to security owners. To the extent that financial institutions use pass-through securities to finance mortgage holdings, they can insulate their profit margin from interest rate fluctuations. The interest and principal payments to owners of pass-through securities can vary over time. For example, if a higher-than-normal proportion of the mortgages backing the securities are prepaid in a specific period, the payments received by the financial institution will be passed through (after deducting a servicing fee) to the security owners.

Prepayment Risk on Mortgage-Backed Securities Although exposure to interest rate risk is reduced, the owners of pass-through securities are exposed to prepayment risk. The primary source of prepayment risk associated with a mortgage pool obviously arises from a borrower's right to prepay a mortgage in part or in full without penalty, which alters the expected life of mortgages depending upon market rates. Some amount of prepayments may occur naturally. When interest rates decline, however, prepayments are accelerated, and the owners of these securities are adversely affected.

ILLUSTRATION Consider a mortgage pass-through security with a par value of $1 million yielding 10 percent for 30 years. Assume the market rate is 10 percent and that normal prepayments on the mortgage pool are expected to be $500 monthly. The monthly minimum required payment on the security is $8,775. Including the $500 prepayment, the total monthly cash flow from this security is $9,275. The payments to the owner of this pass-through security will be completed after about 23 years. If the market interest rate is expected to remain at 10 percent, the security will still be valued at $1 million even if there are prepayments.

Now reconsider this example but assume that the market interest rate immediately declines from 10 percent to 9 percent. At this lower interest rate, prepayments will increase because borrowers will refinance at the new lower rates and pay off their old mortgages. Assume the expected monthly prepayment amount increases to $800 for a total monthly cash flow of $9,575 on the mortgage pass-through security, or $300 more than in the original example. At this accelerated prepayment rate, the payments to the owner of the mortgage pass-through security will be completed after about 20 years. Thus, the expected life of the security is three years shorter because of the accelerated prepayments. At a market interest rate of 9 percent, the present value of the payments is $1,073,734. The value of the security increased as a result of the decline in market interest rates, but the increase in value is limited because of the prepayments. ■

Owners of mortgage-backed securities are also subject to the possibility that prepayments will decelerate in response to rising interest rates.

ILLUSTRATION Reconsider the previous example but assume that the market rate increases from 10 percent to 11 percent. The monthly prepayment at this higher interest rate will be smaller because individuals are less likely to prepay their mortgages when their mortgage rate is lower than market interest rates. Assume the expected monthly prepayment is only $200 per month, which means the total monthly payment is equal to $8,975, and the security's expected life is about 26 years. Thus, the expected life of the mortgage pass-through security is extended. This is a disadvantage to the owner because the new market interest rate at which funds could be reinvested is higher than the rate the owner is earning on the security. ∎

Types of Mortgage Pass-Through Securities

Five of the more common types of mortgage pass-through securities are the following:

- Ginnie Mae mortgage-backed securities
- Fannie Mae mortgage-backed securities
- Publicly issued pass-through securities
- Participation certificates
- Collateralized mortgage obligations (CMOs)

Each type is described in turn.

Ginnie Mae Mortgage-Backed Securities Financial institutions issue securities that are backed by FHA and VA mortgages. Ginnie Mae (Government National Mortgage Association, or GNMA) guarantees timely payment of principal and interest to investors who purchase these securities. The funds received from their sale are used to finance the mortgages. All mortgages pooled together to back Ginnie Mae pass-throughs must have the same interest rate. The interest rate received by purchasers of the pass-throughs is slightly less (typically 50 basis points) than that rate. This difference reflects a fee to the financial institution servicing the loan and to Ginnie Mae for guaranteeing full payment of interest and principal to the security purchasers. The outstanding balance of Ginnie Mae pass-throughs has grown substantially in recent years.

Fannie Mae Mortgage-Backed Securities Fannie Mae (Federal National Mortgage Association, or FNMA) issues mortgage-backed securities and uses the funds to purchase mortgages. In essence, Fannie Mae channels funds from investors to financial institutions that desire to sell their mortgages. These financial institutions may continue to service the mortgages and earn a fee for this service, while Fannie Mae receives a fee for guaranteeing timely payment of principal and interest to the holders of the mortgage-backed securities. The mortgage payments on mortgages backing these securities are sent to the financial institutions that service the mortgages. The payments are channeled through to the purchasers of mortgage-backed securities, which may be collateralized by conventional or federally insured mortgages.

Some mortgage-backed securities issued by Fannie Mae are stripped by separating the principal and interest payments streams and selling them as separate securities. For investors who purchase these securities, the timing of the payments is uncertain because many mortgages are prepaid when interest rates decline, as described earlier.

Publicly Issued Pass-Through Securities (PIPs) Another type of pass-through security, the publicly issued pass-through security (PIP), is similar to Ginnie Mae mortgage-backed securities, except that it is backed by conventional rather than FHA or VA mortgages. The mortgages backing the securities are insured through private insurance companies.

Participation Certificates (PCs) Freddie Mac (Federal Home Loan Mortgage Association) sells **participation certificates (PCs)** and uses the proceeds to finance the origination of conventional mortgages from financial institutions. This provides another outlet (in addition to Fannie Mae) for savings institutions and savings banks that desire to sell their conventional mortgages in the secondary market.

http://mtgprofessor.com/
secondary_markets.htm
Detailed information on
the secondary mortgage
markets.

Collateralized Mortgage Obligations (CMOs) **Collateralized mortgage obligations (CMOs)** were developed in 1983. They have semiannual interest payments, unlike other mortgage-backed securities, which have monthly payments. The CMOs that represent a particular mortgage pool are segmented into classes (or tranches). The first class has the quickest payback. Any repaid principal is initially sent to owners of the first-class CMOs until the total principal amount representing that class is fully repaid. Then any further principal payments are sent to owners of the second-class CMOs until the total principal amount representing that class is fully repaid. This process continues until principal payments are made to owners of the last-class CMOs. CMO issues commonly have between 3 and 10 classes. Individual CMOs have a maximum average life of 10 years.

The attractive feature of CMOs is that investors can choose a class that fits their maturity desires. Even though investors are still uncertain as to when the securities will mature, they have a better feel for the maturity structure than with other pass-through securities. Investors who purchase third-class CMOs know that they will not receive any principal payments until the first- and second-class CMO owners are completely paid off.

One concern about CMOs is the speed of payback in response to lower interest rates. When interest rates decline, mortgages are prepaid, which accelerates the payments back to the holders of CMOs. This forces investors to reinvest their funds elsewhere under the prevailing (low interest rate) conditions. In some periods, massive mortgage prepayments caused accelerated payments on CMOs. Given the uncertainty about CMOs' maturity (because of the possible prepayment), determining the market valuation of CMOs is very difficult.

CMOs are sometimes segmented into "interest-only" (IO) and "principal-only" (PO) classes. Investors in interest-only CMOs receive only interest payments that are paid on the underlying mortgages. When mortgages are prepaid, the interest payments on the underlying mortgages are terminated, and so are payments to investors in interest-only CMOs. For example, mortgage prepayments may cut off the interest rate payments on the CMO after a few years, even though these payments were initially expected to last five years or more. Consequently, investors in these CMOs could lose 50 percent or more of their initial investment. The relatively high yields offered on interest-only CMOs are attributed to their high degree of risk.

Because investors in the principal-only CMO receive principal payments only, they generally receive payments further into the future. Even though the payments to these investors represent principal, the maturity is uncertain because of possible prepayment of the underlying mortgages. For these investors, accelerated prepayment of mortgages is beneficial because they receive their complete payments earlier than expected.

Although CMOs can be a useful investment, their risks must be recognized. Coastal States Life Insurance Company invested much of its available funds in CMOs and failed in 1992 when the market value of its CMOs declined. Insurance regulators are now closely monitoring insurance companies that may have excessive exposure in CMOs. In addition, many mutual funds that invest in CMOs are reassessing their potential risk. Just as loans to less developed countries and high-yield (junk) bonds received more attention after their performance declined, CMOs are now receiving much more attention. Given their popularity in recent years and the difficulty in measuring their market value, regulators are concerned that a pronounced decline in CMO values could have a severe effect on many financial institutions.

Mortgage-Backed Securities for Small Investors

Pass-through securities have been historically restricted to large investors. Ginnie Mae pass-throughs, for example, come in minimum denominations of $25,000, with $5,000 increments above. In recent years, however, unit trusts have been created that allow small investors to participate. For example, a portfolio of Ginnie Mae pass-through securities is sold in $1,000 pieces. Each piece represents a tiny fraction of the overall portfolio of securities. These unit trusts have become very popular in recent years. The composition of the portfolio is not adjusted over time.

Some mutual funds offer Ginnie Mae funds, which, like the unit trusts, represent a portfolio of GNMA pass-through securities. Unlike a unit trust, the composition of a mutual fund's portfolio can be actively managed (adjusted) by the securities firm over time. As would be expected, the market values of Ginnie Mae unit trusts and mutual funds are inversely related to interest rate movements. A Ginnie Mae unit trust is more sensitive to rising interest rates because its composition cannot be adjusted. A mutual fund can modify the composition of its Ginnie Mae portfolio (shift to shorter-term maturities) if it anticipates increasing interest rates. Some mutual funds also invest in Fannie Mae mortgage-backed securities and PCs (participation certificates), allowing the small investor access to them.

Globalization of Mortgage Markets

GL**🌐**BALASPECTS Mortgage market activity is not confined within a single country. For example, non-U.S. financial institutions hold mortgages on U.S. property, and vice versa. Large U.S. banks often maintain mortgage-banking subsidiaries in foreign countries. In addition, the use of interest rate swaps to hedge mortgages in the United States often involves a non-U.S. counterpart. Although investment banking firms may serve as the financial intermediary, they commonly search for a non-U.S. financial institution that desires to swap variable-rate payments in exchange for fixed-rate payments.

Participants in mortgage markets closely follow international economic conditions because of the potential impact on interest rates. Bond and mortgage portfolio decisions are highly influenced by announcements related to the value of the dollar. In general, any announcements that imply a potentially weaker dollar tend to cause expectations of higher U.S. inflation and therefore higher U.S. interest rates. The demand for fixed-rate mortgages will likely decline in response to such announcements. Announcements that imply a potentially stronger dollar tend to cause the opposite expectations and effects. It is difficult to show evidence of these relationships, however, because expectations do not always occur and often change from one day to the next.

Summary

■ Residential mortgages can be characterized by whether they are federally insured, the type of interest rate used (fixed or floating), and the maturity. Quoted interest rates on mortgages vary at a given point in time, depending on these characteristics.

■ Various types of residential mortgages are available including fixed-rate mortgages, adjustable-rate mortgages, graduated-payment mortgages, growing-equity mortgages, second mortgages, and shared-appreciation mortgages.

■ Mortgage pass-through securities represent mortgages that are serviced by the financial institutions that originated them, but are held by other investors. Five of the more popular types of mortgage pass-through securities are Ginnie Mae securities, Fannie Mae securities, publicly issued securities, participation certificates, and collateralized mortgage obligations (CMOs).

Point Counter-Point

Is the Trading of Mortgages Similar to the Trading of Corporate Bonds?

Point Yes. In both cases, the issuer's ability to repay the debt is based on income. Both types of debt securities are highly influenced by interest rate movements.

Counter-Point No. The assessment of corporate bonds requires an analysis of financial statements representing the firms that issued the bonds. The assessment

of mortgages requires an understanding of the structure of the mortgage market (CMOs, etc.).

Who Is Correct? Use the Internet to learn more about this issue. Offer your own opinion on this issue.

Questions and Applications

1. **FHA Mortgages** Distinguish between FHA and conventional mortgages.

2. **Mortgage Rates and Risk** What is the general relationship between mortgage rates and long-term government security rates? Explain how mortgage lenders can be affected by interest rate movements. Also explain how they can insulate against interest rate movements.

3. **ARMs** How does the initial rate on adjustable-rate mortgages (ARMs) differ from the rate on fixed-rate mortgages? Why? Explain how caps on ARMs can affect a financial institution's exposure to interest rate risk.

4. **Mortgage Maturities** Why is the 15-year mortgage attractive to homeowners? Is the interest rate risk to the financial institution higher for a 15-year or a 30-year mortgage? Why?

5. **Balloon-Payment Mortgage** Explain the use of a balloon-payment mortgage. Why might a financial institution prefer to offer this type of mortgage?

6. **Graduated-Payment Mortgage** Describe the graduated-payment mortgage. What type of homeowners would prefer this type of mortgage?

7. **Growing-Equity Mortgage** Describe the growing-equity mortgage. How does it differ from a graduated-payment mortgage?

8. **Second Mortgages** Why are second mortgages offered by some home sellers?

9. **Shared-Appreciation Mortgage** Describe the shared-appreciation mortgage.

10. **Exposure to Interest Rate Movements** Mortgage lenders with fixed-rate mortgages should benefit when interest rates decline, yet research has shown that such a favorable impact is dampened. By what?

11. **Mortgage Valuation** Describe the factors that affect mortgage prices.

12. **Selling Mortgages** Explain why some financial institutions prefer to sell the mortgages they originate.

13. **Secondary Market** Compare the secondary market activity for mortgages to the activity for other capital market instruments (such as stocks and bonds). Provide a general explanation for the difference in the activity level.

14. **Financing Mortgages** What type of financial institution finances the majority of one- to four-family mortgages? What type of financial institution finances the majority of commercial mortgages?

15. **Mortgage Companies** Explain how a mortgage company's degree of exposure to interest rate risk differs from that of other financial institutions.

Advanced Questions

16. **Mortgage Pass-Through Securities** Describe how mortgage pass-through securities are used. How can the use of pass-through securities reduce a financial institution's interest rate risk?

17. **CMOs** Describe how collateralized mortgage obligations (CMOs) are used and why they have been popular.

18. **Maturities of Pass-Through Securities** Explain how the maturity on pass-through securities can be affected by interest rate movements.

19. **How Secondary Mortgage Prices May Respond to Prevailing Conditions** Consider current conditions that could affect interest rates, including inflation (including oil prices), the economy, the budget deficit, and the Fed's monetary policy. Based on prevailing conditions, do you think the values of mortgages that are sold in the secondary market will increase or decrease during this semester? Offer some logic to support your answer. Which factor do you think will have the biggest impact on the values of existing mortgages?

Interpreting Financial News

Interpret the following comments made by Wall Street analysts and portfolio managers:

a. "If interest rates continue to decline, the interest-only CMOs will take a hit."

b. "Estimating the proper value of CMOs is like estimating the proper value of a baseball player; the proper value is much easier to assess five years later."

c. "When purchasing principal-only CMOs, be ready for a bumpy ride."

Managing in Financial Markets

CMO Investment Dilemma As a manager of a savings institution, you must decide whether to invest in collateralized mortgage obligations (CMOs). You can purchase interest-only (IO) or principal-only (PO) classes. You anticipate that economic conditions will weaken in the future and that government spending (and therefore government demand for funds) will decrease.

a. Given your expectations, would IOs or POs be a better investment?

b. Given the situation, is there any reason why you might not purchase the class of CMOs that you selected in the previous question?

c. Your boss suggests that since CMOs typically have semiannual interest payments, their value at any point in time should be the present value of their future payments. Your boss also says that the valuation of CMOs should be simple. Why is your boss wrong?

Problem

1. **Amortization** Use an amortization table that determines the monthly mortgage payment based on a specific interest rate and principal with a 15-year maturity and then for a 30-year maturity. Is the monthly payment for the 15-year maturity twice the amount for the 30-year maturity or less than twice the amount? Explain.

Flow of Funds Exercise

Mortgage Financing

Carson Company currently has a mortgage on its office building through a savings institution. It is attempting to determine whether it should convert its mortgage from a floating rate to a fixed rate. Recall that the yield curve is currently upward sloping. Also recall that Carson is concerned about a possible slowing of the economy because of potential Fed actions to reduce inflation. The fixed rate that it would pay if it refinances is higher than the prevailing short-term rate, but lower than the rate it would pay from issuing bonds.

a. What macroeconomic factors could affect interest rates and therefore affect the mortgage refinancing decision?

b. If Carson refinances its mortgage, it also must decide on the size of a down payment. If it uses more funds for a larger down payment, it will need to borrow more funds to finance its expansion. Should Carson make a minimum down payment or a larger down payment if it refinances the mortgage? Why?

c. Who is indirectly providing the money that is used by companies such as Carson to purchase office buildings? That is, where does the money that the savings institutions channel into mortgages come from?

Internet/Excel Exercise

1. Assess a mortgage payment schedule such as http://realestate.yahoo.com/realestate/calculators/amortization.html. Assume a loan amount of $120,000, an interest rate of 7.4 percent, and a 30-year maturity. Given this information, what is the monthly payment? In the first month, how much of the monthly payment is interest, and how much is principal? What is the outstanding balance after the first year? In the last month of payment, how much of the monthly payment is interest, and how much is principal? Why is there such a difference in the composition of the principal versus interest payment over time?

WSJ Exercise

Explaining Mortgage Rate Premiums

Review the "Corporate Borrowing Rates and Yields" table next to the "Credit Markets" section of a recent issue of *The Wall Street Journal* to determine the Treasury bond yield. How do these rates compare to the Fannie Mae yield quoted in the "Borrowing Benchmarks" section? Why do you think there is a difference between the Fannie Mae rate and Treasury bond yields?

Part 4: Equity Markets

Equity markets facilitate the flow of funds from individual or institutional investors to corporations. Thus, they enable corporations to finance their investments in new or expanded business ventures. They also facilitate the flow of funds between investors. Chapter 10 describes stock offerings and explains how participants in the stock market monitor firms that have publicly traded stock. Chapter 11 explains the valuation of stocks, describes investment strategies involving stocks, and indicates how a stock's performance is measured. Chapter 12 describes the stock market microstructure and explains how orders are placed and executed on stock exchanges.

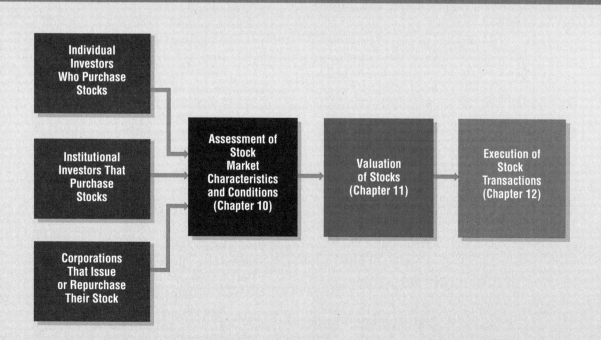

Chapter 10: Stock Offerings and Investor Monitoring

Stock markets facilitate equity investment into firms and the transfer of equity investments between investors.

The specific objectives of this chapter are to:

- explain how stock markets facilitate secondary market trading,
- describe investor participation in the stock markets,
- describe the process of initial public offerings,
- describe the process of secondary offerings,
- explain how the stock market is used to monitor and control firms, and
- describe the globalization of stock markets.

Private Equity

When a firm is created, its founders typically invest their own money in the business. The founders may also invite some family or friends to invest equity in the business. This is referred to as private equity, as the business is privately held, and the owners cannot sell their shares to the public. Young businesses use debt financing from financial institutions and are better able to obtain loans if they have substantial equity invested. Over time, businesses commonly retain a large portion of their earnings and reinvest it to support expansion. This serves as another means of building equity in the firm.

The founders of many firms dream of going public someday so that they can obtain a large amount of financing to support the firm's growth. They may also hope to "cash out" by selling their original equity investment to others. Normally, however, a firm's owners do not consider going public until they want to sell at least $50 million in stock. A public offering of stock may be feasible only if the firm will have a large enough shareholder base to support an active secondary market. With an inactive secondary market, the shares would be illiquid. Investors who own shares and want to sell them would be forced to sell at a discount from the fundamental value, almost as if the firm was not publicly traded. This defeats the purpose of being public. In addition, there are many fixed costs associated with going public, and these costs will be prohibitive for a firm that is raising only a small amount of funds.

Financing by Venture Capital Funds

Even if a firm wants to sell at least $50 million of stock to the public, it may not have a long enough history of stable business performance to be able to raise money from a large number of investors. Private firms that need a large equity investment but are not yet in a position to go public may attempt to obtain funding from a venture capital (VC) fund. VC funds receive money from wealthy investors and from pension funds that are willing to maintain the investment for a long-term period, such as 5 or 10 years. These investors are not allowed to withdraw their money before a specified deadline. VC funds have participated in a number of businesses that ultimately went public and became very successful, including Apple, Microsoft, and Oracle Corporation.

Venture Capital Market The venture capital market brings together the private businesses that need equity funding and the VC funds that can provide funding. One way of doing this is through venture capital conferences where each business briefly makes its pitch as to why it will be very successful (and generate high returns to the VC fund) if it receives equity funding. Alternatively, businesses may submit proposals to VC funds. If a VC fund identifies a proposal that it believes has much potential, it may arrange a meeting with the business's owners and request more detailed information. Most proposals are rejected, however, as VC funds recognize that the majority of new businesses ultimately fail.

Terms of a Venture Capital Deal When a VC fund decides to invest in a business, it will negotiate the terms of its investment, including the amount of funds it is willing to invest. It will also set out clear requirements that the firm must meet, such as providing detailed periodic progress reports. When a VC fund invests in a firm, the fund's managers have an incentive to ensure that the business performs well. Thus, the VC fund managers may serve as advisers to the business. They may also insist on having a seat on the board of directors so that they can influence the firm's future progress. Often, the VC fund provides its funding in stages, based on various conditions that the firm must satisfy. In this way, the VC fund's total investment is aligned with the firm's ability to meet specified financial goals.

Exit Strategy of VC Funds A VC fund typically plans to exit from its original investment within about four to seven years. One common exit strategy is to sell its equity stake to the public after the business engages in a public stock offering. Many VC funds sell their shares of the businesses in which they invest during the first 6 to 24 months after the business goes public. Alternatively, the VC fund may cash out if the company is acquired by another firm, as the acquirer will purchase the shares owned by the VC fund. Thus, the VC fund commonly serves as a bridge for financing the business until the business either goes public or is acquired.

Financing by Private Equity Funds

Private equity funds pool money provided by institutional investors (such as pension funds and insurance companies) and invest in businesses. They also rely heavily on debt to finance their investments. Unlike VC funds, private equity funds commonly take over businesses and manage them. Their managers typically take a percentage of the profits they earn from their investments in return for managing the fund. They also charge an annual fee for managing the fund. Since they commonly purchase a majority stake or all of a business, they have control to restructure the business as they wish. They sell their stake in the business after several years. If they were able to improve the business substantially while they managed it, they should be able to sell their stake to another firm for a much higher price than they paid for it. Alternatively, they may be able to take the business public through an initial public offering (IPO) and cash out at that time.

Public Equity

When a firm goes public, it issues stock in the **primary market** in exchange for cash. Going public has two effects on the firm. First, it changes the firm's ownership structure by increasing the number of owners. Second, it changes the firm's capital structure by increasing the equity investment in the firm, which allows the firm to either pay off some of its debt, or expand its operations, or both.

The stock that the firm issues is a certificate representing partial ownership in the firm. Like debt securities, common stock is issued by firms in the primary market to obtain long-term funds. The purchaser of stock becomes a part owner of the firm, rather than a creditor, however. This ownership feature attracts many investors who want to have an equity interest in a firm, but do not necessarily want to manage their own firm. Owners of stock can benefit from the growth in the value of the firm and therefore have more to gain than creditors. However, they are also susceptible to large losses, as the values of even the most respected corporations have declined substantially in some periods.

The means by which stock markets facilitate the flow of funds are illustrated in Exhibit 10.1. The stock markets are like other financial markets in that they link the surplus units (that have excess funds) with deficit units (that need funds). Corporations issue new stock so that they have sufficient funds to expand their operations. Thus, stock markets allow corporations to increase their expenditures and thereby finance economic growth. Stock issued by corporations may be purchased directly by households. Alternatively, households may invest in shares of stock mutual funds, and the managers of these funds use the proceeds to invest in stocks. Other institutional investors such as pension funds and insurance companies also purchase stocks. The massive growth in the stock market has enabled many corporations to expand to a much greater degree and has allowed investors to share in the profitability of corporations.

In addition to the primary market, which facilitates new financing for corporations, there is also a **secondary market** that allows investors to sell the stock they previously purchased to other investors who want to buy the stock. Thus, the secondary market creates liquidity for investors who invest in stocks. In addition to realizing potential gains when they sell their stock, investors may also receive dividends on a quarterly basis from the corporations in which they invest. Some corporations distribute a portion

Exhibit 10.1   How Stock Markets Facilitate the Flow of Funds

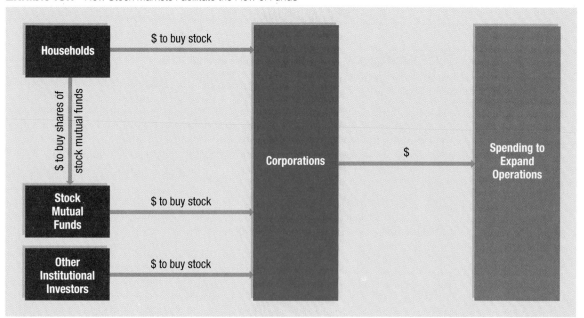

of their earnings to shareholders in the form of dividends, but others reinvest all of their earnings so that they can achieve greater growth.

Ownership and Voting Rights

The owners of small companies also tend to be the managers. In publicly traded firms, however, most of the shareholders are not managers. Thus, they must rely on the firm's managers to serve as agents and to make decisions in the shareholders' best interests.

The ownership of **common stock** entitles shareholders to a number of rights not available to other individuals. Normally, only the owners of common stock are permitted to vote on certain key matters concerning the firm, such as the election of the board of directors, authorization to issue new shares of common stock, approval of amendments to the corporate charter, and adoption of bylaws. Many investors assign their vote to management through the use of a proxy. Many other shareholders simply fail to vote at all. As a result, management normally receives the majority of the votes and can elect its own candidates as directors.

Preferred Stock

Preferred stock represents an equity interest in a firm that usually does not allow for significant voting rights. Preferred shareholders technically share the ownership of the firm with common shareholders and are therefore compensated only when earnings have been generated. Thus, if the firm does not have sufficient earnings from which to pay the preferred stock dividends, it may omit the dividend without fear of being forced into bankruptcy. A cumulative provision on most preferred stock prevents dividends from being paid on common stock until all preferred stock dividends (both current and those previously omitted) have been paid. Normally, the owners of preferred stock do not participate in the profits of the firm beyond the stated fixed annual dividend. All profits above those needed to pay dividends on preferred stock belong to the owners of common stock.

Because the dividends on preferred stock can be omitted, a firm assumes less risk when issuing it than when issuing bonds. If a firm omits preferred stock dividends, however, it may be unable to raise new capital until the omitted dividends have been paid, because investors will be reluctant to make new investments in a firm that is unable to compensate its existing sources of capital.

From a cost perspective, preferred stock is a less desirable source of capital for a firm than bonds. Because a firm is not legally required to pay preferred stock dividends, it must entice investors to assume the risk involved by offering higher dividends. In addition, preferred stock dividends are technically compensation to owners of the firm. Therefore, the dividends paid are not a tax-deductible expense to the firm, whereas interest paid on bonds is tax deductible. Because preferred stock normally has no maturity, it represents a permanent source of financing.

Participation in Stock Markets

Investors can be classified as individual or institutional. The investment by individuals in a large corporation commonly exceeds 50 percent of the total equity. Each individual's investment is typically small, however, causing the ownership to be scattered among numerous individual shareholders.

The various types of institutional investors that participate in the stock markets are summarized in Exhibit 10.2. Because some financial institutions hold large amounts of stock, their collective sales or purchases of stocks can significantly affect stock market prices. Institutional investors also have more resources to monitor a corporation, so corporations recognize that they must respond to advice or complaints by institutional investors in order to keep them as investors. Many institutional investors own millions of shares of a single firm and therefore are willing to spend time to ensure that managers serve the shareholders' interests.

Financial institutions not only participate in stock markets by investing funds, but sometimes issue their own stock as a means of raising funds. Many stock market transactions involve two financial institutions. For example, an insurance company may purchase the newly issued stock of a commercial bank. If the insurance company someday sells this stock in the secondary market, a mutual fund or pension fund may act as the purchaser.

How Investor Decisions Affect Stock Prices Investors make decisions to buy a stock when its market price is below their valuation, which means they believe the stock is undervalued. They may sell their holdings of a stock when the market price is above their valuation, which means they believe the stock is overvalued. Thus, stock valuation drives their investment decisions. Investors commonly disagree on how to value a stock (as explained in Chapter 11). Thus, some investors may believe a stock is undervalued while others believe it is overvalued. This difference in opinions allows for market trading, because it means that there will be buyers and sellers of the same stock at a given point in time.

When there is a shift in the demand for shares or the supply of shares for sale, the equilibrium price changes. When investors revise their expectations of a firm's performance upward, they revise their valuations upward. If the consensus among investors is a favorable revision of expected performance, there are more buy orders for the stock. Demand for shares exceeds the supply of shares for sale, placing upward pressure on the market price. Conversely, if the consensus among investors is lowered expectations of the firm's future performance, there are more sell orders for the stock. The supply of shares for sale exceeds the demand for shares, placing downward pressure on the market price. Overall, the prevailing market price is determined by the participation of investors in aggregate. Stock transactions between investors in the

Exhibit 10.2
Institutional Use of Stock Markets

Type of Financial Institution	Participation in Stock Markets
Commercial banks	• Issue stock to boost their capital base. • Manage trust funds that usually contain stocks.
Stock-owned savings institutions	• Issue stock to boost their capital base.
Savings banks	• Invest in stocks for their investment portfolios.
Finance companies	• Issue stock to boost their capital base.
Stock mutual funds	• Use the proceeds from selling shares to individual investors to invest in stocks.
Securities firms	• Issue stock to boost their capital base. • Place new issues of stock. • Offer advice to corporations that consider acquiring the stock of other companies. • Execute buy and sell stock transactions of investors.
Insurance companies	• Issue stock to boost their capital base. • Invest a large proportion of their premiums in the stock market.
Pension funds	• Invest a large proportion of pension fund contributions in the stock market.

secondary market do not affect the capital structure of the issuer, but merely transfer shares from one investor to another.

Investor Reliance on Information Investors respond to the release of new information that affects their opinions about the firm's future performance. In general, favorable news about the performance of a firm will make investors believe that the firm's stock is undervalued at its prevailing price. The demand for shares of that stock will increase, placing upward pressure on the stock's price. Unfavorable news about the performance of a firm will make investors believe that the firm's stock is overvalued at its prevailing price. Some investors will sell their holdings of that stock, placing downward pressure on the stock's price. Thus, information is incorporated into stock prices through its impact on investors' demand for shares and the supply of shares for sale by investors.

Each stock has its own demand and supply conditions and therefore has a unique market price. Nevertheless, new information about macroeconomic conditions commonly causes expectations for many firms to be revised in the same direction and therefore cause stock prices to move in the same direction.

Investors continually respond to new information in their attempt to purchase stocks that are undervalued or sell any of their stock holdings that are overvalued. When investors properly determine which stocks are undervalued, they can achieve abnormally high returns from investing in those stocks. Thus, the valuation process used by an investor can have a strong influence on the investor's investment performance.

Initial Public Offerings

A corporation first decides to issue stock to the public in order to raise funds. It engages in an **initial public offering (IPO),** which is a first-time offering of shares by a specific firm to the public. An IPO is commonly used not only to obtain new funding but also to offer some founders and VC funds a way to cash out their investment. Even after a firm has gone public, it may need to raise additional equity to support its growth. In that case, it can engage in a secondary offering by issuing additional shares of stock to the public. Some firms have had several secondary offerings to support their expansion. This section describes initial public offerings, and the following section describes secondary offerings.

Process of Going Public

Since firms that engage in an IPO are not well known to investors, they must provide detailed information about their operations and their financial condition. A firm planning on going public normally hires a securities firm (or investment bank) that serves as the lead underwriter for the IPO. The lead underwriter is involved in the development of the prospectus and the pricing and placement of the shares.

Developing a Prospectus A few months before the IPO, the issuing firm (with the help of the lead underwriter) develops a prospectus and files it with the **Securities and Exchange Commission (SEC).** The **prospectus** contains detailed information about the firm and includes financial statements and a discussion of the risks involved. It is intended to provide potential investors with the information they need to decide whether to invest in the firm. Within about 30 days, the SEC will assess the prospectus and determine whether it contains all the necessary information. In many cases, before approving the prospectus, the SEC recommends some changes that provide more information about the firm's financial condition.

Once the SEC approves the prospectus, it is sent to institutional investors who may want to invest in the IPO. In addition, the firm's management and the underwriters of the IPO meet with institutional investors. In many cases, the meetings occur in the form of a road show; the firm's managers travel to various cities and put on a presentation for large institutional investors in each city. The institutional investors are informed of the road show in advance so that they can attend if they may be interested in purchasing shares of the IPO. Some institutional investors may even receive separate individual presentations. Institutional investors are targeted because they may be willing to buy large blocks of shares at the time of the IPO. For this reason, they typically have priority over individual investors in purchasing shares during an IPO.

Pricing The lead underwriter must determine the so-called offer price at which the shares will be offered at the time of the IPO. The price that investors are willing to pay per share is influenced by prevailing market and industry conditions. If other publicly traded firms in the same industry are priced high relative to their earnings or sales, then the price assigned to shares in the IPO will be relatively high.

Before a firm goes public, it attempts to gauge the price that will be paid for its shares. During the road show, the lead underwriter solicits indications of interest in the IPO by institutional investors as to the number of shares that they may demand at various possible offer prices. This process is referred to as bookbuilding.

ILLUSTRATION Saint Louis Company has hired Bucknell Investment Company as its lead underwriter for its IPO. Bucknell organizes a road show for a large set of institutional investors that commonly invest in IPO shares. At the road show, managers from St. Louis Company explain the firm's business and how it will use the IPO proceeds. Then Bucknell contacts the investors to request indications of interest. A summary of its findings is provided in Exhibit 10.3. Based on the feedback received, Bucknell decides that an initial offer price of $11 would be appropriate. This price is low enough that it will almost surely result in sufficient demand for 4 million shares, which would provide $44 million to St. Louis Company. Bucknell is concerned that if it sets the price higher, it might not be able to place all of the shares in the IPO. ■

As a result of the bookbuilding process for setting an offer price, many institutional investors pay a lower price than they would have been willing to pay for the shares. In the preceding example, some institutional investors would have paid $13, but the underwriter used an offer price of $11 for all investors to ensure that at least 4 million shares would be sold. Should the issuing firm be satisfied as long as all the shares are placed? What if St. Louis Company firmly believes that all 4 million shares could have been sold at an offer price of $13 per share? In this case, the firm would have received $52 million (4 million shares × $13 per share), but received only $44 million. It gave up $8 million because the underwriter sold the shares for

Exhibit 10.3
Summary of Bookbuilding Process Just before the IPO

Possible Offer Price	Total Shares Demanded	Total Proceeds to Issuer
$13	3,000,000	$39,000,000
$12	3,500,000	$42,000,000
$11	4,000,000	$44,000,000
$10	4,300,000	$43,000,000

a lower price. In finance terminology, this is referred to as "leaving money on the table." Some issuing firms may be especially concerned that they left money on the table when the market price rises substantially on the day of the IPO, because the price increase may suggest that the demand for shares exceeded the supply of shares for sale on that day. Investment banks might counter that selling the shares at a lower price is appropriate to ensure that all shares can be sold at the offering. If the stock price rises over time (which means that the IPO investors benefit from their investment), the issuing firm may be able to more easily engage in another stock offering in the future because it has gained the trust of the investors.

Some critics suggest that setting a lower offer price provides institutional investors with special favors and may be a way for the investment bank that is underwriting the IPO to attract other business from institutional investors. To the extent that the shares were essentially discounted from their appropriate price, the proceeds that the issuing firm receives from the IPO are lower than it deserves.

In some other countries, an auction process is used for IPOs, and investors pay whatever they bid for the shares. The top bidder's order is accommodated first, followed by the next highest bidder, and so on, until all shares are issued. The issuer can set a minimum price at which the bidding must occur for shares to be issued. This process prevents the underwriter from setting the offer price at a level that is intended to please specific institutional investors.

Allocation of IPO Shares The lead underwriter may rely on a group (called a syndicate) of other securities firms to participate in the underwriting process and share the fees to be received for the underwriting. Each underwriter in the syndicate contacts institutional investors and informs them of the offering. Most of the shares are sold to institutional investors, as it is more convenient for the underwriting syndicate to sell shares in large chunks. Brokerage firms may receive a very small portion (such as 2 percent) of the IPO shares, which they can sell to their individual investors. They normally give priority to their biggest customers.

Transaction Costs The transaction cost to the issuing firm is usually 7 percent of the funds raised. For example, an IPO of $50 million would result in a transaction cost of $3.5 million (7% × $50 million). In addition, the issuer incurs other costs, such as the cost of assessing whether to go public, compiling data for the prospectus, and ensuring that the prospectus is properly written. It also incurs fees from hiring legal or financial advisers during this process. Thus, the total cost of engaging in an IPO may be close to 10 percent of the total offering.

Underwriter Efforts to Ensure Price Stability

The lead underwriter's performance can be partially measured by the movement in the IPO firm's share price following the IPO. If investors quickly sell an IPO stock in the secondary market, there will be downward pressure on the stock's price. If most stocks placed by a particular underwriter perform poorly after the IPO, institutional investors may no longer want to purchase shares underwritten by that underwriter.

Lockup The lead underwriter attempts to ensure stability in the stock's price after the offering by requiring a lockup provision, which prevents the original owners of the firm and the VC firms from selling their shares for a specified period (usually six months from the date of the IPO). The purpose of the lockup provision is to prevent downward pressure that could occur if the original owners or VC firms sold their shares in the secondary market. In reality, however, the provision simply defers the possible excess supply of shares sold in the secondary market. When the lockup period expires, the number of shares for sale in the secondary market may increase abruptly, and the share price commonly declines significantly. In fact, some investors who are allowed to sell their shares before the lockup expiration date now recognize this effect and sell their IPO shares just before the expiration date. Consequently, the stock price begins to decline shortly before that date. Some investment banks attempted to have their analysts provide a positive report just before the lockup expiration date, but the SEC mandated a quiet period to prevent such biased reports before the lockup expiration.

Timing of IPOs

IPOs tend to occur more frequently during bullish stock markets, when potential investors are more interested in purchasing new stocks. Prices of stocks tend to be higher in these periods, and issuing firms attempt to capitalize on such prices.

ILLUSTRATION In the late 1990s, stocks of most firms were priced high relative to their respective earnings or revenues. Investor demand for new stocks was strong. Firms were more willing to engage in IPOs because they were confident that they could sell all of their shares at relatively high prices.

In 2001, the stock market weakened, reducing the valuation of stocks relative to earnings or revenues. For this reason, some firms that planned to go public withdrew their plans. They recognized that their shares would have to be sold for a lower price than they desired. In addition, as economic conditions weakened, some firms cut back on their expansion plans and therefore reduced their need for additional funds. These firms recognized that they should defer their offering until economic conditions were more favorable and stock prices were higher. ∎

Initial Returns of IPOs

The initial (first-day) return of IPOs in the United States has averaged about 20 percent over the last 30 years. Such a return is unusual for a single day and exceeds the typical return earned on stocks over an entire year. The initial return on IPOs was especially high for Internet firms during the 1996–1999 period. During 1998, for example, the mean increase in price on the first trading day following the IPO was 84 percent for Internet stocks. Thus, a $1 million investment in each of the Internet IPOs in 1998 would have resulted in a one-day gain of $840,000. Such a high initial return may indicate that the IPO was underpriced, implying that the offer price was lower than it should have been. In that case, the issuer received less than it should have from issuing the shares. The beneficiaries were the institutional investors that were able to purchase the shares at the low offer price.

ILLUSTRATION On January 15, 1999, an IPO by an Internet stock called Market Watch .com jumped from the initial offer price of $17 per share to $130 per share within the first two hours of trading (a return of about 665 percent at that point) and then declined to $97.50 per share by the end of the day. The one-day return for investors who purchased shares at the offer price was about 474 percent. On December 9, 1999, the IPO for VA Linux had an offer price of $30 per share. By the end of the first day, the price was $239, providing for an initial return of 697 percent for investors who purchased shares at the offer price and sold their shares after one day. ∎

The media attention given to some successful IPOs of Internet firms that turned some small investors into millionaires attracted many other investors who had never invested in the stock market before. Some investors were investing money that they

Results from selected IPOs like those shown here are provided by *The Wall Street Journal.* It identifies firms that went public in the last few weeks and provides their return since the time of the offer price and at the time of the first-day closing price. In many cases, individual investors are unable to obtain shares at the offer price, so the return since the time of the first-day closing may be a more reliable measure of their return. Institutional investors commonly purchase the shares at the offer price. Notice the large difference in the return based on the offer price versus the return based on the first-day closing price. For most IPOs, the return is much higher relative to the offer price. This implies that the stock price rises substantially from the time of the offer until the close of the first day. If the stock price drifts downward over time, however, the returns can be negative even for investors who purchase shares at the offer price.

Source: Reprinted with permission of Dow Jones & Company, Inc., from *The Wall Street Journal,* April 12, 2007; permission conveyed through the Copyright Clearance Center, Inc.

IPO Scorecard
Performance of selected recent IPOs

Company SYMBOL IPO date/Offer price	Wed's close ($)	PCT CHG FROM Offer price	PCT CHG FROM 1st-day close	Company SYMBOL IPO date/Offer price	Wed's close ($)	PCT CHG FROM Offer price	PCT CHG FROM 1st-day close
Veraz Networks **VRAZ** April 5/$8.00	7.00	−12.5	−10.3	Super Micro Cmptr **SMCI** March 29/$8.00	9.54	19.3	8.9
Flagstone Reinsurance **FSR** March 30/$13.50	13.46	−0.3	−0.1	eTelecare Global Sol **ETEL** March 28/$13.50	16.78	24.3	15.3
Capital Prd Ptnrs **CPLP** March 30/$21.50	26.32	22.4	−1.6	Aruba Networks **ARUN** March 27/$11.00	13.52	22.9	−4.5
SenoRx **SENO** March 29/$8.00	8.28	3.5	1.2	CastlePoint **CPHL** March 23/$14.50	15.41	6.3	−4.6
GSI Tech **GSIT** March 29/$5.50	5.24	−4.7	−0.9	Glu Mobile **GLUU** March 22/$11.50	10.14	−11.8	−17.5

Sources: WSJ Market Data Group; Reuters

could not afford to lose, without recognizing the risk involved in investing in Internet stocks. Many of the Internet firms wasted the proceeds of their IPOs and ultimately went bankrupt. The investors who invested in their IPOs lost their entire investments.

Flipping Shares Some investors who know about the unusually high initial returns on IPOs attempt to purchase the stock at its offer price and sell the stock shortly afterward. This strategy is referred to as flipping. Investors who engage in flipping have no intention of investing in the firm over the long run and are simply interested in capitalizing on the initial return that occurs for many IPOs. If many institutional investors flip their shares, they may cause the market price of the stock to decline shortly after the IPO. Thus, underwriters are concerned that flipping may place excessive downward pressure on the stock's price. To discourage flipping, some securities firms make more shares of future IPOs available to institutional investors that retain shares for a relatively long period of time. The securities firms may also prevent institutional investors that engage in flipping from participating in any subsequent IPOs that they underwrite.

Google's IPO

On August 18, 2004, Google engaged in an IPO that attracted massive media attention because of Google's name recognition. Google generated $1.6 billion from the offering, more than four times the value of the combined IPOs by Amazon.com, America Online, Microsoft, Netscape, and Priceline.com. The two co-founders, Larry Page and Sergey Brin, sold a portion of their shares within the IPO for about $40 million each, but retained shares valued at $3 billion each. The Google IPO offers interesting insight into the process by which firms obtain equity funding from investors.

Estimating the Stock's Value Investors attempt to determine the value of the stock that is to be issued so that they can decide whether to invest in the IPO. In the case of Google, some investors used Yahoo! as a benchmark because Yahoo! stock has been publicly traded since 1996. To determine the appropriate price of Google's stock, investors multiplied Google's earnings per share by Yahoo!'s price-earnings ratio. This method has some major limitations, however. First, Google and Yahoo! are not exactly the same type of business. Some investors might argue that Microsoft would be a better benchmark than Yahoo! for Google. If Google has more growth potential than Yahoo!, it may deserve a higher multiple. In addition, Yahoo! and Google use different accounting methods, so estimating a value by comparing the earnings of the two firms is subject to error. These limitations of valuation are discussed in more detail in Chapter 11, but the main point here is that stock valuations are subject to error, especially for IPOs, because their prices were not market determined in the past.

Even the firm issuing stock in an IPO is unsure of its market value, because it is difficult to judge what investors will be willing to pay for the newly issued stock. Google initially expected that its stock would sell for between $118 and $135 per share, but then revised its estimate to below $100 before the IPO.

Google's Communication to Investors before the IPO Like any firm that is about to engage in an IPO, Google provided substantial financial information about its operations and recent performance. However, Google was unique in that it communicated in terms that most investors could easily understand. In addition, it emphasized that it would concentrate on long-term growth rather than on short-term goals such as meeting quarterly earnings targets. Many firms focus on meeting short-term earnings targets, because they know that investors obsess over quarterly earnings and that their stock valuations are influenced by earnings. Google maintained that it could make better decisions if it was not subject to the continual strain of having to satisfy a particular short-term earnings target.

The Auction Process Google's IPO was unique in that it used a Dutch auction process instead of relying almost exclusively on institutional investors. Specifically, it allowed all investors to submit a bid for its stock by a specific deadline. It then ranked the bid prices and determined the minimum price at which it would be able to sell all of the shares that it wished to issue. All bids that were equal to or above that minimum price were accepted, and all bids below the minimum price were rejected.

More than 30 investment banks were involved in the IPO and served as intermediaries between Google and the investors. In a traditional IPO, the investment banks have more responsibility to place the shares, and they tend to focus on placing the shares with institutional investors. Thus, individual investors rarely have access to an IPO. They commonly obtain shares later on the day of the IPO when some of the institutional investors flip their shares. Typically, the individual investors pay a higher price than the offer price paid by institutional investors.

By using a Dutch auction process, Google allowed individual investors to participate directly in the IPO and therefore to obtain shares at the initial offer price. Nevertheless, some interested individual investors decided not to submit a bid during Google's Dutch auction because of the complicated registration process required to purchase the shares. To participate in the auction, they had to complete forms to prove to their respective investment banks that they were financially qualified. Also, some individual investors preferred to wait until after an initial equilibrium price of the stock was established. Consequently, some of these investors decided to buy shares after the auction was completed.

From Google's perspective, the benefit of the auction process was lower costs (as a percentage of proceeds) than with a traditional IPO. The auction process may have saved Google about $20 million in fees. In addition, the auction process allowed Google to attract a diversified investor base, including many individual investors. However, such an auction process is unlikely to be as successful for firms that are not as well known to individual investors as Google.

Results of Google's Dutch Auction Google's auction process resulted in a price of $85 per share, meaning that all investors whose bids were accepted paid $85 per share. Google was able to sell all of its 19.6 million shares at this price, which generated proceeds of $1.67 billion. Recall that Google initially hoped to sell the shares for between $118 and $135 per share. If it could have sold its shares for $120 per share instead of $85 per share, it would have generated an additional $686 million in proceeds from the IPO.

Trading after the Auction Any transactions that occurred after the auction was completed took place in the secondary market, meaning that investors were buying shares that were previously purchased by other investors. Some investors who obtained shares at the time of the IPO sold (flipped) their shares in the secondary market shortly after the auction was completed. The share price increased by 18 percent to $100.34 by the end of the first day, so investors who obtained shares through the auction process and sold their shares at the end of the first day earned an 18 percent return. This also means that investors who purchased their shares at the end of the first day paid 18 percent more than if they had purchased the shares through the auction process.

During the first two days of trading, the trading volume in the secondary market was about 1.7 times the shares issued in the IPO. Clearly, many investors were flipping their shares to benefit from the increased market price after the auction. As of June 2007, Google stock was selling for about $500 per share, or more than five times its original offer price in 2004. Thus, a $10,000 investment in Google stock at the time of the IPO was worth almost $59,000 in less than three years.

Abuses in the IPO Market

BEHAVIORAL FINANCE IPOs have received negative publicity because of several abuses. In 2003, regulators issued new guidelines in an effort to prevent such abuses in the future. Some of the more common abuses are described here.

- *Spinning.* Spinning occurs when an investment bank allocates shares from an IPO to corporate executives who may be considering an IPO or other business that will require the help of an investment bank. The bankers hope that the executives will remember the favor and hire the investment bank in the future.

- *Laddering.* When there is substantial demand for an IPO, some brokers engage in laddering; that is, they encourage investors to place first-day bids for the shares that are above the offer price. This helps to build upward price momentum. Some investors may be willing to participate to ensure that the broker will reserve some shares of the next hot IPO for them.

- *Excessive commissions.* Some brokers have also charged excessive commissions when demand was high for an IPO. Investors were willing to pay the price because they could normally recover the cost from the return on the first day. Since the investment bank set an offer price significantly below the market price that would occur by the end of the first day of trading, investors were willing to accommodate brokers. The gain to the broker was a loss to the issuing firm, however, because its proceeds were less than they would have been if the offer price had been set higher. ■

Long-Term Performance Following IPOs

There is strong evidence that IPOs of firms perform poorly on average over a period of a year or longer. Thus, from a long-term perspective, many IPOs are overpriced at the time of the issue. Investors may be overly optimistic about firms that go public. To the extent that the investors base their expectations on the firm's performance before the IPO, they should be aware that firms do not perform as well after going public as they did before.

ILLUSTRATION Consider the case of MarketWatch.com, whose stock price jumped from the offer price of $17 to $97.50 at the close of the first day. The stock price consistently declined to less than $3 per share or by more than 90 percent within a few years. ■

There is evidence of poor long-term performance on average even when considering all IPOs over various time periods. The weak performance of IPOs may be partially attributed to irrational valuations at the time of the IPO, which were corrected over time. In addition, it may be partially attributed to the firm's managers, who may spend excessively and are less efficient with the firm's funds than they were before the IPO.

Impact of the Sarbanes-Oxley Act on IPOs

The Sarbanes-Oxley Act of 2002 was intended to improve the accuracy of firms' financial statements. Some of its provisions (discussed in more detail later in the chapter) apply to a firm's reporting process at the time of its IPO. The act requires that a firm have an internal control process in place one year before going public. This requirement has improved the quality of the financial reporting. Since it went into effect, investors have made their decisions based on financial information rather than hype. Another factor that has led to more rational investing in IPOs is the media attention given to all the naïve investors who lost money investing in IPOs without understanding them. Since 2002, initial returns on investments in IPOs have generally been smaller, because the demand for IPO shares is not as excessive. At the same time, however, since the initial pricing is more rational, IPO shares have not experienced the long-term downward corrections that prevailed in the late 1990s.

Secondary Stock Offerings

A **secondary stock offering** is a new stock offering by a specific firm whose stock is already publicly traded. Firms engage in secondary stock offerings to raise more equity so that they can more easily expand their operations. A firm that wants to engage in a secondary stock offering must file the offering with the SEC. It will likely hire a securities firm to advise on the number of shares it can sell, to help develop the prospectus submitted to the SEC, and to place the new shares with investors.

Since there is already a market price for the stock of a firm that engages in a secondary offering, the firm hopes that it can issue shares at the existing market price. Given that a secondary offering may involve millions of shares, however, there may not be sufficient demand by investors at the prevailing market price. In this case, the underwriter will have to reduce the price so that it can sell all the new shares. Many secondary offerings cause the market price to decline by 1 to 4 percent on the day of the offering, which reflects the new price at which the increased supply of shares in the market is equal to the demand for the shares. Because of the potential for a decline in the equilibrium price of all of its shares, firms tend to monitor stock market movements when deciding the best time to engage in a secondary stock offering. They are more willing to issue new stock when the market price of their outstanding shares is relatively high and the general outlook for the firm is favorable. Under these conditions, they can issue new shares at a relatively high price, which allows them to generate more funds for a given amount of shares issued.

Corporations sometimes direct their sales of stock toward a particular group, such as their existing shareholders, by giving them **preemptive rights** (first priority) to purchase the new stock. By placing newly issued stock with existing shareholders, the firm avoids diluting ownership. Preemptive rights are exercised by purchasing new shares during the subscription period (which normally lasts a month or less) at the price specified by the rights. Alternatively, the rights can be sold to someone else.

Shelf-Registration

Corporations can publicly place securities without the time lag often caused by registering with the SEC. With this so-called **shelf-registration,** a corporation can fulfill SEC requirements up to two years before issuing new securities. The registration statement contains financing plans over the upcoming two years. The securities are, in a sense, shelved until the firm needs to issue them. Shelf-registrations allow firms quick access to funds without repeatedly being slowed by the registration process. Thus, corporations anticipating unfavorable conditions can quickly lock in their financing costs. Although this is beneficial to the issuing corporation, potential purchasers must realize that the information disclosed in the registration is not continually updated and therefore may not accurately reflect the firm's status over the shelf-registration period.

Stock Exchanges

Any shares of stock that have been issued as a result of an initial public offering or a secondary offering can be traded by investors in the secondary market. In the United States, stock trading between investors occurs on the organized stock exchanges and the over-the-counter (OTC) market.

Organized Exchanges

http://www.nyse.com
New York Stock Exchange market summary, quotes, financial statistics, etc.

Each **organized exchange** has a trading floor where floor traders execute transactions in the secondary market for their clients. Among the most popular organized stock exchanges are the New York Stock Exchange, the American Stock Exchange, the Midwest Stock Exchange, and the Pacific Stock Exchange. The New York Stock Exchange (NYSE) is by far the largest, controlling 80 percent of the value of all organized exchange transactions in the United States. The firms listed on the NYSE are typically much larger than those listed on the other exchanges. For some firms, more than 5 million shares are traded on a daily basis.

Individuals or firms that purchase a seat on a stock exchange become members of the exchange and obtain the right to trade securities there. The term *seat* is somewhat misleading because all trading is carried out by individuals standing in groups. There are 1,366 seats on the NYSE. The price of a seat on the NYSE has exceeded $1 million since 1995. In 2007, the price of a seat was $1.5 million.

The NYSE has two broad types of members: floor brokers and specialists. **Floor brokers** are either commission brokers or independent brokers. **Commission brokers** are employed by brokerage houses and execute orders for clients on the floor of the NYSE. Independent brokers trade for their own account and are not employed by any particular brokerage house. However, they sometimes handle the overflow for brokerage houses and handle orders for brokerage houses that do not employ full-time brokers. The fee independent brokers receive depends on the size and liquidity of the order they trade.

Specialists can match orders of buyers and sellers. In addition, they can buy or sell stock for their own account and therefore create more liquidity for the stock.

The Trading Floor Each organized exchange has a trading floor where the buying and selling of securities take place. The trading floor at the NYSE consists of trading posts and trading booths. The specialists and their clerks maintain 20 trading posts. Above each post, computer monitors display the stocks traded there and the last price for each stock traded at that post. Along the perimeter of the trading floor are about 1,500 trading booths where brokers obtain orders. Once an order is received, the broker will represent that order as an agent at the appropriate trading post. Member firms can also send orders directly to the trading posts through the SuperDot system, which is an electronic system for matching up buy and sell orders for small trades.

The trading that takes place on the floor of an exchange resembles an auction. Any member of the exchange can act as both a seller and a buyer. Those members of the exchange attempting to sell a client's stock strive to obtain the highest price possible, while members purchasing stock for their clients aim for the lowest price possible. When members of the exchange announce the sale of a certain number of shares of a certain stock, they receive bids for that stock by other members. The sellers either accept the highest bid immediately or wait until an acceptable bid is offered.

ILLUSTRATION Maria contacts her brokerage firm (which is a member of the NYSE) and says that she wishes to sell 100 shares of IBM. The broker stores the order and transmits it to the NYSE trading floor either directly through a computer or by telephone. On the floor of the NYSE, the order is initially stored in the SuperDot system. Then, depending on the order details, the order is either routed directly to the specialist's trading post or to the broker's trading booth.

If the order is transmitted directly to the trading post from the SuperDot system, the order will appear on the specialist's display book screen. The specialist can use his own funds to purchase the stock at the prevailing market price if he desires. If the order is transmitted to the broker's trading booth, the brokerage firm's clerk receiving the order will inform its floor broker on the NYSE that a new order has arrived. The floor broker takes the order to the appropriate trading post and can execute the sale of 100 shares of IBM. ■

Trades are now commonly executed electronically at the NYSE.

Listing Requirements The NYSE imposes listing requirements for corporations whose stock is listed there, such as a minimum number of shares outstanding and a minimum level of earnings, cash flow, and revenue over a recent period. Once a stock is listed, the exchange also requires that the share price of the stock be at least $1 per share.

The requirement of a minimum number of shares outstanding is intended to ensure adequate liquidity. For a stock to be liquid, there should be many willing buyers and sellers at any time so that an investor can easily buy or sell the stock at the prevailing market price. In a liquid market, the bid price that brokers are willing to pay for a stock should be just slightly less than the ask price at which they would sell the stock.

The organized stock exchanges charge an initial fee to firms that wish to have their stock listed and meet the requirements. The fee is dependent on the size of the firm. The American Stock Exchange (Amex) also has listing requirements, but they are not as stringent as the NYSE requirements.

As time passes, some new listings occur, along with some delistings. The Amex was about as large as the NYSE in 1970, when about 1,200 firms were listed on each exchange. Since then, listings on the NYSE have increased to more than 2,700, while listings on the Amex have declined to about 800.

Over-the-Counter Market

Stocks not listed on the organized exchanges are traded in the **over-the-counter (OTC) market.** Like the organized exchanges, the OTC market also facilitates secondary market transactions. Unlike the organized exchanges, the OTC market does not have a trading floor. Instead, the buy and sell orders are completed through a telecommunications network. Because there is no trading floor, it is not necessary to buy a seat to trade on this exchange, but it is necessary to register with the SEC.

http://www.nasdaq.com
Trends and other statistical information on various Nasdaq indexes.

Nasdaq Many stocks in the OTC market are served by the **National Association of Securities Dealers Automatic Quotations (Nasdaq),** which is an electronic quotation system that provides immediate price quotations. Firms that wish to have their prices quoted by the Nasdaq must meet specific requirements on minimum assets, capital, and number of shareholders. About 5,000 stocks trade on the Nasdaq. Although most stocks listed in the Nasdaq market are relatively small firms, stocks of some very large firms such as Apple and Intel are also traded there. Transaction costs as a percentage of the investment tend to be higher on the Nasdaq than on the NYSE or the Amex.

The Nasdaq market is composed of two segments, the Nasdaq National Market and the Nasdaq Small Cap Market. The Nasdaq National Market facilitates the trading of large stocks such as Apple and Intel.

Although more stocks are listed on the Nasdaq than on the NYSE, the market value of these stocks is typically much lower than that of stocks listed on the NYSE. The aggregate market value of stocks traded on the Nasdaq is less than one-fourth the aggregate market value of all stocks listed on the NYSE.

In March 1998, the Nasdaq and Amex merged. The Amex is an auction market like the NYSE, while the Nasdaq uses a computerized system. Small companies that are less liquid may benefit from an auction market because the orders are channeled to a trader who stands ready to make a market in that stock. Other stocks may be most easily traded on Nasdaq's computerized telecommunications system. The merger of the Amex and Nasdaq allows investors to have some trades executed automatically on this exchange. For example, an electronic order to purchase 100 shares of a specific firm's stock will be matched with an electronic offer to sell 100 shares of that stock.

In 2007, the NYSE and Nasdaq agencies that regulate trading merged. This reduced the overlap between the rules imposed on firms that execute trades on those exchanges. The firms that execute transactions are now subject to one set of regulations, which makes it easier for them to comply.

OTC Bulletin Board The OTC Bulletin Board lists stocks that have a price below $1 per share. These stocks are sometimes referred to as penny stocks. More than 3,500 stocks are listed here. Many of these stocks were traded in the Nasdaq market but no longer meet Nasdaq requirements. These stocks are less liquid than those traded on exchanges, as there is a very limited amount of trading. They are typically traded by individual investors only. Institutional investors tend to focus on more liquid stocks that can be easily sold in the secondary market at any time.

Pink Sheets In addition, the OTC market has another segment known as the "pink sheets" where even smaller stocks are traded. Like the stocks on the OTC Bulletin Board, these stocks typically do not satisfy the Nasdaq's listing requirements. Financial data on them are very limited, if available at all. Even brokers may not be able to obtain information on many of these firms. Families and officers of these firms commonly control much of the stock.

The pink-sheets market provides quotes for about 5,000 stocks. Because the pink-sheets market does not have the regulatory oversight that exists on other exchanges, fraudulent trading is a serious concern. Companies whose stocks are traded on the pink-sheets market do not have to register with the SEC. Some of the stocks have very little trading volume and may not be traded at all for several weeks. In 2007, firms listed there can qualify for a QX designation if they have continuing business operations that comply with U.S. generally accepted accounting principles (or with accepted accounting principles in their home country). They must report their financial information in English. There are different tiers of a QX designation, depending on whether the stocks also meet additional requirements related to minimum stock price and a minimum number of shareholders. More information about qualifying for the QX designation is provided at http://www.otcqx.com.

Electronic Stock Exchanges

In the mid-1990s, several electronic stock exchanges were created to execute stock transactions electronically. These electronic exchanges, which are known as electronic communications networks (ECNs), are discussed in more detail in Chapter 12. Two of the best-known ECNs are Instinet and Archipelago, which became very popular because of their ability to execute orders efficiently. In April 2005, Nasdaq acquired Instinet. This enhanced Nasdaq's electronic trading efficiency by making its technological platform more competitive. As a result, Nasdaq may be able to attract more new firms to list there after going public.

Archipelago executed orders of Nasdaq and NYSE stocks. Thus, it commonly competed against the NYSE for orders to trade stocks on the NYSE. In January 2006, the NYSE merged with Archipelago. The merger enhanced the NYSE's ability to execute orders efficiently. The merged company is also able to trade Nasdaq-listed stocks through Archipelago's electronic trading system.

Extended Trading Sessions

The NYSE, Amex, and Nasdaq market offer extended trading sessions beyond normal trading hours. A late trading session enables investors to buy or sell stocks after the market closes, and an early morning session (sometimes referred to as a pre-market session) enables them to buy or sell stocks just before the market opens on the following day. Beyond the sessions offered by the exchanges, some ECNs allow for trading at any time. Since many announcements about firms are made after normal trading hours, investors can attempt to take advantage of this information before the market opens the next day. However, the market liquidity during the extended trading sessions is limited. For example, the total trading volume of a widely traded stock at night may be about 5 percent (or less) of its trading volume during the day. Some stocks are rarely traded at all during the night. Thus, a large trade is more likely to jolt the stock price during an extended trading session because a large price adjustment may be necessary to entice other investors to take the opposite position. Some investors attempt to take advantage of unusual stock price movements during extended trading sessions, but are exposed to the risk that the market price will not adjust in the manner that they anticipated.

Stock Quotations Provided by Exchanges

http://www.nasdaq.com
U.S. stock quotes and
charts.

The trading of stocks between investors in the secondary market can cause any stock's price to change. Investors can monitor stock price quotations in financial websites and newspapers. Although the format varies among sources, most quotations provide similar information. Stock prices are always quoted on a per share basis, as in the example in Exhibit 10.4. Use the exhibit to supplement the following discussion of other information in stock quotations.

52-Week Price Range The stock's highest price and lowest price over the previous 52 weeks are commonly listed just to the left of the stock's name. The high and low prices indicate the range for the stock's price over the last year. Some investors use this range as an indicator of how much the stock price fluctuates. Other investors compare this range to the prevailing stock price because they wish to purchase a stock only when its prevailing price is below its 52-week high.

Notice that IBM's 52-week high price was $121.88 and its low price was $80.06 per share. The low price is about 34 percent below the high price, which suggests a wide difference over the last year. When IBM's stock price hit its 52-week low, the company's market value was more than one-third less than it was when the price reached its 52-week high.

Symbol Each stock has a specific symbol that is used to identify the firm. This symbol may be used to communicate trade orders to brokers. Ticker tapes at brokerage firms or on financial news television shows use the symbol to identify each firm. If included in the stock quotations, the symbol normally appears just to the right of the firm's name. Each symbol is usually composed of two to four letters. IBM's ticker symbol is the same as its name. Nike's symbol is NKE, the symbol for Home Depot is HD, and the symbol for Motorola is MOT.

Dividend The annual dividend (DIV) is commonly listed to the right of the firm's name and symbol. It shows the dividends distributed to stockholders over the last year on a per share basis. IBM's dividend is $.56 per share, which indicates an average of $.14 per share for each quarter. The annual dollar amount of dividends paid can be determined by multiplying the dividends per share times the number of shares outstanding.

Dividend Yield Next to the annual dividend, some stock quotation tables also show the dividend yield (Yld), which is the annual dividend per share as a percentage

Exhibit 10.4   Example of Stock Price Quotations

YTD % change	Hi	Lo	Stock	Sym	DIV	Yld%	PE	Vol 100s	Last	Net Chg
+10.3	121.88	80.06	IBM	IBM	.56	.6	20	71979	93.77	+1.06
Year-to-date percentage change in stock price	Highest price of the stock in this year	Lowest price of the stock in this year	Name of stock	Stock symbol	Annual dividend paid per year	Dividend yield, which represents the annual dividend as a percentage of the prevailing stock price	Price-earnings ratio based on the prevailing stock price	Trading volume during the previous trading day	Closing stock price	Change in the stock price on the previous trading day from the close on the day before

of the stock's prevailing price. Since IBM's annual dividend is $.56 per share and its prevailing stock price is $93.77, its stock's dividend yield is

$$\text{Dividend yield} = \frac{\text{Dividends paid per share}}{\text{Prevailing stock price}}$$

$$= \frac{\$.56}{\$93.77}$$

$$= .60\%$$

Some firms attempt to provide a somewhat stable dividend yield over time, but other firms do not.

Price-Earnings Ratio Most stock quotations include the stock's price-earnings (PE) ratio, which represents its prevailing stock price per share divided by the firm's earnings per share (earnings divided by number of existing shares of stock) generated over the last year. IBM's PE ratio of 20 in Exhibit 10.4 is derived by dividing its stock price of $93.77 by the previous year's earnings. PE ratios are closely monitored by some investors who believe that a low PE ratio (relative to other firms in the same industry) signals that the stock is undervalued based on the company's earnings.

Volume Stock quotations also usually include the volume (referred to as "Vol" or "Sales") of shares traded on the previous day. The volume is normally quoted in hundreds of shares. It is not unusual for 1 million shares of a large firm's stock to be traded on a single day. Exhibit 10.4 shows that more than 7 million shares of IBM were traded. Some newspapers also show the percentage change in the volume of trading from the previous day.

Previous Day's Price Quotations Stock quotations show the closing price ("Last") on the previous day. In addition, the change in the price ("Net Chg") is typically provided and indicates the increase or decrease in the stock price from the closing price on the day before.

Stock Index Quotations

http://finance.yahoo.com/?u
Quotations on various U.S. stock market indexes.

Stock indexes serve as performance indicators of specific stock exchanges or of particular subsets of the market. The indexes allow investors to compare the performance of individual stocks with more general market indicators. Some of the more closely monitored indexes are identified next.

Dow Jones Industrial Average The **Dow Jones Industrial Average (DJIA)** is a price-weighted average of stock prices of 30 large U.S. firms. ExxonMobil, IBM, and the Coca-Cola Company are among the stocks included in the index. Although this index is commonly monitored, it has some limitations as a market indicator. First, because the index is price weighted, it assigns a higher weight over time to those stocks that experience higher prices. Therefore, the index tends to have an upward bias in its estimate of the market's overall performance. Second, because the DJIA is based on only 30 large stocks, it does not necessarily serve as an adequate indicator of the overall market or especially of smaller stocks.

Standard & Poor's (S&P) 500 The **Standard & Poor's (S&P) 500 index** is a value-weighted index of stock prices of 500 large U.S. firms. Because this index contains such a large number of stocks, it is more representative of the U.S. stock market

The Wall Street Journal provides a table of quotations on various stock indexes, representing industrial stocks, transportation stocks, utility stocks, a Nasdaq composite, and an index of stocks with small market capitalization. For each stock index, the table discloses the high, low, and closing value based on the previous trading day. The net change and the percentage change in the index value from the day before are also disclosed. In addition, the table provides a range of the index over the previous year and reports the year-to-date (from beginning of the year to present) return and the return over the last three years. Market participants can use this table to compare the past performance of various types of stocks. This comparison may influence their decision regarding what stocks they should sell or buy.

Source: Reprinted with permission of Dow Jones & Company, Inc., from *The Wall Street Journal,* April 6, 2007; permission conveyed through the Copyright Clearance Center, Inc.

Major U.S. Stock-Market Indexes

| | LATEST | | | | | 52-WEEK RANGE | | | %CHG | |
	High	Low	Close	Net chg	%chg	High	Low	%chg	YTD	3-yr. ann.
Dow Jones										
Industrial Average	12572.47	12500.39	12560.20	30.15	0.24	12786.64	10706.14	12.0	0.8	6.0
Transportation Avg	4920.22	4854.85	4917.06	25.29	0.52	5178.37	4141.62	4.0	7.8	18.5
Utility Average	510.84	506.92	510.34	2.11	0.42	510.34	382.49	29.8	11.7	21.8
Wilshire 5000	14650.43	14573.56	14640.38	45.28	0.31	14796.54	12296.92	10.3	2.7	9.1
Nasdaq Stock Market										
Nasdaq Composite	2471.34	2455.60	2471.34	12.65	0.51	2524.94	2020.39	4.7	2.3	5.9
Nasdaq 100	1812.94	1798.53	1812.94	11.20	0.62	1846.34	1451.88	4.2	3.2	6.3
Standard & Poor's										
500 Index	1444.88	1436.67	1443.76	4.39	0.30	1459.68	1223.69	10.3	1.8	7.9
MidCap 400	863.20	858.65	861.79	2.44	0.28	867.61	712.86	7.7	7.1	11.8
SmallCap 600	418.55	416.84	418.17	0.99	0.24	422.69	348.69	5.7	4.5	12.5
Other Indexes										
Russell 2000	813.90	810.35	813.35	2.56	0.32	829.44	671.94	6.1	3.3	10.3
NYSE Composite	9435.20	9386.91	9426.57	28.01	0.30	9453.93	7719.78	12.8	3.1	12.0
NYSE Arca Tech 100	902.29	896.14	902.27	5.29	0.59	916.51	733.86	2.0	3.1	6.5
Value Line	479.95	477.75	479.59	1.69	0.35	484.79	396.73	6.5	4.8	7.4
Amex Biotech	791.61	778.58	791.48	11.49	1.47	791.48	622.13	15.0	4.9	12.5
Amex Pharmaceutical	350.65	347.83	350.03	1.96	0.56	362.26	318.92	6.8	1.4	2.3
PHLX§ KBW Bank	113.67	112.76	113.52	0.35	0.31	121.06	105.34	5.6	-3.4	4.1
PHLX§ Gold/Silver	144.16	142.37	142.61	-0.37	-0.26	168.62	120.08	-4.4	0.3	11.9
PHLX§ Oil Service	221.16	218.69	219.83	0.44	0.20	235.34	173.36	1.6	10.0	29.5
PHLX§ Semiconductor	476.48	472.70	475.60	2.58	0.55	529.30	384.88	-9.3	1.6	-2.9
CBOE Volatility	13.66	12.69	13.23	-0.01	-0.08	23.81	9.89	15.5	14.4	-4.0

§Philadelphia Stock Exchange

Sources: **Reuters**; WSJ Market Data Group

than the DJIA. However, because the S&P 500 index focuses on large stocks, it does not serve as a useful indicator for stock prices of smaller firms.

Wilshire 5000 Total Market Index The Wilshire 5000 Total Market Index was created in 1974 to reflect the values of 5,000 U.S. stocks. Since more stocks have been added over time, the index now contains more than 5,000 stocks. It represents the broadest index of the U.S. stock market. It is widely quoted in financial media and closely monitored by the Federal Reserve and many financial institutions.

The Wall Street Journal provides detailed information beyond stock index quotations that can be used to review stock market conditions during the previous day.

- The proportion of stocks that advanced versus the proportion that declined (useful for determining the general market sentiment).
- Biggest percentage of gainers and losers (these stocks may be the subject of major news on the previous day, causing a large stock price response).
- Stocks with the biggest dollar gains and losses in the previous day.

- Most active stocks (these stocks usually represent large firms and they may also be the subject of major news).
- Volume movers, which are stocks that suddenly experienced a much larger amount of trading volume than their norm.
- Most widely held stocks (these stocks receive more attention since they are so popular among investors).
- Highs/Lows. This table lists:
  - Stocks that reached their highest price on the previous trading day based on prices over the last year.
  - Stocks that reached their lowest price on the previous trading day based on prices over the last year.

New York Stock Exchange Indexes The NYSE provides quotations on indexes that it created. The Composite Index represents the average of all stocks traded on the NYSE. This is an excellent indicator of the general performance of stocks traded on the NYSE, but because these stocks represent mostly large firms, the Composite Index is not an appropriate measure of small stock performance. In addition to the Composite Index, the NYSE also provides indexes for four sectors:

1. Industrial
2. Transportation
3. Utility
4. Financial

These indexes are commonly used as benchmarks for comparison to an individual firm or portfolio in that respective sector. Although the indexes are positively correlated, there are substantial differences in their movements during some periods.

Other Stock Indexes The Amex provides quotations on several indexes of stocks traded on its exchange, including several sectors. The **National Association of Securities Dealers** provides quotations on indexes of stocks traded on the Nasdaq. These indexes are useful indicators of small stock performance because many small stocks are traded on the Nasdaq.

Monitoring by Investors

Since a firm's stock price is normally related to the firm's performance, the return to investors is dependent on how well the firm is managed. A firm's managers serve as agents for shareholders by making decisions that are supposed to maximize the stock's price. The separation of ownership (by shareholders) and control (by managers) can result in agency problems because of conflicting interests. Managers may be tempted to serve their own interests rather than those of the investors who own the firm's stock. To attempt to solve these agency problems, various forms of corporate governance are used to monitor managers of coporations. Investors rely on the board of directors of each firm to ensure that its managers make decisions that enhance the firm's performance and maximize the stock price. Shareholders monitor their stock's price movements to assess whether the managers are achieving the goal of share price maximization. If the stock price is lower than expected, shareholders may attempt to take action to improve the management of the firm.

The easiest way for shareholders to monitor the firm is to monitor changes in its value (as measured by its share price) over time. Since the share price is continuously available, shareholders can quickly detect any abrupt changes in the value of the firm. The return to shareholders is directly influenced by changes in the stock's price over time. When the stock price declines or does not rise as high as shareholders expected, shareholders may blame the weak performance on the firm's managers.

Accounting Irregularities

BEHAVIORAL FINANCE To the extent that managers can manipulate the financial statements, they may be able to hide information from investors. In recent years, many firms (including Enron, Tyco, and WorldCom) used unusual accounting methods to create their financial statements. As a result, it was very difficult for investors to ascertain the true financial condition of these firms and therefore to monitor them. The problem was compounded because the auditors hired to audit the financial statements of some firms allowed them to use these irregular accounting methods. A subset of a firm's board members serve on an audit committee, which is supposed to ensure that the audit is done properly, but in some firms, the committee failed to monitor the auditors. Overall, investors' monitoring of some firms was limited because the accountants distorted the financial statements, the auditors did not properly audit, and the audit committees of those firms did not oversee the audit properly. ■

Sarbanes-Oxley Act

As mentioned earlier, the Sarbanes-Oxley Act was enacted in 2002 to ensure more accurate disclosure of financial information to investors. The act attempts to force accountants to conform to regular accounting standards in preparing a firm's financial statements and to force auditors to take their auditing role seriously. To the extent that the act ensures more accurate financial reporting, it allows investors to more effectively monitor firms and detect when managers are not serving the interests of shareholders. In particular, the act does the following:

- Prevents a public accounting firm from auditing a client firm whose chief executive officer (CEO), chief financial officer (CFO), or other employees with similar job descriptions were employed by the accounting firm within one year prior to the audit. This provision maintains some distance between the audit firm and the client.

- Requires that only outside board members of a firm be on the firm's audit committee, which is responsible for making sure that the audit is conducted in an unbiased manner. Outside board members are more likely to serve the interests of existing and prospective shareholders than inside board members who are part of the firm's management.

- Prevents the members of a firm's audit committee from receiving consulting or advising fees or other compensation from the firm beyond that earned from serving on the board. This provision prevents a firm from providing excessive compensation to the members of an audit committee as a means of paying them off so that they do not closely oversee the audit.

- Requires that the CEO and CFO of firms that are of at least a specified size certify that the audited financial statements are accurate. This provision forces the CFO and CEO to be accountable.

- Specifies major fines or imprisonment for employees who mislead investors or hide evidence. This provision attempts to ensure that a firm's employees will be penalized for their role in distorting the accounting statements.

- Allows public accounting firms to offer nonaudit consulting services to an audit client only if the client's audit committee pre-approves the nonaudit services to be rendered before the audit begins. This provision attempts to ensure that a firm does not pay off an auditor with extra fees for consulting services in return for the auditor's certification that the firm's financial statements are accurate.

The act essentially contains a set of provisions related to a firm's process of recording, auditing, and reporting financial information. It attempts to prevent breakdowns in the process, so that investors can have more confidence in the accuracy of financial statements. Since the act prevents some forms of accounting abuses by publicly traded firms, it should improve the ability of existing and prospective shareholders to monitor these firms.

ILLUSTRATION Several managers of Taos Company own shares of the company and would like to cash out soon. Currently, however, the firm's stock price is low because Taos's performance has been weak. As the CFO prepares the income statement for this year, she considers overstating the firm's earnings because she believes this could improve the stock price and allow her to sell her shares for more money. But she is discouraged by several provisions of the Sarbanes-Oxley Act. First, as a result of the process that Taos Company created to comply with the act, the trail of recorded financial information from various employees to the CFO is now very transparent. Thus, she cannot make up numbers because the paper trail will lead back to her. Second, the auditors are more likely to detect any discrepancy because the process for estimating the earnings is more transparent. Third, the auditors are less likely to purposely overlook such a discrepancy because the act attempts to prevent auditors from ignoring discrepancies in exchange for receiving higher fees. Fourth, the act requires the CFO to sign off on the financial statements. She is subject to criminal charges and fines if the financial statements are determined to be misleading. Thus, she cannot pretend that she did not review the financial statements. ■

Cost of Being Public Establishing a process that satisfies the Sarbanes-Oxley provisions can be very costly. For many firms, the cost of adhering to the guidelines of the Sarbanes-Oxley Act exceeds $1 million per year. Consequently, many small publicly traded firms decided to revert back to private ownership as a result of the act. These firms perceived that they would have a higher value if they were private rather than publicly held because they could avoid the substantial reporting costs that are required of publicly traded firms.

Shareholder Activism

If shareholders are displeased with the way managers are managing a firm, they have three general choices. The first is to do nothing and retain the shares in the hope that management's actions will ultimately lead to strong stock price performance. A second choice is to sell the stock. This choice is common among shareholders who do not believe that they can change the firm's management or do not wish to spend the time and money needed to bring about change. A third choice is to engage in **shareholder activism.** Some of the more common types of shareholder activism are examined here.

Communication with the Firm Shareholders can communicate their concerns to other investors in an effort to place more pressure on the firm's managers or its board members. For example, shareholders may voice concerns about a firm that expands outside its core businesses, attempts to acquire other companies at excessive prices, or defends against a takeover that the shareholders believe would be beneficial.

Institutional investors commonly communicate with high-level corporate managers and have opportunities to offer their concerns about the firm's operations. The managers may be willing to consider the changes suggested by large institutional investors because they do not want those investors to sell their holdings of the firm's stock.

Some institutional investors have become much more involved in monitoring management, as they have realized that they can enhance the value of their security portfolios by ensuring that the firms in which they invest are properly managed. An institutional investor such as a pension fund, a life insurance company, or a mutual fund that holds a substantial amount of a corporation's stock may request a seat on the corporation's board of directors. Alternatively, the investor may request that the corporation at least replace one of the executives on the board with an outside investor to ensure that the board makes decisions to satisfy shareholders. The hope is that any changes suggested by shareholders result in stronger performance and a higher stock price for the firm.

ILLUSTRATION The California Public Employees' Retirement System (CALPERS) manages the pensions for employees of the state of California. It manages more than $80 billion of securities and commonly maintains large stock positions in some firms. When CALPERS believes that these firms are not being managed properly, it communicates its concerns and sometimes proposes solutions. Some of the firms adjust their management to accommodate CALPERS.

CALPERS periodically announces a list of firms that it believes have serious agency problems. These firms may have been unwilling to respond to CALPERS's concerns about their management style. ■

Firms are especially responsive when institutional investors communicate as a team. Institutional Shareholder Services (ISS), Inc. is a firm that organizes institutional shareholders to push for a common cause. After receiving feedback from institutional investors about a particular firm, ISS organizes a conference call with high-ranking executives of the firm so that it can obtain information from the firm. It then announces the time of the conference call to investors and allows them to listen in on the call. The questions focus on institutional shareholders' concerns about the firm's management. Unlike earnings conference calls, which are controlled by firms, ISS runs the conference call. Common questions asked by ISS include:

- Why is your CEO also the chair of the board?
- Why is your executive compensation much higher than the industry norm?
- What is your process for nominating new board members?

Transcripts of the conference calls are available within 48 hours after the call.

Proxy Contest Shareholders may also engage in proxy contests in an attempt to change the composition of the board. This is a more formal effort than communicating with the firm and is normally considered only if an informal request for a change in the board (through communication with the board) is ignored. A change in the board may be beneficial if it forces the board to make decisions that are more focused on maximizing the stock price. If the dissident shareholders gain enough votes, they can elect one or more directors who share their views. In this case, shareholders are truly exercising their control.

ILLUSTRATION As a classic example of the influence of a proxy, the directors of UAL were forced to sell the parent company of United Airlines to its employees. If they had not agreed to this, they could have been replaced through a proxy campaign led by Coniston Partners of New York, which owned about 12 percent of UAL. Even when managers win a proxy contest, they usually leave a company within three years after the contest. ∎

The ISS may recommend that shareholders vote a certain way on specific proxy issues. As a result of these more organized efforts, institutional shareholders are becoming more influential on management decisions. At some firms, they have succeeded in implementing changes that can enhance shareholder value, such as:

- Limiting severance pay for executives who are fired.
- Revising the voting guidelines on the firm's executive compensation policy.
- Requiring more transparent reporting of financial information.
- Imposing ceilings on the CEO's salary and bonus.
- Removing bylaws that prevented takeovers by other firms.
- Allowing for an annual election of all directors so that ineffective directors can be quickly removed from the board.

Shareholder Lawsuits

BEHAVIORAL FINANCE Investors may sue the board if they believe that the directors are not fulfilling their responsibilities to shareholders. This action is intended to force the board to make decisions that are aligned with shareholders' interests. Many lawsuits have been filed when corporations prevent takeovers, pursue acquisitions, or make other restructuring decisions that some shareholders believe will reduce the stock's value.

A firm's board of directors is responsible for supervising the business and affairs of a corporation. The board attempts to ensure that the business is managed in a way that serves the shareholders. Directors also have the responsibility of monitoring operations and ensuring that the firm complies with the laws. They cannot oversee every workplace decision, but they can ensure that the firm has a process that can guide some decisions about moral and ethical conduct. They can also ensure that the firm has a system for internal control and reporting. At some firms, the boards have been negligent in representing the shareholders. Nevertheless, since business performance is subject to uncertainty, directors cannot be held responsible every time a key business decision has an unsatisfactory outcome. When directors are sued, the court system typically focuses on whether the directors' decisions were reasonable, rather than on whether they increased the firm's profitability. Thus, from the court's perspective, the directors' decision-making process is more relevant than the outcome. ∎

Monitoring by Financial Managers

Financial managers of firms closely monitor their own firm's stock price and the stock prices of related companies. If they believe that the stock is undervalued, they may attempt to capitalize on this discrepancy, as explained below.

Stock Repurchases

The notion of asymmetric information means that a firm's managers have information about the firm's future prospects that is not known by the firm's investors. When corporate managers believe that their firm is undervalued, they can use the firm's excess cash to purchase a portion of their shares in the market at a relatively low price based on their valuation of what the shares are really worth. For example, several firms repurchased some of their shares in the 2001–2002 period, when share prices were at very low levels.

Stock repurchases are common even when the stock market is performing well, as long as firms believe that their stock is undervalued. In 2004 (when stock prices were already high), many U.S. firms announced plans to repurchase stock.

In general, studies have found that stock prices respond favorably to stock repurchase announcements, which implies that the announcement signals management's perception that the share price is undervalued. The market responds favorably to this signal.

ILLUSTRATION Reebok International Ltd. announced that it would repurchase one-third of its stock (24 million shares) at an expected cost of about $864 million. Consequently, Reebok would use a higher proportion of debt to finance its business operations. Reebok's stock price immediately increased by 11 percent in response to the stock repurchase announcement. ∎

Although many stock repurchase plans are viewed as a favorable signal, investors may question why the firm does not use its funds to expand its business instead of buying back its stock. Thus, investors' response to a stock repurchase plan varies with the firm's characteristics.

Market for Corporate Control

When corporate managers notice that another firm in the same industry has a low stock price as a result of poor management, they may attempt to acquire that firm. They hope to purchase the business at a low price and improve its management so that they can increase the value of the business. In addition, the combination of the two firms may reduce redundancy in some operations and allow for synergistic benefits. In this way, the managers of the acquiring firm may earn a higher return than if they used their funds for some other type of expansion. In essence, weak businesses are subject to a takeover by more efficient corporations and are therefore subject to the "market for corporate control." Thus, if a firm's stock price is relatively low because of poor performance, it may become an attractive target for other corporations.

A firm may especially benefit from acquisitions when its own stock price has risen. It can use its stock as currency to acquire the shares of a target by exchanging some of its own shares for the target's shares. Some critics claim that acquisitions of inefficient firms typically lead to layoffs and are unfair to employees. The counter to this argument is that without the market for corporate control, firms would be allowed to be inefficient, which is unfair to the shareholders who invested in them. Managers recognize that if their poorly performing business is taken over, they may lose their jobs. Thus, the market for corporate control can encourage managers to make decisions that maximize the stock's value so that they can discourage takeovers.

In general, studies have found that the share prices of target firms react very positively, but that the share prices of acquiring firms are not favorably affected. Investors may not expect the acquiring firm to achieve its objectives. For example, there is some evidence that firms engaging in acquisitions do not eliminate inefficient operations after the acquisitions, perhaps because of the potential low morale that results from layoffs.

Leveraged Buyouts The market for corporate control is enhanced by the use of **leveraged buyouts (LBOs),** which are acquisitions that require substantial amounts of borrowed funds. That is, the acquisition requires a substantial amount of financial leverage. Some so-called buyout firms identify poorly managed firms, acquire them (mostly with the use of borrowed funds), improve their management, and then sell them at a higher price than they paid. Alternatively, a group of managers who work for the firm may believe that they can restructure the firm's operations to improve cash flows. The managers may attempt an LBO in the hope that they can improve the firm's performance.

The use of debt to retire a company's stock creates a very highly leveraged capital structure. One favorable aspect of such a revised capital structure is that the ownership of the firm is normally reduced to a small group of people, who may be managers of the firm. Thus, agency costs should be reduced when managers act in their own interests instead of the firm's. A major concern about LBOs, however, is that the firm will experience cash flow problems over time because of the high periodic debt payments that result from the high degree of financial leverage. A firm financed in this way has a high potential return but is risky.

Some firms that engage in LBOs issue new stock after improving the firm's performance. This process is referred to as a **reverse leveraged buyout (reverse LBO).** Whereas an LBO may be used to purchase all the stock of a firm that has not achieved its potential performance (causing its stock to be priced low), a reverse LBO is normally desirable when the stock can be sold at a high price. In essence, the owners hope to issue new stock at a much higher price than they paid when enacting the LBO. The volume of reverse LBOs was relatively low in the late 1980s, when stock prices were low shortly after the 1987 stock market crash. The volume increased during the bullish stock market in the late 1990s, however.

Barriers to the Market for Corporate Control

The power of corporate control to eliminate agency problems is limited due to barriers that can make it more costly for a potential acquiring firm to acquire another firm whose managers are not serving the firm's shareholders. Some of the more common barriers to corporate control are identified next.

Antitakeover Amendments Some firms have added **antitakeover amendments** to their corporate charter. There are various types of antitakeover amendments. For example, an amendment may require that at least two-thirds of the shareholder votes approve a takeover before the firms can be acquired. Antitakeover amendments are supposed to be enacted to protect shareholders against an acquisition that will ultimately reduce the value of their investment in the firm. However, it may be argued that shareholders are adversely affected by antitakeover amendments.

Poison Pills **Poison pills** are special rights awarded to shareholders or specific managers on the occurrence of specified events. They can be enacted by a firm's board of directors without the approval of shareholders. Sometimes a target enacts a poison pill to defend against takeover attempts. For example, a poison pill might give all shareholders the right to be allocated an additional 30 percent of shares (based on their existing share holdings) without cost whenever a potential acquirer attempts to acquire the firm. The poison pill makes it more expensive and more difficult for a potential acquiring firm to acquire the target.

Golden Parachutes A **golden parachute** specifies compensation to managers in the event that they lose their jobs or there is a change in the control of the firm. For example, all managers might have the right to receive 100,000 shares of the firm's stock whenever the firm is acquired. It can be argued that a golden parachute provides managers with security so that they can make decisions that will improve the long-term performance of the firm. That is, managers protected by a golden parachute may be more willing to make decisions that enhance shareholder wealth over the long run even though the decisions adversely affect the stock price in the short run. The counterargument, however, is that a golden parachute allows managers to serve their own interests, rather than shareholder interests, because they receive large compensation even if they are fired.

Golden parachutes can discourage takeover attempts by increasing the cost of the acquisition. A potential acquiring firm recognizes that it will incur the expense associated with the golden parachutes if it acquires a particular target that has enacted golden parachutes prior to the takeover attempt. To the extent that this (or any) defense against takeovers is effective, it disrupts the market for corporate control by allowing managers of some firms to be protected while serving their own interests rather than shareholder interests.

Globalization of Stock Markets

GL🌐BALASPECTS Stock markets are becoming globalized in the sense that barriers between countries have been removed or reduced. Thus, firms in need of funds can tap foreign markets, and investors can purchase foreign stocks. In recent years, many firms have obtained funds from foreign markets through international stock offerings. This strategy may represent an effort by a firm to enhance its global image. Alternatively, because the issuing firm is tapping a larger pool of potential investors, it may more easily place the entire issue of new stock.

Foreign Stock Offerings in the United States

Many of the recent stock offerings in the United States by non-U.S. firms have resulted from privatization programs in Latin America and Europe, whereby businesses that were previously government owned are sold to U.S. shareholders. Some of these businesses are so large that the local stock markets cannot digest the stock offerings. Consequently, U.S. investors are financing many privatized businesses based in foreign countries.

When a non-U.S. firm issues stock in its own country, its shareholder base is quite limited because a few large institutional investors may own most of the shares. By issuing stock in the United States, the firm diversifies its shareholder base; such diversification can reduce share price volatility when large investors sell shares.

Although some large non-U.S. firms have developed a market for their stock in the United States, others are unwilling to do so because of SEC regulations. The SEC requires that any firms desiring to list their stock on a U.S. stock exchange must provide financial statements that satisfy U.S. accounting standards and are compatible with the financial statements of U.S. firms. Non-U.S. firms can avoid the expense of providing these statements if they choose not to list on U.S. exchanges.

Some non-U.S. firms obtain equity financing by using **American depository receipts (ADRs),** which are certificates representing shares of non-U.S. stock. The use of ADRs circumvents some disclosure requirements imposed on stock offerings in the United States, yet enables non-U.S. firms to tap the U.S. market for funds. The ADR market grew after businesses were privatized in the early 1990s because some of them issued ADRs to obtain financing.

International Placement Process

Investment banks facilitate the international placement of new stock through one or more syndicates across countries. Many investment banks and commercial banks based in the United States provide underwriting and other investment banking services in foreign countries.

The ability of investment banks to place new shares in foreign markets is somewhat dependent on the stock's perceived liquidity in those markets. A secondary market for the stock must be established in foreign markets to enhance liquidity and make newly issued stocks more attractive. Listing stock on a foreign stock exchange not only enhances the stock's liquidity but may also increase the firm's perceived financial standing when the exchange approves the listing application. Listing on foreign stock exchanges can also protect a firm against hostile takeovers because it disperses ownership and makes it more difficult for other firms to gain a controlling interest. Listing on a foreign stock exchange entails some costs, such as expenses for converting financial data in an annual report into a foreign currency and making financial statements compatible with the accounting standards used in that country.

Global Stock Exchanges

A summary of the world's major stock markets is provided in Exhibit 10.5. Numerous other exchanges also exist. In the past, the growth of many foreign stock markets was limited because their firms relied more on debt financing than equity financing. Recently, however, firms outside the United States have been issuing stock more frequently, which has allowed for substantial growth of non-U.S. stock markets. The percentage of individual versus institutional ownership of shares varies across stock markets. Financial institutions and other firms own a large proportion of the shares outside the United States, and individual investors own a relatively small proportion.

Exhibit 10.5   Comparison of Global Stock Exchanges

Country	Market Capitalization (in millions of $)	Number of Listed Domestic Companies	Country	Market Capitalization (in millions of $)	Number of Listed Domestic Companies
Argentina	61,478	101	Italy	789,563	269
Australia	776,403	1,515	Japan	3,678,262	3,220
Austria	85,815	99	Jamaica	37,639	39
Belgium	768,377	170	Malaysia	180,346	1,020
Brazil	474,647	381	Mexico	239,128	151
Canada	1,177,518	3,597	Netherlands	622,284	234
Chile	136,446	245	Poland	93,873	248
China	780,763	1,387	Singapore	171,555	489
Czech Republic	38,345	36	Spain	940,673	3,272
Finland	183,765	134	Sweden	376,781	256
Germany	1,194,517	660	Switzerland	825,849	282
Hong Kong	861,463	1,086	Thailand	123,539	468
India	553,074	4,763	U.K.	2,815,928	2,486
Ireland	114,085	53	U.S.	16,323,726	5,231
Israel	120,114	572			

Source: World Development Indicators, World Bank.

Variation in Characteristics across Stock Markets The volume of trading activity in each stock market is influenced by legal and other characteristics of the country. Shareholder rights vary among countries, as shareholders in some countries have more voting power and can have a stronger influence on corporate management.

The legal protection of shareholders also varies substantially among countries. Shareholders in some countries can more effectively sue publicly traded firms if their executives or directors commit financial fraud. In general, common law countries such as the United States, Canada, and the United Kingdom allow for more legal protection than civil law countries such as France and Italy.

The government's enforcement of securities laws also varies among countries. If a country has laws to ptotect shareholders but does not enforce the laws, shareholders are not protected. Some countries tend to have less corporate corruption than others; in these countries, shareholders are less exposed to major losses due to corruption.

In addition, the degree of financial information that must be provided by public companies varies among countries. The variation may be due to the accounting laws set by the government for public companies or to reporting rules enforced by local stock exchanges. Shareholders are less susceptible to losses due to a lack of information if public companies are required to be more transparent in their financial reporting.

In general, more investors are attracted to stock markets in countries that provide voting rights and legal protection for shareholders, strictly enforce the laws, do not tolerate corruption, and impose stringent accounting requirements. These conditions encourage investors to have more confidence in the stock market and allow for greater pricing efficiency. In addition, companies are attracted to the stock market when there are many investors, because they can easily raise funds in the market under these conditions. Conversely, if a stock market does not attract investors, it will not attract companies that need to raise funds. These companies will have to rely on stock markets in other countries or on credit markets to raise funds.

Euronext In 2000, the Amsterdam, Brussels, and Paris stock exchanges merged to create the Euronext market. Since then, the Lisbon stock exchange has joined Euronext as well. The Euronext market has about 1,500 firms listed, and about 300 of those firms are from other countries. Most of the largest firms based in Europe have listed their stock on the Euronext market. This market is likely to grow over time as other stock exchanges may join this market as well. A single European stock market would make it easier for investors who may want to do all of their trading in one market, which has similar guidelines for all stocks regardless of their home country. At this point, the guidelines have not been completely standardized across the stocks listed.

In 2006, the NYSE merged with Euronext. The combined exchanges facilitate more than $2 trillion in stock trades every month. This is expected to result in a single platform in which stocks, bonds, and derivative contracts are traded around the clock. The stocks listed on these two exchanges have a market capitalization of about $27 trillion, $22 trillion due to NYSE and $5 trillion due to Euronext. The merger is expected to simplify the cross-border trading of stocks.

Emerging Stock Markets

Emerging markets enable foreign firms to raise large amounts of capital by issuing stock. These markets also provide a means for investors from the United States and other countries to invest their funds.

Some emerging stock markets are relatively new and small and may not be as efficient as the U.S. stock market. Thus, some stocks may be undervalued, a possibility

The Wall Street Journal provides a summary of European stock performance under the heading "Dow Jones Stoxx 50." It lists the stocks in Europe that performed very well during the previous trading day. It also identifies stocks in Europe that performed very poorly during the previous trading day. This section also provides a summary of the major stocks traded in Europe.

that has attracted investors to these markets. Because some of these markets are small, however, they may be susceptible to manipulation by large traders. Furthermore, insider trading is more prevalent in many foreign markets because rules against it are not enforced. In general, large institutional investors and insiders based in the foreign markets may have some advantages.

Although international stocks can generate high returns, they also may exhibit high risk. Some of the emerging stock markets are often referred to as casinos because of the wild gyrations in gains and losses the panic trading that occurs.

The emerging markets experience large price swings because of two characteristics. First, the small number of shares for some firms allows large trades to jolt the equilibrium price. Second, valid financial information about firms is sometimes lacking, causing investors to trade according to rumors. Trading patterns based on continual rumors are more volatile than trading patterns based on factual data.

Methods Used to Invest in Foreign Stocks

Investors can obtain foreign stocks by purchasing shares directly, purchasing American depository receipts (ADRs), investing in international mutual funds, and purchasing exchange-traded funds (ETFs). Each of these methods is explained in turn.

Direct Purchases Investors can easily invest in stocks of foreign companies that are listed on the local stock exchanges. However, this set of stocks is quite limited. Foreign stocks not listed on local stock exchanges can be purchased through some full-service brokerage firms that have offices in foreign countries, but the transaction costs incurred from purchasing foreign stocks in this manner are high.

American Depository Receipts An alternative means of investing in foreign stocks is by purchasing ADRs, which, as mentioned earlier, are certificates that represent shares of non-U.S. stocks. Many non-U.S. companies established ADRs in order to develop name recognition in the United States. In addition, some companies wanted to raise funds in the United States.

ADRs are attractive to U.S. investors for the following reasons. First, they are closely followed by U.S. investment analysts. Second, companies represented by ADRs are required by the SEC to file financial statements consistent with generally accepted accounting principles in the United States. These statements may not be available for other non-U.S. companies. Third, reliable quotes on ADR prices are consistently available, with existing currency values factored in to translate the price into dollars. A disadvantage, however, is that the selection of ADRs is limited. Also, the ADR market is less active than other stock markets, so ADRs are less liquid than most listed U.S. stocks.

International Mutual Funds Another way to invest in foreign stocks is to purchase shares of **international mutual funds (IMFs),** which are portfolios of international stocks created and managed by various financial institutions. Thus, individuals can diversify across international stocks by investing in a single IMF. Some IMFs focus on a specific foreign country, while others contain stocks across several countries or even several continents.

International Exchange-Traded Funds Exchange-traded funds (ETFs) are passive funds that track a specific index. International ETFs represent international stock indexes. They have become very popular in the last few years. By investing in an international ETF, investors can invest in a specific index representing a foreign country's stock market. An ETF trades like a stock, as it is listed on an exchange, and its value changes in response to trading activity. Although ETFs are denominated in dollars, the net asset value of an international ETF is determined by translating the foreign currency value of the foreign securities into dollars.

Some international ETFs have been called different names, such as world equity benchmark shares (WEBS) or iShares, by their sponsors. A major difference between ETFs and IMFs is that IMFs are managed, whereas ETFs simply represent an index. If investors prefer that the portfolio be rebalanced by portfolio managers over time, they may prefer an IMF. However, ETFs have lower expenses because they avoid the cost of active portfolio management. The difference in expense ratios between an IMF and an ETF may be 2 percent annually or more.

http://finance.yahoo.com/?u
Quotations on various stock market indexes around the world.

While the price of a share of each international ETF is denominated in dollars, the underlying securities that make up the index are denominated in non-U.S. currencies. Thus, the return on the ETF will be influenced by the movement of the foreign country's currency against the dollar. This is also true for IMFs. If the foreign currency **appreciates** (increases in value), this will boost the value of the index as measured in dollars. Conversely, if the foreign currency **depreciates** (decreases in value), this will reduce the value of the index as measured in dollars.

Summary

■ Stock markets facilitate the transfer of stock ownership between investors. The trading of a stock in the stock market determines its equilibrium price.

■ Investors are commonly classified as individual or institutional. The proportion of a firm's shares held by any individual investor tends to be small, which limits the ability of an individual investor to influence the firm's management. Institutional investors have larger equity positions and therefore are more capable of influencing the firm's management. Stock mutual funds, pension funds, and insurance companies are the major institutional investors in the stock market. Securities firms serve as brokers by matching up buyers and sellers in the stock market.

■ An initial public offering (IPO) is a first-time offering of shares by a specific firm to the public. Many firms engage in an IPO when they have feasible business expansion plans, but are already near their debt capacity. A firm that engages in an IPO must develop a prospectus that is filed with the SEC and does a

road show to promote its offering. It hires an underwriter to help with the prospectus and road show and to place the shares with investors.

■ A secondary stock offering is an offering of shares by a firm that already has publicly traded stock. Firms engage in secondary offerings when they need more equity funding to support additional expansion.

■ Corporations sometimes serve as investors when they believe that their own business or another business is undervalued. If they believe their own business is undervalued, they can repurchase shares of stock in the secondary market at a relatively low price. If they believe that another poorly performing business is undervalued, they may consider acquiring the shares of that business and then reorganizing the business (replacing managers) to improve its value. This makes poorly performing businesses subject to the market for corporate control.

■ Many U.S. firms issue shares in foreign countries, as well as in the United States, so that they can spread their shares among a larger set of investors. In a similar manner, many non-U.S. firms not only issue shares in their own markets but also tap the U.S. market for funds. This strategy not only enlarges the investor base, but also may enhance the global name recognition of a firm.

Global stock exchanges exist to facilitate the trading of stocks around the world. U.S. investors invest in foreign stocks by direct purchases on foreign stock exchanges, by purchasing ADRs, by investing in international mutual funds, and by investing in international exchange-traded funds.

Point Counter-Point

Should a Stock Exchange Enforce Some Governance Standards on the Firms Listed on the Exchange?

Point No. Governance is the responsibility of the firms, and not the stock exchange. The stock exchange should simply ensure that the trading rules of the exchange are enforced and should not intervene in the firms' governance issues.

Counter-Point Yes. When a stock exchange enforces governance standards such as requiring a firm

to have a majority of outside members on its board of directors, it can enhance the credibility of the exchange.

Who Is Correct? Use the Internet to learn more about this issue. Offer your own opinion on this issue.

Questions and Applications

1. **Shareholder Rights** Explain the rights of common stockholders that are not available to other individuals.

2. **Stock Offerings** What is the danger of issuing too much stock? What is the role of the investment bank that serves as the underwriter, and how can it ensure that the firm does not issue too much stock?

3. **IPOs** Why do firms engage in IPOs? What is the amount of fees that the lead underwriter and its syndicate charge a firm that is going public? Why are there many IPOs in some periods and few IPOs in other periods?

4. **Venture Capital** Explain the difference between obtaining funds from a venture capital firm and engaging in an IPO. Explain how the IPO may serve as a means by which the venture capital firm can cash out.

5. **Prospectus and Road Show** Explain the use of a prospectus developed before an IPO. Why does a firm do a road show before its IPO? What factors influence the offer price of stock at the time of the IPO?

6. **Bookbuilding** Describe the process of bookbuilding. Why is bookbuilding sometimes criticized as a means of setting the offer price?

7. **Lockups** Describe a lockup provision and explain why it is required by the lead underwriter.

8. **Initial Return** What is the meaning of an initial return for an IPO? Were initial returns of Internet IPOs in the late 1990s higher or lower than normal? Why?

9. **Flipping** What is the meaning of "flipping" shares? Why would investors want to flip shares?

10. **Performance of IPOs** How do IPOs perform over the long run?

11. **Asymmetric Information** Discuss the concept of asymmetric information and explain how it may cause corporate managers to serve as investors.

12. **Stock Repurchases** Explain why the stock price of a firm may rise when the firm announces that it is repurchasing its shares.

13. **Corporate Control** Describe how the interaction between buyers and sellers affects the market value of a firm, and explain how that can subject a firm to the market for corporate control.

14. **ADRs** Explain how ADRs enable U.S. investors to become part owners of foreign companies.

15. **NYSE** Explain why stocks traded on the NYSE exhibit lower risk than stocks that are traded on other exchanges.

16. **Role of Organized Exchanges** Are organized stock exchanges used to place newly issued stock? Explain.

Advanced Questions

17. **Role of IMFs** How have international mutual funds (IMFs) increased the international integration of capital markets among countries?

18. **Spinning and Laddering** Describe spinning and laddering in the IPO market. How do you think these actions influence the price of a newly issued stock? Who is adversely affected as a result of these actions?

19. **Impact of Accounting Irregularities** How do you think accounting irregularities affect the pricing of corporate stock in general? From an investor's viewpoint, how do you think the information used to price stocks changes given that accounting irregularities exist?

20. **Impact of Sarbanes-Oxley Act** Briefly describe the provisions of the Sarbanes-Oxley Act. Discuss how this act affects the monitoring by shareholders.

21. **IPO Dilemma** Denton Company plans to engage in an IPO and will issue 4 million shares of stock. It is hoping to sell the shares for an offer price of $14. It hires an investment bank that suggests that the offer price for the stock should be $12 per share to ensure that all the shares will be easily sold. Explain the dilemma for Denton Company. What is the advantage of following the advice of the investment bank? What is the disadvantage? Is the investment bank's incentive to place the shares aligned with that of Denton Company?

22. **Variation in Investor Protection among Countries** Explain how shareholder protection varies among countries. Explain how enforcement of securities laws varies among countries. Why do these characteristics affect the valuations of stocks?

23. **International ETFs** Describe international ETFs. Explain how ETFs are exposed to exchange rate risk. How do you think an investor decides whether to purchase an ETF representing Japan, Spain, or some other country?

Interpreting Financial News

Interpret the following statements made by Wall Street analysts and portfolio managers:

a. "The recent wave of IPOs is an attempt by many small firms to capitalize on the recent runup in stock prices."
b. "IPOs transfer wealth from unsophisticated investors to large institutional investors who get in at the offer price and get out quickly."
c. "Firms must be more accountable to the market when making decisions because they are subject to indirect control by institutional investors."

Managing in Financial Markets

Investing in an IPO As a portfolio manager of a financial institution, you are invited to numerous road shows in which firms that are going public promote themselves and the lead underwriter invites you to invest in the IPO. Beyond any specific information about the firm, what other information would you need to decide whether to invest in the upcoming IPO?

Problem

1. **Dividend Yield** Over the last year, Calzone Corporation paid a quarterly dividend of $0.10 in each of the four quarters. The current stock price of Calzone Corporation is $39.78. What is the dividend yield for Calzone stock?

Flow of Funds Exercise

Contemplating an Initial Public Offering (IPO)

Recall that if the economy continues to be strong, Carson Company may need to increase its production capacity by about 50 percent over the next few years to satisfy demand. It would need financing to expand and accommodate the increase in production. Recall that the yield curve is currently upward sloping. Also recall that Carson is concerned about a possible slowing of the economy because of potential Fed actions to reduce inflation. It is also considering issuing stock or bonds to raise funds in the next year.

a. If Carson issued stock now, it would have the flexibility to obtain more debt and would also be able to reduce its cost of financing with debt. Why?

b. Why would an IPO result in heightened concerns in financial markets about Carson Company's potential agency problems?

c. Explain why institutional investors such as mutual funds and pension funds that invest in stock for long-term periods (at least a year or two) may be more interested in investing in some IPOs than they are in purchasing other stocks that have been publicly traded for several years.

d. Given that institutional investors such as insurance companies, pension funds, and mutual funds are the major investors in IPOs, explain the flow of funds that results from an IPO. That is, what is the original source of the money that is channeled through the institutional investors and provided to the firm going public?

Internet/Excel Exercises

Go to http://ipoportal.edgar-online.com/ipo/home .asp. Review an IPO that is scheduled for the near future. Review the deal information about this IPO.

1. What is the offer amount? How much are total expenses? How much are total expenses as a percentage of the deal amount? How many shares are issued? How long is the lockup period?

2. Review some additional IPOs that are scheduled. What is the range for the offer amount? What is the range for the lockup period length?

WSJ Exercise

Assessing Stock Market Movements

Review the section "Abreast of the Market" in a recent issue of *The Wall Street Journal*. Indicate whether the market prices increased or decreased, and explain what caused the market's movement.

Part 5: Derivative Security Markets

Derivatives are financial contracts whose values are derived from the values of underlying assets. They are widely used to speculate on future expectations or to reduce a security portfolio's risk. The chapters in Part 5 focus on derivative security markets. Each chapter explains how institutional portfolio managers and speculators use these markets. Many financial market participants simultaneously use all these markets, as is emphasized throughout the chapters.

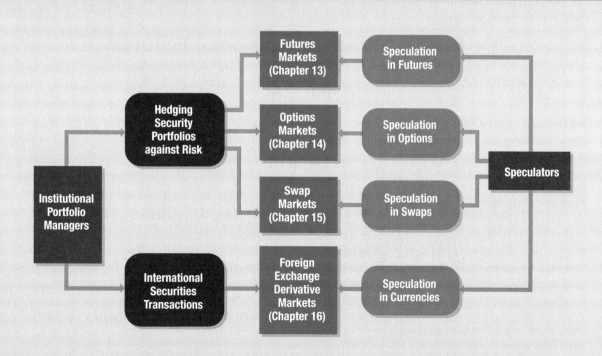

Chapter 13: Financial Futures Markets

In recent years, financial futures markets have received much attention because they have the potential to generate large returns to speculators and because they entail a high degree of risk. However, these markets can also be used to reduce the risk of financial institutions and other corporations. Financial futures markets facilitate the trading of financial futures contracts.

The specific objectives of this chapter are to:

■ explain how financial futures contracts are valued,

■ explain how interest rate futures contracts are used to speculate or hedge, based on anticipated interest rate movements,

■ explain how stock index futures contracts are used to speculate or hedge, based on anticipated stock price movements, and

■ describe how financial institutions participate in the financial futures markets.

Background on Financial Futures

A **financial futures contract** is a standardized agreement to deliver or receive a specified amount of a specified financial instrument at a specified price and date. The buyer of a financial futures contract buys the financial instrument, while the seller of a financial futures contract delivers the instrument for the specified price. Financial futures contracts are traded on organized exchanges, which establish and enforce rules for such trading. Futures exchanges provide an organized marketplace where futures contracts can be traded. They clear, settle, and guarantee all transactions that occur on their exchanges.

http://www.cftc.gov/
Detailed information on the CFTC.

The operations of financial futures exchanges are regulated by the Commodity Futures Trading Commission (CFTC). The CFTC approves futures contracts before they can be listed by futures exchanges and imposes regulations to prevent unfair trading practices.

Many of the popular financial futures contracts are on debt securities such as Treasury bills, Treasury notes, Treasury bonds, and Eurodollar CDs. These contracts are referred to as **interest rate futures.** There are also financial futures contracts on stock indexes, which are referred to as **stock index futures.** For each type of contract, the settlement dates at which delivery would occur are in March, June, September, and December.

Purpose of Trading Financial Futures

Financial futures are traded either to speculate on prices of securities or to hedge existing exposure to security price movements. **Speculators** in financial futures markets take positions to profit from expected changes in the price of futures contracts over time. **Hedgers** take positions to reduce their exposure to future movements in interest rates or stock prices.

Many hedgers who maintain large portfolios of stocks or bonds take a futures position to hedge their risk. Speculators commonly take the opposite position and therefore serve as the counterparty on many futures transactions. Thus, speculators provide liquidity to the futures market.

Speculators in futures can be classified according to their methods. **Day traders** attempt to capitalize on price movements during a single day; normally, they close out their futures positions on the same day the positions were initiated. **Position traders** maintain their futures positions for longer periods of time (for weeks or months) and thus attempt to capitalize on expected price movements over a longer time horizon.

Structure of the Futures Market

Most financial futures contracts in the United States are traded on the Chicago Board of Trade (CBOT) or the Chicago Mercantile Exchange (CME). The trading floor for most futures contracts is open from 8:30 A.M. to 3:15 P.M. Only the members of a futures exchange (or persons to whom members have leased their privileges) can engage in futures transactions on the exchange floor. A person becomes a member by purchasing a seat on the exchange. The price of a seat on any exchange fluctuates over time, in accordance with the demand for seats and supply of seats for sale.

Members of a futures exchange can be classified as either **commission brokers** (also called floor brokers) or **floor traders.** Commission brokers execute orders for their customers. Many of them are employees of brokerage firms, but others work independently. Floor traders (also called **locals**) trade futures contracts for their own account.

Over-the-Counter Trading Many types of futures contracts and other derivative contracts are now being sold over the counter, whereby a financial intermediary (such as a commercial bank or an investment bank) finds a counterparty or serves as the counterparty. These over-the-counter arrangements are more personalized and can be tailored to the specific preferences of the parties involved. Such tailoring is not possible for the more standardized futures contracts sold on the exchanges.

Electronic Trading Some futures contracts are now traded electronically. The Chicago Mercantile Exchange has an electronic trading platform called GLOBEX that complements its floor trading. Some futures contracts are traded both on the trading floor and on GLOBEX, while others are traded only on GLOBEX. Transactions can occur on GLOBEX virtually around the clock (closed about one hour per day for maintenance) and on weekends. In 2004, the Chicago Board of Options Exchange (CBOE) opened a fully electronic futures exchange.

Consolidation The CME specialized in futures contracts on money market securities, stock indexes, and currencies. The CBOT specialized in futures contracts on Treasury bonds and agricultural products, and also traded stock options (described in the next chapter). The CME went public in 2002, while the CBOT went public in 2005. In October 2006, the CME proposed merging with the CBOT. At that time, the combined market value of the two exchanges was $25 billion. The combined exchanges have an average trading volume of about 9 million contracts, with an underlying value of $4.2 billion. By allowing for one trading platform and the elimination of some overlapping staff positions, the combination is expected to improve efficiency and achieve cost savings of more than $100 million per year. While this merger was awaiting approval from regulators and shareholders, the CBOT received a competing

http://www.nfa.futures.org/
Information for investors who wish to trade futures contracts.

http://www.cbot.com/
Offers details about the products offered by the CBOT and also provides price quotations of the various futures contracts.

bid from the Intercontinental Exchange (ICE), which facilitates the trading of global futures contracts. However, it agreed to the bid by the CME in July 2007.

Trading Futures

Customers who desire to buy or sell futures contracts open accounts at brokerage firms that execute futures transactions. Under exchange requirements, a customer must establish a margin deposit with the broker before a transaction can be executed. This so-called **initial margin** is typically between 5 percent and 18 percent of a futures contract's full value. Brokers commonly require margin deposits above those required by the exchanges. As the futures contract price changes on a daily basis, its value is "marked to market," or revised to reflect the prevailing conditions. When the value of a customer's contract moves in an unfavorable direction, that customer may receive a margin call from the broker, requiring additional funds to be deposited in the margin account. The margin requirements reduce the risk that customers will later default on their obligations.

Type of Orders Customers can place a market order or a limit order. With a market order, the trade will automatically be executed at the prevailing price of the futures contract. With a limit order, the trade will be executed only if the price is within the limit specified by the customer. For example, a customer may place a limit order to buy a particular futures contract if it is priced no higher than a specified price. Similarly, a customer may place an order to sell a futures contract if it is priced no lower than a specified minimum price.

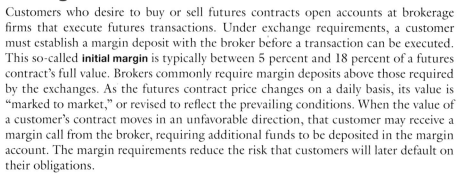

How Orders Are Executed The brokerage firm communicates its customers' orders to telephone stations located near the trading floor of the futures exchange. The floor brokers accommodate these orders. Each type of financial futures contract is traded in a particular location on the trading floor. The floor brokers make their offers to trade by open outcry, specifying the quantity of contracts they wish to buy or sell. Other floor brokers and traders interested in trading the particular type of futures contract can respond to the open outcry. When two traders on the trading floor reach an agreement, each trader documents the specifics of the agreement (including the price), and the information is transmitted to the customers.

Floor brokers receive transaction fees in the form of a bid-ask spread. That is, they purchase a given futures contract for one party at a slightly lower price than the price at which they sell the contract to another party. For every buyer of a futures contract, there must be a corresponding seller.

The futures exchange facilitates the trading process but does not take buy or sell positions on the futures contract. Instead, the exchange acts as a clearinghouse. A clearinghouse facilitates the trading process by recording all transactions and guaranteeing timely payments on the futures contracts. This precludes the need for a purchaser of a futures contract to check the creditworthiness of the contract seller. In fact, purchasers of contracts do not even know who the sellers are, and vice versa. The clearinghouse also supervises the delivery of contracts as of the settlement date.

Interpreting Financial Futures Tables

Prices of interest rate futures contracts vary from day to day and are reported in the financial pages of newspapers. Assume the information in Exhibit 13.1 appears on a particular day in May 2008 and refers to the previous trading day. From this exhibit, the futures contract specifying delivery of the Treasury bills for June opened at 94.00 (per $100 par value). The highest trading price for the day was 94.26, the low

Exhibit 13.1
Example of Treasury Bill
Futures Quotations

Treasury Bill Futures						
(1)	(2)	(3)	(4)	(5)	(6)	(7)
				Discount		
	Open	High	Low	Settle	Change	Settle
June 2008	94.00	94.26	94.00	94.20	+.30	5.80
Sept 2008	93.80	94.05	93.80	94.05	+.28	5.95
Dec 2008	93.62	93.79	93.62	93.75	+.24	6.25
Mar 2009	93.45	93.60	93.45	93.60	+.23	6.40

was 94.00, and the closing price (settle price in Column 5) at the end of the day was 94.20. The change in Column 6 is the difference between the settle price and the quoted settle price on the previous trading day.

Exhibit 13.1 provides information for T-bill futures contracts with four different settlement months. Once the June settlement date passes, the other months will move up one row in the table, and information on T-bill futures with a settlement date for the following June will appear in the fourth row.

Futures on Treasury bonds and notes are also available and can be used for hedging portfolio positions or for speculation. Specific characteristics of these contracts are shown in Exhibit 13.2. Both Treasury bond and note futures represent a face value of $100,000, which is substantially less than the $1 million face value of securities underlying the T-bill futures contracts.

Valuation of Financial Futures

http://www.cme.com
Quotations for futures
contracts.

If there are more traders with buy offers than sell offers for a particular contract, the futures price will rise until this imbalance is removed. Price changes on financial futures contracts are indicated on quotation tickers.

Exhibit 13.2
Characteristics of
Treasury Bond and
Note Futures

Characteristic of Futures Contract	U.S. Treasury Bond Futures	U.S. Treasury Note Futures
Size	$100,000 face value.	$100,000 face value.
Deliverable grade	U.S. Treasury bonds maturing at least 15 years from date of delivery if not callable; coupon is 8%. (The coupon rate on new contracts is periodically adjusted to reflect market interest rate levels.)	U.S. Treasury notes maturing at least 6½ years but not more than 10 years from the first day of the delivery month; coupon rate is 6%. [The coupon rate on new contracts is periodically adjusted to reflect market interest rate levels.]
Price quotation	In points ($1,000) and thirty-seconds of a point.	In points ($1,000) and thirty-seconds of a point.
Minimum price fluctuation	One thirty-second ($\frac{1}{32}$) of a point, or $31.25 per contract.	One thirty-second ($\frac{1}{32}$) of a point, or $31.25 per contract.
Daily trading limits	Three points ($3,000) per contract above or below the previous day's settlement price.	Three points ($3,000) per contract above or below the previous day's settlement price.
Settlement months	March, June, September, December.	March, June, September, December.

The price of any financial futures contract generally reflects the expected price of the underlying security (or index) as of the settlement date. Thus, any factors that influence that expected value should influence the current prices of financial futures. A primary factor is the current price of the underlying security (or index), which normally serves as a somewhat useful indicator of the future price. As the market price of the financial asset represented by the financial futures contract changes, so will the value of the contract. For example, if the prices of Treasury bonds rise, the value of an existing Treasury bond futures contract should rise because the contract has locked in the price at which Treasury bonds can be purchased.

In addition, some information about economic or market conditions may influence the futures price even though it does not affect the current price. For example, a particular regulatory event anticipated six months from now could possibly affect the futures price even though it does not affect the price of the underlying security. Thus, the futures price is mainly a function of the prevailing price of the underlying security plus an expected adjustment in that price by the settlement date. The futures price should change in response to either changes in the prevailing price or changes in the expected adjustment in that price by the settlement date.

Impact of the Opportunity Cost

Another factor that influences the futures price is the opportunity cost (or benefits) involved in holding a futures contract rather than owning the underlying security. An investor who purchases stock index futures rather than the stocks themselves does not receive the dividends. By itself, this factor would cause the stock index futures to be priced lower than the stocks themselves. However, because the investor's initial investment is much smaller when purchasing the stock index futures, the investor may be able to generate interest income on the remaining funds. By itself, this factor would cause the stock index futures to be priced higher than the stocks themselves. When both factors are considered, the effects are somewhat offsetting.

Explaining Price Movements of Bond Futures Contracts

Price movements of bond futures contracts are driven by economic conditions. A framework for explaining movements in bond futures prices is provided in Exhibit 13.3.

Since Treasury bond futures prices tend to move with the prices of Treasury bonds, participants in the Treasury bond futures market closely monitor the same economic indicators monitored by participants in the Treasury bond market. These indicators may signal future changes in the strength of the economy, which signal changes in the risk-free interest rate and in the required return from investing in bonds. Some of the more closely monitored indicators of economic growth include employment, gross domestic product, retail sales, industrial production, and consumer confidence. When indicators signal an increase in economic growth, participants anticipate an increase in interest rates, which places downward pressure on bond prices and therefore also on Treasury bond futures prices. Conversely, when indicators signal a decrease in economic growth, participants anticipate lower interest rates, which places upward pressure on bond prices and therefore also on Treasury bond futures.

Participants in the Treasury bond futures market also closely monitor indicators of inflation, such as the consumer price index and the producer price index. In general, an unexpected increase in these indexes tends to create expectations of higher interest rates and places downward pressure on bond prices and therefore also on Treasury bond futures prices.

Exhibit 13.3
Framework for
Explaining Changes
in Treasury Bond and
Treasury Bill Futures
Prices over Time

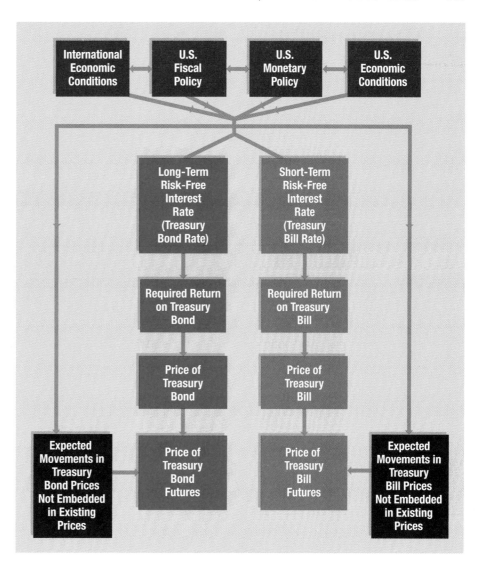

Indicators that reflect the amount of long-term financing are also monitored. For example, announcements about the government deficit or the amount of money that the Treasury hopes to borrow in a Treasury bond auction are closely monitored. Any information that implies more government borrowing than expected tends to signal upward pressure on the long-term risk-free interest rate (the Treasury bond rate), downward pressure on bond prices, and therefore downward pressure on Treasury bond futures prices.

Speculating with Interest Rate Futures

The following example explains how speculators use interest rate futures.

ILLUSTRATION   In February, Jim Sanders forecasts that interest rates will decrease over the next month. If his expectation is correct, the market value of T-bills should increase. Sanders calls a broker and purchases a T-bill futures contract. Assume that the price of the contract was 94.00 (a 6 percent discount) and that the price of T-bills as of the March settlement date is 94.90 (a 5.1 percent discount). Sanders can accept delivery of the T-bills and sell them for more than he paid for them. Because T-bill futures represent $1 million of par value, the nominal profit from this speculative strategy is

Selling price	$949,000	(94.90% of $1,000,000)
− Purchase price	− 940,000	(94.00% of $1,000,000)
= Profit	$9,000	(0.90% of $1,000,000) ∎

In this example, Sanders benefited from his speculative strategy because interest rates declined from the time he took the futures position until the settlement date. If interest rates had risen over this period, the price of T-bills as of the settlement date would have been below 94.00 (reflecting a discount above 6 percent), and Sanders would have incurred a loss.

ILLUSTRATION Assume that the price of T-bills as of the March settlement date is 92.50 (representing a discount of 7.5 percent). In this case, the nominal profit from Sander's speculative strategy is

Selling price	$925,000	(92.50% of $1,000,000)
− Purchase price	− 940,000	(94.00% of $1,000,000)
= Profit	− $15,000	(−1.50% of $1,000,000)

Now suppose instead that, as of February, Sanders had anticipated that interest rates would rise by March. He therefore sold a T-bill futures contract with a March settlement date, obligating him to provide T-bills to the purchaser as of the delivery date. When T-bill prices declined by March, Sanders was able to obtain T-bills at a lower market price in March than the price at which he was obligated to sell those bills. Again, there is always the risk that interest rates (and therefore T-bill prices) will move contrary to expectations. In that case, Sanders would have paid a higher market price for the T-bills than the price at which he could sell them. ∎

The potential payoffs from trading futures contracts are illustrated in Exhibit 13.4. The left graph represents a purchaser of futures, and the right graph represents a seller of futures. The S on each graph indicates the initial price at which a futures position is created. The horizontal axis represents the market value of the securities represented by a futures contract as of the delivery date. The maximum possible loss when purchasing futures is the amount to be paid for the securities, but this loss will occur only if the market value of the securities falls to zero. The amount of gain (or loss) to

Exhibit 13.4
Potential Payoffs from Speculating in Financial Futures

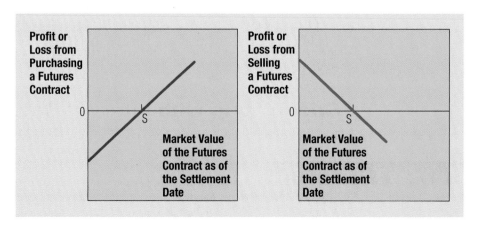

a speculator who initially purchased futures will equal the loss (or gain) to a speculator who initially sold futures on the same date (assuming zero transaction costs).

Impact of Leverage

Since investors commonly use a margin account to take futures positions, the return from speculating in interest rate futures should reflect the degree of financial leverage involved. The return is magnified substantially when considering the relatively small margin maintained by many investors.

ILLUSTRATION In the example where Jim Sanders earned a profit of $9,000 on a futures contract, this profit represents 0.90 percent of the value of the underlying contract par value. Consider that Sanders could have taken the interest rate futures position with an initial margin of perhaps $10,000. Under these conditions, the $9,000 profit represents a return of 90 percent over the period of less than two months in which he maintained the futures position.

Just as financial leverage magnifies positive returns, it also magnifies losses. In the example where Sanders lost $15,000 on a futures contract, he would have lost 100 percent of his initial margin and would have been required to add more funds to his margin account when the value of the futures position began to decline. ■

Closing Out the Futures Position

Most buyers and sellers of financial futures contracts do not actually make or accept delivery of the financial instrument; instead, they offset their positions by the settlement date. For example, speculators who purchased Treasury bond futures contracts could sell similar futures contracts by the settlement date. Because they now own a contract to receive and a contract to deliver, the obligations net out. The gain or loss from involvement in futures positions depends on the futures price at the time of the purchase versus the futures price at the time of the sale. If the price of the securities represented by the futures contract has risen over the period of concern, speculators who initially purchased interest rate futures will likely have paid a lower futures price than the price at which they can sell the futures contract. Thus, a positive gain will have resulted, and the size of the gain will depend on the degree of movement in the prices of the securities underlying the contract.

Consider the opposite situation (referred to as a "short" position) where the sale of futures is followed by a purchase of futures a few months later to offset the initial short position. If security prices have risen over this period, the earlier contract to sell futures will be priced lower than the later contract to purchase futures. Thus, the speculator will have a loss.

ILLUSTRATION Assume that a speculator purchased a futures contract on Treasury bonds at a price of 90–00. One month later, the speculator sells the same futures contract in order to close out the position. At this time, the futures contract specifies 92–10, or 92 and $^{10}/_{32}$ percent of the par value, as the price. Given that the futures contract on Treasury bonds specifies a par value of $100,000, the nominal profit is

Selling price	$92,312	($92^{10}/_{32}$% of $100,000)
− Purchase price	− 90,000	(90.00% of $100,000)
= Profit	$2,312	($2^{10}/_{32}$% of $100,000)

When the initial position is a sale of the futures contract, a purchase of that same type of contract will close out the position. For example, assume a speculator took an initial short position. Using the numbers above, a loss of $2,312 (ignoring transaction costs) will result from closing out the short position one month later. Participants close out a position when they expect that a larger loss will occur if the position is not closed out. If the short position is not closed out before the settlement date, the investor taking that position is obligated to deliver the securities underlying the futures contract at that time. ■

According to estimates, only 2 percent of all futures contracts actually involve delivery, yet this does not reduce their effectiveness for speculation or hedging. Because the contract prices move with the financial instrument representing the contract, an offsetting position at the settlement date generates the same gain or loss as if the instrument were delivered.

Hedging with Interest Rate Futures

Financial institutions can classify their assets and liabilities by the sensitivity of their market value to interest rate movements. The difference between a financial institution's volume of rate-sensitive assets and rate-sensitive liabilities represents its exposure to interest rate risk. Over the long run, an institution may attempt to restructure its assets or liabilities to balance the degree of rate sensitivity. Restructuring the balance sheet takes time, however. In the short run, the institution may consider using financial futures to hedge its exposure to interest rate movements. A variety of financial institutions use financial futures to hedge their interest rate risk, including mortgage companies, securities dealers, commercial banks, savings institutions, pension funds, and insurance companies.

Using Interest Rate Futures to Create a Short Hedge

Financial institutions most commonly use interest rate futures to create a **short hedge.** Consider a commercial bank that currently holds a large amount of corporate bonds and long-term fixed-rate commercial loans. Its primary source of funds has been short-term deposits. The bank will be adversely affected if interest rates rise in the near future because its liabilities are more rate-sensitive than its assets. Although the bank believes that its bonds are a reasonable long-term investment, it anticipates that interest rates will rise temporarily. Therefore, it hedges against the interest rate risk by selling futures on securities that have characteristics similar to the securities it is holding, so the futures prices will change in tandem with these securities. One possible strategy is to sell Treasury bond futures because the price movements of Treasury bonds are highly correlated with movements in corporate bond prices.

If interest rates rise as expected, the market value of existing corporate bonds held by the bank will decline. Yet, this decline could be offset by the favorable impact of the futures position. The bank locked in the price at which it could sell Treasury bonds. It can purchase Treasury bonds at a lower price just prior to settlement of the futures contract (because the value of bonds will have decreased) and profit from fulfilling its futures contract obligation. Alternatively, it could offset its short position by purchasing futures contracts similar to the type that it sold earlier.

ILLUSTRATION Assume that Charlotte Insurance Company plans to satisfy cash needs in six months by selling its Treasury bond holdings for $5 million at that time. It is concerned that interest rates might increase over the next three months, which would reduce the market value of the bonds by the time they are sold. To hedge against this possibility, Charlotte plans to sell Treasury bond futures. It sells

50 Treasury bond futures contracts with a par value of $5 million ($100,000 per contract) for 98–16 (or 98 and $^{16}/_{32}$ percent of par value).

Suppose that the actual price of the futures contract declines to 94–16 because of an increase in interest rates. Charlotte can close out its short futures position by purchasing contracts identical to those it has sold. If it purchases 50 Treasury bond futures contracts at the prevailing price of 94–16, its profit per futures contract will be

Selling price	$98,500	(98.50% of $100,000)
− Purchase price	− 94,500	(94.50% of $100,000)
= Profit	$4,000	(4.00% of $100,000)

Charlotte had a position in 50 futures contracts, so its total profit from its position will be $200,000 ($4,000 per contract × 50 contracts). This gain on the futures contract position will help offset the reduced market value of Charlotte's bond holdings. Charlotte could also have earned a gain on its position by purchasing an identical futures contract just before the settlement date.

If interest rates rise by a greater degree over the six-month period, the market value of Charlotte's Treasury bond holdings will decrease further. However, the price of Treasury bond futures contracts will also decrease by a greater degree, creating a larger gain from the short position in Treasury bond futures. If interest rates decrease, the futures prices will rise, causing a loss on Charlotte's futures position. But this will be offset by a gain in the market value of Charlotte's bond holdings. In this case, the firm would have experienced better overall performance without the hedge. Firms cannot know whether a hedge of interest rate risk will be beneficial in a future period because they cannot always predict the direction of future interest rates. ■

The preceding example presumes that the **basis,** or the difference between the price of a security and the price of a futures contract, remains the same. In reality, the price of the security may fluctuate more or less than the futures contract used to hedge it. If so, a perfect offset will not result when a given face value amount of securities is hedged with the same face value amount of futures contracts.

Tradeoff from Using a Short Hedge When one considers both the rising and the declining interest rate scenarios, the advantages and disadvantages of interest rate futures are obvious. Interest rate futures can hedge against both adverse and favorable events. Exhibit 13.5 compares two probability distributions of returns generated by a financial institution whose liabilities are more rate-sensitive than its assets. If the institution hedges its exposure to interest rate risk, its probability distribution of returns is narrower than if it does not hedge. The return from hedging would have been higher than without hedging if interest rates increased (see the left side of the graph) but lower if interest rates decreased (see the right side of the graph).

A financial institution that hedges with interest rate futures is less sensitive to economic events. Thus, financial institutions that frequently use interest rate futures may be able to reduce the variability of their earnings over time, which reflects a lower degree of risk. Nevertheless, it should be recognized that hedging is unlikely to remove all uncertainty because it is virtually impossible to perfectly hedge the sensitivity of all cash flows to interest rate movements.

Cross-Hedging Financial institutions sometimes want to hedge the interest rate risk of assets that cannot be perfectly matched by interest rate futures contracts. In this case, they attempt to identify an asset represented by futures contracts whose market value moves closely in tandem with that of the assets they want to hedge. The use of a futures contract on one financial instrument to hedge a position in a

Exhibit 13.5
Comparison of
Probability Distributions
of Returns; Hedged
versus Unhedged
Positions.

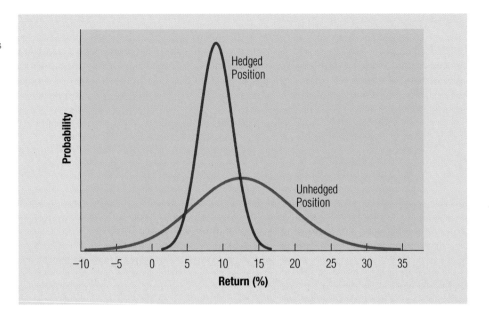

different financial instrument is known as **cross-hedging.** The effectiveness of a cross-hedge depends on the degree of correlation between the market values of the two financial instruments. If the price of the underlying security of the futures contract moves closely in tandem with the security hedged, the futures contract can provide an effective hedge.

For example, a financial institution may take a short position in Treasury bond futures contracts to hedge the interest rate risk of a portfolio of corporate bonds. The Treasury bonds and corporate bonds may be similarly sensitive to interest rate movements (assuming their maturities and coupon payment structures are similar). However, shifts in credit conditions could sever the close relationship between Treasury bond and corporate bond prices because the prices may be affected differently by economic conditions that influence the probability of default. For example, news that signals the possibility of a recession could cause investors to shift from corporate bonds to Treasury bonds. During this transition, the market value of the institution's corporate bond portfolio may decline, while Treasury bond prices are rising. Thus, the sale of Treasury bond futures to hedge against the expected temporary decline in the market value of a corporate bond portfolio would not have been effective.

Even when the futures contract is highly correlated with the portfolio being hedged, the value of the futures contract may change by a higher or lower percentage than the portfolio's market value. If the futures contract value is less volatile than the portfolio value, hedging will require a greater amount of principal represented by the futures contracts. For example, assume that for every percentage movement in the price of the futures contract, the value of the portfolio moves by 1.25 percent. In this case, the value of futures contracts to fully hedge the portfolio would be 1.25 times the principal of the portfolio.

Using Interest Rate Futures to Create a Long Hedge

Some financial institutions use a **long hedge** to reduce exposure to the possibility of declining interest rates. Consider government securities dealers who plan to purchase long-term bonds in a few months. If the dealers are concerned that prices of these

The Wall Street Journal provides price quotations for various interest rate futures contracts, including Treasury bond futures, Treasury note futures, and federal funds futures. The table contains the open price, high price, low price, and closing (settle) price for interest rate futures contracts that have a settlement date in the near future. The settlement month is listed just below the name of the contract. This table also lists the net change in price from the previous day and the open interest (number of existing contracts that have not been offset). The open interest is generally much larger for the interest rate futures contracts with settlement dates in the near future. Market participants can use this table to monitor their existing positions in interest rate futures or when considering a new position in interest rate futures.

Source: Reprinted with permission of Dow Jones & Company, Inc., from *The Wall Street Journal,* April 6, 2007; permission conveyed through the Copyright Clearance Center, Inc.

Interest Rate Futures

Treasury Bonds (CBT)-$100,000; pts 32nds of 100%

June	111-10	111-13	110-30	**111-01**	−8	836,419
Sept	111-08	111-08	110-31	**111-00**	−8	5,252

Treasury Notes (CBT)-$100,000; pts 32nds of 100%

June	108-040	108-060	107-290	**107-305**	−5.5	2,468,043
Sept	108-045	108-050	107-315	**108-005**	−5.5	41,673

5 Yr. Treasury Notes (CBT)-$100,000; pts 32nds of 100%

June	105-245	105-255	105-200	**105-215**	−2.5	1,531,475

2 Yr. Treasury Notes (CBT)-$200,000; pts 32nds of 100%

June	102-130	102-135	102-110	**102-117**	−1.0	952,293

30 Day Federal Funds (CBT)-$5,000,000; 100 - daily avg.

April	94.755	94.755	94.750	**94.750**	...	186,431
June	94.765	94.770	94.760	**94.765**	...	159,637

1 Month Libor (CME)-$3,000,000; pts of 100%

April	94.6800	94.6825	94.6800	**94.6800**	...	26,067
May	94.6875	94.6875	94.6850	**94.6850**	...	37,875

Eurodollar (CME)-$1,000,000; pts of 100%

April	94.6550	94.6575	94.6525	**94.6550**	...	50,840
June	94.7200	94.7250	94.7050	**94.7100**	−.0050	1,605,231
Sept	94.8900	94.9000	94.8600	**94.8700**	−.0200	1,394,444
Dec	95.0900	95.1050	95.0550	**95.0700**	−.0200	1,662,580

securities will rise before the time of their purchases, they may purchase Treasury bond futures contracts. These contracts lock in the price at which Treasury bonds can be purchased, regardless of what happens to market rates prior to the actual purchase of the bonds.

As another example, consider a bank that has obtained a significant portion of its funds from large CDs with a maturity of five years. Also assume that most of its assets represent loans with rates that adjust every six months. This bank would be adversely affected by a decline in interest rates because interest earned on assets would be more sensitive than interest paid on liabilities. To hedge against the possibility of lower interest rates, the bank could purchase T-bill futures to lock in the price on T-bills at a specified future date. If interest rates decline, the gain on the futures position could partially offset any reduction in the bank's earnings due to the reduction in interest rates.

Hedging Net Exposure

Because interest rate futures contracts entail transaction costs, they should be used only to hedge **net exposure,** which reflects the difference between asset and liability positions. Consider a bank that has $300 million in long-term assets and $220 million worth of long-term fixed-rate liabilities. If interest rates rise, the market value of the long-term assets will decline, but the bank will benefit from the fixed rate on the $220 million in long-term liabilities. Thus, the net exposure is only $80 million (assuming that the long-term assets and liabilities are similarly affected by rising interest rates). The financial institution should therefore focus on hedging its net exposure of $80 million by creating a short hedge.

Bond Index Futures

A bond index futures contract allows for the buying and selling of a bond index for a specified price at a specified date. For financial institutions that trade in municipal bonds, the Chicago Board of Trade offers **Municipal Bond Index (MBI) futures.** The index is based on the **Bond Buyer Index** of 40 actively traded general obligation and revenue bonds. The specific characteristics of MBI futures are shown in Exhibit 13.6. Because MBI futures are based on an index rather than on the bonds themselves, there is no physical exchange of bonds. Instead, these futures contracts are settled in cash.

ILLUSTRATION Palm Insurance Company will be receiving large cash flows in the near future. Although it plans to use some of the incoming funds to purchase municipal bonds, Palm is concerned that because of the likely downward trend in interest rates, municipal bond prices may increase before it can purchase them. Thus, it purchases MBI futures. If Palm's expectation is correct, the futures position will generate a gain, which can be used to pay for the higher-priced bonds once it has sufficient funds. Conversely, if bond prices fall, Palm will incur a loss from its futures position, but it will be able to purchase bonds at a lower price.

Meanwhile Evergreen Securities has agreed to underwrite bonds for various municipalities. It expects the market prices of bonds to decline in the near future. Such an event could reduce underwriting profits if the market price falls before these bonds are sold. To hedge this risk, Evergreen sells MBI futures. The futures position will generate a gain and offset the reduced underwriting profits if the firm's expectations are correct. ■

Stock Index Futures

A stock index futures contract allows for the buying and selling of a stock index for a specified price at a specified date. Futures for various stock indexes are traded on the Chicago Mercantile Exchange. Exhibit 13.7 shows the contracts that are available and their valuation.

ILLUSTRATION The S&P 500 index futures contract is valued as the index times $250, so if the index is valued at 1600, the contract is valued at $1600 \times \$250 = \$400,000$. Mini S&P 500 index futures contracts are available for small investors. These contracts are valued at $50 times the index, so if the index is valued at 1600, the contract is valued at $1600 \times \$50 = \$80,000$. ■

Exhibit 13.6   Characteristics of Municipal Bond Index Futures

Characteristics of Futures Contract	Municipal Bond Index Futures
Trading unit	1,000 times the Bond Buyer Municipal Bond Index. A price of 90–00 represents a contract size of $90,000.
Price quotation	In points and thirty-seconds of a point.
Minimum price fluctuation	One thirty-second ($\frac{1}{32}$) of a point, or $31.25 per contract.
Daily trading limits	Three points ($3,000) per contract above or below the previous day's settlement price.
Settlement months	March, June, September, December.
Settlement procedure	Municipal Bond Index futures settle in cash on the last day of trading.

Exhibit 13.7
Stock Index Futures
Contracts

Type of Stock Index Futures Contract	Contract Is Valued As
S&P 500 index	$250 times index
Mini S&P 500 index	$50 times index
S&P Midcap 400 index	$500 times index
S&P Small Cap index	$200 times index
Nasdaq 100 index	$100 times index
Mini Nasdaq 100 index	$20 times index
Mini Nasdaq Composite index	$20 times index
Russell 2000 index	$500 times index
Nikkei (Japan) 225 index	$5 times index

A futures contract on the S&P 500 index represents a composite of 500 large corporations. The purchase of an S&P 500 futures contract obligates the purchaser to purchase the S&P 500 index at a specified settlement date for a specified amount. Thus, participants who expect the stock market to perform well before the settlement date may consider purchasing S&P 500 index futures. Conversely, participants who expect the stock market to perform poorly before the settlement date may consider selling S&P 500 index futures.

Stock index futures contracts have four settlement dates in a given year—the third Friday in March, June, September, and December. The securities underlying the stock index futures contracts are not deliverable; settlement occurs through a cash payment. On the settlement date, the futures contract is valued according to the quoted stock index. The net gain or loss on the stock index futures contract is the difference between the futures price when the initial position was created and the value of the contract as of the settlement date.

Like other financial futures contracts, stock index futures can be closed out before the settlement date by taking an offsetting position. For example, if an S&P 500 futures contract with a December settlement date is purchased in September, this position can be closed out in November by selling an S&P 500 futures contract with the same December settlement date. When a position is closed out prior to the settlement date, the net gain or loss on the stock index futures contract is the difference between the futures price when the position was created and the futures price when the position is closed out.

Some speculators prefer to trade stock index futures rather than actual stocks because of the smaller transaction costs. The commission for a purchase and subsequent sale of S&P 500 futures contracts is substantially less than the commission for purchasing and selling the equivalent stocks in the S&P 500.

Valuing Stock Index Futures Contracts

The value of a stock index futures contract is highly correlated with the value of the underlying stock index. Nevertheless, the value of the stock index futures contract commonly differs from the price of the underlying asset because of unique features of the stock index futures contract.

ILLUSTRATION Consider that an investor can buy either a stock index or a futures contract on the stock index with a settlement date of six months from now. In either case, the investor will own the stock index in six months, but buying the

The *Wall Street Journal* provides futures price quotations for various stock indexes, including the Dow Jones (DJ) Industrial Average, the S&P 500, and the Nasdaq 100. The table contains the open price, high price, low price, and closing (settle) price for index futures that have a settlement date in the near future. The settlement month is listed just below the name of the index. This table also provides the change in price from the previous day and the open interest (number of existing contracts that have not been offset). The open interest is generally much larger for the index futures contracts with settlement dates in the near future. Market participants can use this table to monitor their existing positions in index futures or when considering a new position in index futures. Some market participants monitor the futures price in comparison to the prevailing index level because they interpret it as the market's general forecast of the index.

Source: Reprinted with permission of Dow Jones & Company, Inc., from *The Wall Street Journal,* April 6, 2007; permission conveyed through the Copyright Clearance Center, Inc.

Index Futures

DJ Industrial Average (CBT)-$10 x index

	Open	High	Low	Settle	Chg	Open Int
June	12591	12643	12573	**12622**	27	40,370
Sept	12700	12735	12700	**12725**	27	42

Mini DJ Industrial Average (CBT)-$5 x index

June	12594	12643	12571	**12622**	27	75,016
Sept	12692	12692	12692	**12725**	27	38

S&P 500 Index (CME)-$250 x index

June	1448.20	1454.70	1446.30	**1452.70**	4.20	605,349
Sept	1466.00	1467.90	1459.90	**1466.10**	4.20	15,118

Mini S&P 500 (CME)-$50 x index

June	1448.00	1454.75	1446.25	**1452.75**	4.25	1,872,145
Sept	1462.00	1468.00 ▲	1460.00	**1466.00**	4.00	9,054

Nasdaq 100 (CME)-$100 x index

June	1818.25	1831.50	1814.00	**1828.25**	9.00	46,570

Mini Nasdaq 100 (CME)-$20 x index

June	1818.3	1831.5	1814.5	**1828.3**	9.0	351,449
Sept	1842.0	1853.8	1838.5	**1851.0**	9.0	105

Russell 1000 (NYBOT)-$500 x index

June	790.50	793.50 ▲	790.50	**793.50**	2.25	67,747

U.S. Dollar Index (NYBOT)-$1,000 x index

June	82.73	82.78	82.37	**82.45**	-.26	27,906
Sept	82.42	82.16	82.16	**82.21**	-.26	2,080

Source: Reuters

index rather than the index futures offers distinct advantages and disadvantages. On the favorable side, the buyer of the index receives dividends, whereas the buyer of the index futures does not. On the unfavorable side, the buyer of the index must use funds to buy the index, whereas the buyer of index futures can engage in the futures contract simply by establishing a margin deposit with a relatively small amount of assets (such as Treasury securities) that may generate interest while they are used to satisfy margin requirements.

Assume that the index will pay dividends equal to 3 percent over the next six months. Also assume that the purchaser of the index will borrow funds to purchase the index, at an interest rate of 2 percent over the six-month period. In this example, the advantage of holding the index (a 3 percent dividend yield) relative to holding a futures contract on the index more than offsets the 2 percent cost of financing the purchase of the index. The so-called net financing cost (also called cost of carry) to the purchaser of the underlying assets (the index) is the 2 percent cost of financing minus the 3 percent yield earned on the assets, or −1 percent. A negative cost of carry indicates that the cost of financing is less than the yield earned from dividends.

If the spot price of the index is the same as the futures price, the futures price will be more attractive. In fact, given the information in this example, speculators can engage in arbitrage whereby they earn a risk-free profit without tying up their funds. Specifically, they use borrowed funds to purchase the index at the spot price and simultaneously sell index futures. This strategy generates a 3 percent gain due to the dividend yield and incurs a 2 percent cost of financing, or a net gain of 1 percent without tying up any funds over the six-month period. Such arbitrage puts upward pressure on the spot price of the index (because of the purchases of the index) and downward pressure on the index futures price. Once the futures price is 1 percent less than the spot price, arbitrage will no longer be possible because the 3 percent gain from dividends is offset by the 2 percent cost of financing and the 1 percent discount on the futures price. That is, the -1 percent cost of carry is offset by selling index futures at 1 percent less than the spot rate at which the index was purchased. As this example illustrates, the price of the index futures contract is driven by the underlying index, along with the cost of carry. Arbitrage ensures that as the index value and the cost of carry change over time, so will the price of the index futures contract. In general, the underlying security (or index) tends to change by a much greater degree than the cost of carry, so changes in financial futures prices are primarily attributed to changes in the values of the underlying securities (or indexes). ■

Indicators of Stock Index Futures Prices Since stock index futures prices are primarily driven by movements in the corresponding stock indexes, participants in stock index futures monitor indicators that may signal changes in the stock indexes. These investors monitor some of the same economic indicators as bond futures participants, but do not necessarily respond to new information in the same way. Furthermore, index futures participants tend to have divergent views on how the new information will affect a stock index. Consequently, although the new information may cause substantial trading of stock index futures, the expected effects on index prices may vary. Thus, the impact of new information on the prices of stock index futures cannot be easily anticipated.

Speculating with Stock Index Futures

Stock index futures can be traded to capitalize on expectations about general stock market movements.

ILLUSTRATION Boulder Insurance Company plans to purchase a variety of stocks for its stock portfolio in December, once cash inflows are received. Although the company does not have cash to purchase the stocks immediately, it is anticipating a large jump in stock market prices before December. Given this situation, it decides to purchase S&P 500 index futures. The futures price on the S&P 500 index with a December settlement date is 1500. The value of an S&P 500 futures contract is $250 times the index. Because the S&P 500 futures prices should move with the stock market, it will rise over time if the company's expectations are correct. Assume that the S&P 500 index rises to 1600 on the settlement date.

In this example, the nominal profit on the S&P 500 index futures is

Selling price	$400,000	(Index value of 1600 × $250)
− Purchase price	− 375,000	(Index value of 1500 × $250)
= Profit	$25,000	■

Thus, Boulder was able to capitalize on its expectations even though it did not have sufficient cash to purchase stock. If stock prices had declined over the period of concern, the S&P 500 futures price would have decreased, and Boulder would have incurred a loss on its futures position.

Hedging with Stock Index Futures

Stock index futures are also commonly used to hedge the market risk of an existing stock portfolio.

ILLUSTRATION Glacier Stock Mutual Fund expects the stock market to decline temporarily, causing a temporary decline in its stock portfolio. The fund could sell its stocks with the intent to repurchase them in the near future, but it would incur excessive transaction costs. A more efficient solution is to sell stock index futures. If the fund's stock portfolio is similar to the S&P 500 index, Glacier can sell futures contracts on that index. If the stock market declines as expected, Glacier will generate a gain when closing out the stock index futures position, which will somewhat offset the loss on its stock portfolio. ■

This hedge is more effective when the investor's portfolio is diversified like the S&P 500 index. The value of a less diversified stock portfolio will correlate less with the S&P 500 index, so a gain from selling index futures may not completely offset the loss in the portfolio during a market downturn. Assuming that the stock portfolio moves in tandem with the S&P 500, a full hedge would involve the sale of the amount of futures contracts whose combined underlying value is equal to the market value of the stock portfolio being hedged.

ILLUSTRATION Assume that a portfolio manager has a stock portfolio valued at $400,000. Also assume that S&P 500 index futures contracts are available for a settlement date one month from now at a level of 1600, which is about equal to today's index value. The manager could sell S&P 500 futures contracts to hedge the stock portfolio. Since the futures contract is valued at $250 times the index level, the contract will result in a payment of $400,000 at settlement date. One index futures contract will be needed to match the existing value of the stock portfolio. Assuming that the stock index moves in tandem with the manager's stock portfolio, any loss on the portfolio should be offset by the gain on the futures contract. For example, if the stock portfolio declines by about 5 percent over one month, this reflects a loss of $20,000 (5% of $400,000 = $20,000). Yet, the S&P 500 index should also have declined by 5 percent (to a level of 1520). Consequently, the S&P 500 index futures contract that was sold by the manager should result in a gain of $20,000 [(1600 − 1520) × $250], which offsets the loss on the stock portfolio. ■

If the stock market experiences higher prices over the month, the S&P 500 index will rise, creating a loss on the futures contract. The value of the manager's stock portfolio will have increased to offset the loss, however.

Test of Suitability of Stock Index Futures The suitability of using stock index futures to hedge can be assessed by measuring the sensitivity of the portfolio's performance to market movements over a period prior to taking a hedge position. The sensitivity of a hypothetical position in futures to those same market movements in that period could also be assessed. A general test of suitability is to determine whether the hypothetical derivative position would have offset adverse market effects on the portfolio's performance. Although it may be extremely difficult to perfectly hedge all of a portfolio's exposure to market risk, for a hedge to be suitable there should be some evidence that such a hypothetical hedge would have been moderately effective for that firm. That is, if the position in financial derivatives would not have provided an effective hedge of market risk over a recent period, a firm should not expect that it will provide an effective hedge in the future. This test of suitability uses only data that were available at the time the hedge was to be enacted.

Determining the Proportion of the Portfolio to Hedge Portfolio managers do not necessarily hedge their entire stock portfolio, because they may wish to be partially exposed in the event that stock prices rise. For instance, if the portfolio in the preceding example was valued at $1.2 million, the portfolio manager could have hedged one-third of the stock portfolio by selling one stock index futures contract. The short position in one index futures contract would reflect one-third of the value of the stock portfolio. Alternatively, the manager could have hedged two-thirds of the stock portfolio by selling two stock index futures contracts. The higher the proportion of the portfolio that is hedged, the more insulated the manager's performance is from market conditions, whether those conditions are favorable or unfavorable. Exhibit 13.8 illustrates the net gain (including the gain on the futures and the gain on the stock portfolio) to the portfolio manager under five possible scenarios for the market return (shown in the first column). If the stock market declines, any degree of hedging is beneficial, but the benefits are greater if a higher proportion of the portfolio was hedged. If the stock market performs well, any degree of hedging reduces the net gain, but the reduction is greater if a higher proportion of the portfolio was hedged. In essence, hedging with stock index futures reduces the sensitivity to both unfavorable and favorable market conditions.

Dynamic Asset Allocation with Stock Index Futures

Institutional investors are increasingly using **dynamic asset allocation,** in which they switch between risky and low-risk investment positions over time in response to changing expectations. This strategy allows managers to increase the exposure of their portfolios when they expect favorable market conditions, and to reduce their exposure when they expect unfavorable market conditions. When they anticipate favorable market movements, stock portfolio managers can purchase stock index futures, which intensify the effects of market conditions. Conversely, when they anticipate unfavorable market movements, they can sell stock index futures to reduce the effects that market conditions will have on their stock portfolios. As expectations change frequently, portfolio managers commonly alter their degree of exposure. Stock index futures allow portfolio managers to alter their risk-return position without restructuring their existing stock portfolios. Using dynamic asset allocation in this way avoids the substantial transaction costs that would be associated with restructuring the stock portfolios.

Prices of Stock Index Futures versus Stocks

The prices of index futures and the prices of the stocks representing the index can differ to some degree. To understand why, consider a situation in which many institutional investors anticipate a temporary decline in stock prices. Because they expect the decline to be only temporary, the investors prefer not to liquidate their stock

Exhibit 13.8
Net Gain (on Stock Portfolio and Short Position in Stock Index Futures) for Different Degrees of Hedging

| Scenario for Market Return | Proportion of Stock Portfolio Hedged | | | |
	0%	33%	67%	100%
−20%	−20%	−13.4%	−6.7%	0%
−10	−10	−6.7	−3.3	0
0	0	0	0	0
10	+10	+6.7	+3.3	0
20	+20	+13.4	+6.7	0

Note: Numbers are based on the assumption that the stock portfolio moves in perfect tandem with the market.

portfolios. As a form of portfolio insurance, they sell stock index futures so that any decline in the market value of their stock portfolio will be offset by a gain on their futures position. When numerous institutional investors sell index futures instead of selling stocks to prepare for a market decline, their actions can cause the index futures price to be below the prevailing stock prices.

In some cases, index futures prices may exceed the prices of the stocks that the index comprises. As favorable information about the stock market becomes available, investors can buy either stock index futures or the actual stocks that make up the index. The futures can be purchased immediately with a small up-front payment. Purchasing actual stocks may take longer because of the time needed to select specific stocks. In addition, a larger up-front investment is necessary. This explains why the price of stock index futures may reflect investor expectations about the market more rapidly than stock prices.

Recent studies have found a high degree of correlation between the stock index futures and the index itself. Price movements in the stock index sometimes lag behind movement in the stock index futures by up to 45 minutes. This confirms that the stock index futures more rapidly reflect new information that can influence expectations about the stock market. Even though the index futures price movements frequently precede stock index movements, the relationship is not consistent enough to develop an exploitable trading strategy in which positions in a stock index are taken based on the most recent movement in the futures index.

Arbitrage with Stock Index Futures

The New York Stock Exchange (NYSE) narrowly defines program trading as the simultaneous buying and selling of at least 15 different stocks that in aggregate is valued at more than $1 million. Program trading is commonly used in conjunction with the trading of stock index futures contracts in a strategy known as **index arbitrage.** Securities firms act as **arbitrageurs** by capitalizing on discrepancies between prices of index futures and stocks. Index arbitrage involves the buying or selling of stock index futures with a simultaneous opposite position in the stocks that the index comprises. The index arbitrage is instigated when prices of stock index futures differ significantly from the stocks represented by the index. For example, if the index futures contract is priced high relative to the stocks representing the index, an arbitrageur may consider purchasing the stocks and simultaneously selling stock index futures. Alternatively, if the index futures are priced low relative to the stocks representing the index, an arbitrageur may purchase index futures and simultaneously sell stocks. An arbitrage profit is attainable if the price differential exceeds the costs incurred from trading in both markets.

Index arbitrage does not cause the price discrepancy between the two markets, but rather responds to it. The arbitrageur's ability to detect price discrepancies between stock and futures markets is enhanced by computers. Roughly 50 percent of all program trading activity is for the purpose of index arbitrage.

Some critics suggest that the index arbitrage activity of purchasing index futures while selling stocks adversely affects stock prices. However, if index futures did not exist, institutional investors could not use portfolio insurance. In this case, a general expectation of a temporary market decline would more likely encourage the sales of stocks to prepare for the decline, which would accelerate the drop in prices.

Circuit Breakers on Stock Index Futures

Circuit breakers are trading restrictions imposed on specific stocks or stock indexes. The Chicago Mercantile Exchange imposes circuit breakers on the S&P 500 futures contract.

By prohibiting trading for short time periods when prices decline to specific threshold levels, circuit breakers may allow investors to determine whether circulating rumors are true and to work out credit arrangements if they have received a margin call. If prices are still perceived to be too high when the markets reopen, the prices will decline further. Thus, circuit breakers do not guarantee that prices will turn upward. Nevertheless, they may be able to prevent large declines in prices that would be attributed to panic selling rather than to fundamental forces.

The first test for the circuit breakers was on October 13, 1989, when stocks declined by about 5 percent on average. Exhibit 13.9 shows the price trends of stocks and index futures on this day. At 2:07 P.M., the first circuit breaker tripped as the S&P futures contract declined by 12 points below the previous day's closing price. Stocks were not subject to that circuit breaker, however, and their prices continued to decline while index futures trading was halted. When the index futures market reopened, the index futures price dropped sharply, then increased for a few minutes, and then declined until 2:45 P.M.; at that time, it was 30 points below the previous day's close. Consequently, the second breaker was imposed. It is unclear whether the circuit breakers reduced panic selling on this day, as it is difficult to determine how futures prices would have changed without the circuit breakers.

On July 23, 1990, the circuit breakers were tested once again. Stock market prices plunged in the morning, causing a circuit breaker to be imposed on stock index futures. Meanwhile, the NYSE asked members to temporarily stop index arbitrage trades. The pessimism subsided shortly thereafter. Some traders acknowledged that the market decline could have been much more pronounced without the use of circuit breakers on this day.

Exhibit 13.9 Use of Circuit Breakers during the Mini-Crash on October 13, 1989

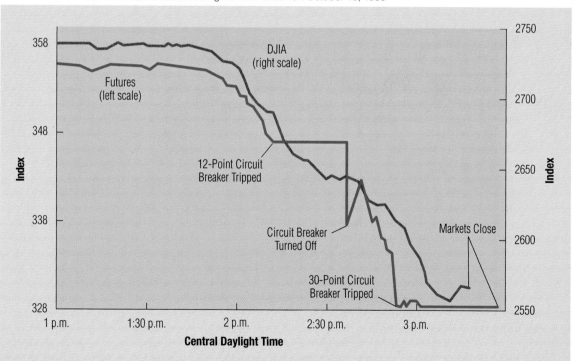

Note: The futures price is the minute-by-minute average of the December 1989 S&P 500 stock index futures contract traded at the Chicago Mercantile Exchange. The stock price is the minute-by-minute average of the Dow Jones Industrial Average.
Source: *Economic Review,* Federal Reserve Bank of Kansas City (March–April 1990): 39.

Single Stock Futures

A single stock futures contract is an agreement to buy or sell a specified number of shares of a specified stock on a specified future date. Such contracts have been traded on futures exchanges in Australia and Europe since the 1990s. In 2001, the Nasdaq market and the London International Financial Futures and Options Exchange (LIFFE) engaged in a joint venture to create a U.S. market for trading single stock futures. The contracts are available for specific stocks that are traded on the Nasdaq market or NYSE. The nominal size of a contract is 100 shares. Investors can buy or sell singles stock futures contracts through their broker. The orders to buy and sell a specific single stock futures contract are matched electronically. Single stock futures have become increasingly popular. They are regulated by the Commodity Futures Trading Commission (CFTC) and the Securities and Exchange Commission (SEC).

Settlement dates are on the third Friday of the delivery month on a quarterly basis (March, June, September, and December) for the next five quarters, as well as the nearest two months. For example, on January 3, an investor could purchase a stock futures contract for the third Friday in the next two months (January or February), or over the next five quarters (March, June, September, December, and March of the following year). Trading hours are from 9:30 A.M. to 4 P.M. eastern standard time. An investor can buy single stock futures on margin.

Investors who expect a particular stock's price to rise over time may consider buying futures on that stock. To obtain a contract to buy March futures on 100 shares of Zyco stock for $5,000 ($50 per share), an investor must submit the $5,000 payment to the clearinghouse on the third Friday in March and will receive shares of Zyco stock on the settlement date. If Zyco stock is valued at $53 at the time of settlement, the investor can sell the stock in the stock market for a gain of $3 per share or $300 for the contract (ignoring commissions). This gain would likely reflect a substantial return on the investment since the investor had to invest only a small margin (perhaps 20 percent of the contract price) to take a position in futures. If Zyco stock is valued at $46 at the time of settlement, the investor would incur a loss of $4 share, which would reflect a substantial percentage loss on the investment. Thus, single stock futures offer potential high returns but also high risk.

Investors who expect a particular stock's price to decline over time can sell futures contracts on that stock. This activity is somewhat similar to selling a stock short, except that single stock futures can be sold without borrowing the underlying stock from a broker as short-sellers must do. To obtain a contract to sell March futures of Zyco stock, an investor must deliver Zyco stock to the clearinghouse on the third Friday in March and will receive the payment specified in the futures contract.

Investors can close out their position at any time by taking the opposite position. For example, assume that shortly after the investor purchased futures on Zyco stock with a March delivery at $50 per share, the stock price declines. Rather than incur the risk that the price could continue to decline, the investor could sell a Zyco futures contract with a March delivery. If this contract specifies a price of $48 per share, the investor's gain will be the difference between the selling price and the buying price, which is −$2 per share or −$200 for the contract.

The Chicago Board of Options Exchange and the Chicago Board of Trade recently engaged in a joint venture called OneChicago, which serves as another market for trading single stock futures. The contract specifications are similar to those established by Nasdaq and LIFFE. The contracts are traded electronically.

Risk of Trading Futures Contracts

Users of futures contracts must recognize the various types of risk exhibited by such contracts and other derivative instruments.

Market Risk

Market risk refers to fluctuations in the value of the instrument as a result of market conditions. Firms that use futures contracts to speculate should be concerned about market risk. If their expectations about future market conditions are wrong, they may suffer losses on their futures contracts. Firms that use futures contracts to hedge are less concerned about market risk because if market conditions cause a loss on their derivative instruments, they should have a partial offsetting gain on the positions that they were hedging.

Basis Risk

A second type of risk is **basis risk,** or the risk that the position being hedged by the futures contracts is not affected in the same manner as the instrument underlying the futures contract. This type of risk applies only to those firms or individuals who are using futures contracts to hedge. For example, consider a bond portfolio manager who uses Treasury bond futures contracts to hedge a portfolio of Treasury bonds that have, on average, five years remaining until maturity. The value of the Treasury bond futures may not necessarily move in tandem with the value of the Treasury bond portfolio, because the maturities (and the duration) of the bond portfolio and the underlying securities in the futures contract are not exactly the same. Therefore, a short position in Treasury bond futures contracts will not perfectly offset the impact of interest rate movements on the Treasury bond portfolio.

Liquidity Risk

A third type of risk is **liquidity risk,** which refers to potential price distortions due to a lack of liquidity. For example, a firm may purchase a particular bond futures contract to speculate on expectations of rising bond prices. However, when it attempts to close out its position by selling an identical futures contract, it may find that there are no willing buyers for this type of futures contract at that time. In this case, the firm will have to sell the futures contract at a lower price. Users of futures contracts may reduce liquidity risk by using only those futures contracts that are widely traded.

Credit Risk

A fourth type of risk is **credit risk,** which is the risk that a loss will occur because a counterparty defaults on the contract. This type of risk exists for over-the-counter transactions, in which a firm or individual relies on the creditworthiness of a counterparty.

The possibility that counterparties will not fulfill their obligations is not a concern when trading futures and other derivatives on exchanges, because the exchanges normally guarantee that the provisions of the contract will be honored. The financial intermediaries that make the arrangements in the over-the-counter market can also take some steps to reduce this type of risk. First, the financial intermediary can require that each party provide some form of collateral to back up its position. Second, the financial intermediary can serve as a guarantor (for a fee) in the event that the counterparty does not fulfill its obligation.

Prepayment Risk

Prepayment risk refers to the possibility that the assets to be hedged may be prepaid earlier than their designated maturity. Suppose a commercial bank sells Treasury bond futures in order to hedge its holdings of corporate bonds, and just after the futures position is created, the bonds are called by the corporation that initially issued them. If interest rates subsequently decline, the bank will incur a loss from its futures position without a corresponding gain from its bond position (because the bonds were called earlier).

As a second example, consider a savings and loan association with large holdings of long-term fixed-rate mortgages that are mostly financed by short-term funds. It sells Treasury bond futures to hedge against the possibility of rising interest rates; then, after the futures position is established, interest rates decline, and many of the existing mortgages are prepaid by homeowners. The savings and loan association will incur a loss from its futures position without a corresponding gain from its fixed-rate mortgage position (because the mortgages were prepaid).

Operational Risk

A sixth type of risk is **operational risk,** which is the risk of losses as a result of inadequate management or controls. For example, firms that use futures contracts to hedge are exposed to the possibility that the employees responsible for their futures positions do not fully understand how values of specific futures contracts will respond to market conditions. Furthermore, those employees may take more speculative positions than the firms desire if the firms do not have adequate controls to monitor their positions.

Regulation in the Futures Markets

Given recent cases in which firms incurred major losses on futures contracts or other derivative securities, there is more awareness about **systemic risk,** or the risk that a particular event (such as financial problems at one particular firm) could spread adverse effects among several firms or among financial markets. The concern about systemic risk stems from the intertwined relationships among firms that engage in derivative securities trading that obligates them to make future payments to each other.

ILLUSTRATION Nexus, Inc. requests several transactions in derivative securities, in which it buys futures on Treasury bonds in an over-the-counter market. Bangor Bank accommodates Nexus by taking the opposite side of the transactions. The bank's positions in these contracts also serve as a hedge against its existing exposure to interest rate risk. As time passes, Nexus experiences financial problems. As interest rates rise and the value of a Treasury bond futures contract declines, Nexus will take a major loss on the futures transactions. It files for bankruptcy, as it is unable to fulfill its obligation to buy the Treasury bonds from Bangor Bank at the settlement date. Bangor Bank was relying on this payment to hedge its exposure to interest rate risk. Consequently, Bangor Bank experiences financial problems and cannot make the payments on other over-the-counter derivatives contracts that it has with three other financial institutions. These financial institutions were relying on those funds to cover their own obligations on derivative contracts with several other firms. These firms may then be unable to honor their payment obligations resulting from derivative contract agreements, causing the adverse effects to spread further. ■

Lengthy delays in payment could also disrupt the financial markets. Systemic risk is more pronounced as a result of the increasing use of over-the-counter markets for the trading of derivative securities.

Various regulators have attempted to reduce systemic risk by ensuring that participants in derivative securities markets have adequate collateral to back their derivative positions and that the participants fully disclose their exposure to risk resulting from derivative positions. For example, the Federal Reserve System monitors the commercial banks that participate in the derivative securities markets to ensure that they have adequate capital.

Furthermore, accounting regulators revised accounting standards in 1994 to require more disclosure about derivative positions. Specifically, firms are now required to report both their objectives in using derivative securities and the means by which they plan to achieve those objectives. The accounting guidelines also encourage firms to measure the impact of various possible economic scenarios on their derivative positions. Some, but not all, types of derivative securities must be reported in the financial statements. Similarly, some, but not all, derivative securities must be valued in financial statements at their market value. There is an ongoing effort to make the accounting rules more consistent among derivative securities in the United States and throughout other countries as well.

Institutional Use of Futures Markets

Exhibit 13.10 summarizes the manner in which various types of financial institutions participate in futures markets. Financial institutions generally use futures contracts to reduce risk, as has already been illustrated by several examples. Some commercial banks and savings institutions use a short hedge to protect against a possible increase in interest rates. Some bond mutual funds, pension funds, and life insurance companies take short positions in interest rate futures to insulate their bond portfolios from a possible increase in interest rates. Stock mutual funds, pension funds, and insurance companies take short positions in stock index futures to partially insulate their respective stock portfolios from adverse stock market movements.

Globalization of Futures Markets

GL🌐BALASPECTS The trading of financial futures also requires the assessment of international financial market conditions. The flow of foreign funds into and out of the United States can affect interest rates and therefore the market value of Treasury bonds, corporate bonds, mortgages, and other long-term debt securities. Portfolio managers assess international flows of funds to forecast changes in interest rate movements, which in turn affect the value of their respective portfolios. Even speculators assess international flows of funds to forecast interest rates so that they can determine whether to take short or long futures positions.

Exhibit 13.10
Institutional Use of
Futures Markets

Type of Financial Institution	Participation in Futures Markets
Commercial banks	• Take positions in futures contracts to hedge against interest rate risk.
Savings institutions	• Take positions in futures contracts to hedge against interest rate risk.
Securities firms	• Execute futures transactions for individuals and firms. • Take positions in futures contracts to hedge their own portfolios against stock market or interest rate movements.
Mutual funds	• Take positions in futures contracts to speculate on future stock market or interest rate movements. • Take positions in futures contracts to hedge their portfolios against stock market or interest rate movements.
Pension funds	• Take positions in futures contracts to hedge their portfolios against stock market or interest rate movements.
Insurance companies	• Take positions in futures contracts to hedge their portfolios against stock market or interest rate movements.

Non-U.S. Participation in U.S. Futures Contracts

Financial futures contracts on U.S. securities are commonly traded by non-U.S. financial institutions that maintain holdings of U.S. securities. These institutions use financial futures to reduce their exposure to U.S. stock market or interest rate movements. The Chicago Board of Trade has allowed more access to non-U.S. customers by expanding its trading hours to cover various time zones.

Foreign Stock Index Futures

Foreign stock index futures have been created to either speculate on or hedge against potential movements in foreign stock markets. Expectations of a strong foreign stock market encourage the purchase of futures contracts on the representative index. Conversely, if firms expect a decline in the foreign market, they will consider selling futures on the representative index. In addition, financial institutions with substantial investment in a particular foreign stock market can hedge against a temporary decline in that market by selling foreign stock index futures.

Some of the more popular foreign stock index futures contracts are identified in Exhibit 13.11. Numerous other foreign stock index futures contracts have been created. In fact, futures exchanges have been established in Ireland, France, Spain, and Italy. Financial institutions around the world can use futures contracts to hedge against temporary declines in their asset portfolios. Speculators can take long or short positions to speculate on a particular market with a relatively small initial investment. Financial futures on debt instruments (such as futures on German government bonds) are also offered by numerous exchanges in non-U.S. markets, including the London International Financial Futures Exchange, Singapore International Monetary Exchange (SIMEX), and Sydney Futures Exchange (SFE). In 2001, the LIFFE was acquired by Euronext, an alliance of European stock exchanges.

Electronic trading of futures contracts is creating an internationally integrated futures market. As mentioned earlier, the Chicago Mercantile Exchange has instituted GLOBEX, a round-the-world electronic trading network. It allows financial futures contracts to be traded even when the trading floor is closed.

Currency Futures Contracts

A **currency futures contract** is a standardized agreement to deliver or receive a specified amount of a specified foreign currency at a specified price (exchange rate) and date. The settlement months are March, June, September, and December. Some companies act as hedgers in the currency futures market by purchasing futures on currencies that they will need in the future to cover payables or by selling futures on currencies that they will receive in the future. Speculators in the currency futures market may purchase futures on a foreign currency that they expect to strengthen against the U.S. dollar or sell futures on currencies that they expect to weaken against the U.S. dollar.

Exhibit 13.11
Popular Foreign Stock Index Futures Contracts

Name of Stock Futures Index	Description
Nikkei 225	225 Japanese stocks
Toronto 35	35 stocks on Toronto stock exchange
Financial Times Stock Exchange 100	100 stocks on London stock exchange
Barclays share price	40 stocks on New Zealand stock exchange
Hang Seng	33 stocks on Hong Kong stock exchange
Osaka	50 Japanese stocks
All Ordinaries share price	307 Australian stocks

Purchasers of currency futures contracts can hold the contract until the settlement date and accept delivery of the foreign currency at that time, or they can close out their long position prior to the settlement date by selling the identical type and number of contracts before then. If they close out their long position, their gain or loss is determined by the futures price when they created the position versus the futures price at the time the position was closed out. Sellers of currency futures contracts either deliver the foreign currency at the settlement date or close out their position by purchasing an identical type and number of contracts prior to the settlement date.

Summary

■ A financial futures contract is a standardized agreement to deliver or receive a specified amount of a specified financial instrument at a specified price and date. As the market value of the underlying instrument changes, so will the value of the financial futures contract. As the market value of the underlying instrument rises, there is a greater demand for the futures contract that has locked in the price of the instrument.

■ An interest rate futures contract locks in the price to be paid for a specified debt instrument. Speculators who expect interest rates to decline can purchase interest rate futures contracts, because the market value of the underlying debt instrument should rise. Speculators who expect interest rates to rise can sell interest rate futures contracts, because the market value of the underlying debt instrument should decrease.

Financial institutions (or other firms) that desire to hedge against rising interest rates can sell interest rate futures contracts. Financial institutions that desire to hedge against declining interest rates can purchase these contracts. If interest rates move in the anticipated direction, the financial institutions will gain from their futures position, which can partially offset any adverse effects of the interest rate movements on their normal operations.

■ Speculators who expect stock prices to increase can purchase stock index futures contracts; speculators who expect stock prices to decrease can sell these contracts. Stock index futures can be sold by financial institutions that expect a temporary decline in stock prices and wish to hedge their stock portfolios.

■ Depository institutions such as commercial banks and savings institutions commonly sell interest rate futures contracts to hedge against a possible increase in interest rates. Bond mutual funds, pension funds, and insurance companies also sell interest rate futures contracts to hedge their bond portfolios against a possible increase in interest rates.

Stock mutual funds, pension funds, and insurance companies frequently sell stock index futures contracts to hedge their stock portfolios against a possible temporary decrease in stock prices.

Point Counter-Point

Has the Futures Market Created More Uncertainty for Stocks?

Point Yes. Futures contracts encourage speculation on indexes. Thus, an entire market can be influenced by the trading of speculators.

Counter-Point No. Futures contracts are commonly used to hedge portfolios and therefore can reduce the effects of weak market conditions. Moreover, investing in stocks is just as speculative as taking a position in futures markets.

Who Is Correct? Use the Internet to learn more about this issue. Offer your own opinion on this issue.

Questions and Applications

1. **Futures Contracts** Describe the general characteristics of a futures contract. How does a clearinghouse facilitate the trading of financial futures contracts?

2. **Futures Pricing** How does the price of a financial futures contract change as the market price of the security it represents changes? Why?

3. **Hedging with Futures** Explain why some futures contracts may be more suitable than others for hedging exposure to interest rate risk.

4. **Treasury Bond Futures** Will speculators buy or sell Treasury bond futures contracts if they expect interest rates to increase? Explain.

5. **Gains from Purchasing Futures** Explain how purchasers of financial futures contracts can offset their position. How is their gain or loss determined? What is the maximum loss to a purchaser of a futures contract?

6. **Gains from Selling Futures** Explain how sellers of financial futures contracts can offset their position. How is their gain or loss determined?

7. **Hedging with Futures** Assume a financial institution has a larger amount of rate-sensitive assets than rate-sensitive liabilities. Would it be more likely to be adversely affected by an increase or a decrease in interest rates? Should it purchase or sell interest rate futures contracts in order to hedge its exposure?

8. **Hedging with Futures** Assume a financial institution has a larger amount of rate-sensitive liabilities than rate-sensitive assets. Would it be more likely to be adversely affected by an increase or a decrease in interest rates? Should it purchase or sell interest rate futures contracts in order to hedge its exposure?

9. **Hedging Decision** Why do some financial institutions remain exposed to interest rate risk, even when they believe that the use of interest rate futures could reduce their exposure?

10. **Long versus Short Hedge** Explain the difference between a long hedge and a short hedge used by financial institutions. When is a long hedge more appropriate than a short hedge?

11. **Impact of Futures Hedge** Explain how the probability distribution of a financial institution's returns is affected when it uses interest rate futures to hedge. What does this imply about its risk?

12. **Cross-Hedging** Describe the act of cross-hedging. What determines the effectiveness of a cross-hedge?

13. **Hedging with Bond Futures** How might a savings and loan association use Treasury bond futures to hedge its fixed-rate mortgage portfolio (assuming that its main source of funds is short-term deposits)? Explain how prepayments on mortgages can limit the effectiveness of the hedge.

14. **Stock Index Futures** Describe stock index futures. How could they be used by a financial institution that is anticipating a jump in stock prices but does not yet have sufficient funds to purchase large amounts of stock? Explain why stock index futures may reflect investor expectations about the market more quickly than stock prices.

15. **Selling Stock Index Futures** Why would a pension fund or insurance company even consider selling stock index futures?

16. **Index Arbitrage** Explain how index arbitrage may be used.

17. **Circuit Breakers** Explain the use of circuit breakers.

Advanced Questions

18. **Hedging with Futures** Elon Savings and Loan Association has a large number of 30-year mortgages with floating interest rates that adjust on an annual basis and obtains most of its funds by issuing five-year certificates of deposit. It uses the yield curve to assess the market's anticipation of future interest rates. It believes that expectations of future interest rates are the major force affecting the yield curve. Assume that a downward-sloping yield curve with a steep slope exists. Based on this information, should Elon consider using financial futures as a hedging technique? Explain.

19. **Hedging Decision** Blue Devil Savings and Loan Association has a large number of 10-year fixed-rate mortgages and obtains most of its funds from short-term deposits. It uses the yield curve to assess the market's anticipation of future interest rates. It believes that expectations of future interest rates are the major force affecting the yield curve. Assume that an upward-sloping yield curve with a steep slope exists. Based on this information, should Blue Devil consider using financial futures as a hedging technique? Explain.

20. **How Futures Prices May Respond to Prevailing Conditions** Consider the prevailing conditions for inflation (including oil prices), the economy, the budget deficit, and other conditions that could

affect the values of futures contracts. Based on prevailing conditions, would you prefer to buy or sell Treasury bond futures at this time? Would you prefer to buy or sell stock index futures at this time? Assume that you would close out your position at the end of your semester. Offer some logic to support your answers. Which factor is most influential on your decision regarding Treasury bond futures and on your decision regarding stock index futures?

Interpreting Financial News

Interpret the following statements made by Wall Street analysts and portfolio managers:

a. "The existence of financial futures contracts allows our firm to hedge against temporary market declines without liquidating our portfolios."
b. "Given my confidence in the market, I plan to use stock index futures to increase my exposure to market movements."
c. "We used currency futures to hedge the exchange rate exposure of our international mutual fund focused on German stocks."

Managing in Financial Markets

Managing Portfolios with Futures Contracts As a portfolio manager, you are monitoring previous investments that you made in stocks and bonds of U.S. firms, as well as stocks and bonds of Japanese firms. Though you plan to keep all of these investments over the long run, you are willing to hedge against adverse effects on your investments that result from economic conditions. You expect that over the next year, U.S. and Japanese interest rates will decline, the U.S. stock market will perform poorly, the Japanese stock market will perform well, and the Japanese yen (the currency) will depreciate against the dollar.

a. Should you consider taking a position in U.S. bond index futures to hedge your investment in U.S. bonds? Explain.
b. Should you consider taking a position in Japanese bond index futures to hedge your investment in Japanese bonds? Explain.
c. Should you consider taking a position in U.S. stock index futures to hedge your investment in U.S. stocks? Explain.
d. Should you consider taking a position in Japanese stock index futures to hedge your investment in Japanese stocks? (Note: The Japanese stock index is denominated in yen and therefore is used to hedge stock movements, not currency movements.)
e. Should you consider taking a position in Japanese yen futures to hedge the exchange rate risk of your investment in Japanese stocks and bonds?

Problems

1. **Profit from T-bill Futures** Spratt Company purchased T-bill futures contracts when the quoted price was 93.50. When this position was closed out, the quoted price was 94.75. Determine the profit or loss per contract, ignoring transaction costs.

2. **Profit from T-bill Futures** Suerth Investments, Inc. purchased T-bill futures contracts when the quoted price was 95.00. When this position was closed out, the quoted price was 93.60. Determine the profit or loss per contract, ignoring transaction costs.

3. **Profit from T-bill Futures** Toland Company sold T-bill futures contracts when the quoted price was 94.00. When this position was closed out, the quoted price was 93.20. Determine the profit or loss per contract, ignoring transaction costs.

4. **Profit from T-bill Futures** Rude Dynamics, Inc. sold T-bill futures contracts when the quoted price was 93.26. When this position was closed out, the quoted price was 93.90. Determine the profit or loss per contract, ignoring transaction costs.

5. **Profit from T-bond Futures** Egan Company purchased a futures contract on Treasury bonds that specified a price of 91–00. When the position was closed out, the price of the Treasury bond futures contract was 90–10. Determine the profit or loss, ignoring transaction costs.

6. **Profit from T-bond Futures** R. C. Clark sold a futures contract on Treasury bonds that specified a price of 92–10. When the position was closed out, the price of the Treasury bond futures contract was 93–00. Determine the profit or loss, ignoring transaction costs.

7. **Profit from Stock Index Futures** Marks Insurance Company sold S&P 500 stock index futures that specified an index of 1690. When the position was closed out, the index specified by the futures contract was 1720. Determine the profit or loss, ignoring transaction costs.

Flow of Funds Exercise

Hedging with Futures Contracts

Recall that if the economy continues to be strong, Carson Company may need to increase its production capacity by about 50 percent over the next few years to satisfy demand. It would need financing to expand and accommodate the increase in production. Recall that the yield curve is currently upward sloping. Also recall that Carson is concerned about a possible slowing of the economy because of potential Fed actions to reduce inflation. Carson currently relies mostly on commercial loans with floating interest rates for its debt financing.

a. How could Carson use futures contracts to reduce the exposure of its cost of debt to interest rate movements? Be specific about whether it would use a short hedge or a long hedge.

b. Will the hedge that you described in the previous question perfectly offset the increase in debt costs if interest rates increase? Explain what drives the profit from the short hedge, versus what drives the higher cost of debt to Carson if interest rates increase.

Internet/Excel Exercises

1. Go to http://www.futuresource.com/. Review the charts for an equity index product such as the S&P 500. Explain how the price pattern moved recently.

2. Now compare that pattern to the actual trend of the S&P 500, which is provided at http://finance.yahoo.com/?u (just click on "S&P 500" there to access the charts). Describe the relationship between the movements in S&P 500 futures and movements in the S&P 500 index.

Midterm Self-Exam

Midterm Review

You have just completed all of the chapters focused on the financial markets. Here is a brief summary of some of the key points in those chapters.

Chapter 1 provides an overview of the types of financial markets, the securities that are traded within those markets, and the financial institutions that serve those markets. Chapter 2 explains how general interest rate levels are driven by factors that affect the demand for loanable funds (such as inflation and economic growth), and the supply of loanable funds (such as the Fed's monetary policy). Chapter 3 explains how interest rates vary among securities due to differences in credit risk, liquidity, tax status, and term to maturity. Chapter 4 describes the Fed's monetary policy, while Chapter 5 explains how the Fed's policy adjusts the supply of loanable funds to affect interest rates and economic conditions.

Chapter 6 explains how money market securities serve investors whose primary need is liquidity rather than high returns. Chapters 7 through 12 describe the characteristics, pricing, and risk of capital market securities. In particular, Chapters 7 through 9 focus on long-term debt securities and explain how sensitive the market values of long-term debt are to interest rate movements. Chapter 10 describes how stocks are placed and how institutional investors attempt to ensure that managers of publicly traded companies make decisions that maximize the stock's value. Chapter 11 shows how the value of a stock is influenced by the factors that influence the firm's future cash flows or risk. Chapter 12 describes how stocks are traded and how the trading is regulated. Because money market securities, long-term debt securities, and stocks have different characteristics, they serve different investors. In addition, the sensitivity of their prices to various factors differs among securities. Therefore, investors are able to allocate their investments in securities to reflect their specific return and risk preferences.

Chapter 13 explains how interest rate futures contracts can be sold to speculate on expectations of rising rates, as well as how these contracts can be sold to speculate on expectations of declining interest rates. It also explains how interest rate futures can be sold to hedge the interest rate risk of portfolios containing long-term debt securities and how stock index futures contracts can be used to hedge the market risk of stock portfolios. Chapter 14 explains how call options can be used to speculate on expectations of rising stock prices, while put options can be used to speculate on expectations of declining stock prices. It also explains how put options on stock indexes can be used to hedge stock portfolios, while put options on bond index futures can be used to hedge long-term debt security portfolios. Chapter 15 explains how interest rate swaps can be used to speculate on expectations of rising or declining interest rates, while Chapter 16 explains how foreign exchange markets are used to facilitate the trading of international securities.

This exam does not cover all of the concepts that have been presented up to this point. It is simply intended to allow you to test yourself on a general overview of key concepts. Try to simulate taking an exam by answering all of the questions without using your book and your notes. The answer key for this exam is provided just after this exam. If you have any wrong answers, you should re-read the related material and then redo any exam questions that you had wrong.

This exam may not necessarily match the level of rigor in your course. Your instructor may provide specific information about how this Midterm Self-Exam relates to the coverage and rigor of the midterm exam in your course.

Midterm Self-Exam

1. Explain the meaning of asymmetric information and how it can have an impact on trading in the stock market.

2. In the last year, the one-year risk-free interest rate increased from 3 to 7 percent.
   a. What is a likely reason for the large increase in the risk-free rate?
   b. In the last year, the 10-year risk-free rate declined from 7 to 6 percent. How can you reconcile the change in the short-term interest rate with the change in the long-term interest rate? What does the shift in the yield curve imply about future interest rates according to expectations theory?

3. The prevailing yield on a B-rated corporate bond is 7 percent. Explain how the yield offered on new B-rated bonds could be affected if economic conditions deteriorate. There are two forces that deserve consideration.

4. Consider the components that determine the prevailing yield of a highly rated corporate bond, such as the risk-free rate, default risk premium, and liquidity premium. The yield offered on a corporate bond in the secondary market changes over time. Which component do you think is typically the main source of changes in the yield offered on a highly rated corporate bond over time? Explain.

5. Recently, economic conditions have weakened. Although consumer prices have not increased in the last year, oil prices have risen by 20 percent in the last month. The Fed wants to show its dedication to controlling inflation and therefore decides to restrict the money supply and increase the target federal funds rate by .5 percent.
   a. If you were on the FOMC, would you support the Fed's decision? Explain.
   b. Explain how prices of money market securities would change in response to this policy. Why might bond prices be more sensitive to the change in the Fed's policy than money market securities? Why might bond prices be less sensitive to change in the Fed's policy than money market securities?

6. Assume that the Fed decided to reduce the federal funds rate by .5 percent today and that this decision was not anticipated by the financial markets.
   a. Why might the change in monetary policy affect the yields paid by corporations when they issue corporate bonds?
   b. Why might the change in monetary policy have no effect on the yields paid by corporations when they issue corporate bonds?

7. Why do bond market participants pay close attention to the fiscal policy decisions of the U.S. government?

8. A Treasury bond's coupon and principal payments are guaranteed. Does this mean that the value of the Treasury bond is almost constant over time? Explain.

9. Offer a logical explanation for why higher expected inflation could affect the yield on new 30-year fixed-rate mortgages. Why are secondary price movements of fixed-rate mortgages correlated with price movements of corporate bonds?

10. Assume that the Fed uses monetary policy to reduce the target federal funds rate. Also assume that the market does not anticipate this reduction. Use the CAPM framework to explain why this policy could enhance the prices of stocks.

11. Assume that the standard deviation of a stock's monthly returns is 4 percent. The expected return of the stock over the next month is zero. Using the VAR method, estimate the maximum expected loss for a month based on a 95 percent confidence level.

12. Based on what you learned in the chapters on the bond markets and stock markets, are these markets complements or substitutes from an issuer's perspective? From an investor's perspective?

13. Explain why a publicly traded firm's ability to place stock in a secondary offering is dependent on the stock's liquidity in the secondary market.

14. Why would a publicly traded firm go private? Why might the Sarbanes-Oxley Act encourage some publicly traded firms to go private?

15. Why does the market for corporate control affect stock valuations? Offer a reason why the market for corporate control will not always force corporate managers to serve shareholders.

16. Charleston Investment Company just purchased Renfro stock for $50. It engages in a covered call strategy in which it sells call options on Renfro stock. A call option on Renfro stock is available with an exercise price of $52, a one-year expiration date, and a premium of $2. Assume the buyers of the call option will exercise the option on the expiration date, if it is feasible to do so. Charleston will sell the stock at the end of one year even if the option is not exercised. Determine the net profit per share for Charleston based on the following possible prices for Renfro stock at the end of one year:
    a. $45
    b. $49
    c. $50
    d. $53
    e. $55

17. a. Compare the purchase of stock index futures versus index options. Why might institutional investors use futures to hedge their stock portfolios in some periods and options to hedge their stock portfolios in other periods?
    b. Explain the tradeoff involved when purchasing a put option with an exercise price that is at the money versus deep out of the money to hedge a stock portfolio.

18. Assume that interest rate parity exists. Assume U.S. investors plan to invest in a government security denominated in a foreign currency.
    a. If the security has a higher interest rate than the U.S. interest rate, will the forward rate of the currency exhibit a discount? Explain.
    b. If the investors engage in covered interest arbitrage, will they achieve a return that is higher than, lower than, or the same as the foreign interest rate? Explain.
    c. If the investors engage in covered interest arbitrage, will they achieve a return that is higher than, lower than, or the same as the U.S. interest rate? Explain.

Answers to Midterm Self-Exam

1. Asymmetric information occurs because managers of publicly traded firms have more information about their firms than investors who do not work at the firm. Consequently, the valuation of firms by investors is limited because there may be private information about the firms that they do not have. This can result in improper pricing of stocks and a wide dispersion among investors regarding the proper valuation of stocks.

2. a. Common reasons for higher interest rates include a stronger economy, higher inflation, and a more restrictive monetary policy.

   b. The yield curve had a steep upward slope one year ago. Now the yield curve has a slight downward slope. According to expectations theory, based on the prevailing yield curve, interest rates are expected to decline in the future.

3. If deteriorating economic conditions cause a decline in the demand for loanable funds, the risk-free interest rate will decline. However, the risk premium should increase because the chance of default by the issuer of the bonds will be higher as a result of the weaker economy.

4. Changes in the risk-free rate can have a major impact on the yield offered on a corporate bond. The default risk premium and liquidity premium may change, but normally they have less impact on the yield offered over time.

5. a. No, because the policy will not necessarily have any impact on oil prices, but it will slow economic growth and the economy is already weak.

   b. Prices of money market securities will decline in response to the Fed's policy change because the interest rate and therefore the required rate of return on short-term securities will increase, and the present value of their cash flows will be reduced. When the Fed reduces the money supply in order to increase the federal funds rate, this shift could also possibly affect long-term interest rates. If so, the required rate of return on bonds will change, and long-term bond prices will decline in response. However, if the Fed's policy has no effect on long-term interest rates, the prices of long-term bonds should not change. In this case, bond prices are less sensitive than money market security prices to the Fed's policy.

6. a. The short-term and long-term markets for debt securities are partially integrated. Therefore, when the Fed increases the money supply in order to reduce the federal funds rate, some of the increased funds in the financial system may be used to invest in bonds. The additional funds supplied to the bond market can reduce the rate that corporations must pay when they borrow by issuing bonds.

   b. Sometimes, when the Fed increases the money supply, most of the additional funds are channeled into short-term debt securities rather than long-term debt securities. In this case, there may be no effect on the yields offered on new corporate bonds.

7. The U.S. government's fiscal policy can affect the budget deficit, which can influence interest rates and thereby affect bond prices.

8. No. Movements in the long-term interest rate cause movements in the required rate of return, which can have a major impact on the valuation of Treasury bonds.

9. The higher inflationary expectations may result in a higher demand for and a smaller supply of loanable funds, which would drive interest rates higher. This results in a higher long-term risk-free interest rate, which is a key component of the required rate of return when investing in long-term fixed-rate mortgages.

10. The lower target federal funds rate may result in a lower long-term risk-free rate, which increases the present value of future cash flows generated by the stock. In addition, the lower interest rate may stimulate borrowing and spending by consumers, which could increase demand for the firm's products and therefore increase cash flows.

11. $0 - (1.64 \times 4\%) = -6.56\%$

12. Issuers may view the markets as complements because they may use both types of markets to raise funds. In some cases, however, the markets serve as substitutes because a firm may tap only one market or the other.

    Investors may view the markets as complements because they may use both types of markets to invest funds. In some cases, however, the markets serve as substitutes because an investor may tap only one market or the other at a given point in time when investing funds.

13. Most investors that purchase publicly traded stock want to be able to sell the stock easily in the secondary market in the future. If a stock is illiquid, investors may not be able to sell the stock easily because there may be no interested investors who are willing to purchase the stock. Thus, investors may have to sell the stock at a discount because of the illiquidity.

14. A publicly traded firm may go private if its managers believe that it is undervalued in the public market. Thus, the managers may suggest that the firm use cash and debt to repurchase all of its outstanding stock. The Sarbanes-Oxley Act increased the reporting requirements for publicly traded firms, which increased the cost of financial reporting by more than $1 million per year for some publicly traded firms. Some firms decided that the benefits of being public were less than the costs of being public, and they went private to avoid the reporting requirements.

15. The market for corporate control may encourage some efficient firms to acquire other inefficient firms whose stock prices are relatively low because these firms have performed poorly. The efficient firms may be able to restructure the firms that they purchase and improve their performance. Thus, the market for corporate control allows for a change in control so that more efficient managers replace weak managers.

    The market for corporate control does not cure every weak firm. There is limited information about firms, which may discourage other firms from trying to acquire them. For example, these weak firms could have many legal problems which might have to be assumed by any firm that acquires them.

16. a. −$3
    b. $1
    c. $2
    d. $4
    e. $4

17. a. Institutional investors may prefer to hedge with stock index futures when they are less confident about stock market conditions, because they forgo the potential gain if market conditions are favorable. Index options may be more desirable when the investors want to hedge but also believe there is a reasonable chance that market conditions will be favorable. They must pay a premium for such flexibility.
    b. When purchasing a stock index option that is deep out of the money in order to hedge against market declines, a lower premium is paid. However, the hedge is less effective because the exercise price is low. The stock portfolio is only hedged against very large losses. Purchasing a stock index put option at the money to hedge against market declines will insulate a stock portfolio even if losses are small. However, the premium paid for this type of option is very high.

18. a. Yes, based on the interest rate parity formula.
    b. Lower, because there is a discount on the forward rate.
    c. The same, based on interest rate parity.

Part 6: Commercial Banking

The chapters in Part 6 focus on commercial banking. Chapter 17 identifies the common sources and uses of funds for commercial banks, and Chapter 18 describes the regulations that are imposed on sources and uses of funds and other banking operations. Chapter 19 explains how banks manage their sources and uses of funds to deal with risk. Chapter 20 explains how commercial bank performance can be measured and monitored to assess previous managerial policies.

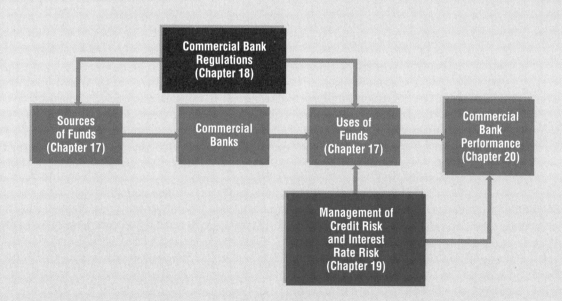

Chapter 17: Commercial Bank Operations

Measured by total assets, commercial banks are the most important type of financial intermediary. Like other financial intermediaries, they perform a critical function of facilitating the flow of funds from surplus units to deficit units.

The specific objectives of this chapter are to:

■ describe the most common sources of funds for commercial banks,

■ explain the most common uses of funds for commercial banks, and

■ describe typical off-balance sheet activities for commercial banks.

Background on Commercial Banks

Up to this point, the text has focused on the role and functions of financial markets. From this point forward, the emphasis is on the role and functions of financial institutions. Recall from Chapter 1 that financial institutions commonly facilitate the flow of funds between surplus units and deficit units. Commercial banks represent a key financial intermediary because they serve all types of surplus and deficit units. They offer deposit accounts with the size and maturity characteristics desired by surplus units. They repackage the funds received from deposits to provide loans of the size and maturity desired by deficit units. They have the ability to assess the creditworthiness of deficit units that apply for loans, so that they can limit their exposure to credit (default) risk on the loans they provide.

Bank Market Structure

In 1985, more than 14,000 banks were located in the United States. Since then, the market structure has changed dramatically. Banks have been consolidating for several reasons. One reason is that interstate banking regulations were changed in 1994 to allow banks more freedom to acquire other banks across state lines. Consequently, banks in a particular region are now subject to competition not only from other local banks but also from any bank that may penetrate that market. This has prompted banks to become more efficient in order to survive. They have pursued growth as a means of capitalizing on economies of scale (lower average costs for larger scales of operations) and enhanced efficiency. Acquisitions have been a convenient way to grow quickly.

As a result of this trend, there are only about half as many banks today as there were in 1985, and consolidation is still occurring. Exhibit 17.1 shows how the number of banks has declined over time, which increased concentration in the banking industry. The largest 100 banks now account for about 75 percent of all bank assets

Exhibit 17.1 Consolidation among Commercial Banks over Time

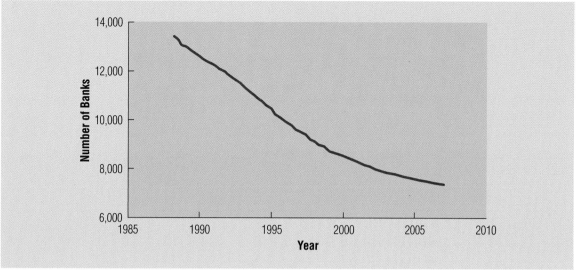

Source: Federal Reserve.

versus about 50 percent in 1985. The largest banks have increased their market share of total commercial and industrial loans. The increased concentration of banking has enhanced the efficiency with which banks offer services. Consumers have benefited from the improved efficiency.

Many banks are owned by bank holding companies, which are companies that own at least 10 percent of a bank. The holding company structure allows more flexibility to borrow funds, issue stock, repurchase the company's own stock, and acquire other firms. Bank holding companies may also avoid some state banking regulations.

The operations, management, and regulation of a commercial bank vary with the types of services offered. Therefore, the different types of financial services (such as banking, securities, and insurance) are discussed in separate chapters. This chapter on commercial bank operations applies to both independent commercial banks and commercial bank units that are part of a financial conglomerate formed by combining a bank and other financial services firms (discussed further in Chapter 18).

Whether they are independent or part of a financial conglomerate, commercial banks play an important role in facilitating the flow of funds through financial markets. They serve individuals by offering various types of deposit accounts and financial services. They channel funds to corporations by providing commercial loans. Their primary operations can be most easily identified by reviewing their main sources of funds, their main uses of funds, and the off-balance sheet activities that they provide, as explained in this chapter.

Bank Sources of Funds

http://

http://www.fdic.gov
Statistics on bank sources
and uses of funds.

To understand how any financial institution (or subsidiary of the institution) obtains funds and uses funds, its balance sheet can be reviewed. Its reported liabilities and equity indicate its sources of funds, while its reported assets indicate its uses of funds. The major sources of commercial bank funds are summarized as follows:

Deposit Accounts
1. Transaction deposits
2. Savings deposits

3. Time deposits
4. Money market deposit accounts

Borrowed Funds

1. Federal funds purchased (borrowed)
2. Borrowing from the Federal Reserve banks
3. Repurchase agreements
4. Eurodollar borrowings

Long-Term Sources of Funds

1. Bonds issued by the bank
2. Bank capital

Each source of funds is briefly described in the following subsections.

Transaction Deposits

A **demand deposit account,** or checking account, is offered to customers who desire to write checks against their account. A conventional demand deposit account requires a small minimum balance and pays no interest. From the bank's perspective, demand deposit accounts are classified as transaction accounts that provide a source of funds that can be used until withdrawn by customers (as checks are written).

Another type of transaction deposit is the **negotiable order of withdrawal (NOW) account,** which pays interest as well as providing checking services. Since 1981, commercial banks and other depository institutions throughout the country have been allowed to offer these accounts. Because NOW accounts at most financial institutions require a larger minimum balance than some consumers are willing to maintain in a transaction account, traditional demand deposit accounts are still popular.

Electronic Transactions Some transactions originating from transaction accounts have become much more efficient as a result of electronic banking. About two-thirds of all employees in the United States have direct deposit accounts, which allow their paychecks to be directly deposited to their transaction account (or other accounts). Most Social Security recipients have their checks directly deposited to their bank accounts. Computer banking enables bank customers to view their bank accounts online, pay bills, make credit card payments, order more checks, and transfer funds between accounts.

Bank customers use automated teller machines (ATMs) to make withdrawals from their transaction accounts, add deposits, check account balances, and transfer funds. ATMs are available around the world and enable customers to access cash in foreign currency. The customer's account balance is then reduced by an amount that reflects the prevailing exchange rate. In essence, customers can obtain foreign currencies at any time and generally at a more favorable exchange rate than if they used the retail foreign exchange shops that are located in many countries.

Debit cards allow bank customers to use a card to make purchases and have their bank account debited to reflect the amount spent. Banks also allow preauthorized debits, in which specific periodic payments are automatically transferred from a customer's bank account to a particular recipient. Preauthorized debits are commonly used to cover monthly utility bills, car loan payments, and mortgage payments.

Savings Deposits

The traditional savings account is the passbook savings account, which does not permit check writing. Until 1986, Regulation Q restricted the interest rate banks could offer on passbook savings. The idea was to prevent excessive competition that could cause bank failures, but in actuality, the ceilings prevented commercial banks from competing for funds during periods of higher interest rates. In 1986, Regulation Q was eliminated. Passbook savings accounts continue to attract savers with a small amount of funds, as such accounts often have no required minimum balance. Although legally customers are required to provide a 30-day written notice to withdraw funds, most banks will allow withdrawals from these accounts on a moment's notice.

Another type of savings account is the **automatic transfer service (ATS)** account, created in November 1978. It allows customers to maintain an interest-bearing savings account that automatically transfers funds to their checking account when checks are written. Only the amount of funds needed is transferred to the checking account. Thus, the ATS provides interest and check-writing ability to customers. Some ATS accounts were eliminated when NOW accounts were established.

Time Deposits

Time deposits are deposits that cannot be withdrawn until a specified maturity date. Although savings deposits are sometimes classified as time deposits because of the legal 30-day notice described above, they are treated separately here because the 30-day notice normally is not enforced. The two most common types of time deposits are certificates of deposit (CDs) and negotiable certificates of deposit.

Certificates of Deposit A common type of time deposit known as a retail **certificate of deposit** (or retail **CD**) requires a specified minimum amount of funds to be deposited for a specified period of time. Banks offer a wide variety of CDs to satisfy depositors' needs. Annualized interest rates offered on CDs vary among banks, and even among maturity types at a single bank. There is no organized secondary market for retail CDs. Depositors must leave their funds in the bank until the specified maturity, or they will normally forgo a portion of their interest as a penalty.

CD rates are easily accessible on numerous websites. For example, Bank-Rate (http://www.bankrate.com) and Bank CD-Rate Scanner (http://www.bankcd.com) identify banks that are paying the highest rates on CDs at any point in time. Because of easy access to CD rate information online, many depositors invest in CDs at banks far away to earn a higher rate than that offered by local banks. Some banks allow depositors to invest in CDs online by providing a credit card number.

The interest rates on retail CDs have historically been fixed. In recent years, however, more exotic retail CDs have been offered. **Bull-market CDs** reward depositors if the stock market performs well and **bear-market CDs** reward depositors if the market performs poorly. These new types of retail CDs typically require a minimum deposit of $1,000 to $5,000. Like more conventional CDs, they qualify for deposit insurance (assuming that the depository institution of concern is insured).

In recent years, some financial institutions have begun to offer CDs with a callable feature (referred to as **callable CDs**). That is, they can be called by the financial institution, forcing an earlier maturity. For example, a bank could issue a callable CD with a five-year maturity, callable after two years. In two years, the financial institution will likely call the CD if it can obtain funds at a lower rate over the following three years than the rate paid on that CD. Depositors who invest in callable CDs earn a slightly higher interest rate, which compensates them for the risk that the CD may be called.

Negotiable Certificates of Deposit Another type of time deposit is the **negotiable CD (NCD),** offered by some large banks to corporations. NCDs are similar to retail CDs in that they require a specified maturity date and require a minimum deposit. Their maturities are typically short term, and their minimum deposit requirement is $100,000. A secondary market for NCDs does exist.

The level of large time deposits is much more volatile than that of small time deposits, because investors with large sums of money frequently shift their funds to wherever they can earn higher rates. Small investors do not have as many options as large investors and are less likely to shift in and out of small time deposits.

Money Market Deposit Accounts

Money market deposit accounts (MMDAs) were created by a provision of the Garn-St Germain Act of December 1982. They differ from conventional time deposits in that they do not specify a maturity. MMDAs are more liquid than retail CDs from the depositor's point of view. Because banks prefer to know how long they will have the use of a depositor's funds, they normally pay a higher interest rate on CDs. MMDAs differ from NOW accounts in that they provide limited check-writing ability (they allow only a limited number of transactions per month); require a larger minimum balance, and offer a higher yield.

The remaining sources of funds to be described are of a nondepository nature. Such sources are necessary when a bank temporarily needs more funds than are being deposited. Some banks use nondepository funds as a permanent source of funds.

Federal Funds Purchased

The federal funds market allows depository institutions to accommodate the short-term liquidity needs of other financial institutions. Federal funds purchased (or borrowed) represent a liability to the borrowing bank and an asset to the lending bank that sells them. Loans in the federal funds market are typically for one to seven days. Such loans can be rolled over so that a series of one-day loans can take place. The intent of federal funds transactions is to correct short-term fund imbalances experienced by banks. A bank may act as a lender of federal funds on one day and as a borrower shortly thereafter, as its fund balance changes on a daily basis.

The interest rate charged in the federal funds market is called the **federal funds rate.** Like other market interest rates, it moves in reaction to changes in demand or supply or both. If many banks have excess funds and few banks are short of funds, the federal funds rate will be low. Conversely, a high demand by many banks to borrow federal funds relative to a small supply of excess funds available at other banks will result in a higher federal funds rate. Whatever rate exists will typically be the same for all banks borrowing in the federal funds market, although a financially troubled bank may have to pay a higher rate to obtain federal funds (to compensate for its higher risk). The federal funds rate is on an annualized basis (using a 360-day year) even though the loans are usually for terms less than one week. The federal funds rate is generally between .25 percent and 1.00 percent above the Treasury bill rate. The difference increases when the perceived risk of banks increases.

The federal funds market is typically most active on Wednesday, because that is the final day of each particular settlement period for which each bank must maintain a specified volume of reserves required by the Fed. Banks that were short of required reserves on average over the period must compensate with additional required reserves before the settlement period ends. Large banks frequently need temporary funds and therefore are common borrowers in the federal funds market.

Borrowing from the Federal Reserve Banks

Another temporary source of funds for banks is the Federal Reserve System, which serves as the U.S. central bank. Along with other bank regulators, the Federal Reserve district banks regulate certain activities of banks. They also provide short-term loans to banks (as well as to some other depository institutions). This form of borrowing by banks is often referred to as borrowing at the discount window. The interest rate charged on these loans is known as the **primary credit lending rate.**

As of January 2003, the primary credit lending rate was to be set at a level above the federal funds rate at any point in time. This was intended to ensure that banks rely on the federal funds market for normal short-term financing and only borrow from the Fed as a last resort.

Loans from the Federal Reserve are short term, commonly from one day to a few weeks. To ensure that the need for funds is justified, banks that wish to borrow at the Federal Reserve must first obtain the Fed's approval. Like the federal funds market, loans from the Fed are mainly used to resolve a temporary shortage of funds. If a bank needs more permanent sources of funds, it will develop a strategy to increase its level of deposits.

The Federal Reserve is intended to be a source of funds for banks that experience unanticipated shortages of reserves. Frequent borrowing to offset reserve shortages implies that the bank has a permanent rather than a temporary need for funds and should therefore satisfy this need with a more permanent source of funds. The Fed may disapprove of continuous borrowing by a bank unless there are extenuating circumstances, such as that the bank was experiencing financial problems and could not obtain temporary financing from other financial institutions.

Repurchase Agreements

A **repurchase agreement (repo)** represents the sale of securities by one party to another with an agreement to repurchase the securities at a specified date and price. Banks often use a repo as a source of funds when they expect to need funds for just a few days. The bank simply sells some of its government securities (such as Treasury bills) to a corporation with a temporary excess of funds and buys those securities back shortly thereafter. The government securities involved in the repo transaction serve as collateral for the corporation providing funds to the bank.

Repurchase agreement transactions occur through a telecommunications network connecting large banks, other corporations, government securities dealers, and federal funds brokers. The federal funds brokers match up firms or dealers that need funds (wish to sell and later repurchase their securities) with those that have excess funds (are willing to purchase securities now and sell them back on a specified date). Transactions are typically in blocks of $1 million. Like the federal funds rate, the yield on repurchase agreements is quoted on an annualized basis (using a 360-day year) even though the loans are for short-term periods. The yield on repurchase agreements is slightly less than the federal funds rate at any given point in time, because the funds loaned out are backed by collateral and are therefore less risky.

Eurodollar Borrowings

If a U.S. bank is in need of short-term funds, it may borrow dollars from those banks outside the United States that accept dollar-denominated deposits, or **Eurodollars.** Some of these so-called Eurobanks are foreign banks or foreign branches of U.S. banks that participate in the Eurodollar market by accepting large short-term deposits and making short-term loans in dollars. Because U.S. dollars are widely used as an international medium of exchange, the Eurodollar market is very active. Some large U.S. banks commonly obtain short-term funds from Eurodollar deposits.

Bonds Issued by the Bank

Like other corporations, banks own some fixed assets such as land, buildings, and equipment. These assets often have an expected life of 20 years or more and are usually financed with long-term sources of funds, such as through the issuance of bonds. Common purchasers of such bonds are households and various financial institutions, including life insurance companies and pension funds. Banks do not finance with bonds as much as most other corporations, because they have fewer fixed assets than corporations that use industrial equipment and machinery for production. Therefore, banks have less need for long-term funds.

Bank Capital

Bank capital generally represents funds attained through the issuance of stock or through retaining earnings. With either form, the bank has no obligation to pay out funds in the future. This distinguishes bank capital from all the other sources of funds, which represent a future obligation by the bank to pay out funds. Bank capital as defined here represents the equity or net worth of the bank. Capital can be classified as primary or secondary. Primary capital results from issuing common or preferred stock or retaining earnings, while secondary capital results from issuing subordinated notes and bonds.

A bank's capital must be sufficient to absorb operating losses in the event that expenses or losses exceed revenues, regardless of the reason for the losses. Although long-term bonds are sometimes considered to be secondary capital, they are a liability to the bank and therefore do not appropriately cushion against operating losses.

The issuance of new stock dilutes the ownership of the bank because the proportion of the bank owned by existing shareholders decreases. In addition, the bank's reported earnings per share are reduced when additional shares of stock are issued, unless earnings increase by a greater proportion than the increase in outstanding shares. For these reasons, banks generally attempt to avoid issuing new stock unless absolutely necessary.

Bank regulators are concerned that banks may maintain a lower level of capital than they should and have therefore imposed capital requirements on them. Because capital can absorb losses, a higher level of capital is thought to enhance a bank's safety and may increase the public's confidence in the banking system. In 1981, regulators imposed a minimum primary capital requirement of 5.5 percent of total assets and a minimum total capital requirement of 6 percent of total assets. Because of regulatory pressure, banks have increased their capital ratios in recent years.

In 1988, regulators imposed new risk-based capital requirements that were completely phased in by 1992. Under this system, the required level of capital for each bank is dependent on its risk. Assets with low risk are assigned relatively low weights, and assets with high risk are assigned high weights. The capital level is set as a percentage of the risk-weighted assets. Therefore, riskier banks are subject to higher capital requirements. The same risk-based capital guidelines have been imposed in several other industrialized countries. Additional details are provided in the next chapter.

Summary of Bank Sources of Funds

Because banks cannot completely control the amount of deposits they receive, they may experience a shortage of funds. For this reason, the nondepository sources of funds are useful. To support the acquisition of fixed assets, long-term funds are obtained by issuing long-term bonds, issuing stock, or retaining a sufficient amount of earnings.

Exhibit 17.2 shows the distribution of fund sources. Transaction and savings deposits make up 48 percent of all bank liabilities. The distribution of bank sources of funds is influenced by bank size. Smaller banks rely more heavily on savings deposits than larger banks do because small banks concentrate on household savings and therefore on small deposits. Much of this differential is made up in large time deposits (such as NCDs) for very large banks. In addition, the larger banks rely more on short-

Exhibit 17.2
Bank Sources of Funds
(as a Proportion of Total
Liabilities)

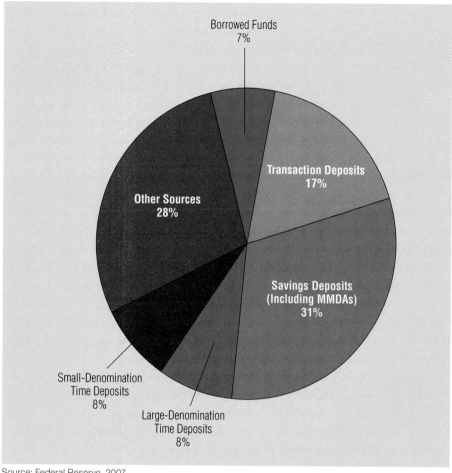

Source: Federal Reserve, 2007.

term borrowings than do small banks. The impact of the differences in composition of fund sources on bank performance is discussed in Chapter 20.

Uses of Funds by Banks

Having identified the main sources of funds, bank uses of funds can be discussed. The more common uses of funds by banks include the following:

- Cash
- Bank loans
- Investment in securities
- Federal funds sold (loaned out)
- Repurchase agreements
- Eurodollar loans
- Fixed assets

Cash

Banks must hold some cash as reserves to meet the reserve requirements enforced by the Federal Reserve. Banks also hold cash to maintain some liquidity and accommodate any withdrawal requests by depositors. Because banks do not earn income from cash, they hold only as much cash as is necessary to maintain a sufficient degree of liquidity. They can tap various sources for temporary funds and therefore are not overly concerned with maintaining excess reserves.

Banks hold cash in their vaults and at their Federal Reserve district bank. Vault cash is useful for accommodating withdrawal requests by customers or for qualifying as required reserves, while cash held at the Federal Reserve district banks represents the major portion of required reserves. The Fed mandates that banks maintain required reserves because they provide a means by which the Fed can control the money supply. The required reserves of each bank depend on the composition of its deposits.

Bank Loans

The main use of bank funds is for loans. The loan amount and maturity can be tailored to the borrower's needs.

Types of Business Loans A common type of business loan is the **working capital loan** (sometimes called a self-liquidating loan), designed to support ongoing business operations. There is a lag between the time when a firm needs cash to purchase raw materials used in production and the time when it receives cash inflows from the sales of finished products. A working capital loan can support the business until sufficient cash inflows are generated. These loans are typically short term, but they may be needed by businesses on a frequent basis.

Banks also offer **term loans,** which are used primarily to finance the purchase of fixed assets such as machinery. With a term loan, a specified amount of funds is loaned out, for a specified period of time and a specified purpose. The assets purchased with the borrowed funds may serve as partial or full collateral on the loan. Maturities on term loans commonly range from 2 to 5 years and are sometimes as long as 10 years. When banks offer term loans, they typically impose **protective covenants,** which specify specific conditions for the borrower that may protect the bank from loan default. For example, a bank may specify a maximum level of dividends that the borrower can pay to its shareholders each year. This protective covenant is intended to ensure that the borrower has sufficient cash to repay its loan on time.

Term loans can be amortized so that the borrower makes fixed periodic payments over the life of the loan. Alternatively, the bank can periodically request interest payments, with the loan principal to be paid off in one lump sum (called a **balloon payment**) at a specified date in the future. This is known as a **bullet loan.** Several combinations of these payment methods are also possible. For example, a portion of the loan may be amortized over the life of the loan, while the remaining portion is covered with a balloon payment.

As an alternative to providing a term loan, the bank may purchase the assets and lease them to the firm in need. This method, known as a **direct lease loan,** may be especially appropriate when the firm wishes to avoid adding more debt to its balance sheet. Because the bank is the owner of the assets, it can depreciate them over time for tax purposes.

A more flexible financing arrangement is the **informal line of credit,** which allows the business to borrow up to a specified amount within a specified period of time. This is useful for firms that may experience a sudden need for funds but do not know precisely when. The interest rate charged on any borrowed funds is typically adjustable in accordance with prevailing market rates. Banks are not legally obligated to provide funds to the business, but they usually honor the arrangement to avoid harming their reputation.

An alternative to the informal line of credit is the **revolving credit loan,** which obligates the bank to offer up to some specified maximum amount of funds over a specified period of time (typically less than five years). Because the bank is committed to provide funds when requested, it normally charges businesses a commitment fee (of about one-half of 1 percent) on any unused funds.

The interest rate charged by banks on loans to their most creditworthy customers is known as the **prime rate.** Banks periodically revise the prime rate in response to changes in market interest rates, which reflect changes in the bank's cost of funds. Thus, the prime rate moves in tandem with the Treasury bill rate. The prime rate in recent years is shown in Exhibit 17.3. It increased in the late 1990s when interest rates were rising. Then, in 2001, it declined in response to the weak economy as the demand for loanable funds decreased and the Fed took actions to reduce the federal funds rate. It increased during the 2004–2007 period in response to economic growth and an increase in demand for business loans. The prime rate tends to adjust in response to changes in other interest rates that influence the bank's cost of funds. When economic conditions are weak, however, the spread between the prime rate and the bank's cost of funds tends to widen because banks require a higher premium to compensate for credit risk.

Loan Participations Some large corporations wish to borrow a larger amount of funds than any individual bank is willing to provide. To accommodate a corporation, several banks may be willing to pool their available funds in what is referred to as a **loan participation.** Loan participations can take various forms, but in the most common form, one of the banks serves as the lead bank by arranging for the documentation, disbursement, and payment structure of the loan. The main role of the other banks is to supply funds that are channeled to the borrower by the lead bank. The borrower may not even realize that much of the funds have been provided by other banks. As interest payments are received, the lead bank passes the payments on to the other participants in proportion to the original loan amounts they provided. The lead bank receives fees for servicing the loan in addition to its share of interest payments.

Exhibit 17.3   Prime Rate over Time

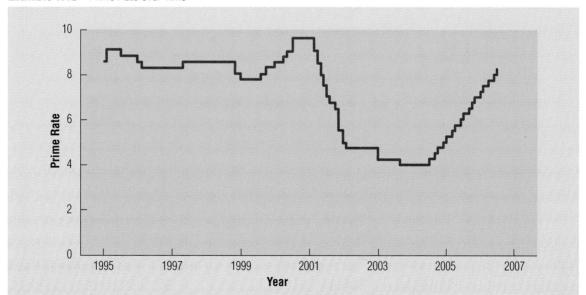

Source: Federal Reserve.

The lead bank is expected to ensure that the borrower repays the loan. Normally, however, the lead bank is not required to guarantee the interest payments. Thus, all participating banks are exposed to credit (default) risk.

Loans Supporting Leveraged Buyouts

Some commercial banks finance leveraged buyouts (LBOs). The loan amount provided by a single bank to support an LBO is usually between $15 million and $40 million. The exposure of some large commercial banks to LBO loans exceeds $1 billion. An attractive feature of LBO financing is the relatively high loan rate that can be charged. In addition, some fee income can be generated from the administrative services performed by commercial banks when financing LBOs.

In a sense, financing part of an LBO is no different than financing other privately held businesses. These businesses are highly leveraged and experience cash flow pressure during periods when sales are lower than normal. Their high degree of financial leverage causes cash outflows to be somewhat sensitive to business cycles.

Firms request LBO financing because they perceive that the market value of certain publicly held shares is too low. It is desirable that these firms have access to equity funds because it can serve as a cushion during periods of poor economic conditions. Although these firms prefer not to go public again during such periods, they are at least capable of doing so. Banks financing these firms can, as a condition of the loan, require that the firms reissue stock if they experience cash flow problems.

Many firms involved in LBOs are diversified conglomerates that will be split into various divisions and sold. This may enable banks to spread their lending base by lending to divisions that have been sold. Businesses may be separated if the sum of the parts appears to be worth more than the whole. A conglomerate could absorb the failure of a single division, but if the division is independent, its failure is absorbed by its creditors.

A commercial bank's risk may rise as its financing of LBOs increases. Banks that reduce their more conservative assets to finance LBOs incur a higher degree of risk. Many LBOs are financed with junk bonds, which suggests a high degree of risk. Thus, banks could be incurring the same risk as if they had purchased junk bonds. With LBO financing, however, the bank-borrower relationship may allow for more personalized guidance of firms experiencing financial problems. In addition, banks may have first claim to the firm's assets if the firm fails. Thus, these bank loans are considered to be less risky.

Some banks originate the loans designed for LBOs and then sell them to other financial institutions, such as insurance companies, pension funds, and foreign banks. In this way, they can generate fee income by servicing the loans while avoiding the credit risk associated with the loans.

Bank regulators now monitor the amount of bank financing provided to corporate borrowers that have a relatively high degree of financial leverage. These loans, known as **highly leveraged transactions (HLTs),** are defined by the Federal Reserve as credit that results in a debt-to-asset ratio of at least 75 percent. In other words, the level of debt is at least three times the level of equity. About 60 percent of HLT funds are used to finance LBOs, while some of the funds are used to repurchase only a portion of the outstanding stock. HLTs are usually originated by a large commercial bank, which provides 10 to 20 percent of the financing itself. Other financial institutions participate by providing the remaining 80 to 90 percent of the funds needed.

Collateral Requirements on Business Loans

Commercial banks are increasingly accepting intangible assets (such as patents, brand names, and licenses to franchises and distributorships) as collateral for commercial loans. This change is especially important to service-oriented companies that do not have tangible assets.

Lender Liability on Business Loans In recent years, businesses that previously obtained loans from banks are filing lawsuits, claiming that the banks terminated further financing without sufficient notice. These so-called lender liability suits have been prevalent in the farming industry. Some farmers have claimed that banks encouraged them to borrow and then refused to provide the additional financing necessary to make their projects successful. As a result, the farmers lost the land and equipment used as collateral. Lender liability lawsuits have also been filed by companies in other industries, including the grocery, clothing, and oil industries.

Volume of Business Loans Exhibit 17.4 shows the volume of business loans provided by commercial banks over time. Notice how the volume increased consistently during the 1990s but declined in the 2001–2003 period. The decline is directly attributed to weak economic conditions, which resulted in a lower aggregate demand for products and services provided by firms. Consequently, firms reduced their demand for loans. When commercial banks experience a lower demand for business loans, they attempt to use more funds for other purposes. In the 2004–2007 period, economic growth increased, resulting in an increase in business loans provided by banks.

http://www.fdic.com
Information about bank loan and deposit volume.

Types of Consumer Loans Commercial banks provide **installment loans** to individuals to finance purchases of cars and household products. These loans require the borrowers to make periodic payments over time.

Banks also provide credit cards to consumers who qualify, enabling them to purchase various goods without having to reapply for credit on each purchase. Credit card holders are assigned a maximum limit, based on their income and employment record, and a fixed annual fee may be charged. This service often involves an agreement with VISA or MasterCard. If consumers pay off the balance each month, they normally are not charged interest. Bank rates on credit card balances are sometimes about double the rate charged on business loans. State regulators can impose **usury laws** that restrict the maximum rate of interest charged by banks, and these laws may be applied to credit card loans as well. A federal law requires that banks abide by the usury laws of the state where they are located rather than the state where the consumer lives.

Exhibit 17.4   Volume of Business Loans Provided by Commercial Banks

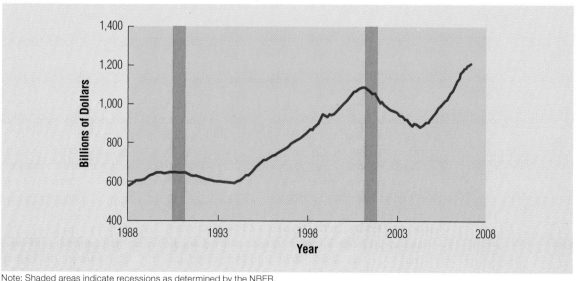

Note: Shaded areas indicate recessions as determined by the NBER.
Source: Federal Reserve.

Assessing the applicant's creditworthiness is much easier for consumer loans than for corporate loans. An individual's cash flow is typically simpler and more predictable than a firm's cash flow. In addition, the average loan amount to an individual is relatively small, warranting a less detailed credit analysis.

Since the interest rate on credit card loans and personal loans is typically much higher than the cost of funds, many commercial banks have pursued these types of loans as a means of increasing their earnings. The most common method of increasing such loans is to use more lenient guidelines when assessing the creditworthiness of potential customers. However, there is an obvious tradeoff between the potential return and exposure to credit risk. When commercial banks experience an increase in defaults on credit card loans and other personal loans, they respond by increasing their standards for extending credit card loans and personal loans. This results in a reduced allocation of funds to credit card loans, which also reduces the potential returns of the bank. As economic conditions improve, commercial banks tend to increase their allocation of funds toward credit card loans.

Real Estate Loans Banks also provide real estate loans. For residential real estate loans, the maturity on a mortgage is typically 15 to 30 years, although shorter-term mortgages with a balloon payment are also common. The loan is backed by the residence purchased. Banks also provide some commercial real estate loans to finance commercial development. In the 2004–2007 period of economic expansion, many banks offered subprime loans to homeowners with questionable credit quality. Many of these loans defaulted in 2007, which caused banks to increase their standards.

Investment in Securities

Banks purchase Treasury securities as well as securities issued by agencies of the federal government. Government agency securities can be sold in the secondary market, but the market is not as active as it is for Treasury securities. Furthermore, government agency securities are not a direct obligation of the federal government. Therefore, credit risk exists, although it is normally thought to be very low. Banks that are willing to accept the slight possibility of credit risk and less liquidity from investing in government agency securities can earn a higher return than on Treasury securities with a similar maturity.

Federal agency securities are commonly issued by federal agencies, such as the Federal Home Loan Mortgage Corporation (called Freddie Mac) and the Federal National Mortgage Association (called Fannie Mae). Funds received by the agencies issuing these securities are used to purchase mortgages from various financial institutions. Such securities have maturities that can range from one month to 25 years. Unlike interest income from Treasury securities, interest income from federal agency securities is subject to state and local income taxes.

Banks also purchase corporate and municipal securities. Although corporate bonds are subject to credit risk, they offer a higher return than Treasury or government agency securities. Municipal bonds exhibit some degree of risk but can also provide an attractive return to banks, especially when their after-tax return is considered. The interest income earned from municipal securities is exempt from federal taxation. Banks purchase only **investment-grade securities,** which are rated as "medium quality" or higher by rating agencies.

Bank Investment in Securities over Time In general, banks hold securities that offer a lower expected return than the loans that the banks provide. However, these securities also tend to offer more liquidity and are subject to a lower risk of default than the loans. During periods of economic growth, the demand for loans by qualified borrowers increases, and banks tend to sell some of their security holdings so that they can provide more loans. They can increase their expected return by accommodating the loan demand, and the risk of default on the loans is relatively low. With favorable economic conditions, the borrowers are likely to have sufficient income to repay their loans.

When the economy weakens, business inventories increase, and firms are unwilling to expand. The demand for loans declines, and banks are unable to provide as many loans to qualified borrowers. Consequently, the banks increase their purchases of securities. Exhibit 17.5 shows the level of banks' investment in securities over time. In the late 1990s when economic growth was strong, banks used a relatively high proportion of their funds to accommodate the large demand for loans and therefore reduced their holdings of securities. In 2002 when the economy was weak, banks reduced their loans and increased their investment in securities. In the 2004–2007 period, banks increased their loans and reduced their investment in securities.

Federal Funds Sold

Some banks often lend funds to other banks in the federal funds market. The funds sold, or lent out, will be returned at the time specified in the loan agreement, with interest. The loan period is typically very short, such as a day or a few days. Small banks are common providers of funds in the federal funds market. If the transaction is executed by a broker, the borrower's cost on a federal funds loan is slightly higher than the lender's return, because the broker matching up the two parties charges a transaction fee.

Exhibit 17.5   Bank Investment in Securities over Time

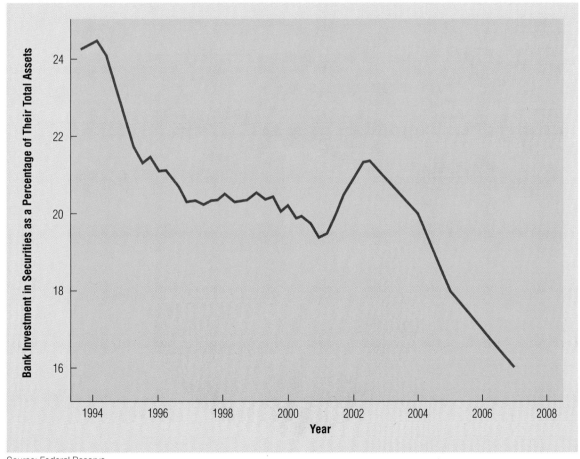

Source: Federal Reserve.

Repurchase Agreements

Recall that from the borrower's perspective, a repurchase agreement (repo) transaction involves repurchasing the securities it had previously sold. From a lender's perspective, the repo represents a sale of securities that it had previously purchased. Banks can act as the lender (on a repo) by purchasing a corporation's holdings of Treasury securities and selling them back at a later date. This provides short-term funds to the corporation, and the bank's loan is backed by these securities.

Eurodollar Loans

Branches of U.S. banks located outside the United States and some foreign-owned banks provide dollar-denominated loans to corporations and governments. These so-called **Eurodollar loans** are common because the dollar is frequently used for international transactions. Eurodollar loans are short term and denominated in large amounts, such as $1 million or more. Some U.S. banks even establish Eurodollar deposits at a foreign bank as a temporary use of funds.

Fixed Assets

Banks must maintain some amount of fixed assets, such as office buildings and land, so that they can conduct their business operations. However, this is not a concern to the bank managers who decide how day-to-day incoming funds will be used. They direct these funds into the other types of assets already identified.

Summary of Bank Uses of Funds

The distribution of bank uses of funds is illustrated in Exhibit 17.6. Loans of all types make up about 60 percent of bank assets, while securities account for about 21 percent of bank assets. The distribution of assets for an individual bank varies with the type of bank. For example, smaller banks tend to have a relatively large amount of household loans and government securities; larger banks have a higher level of business loans (including loans to foreign firms).

Exhibit 17.6   Bank Uses of Funds (as a Proportion of Total Assets)

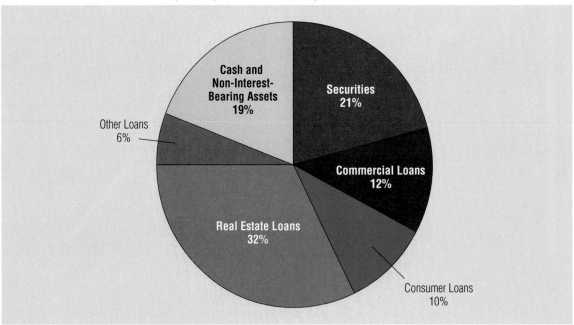

Source: Federal Reserve, 2007.

The distribution of bank uses of funds indicates how commercial banks operate. In recent years, however, banks have begun to provide numerous services that are not indicated on their balance sheet. These services differ distinctly from banks' traditional operations that focused mostly on channeling deposited funds into various types of loans and investments.

The desire by commercial banks to offer nonbanking services escalated in the early 1990s, when very low interest rates caused depositors to withdraw deposits and invest the proceeds in stocks and bonds. Many banks attempted to retain the business of those depositors by having their subsidiaries offer discount brokerage services or mutual fund services. Thus, even though the funds were withdrawn from the banking operations, they were commonly reinvested in the bank's subsidiaries.

Commercial Bank Balance Sheet A commercial bank's sources of funds represent its liabilities or equity, while its uses of funds represent its assets. Each commercial bank determines its own composition of liabilities and assets, which determines its specific operations.

ILLUSTRATION Exhibit 17.7 shows the balance sheet of Hornet Bank. The bank's assets are shown on the left side of the balance sheet. The second column indicates the dollar amount of each asset, and the third column shows the size of each asset in proportion to total assets to illustrate how Hornet Bank distributes its funds. Hornet's main assets are commercial and consumer loans, as well as securities. The balance sheet shows the bank's holdings at a particular point in time. It frequently revises the composition of its assets in response to economic conditions. When the economy improves and creditworthy businesses want to expand, Hornet Bank will sell some of its holdings of Treasury securities and use the funds to provide more corporate loans.

Hornet Bank's liabilities and stockholders' equity are shown on the right side of the balance sheet. Hornet obtains funds from various types of deposits. It incurs some expenses from all types of deposits. In particular, it must hire employees to serve depositors. The composition of Hornet's liabilities determines its interest expenses, because it does not pay interest on demand deposits but pays a relatively high interest rate on large CDs.

Hornet also incurs expenses from managing its assets. Its main expense is the cost of hiring employees to assess the creditworthiness of businesses and households that request loans. In general, Hornet wants to generate enough income from its assets so that it can cover its expenses and provide a reasonable return to its shareholders. Its primary source of income is the interest received on the business loans that it provides. Its capital is shown on the balance sheet as common stock issued and retained earnings. ■

Exhibit 17.8 shows how commercial banks use the key balance sheet items to finance economic growth. They channel funds from their depositors to households and thereby finance household spending. They channel funds from depositors to corporations and thereby finance corporate expansion. They also use some deposits to purchase Treasury and municipal securities and thereby finance spending by the Treasury and municipalities.

Off-Balance Sheet Activities

Banks commonly engage in off-balance sheet activities, which generate fee income without requiring an investment of funds. These activities do create a contingent

Exhibit 17.7 Balance Sheet of Hornet Bank as of June 30, 2008

Assets	Dollar Amount (in Millions)	Proportion of Total Assets	Liabilities and Stockholders' Equity	Dollar Amount (in Millions)	Proportion of Total Liabilities and Stockholders' Equity
Cash (includes required reserves)	$ 50	5%	Demand deposits	$ 250	25%
Commercial loans	400	40%	NOW accounts	60	6%
Consumer loans	250	25%	Money market deposit accounts	200	20%
Treasury securities	80	8%	Short-term CDs	250	25%
Corporate securities	120	12%	CDs with maturities beyond one year	120	12%
Federal funds sold (lent out)	10	1%	Federal funds purchased (borrowed)	0	0%
Repurchase agreements	20	2%	Long-term debt	30	3%
Eurodollar loans	0	0%			
Fixed assets	70	7%	Common stock issued	50	5%
			Retained earnings	40	4%
TOTAL ASSETS	$1,000	100%	TOTAL LIABILITIES AND STOCKHOLDERS' EQUITY	$1,000	100%

Exhibit 17.8 How Commercial Banks Finance Economic Growth

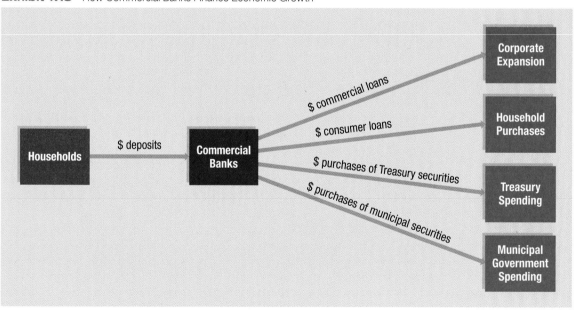

obligation for banks, however. The following are some of the more popular off-balance sheet activities:

- Loan commitments
- Standby letters of credit
- Forward contracts on currencies
- Interest rate swap contracts

Loan Commitments

A **loan commitment** is an obligation by a bank to provide a specified loan amount to a particular firm upon the firm's request. The interest rate and purpose of the loan may also be specified. The bank charges a fee for offering the commitment.

One type of loan commitment is a **note issuance facility (NIF),** in which the bank agrees to purchase the commercial paper of a firm if the firm cannot place its paper in the market at an acceptable interest rate. Although banks earn fees for their commitments, they could experience illiquidity if numerous firms request their loans at the same time.

Standby Letters of Credit

A **standby letter of credit (SLC)** backs a customer's obligation to a third party. If the customer does not meet its obligation, the bank will. The third party may require that the customer obtain an SLC to complete a business transaction. For example, consider a municipality that wants to issue bonds. To ensure that the bonds are easily placed, a bank could provide an SLC that guarantees payment of interest and principal. In essence, the bank uses its credit rating to enhance the perceived safety of the bonds. In return for the guarantee, the bank charges a fee to the municipality. The bank should be willing to provide SLCs only if the fee received compensates for the possibility that the municipality will default on its obligation.

Forward Contracts on Currencies

A forward contract on currency is an agreement between a customer and a bank to exchange one currency for another on a particular future date at a specified exchange rate. Banks engage in forward contracts with customers that desire to hedge their exchange rate risk. For example, a U.S. bank may agree to purchase 5 million euros in one year from a firm for $1.10 per euro. The bank may simultaneously find another firm that wishes to exchange 5 million euros for dollars in one year. The bank can serve as an intermediary and accommodate both requests, earning a transaction fee for its services. However, it is exposed to the possibility that one of the parties will default on its obligation.

Interest Rate Swap Contracts

Banks also serve as intermediaries for interest rate swaps, whereby two parties agree to periodically exchange interest payments on a specified notional amount of principal. Once again, the bank receives a transaction fee for its services. If it guarantees payments to both parties, it is exposed to the possibility that one of the parties will default on its obligation. In that event, the bank must assume the role of that party and fulfill the obligation to the other party.

Some banks facilitate currency swaps (for a fee) by finding parties with opposite future currency needs and executing a swap agreement. Currency swaps are somewhat similar to forward contracts, except that they are usually for more distant future dates.

International Banking

GL🌐BALASPECTS Until historical barriers against interstate banking were largely removed in 1994, some U.S. commercial banks were better able to achieve growth by penetrating foreign markets than by expanding at home. It is somewhat ironic that New York banks historically had branches in Taiwan and Hong Kong but not in New Jersey or Connecticut. Even though interstate expansion within the United States is easier now, many U.S. banks are also expanding internationally to improve their prospects for growth and to diversify so that their business will not be dependent on a single economy.

Global Competition in Foreign Countries

The most common way for U.S. commercial banks to expand internationally is by establishing branches, full-service banking offices that can compete directly with other banks located in a particular area. Before establishing foreign branches, a U.S. bank must obtain the approval of the Federal Reserve Board. Among the factors considered by the Fed are the bank's financial condition and experience in international business. Commercial banks may also consider establishing agencies, which can provide loans but cannot accept deposits or provide trust services.

U.S. banks have recently established foreign subsidiaries wherever they expect more foreign expansion by U.S. firms, such as in Southeast Asia and Eastern Europe. Recently, expansion has also been focused on Latin America. As a result of the North American Free Trade Agreement (NAFTA), U.S. banks have expanded their business in Mexico to help finance the establishment of subsidiaries by U.S-based corporations. The banks offer banker's acceptances, foreign exchange services, credit card services, and other household services in Mexico.

As an example of the diversity in international banking services, consider the case of Citigroup. Citigroup offers a number of key services to firms around the world including foreign exchange transactions, forecasting, risk management, cross-border trade finance, acquisition finance, cash management services, and local currency funding. Citigroup serves not only large multinational corporations, such as Coca-Cola, Dow Chemical, IBM, and Sony, but also small firms that need international banking services. By spreading itself across the world, Citigroup can typically handle the banking needs of all of a multinational corporation's subsidiaries.

Expansion by Foreign Banks in the United States

While U.S. banks have expanded into foreign markets, foreign banks have also entered U.S. markets. Initially, they entered primarily to serve foreign corporations that set up subsidiaries in the United States. Because this is still their primary function, they concentrate on corporate rather than consumer services.

Japanese banks in particular have a very significant presence in the United States. A major reason for their growth is that they offer very competitive corporate loans. They also have been known to provide letters of credit for lower fees than those charged by U.S. banks. They also have a relatively low cost of capital, which allows them to take on ventures that might not be feasible for U.S. banks. Furthermore, the high Japanese savings rate allows for substantial growth in deposits in Japan, which may then be channeled to support operations in the United States.

In addition to establishing full-service branches, since 1913 foreign banks have established **Edge Act corporations** in the United States to specialize in international banking and foreign financial transactions. These corporations can accept deposits and provide loans, as long as these functions are specifically related to international transactions.

Impact of the Euro on Global Competition

The inception of the euro has stimulated increased bank expansion throughout Europe. The use of a single currency in a number of European countries simplifies transactions because the majority of a bank's transactions between those countries are now denominated in euros. Use of the euro also reduces exposure to exchange rate risk, as banks can accept deposits in euros and use euros to lend funds or invest in securities. The use of a single currency throughout many European countries may also encourage firms to engage in a bond or stock offering to support their European business, as the euro can be used to support most of that business. Commercial banks can serve as intermediaries by underwriting and placing the debt or the equity issued by firms.

Given the potential advantages of a single currency, U.S. banks and European banks are expanding throughout Europe by acquiring existing banks. The single currency makes it easier to achieve economies of scale and enables banks' internal reporting systems to be more efficient. As banks expand and capitalize on economies of scale, the global competition has become more intense. Furthermore, the euro enables businesses in Europe to more easily compare the prices of services offered by banks based in different European countries. This also forces banks to be more competitive.

Summary

■ The most common sources of commercial bank funds are deposit accounts, borrowed funds, and long-term sources of funds. The common types of deposit accounts are transaction deposits, savings deposits, time deposits, and money market deposit accounts. These accounts vary in terms of liquidity (for the depositor) and the interest rates offered.

Commercial banks can solve temporary deficiencies in funds by borrowing from other banks (federal funds market), from the Federal Reserve, or from other sources by issuing short-term securities such as repurchase agreements. When banks need long-term funds to support expansion, they may use retained earnings, issue new stock, or issue new bonds.

■ The most common uses of funds by commercial banks are bank loans and investment in securities. Banks can use excess funds by providing loans to other banks or by purchasing short-term securities.

■ Banks engage in off-balance sheet activities such as loan commitments, standby letters of credit, forward contracts, and swap contracts. These types of activities generate fees for commercial banks. However, they also reflect commitments by the banks, which can expose them to more risk.

Point Counter-Point

Should Banks Engage in Other Financial Services Besides Banking?

Point No. Banks should focus on what they do best.

Counter-Point Yes. Banks should increase their value by engaging in other services. They can appeal to customers who want to have all their financial services provided by one financial institution.

Who Is Correct? Use the Internet to learn more about this issue. Offer your own opinion on this issue.

Questions and Applications

1. **Bank Balance Sheet** Create a balance sheet for a typical bank, showing its main liabilities (sources of funds) and assets (uses of funds).

2. **Bank Sources of Funds** What are four major sources of funds for banks? What alternatives does a bank have if it needs temporary funds? What is the most common reason that banks issue bonds?

3. **CDs** Compare and contrast a retail CD and a negotiable CD.

4. **Money Market Deposit Accounts** How does a money market deposit account differ from other bank sources of funds?

5. **Federal Funds** Define federal funds, federal funds market, and federal funds rate. Who sets the federal funds rate? Why is the federal funds market more active on Wednesday?

6. **Federal Funds Market** Explain the use of the federal funds market in facilitating bank operations.

7. **Borrowing from the Federal Reserve** Describe the process of "borrowing at the Federal Reserve." What rate is charged, and who sets it? Why do banks commonly borrow in the federal funds market rather than through the Federal Reserve?

8. **Repurchase Agreements** How does the yield on a repurchase agreement differ from a loan in the federal funds market? Why?

9. **Bullet Loan** Explain the advantage of a bullet loan.

10. **Bank Use of Funds** Why do banks invest in securities, even though loans typically generate a higher return? Explain how a bank decides the appropriate percentage of funds that should be allocated to each type of asset.

11. **Bank Capital** Explain the dilemma faced by banks when determining the optimal amount of capital to hold. A bank's capital is less than 10 percent of its assets. How do you think this percentage would compare to that of manufacturing corporations? How would you explain this difference?

12. **HLTs** Would you expect a bank to charge a higher rate on a term loan or a highly leveraged transaction (HLT) loan? Why?

13. **International Banking** Explain the operations of foreign branches of U.S. banks.

Interpreting Financial News

Interpret the following comments made by Wall Street analysts and portfolio managers:

a. "Lower interest rates may reduce the size of banks."

b. "Banks are no longer as limited when competing with other financial institutions for funds targeted for the stock market."

c. "If the demand for loans rises substantially, interest rates will adjust to ensure that commercial banks can accommodate the demand."

Managing in Financial Markets

Managing Sources and Uses of Funds As a consultant, you have been asked to assess a bank's sources and uses of funds and to offer recommendations on how it can restructure its sources and uses of funds to improve its performance. This bank has traditionally focused on attracting funds by offering certificates of deposit (CDs). It offers checking accounts and money market deposit accounts (MMDAs), but it has not advertised these accounts because it has obtained an adequate amount of funds from the CDs. It pays about 3 percentage points more on its CDs than on its MMDAs, but the bank prefers to know the precise length of time it can use the deposited funds. (The CDs have a specified maturity while the MMDAs do not.) Its cost of funds has historically been higher than that of most banks, but it has not been concerned because its earnings have been relatively high. The bank's use of funds has historically focused on local real estate loans to build shopping malls and apartment complexes. The real estate loans have provided a very high return over the last several years. However, the demand for real estate in the local area has slowed.

a. Should the bank continue to focus on attracting funds by offering CDs, or should it push its other types of deposits?

b. Should the bank continue to focus on real estate loans? If the bank reduces its real estate loans, where should the funds be allocated?

c. How will the potential return on the bank's uses of funds be affected by your restructuring of the asset portfolio? How will the cost of funds be affected by your restructuring of the bank's liabilities?

Flow of Funds Exercise

Services Provided by Financial Conglomerates

Carson Company is attempting to compare the services offered by different banks, as it would like to have all services provided by one bank.

a. Explain the different types of services provided by a financial institution that may allow Carson Company to obtain funds or to hedge its risk.

b. Review the services that you listed in the previous question. What services could provide financing to Carson Company? What services could hedge Carson's exposure to risk?

Internet/Excel Exercise

1. Go to the website http://www.chase.com. List the various services offered by Chase that were listed in this chapter. For each, state whether the service provided by the bank reflects an asset (use of funds) or a liability (source of funds) for the bank. What interest rates does Chase offer on its CDs?

Chapter 18: Bank Regulation

Bank regulations are designed to maintain public confidence in the financial system by preventing commercial banks from becoming too risky.

The specific objectives of this chapter are to:

■ describe the key regulations imposed on commercial banks,

■ explain how regulators monitor banks, and

■ describe the main provisions of the Federal Deposit Insurance Corporation Improvement Act (FDICIA).

Background

http://

http://www.federalreserve.gov Detailed descriptions of bank regulations from the Federal Reserve Board.

The banking industry has experienced substantial changes in recent years. The industry has become more competitive due to deregulation. Today, banks have considerable flexibility in the services they offer, the locations where they operate, and the rates they pay depositors for deposits. Although generally viewed as favorable, this flexibility is creating intense competition among banks and even between banks and other financial institutions that now offer bank services.

Many banks have expanded across the country by opening new branches or making acquisitions in an attempt to use their resources efficiently. Others have diversified across services to capitalize on economies of scope. Many banks have expanded beyond their traditional banking business and now offer other financial services. Bank regulators have attempted to manage the speed of integration between banks and other financial service firms.

Bank regulation is needed to protect customers who supply funds to the banking system. By preventing bank runs that might occur if customers became concerned about the safety of their deposits, regulation ensures a safer banking environment. Regulators also attempt to enhance the safety of the banking system by overseeing individual banks. The regulators do not attempt to manage individual banks, but do impose some discipline so that banks assuming more risk are forced to create their own form of protection against the possibility that they will default. In this way, regulators are shifting more of the burden of risk assessment to the individual banks themselves. This chapter explains the regulatory structure and the key regulatory events that have had the greatest impact on commercial banking operations.

Regulatory Structure

http://

http://www.federalreserve.gov/banknreg.htm Key bank regulations from the website of the Board of Governors of the Federal Reserve System.

The regulatory structure of the banking system in the United States is dramatically different from that of other countries. It is often referred to as a **dual banking system** because it includes both a federal and a state regulatory system. There are more than 6,000 separately owned commercial banks in the United States, supervised by three federal agencies and 50 state agencies. The regulatory structure in other countries is much simpler.

A charter from either a state or the federal government is required to open a commercial bank in the United States. A bank that obtains a state charter is referred to as a state bank; a bank that obtains a federal charter is known as a national bank. All national banks are required to be members of the Federal Reserve System (the Fed). The federal charter is issued by the Comptroller of the Currency. An application for a bank charter must be submitted to the proper supervisory agency, should provide evidence of the need for a new bank, and should disclose how the bank will be operated. Regulators determine if the bank satisfies general guidelines to qualify for the charter.

State banks may decide whether they wish to be members of the Federal Reserve System. The Fed provides a variety of services for commercial banks and controls the amount of funds within the banking system. About 35 percent of all banks are members of the Federal Reserve. These banks are generally larger than the norm; their combined deposits make up about 70 percent of all bank deposits. Both member and nonmember banks can borrow from the Fed, and both are subject to the Fed's reserve requirements.

Regulators

National banks are regulated by the Comptroller of the Currency, while state banks are regulated by their respective state agency. Banks that are insured by the **Federal Deposit Insurance Corporation (FDIC)** are also regulated by the FDIC. Because all national banks must be members of the Federal Reserve and all Fed member banks must hold FDIC insurance, national banks are regulated by the Comptroller of the Currency, the Fed, and the FDIC. State banks are regulated by their respective state agency, the Fed (if they are Fed members), and the FDIC. The Comptroller of the Currency is responsible for conducting periodic evaluations of national banks, the Fed holds the same responsibility for state-chartered banks that are members of the Fed, and the FDIC is responsible for state-chartered banks that are not members of the Fed.

Because of the regulatory overlap, it has often been argued that a single regulatory agency should be assigned the role of regulating all commercial banks and savings institutions. The momentum for consolidation increased in 1989, when the Financial Institutions Reform, Recovery, and Enforcement Act (FIRREA) was passed. One of the provisions of FIRREA allows commercial banks to acquire either healthy or failing savings and loan associations (S&Ls). Prior to the Act, banks could not acquire S&Ls. With the merging of commercial banks and S&Ls resulting from the Act, there is even more rationale for a single regulatory agency that would oversee both industries.

Regulation of Bank Ownership

Commercial banks can be either independently owned or owned by a **bank holding company (BHC).** Although some multibank holding companies (owning more than one bank) exist, one-bank holding companies are more common. More banks are owned by holding companies than are owned independently. The popularity of the holding company structure stems from 1970, when amendments to the Bank Holding Company Act of 1956 were enacted, allowing BHCs to participate in various nonbanking activities, such as leasing, mortgage banking, and data processing. As a result, BHCs have greater potential for product diversification.

Regulation of Bank Deposits

Federal deposit insurance has existed since the creation of the FDIC in 1933 as a response to the bank runs that occurred in the late 1920s and early 1930s. During the

Great Depression period of 1930–1932, about 5,100 banks failed, representing more than 20 percent of the existing banks at that time. The initial wave of failures caused depositors to withdraw their deposits from other banks, fearing that failures would spread. Their actions actually caused more banks to fail. If deposit insurance had been available, depositors might not have removed their deposits, and some bank failures might have been avoided.

The FDIC preserves public confidence in the U.S. financial system by providing deposit insurance to commercial banks and savings institutions. The FDIC is managed by a board of five directors, who are appointed by the president. Its headquarters is in Washington, D.C., but it has six regional offices and other field offices throughout the country. Today, the FDIC's insurance funds are responsible for insuring deposits of more than $3 trillion.

The specified amount of deposits per person insured by the FDIC has increased from $2,500 in 1933 to $100,000 today. The insured deposits make up 80 percent of all commercial bank balances, as very large deposit accounts are insured only up to the $100,000 limit. Deposits in foreign branches of U.S. banks are not insured by the FDIC, however. Federal deposit insurance continues to be instrumental in preventing bank runs. Depositors are not so quick to remove their deposits because of a rumor about a bank or the banking system when they realize that their deposits are insured by the federal government.

The pool of funds used to cover insured depositors is now referred to as the **Bank Insurance Fund.** This fund is entirely supported by annual insurance premiums paid by commercial banks. The annual premium ranges from 23¢ to 31¢ per $100 of deposits, depending on the specific bank's financial condition. In 2003, only three banks insured by the fund failed, and their total assets were $1.1 billion. No banks have failed in recent years. As of 2007, the fund's balance was about $49 billion.

Until 1991, all banks obtained insurance for their depositors at the same rate as safer banks. Because the riskiest banks were more likely to fail, they were being indirectly subsidized by safer banks. This system encouraged some banks to assume more risk because they could still attract deposits from depositors who knew they would be covered regardless of the bank's risk. The act of insured banks taking on more risk because their depositors are protected is referred to as a **moral hazard problem.** As a result of many banks taking excessive risks, bank failures increased during the 1980s and early 1990s. The balance in the FDIC's insurance fund declined because the FDIC had to reimburse depositors who had deposits at the banks that failed.

The moral hazard problem prompted bank regulators and Congress to search for a way to discourage banks from taking excessive risk and to replenish the Bank Insurance Fund. As a result of the Federal Deposit Insurance Corporation Improvement Act (FDICIA) of 1991, risk-based deposit insurance premiums were phased in. Consequently, bank insurance premiums are now aligned with the risk of banks, thereby reducing the moral hazard problem.

Deregulation Act of 1980

For many years, discussions by Congress, the regulatory agencies, and depository institutions focused on reducing bank regulations. In 1980, the **Depository Institutions Deregulation and Monetary Control Act (DIDMCA)** was enacted to achieve these objectives. The Act contained a wide variety of provisions, but the main ones can be divided into two categories: (1) those intended to deregulate the banking (and other depository institutions) industry and (2) those intended to improve monetary control. Because this chapter focuses on regulation and deregulation, only the first category is discussed here.

The DIDMCA was a major force in deregulating the banking industry and increasing competition among banks. Its main deregulatory provisions are as follows:

- The interest rate ceilings (enforced by **Regulation Q**) on time and savings deposits of depository institutions were phased out, allowing banks to make their own decisions on what interest rates to offer for time and savings deposits.

- All depository institutions were allowed to offer NOW accounts. Because NOW accounts normally require a higher minimum balance, they are not suitable for all consumers; however, their ability to pay interest has attracted those who can afford the minimum balance.

- Depository institutions were allowed more flexibility to engage in various types of lending. For example, savings and loan associations were allowed to offer a limited amount of commercial and consumer loans. Consequently, competition among depository institutions for consumer and commercial loans increased, and the asset mix of different depository institutions has become more similar over time.

- In an effort to improve efficiency in the banking system, the DIDMCA required that the Fed explicitly charge for its services and offer them to any depository institutions that desired them.

Beyond these deregulatory provisions, the DIDMCA called for an increase in the maximum deposit insurance level from $40,000 to $100,000 per depositor at each given bank to reduce the chances of deposit runs.

The DIDMCA has had a significant impact on the banking industry, most importantly by increasing competition among depository institutions. In addition, there has been a shift from conventional demand deposits to NOW accounts. Consumers have also shifted funds from conventional passbook savings accounts to various types of CDs that pay market interest rates.

Garn-St Germain Act

Banks and other depository institutions were further deregulated in 1982 as a result of the **Garn-St Germain Act.** The Act came at a time when some depository institutions (especially savings and loan associations) were experiencing severe financial problems. One of its more important provisions permitted depository institutions to offer money market deposit accounts (MMDAs), which have no minimum maturity and no interest ceiling. These accounts allow a maximum of six transactions per month (three by check). They are very similar to the traditional accounts offered by **money market mutual funds** (whose main function is to sell shares and pool the funds to purchase short-term securities that offer market-determined rates). Because MMDAs offer savers similar benefits, they allow depository institutions to compete against money market funds in attracting savers' funds.

A second key deregulatory provision of the Garn-St Germain Act permitted depository institutions to acquire failing institutions across geographic boundaries. The intent was to reduce the number of failures that require liquidation, as the chances of finding a potential acquirer for a failing institution improve when geographic barriers are removed. Also, competition was expected to increase, as depository institutions previously barred from entering specific geographic areas could do so by acquiring failing institutions.

Although the proper degree of deregulation is disputed, consumers appear to have benefited from these deregulatory moves. They now have a greater variety of financial services from which to choose, and the pricing of services is controlled by intense competition.

Regulation of Operations

Bank regulations govern many operations of commercial banks, including bank assets, the provision of securities services, and the provision of insurance services.

Regulation of Bank Assets

As a result of concern about the popularity of highly leveraged loans (for supporting leveraged buyouts and other activities), bank regulators monitor the amount of highly leveraged transactions (HLTs). HLTs are commonly defined as loan transactions in which the borrower's liabilities are valued at more than 75 percent of total assets.

Regulators also monitor a bank's exposure to debt of foreign countries. Because banks are required by regulators to report significant exposure to foreign debt, investors and creditors have access to more detailed information about the composition of bank loan portfolios.

Banks are restricted to a maximum loan amount of 15 percent of their capital to any single borrower (up to 25 percent if the loan is adequately collateralized). This forces them to diversify their loans to a degree.

Banks are also regulated to ensure that they attempt to accommodate the credit needs of the communities in which they operate. The Community Reinvestment Act (CRA) of 1977 (revised in 1995) requires that banks meet the credit needs of qualified borrowers in their community, even those with low or moderate incomes. The CRA is not intended to force banks to make high-risk loans but rather to ensure that lower-income (and qualified) borrowers receive the loans that they request. Each bank's performance in this regard is evaluated periodically by its respective regulator.

Banks are not allowed to use borrowed or deposited funds to purchase common stock, although they can manage stock portfolios through trust accounts that are owned by individuals. Banks can invest only in bonds that are investment-grade quality (as measured by a Baa rating or higher by Moody's or a BBB rating or higher by Standard & Poor's). These regulations are intended to prevent banks from taking excessive risks.

Regulation of Securities Services

The Banking Act of 1933 (better known as the **Glass-Steagall Act**) separated banking and securities activities. The Act was prompted by problems during 1929 when some banks sold some of their poor-quality securities to their trust accounts established for individuals. Some banks also engaged in insider trading, buying or selling corporate securities based on confidential information provided by firms that had requested loans. The Glass-Steagall Act prevented any firm that accepted deposits from underwriting stocks and bonds of corporations. Banks could underwrite general obligation bonds of states and municipalities or purchase and sell securities for their trust accounts. In addition, they could hold investment-grade corporate bonds within their asset portfolio. In this case, the bank was acting as a creditor and not as a shareholder.

The separation of securities activities from banking activities was intended to prevent potential conflicts of interest. For example, the belief was that if a bank was allowed to underwrite securities, it might advise its corporate customers to purchase these securities and could threaten to cut off future loans if the customers did not oblige. Furthermore, it might provide loans to customers with the understanding that a portion of the funds would be used to purchase securities underwritten by the bank.

Banks suggested, however, that any potential conflicts of interest could be prevented by regulators. Furthermore, banks argued that if they could engage in securities activities, they might have easier access to marketing, technological, and managerial resources and could reduce the prices of securities-related services to consumers. In addition, banks could become financial supermarkets, providing securities activities as well as normal banking services. This would be an added convenience to customers. Finally, the increased competition could force all firms providing securities activities to be more efficient.

http://www.federalreserve
.gov/banknreg.htm Links to
regulations of securities
services offered by banks.

The Financial Services Modernization Act
In 1999, Congress passed the **Financial Services Modernization Act** (also called the Gramm-Leach-Bliley Act), which essentially repealed the Glass-Steagall Act. The 1999 Act allows affiliations between banks, securities firms, and insurance companies. It also allows bank holding companies to engage in any financial activity through their ownership of subsidiaries. Consequently, a single holding company can engage in traditional banking activities, securities trading, underwriting, and insurance. The Act also requires that the holding company be well managed and have sufficient capital in order to expand its financial services. The Securities and Exchange Commission (SEC) regulates any securities products that are created, but the bank subsidiaries that offer the securities products are regulated by bank regulators.

Although many commercial banks had previously pursued securities services, the 1999 Act increased the degree to which banks can offer these services. Furthermore, it allowed securities firms and insurance companies to acquire banks. Under the Act, commercial banks must have a strong rating in community lending (meaning that they have been willing to actively provide loans in lower-income communities) in order to pursue additional expansion in securities and other nonbank activities.

Now that banks have more freedom to pursue securities and insurance activities and securities and insurance companies can more easily acquire banks, more consolidation among banks, securities firms, and insurance companies is occurring. Although this trend began earlier, the 1999 Act has enabled financial institutions to engage in consolidation without having to sell off specific subsidiaries because of barriers prohibiting them from combining all financial services under a single ownership.

Benefits of Diversification to Customers
The diversification made possible by the 1999 Act offers benefits to a financial institution's clients, whether they are individuals or firms. Since individuals commonly use financial institutions to deposit funds, obtain mortgage loans and consumer loans (such as an automobile loan), purchase shares of mutual funds, order stock transactions (brokerage), and purchase insurance, they can obtain all their financial services from a single financial conglomerate. Since firms commonly use financial institutions to maintain a business checking account, obtain loans, issue stocks or bonds, have their pension fund managed, and purchase insurance services, they can receive all of their financial services from a single financial conglomerate. Some financial conglomerates can provide virtually every financial service that individuals or firms might desire. Other financial conglomerates specialize in the services desired by a particular type of client, such as individuals or large firms.

Benefits of Diversification to Financial Institutions
Diversification also offers benefits to financial institutions. By offering more diversified services, financial institutions can reduce their reliance on the demand for any single service that they offer. This diversification may result in less risk for the institution's consolidated business, assuming that the new services are not subject to a much higher degree of risk than its traditional services. A recent annual report of Bank of America summarized this concept:

> *"To further diversify risk, Bank of America continues to diversify its revenue stream—complementing the deposit and lending base by increasing income from value-added fee-based services our customers want."*

The individual units of a financial conglomerate may generate some new business simply because they are part of the conglomerate and offer convenience to clients who already rely on its other services. Each financial unit's list of existing clients represents a potential source of new clients for the other financial units to pursue.

Regulation of Insurance Services

As with securities services, banks have been eager to offer insurance services. The arguments for and against bank involvement in insurance are quite similar to those regarding bank involvement in securities. Banks could increase competition in the insurance industry, as they would be able to offer services at a lower cost. In addition, they could offer their customers the convenience of one-stop shopping (especially if the bank could also offer securities services).

Before the late 1990s, banks were involved in insurance in various limited ways. Banks that had participated in insurance activities before 1971 were allowed to continue to do so. In addition, some banks leased space in their buildings to insurance companies in exchange for a payment equal to a percentage of the insurance company's sales. Banks also engaged in cooperative agreements with insurance companies; the banks would sell insurance to their customers, but the insurance company served as the insurer. The bank received a fee for generating business for the insurance company.

In 1995, the Supreme Court ruled that national banks could sell annuities. With an **annuity,** customers pay a premium in exchange for a future stream of annual payments. Since annuities had previously been sold only by insurance companies, the decision provided another way for banks to penetrate the insurance industry.

In 1998, regulators allowed the merger between Citicorp and Traveler's Insurance Group, which essentially paved the way for the consolidation of bank and insurance services. Passage of the Financial Services Modernization Act in the following year confirmed that banks and insurance companies could merge and consolidate their operations. These events encouraged banks and insurance companies to pursue mergers as a means of offering a full set of financial services.

Regulation of Off-Balance Sheet Transactions

Banks offer a variety of off-balance sheet commitments. For example, banks provide letters of credit to back commercial paper issued by corporations. They also act as the intermediary on interest rate swaps and usually guarantee payments over the specified period in the event that one of the parties defaults on its payments.

Various off-balance sheet transactions have become popular because they provide fee income. That is, banks charge a fee for guaranteeing against the default of another party and for facilitating transactions between parties. Nevertheless, off-balance sheet transactions also expose the banks to risk. If, during a severe economic downturn, many corporations should default on their commercial paper or on payments specified by interest rate swap agreements, the banks that provided guarantees would incur large losses.

Bank exposure to off-balance sheet activities has become a major concern of regulators. Banks could be riskier than their balance sheets indicate because of these transactions. The risk-based capital requirements are higher for banks that conduct more off-balance sheet activities. In this way, regulators discourage banks from excessive off-balance sheet activities.

Regulation of the Accounting Process

BEHAVIORAL FINANCE Publicly traded banks, like other publicly traded companies, are required to provide financial statements that indicate their recent financial position and performance. In the 2001–2002 period, the accounting scandals at Enron, WorldCom, and some other firms caused a lack of confidence in the financial information disclosed by firms. In some cases, executives sold their holdings of their firm's stock during a period when the firm's reported earnings were exaggerated, causing the stock's market price to be higher than the firm's actual earnings warranted. Investors are less willing to invest in firms whose earnings may be exaggerated. The Sarbanes-Oxley (SOX) Act was enacted in 2002 to ensure a more transparent process for reporting on a firm's productivity and financial condition. The Act requires firms to implement an internal reporting process that can be easily monitored by executives and makes it impossible for executives to pretend that they did not know about fraudulent reporting. Although publicly traded banks were not the cause of the accounting scandals, they must also follow the guidelines specified in the SOX Act.

Some of the key provisions of the Act require banks to improve their internal control processes and establish a centralized database of information. They must implement a system that automatically checks data for unusual discrepancies relative to norms. They must speed the process by which all departments and all subsidiaries have access to the data that they need. Executives are now more accountable for a bank's financial statements because they must personally verify the accuracy of the statements. In addition, the more complete reporting process provides an electronic paper trail so that major decisions by banks (such as acquisitions and other forms of restructuring) must be more clearly justified. One negative effect of the SOX Act is that publicly traded banks have incurred expenses of more than $1 million per year to comply with its provisions. Nevertheless, investors may have more confidence in the financial statements now that there is greater accountability that could discourage fraudulent accounting. Although privately held banks are not directly subject to the SOX guidelines, bank regulators have asked these banks to review their accounting processes and ensure that their disclosure of financial information is accurate and complete. ■

Regulation of Interstate Expansion

The **McFadden Act of 1927** prevented banks from establishing branches across state lines, regardless of their intrastate branching status. The Douglas Amendment to the Bank Holding Company Act of 1956 complemented the McFadden Act by preventing interstate acquisitions of banks by bank holding companies.

Because banks were historically restricted from crossing state lines, no single bank could control the entire market for bank deposits. Thus, geographic restrictions effectively limited the concentration of any bank in obtaining deposited funds. Similarly, because banks had limited deposit-accepting capabilities, no single bank could control the entire loan market. Furthermore, geographic restrictions discouraged banks from offering consumer loans or small business loans outside their boundaries. The cost of providing such services long distance did not allow these banks to be competitive with local banks. For large commercial loans, however, the amount of the loan transaction overshadowed the cost of long-distance servicing. Thus, the market for large commercial loans was nationwide, even with geographic restrictions on branching.

Interstate Banking Act

By 1994, most states had approved nationwide interstate banking. Some of these states required a reciprocal arrangement; that is, they allowed acquisitions by out-of-state banks if those banks were located in states that also permitted out-of-state acquisitions. Under these conditions, most interstate expansion was achieved through bank acquisitions.

In September 1994, however, federal guidelines were revised as Congress passed a banking bill that removed interstate branching restrictions. This legislation, known as the Reigle-Neal Interstate Banking and Branching Efficiency Act of 1994, eliminated most restrictions on interstate bank mergers and allowed commercial banks to open branches nationwide. Shortly after the Act was passed, many interstate banks consolidated their operations so that their branches reported to the main holding company, rather than to state subsidiaries.

Banks became more efficient as a result of the Act because they were no longer required to maintain separate banking companies in each state to report to bank regulators. Previously, commercial banks operating in multiple states had to establish separate corporations in each state, with separate boards of directors. Banks with operations across several states reduced their costs as a result of the Act. In particular, reporting costs of banks were reduced over time. Furthermore, banks reduced their costs as a result of consolidating their operations. The reduction in the operating costs was even more pronounced than the reduction in reporting costs.

Bank customers have benefited not only because of lower costs to banks, but also because of convenience. Customer bank accounts are no longer restricted to a particular state. Customers can make deposits or withdraw funds from their accounts even when they are outside their home state. In fact, customers can now deposit checks or obtain a loan in any state where their bank has a branch.

One benefit of nationwide interstate banking is that it allows banks to grow and reduce operating costs per unit of output as output increases. This is commonly referred to as **economies of scale.** Interstate banking has also allowed banks in stagnant markets to penetrate markets where economic conditions are more favorable. In addition, banks in all markets have been pressured to become more efficient as a result of the increased competition.

Regulation of Capital

Banks are subject to capital requirements, which force them to maintain a minimum amount of **capital** (or equity) as a percentage of total assets. This regulation has been the focus of numerous controversies. In general, banks would prefer to maintain a low amount of capital to boost their return on equity ratio, whereas regulators have argued that banks need a sufficient amount of capital to absorb potential operating losses. In this way, the number of bank failures may be reduced, enhancing depositors' confidence in the banking system.

Minimum capital requirements were imposed on U.S. banks in 1981 by three different regulatory agencies. In 1985, the requirements were made uniform across agencies. Nevertheless, there were still two discrepancies. First, all banks with more than $150 million in assets were subject to the same requirements, even though some banks were taking much more risk than others. Second, banks outside the United States were subject to their respective country's capital requirements. This created an unequal global playing field, because banks with lower capital requirements had a competitive advantage. These banks could achieve an acceptable return on equity with smaller profit margins because of their lower capital level. Thus, they could gain market share by underpricing their competitors that were subject to higher capital requirements.

Basel Accord

In the Basel Accord in 1988, the central banks of 12 major countries agreed to uniform capital requirements. This accord was facilitated by the Bank for International Settlements (BIS), which is based in Basel, Switzerland. The BIS was established in 1930 to facilitate international monetary cooperation among countries. In the 1980s, it focused on facilitating solutions to the international debt problems. It played a major role in drafting the accord and in more recent efforts to refine it.

A key change made by the Basel Accord was to base the capital requirements on a bank's risk level. Thus, it forced banks with greater risk to maintain a higher level of capital and thereby discouraged banks from excessive exposure to credit risk. The capital requirements were phased in so that banks deficient in capital would have time to build their capital base. By the end of 1992, banks were required to have a capital ratio of at least 8 percent of risk-weighted assets, with a minimum Tier 1 capital ratio of 4 percent. Tier 1 capital consists mostly of shareholders' equity, retained earnings, and preferred stock, while Tier 2 capital includes loan loss reserves (up to a specified maximum) and subordinated debt.

Assets are weighted according to risk. Very safe assets such as cash are assigned a zero weight, while very risky assets are assigned a 100 percent weight. Because the required capital is set as a percentage of risk-weighted assets, riskier banks are subject to more stringent capital requirements.

In 1996, the Basel Accord was amended so that other factors that affect bank risk are also considered. The amendment mandates that a bank's capital level also account for its sensitivity to market conditions, such as stock prices, interest rates, and exchange rates.

The trend of the average Tier 1 and Tier 2 capital levels among banks is shown in Exhibit 18.1. Before the Basel Accord, capital levels were lower for many banks. Exhibit 18.1 illustrates that since the amendment to the Basel Accord in 1996, the Tier 1 and Tier 2 capital levels have been somewhat stable.

Basel II Accord

In recent years, banking regulators who form the so-called Basel Committee have been working on a new accord (called Basel II) that will refine the risk measures and increase the transparency of a bank's risk to its customers. The goal is to properly account for a bank's risk so that the bank's capital requirements are in line with its corresponding risk. This is a major challenge because different banks may have different

Exhibit 18.1   Trend of Tier 1 and Tier 2 Capital over Time at U.S. Banks

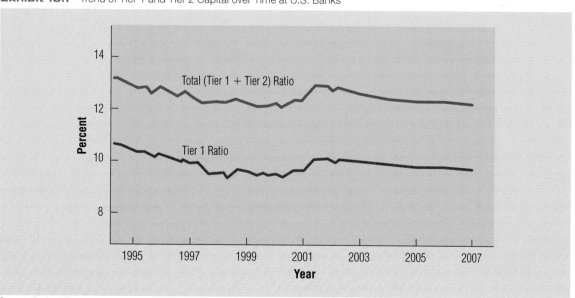

Source: Federal Reserve.

risk levels even though they all have the same composition of corporate loans, household mortgage loans, and other types of loans. Risk levels could differ if, for example, some banks required better collateral to back their loans. In addition, some banks may take positions in derivative securities that can reduce their credit risk, while other banks may have positions in derivative securities that increase their credit risk. The Basel II Accord attempts to account for such differences among banks.

Specifically, the Basel II Accord has three major parts:

1. Revise the measurement of credit risk.
2. Explicitly account for operational risk.
3. Require more disclosure for market participants.

Revised Measures of Credit Risk Banks can continue to use the traditional standardized approach to calculating credit risk, in which they categorize their assets and assign risk weights to the categories. To improve the calculation, however, the categories are being refined to account for possible differences in risk levels of loans within a category.

ILLUSTRATION As a result of Basel II, a bank's loans that are past due will be assigned a higher weight. This adjustment inflates the size of these assets for the purpose of determining minimum capital requirements, so that banks with more loans that are past due will be forced to maintain a higher level of capital (other things being equal). ■

An alternative method of calculating credit risk, called the internal ratings-based (IRB) approach, would also be available. A bank would provide summary statistics about its loans to the Basel Committee, which would apply preexisting formulas to the statistics to determine the required capital level for that bank.

Accounting for Operational Risk The Basel Committee defines operational risk as the risk of losses resulting from inadequate or failed internal processes or systems. The Basel Accord did not explicitly account for this type of risk. The Basel Committee wants to encourage banks to improve their techniques for controlling operational risk because doing so could reduce failures in the banking system. By imposing higher capital requirements on banks with higher levels of operational risk, Basel II would provide an incentive for banks to reduce their operational risk. Initially, banks will be allowed to use their own methods for assessing their exposure to operational risk. The Basel Committee suggests that a bank's average annual income over the last three years may serve as an indicator. The annual income represents the size of a bank's operations and thus may reflect the degree of the bank's operational risk. However, the Basel Committee plans to develop a more sophisticated process to assess operational risk over time.

Public Disclosure of Risk Indicators The Basel Committee plans to require banks to provide more information to existing and prospective shareholders about their exposure to different types of risk. Whereas the other provisions of Basel II focus on ensuring that a bank's capital requirements are based on its risk, this provision would increase the information available about a bank's risk. By making banks' risk more transparent to investors, this provision may cause banks to use more conservative management.

Implementation of the Basel II Accord Some countries implemented the Basel II Accord in 2008, with a focus on their international banks. The provisions of the Basel II Accord are not directly enforceable. However, countries established new guidelines for their banks that are adapted from some parts of the accord. In particular, banks in some countries such as the United States, Canada, and those in the European Union have created regulations that conform to some parts of the Basel II Accord. Many Asian countries plan to implement the Basel II guidelines over time. Others, such as China, are unlikely to implement the accord because their banking system is less developed. The approaches used by banks to assess their exposure to risk vary among countries.

Use of the Value-at-Risk Method to Determine Capital Requirements

Under the 1996 amendment to the Basel Accord, the capital requirements on large banks that have substantial trading businesses (such as interest rate derivatives, foreign exchange derivatives, and underwriting services) were adjusted to incorporate their own internal measurements of general market risk, which reflects exposure to movements in market forces such as interest rates, stock prices, and exchange rates. The capital requirements imposed to cover general market risk are based on the bank's own assessment of risk when applying a value-at-risk (VAR) model. Recall that participants in the stock market commonly use this model to assess the risk of a stock portfolio. It is used in a somewhat similar manner to assess the risk of a bank.

The VAR model can be applied in various ways to determine capital requirements. In general, a bank defines the VAR as the estimated potential loss from its trading businesses that could result from adverse movements in market prices. Banks typically use a 99 percent confidence level, meaning that there is a 99 percent chance that the loss on a given day will be more favorable than the VAR estimate. When applied to a daily time horizon, the actual loss from a bank's trading businesses should not exceed the VAR estimated loss on more than 1 out of every 100 days. Banks estimate the VAR by assessing the probability of specific adverse market events (such as an abrupt change in interest rates) and the possible sensitivity in response to those events. Banks with a higher maximum loss based on a 99 percent confidence interval are subject to higher capital requirements.

This focus on daily price movements forces banks to continuously monitor their trading positions so that they are immediately aware of any losses. Many banks now have access to the market values of their trading businesses at the end of every day. If banks used a longer-term horizon (such as a month), larger losses might build up before being recognized.

Testing the Validity of a Bank's VAR The validity of a bank's estimated VAR is assessed with backtests in which the actual daily trading gains or losses are compared to the estimated VAR over a particular period. If the VAR is estimated properly, only 1 percent of the actual daily trading days should show results that are worse than the estimated VAR. In reality, banks may not be very concerned if all their trading results exceed their estimated VAR, because this suggests that their risk may have been overestimated for that period. However, they would be concerned (as would regulators) if the actual results from the trading businesses were frequently worse than the estimated VAR.

Related Stress Tests Some banks supplement the VAR estimate with stress tests.

ILLUSTRATION Georgia Bank wants to estimate the loss that would occur in response to an extreme adverse market event. First, it identifies an extreme event that could occur, such as an increase in interest rates on one day that is 10 standard deviations from the mean daily change in interest rates. The mean and standard deviation of daily interest rate movements may be based on a recent historical period, such as the last 300 days. Georgia Bank then uses this scenario along with the typical sensitivity of its trading businesses to such a scenario to estimate the loss on its trading businesses as a result. It may then repeat this exercise based on a scenario of a decline in the market value of stocks that is 10 standard deviations from the mean daily change in stock prices. It may even estimate the possible losses in its trading businesses from an adverse scenario in which interest rates increase and stock prices decline substantially on a given day. ■

How Regulators Monitor Banks

http://www.fdic.gov
Information about specific bank regulations.

Bank regulators typically conduct an on-site examination of each commercial bank at least once a year. During the examination, regulators assess the bank's compliance with existing regulations and its financial condition. In addition to on-site examinations, regulators periodically monitor commercial banks with computerized monitoring systems, based on data provided by the banks on a quarterly basis.

Regulators monitor banks to detect any serious deficiencies that might develop so that they can correct the deficiencies before the bank fails. The more failures they can prevent, the more confidence the public will have in the banking industry. The evaluation approach described here is used by the FDIC, the Federal Reserve, and the Comptroller of the Currency.

The single most common cause of bank failure is poor management. Unfortunately, no reliable measure of poor management exists. Therefore, the regulators rate banks on the basis of six characteristics, which together comprise the **CAMELS ratings,** so named for the acronym that identifies the six characteristics:

- Capital adequacy
- Asset quality
- Management
- Earnings
- Liquidity
- Sensitivity

Each of the CAMELS characteristics is rated on a 1-to-5 scale, with 1 indicating outstanding and 5 very poor. A composite rating is determined as the mean rating of the six characteristics. Banks with a composite rating of 4.0 or higher are considered to be problem banks. They are closely monitored, because their risk level is perceived as very high.

Capital Adequacy

Because adequate bank capital is thought to reduce a bank's risk, regulators determine the **capital ratio** (typically defined as capital divided by assets). Regulators have become increasingly concerned that some banks do not hold enough capital and have increased capital requirements. If banks hold more capital, they can more easily absorb potential losses and are more likely to survive. Banks with higher capital ratios are therefore assigned a higher capital adequacy rating. Even a bank with a relatively high level of capital could fail, however, if the other components of its balance sheet have not been properly managed. Thus, regulators must evaluate other characteristics of banks in addition to capital adequacy.

Asset Quality

Each bank makes its own decisions as to how deposited funds should be allocated, and these decisions determine its level of credit (default) risk. Regulators therefore evaluate the quality of the bank's assets, including its loans and its securities.

ILLUSTRATION   The Fed considers the 5 Cs to assess the quality of the loans extended by Skyler Bank, which it is examining:

- Capacity—the borrower's ability to pay.
- Collateral—the quality of the assets that back the loan.
- Condition—the circumstances that led to the need for funds.
- Capital—the difference between the value of the borrower's assets and its liabilities.
- Character—the borrower's willingness to repay loans, as measured by its payment history on the loan and credit report.

From an assessment of a sample of Skyler Bank's loans, the Fed determines that the borrowers have excessive debt, minimal collateral, and low capital levels. Thus, the Fed concludes that Skyler Bank's asset quality is weak. ■

Rating an asset portfolio can be difficult, however, as the following example illustrates.

ILLUSTRATION   A bank currently has 1,000 loans outstanding to firms in a variety of industries. Each loan has specific provisions as to how it is secured (if at all) by the borrower's assets; some of the loans have short-term maturities, while others are for longer terms. Imagine the task of assigning a rating to this bank's asset quality. Even if all the bank's loan recipients are current on their loan repayment schedules, this does not guarantee that the bank's asset quality deserves a high rating. The economic conditions existing during the period of prompt loan repayment may not persist in the future. Thus, an appropriate examination of the bank's asset portfolio should incorporate the portfolio's exposure to potential events (such as a recession). The reason for the regulatory examination is not to grade past performance, but to detect any problem that could cause the bank to fail in the future. ■

Because of the difficulty in assigning a rating to a bank's asset portfolio, it is possible that some banks will be rated lower or higher than they deserve.

Management

Each of the characteristics examined relates to the bank's management. In addition, regulators specifically rate the bank's management according to administrative skills, ability to comply with existing regulations, and ability to cope with a changing environment. They also assess the bank's internal control systems, which may indicate how well the bank's management would detect its own financial problems. This evaluation is clearly subjective.

Earnings

Although the CAMELS ratings are mostly concerned with risk, earnings are very important. Banks fail when their earnings become consistently negative. A profitability ratio commonly used to evaluate banks is **return on assets (ROA),** defined as earnings after taxes divided by assets. In addition to assessing a bank's earnings over time, it is also useful to compare the bank's earnings with industry earnings. This allows for an evaluation of the bank relative to its competitors. In addition, regulators are concerned about how a bank's earnings would change if economic conditions change.

Liquidity

Some banks commonly obtain funds from some outside sources (such as the Federal Reserve or the federal funds market), but regulators would prefer that banks not consistently rely on these sources. Such banks are more likely to experience a liquidity crisis whereby they are forced to borrow excessive amounts of funds from outside sources. If existing depositors sense that the bank is experiencing a liquidity problem, they may withdraw their funds, compounding the problem.

Sensitivity

Regulators also assess the degree to which a bank might be exposed to adverse financial market conditions. Two banks could be rated similarly in terms of recent earnings, liquidity, and other characteristics, and yet one bank may be much more sensitive than the other to financial market conditions. Regulators began to explicitly consider banks' sensitivity to financial market conditions in 1996 and added this characteristic to what were previously referred to as the CAMEL ratings. In particular, regulators place much emphasis on a bank's sensitivity to interest rate movements. Many banks have liabilities that are repriced more frequently than their assets and are therefore adversely affected by rising interest rates. Banks that are more sensitive to rising interest rates are more likely to experience financial problems.

Limitations of the CAMELS Rating System

The CAMELS rating system is essentially a screening device. Because there are so many banks, regulators do not have the resources to closely monitor each bank on a frequent basis. The rating system identifies what are believed to be problem banks. Over time, some problem banks improve and are removed from the "problem list," while others may deteriorate further and ultimately fail. Still other banks are added to the problem list.

Although examinations by regulators may help detect problems experienced by some banks in time to save them, many problems still go unnoticed, and by the time they are detected, it may be too late to find a remedy. Because financial ratios measure current or past performance rather than future performance, they do not always detect problems in time to correct them. Thus, although an analysis of financial ratios can be useful, the task of assessing a bank is as much an art as it is a science. Subjective opinion must complement objective measurements to provide the best possible evaluation of a bank.

Any system used to detect financial problems may err in one of two ways. It may classify a bank as safe when in fact it is failing or as very risky when in fact it is safe. The first type of mistake is more costly, because some failing banks are not identified in time to help them. To avoid this mistake, bank regulators could lower their benchmark composite rating. However, if they did, many more banks would be on the problem list requiring close supervision, and regulators would have to spread their limited resources too thin.

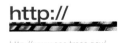

Corrective Action by Regulators

When a bank is classified as a problem bank, regulators thoroughly investigate the cause of its deterioration. Corrective action is often necessary. Regulators may examine such banks frequently and thoroughly and discuss with bank management possible remedies to cure the key problems. For example, regulators may request that a bank boost its capital level or delay its plans to expand. They can require that additional financial information be periodically updated to allow continued monitoring. They have the authority to remove particular officers and directors of a problem bank if doing so would enhance the bank's performance. They even have the authority to take legal action against a problem bank if the bank does not comply with their suggested remedies. Such a drastic measure is rare, however, and would not solve the existing problems of the bank.

Funding the Closure of Failing Banks

The FDIC is responsible for the closure of failing banks. It must decide whether to liquidate the failed bank's assets or to facilitate the acquisition of that bank by another bank. When liquidating a failed bank, the FDIC draws from its Bank Insurance Fund to reimburse insured depositors. Although the FDIC insures deposits of commercial banks and savings and loan associations, its Bank Insurance Fund is specifically targeted to commercial banks. After reimbursing depositors of the failed bank, the FDIC attempts to sell any marketable assets (such as securities and some loans) of the failed bank. The cost to the FDIC of closing a failed bank is the difference between the reimbursement to depositors and the proceeds received from selling the failed bank's assets.

An alternative solution is for the FDIC to provide some financial support to facilitate another bank's acquisition of the failed bank. The acquiring bank recognizes that the market value of the failed bank's assets is less than its liabilities. Nevertheless, the potential acquirer may consider acquiring the failed bank if it is given sufficient funds by the FDIC. The FDIC may be willing to provide funding if doing so would be less costly than liquidating the failed bank. Whether a failing bank is liquidated or acquired by another bank, it loses its identity.

On November 27, 1991, Congress passed the **Federal Deposit Insurance Corporation Improvement Act (FDICIA),** which was intended to penalize banks that engage in high-risk activities and also to reduce the regulatory costs of closing troubled banks. The more significant provisions of this act were as follows:

1. Regulators were required to act more quickly in forcing banks with inadequate capital to correct the deficiencies. Regulators classify a bank's capital position in one of five categories, ranging from well capitalized to critically undercapitalized. Three of the five categories reflect some deficiency in capital. Any banks that are classified in one of these three categories must meet specific requirements to boost their capital. This provision of the FDICIA forces banks with inadequate capital to correct their deficiencies. Consequently, the regulatory costs of closing the banks that ultimately fail should be reduced. At the time these categories were developed, less than 2 percent of all banks were classified in one of the three categories that call for specific corrective action.

2. Regulators were required to close troubled banks more quickly, rather than provide financial support to such banks over extended periods of time. This provision was intended to minimize the losses that may otherwise accumulate if troubled banks are allowed to remain open.

3. Deposits exceeding the insured limit ($100,000) are not to be covered when a bank fails. This provision forces large depositors to consider the risk of a bank before depositing funds there. Because the larger banks typically obtain more funds in the form of large deposits, they are affected to a greater degree by this provision. In the past, larger banks were perceived to be protected from failure because so many uninsured depositors were exposed. Because these banks are no longer

protected, their ability to obtain large deposits is now more closely linked to their financial condition. Banks with excessive risk have to pay higher interest rates (due to a higher risk premium) on large deposits.

4. Deposit insurance premiums were to be based on the risk of banks, rather than on the traditional fixed rate. Thus, riskier banks incur higher deposit insurance premiums. The risk-based deposit insurance premiums charged to financial institutions are based on a regulatory rating and the financial institution's capital level. The lower the financial institution's rating and the lower the capital level, the higher the annual deposit insurance premium that it must pay.

5. The FDIC was granted the right to borrow $30 billion from the Treasury to cover bank failures and an additional $45 billion to finance working capital needs (from the time the FDIC reimburses depositors until it is able to liquidate the assets). The extra funding gives the FDIC more flexibility in the event that its Bank Insurance Fund is depleted, so that it can continue to operate effectively. Without such flexibility, the FDIC could be forced to let troubled banks remain open, if its funding was not adequate to finance the bank closings. Thus, the costs of closing these banks later on would likely be higher. In fact, another objective of the FDICIA was to increase the size of the Bank Insurance Fund over time, and this goal has been achieved.

Some additional provisions of the FDICIA complement those just described. The Act requires more complete disclosure by commercial banks, which is intended to help regulators detect financial problems at an early stage. This provision can reduce bank losses and may allow some banks to resolve problems before it is too late. Another provision limits the amount of loans that can be provided by the Fed to undercapitalized institutions. This complements other provisions that enforce capital standards. The FDICIA also requires that regulators enforce standards on real estate loans. This provision is intended to prevent institutions from excessive exposure to the real estate market.

In general, the provisions of the FDICIA attempt to tie a bank's operating costs to its risk level. This is a distinct change from the previous system, which did not link some costs (such as interest paid on large deposits and insurance premiums) to the bank's risk. Because the FDICIA provisions link costs with risks, banks may be discouraged from taking excessive risks. Thus, fewer banks may fail, thereby reducing the costs incurred by the FDIC (and ultimately the taxpayers). Furthermore, the provisions on capital deficiencies and quicker closings of troubled banks can reduce the costs to the FDIC of closing troubled banks.

Preferential Regulatory Treatment

Some troubled banks have received preferential treatment from bank regulators. The most obvious example is Continental Illinois Bank, which was rescued by the federal government in 1984. Continental Illinois Bank had experienced serious loan default problems in 1983 and 1984. Continental's problems intensified as its depositors began to withdraw their funds. This is a common scenario when a bank fails. In contrast to most other situations, however, the bank regulators intervened. As massive deposit withdrawals occurred in May 1984, the FDIC announced that it would guarantee *all* deposits (and nondeposit liabilities) of Continental, even those beyond the normal $100,000 limit. This was an attempt to prevent further deposit withdrawals until some arrangements could be made to rescue Continental. In July 1984, the FDIC arranged for a rescue plan whereby it would support Continental by purchasing some of its existing loan commitments and providing capital, with the total support amounting to more than $5 billion.

During this same time period, other troubled banks were failing without any rescue attempt from the federal government. The reason for the Continental rescue plan was that, as one of the largest banks in the country, Continental's failure could have reduced public confidence in the banking system. Also, the rescue effort was less expensive to the FDIC than dealing with Continental's failure. But even if the direct costs to the FDIC had been higher, the potential indirect costs (such as the possible chain reaction of deposit withdrawals at other large banks) of letting the bank fail could have been too great to risk. Regardless of the reason for the FDIC's rescue, the fact remains that Continental Illinois Bank was rescued, while troubled smaller banks were not. This has important implications for the banking industry, identified in the following arguments for and against a government rescue.

Argument for Government Rescue

If the federal government had not intervened and Continental had failed and been liquidated, only depositors with less than $100,000 would have been assured full reimbursement. Then depositors with more than $100,000 at other banks could have become more concerned about their risk, and other large banks that were also experiencing serious loan default problems would have been likely candidates for runs on their deposit accounts. Even if other large banks were financially sound, a false rumor could have heightened depositors' worries and caused a run on deposits.

Argument against Government Rescue

A federal government bailout can be expensive. In January 1987, Continental Illinois Bank stated that the FDIC would recover as little as $1.1 billion of the $2.81 billion of troubled loans that it had assumed in 1984, depleting the FDIC's reserve fund.

When the federal government rescues a large bank, it sends a message to the banking industry that large banks will not be allowed to fail. Consequently, large banks may take excessive risks without concern about failure. If a large bank's risky ventures (such as loans to very risky borrowers) pay off, the return will be high. If they do not pay off, the federal government will bail the bank out. This argument has also been used in regard to international debt. On several occasions, large banks with risky loans to less developed countries (LDCs) have been aided by U.S. government financial support of the LDCs (increasing the chance that the LDCs would repay the U.S. banks). If large banks can be sure that they will be rescued, their shareholders will benefit because they face limited downside risk.

Proposals for Government Rescue

There may never be complete agreement as to whether the federal government should have bailed out Continental. The critical question is how the federal government should react in the future if another large bank is failing. An ideal solution would prevent a run on deposits of other large banks, yet not reward a poorly performing bank with a bailout. One possible solution would be for regulators such as the Federal Reserve and the FDIC to play a greater role in assessing bank financial conditions over time. In this way, they might be able to recognize problems before they become too severe. But there is no guarantee that increased regulatory reviews would have prevented Continental's financial problems. Bankers might suggest that regulators cannot contribute anything beyond what they already know. Thus, the role of a regulator should be more of a police officer (watching for illegal operations) than a consultant. In addition, increased regulatory reviews would result in an additional cost to the federal government.

Global Bank Regulations

GL◯BALASPECTS Although the division of regulatory power between the central bank and other regulators varies among countries, each country has a system for monitoring and regulating commercial banks. Most countries also maintain different guidelines for deposit insurance. Differences in regulatory restrictions can allow some banks a competitive advantage in a global banking environment.

Canada's banks tend to be subject to fewer banking regulations than U.S. banks. For instance, Canadian banks can expand throughout Canada, allowing the larger Canadian banks to control much of the market share. Historically, Canadian banks were not as restricted in investment banking activities as U.S. banks and therefore control much of the Canadian securities industry. Recently, Canadian banks have begun to enter the insurance industry.

European banks have had much more freedom than U.S. banks in offering investment banking services such as underwriting corporate securities. In fact, many European branches of U.S. banks provided investment banking services in Europe that were not allowed in the United States. European banks have penetrated the insurance industry in recent years by acquiring numerous insurance companies. Many European banks are allowed to invest in stocks.

Japanese commercial banks have some flexibility to provide investment banking services, but not as much as European banks. Perhaps the most obvious difference between Japanese and U.S. bank regulations is that Japanese banks are allowed to use depositor funds to invest in stocks of corporations. Thus, Japanese banks are not only creditors of firms, but are also their shareholders.

Uniform Global Regulations

The standardization of some regulations around the world has contributed to the globalization of markets and other financial services. Three of the more significant regulatory events allowing for a more competitive global playing field are (1) the International Banking Act, which placed U.S. and foreign banks operating in the United States under the same set of rules; (2) the Single European Act, which placed all European banks operating in many European countries under the same set of rules; and (3) the uniform capital adequacy guidelines, which forced banks of 12 industrialized nations to abide by the same minimum capital constraints. A discussion of each of these key events follows.

http://

http://www.law.cornell.edu Text of the IBA can be found through a search.

Uniform Regulations for Banks Operating in the United States
A key act related to international banking was the International Banking Act (IBA) of 1978, which was designed to impose similar regulations across domestic and foreign banks doing business in the United States. Prior to the Act, foreign banks had more flexibility to cross state lines in the United States than U.S.-based banks had. The IBA required foreign banks to identify one state as their home state so that they would be regulated like other U.S.-based banks residing in that state.

Uniform Regulations across Europe
One of the most significant events affecting international banking markets has been the **Single European Act of 1987,** which was phased in throughout many European countries. The following are some of the more relevant provisions of the Act for the banking industry:

- Capital can flow freely throughout the participating countries.
- Banks can offer a wide variety of lending, leasing, and securities activities in the participating countries.

- Regulations regarding competition, mergers, and taxes are similar throughout these countries.
- A bank established in any participating European country has the right to expand into any or all of the other participating countries.

As a result of the Single European Act, a common market has been established for many European countries. One of the key objectives of the Act is to facilitate the free flow of capital across countries in order to enhance financial market efficiency. To this end, the Act eliminated capital controls imposed by individual European countries on services such as deposit taking, lending, leasing, portfolio management advice, and credit references.

As a result, European banks have begun to consolidate across countries. Efficiency in the European banking markets is increasing as banks can more easily cross countries without concern about country-specific regulations that prevailed in the past.

Another key provision of the Act is that banks can enter Europe and receive the same banking powers as other banks there. Similar provisions apply to non-U.S. banks that enter the United States.

Even some European savings institutions have been affected by the more uniform regulations. Savings institutions throughout the participating countries are now evolving into full-service institutions, expanding into services such as insurance, brokerage, and mutual fund management.

The inception of a single currency (the euro) in 1999 has expedited the integration among participating European countries. With one currency, consolidation of financial services among countries is easier.

Uniform Capital Adequacy Guidelines around the World

Before 1988, capital standards imposed on banks varied across countries, which allowed some banks to have a comparative global advantage over others. The Basel Accord (discussed earlier) resulted in more uniform capital requirements among countries. Even with uniform capital requirements across countries, some analysts still contend that some banks are at a competitive disadvantage because they are subject to different accounting and tax provisions. Nevertheless, the uniform capital requirements represent significant progress toward a more level global field.

Summary

■ Banks are regulated on the deposit insurance that they must maintain, the disclosure of their loan composition, the bonds that they are allowed to purchase, the minimum capital level they must maintain, the locations where they can operate, and the services that they can offer. Although capital requirements have become more stringent, regulations on where banks can operate and what services they can offer have been loosened. Most regulations are intended to enhance the safety and soundness of the banking system, without hampering efficiency.

■ Bank regulators monitor banks by focusing on six criteria: capital, asset quality, management, earnings, liquidity, and sensitivity to financial market conditions. The regulators assign ratings to these criteria to determine whether corrective action is necessary.

■ In 1991, Congress passed the Federal Deposit Insurance Corporation Improvement Act (FDICIA), which gave regulators the power to act quickly in taking corrective action. Specifically, regulators could force banks with inadequate capital to boost capital levels. Regulators were also required to close troubled banks more quickly.

Point Counter-Point

Should Regulators Intervene to Take Over Weak Banks?

Point Yes. Intervention could turn a bank around before weak management results in failures. Bank failures require funding from the FDIC to reimburse depositors up to the deposit insurance limit. This cost could be avoided if the bank's problems are corrected before it fails.

Counter-Point No. Regulators will not necessarily manage banks any better. Also, this would lead to excessive government intervention each time a bank

experienced problems. Banks would use a very conservative management approach to avoid intervention, but this approach would not necessarily appeal to their shareholders who want high returns on their investment.

Who Is Correct? Use the Internet to learn more about this issue. Offer your own opinion on this issue.

Questions and Applications

1. **Regulation of Bank Sources and Uses of Funds** How are a bank's balance sheet decisions regulated?

2. **Off-Balance Sheet Activities** Provide examples of off-balance sheet activities. Why are regulators concerned about them?

3. **Regulatory Acts about Interstate Banking** Briefly describe the McFadden Act of 1927, the Douglas Amendment to the Bank Holding Company Act of 1956, and the Riegle-Neal Interstate Banking Act of 1994.

4. **FDIC Insurance** What led to the establishment of FDIC insurance?

5. **Glass-Steagall Act** Briefly describe the Glass-Steagall Act. Then explain how the related regulations have changed.

6. **DIDMCA** Describe the main provisions of the DIDMCA that relate to deregulation.

7. **CAMELS Ratings** Explain how the CAMELS ratings are used.

8. **Uniform Capital Requirements** Explain how the uniform capital requirements in 1988 created a more equal global playing field. Explain how the uniform capital requirements can discourage banks from taking excessive risk.

9. **FIRREA** Explain how the Financial Institutions Reform, Recovery, and Enforcement Act (FIRREA) has resulted in increasing integration between the commercial banking industry and the savings institution industry.

10. **HLTs** Describe highly leveraged transactions (HLTs), and explain why a bank's exposure to HLTs is closely monitored by regulators.

11. **Bank Underwriting** Why might banks be even more interested in underwriting corporate debt issues since the higher capital requirements were imposed on them?

12. **Moral Hazard** Explain the "moral hazard" problem as it relates to deposit insurance.

13. **Economies of Scale** How do economies of scale in banking relate to the issue of interstate banking?

14. **Contagion Effects** How can the financial problems of one large bank affect the market's risk evaluation of other large banks?

15. **Regulating Bank Failures** Why are bank regulators more concerned about a large bank failure than a small bank failure, aside from the difference in direct cost to the FDIC?

16. **Financial Services Modernization Act** Describe the Financial Services Modernization Act of 1999. Explain how it affected commercial bank operations and changed the competitive landscape among financial institutions.

17. **IBA** What was the purpose of the International Banking Act (IBA)?

18. **Single European Act** Explain how the Single European Act affected international banking.

19. **Impact of SOX on Banks** Explain how the Sarbanes-Oxley Act improved the transparency of banks. Why could the act have a negative impact on some banks?

Interpreting Financial News

Interpret the following comments made by Wall Street analysts and portfolio managers:

a. "The FDIC recently subsidized a buyer for a failing bank, which had different effects on FDIC costs than if the FDIC closed the bank."

b. "Bank of America has pursued the acquisition of many failed banks because it sees potential benefits."

c. "By allowing a failing bank time to resolve its financial problems, the FDIC imposes an additional tax on taxpayers."

Managing in Financial Markets

Effect of Bank Strategies on Bank Ratings A bank has asked you to assess various strategies it is considering and explain how they could affect its regulatory review. Regulatory reviews include an assessment of capital, asset quality, management, earnings, liquidity, and sensitivity to financial market conditions. Many types of strategies can result in more favorable regulatory reviews based on some criteria but less favorable reviews based on other criteria. The bank is planning to issue more stock, retain more of its earnings, increase its holdings of Treasury securities, and reduce its business loans. The bank has historically been rated favorably by regulators, but believes that these strategies will result in an even more favorable regulatory assessment.

a. Which regulatory criteria will be affected by the bank's strategies? How?

b. Do you believe that the strategies planned by the bank will satisfy shareholders? Is it possible for the bank to use strategies that would satisfy both regulators and shareholders? Explain.

c. Do you believe that the strategies planned by the bank will satisfy the bank's managers? Explain.

Flow of Funds Exercise

Impact of Regulation and Deregulation on Financial Services

Carson Company relies heavily on commercial banks for funding and for some other services.

a. Explain how the services provided by a commercial bank (just the banking, not the nonbank, services) to Carson may be limited due to bank regulation.

b. Explain the types of nonbank services that Carson Company can receive from the subsidiaries of a commercial bank as a result of recent deregulation.

c. How might Carson Company be affected by the deregulation that allows subsidiaries of a commercial bank to offer nonbank services?

Internet/Excel Exercise

1. Browse the most recent Quarterly Banking Profile at http://www.fdic.gov/bank/analytical/index.html. Click on "Industry Analysis" and then on "Failed Banks." Describe how regulators responded to one recent bank failure listed here.

WSJ Exercise

Impact of Bank Regulations

Using a recent issue of *The Wall Street Journal,* summarize an article that discussed a particular commercial bank regulation that has recently been passed or is currently being considered by regulators. (You may wish to use *The Wall Street Journal Index* in the library to identify a specific article on a commercial banking regulation or bill.) Would this regulation have a favorable or unfavorable impact on commercial banks? Explain.

Chapter 19: Bank Management

The performance of any commercial bank depends on the management of the bank's assets, liabilities, and capital. Increased competition has made efficient management essential for survival.

The specific objectives of this chapter are to:

- describe the underlying goal of bank management,
- explain how banks manage liquidity,
- explain how banks manage interest rate risk,
- explain how banks manage credit risk, and
- explain how banks manage capital.

Bank Management

The underlying goal behind the managerial policies of a bank is to maximize the wealth of the bank's shareholders. Thus, bank managers should make decisions that maximize the price of the bank's stock.

In some cases, managers are tempted to make decisions that are in their own best interests rather than shareholder interests. For example, decisions that result in growth may be intended to increase employee salaries, as larger banks tend to provide more employee compensation. In addition, the compensation to a bank's loan officers may be tied to loan volume, which encourages a loan department to extend loans without concern about risk. As these examples suggest, banks can incur agency costs, or costs resulting from managers maximizing their own wealth instead of shareholder wealth. To prevent agency problems, some banks provide stock as compensation to managers. These managers may be more likely to maximize shareholder wealth because they are shareholders as well. Also, if managerial decisions conflict with the goal of maximizing shareholder wealth, the share price will not achieve its maximum. Therefore, the bank may become a takeover target, as other banks perceive it as undervalued, with the potential to improve under their own management. In this way, managers can be disciplined to maximize shareholder wealth.

Board of Directors

A bank's board of directors oversees the operations of the bank and attempts to ensure that managerial decisions are in the best interests of the shareholders. Bank boards tend to have more directors and a higher percentage of outside directors than boards of other types of firms. Some of the more important functions of bank directors are to

- Determine a compensation system for the bank's executives.
- Ensure proper disclosure of the bank's financial condition and performance to investors.

- Oversee growth strategies such as acquisitions.

- Oversee policies for changing the capital structure, including decisions to raise capital or to engage in stock repurchases.

- Assess the bank's performance and ensure that corrective action is taken if the performance is weak due to poor management.

Bank directors are liable if they do not fulfill their duties. In the mid-1980s, several banks failed because of inappropriate lending. For example, some banks engaged in various forms of insider lending in which employees were given loans at favorable interest rates. These loans were clearly not intended to serve shareholder interests. The Federal Deposit Insurance Corporation (FDIC) filed numerous lawsuits against bank directors for being negligent in their oversight of bank lending behavior. In recent years, shareholders have taken the initiative and filed lawsuits against bank directors who were negligent in monitoring management decisions.

The Sarbanes-Oxley (SOX) Act, described in the previous chapter, has had a major effect on the monitoring conducted by the board members of commercial banks. Recall that this act requires publicly traded firms to implement a more thorough internal control process to ensure more accurate financial reporting to shareholders. As a result of the SOX Act, directors are now held more accountable for their oversight because the internal process requires them to document their assessment and opinion of key decisions made by the bank's executives. Furthermore, directors more frequently hire outside legal and financial advisers to aid in assessing key decisions (such as acquisitions) by bank executives to determine whether the decisions are justified.

Managing Liquidity

Banks can experience illiquidity when cash outflows (due to deposit withdrawals, loans, etc.) exceed cash inflows (new deposits, loan repayments, etc.). They can resolve any cash deficiency either by creating additional liabilities or by selling assets. Banks have access to various forms of borrowing, such as the federal funds market. They also maintain some assets that can readily be sold in the secondary market. The decision on how to obtain funds depends on the situation. If the need for funds is temporary, an increase in short-term liabilities (from the federal funds market) may be appropriate. If the need is permanent, however, a policy for increasing deposits or selling liquid assets may be appropriate.

Because some assets are more marketable than others, the bank's asset composition can affect its degree of liquidity. At an extreme, banks could ensure sufficient liquidity by using most of their funds to purchase Treasury securities. However, they must also be concerned with achieving a reasonable return on their assets, which often conflicts with the liquidity objective. Although Treasury securities are liquid, their yield is low relative to bank loans or investments in other securities. Recent research has shown that high-performance banks are able to maintain relatively low (but sufficient) liquidity. Banks should maintain the level of liquid assets that will satisfy their liquidity needs but use their remaining funds to satisfy their other objectives. As the secondary market for loans has become active, banks are better able to satisfy their liquidity needs with a higher proportion of loans while striving for higher profitability.

Use of Securitization to Boost Liquidity

The ability to securitize assets such as automobile and mortgage loans can enhance a bank's liquidity position. The process of securitization commonly involves the sale of assets by the bank to a trustee, who issues securities that are collateralized by the assets. The bank may still service the loans, but it passes through the interest and principal payments received to the investors who purchased the securities. Banks are more liquid as a result of securitization because they effectively convert future cash flows into immediate cash. In most cases, the process includes a guarantor who, for a fee, guarantees future payments to investors who purchased the securities. The loans that collateralize the securities normally exceed the amount of the securities issued or are backed by an additional guarantee from the bank that sells the loans.

Collateralized Loan Obligations (CLOs). As one form of securitization, commercial banks can obtain funds by packaging their commercial loans with those of other financial institutions as collateralized loan obligations (CLOs) and then selling securities that represent ownership of these loans. The banks earn a fee for selling these loans. More than $100 billion was raised in 2006 from the creation of CLOs. The pool of loans is less risky than a typical individual loan within the pool because the loans were provided to a diversified set of borrowers. The securities that are issued to investors who invest in the loan pool represent various classes. For example, one class of notes issued to investors may be BB-rated notes, which offer an interest rate of LIBOR (London Interbank Offer Rate) plus 3.5 percent. If there are loan defaults by the corporate borrowers whose loans are in the pool, this group of investors will be the first to suffer losses. Another class may consist of BBB-rated notes that offer a slightly lower interest rate. Investors in these notes are slightly less exposed to defaults on the loans. The AAA-rated notes offer investors the most protection against loan defaults but provide the lowest interest rate, such as LIBOR plus .25 percent. Insurance companies and pension funds are common investors in CLOs.

Managing Interest Rate Risk

The performance of a bank is highly influenced by the interest payments earned on its assets relative to the interest paid on its liabilities (deposits). The difference between interest payments received versus interest paid is measured by the **net interest margin** (also referred to sometimes as "spread"):

$$\text{Net interest margin} = \frac{\text{Interest revenues} - \text{Interest expenses}}{\text{Assets}}$$

In some cases, net interest margin is defined to include only the earning assets, excluding any assets that do not generate a return to the bank (such as required reserves). Because the rate sensitivity of a bank's liabilities normally does not perfectly match that of the assets, the net interest margin changes over time. The change depends on whether bank assets are more or less rate sensitive than bank liabilities, the degree of difference in rate sensitivity, and the direction of interest rate movements.

The composition of a bank's balance sheet will determine how its profitability is influenced by interest rate fluctuations. If a bank expects interest rates to consistently decrease over time, it will consider allocating most of its funds to rate-insensitive assets, such as long-term and medium-term loans (all with fixed rates) as well as long-term securities. These assets will continue to provide the same periodic yield. As interest rates decline, the bank's cost of funds will decrease, and its overall return will increase.

If a bank expects interest rates to consistently increase over time, it will consider allocating most of its funds to rate-sensitive assets such as short-term commercial and consumer loans, long-term loans with floating interest rates, and short-term securities. The short-term instruments will mature soon, so reinvestment will be at a higher rate if interest rates increase. The longer-term instruments will continue to exist, so the bank will benefit from increasing interest rates only if it uses floating rates.

During a period of rising interest rates, a bank's net interest margin will likely decrease if its liabilities are more rate sensitive than its assets, as illustrated in Exhibit 19.1. Under the opposite scenario, where market interest rates are declining over time, rates offered on new bank deposits, as well as those earned on new bank loans, will be affected by the decline in interest rates. The deposit rates will typically be more sensitive if their turnover is quicker, as illustrated in Exhibit 19.2.

To manage interest rate risk, a bank measures the risk and then uses its asessment of future interest rates to decide whether and how to hedge the risk. Methods of assessing the risk are described next, followed by a discussion of the hedging decision and methods of reducing interest rate risk.

Methods Used to Assess Interest Rate Risk

No method of measuring interest rate risk is perfect, so commercial banks use a variety of methods to assess their exposure to interest rate movements. The following are the most common methods of measuring interest rate risk:

- Gap analysis
- Duration analysis
- Regression analysis

Exhibit 19.1

Impact of Increasing Interest Rates on a Bank's Net Interest Margin (If the Bank's Liabilities Are More Rate Sensitive Than Its Assets)

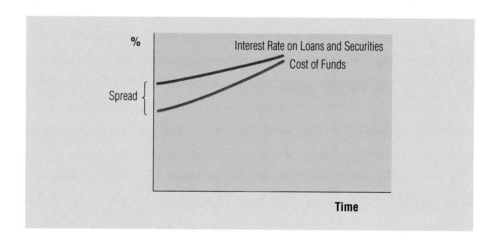

Exhibit 19.2

Impact of Decreasing Interest Rates on a Bank's Net Interest Margin (If the Bank's Liabilities Are More Rate Sensitive Than Its Assets)

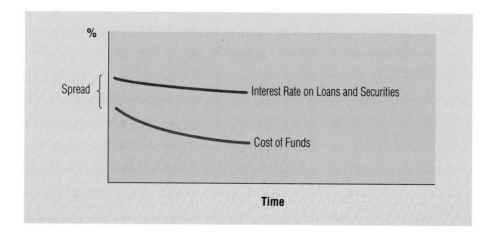

Gap Analysis Banks can attempt to determine their interest rate risk by monitoring their **gap** over time, defined here as

$$\text{Gap} = \text{Rate-sensitive assets} - \text{Rate-sensitive liabilities}$$

An alternative formula is the **gap ratio,** which is measured as the volume of rate-sensitive assets divided by rate-sensitive liabilities. A gap of zero (or gap ratio of 1.00) indicates that rate-sensitive assets equal rate-sensitive liabilities, so the net interest margin should not be significantly influenced by interest rate fluctuations. A negative gap (or gap ratio of less than 1.00) indicates that rate-sensitive liabilities exceed rate-sensitive assets. Banks with a negative gap are typically concerned about a potential increase in interest rates, which could reduce their net interest margin.

ILLUSTRATION Kansas City (K.C.) Bank had interest revenues of $80 million last year and $35 million in interest expenses. About $400 million of its $1 billion in assets are rate sensitive, while $700 million of its liabilities are rate sensitive. K.C. Bank's net interest margin is

$$\text{Net interest margin} = (\$80{,}000{,}000 - \$35{,}000{,}000)/\$1{,}000{,}000{,}000$$
$$= .045, \text{ or } 4.5\%$$

K.C. Bank's gap is

$$\text{Gap} = \$400{,}000{,}000 - \$700{,}000{,}000$$
$$= -\$300{,}000{,}000$$

K.C. Bank's gap ratio is

$$\text{Gap ratio} = \$400{,}000{,}000/\$700{,}000{,}000$$
$$= .5714, \text{ or } 57.14\%$$

Based on the gap analysis of K.C. Bank, an increase in market interest rates would cause its net interest margin to decline from its recent level of 4.5 percent. Conversely, a decrease in interest rates would cause its net interest margin to increase above 4.5 percent. ■

Many banks classify interest-sensitive assets and liabilities into various categories based on the time of repricing. Then the bank can determine the gap in each category so that its exposure to interest rate risk can be assessed.

ILLUSTRATION Deacon Bank compares the interest rate sensitivity of its assets versus its liabilities as shown in Exhibit 19.3. It has a negative gap in the less-than-1-month maturity range, the 3- to 6-month range, and the 6- to 12-month range. Thus, the bank may hedge this gap if it believes that interest rates are rising. ■

Although the gap as described here is an easy method for measuring a bank's interest rate risk, it has limitations. Banks must decide how to classify their liabilities and assets as rate sensitive versus rate insensitive. For example, should a Treasury security with a year to maturity be classified as rate sensitive or rate insensitive? How short must a maturity be to qualify for the rate-sensitive classification?

Each bank may have its own classification system, because there is no perfect measurement of the gap. Whatever system is used, there is a possibility that the measurement will be misinterpreted.

ILLUSTRATION Spencer Bank obtains much of its funds by issuing CDs with seven-day and one-month maturities as well as money market deposit accounts

Exhibit 19.3
Interest-Sensitive
Assets and Liabilities:
Illustration of the Gap
Measured for Various
Maturity Ranges for
Deacon Bank

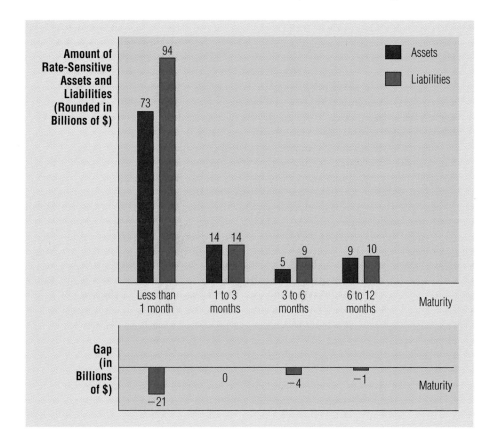

(MMDAs). Assume that it typically uses these funds to provide loans with a floating rate, adjusted once per year. These sources of funds and uses of funds will likely be classified as rate sensitive. Thus, the gap will be close to zero, implying that the bank is not exposed to interest rate risk. Yet, there is a difference in the *degree* of rate sensitivity between the bank's sources and uses of funds. The rates paid by the bank on its sources of funds will change more frequently than the rates earned on its uses of funds. Thus, Spencer Bank's net interest margin would likely be reduced during periods of rising interest rates. This exposure would not be detected by the gap measurement. ■

Duration Measurement An alternative approach to assessing interest rate risk is to measure duration. Some assets or liabilities are more rate sensitive than others, even if the frequency of adjustment and the maturity are the same. A 10-year zero-coupon bond is more sensitive to interest rate fluctuations than a 10-year bond that pays coupon payments. Thus, the market value of assets in a bank that has invested in zero-coupon bonds will be very susceptible to interest rate movements. The duration measurement can capture these different degrees of sensitivity. In recent years, banks and other financial institutions have used the concept of **duration** to measure the sensitivity of their assets to interest rate movements. There are various measurements for an asset's duration; one of the more common is

$$\text{DUR} = \frac{\displaystyle\sum_{t=1}^{n} \frac{C_t(t)}{(1+k)^t}}{\displaystyle\sum_{t=1}^{n} \frac{C_t}{(1+k)^t}}$$

where C_t represents the interest or principal payments of the asset, t is the time at which the payments are provided, and k is the required rate of return on the asset, which reflects the asset's yield to maturity. The duration of each type of bank asset can be determined, and the duration of the asset portfolio is the weighted average (based on the relative proportion invested in each asset) of the durations of the individual assets.

The duration of each type of bank liability can also be estimated; the duration of the portfolio is estimated as the weighted average of the durations of the liabilities. The bank can then estimate its **duration gap,** which is commonly measured as the difference between the weighted duration of the bank's assets and the weighted duration of its liabilities, adjusted for the firm's asset size:

$$\text{DURGAP} = \frac{(\text{DURAS} \times \text{AS})}{\text{AS}} - \frac{(\text{DURLIAB} \times \text{LIAB})}{\text{AS}}$$

$$= \text{DURAS} - [\text{DURLIAB} \times (\text{LIAB/AS})]$$

where DURAS is the average duration of the bank's assets, DURLIAB is the weighted average of the bank's liabilities, AS represents the market value of the assets, and LIAB represents the market value of the liabilities. A duration gap of zero suggests that the bank's value should be insensitive to interest rate movements, meaning that the bank is not exposed to interest rate risk. For most banks, the average duration of assets exceeds the average duration of liabilities, so the duration gap is positive. This implies that the market value of the bank's assets is more sensitive to interest rate movements than the value of its liabilities because the asset durations are higher on average. Thus, if interest rates rise, banks with positive duration gaps will be adversely affected. Conversely, if interest rates decline, banks with positive duration gaps will benefit. The larger the duration gap, the more sensitive the bank should be to interest rate movements.

Other things being equal, assets with shorter maturities have shorter durations; also, assets that generate more frequent coupon payments have shorter durations than those that generate less frequent payments. Banks and other financial institutions concerned with interest rate risk use duration to compare the rate sensitivity of their entire asset and liability portfolios. Because duration is especially critical for a savings institution's operations, a numerical example showing the measurement of the duration of a savings institution's entire asset and liability portfolio is provided in Chapter 21.

Although duration is a valuable technique for comparing the rate sensitivity of various securities, its capabilities are limited when applied to assets that can be terminated on a moment's notice. For example, consider a bank that offers a fixed-rate five-year loan that can be paid off early without penalty. If the loan is not paid off early, it is perceived as rate insensitive. Yet, there is the possibility that the loan will be terminated anytime over the five-year period. In this case, the bank would reinvest the funds at a rate dependent on market rates at that time. Thus, the funds used to provide the loan *can* be sensitive to interest rate movements, but the degree of sensitivity depends on when the loan is paid off. In general, loan prepayments are more common when market rates decline, because borrowers refinance by obtaining lower-rate loans to pay off existing loans. The point here is that the possibility of prepayment makes it impossible to perfectly match the rate sensitivity of assets and liabilities.

Regression Analysis Gap analysis and duration analysis are based on the bank's balance sheet composition. Alternatively, a bank can assess interest rate risk by simply determining how performance has historically been influenced by interest rate movements. To do this, a proxy must be identified for bank performance and for prevailing interest rates, and a model that can estimate the relationship between the proxies must be chosen. A common proxy for performance is return on assets, return on equity, or the percentage change in stock price. To determine how performance is affected by interest rates, regression analysis can be applied to historical data. For example, using an interest rate proxy called i, the S&P 500 stock index as the market and the bank's stock return (R) as the performance proxy, the following regression model could be used:

$$R = B_0 + B_1 R_m + B_2 i + \mu$$

where R_m is the return on the market, B_0, B_1, and B_2 are regression coefficients, and μ is an error term. The regression coefficient B_2 in this model can also be called the interest rate coefficient, because it measures the sensitivity of the bank's performance to interest rate movements. A positive (negative) coefficient suggests that performance is favorably (adversely) affected by rising interest rates. If the interest rate coefficient is not significantly different from zero, this suggests that the bank's stock returns are insulated from interest rate movements.

Models similar to that just described have been tested for the portfolio of all publicly traded banks to determine whether bank stock levels are affected by interest rate movements. The vast majority of this research has found that bank stock levels are inversely related to interest rate movements (the B_2 coefficient is negative and significant). These results can be attributed to the common imbalance between a bank's rate-sensitive liabilities and its assets. Because banks tend to have a negative gap (their liabilities are more rate sensitive than their assets), rising interest rates reduce bank performance. These results are generalized for the banking industry and do not apply to every bank.

Because a bank's assets and liabilities are replaced over time, exposure to interest rate risk must be continually reassessed. As exposure changes, the reaction of bank performance to a particular interest rate pattern will change.

When a bank uses regression analysis to determine its sensitivity to interest rate movements, it may combine this analysis with the so-called value-at-risk (VAR) method to determine how its market value would change in response to specific interest rate movements. The VAR method can be applied by combining a probability distribution of interest rate movements with the interest rate coefficient (measured from the regression analysis) to determine a maximum expected loss due to adverse interest rate movements. For example, if the bank determines from applying the regression model to monthly data that its interest rate regression coefficient is -2.4, this implies that for a 1 percentage point increase in interest rates, the value of the bank would decline by 2.4 percent. Assume that the bank determines at the 99 percent confidence level that the change in the interest rate should be no worse than an increase of 2.0 percent. For a 2 percentage point increase, the value of the bank is expected to decline by 4.8 percent (computed as 2.0 percent multiplied by the regression coefficient of -2.4). Thus, the maximum expected loss due to interest rate movements (based on a 99 percent confidence level) is a 4.8 percent loss in market value.

Determining Whether to Hedge Interest Rate Risk

A bank can consider its measurement of its interest rate risk along with its forecast of interest rate movements to determine whether it should consider hedging its risk. The general conclusions resulting from a bank's analysis of its interest rate risk are presented in Exhibit 19.4. This exhibit shows the three methods that are commonly used by banks to measure their interest rate risk. Since none of these measures is perfect for all situations, some banks measure interest rate risk using all three methods. Other

Exhibit 19.4
Framework for
Managing Interest
Rate Risk

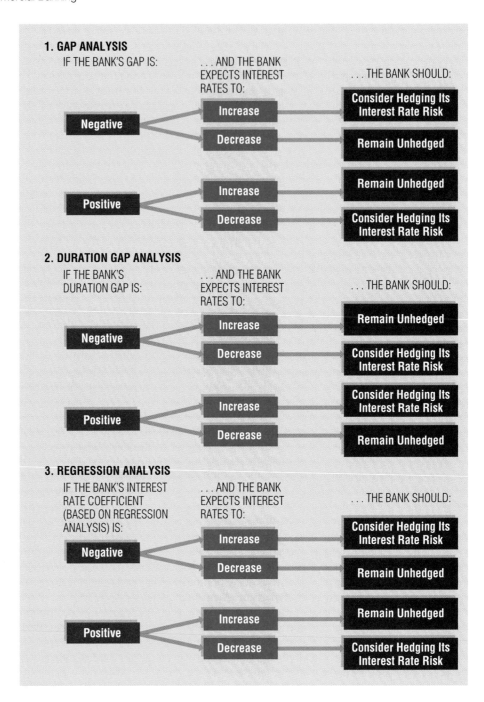

banks prefer just one of the methods. The use of any method along with an interest rate forecast can help a bank determine whether it should consider hedging its interest rate risk.

In general, the three methods should lead to a similar conclusion. If a bank has a negative gap, its average asset duration is probably larger than its liability duration (positive duration gap), and its past performance level is probably inversely related to interest rate movements. If the bank recently revised the composition of its assets or liabilities, however, it may wish to focus on the gap or the duration gap, as regression analysis is based on a historical relationship that may no longer exist. Banks use their analysis of gap along with their forecast of interest rates to make their hedging decision. The specific methods of hedging interest rate risk are described next.

Methods Used to Reduce Interest Rate Risk

Banks have monitored interest rate risk since the late 1970s, as interest rate movements have been very volatile. Interest rate risk can be reduced by

- Maturity matching
- Using floating-rate loans
- Using interest rate futures contracts
- Using interest rate swaps
- Using interest rate caps

Maturity Matching One obvious method of reducing interest rate risk is to match each deposit's maturity with an asset of the same maturity. For example, if the bank receives funds for a one-year CD, it could provide a one-year loan or invest in a security with a one-year maturity. Although this strategy would avoid interest rate risk, it cannot be implemented effectively. Banks receive a large volume of short-term deposits and would not be able to match up maturities on deposits with the longer loan maturities. Borrowers rarely request funds for a period as short as one month or even six months. In addition, the deposit amounts are typically small relative to the loan amounts. A bank would have difficulty combining deposits with a particular maturity to accommodate a loan request with the same maturity.

Using Floating-Rate Loans An alternative solution is to use floating-rate loans, which allow banks to support long-term assets with short-term deposits without overly exposing themselves to interest rate risk. Floating-rate loans cannot, however, completely eliminate the risk. If the cost of funds is changing more frequently than the rate on assets, the bank's net interest margin is still affected by interest rate fluctuations.

When banks reduce their exposure to interest rate risk by replacing long-term securities with more floating-rate commercial loans, they increase their exposure to credit risk, because the commercial loans provided by banks typically have a higher frequency of default than the securities they hold. In addition, bank liquidity risk would increase, because loans are not as marketable as securities.

Using Interest Rate Futures Contracts Large banks frequently use interest rate futures and other types of derivative instruments to hedge interest rate risk. A common method of reducing interest rate risk is to use interest rate futures contracts, which lock in the price at which specified financial instruments can be purchased or sold on a specified future settlement date. Recall that the sale of a futures contract on Treasury bonds prior to an increase in interest rates will result in a gain, because an identical futures contract can be purchased later at a lower price once interest rates rise. Thus, a gain on the Treasury bond futures contracts can offset the adverse effects of higher interest rates on a bank's performance. The size of the bank's position in Treasury bond futures is dependent on the size of its asset portfolio, the degree of its exposure to interest rate movements, and its forecasts of future interest rate movements.

Exhibit 19.5 illustrates how the use of financial futures contracts can reduce the uncertainty about a bank's net interest margin. The sale of CD futures, for example, reduces the potential adverse effect of rising interest rates on the bank's interest

Exhibit 19.5
Effect of Financial Futures on the Net Interest Margin of Banks That Have More Rate-Sensitive Liabilities Than Assets

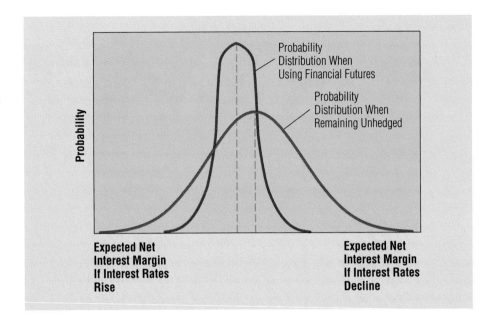

expenses. Yet, it also reduces the potential favorable effect of declining interest rates on the bank's interest expenses. Assuming that the bank initially had more rate-sensitive liabilities, its use of futures would reduce the impact of interest rates on its net interest margin.

Using Interest Rate Swaps Commercial banks can hedge interest rate risk by engaging in an interest rate swap, which is an arrangement to exchange periodic cash flows based on specified interest rates. A fixed-for-floating swap allows one party to periodically exchange fixed cash flows for cash flows that are based on prevailing market interest rates.

A bank whose liabilities are more rate sensitive than its assets can swap payments with a fixed interest rate in exchange for payments with a variable interest rate over a specified period of time. If interest rates rise, the bank benefits because the payments to be received from the swap will increase while its outflow payments are fixed. This can offset the adverse impact of rising interest rates on the bank's net interest margin. In 2004, interest rates were unusually low, causing banks to take swap positions that protected against a possible increase in interest rates. These banks benefited from their swap positions as interest rates rose in the 2005–2007 period.

An interest rate swap requires another party that is willing to provide variable-rate payments in exchange for fixed-rate payments. Financial institutions that have more rate-sensitive assets than liabilities may be willing to assume such a position, because they could reduce their exposure to interest rate movements in this manner. A financial intermediary is typically needed to match up the two parties that desire an interest rate swap. Some investment banking firms and large commercial banks serve in this role.

ILLUSTRATION Assume that Denver Bank (DB) has large holdings of 11 percent fixed-rate loans. Because its sources of funds are mostly interest rate sensitive, DB desires to swap fixed-rate payments in exchange for variable-rate payments. It informs Colorado Bank of its situation, because it knows that this bank commonly engages in swap transactions. Colorado Bank searches for a client and finds that

Brit Eurobank desires to swap variable-rate dollar payments in exchange for fixed dollar payments. Colorado Bank then develops the swap arrangement illustrated in Exhibit 19.6. DB will swap fixed-rate payments in exchange for variable-rate payments based on LIBOR (the rate charged on loans between Eurobanks). Because the variable-rate payments will fluctuate with market conditions, DB's payments received will vary over time. The length of the swap period and the notional amount (the amount to which the interest rates are applied to determine the payments) can be structured to the participants' desires. Colorado Bank, the financial intermediary conducting the swap, charges a fee, such as .1 percent of the notional amount per year. Some financial intermediaries for swaps may act as the counterparty and exchange the payments desired, rather than just match up two parties.

Now assume that the fixed payments to be paid are based on a fixed rate of 9 percent. Also assume that LIBOR is initially 7 percent and that DB's cost of funds is 6 percent. Exhibit 19.7 shows how DB's spread is affected by various possible interest rates when unhedged versus when hedged with an interest rate swap. If LIBOR remains at 7 percent, DB's spread would be 5 percent if unhedged and only 3 percent when using a swap. However, if LIBOR increases beyond 9 percent, the spread when using the swap exceeds the unhedged spread because the higher cost of funds causes a lower unhedged spread. The swap arrangement would provide DB with increased

Exhibit 19.6
Illustration of an Interest Rate Swap

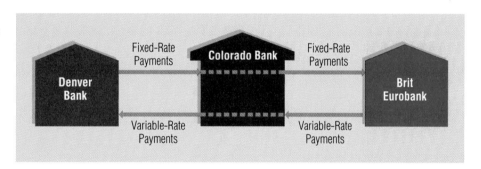

Exhibit 19.7   Comparison of Denver Bank's Spread: Unhedged versus Hedged

	Possible LIBOR Rates in the Future					
Unhedged Strategy	7%	8%	9%	10%	11%	12%
Average rate on existing mortgages	11%	11%	11%	11%	11%	11%
Average cost of deposits	6	7	8	9	10	11
Spread	5	4	3	2	1	0
Hedging with an Interest Rate Swap						
Fixed interest rate earned on fixed-rate mortgages	11	11	11	11	11	11
Fixed interest rate owed on swap arrangement	9	9	9	9	9	9
Spread on fixed-rate payments	2	2	2	2	2	2
Variable interest rate earned on swap arrangement	7	8	9	10	11	12
Variable interest rate owed on deposits	6	7	8	9	10	11
Spread on variable-rate payments	1	1	1	1	1	1
Combined total spread when using the swap	3	3	3	3	3	3

payments that offset the higher cost of funds. The advantage of a swap is that it can lock in the spread to be earned on existing assets, or at least reduce the possible variability of the spread. ■

When interest rates decrease, a bank's outflow payments would exceed inflow payments on a swap. However, the spread between the interest rates received on existing fixed-rate loans and those paid on deposits should increase, offsetting the net outflow from the swap. During periods of declining interest rates, fixed-rate loans are often prepaid, which could result in a net outflow from the swap without any offsetting effect.

Using Interest Rate Caps An alternative method of hedging interest rate risk is an interest rate cap, an agreement (for a fee) to receive payments when the interest rate of a particular security or index rises above a specified level during a specified time period. Various financial intermediaries (such as commercial banks and brokerage firms) offer interest rate caps. During periods of rising interest rates, the cap provides compensation, which can offset the reduction in the spread during such periods.

International Interest Rate Risk

When a bank has foreign currency balances, the strategy of matching the overall interest rate sensitivity of assets to that of liabilities will not automatically achieve a low degree of interest rate risk.

ILLUSTRATION California Bank has deposits denominated mostly in euros, while its floating-rate loans are denominated mostly in dollars. It matches its average deposit maturity with its average loan maturity. However, the difference in currency denominations creates interest rate risk. The deposit and loan rates are dependent on the interest rate movements of the respective currencies. The performance of California Bank will be adversely affected if the interest rate on the euro increases and the U.S. interest rate decreases. ■

Even though a bank matches the mix of currencies in its assets and its liabilities, it can still be exposed to interest rate risk if the rate sensitivities differ between assets and liabilities for each currency.

ILLUSTRATION Oklahoma Bank uses its dollar deposits to make dollar loans and its euro deposits to make euro loans. It has short-term dollar deposits and uses the funds to make long-term dollar loans. It also has medium- and long-term fixed-rate deposits in euros and uses those funds to make euro loans with adjustable rates. An increase in U.S. rates will reduce the spread on Oklahoma Bank's dollar loans versus deposits, because the dollar liabilities are more rate sensitive than the dollar assets. In addition, a decline in interest rates on the euro will decrease the spread on the euro loans versus deposits, because the euro assets are more rate sensitive than the euro liabilities. Thus, exposure to interest rate risk can be minimized only if the rate sensitivities of assets and liabilities are matched for each currency. ■

Managing Credit Risk

Most of a bank's funds are used either to make loans or to purchase debt securities. For either use of funds, the bank is acting as a creditor and is subject to credit (default) risk, or the possibility that credit provided by the bank will not be repaid. The types of loans provided and the securities purchased will determine the overall credit risk of the asset portfolio. A bank can also be exposed to credit risk if it serves as a guarantor on interest rate swaps and other derivative contracts in which it is the intermediary.

Tradeoff between Credit Risk and Expected Return

If a bank wants to minimize credit risk, it can use most of its funds to purchase Treasury securities, which are virtually free of credit risk. However, these securities may not generate a much higher yield than the average overall cost of obtaining funds. In fact, some bank sources of funds can be more costly to banks than the yield earned on Treasury securities.

At the other extreme, a bank concerned with maximizing its return could use most of its funds for consumer and small business loans. Such an asset portfolio would be subject to a high degree of credit risk, however. If economic conditions deteriorate, a relatively large amount of high-risk loans may default.

Ideally, a bank will manage its assets so as to simultaneously maximize return on assets and minimize credit risk. But, obviously, both objectives cannot be achieved simultaneously. The return on any bank asset depends on the risk involved. Because riskier assets offer higher returns, a bank's strategy to increase its return on assets will typically entail an increase in the overall credit risk of its asset portfolio.

Because a bank cannot simultaneously maximize return and minimize credit risk, it must compromise. That is, it will select some assets that generate high returns but are subject to a relatively high degree of credit risk and also some assets that are very safe but offer a lower rate of return. This way the bank attempts to earn a *reasonable* return on its overall asset portfolio and maintain credit risk at a *tolerable* level. What return level is reasonable? What level of credit risk is tolerable? There is no consensus on the answers. The actual degree of importance attached to a high return versus low credit risk is dependent on the risk-return preferences of a bank's shareholders and managers.

How the Loan Allocation Decision Affects Return and Risk

A bank must develop a plan for allocating funds across different types of loans. The loan composition has a major influence on the bank's expected return and its exposure to credit risk. The top of Exhibit 19.8 compares the returns among types of bank loans, while the bottom of the exhibit compares risk among types of bank loans. Of the loan types in the top of Exhibit 19.8, credit cards offer the highest net interest margin above the bank's cost of funds. Consumer loans provide the next highest interest margin above the bank's cost of funds. Thus, if banks focus on credit card or consumer loans, they will earn a very high rate of return if all of these loans are repaid fully and on time.

In reality, however, credit card and consumer loans experience more defaults than other types of loans. The bottom of Exhibit 19.8 compares loan loss levels (in proportion to loan value) among banks with different specializations. Notice how high the loan loss level is for banks that specialize in credit card loans. Banks that pursue the high potential returns associated with credit card loans must accept a high degree of credit risk.

Despite the risk, many banks have increased their credit card business in recent years. This is a typical example of increasing credit risk in an attempt to increase return. Many banks have also adopted more lenient credit standards in order to generate a greater amount of credit card business. Consequently, more undeserving consumers have obtained credit cards, and the delinquency rate has increased. For those banks that were too lenient, the wide spread between the return on credit card loans and the cost of funds has been offset by a high level of bad debt (default) expenses.

Exhibit 19.8 Return and Risk Tradeoff among Types of Loans

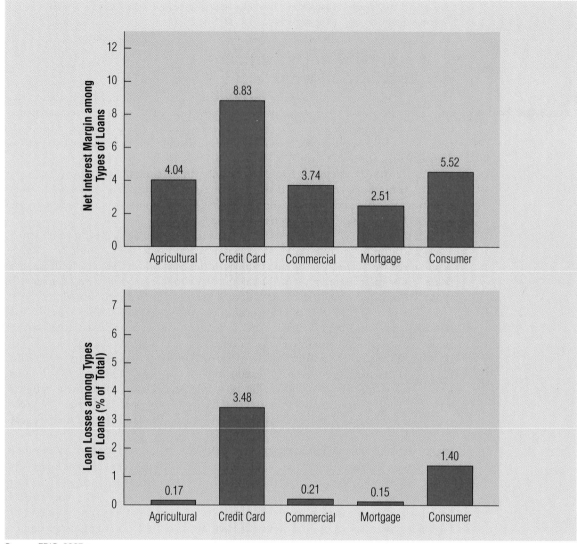

Source: FDIC, 2007.

Changes in Expected Return and Risk Over time, economic conditions change, causing the potential return and risk of assets to change. Banks adjust their asset portfolios accordingly. They tend to provide a larger than normal volume of loans during an economic upswing. Banks generally reduce loans and increase their purchases of low-risk securities when the economy is weak.

Measuring Credit Risk

An important part of managing credit risk is to measure it. This requires a credit assessment of loan applicants. Banks employ credit analysts who review the financial information of corporations applying for loans and evaluate their creditworthiness. The evaluation should indicate the probability that a firm can meet its loan payments so that the bank can decide whether to grant the loan.

Determining the Collateral When a bank assesses a request for credit, it must decide whether to require collateral that can back the loan in the event that the borrower is unable to repay it. For example, a loan extended to a firm that needs machinery may specify that the machinery serve as collateral. When a bank serves as an intermediary and a guarantor on derivative contracts, it commonly attempts to require collateral such as securities owned by the client.

Determining the Loan Rate If the bank decides to grant the loan, it can then use its evaluation of the firm to determine the appropriate interest rate. Loan applicants deserving of a loan may be rated on a basis of 1 to 5 (1 being the highest quality), reflecting their degree of credit risk. The rating dictates the premium to be added to the base rate. For example, a rating of 5 may dictate a 2 percentage point premium above the prime rate (the rate a bank offers to its most creditworthy customers), while a rating of 3 may dictate a 1 percentage point premium. Given the current prime rate along with a rating of the potential borrower, the loan rate can be determined.

Some loans to high-quality (low-risk) customers are commonly offered at rates below the prime rate. This does not necessarily mean that banks have reduced their spread. It may instead imply that the banks have redefined the prime rate to represent the appropriate loan rate for borrowers with a moderate risk rating. Thus, a discount would be attached to the prime rate when determining the loan rate for borrowers with a superior rating.

Reducing Credit Risk

Although all consumer and commercial loans exhibit some credit risk, banks can use several methods to manage this risk. Banks should diversify their loans to ensure that their customers are not dependent on a common source of income. For example, a bank in a small farming town that provides consumer loans to farmers and commercial loans to farm equipment manufacturers is highly susceptible to credit risk. If the farmers experience a bad growing season because of poor weather conditions, they may be unable to repay their consumer loans. Furthermore, the farm equipment manufacturers would simultaneously experience a drop in sales and may be unable to repay their commercial loans.

Industry Diversification of Loans When a bank's loans are too heavily concentrated in a specific industry, it should attempt to expand its loans into other industries. In this way, if one particular industry experiences weakness (which will lead to loan defaults by firms in that industry), loans provided to other industries will be insulated from that industry's conditions. However, a bank's loan portfolio may still be subject to high credit risk even though its loans are diversified across industries.

For example, consider a bank in a city that provides most of its commercial loans to firms in that city and has diversified its loans across various industries to avoid the problem just described. Assume that this city is the home of a large naval base. If, for some reason, the naval personnel employed at that base are sent out to sea, the city's firms may not be able to generate sufficient business to repay their loans. This example illustrates how corporate borrowers from different industries but from the same geographic region can be similarly affected by a particular event.

International Diversification of Loans Many banks reduce their exposure to U.S. economic conditions by diversifying their loan portfolio internationally. They use a country risk assessment system to assess country characteristics that may influence the ability of a government or corporation to repay its debt. In particular, the country risk assessment focuses on a country's financial and political conditions. Banks tend to focus on countries to which they have assigned a high country risk rating. Once a bank establishes a branch in a foreign country, however, it is committed to international loans in that country. After extending loans, a bank cannot recall them just because country conditions have deteriorated.

Diversifying loans across countries can often reduce the loan portfolio's exposure to any single economy or event. If diversification across geographic regions means that the bank must accept loan applicants with very high risk, however, the bank is defeating its purpose.

Selling Loans Banks can eliminate loans that are causing excessive risk to their loan portfolios by selling them in the secondary market. Most loan sales enable the bank originating the loan to continue servicing the loan by collecting payments and monitoring the borrower's collateral. However, the bank that originated the loan is no longer funding the loan, and the loan is therefore removed from the bank's assets. Bank loans are commonly purchased by other banks and some other financial institutions, such as pension funds and insurance companies, and some mutual funds.

Revising the Loan Portfolio in Response to Economic Conditions Banks continuously assess both the overall composition of their loan portfolios and the economic environment. As economic conditions change, so does the risk of a bank's loan portfolio. A bank is typically more willing to extend loans during strong economic conditions, since businesses are more likely to meet their loan payments under those conditions. During weak economic conditions, the bank is more cautious and reduces the amount of new loans that are extended to businesses. Under these conditions, the bank typically increases the credit it extends to the Treasury by purchasing more Treasury securities. Nevertheless, its loan portfolio may still be heavily exposed to economic conditions because some of the businesses that have already borrowed may be unable to repay their loans.

Managing Market Risk

http://www.fdic.gov
Analytical assessment of the banking industry, including the recent performance of banks.

From a bank management perspective, market risk results from changes in the value of securities due to changes in financial market conditions such as interest rate movements, exchange rate movements, and equity prices. As banks pursue new services related to the trading of securities, they have become much more susceptible to market risk. For example, some banks now provide loans to special partnerships called hedge funds, which use the borrowed funds to invest in stocks or derivative securities. Thus, these loans may not be repaid if the prices of the stocks or derivative securities held by the hedge funds decline substantially.

The increase in banks' exposure to market risk is also attributed to their increased participation in the trading of derivative contracts. Many banks now serve as intermediaries between firms that take positions in derivative securities and will be exchanging payments in the future. For some of these transactions, a bank serves as a guarantor to one of the parties if the counterparty in the transaction does not fulfill its payment obligation. If derivative security prices change abruptly and cause several parties involved in these transactions to default, a bank that served as a guarantor will suffer major losses. Furthermore, banks that purchase debt securities issued in developing countries are subject to abrupt losses as a result of abrupt swings in the economic or currency conditions in those countries.

The need to monitor the positions of banks with substantial trading businesses was reinforced by the shocking $488 million loss reported by Bankers Trust (now part of Deutsche Bank) in October 1998. The loss was attributed to markdowns on

Russian and Latin American debt securities held by Bankers Trust, adverse currency movements, and a reduction in its securities underwriting business. If Bankers Trust had been using a system that monitored the market values of its positions on a daily basis, it might have been able to reduce its losses.

Measuring Market Risk

Banks commonly measure their exposure to market risk by applying the value-at-risk (VAR) method, which involves determining the largest possible loss that would occur as a result of changes in market prices based on a specified percent confidence level. To estimate this loss, the bank first determines an adverse scenario (such as a 9 percent decline in stock prices or a 30 percent decline in derivative security prices) for market prices that has a 1 percent chance of occurring. Then it estimates the impact of that scenario on its positions, based on the sensitivity of the values of its positions to the scenario. All of the losses that would occur from existing positions are summed to determine the estimated total loss to the bank under this scenario. This estimate reflects the largest possible loss at the 99 percent confidence level, as there is only a 1-in-100 chance that such an unfavorable scenario would occur. By determining its exposure to market risk, the bank can ensure that it has sufficient capital to cushion against the adverse effects of such an event.

Bank Revisions of Market Risk Measurements
Banks continually revise their estimate of market risk in response to changes in their investment and credit positions and to changes in market conditions. When market prices become more volatile, banks recognize that market prices could change to a greater degree and typically increase their estimate of their potential losses due to market conditions. For example, in the fall of 1998, market conditions across countries were unusually volatile due to the Russian debt default. There was more uncertainty about exchange rates, interest rates, and equity prices. Many banks recognized that their market risk had increased (even if their existing investment and credit positions had not changed), and reestimated their potential loss due to market risk by adjusting the potential magnitude of foreign exchange, interest rate, and equity price movements.

How J.P. Morgan Assesses Market Risk
Banks commonly disclose their estimate of market risk and their method of measuring it in their annual report. For example, J.P. Morgan & Co. (part of J.P. Morgan Chase, one of the largest U.S. banks) uses a 95 percent confidence level to determine the maximum expected one-day loss in its investments and credit instruments due to changes in interest rates, foreign exchange rates, equity prices, and commodity prices. If its measure of market risk is $35 million, under normal market conditions (95 percent of the time), market price movements should result in a one-day loss on its positions of no more than $35 million.

Diversification effects are considered because any potential adverse effects would not be expected to occur simultaneously for all types of market prices. For example, some of J.P. Morgan's investment positions might be adversely affected by adverse interest rate movements, but some of its other positions would not be adversely affected by foreign exchange prices as long as no unusual movement in foreign exchange prices occurred at the same time as the unusual interest rate movement.

Relationship between a Bank's Market Risk and Interest Rate Risk
A bank's market risk is partially dependent on its exposure to interest rate risk. Banks give special attention to interest rate risk, however, because it is commonly the most important component of market risk. Moreover, many banks assess

interest rate risk by itself when evaluating their positions over a longer time horizon. For example, a bank might assess interest rate risk by itself over the next year using the methods described earlier in the chapter. In this case, the bank might use the assessment to alter the maturities on the deposits it attempts to obtain or on its uses of funds. Conversely, banks' assessment of market risk tends to be focused on a shorter-term horizon, such as the next month. Nevertheless, they may still use their assessment of market risk to alter their operations, as explained next.

Methods Used to Reduce Market Risk

If a bank determines that its exposure to market risk is excessive, it can reduce its involvement in the activities that cause the high exposure. For example, it could reduce the amount of transactions in which it serves as guarantor for its clients or reduce its investment in foreign debt securities that are subject to adverse events in a specific region. Alternatively, it could attempt to take some trading positions to offset some of its exposure to market risk. It could also sell some of its securities that are heavily exposed to market risk.

Operating Risk

Operating risk is the risk resulting from a bank's general business operations. Banks are subject to risk related to information (sorting, processing, transmitting through technology), execution of transactions, damaged relationships with clients, legal issues (lawsuits by employees and customers), and regulatory issues (increased costs due to new compliance requirements or penalties due to lack of compliance). Although these forms of risk are not closely related to the financial forms of risk discussed so far, they should at least be recognized since they can affect a bank's value.

Managing Risk of International Operations

Banks that are engaged in international banking face additional types of risk.

Exchange Rate Risk

http://
http://www.risknews.net
Links to risk-related information in international banking.

When a bank providing a loan requires that the borrower repay in the currency denominating the loan, it may be able to avoid exchange rate risk. However, some international loans contain a clause that allows repayment in a foreign currency, thus allowing the borrower to avoid exchange rate risk.

In many cases, banks convert available funds (from recent deposits) to whatever currency corporations want to borrow. Thus, they create an asset denominated in that currency, while the liability (deposits) is denominated in a different currency. If the liability currency appreciates against the asset currency, the bank's profit margin is reduced.

All large banks are exposed to exchange rate risk to some degree. They can attempt to hedge this risk in various ways.

ILLUSTRATION Cameron Bank, a U.S. bank, converts dollar deposits into a British pound (£) loan for a British corporation, which will pay £50,000 in interest per year. Cameron Bank may attempt to engage in forward contracts to sell £50,000 forward for each date when it will receive those interest payments. That is, it will search for corporations that wish to purchase £50,000 on the dates of concern. ■

In reality, a large bank will not hedge every individual transaction, but will instead net out the exposure and be concerned only with net exposure. Large banks enter into several international transactions on any given day. Some reflect future cash inflows in a particular currency, while others reflect cash outflows in that currency. The bank's exposure to exchange rate risk is determined by the net cash flow in each currency.

Settlement Risk

International banks that engage in large currency transactions are exposed not only to exchange rate risk as a result of their different currency positions, but also to settlement risk, or the risk of a loss due to settling their transactions. For example, a bank may send its currency to another bank as part of a transaction agreement, but it may not receive any currency from the other bank if that bank defaults before sending its payment.

The failure of a single large bank could create more losses if other banks were relying on receivables from the failed bank to make future payables of their own. Consequently, there is concern about systemic risk, or the risk that many participants will be unable to meet their obligations because they did not receive payments on obligations due to them.

Bank Capital Management

Like other corporations, banks must determine the level of capital that they should maintain. Bank operations are distinctly different from other types of firms because the majority of their assets (such as loans and security holdings) generate more predictable cash flows. Thus, banks can use a much higher degree of financial leverage than other types of firms. The FDIC, which insures depositors, bears most of the risk in the event of failure. Depositors who are fully insured normally do not penalize banks for taking excessive risk, which could encourage some banks to use a high degree of financial leverage.

Banks must also consider the minimum capital ratio required by regulators. This minimum could possibly force a bank to maintain more capital than it believes is optimal. To please shareholders, banks typically attempt to maintain only the amount of capital that is sufficient to support bank operations. If a bank has too much capital as a result of issuing excessive amounts of stock, each shareholder will receive a smaller proportion of any distributed earnings.

A common measure of the return to the shareholders is the **return on equity (ROE),** measured as

$$ROE = \frac{\text{Net profit after taxes}}{\text{Equity}}$$

The term *equity* represents the bank's capital. The return on equity can be broken down as follows:

$$ROE = \text{Return on assets (ROA)} \times \text{Leverage measure}$$

$$\frac{\text{Net profit after taxes}}{\text{Equity}} = \frac{\text{Net profit after taxes}}{\text{Assets}} \times \frac{\text{Assets}}{\text{Equity}}$$

The ratio (assets/equity) is sometimes called the **leverage measure,** because leverage reflects the volume of assets a firm supports with equity. The greater the leverage measure, the greater the amount of assets per dollar's worth of equity. The above breakdown of ROE is useful because it can demonstrate how excessive capital can lower a bank's ROE.

Consider two banks called Hilev and Lolev, each of which has a return on assets (ROA) of 1 percent. Hilev Bank has a leverage measure of 15, while Lolev Bank has a leverage measure of 10. The ROE for each bank is determined as follows:

$$\text{ROE} = \text{ROA} \times \text{Leverage measure}$$
$$\text{ROE for Hilev Bank} = 1\% \times 15$$
$$= 15\%$$
$$\text{ROE for Lolev Bank} = 1\% \times 10$$
$$= 10\%$$

Even though each bank's assets are generating a 1 percent ROA, the ROE of Hilev Bank is much higher, because Hilev Bank is supporting its assets with a smaller proportion of capital. ■

Bank regulators require banks to hold a minimum amount of capital, because capital can be used to absorb losses. Banks, however, generally prefer to hold a relatively low amount of capital for the reasons just expressed.

Because required capital is specified as a proportion of loans (and some other assets), banks can reduce the required level of capital by selling some of their loans in the secondary market. They can still service the loans to generate fee income but would be subject to a lower capital constraint as a result of removing loans from their asset portfolio.

If banks are holding an excessive amount of capital, they can reduce it by distributing a high percentage of their earnings to shareholders (as dividends). Thus, capital management is related to the bank's dividend policy.

A growing bank may need more capital to support construction of new buildings, Internet services, office equipment, and other expenses. It will therefore need to retain a larger proportion of its earnings than a bank that has no plans for future growth. If the growing bank prefers to provide existing shareholders with a sizable dividend, it will then have to obtain the necessary capital by issuing new stock. This strategy allows the bank to distribute dividends but dilutes the proportional ownership of the bank. An obvious tradeoff exists here. The solution is not so obvious. A bank in need of capital must assess the tradeoff involved and follow a policy that it believes will maximize the wealth of shareholders.

Management Based on Forecasts

Some banks position themselves to significantly benefit from an expected change in the economy. Exhibit 19.9 provides possible policy decisions for four different forecasts and suggests how a bank might react to each. This exhibit is simplified in that it does not consider future economic growth and interest rate movements simultaneously. Furthermore, it does not consider other economic forecasts that banks would also consider. Nevertheless, it illustrates the type of risk-return tradeoff constantly faced by bank managers. For example, if managers expect a strong economy, they can boost earnings by shifting into relatively risky loans and securities that pay a high return. If the economy is strong as expected, only a small percentage of the loans and securities will default, and the bank's strategy will result in improved earnings. However, if the bank's forecast turns out to be wrong, its revised asset portfolio will be

Exhibit 19.9 Bank Management of Liabilities and Assets Based on Economic Forecasts

Economic Forecast by the Bank	Appropriate Adjustment to Liability Structure Based on the Forecast	Appropriate Adjustment to Asset Structure Based on the Forecast	General Assessment of Bank's Adjusted Balance Sheet Structure
1. Strong economy		Concentrate more heavily on loans; reduce holdings of low-risk securities.	Increased potential for stronger earnings; increased exposure of bank earnings to credit risk.
2. Weak economy		Concentrate more heavily on risk-free securities and low-risk loans; reduce holdings of risky loans.	Reduced credit risk; reduced potential for stronger earnings if the economy does not weaken.
3. Increasing interest rates	Attempt to attract CDs with long-term maturities.	Apply floating interest rates to loans whenever possible; avoid long-term securities.	Reduced interest rate risk; reduced potential for stronger earnings if interest rates decrease.
4. Decreasing interest rates	Attempt to attract CDs with short-term maturities.	Apply fixed interest rates to loans whenever possible; concentrate on long-term securities or loans.	Increased potential for stronger earnings; increased interest rate risk.

more susceptible to a weak economy. The bank could be severely damaged during a weak economy, because several borrowers are likely to default on their loans and securities.

An inaccurate forecast of the economy will have less effect on more conservative banks that maintain a sizable portion of very safe loans and securities. If the economy strengthens as predicted, however, these banks also will not benefit as much as the bank that assumed more risk. The degree to which a bank is willing to revise its balance sheet structure in accordance with economic forecasts depends on its confidence in those forecasts and its willingness to incur risk.

Because the first two forecasts shown in Exhibit 19.9 are on economic growth, they relate to credit risk. The last two forecasts are on interest rates and therefore relate to interest rate risk. Banks cannot completely adjust their balance sheet structure in accordance with economic forecasts. For example, they cannot implement a policy of accepting only long-term CDs just because they believe interest rates will rise. Nevertheless, they could attract a greater than normal amount of long-term CDs by offering an attractive interest rate on long-term CDs and advertising this rate to potential depositors.

The bank's balance sheet management will affect its performance (as measured from its income statement) in the following ways. First, its liability structure will influence its interest and noninterest expenses on the income statement. If it obtains a relatively large portion of its funds from conventional demand deposits, interest expenses should be relatively low, while its noninterest expenses (due to check clearing, processing, etc.) should be relatively high. A bank's asset structure can also affect expenses. If a bank maintains a relatively large portion of commercial loans, its noninterest expenses should be high because of the labor cost of assessing the borrower's credit along with loan-processing costs. Nevertheless, banks with the heaviest concentration in commercial loans expect their additional interest revenues to more than offset the additional noninterest expenses incurred. Their strategy will pay off only if they can avoid a sizable number of defaulted loans. Of course, this is the risk they must take in striving for a high return.

Ideally, banks would use an aggressive approach when they can capitalize on favorable economic conditions but insulate themselves during adverse economic conditions. Because economic conditions cannot always be accurately forecasted for several years in advance, even well-managed banks will experience defaults on loans. This is a cost of doing business. Banks attempt to use proper diversification so that a domino effect of defaulted loans will not occur within their loan portfolio. Similarly, interest rate movements cannot always be accurately forecasted. Thus, banks should not be overly aggressive in attempting to capitalize on interest rate forecasts. They should assess the sensitivity of their future performance to each possible interest rate scenario that could occur to ensure that their balance sheet is structured to survive any possible scenario.

http://

http://www.fdic.gov
Statistical overview of how
banks have performed in
recent years.

Bank Restructuring

Bank operations change in response to changing regulations and economic conditions and to managerial policies designed to hedge various forms of risk. For example, in recent years banks have expanded across state lines, diversified their asset portfolios, boosted their capital ratios, and expanded their operations into services such as insurance, brokerage, underwriting of securities, and sales of mutual funds. Large changes in bank operations typically require restructuring, which normally must be assessed and approved by the bank's executives and board of directors.

Decisions to restructure are complex because of their effects on customers, shareholders, and employees. A strategic plan to satisfy customers and shareholders will not necessarily satisfy the majority of employees. During the early 1990s, many banks downsized their operations because their business had declined in response to poor economic conditions. Downsizing forced consolidation of some divisions and layoffs as well. Although downsizing may be unavoidable in some periods, the plan for restructuring should consider the potential effects on employee morale.

Bank Acquisitions

A common form of bank restructuring is growth through acquisitions of other banks. Growth can be achieved more quickly with acquisitions than by establishing new branches.

Bank acquisitions offer several potential advantages. First, some banks may be able to achieve economies of scale by acquiring other banks. If the costs of some operations are mostly fixed, an increase in the size of those operations should create efficiencies because the costs in proportion to total assets decline. A related advantage is that bank acquisitions can remove redundant operations. For example, if branches of the acquiring bank are next to branches of the target bank, some of these branches can be closed without a loss of convenience to customers.

Bank acquisitions can also achieve diversification benefits as the acquirer can offer loans in some new industries. Furthermore, an acquiring bank may have some managerial advantages over a target, which should allow the acquirer to improve the target's performance after the acquisition.

Along with the potential advantages, some potential disadvantages are associated with bank acquisitions. First, some acquisitions are motivated by highly optimistic projections of the cost efficiencies that will result from combining the operations of the target and acquirer. Thus, an acquirer may pay an excessive price for the target bank. Second, the reorganization of operations after an acquisition can lead to significant employee morale problems and high employee turnover.

Are Bank Acquisitions Worthwhile? Numerous studies have assessed the stock price reaction of banks that acquire other banks. If investors believe that the acquiring bank will benefit from the acquisition, the stock price should rise in response to the acquisition announcement. Most of the studies have found that the acquiring bank's stock price either does not change or reacts negatively. These results suggest that the market does not expect the acquisition to be favorable. One possible explanation is that the acquiring bank will never achieve the expected efficiencies that motivated the acquisition. Second, personnel clashes among the units to be merged could result in high turnover and low morale. Third, the acquiring bank may simply be paying too much for the target bank.

Integrated Bank Management

Bank management of assets, liabilities, and capital is integrated. A bank's asset growth can be achieved only if it obtains the necessary funds. Furthermore, growth may require an investment in fixed assets (such as additional offices) that will require an accumulation of bank capital. Integration of asset, liability, and capital management ensures that all policies will be consistent with a cohesive set of economic forecasts. An integrated management approach is necessary to manage liquidity risk, interest rate risk, and credit risk.

Example

Assume that you are hired as a consultant by Atlanta Bank to evaluate its favorable and unfavorable aspects. Atlanta Bank's balance sheet is shown in Exhibit 19.10. A bank's balance sheet can best be evaluated by converting the actual dollar amounts of balance sheet components to a percentage of assets. This conversion enables the bank to be compared with its competitors. Exhibit 19.11 shows each balance sheet component as a percentage of total assets for Atlanta Bank (derived from Exhibit 19.10). To the right of each bank percentage is the assumed industry average percentage for a sample of banks with a similar amount of assets. For example, the bank's required reserves are 4 percent of assets (the same as the industry average), its floating-rate commercial loans are 30 percent of assets (versus an industry average of 20 percent), and so on. The same type of comparison is provided for liabilities and capital on the right side of the exhibit. A comparative analysis relative to the industry can indicate the management style of Atlanta Bank.

It is possible to evaluate the potential level of interest revenues, interest expenses, noninterest revenues, and noninterest expenses for Atlanta Bank relative to the industry. Furthermore, it is possible to assess the bank's exposure to credit risk and interest rate risk as compared to the industry.

A summary of Atlanta Bank based on the information in Exhibit 19.11 is provided in Exhibit 19.12. Although its interest expenses are expected to be above the industry average, so are its interest revenues. Thus, it is difficult to determine whether Atlanta Bank's net interest margin will be above or below the industry average. Because it is more heavily concentrated in risky loans and securities, its credit risk is higher than that of the average bank; yet, its interest rate risk is less because of its relatively high concentration of medium-term CDs and floating-rate loans. A gap measurement of Atlanta Bank can be conducted by first identifying the rate-sensitive liabilities and assets, as follows:

Rate-Sensitive Assets	Amount (in Millions)	Rate-Sensitive Liabilities	Amount (in Millions)
Floating-rate loans	$3,000	NOW accounts	$1,200
Floating-rate mortgages	500	MMDAs	2,000
Short-term Treasury securities	1,000	Short-term CDs	1,500
	$4,500		$4,700

Exhibit 19.10
Balance Sheet of
Atlanta Bank (in Millions
of Dollars)

Assets			Liabilities and Capital		
Required reserves		$ 400	Demand deposits		$ 500
Commercial loans			NOW accounts		1,200
Floating-rate	3,000		MMDAs		2,000
Fixed-rate	1,100		CDs		
Total		4,100	Short-term	1,500	
Consumer loans		2,500	From 1 to 5 yrs.	3,800	
Mortgages			Total		5,300
Floating-rate	500		Long-term bonds		200
Fixed-rate	None		CAPITAL		800
Total		500			
Treasury securities					
Short-term	1,000				
Long-term	None				
Total		1,000			
Corporate securities					
High-rated	None				
Moderate-rated	1,000				
Total		1,000			
Municipal securities					
High-rated	None				
Moderate-rated	None				
Total		None			
Fixed assets		500			
TOTAL ASSETS		$10,000	TOTAL LIABILITIES AND CAPITAL		$10,000

$$\text{Gap} = \$4{,}500 \text{ million} - \$4{,}700 \text{ million}$$
$$= -\$200 \text{ million}$$

$$\text{Gap ratio} = \frac{\$4{,}500 \text{ million}}{\$4{,}700 \text{ million}}$$
$$= .957$$

The gap measurements suggest somewhat similar rate sensitivity on both sides of the balance sheet.

The future performance of Atlanta Bank relative to the industry depends on future economic conditions. If interest rates rise, it will be more insulated than other banks. If interest rates fall, other banks will likely benefit to a greater degree. Under conditions of a strong economy, Atlanta Bank would likely benefit more than other banks because of its aggressive lending approach. Conversely, an economic slowdown could cause more loan defaults, and Atlanta Bank would be more susceptible to

Exhibit 19.11 Comparative Balance Sheet of Atlanta Bank

Assets			Liabilities and Capital		
	Percentage of Assets for Atlanta Bank	Average Percentage for Industry		Percentage of Total for Atlanta Bank	Average Percentage for Industry
Required reserves	4%	4%	Demand deposits	5%	17%
Commercial loans			NOW accounts	12	8
Floating-rate	30	20	MMDAs	20	20
Fixed-rate	11	11	CD		
Total	41	31	Short-term	15	35
Consumer loans	25	20	From 1 to 5 yrs.	38	10
Mortgages			Long-term bonds	2	2
Floating-rate	5	7	CAPITAL	8	8
Fixed-rate	0	3			
Total	5	10			
Treasury securities					
Short-term	10	7			
Long-term	0	8			
Total	10	15			
Corporate securities					
High-rated	0	5			
Moderate-rated	10	5			
Total	10	10			
Municipal securities					
High-rated	0	3			
Moderate-rated	0	2			
Total	0	5			
Fixed assets	5	5			
TOTAL ASSETS	100%	100%	TOTAL LIABILITIES AND CAPITAL	100%	100%

Exhibit 19.12 Evaluation of Atlanta Bank Based on Its Balance Sheet

	Main Influential Components	Evaluation of Atlanta Bank Relative to Industry
Interest expenses	All liabilities except demand deposits.	Higher than industry average because it concentrates more on high-rate deposits than the norm.
Noninterest expenses	Loan volume and checkable deposit volume.	Possibly higher than the norm; its checkable deposit volume is less than the norm, but its loan volume is greater than the norm.
Interest revenues	Volume and composition of loans and securities.	Potentially higher than industry average because its assets are generally riskier than the norm.
Exposure to credit risk	Volume and composition of loans and securities.	Higher concentration of loans than industry average; it has a greater percentage of risky assets than the norm.
Exposure to interest rate risk	Maturities on liabilities and assets; use of floating-rate loans.	Lower than the industry average; it has more medium-term liabilities, fewer assets with very long maturities, and more floating-rate loans.

Exhibit 19.13
Participation of
Commercial Banks
in Financial Markets

Financial Market	Participation by Commercial Banks
Money markets	As banks offer deposits, they must compete with other financial institutions in the money market along with the Treasury to obtain short-term funds. They serve households that wish to invest funds for short-term periods.
Mortgage markets	Some banks offer mortgage loans on homes and commercial property and therefore provide financing in the mortgage market.
Bond markets	Commercial banks purchase bonds issued by corporations, the Treasury, and municipalities.
Futures markets	Commercial banks take positions in futures to hedge interest rate risk.
Options markets	Commercial banks take positions in options on futures to hedge interest rate risk.
Swaps markets	Commercial banks engage in interest rate swaps to hedge interest rate risk.

possible defaults than other banks. This could be confirmed only if more details were provided (such as a more comprehensive breakdown of the balance sheet).

Participation in Financial Markets

In order to manage their operations, commercial banks rely heavily on financial markets, as explained in Exhibit 19.13. They rely on the money markets to obtain funds, the mortgage and bond markets to use some of their funds, and the futures, options, and swaps markets to hedge their risk.

Summary

■ The underlying goal of bank management is to maximize the wealth of the bank's shareholders, which implies maximizing the price of the bank's stock (if the bank is publicly traded).

■ Banks manage liquidity by maintaining some liquid assets such as short-term securities and ensuring easy access to funds (through the federal funds market).

■ Banks measure their sensitivity to interest rate movements so that they can assess their exposure to interest rate risk. Common methods of measuring interest rate risk include gap analysis and duration analysis. Some banks use regression analysis to determine the sensitivity of their earnings or stock returns to interest rate movements.

Banks can reduce their interest rate risk by matching maturities of their assets and liabilities or by using floating-rate loans to create more rate sensitivity in their assets. Alternatively, they may use

interest rate futures contracts or interest rate swaps instead. If they are adversely affected by rising interest rates, they could sell financial futures contracts or engage in a swap of fixed-rate payments for floating-rate payments.

■ Banks manage credit risk by carefully assessing the borrowers who apply for loans. They also diversify their loans across borrowers of different regions and industries so that the loan portfolio is not heavily susceptible to financial problems in any single region or industry.

■ Banks attempt to maintain sufficient capital to satisfy regulatory constraints. However, they generally prefer to avoid holding excessive capital because a high level of capital can reduce their return on equity. If banks need to raise capital, they can attempt to retain more earnings (reduce dividends) or issue new stock.

Point Counter-Point

Can Bank Failures Be Avoided?

Point No. Banks are in the business of providing credit. When economic conditions deteriorate, there will be loan defaults and some banks will not be able to survive.

Counter-Point Yes. If banks focus on providing loans to creditworthy borrowers, most loans will not default even during recessionary periods.

Who Is Correct? Use the Internet to learn more about this issue. Offer your own opinion on this issue.

Questions and Applications

1. **Integrating Asset and Liability Management** What is accomplished when a bank integrates its liability management with its asset management?

2. **Liquidity** Given the liquidity advantage of holding Treasury bills, why do banks hold only a relatively small portion of their assets as T-bills?

3. **Illiquidity** How do banks resolve illiquidity problems?

4. **Managing Interest Rate Risk** If a bank expects interest rates to decrease over time, how might it alter the rate sensitivity of its assets and liabilities?

5. **Rate Sensitivity** List some rate-sensitive assets and some rate-insensitive assets of banks.

6. **Managing Interest Rate Risk** If a bank is very uncertain about future interest rates, how might it insulate its future performance from future interest rate movements?

7. **Net Interest Margin** What is the formula for the net interest margin? Explain why it is closely monitored by banks.

8. **Managing Interest Rate Risk** Assume that a bank expects to attract most of its funds through short-term CDs and would prefer to use most of its funds to provide long-term loans. How could it follow this strategy and still reduce interest rate risk?

9. **Bank Exposure to Interest Rate Movements** According to this chapter, have banks been able to insulate themselves against interest rate movements? Explain.

10. **Gap Management** What is a bank's gap, and what does it attempt to determine? Interpret a negative gap. What are some limitations of measuring a bank's gap?

11. **Duration** How do banks use duration analysis?

12. **Measuring Interest Rate Risk** Why do loans that can be prepaid on a moment's notice complicate the bank's assessment of interest rate risk?

13. **Bank Management Dilemma** Can a bank simultaneously maximize return and minimize default risk? If not, what can it do instead?

14. **Bank Exposure to Economic Conditions** As economic conditions change, how do banks adjust their asset portfolio?

15. **Bank Loan Diversification** In what two ways should a bank diversify its loans? Why? Is international diversification of loans a viable solution to credit risk? Defend your answer.

16. **Commercial Borrowing** Do all commercial borrowers receive the same interest rate on loans?

17. **Bank Dividend Policy** Why might a bank retain some excess earnings rather than distribute them as dividends?

18. **Managing Interest Rate Risk** If a bank has more rate-sensitive liabilities than rate-sensitive assets, what will happen to its net interest margin during a period of rising interest rates? During a period of declining interest rates?

19. **Floating-Rate Loans** Does the use of floating-rate loans eliminate interest rate risk? Explain.

20. **Managing Exchange Rate Risk** Explain how banks become exposed to exchange rate risk.

Advanced Questions

21. **Bank Exposure to Interest Rate Risk** Oregon Bank has branches overseas that concentrate on short-term deposits in dollars and floating-rate loans in British pounds. Because it maintains rate-sensitive assets and liabilities of equal amounts, it believes it has essentially eliminated its interest rate risk. Do you agree? Explain.

22. **Managing Interest Rate Risk** Dakota Bank has a branch overseas with the following balance sheet characteristics: 50 percent of the liabilities are rate sensitive and denominated in Swiss francs; the remaining 50 percent of liabilities are rate insensitive and are denominated in dollars. With regard to assets, 50 percent are rate sensitive and are denominated in dollars; the remaining 50 percent of assets are rate insensitive and are denominated in Swiss francs.

    a. Is the performance of this branch susceptible to interest rate movements? Explain.

    b. Assume that Dakota Bank plans to replace its short-term deposits denominated in U.S. dollars with short-term deposits denominated in Swiss francs, because Swiss interest rates are currently lower than U.S. interest rates. The asset composition would not change. This strategy is intended to widen the spread between the rate earned on assets and the rate paid on liabilities. Offer your insight on how this strategy could backfire.

    c. One consultant has suggested to Dakota Bank that it could avoid exchange rate risk by making loans in whatever currencies it receives as deposits. In this way, it will not have to exchange one currency for another. Offer your insight on whether there are any disadvantages to this strategy.

Interpreting Financial News

Interpret the following comments made by Wall Street analysts and portfolio managers:

a. "The bank's biggest mistake was that it did not recognize that its forecasts of a strong local real estate market and declining interest rates could be wrong."

b. "Banks still need some degree of interest rate risk to be profitable."

c. "The bank used interest rate swaps so that its spread is no longer exposed to interest rate movements. However, its loan volume and therefore its profits are still exposed to interest rate movements."

Managing in Financial Markets

Hedging with Interest Rate Swaps As a manager of Stetson Bank, you are responsible for hedging Stetson's interest rate risk. Stetson has forecasted its cost of funds as follows:

Year	Cost of Funds
1	6%
2	5%
3	7%
4	9%
5	7%

It expects to earn an average rate of 11 percent on some assets that charge a fixed interest rate over the next five years. It considers engaging in an interest rate swap in which it would swap fixed payments of 10 percent in exchange for variable-rate payments of LIBOR plus 1 percent. Assume LIBOR is expected to be consistently 1 percent above Stetson's cost of funds.

a. Determine the spread that would be earned each year if Stetson uses an interest rate swap to hedge all of its interest rate risk. Would you recommend that Stetson use an interest rate swap?

b. Although Stetson has forecasted its cost of funds, it recognizes that its forecasts may be inaccurate. Offer a method that Stetson can use to assess the potential results from using an interest rate swap while accounting for the uncertainty surrounding future interest rates.

c. The reason for Stetson's interest rate risk is that it uses some of its funds to make fixed-rate loans, as some borrowers prefer fixed rates. An alternative method of hedging interest rate risk is to use adjustable-rate loans. Would you recommend that Stetson use only adjustable-rate loans to hedge its interest rate risk? Explain.

Problems

1. **Net Interest Margin** Suppose a bank earns $201 million in interest revenue but pays $156 million in interest expense. It also has $800 million in earning assets. What is its net interest margin?

2. **Calculating Return on Assets** If a bank earns $169 million net profit after tax and has $17 billion invested in assets, what is its return on assets?

3. **Calculating Return on Equity** If a bank earns $75 million net profits after tax and has $7.5 billion invested in assets and $600 million equity investment, what is its return on equity?

4. **Managing Risk** Use the balance sheet for San Diego Bank in Exhibit A and the industry norms in Exhibit B to answer the following questions:

   a. Estimate the gap and the gap ratio and determine how San Diego Bank would be affected by an increase in interest rates over time.

Exhibit A Balance Sheet for San Diego Bank (in Millions of Dollars)

Assets			Liabilities and Capital		
Required reserves		$ 800	Demand deposits		$ 800
Commercial loans			NOW accounts		2,500
Floating-rate	None		MMDAs		6,000
Fixed-rate	7,000		CDs		
Total		7,000	Short-term	9,000	
Consumer loans		5,000	From 1 to 5 yrs.	None	
Mortgages			Total		9,000
Floating-rate	None		Federal funds		500
Fixed-rate	2,000		Long-term bonds		400
Total		2,000	CAPITAL		800
Treasury securities					
Short-term	None				
Long-term	1,000				
Total		1,000			
Long-term corporate securities					
High-rated	None				
Moderate-rated	2,000				
Total		2,000			
Long-term municipal securities					
High-rated	None				
Moderate-rated	1,700				
Total		1,700			
Fixed assets		500			
TOTAL ASSETS		$20,000	TOTAL LIABILITIES and CAPITAL		$20,000

Exhibit B Industry Norms in Percentage Terms

Assets		Liabilities and Capital	
Required reserves	4%	Demand deposits	17%
Commercial loans		NOW accounts	10
Floating-rate	20	MMDAs	20
Fixed-rate	11	CDs	
Total	31	Short-term	35
Consumer loans	20	From 1 to 5 yrs.	10
Mortgages		Total	45
Floating-rate	7	Long-term bonds	2
Fixed-rate	3	CAPITAL	6
Total	10		
Treasury securities			
Short-term	7		
Long-term	8		
Total	15		
Long-term corporate securities			
High-rated	5		
Moderate-rated	5		
Total	10		
Long-term municipal securities			
High-rated	3		
Moderate-rated	2		
Total	5		
Fixed assets	5		—
TOTAL ASSETS	100%	TOTAL LIABILITIES and CAPITAL	100%

b. Assess San Diego's credit risk. Does it appear high or low relative to the industry? Would San Diego Bank perform better or worse than other banks during a recession?

c. For any type of bank risk that appears to be higher than the industry, explain how the balance sheet could be restructured to reduce the risk.

5. **Measuring Risk** Montana Bank wants to determine the sensitivity of its stock returns to interest rate movements, based on the following information:

Quarter	Return on Montana Stock	Return on Market	Interest Rate
1	2%	3%	6.0%
2	2	2	7.5
3	−1	−2	9.0
4	0	−1	8.2
5	2	1	7.3
6	−3	−4	8.1

Quarter	Return on Montana Stock	Return on Market	Interest Rate
7	1	5	7.4
8	0	1	9.1
9	−2	0	8.2
10	1	−1	7.1
11	3	3	6.4
12	6	4	5.5

Use a regression model in which Montana's stock return is dependent on the stock market return and the interest rate. Determine the relationship between the interest rate and Montana's stock return by assessing the regression coefficient applied to the interest rate. Is the sign of the coefficient positive or negative? What does it suggest about the bank's exposure to interest rate risk? Should Montana Bank be concerned about rising or declining interest rate movements in the future?

Flow of Funds Exercise

Managing Credit Risk

Recall that Carson Company relies heavily on commercial banks for loans. When the company was first established with equity funding from its owners, Carson Company could easily obtain debt financing, as the financing was backed by some of the firm's assets. However, as Carson expanded, it continually relied on extra debt financing, which increased its ratio of debt to equity. Some banks were unwilling to provide more debt financing because of the risk that Carson would not be able to repay additional loans. A few banks were still willing to provide funding, but they required an extra premium to compensate for the risk.

a. Explain the difference in the willingness of banks to provide loans to Carson Company. Why is there a difference between banks when they are assessing the same information about a firm that wants to borrow funds?

b. Consider the flow of funds for a publicly traded bank that is a key lender to Carson Company. This bank received equity funding from shareholders, which it uses to establish its business. It channels bank deposit funds, which are insured by the FDIC, to provide loans to Carson Company and other firms. The depositors have no idea how the bank uses their funds, as their deposits are insured, yet the FDIC is not preventing the bank from making risky loans. So who is monitoring the bank? Do you think the bank is taking more risk than its shareholders desire? How does the FDIC discourage the bank from taking too much risk? Why might the bank ignore the FDIC's efforts to discourage excessive risk taking?

Internet/Excel Exercises

1. Assess the services offered by an Internet bank, using the website http://www.netbank.com. Describe the types of online services offered by the bank. Do you think an Internet bank such as this offers higher or lower interest rates than a "regular" commercial bank? Why or why not?

2. Go to http://finance.yahoo.com/, enter the symbol BK (Bank of New York), and click on "Get Quotes." Click on "5y" just below the stock price trend to review the stock price movements over the

last five years. Check the S&P box just above the graph and click on "Compare" in order to compare the trend of Bank of New York with the movements in the S&P stock index. Has Bank of New York performed better or worse than the index? Offer an explanation for its performance.

3. Go to http://finance.yahoo.com/, enter the symbol WB (Wachovia Corporation), and click on "Get Quotes." Retrieve stock price data at the beginning of the last 20 quarters. Then go to

http://research.stlouisfed.org/fred2/ and retrieve interest rate data at the beginning of the last 20 quarters for the three-month Treasury bill. Record the data on an Excel spreadsheet. Derive the quarterly return of Wachovia. Derive the quarterly change in the interest rate. Apply regression analysis in which the quarterly return of Wachovia is the dependent variable and the quarterly change in the interest rate is the independent variable (see Appendix B for more information about using regression analysis). Is there a positive or negative relationship between the interest rate movement and the return of Wachovia stock? Is the relationship significant? Offer an explanation for this relationship.

WSJ Exercise

Bank Management Strategies

Summarize an article in *The Wall Street Journal* that discussed a recent change in managerial strategy by a particular commercial bank. (You may wish to do an Internet search in the online version of *The Wall Street Journal* to identify an article on a commercial bank's change in strategy.) Describe the change in managerial strategy. How will the bank's balance sheet be affected by this change? How will the bank's potential return and risk be affected? What reason does the article give for the bank's decision to change its strategy?

Chapter 20: Bank Performance

A commercial bank's performance is examined for various reasons. Bank regulators identify banks that are experiencing severe problems so that they can be remedied. Shareholders need to determine whether they should buy or sell the stock of various banks. Investment analysts must be able to advise prospective investors on which banks to select for investment. Commercial banks also evaluate their own performance over time to determine the outcomes of previous management decisions so that changes can be made where appropriate. Without persistent monitoring of performance, existing problems can remain unnoticed and lead to financial failure in the future.

The specific objectives of this chapter are to:

- identify the factors that affect the valuation of a commercial bank,
- compare the performance of banks in different size classifications over recent years, and
- explain how to evaluate the performance of banks based on financial statement data.

Valuation of a Commercial Bank

Commercial banks (or commercial bank units that are part of a financial conglomerate) are commonly valued by their managers as part of their efforts to monitor performance over time and to determine the proper mix of services that will maximize the value of the bank. Banks may also be valued by other financial institutions that are considering an acquisition. An understanding of commercial bank valuation is useful because it identifies the factors that determine a commercial bank's value. The value of a commercial bank can be modeled as the present value of its future cash flows:

$$V = \sum_{t=1}^{n} \frac{E(CF_t)}{(1 + k)^t}$$

where $E(CF_t)$ represents the expected cash flow to be generated in period t, and k represents the required rate of return by investors who invest in the commercial bank. Thus, the value of a commercial bank should change in response to changes in its expected cash flows in the future and to changes in the required rate of return by investors:

$$\Delta V = f[\Delta E(CF), \Delta k]$$
$$\quad\quad\quad + \quad\quad -$$

Factors That Affect Cash Flows

The change in a commercial bank's expected cash flows may be modeled as

$$\Delta E(CF) = f(\Delta ECON, \Delta R_f, \Delta INDUS, \Delta MANAB)$$
$$ + - ? +$$

where ECON represents economic growth, R_f represents the risk-free interest rate, INDUS represents prevailing bank industry conditions (including regulations and competition), and MANAB represents the abilities of the commercial bank's management.

Change in Economic Growth Economic growth can enhance a commercial bank's cash flows by increasing the household or business demand for loans. During periods of strong economic growth, loan demand tends to be higher, allowing commercial banks to provide more loans. Since loans tend to generate better returns to commercial banks than investment in Treasury securities or other securities, expected cash flows should be higher. Another reason cash flows may be higher is that fewer loan defaults normally occur during periods of strong economic growth.

Furthermore, the demand for other financial services provided by commercial banks tends to be higher during periods of strong economic growth. For example, brokerage, insurance, and financial planning services typically receive more business when economic growth is strong, because households have relatively high levels of disposable income.

Change in the Risk-Free Interest Rate Interest rate movements may be inversely related to a commercial bank's cash flows. If the risk-free interest rate decreases, other market rates may also decline, which may result in a stronger demand for the commercial bank's loans. Second, commercial banks rely heavily on short-term deposits as a source of funds, and the rates paid on these deposits are typically revised in accordance with other interest rate movements. Banks' uses of funds (such as loans) are normally also sensitive to interest rate movements, but to a smaller degree. Therefore, when interest rates fall, the depository institution's cost of obtaining funds declines more than the decline in the interest earned on its loans and investments. Conversely, an increase in interest rates could reduce a commercial bank's expected cash flows because the interest paid on deposits may increase to a greater degree than the interest earned on loans and investments.

Change in Industry Conditions One of the most important industry characteristics that can affect a commercial bank's cash flows is regulation. If regulators reduce the constraints imposed on commercial banks, banks' expected cash flows should increase. For example, when regulators eliminated certain geographic constraints, commercial banks were able to expand across new regions in the United States. As regulators reduced constraints on the types of businesses that commercial banks could pursue, the banks were able to expand by offering other financial services (such as brokerage and insurance services).

Another important industry characteristic that can affect a bank's cash flows is technological innovation, which can improve efficiencies and therefore enhance cash flows. The level of competition is an additional industry characteristic that can affect cash flows, because a high level of competition may reduce the bank's volume of business or reduce the prices it can charge for its services. As regulation has been reduced, competition has intensified. While some commercial banks benefit, other banks may lose some of their market share.

Change in Management Abilities Of the four characteristics that commonly affect the cash flows, the only one over which the bank has control is management skills. It cannot dictate economic growth, interest rate movements, or regulations, but it can select its managers and its organizational structure. The managers can attempt to make internal decisions that will capitalize on the external forces (economic growth, interest rates, regulatory constraints) that the bank cannot control.

As the management skills of a commercial bank improve, so should its expected cash flows. For example, skillful managers will recognize how to revise the composition of the bank's assets and liabilities to capitalize on existing economic or regulatory conditions. They can capitalize on economies of scale by expanding specific types of businesses and by offering a diversified set of services that accommodate specific customers. They may restructure operations and use technology in a manner that can reduce expenses. They may also use derivative securities to alter the bank's potential return and risk. Thus, even if the other external forces are unchanged, a commercial bank's expected cash flows (and therefore value) can change in response to a change in its management skills.

Factors That Affect the Required Rate of Return by Investors

The required rate of return by investors who invest in a commercial bank can be modeled as

$$\Delta k = f(\Delta R_f, \Delta RP)$$
$$+ \quad +$$

where R_f represents a change in the risk-free interest rate, and RP represents the risk premium of the bank.

Change in the Risk-Free Rate When the risk-free rate increases, so does the return required by investors. Recall that the risk-free rate of interest is driven by inflationary expectations (INF), economic growth (ECON), the money supply (MS), and the budget deficit (DEF):

$$\Delta R_f = f(\Delta INF, \Delta ECON, \Delta MS, \Delta DEF)$$
$$+ \qquad + \qquad - \qquad +$$

High inflation, economic growth, and a high budget deficit place upward pressure on interest rates, while money supply growth places downward pressure on interest rates (assuming it does not cause inflation).

Change in the Risk Premium If the risk premium on a commercial bank rises, so will the required rate of return by investors who invest in the bank. The risk premium can change in response to changes in economic growth, industry conditions, or management abilities:

$$\Delta RP = f(\Delta ECON, \Delta INDUS, \Delta MANAB)$$
$$- \qquad\quad ? \qquad\quad -$$

High economic growth results in less risk for a commercial bank because its loans and investments in debt securities are less likely to default.

Bank industry characteristics such as regulatory constraints, technological innovations, and the level of competition can affect the risk premium on banks. Regulatory constraints may include a minimum level of capital required of banks. The most prominent regulatory change in recent years has been the reduction in constraints on services, which has allowed commercial banks to diversify their offerings to reduce risk. Conversely, this change may allow commercial banks to engage in some services that are riskier than their traditional services and to pursue some services that they cannot provide efficiently. Thus, the reduction in regulatory constraints could increase the risk premium required by investors.

An improvement in management skills may reduce the perceived risk of a commercial bank. To the extent that more skillful managers allocate funds to assets that exhibit less risk, they may reduce the risk premium required by investors who invest in the bank.

Exhibit 20.1 provides a framework for valuing a commercial bank, based on the preceding discussion. In general, the valuation is favorably affected by economic growth, lower interest rates, a reduction in regulatory constraints (assuming the bank focuses on services that it can provide efficiently), and an improvement in the bank's management abilities.

Performance of Banks

http://www.fdic.gov
Information about the performance of commercial banks.

Exhibit 20.2 summarizes the performance of all U.S.-chartered insured commercial banks during particular years. Each item is measured as a percentage of assets to control for growth when assessing the changes in each characteristic over time. Exhibit 20.2 serves as a useful reference point for assessing each of the performance proxies discussed throughout this chapter. Bank performance is shown over time to illustrate how performance can change. The following discussion examines the items in the first column of Exhibit 20.2 in the order listed; these income statement items are also the key income and expense items that affect a bank's performance.

Exhibit 20.1   Framework for Valuing a Commercial Bank

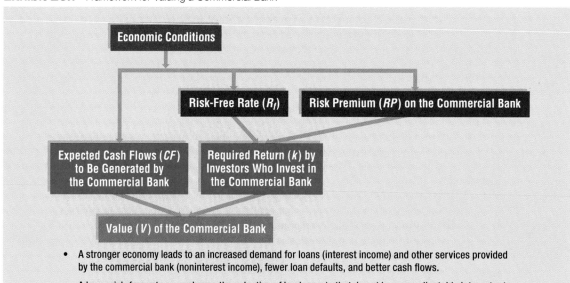

- A stronger economy leads to an increased demand for loans (interest income) and other services provided by the commercial bank (noninterest income), fewer loan defaults, and better cash flows.

- A lower risk-free rate can enhance the valuation of bank assets that do not have an adjustable interest rate, such as some consumer and mortgage loans. It can also increase the valuations of bonds. Commercial banks that have a higher proportion of these types of assets will benefit more from a decline in the risk-free rate and will be adversely affected to a greater degree by an increase in the risk-free rate.

- The valuation is also influenced by industry conditions and the commercial bank's management (not shown in the diagram). These factors affect the risk premium (and therefore the required return by investors) and the expected cash flows to be generated by the commercial bank.

Exhibit 20.2 Performance Summary of All Insured Commercial Banks (1995–2006). All items in the exhibit are estimated as a proportion of total assets

Item	1995	1998	2001	2002	2003	2006
1. Gross interest income	7.30%	6.65%	6.40%	5.30%	4.66%	5.20%
2. Gross interest expenses	3.58	3.29	2.98	1.80	1.32	1.81
3. Net interest income	3.72	3.36	3.42	3.50	3.32	3.39
4. Noninterest income	2.02	2.27	2.51	2.53	2.57	2.38
5. Loan loss provision	.30	.41	.68	.68	.47	.26
6. Noninterest expenses	3.64	3.57	3.56	3.46	3.42	3.36
7. Securities gains (losses)	.01	.06	.07	.10	.08	.00
8. Income before tax	1.81	1.66	1.77	1.98	2.08	1.95
9. Taxes	.63	.59	.59	.65	.67	.32
10. Net income	1.18	1.13	1.17	1.33	1.41	1.33
11. Cash dividends provided	.75	.76	.87	1.01	1.08	.78
12. Retained earnings	.43	.37	.30	.31	.33	.55

Source: Federal Reserve.

Interest Income and Expenses

Gross interest income (in Row 1 of Exhibit 20.2) is interest income generated from all assets. It is affected by market rates and the composition of assets held by banks. Gross interest income increased from 2003 to 2006 for all types of banks because of the general increase in market interest rates.

A comparison of gross interest income levels among four bank size classifications is shown in Exhibit 20.3. The size classifications include "money center" banks, which are the 10 largest banks that serve money centers such as New York and San Francisco; large banks (ranked 11 to 100 in size); medium banks (ranked 101 to 1,000 in size); and small banks (ranked lower than 1,000 in size). In recent years, the gross interest income of small and medium banks has typically been higher than that of other banks. They have been able to charge higher interest rates on their loans than large banks or money center banks because they face less competition on loans to small local businesses. Money center banks and large banks tend to provide more loans to larger firms, which have various options available to obtain funds.

Gross interest expenses (in Row 2) represent interest paid on deposits and on other borrowed funds (from the federal funds market). These expenses are affected by market rates and the composition of the bank's liabilities. Since NOW accounts and money market deposit accounts (MMDAs) have become popular, banks are attracting a smaller percentage of funds through traditional non-interest-bearing demand deposit accounts. In addition, low interest rate passbook savings accounts are drawing fewer funds because of the alternative certificates of deposit (CDs) available. A large percentage of banks' sources of funds have market-determined interest rates.

A comparison of gross interest expenses among the four bank size classes is presented in Exhibit 20.4. In recent years, gross interest expenses have been similar among banks. Interest expenses of commercial banks tend to move in line with the general movement in market interest rates.

Net interest income (in Row 3) is the difference between gross interest income and interest expenses and is measured as a percentage of assets. This measure is commonly referred to as net interest margin. It has a major effect on the bank's performance.

Exhibit 20.3   Comparison of Gross Interest Income among Bank Classes

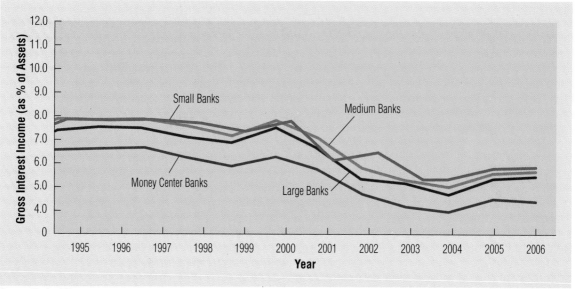

Source: Federal Reserve.

Exhibit 20.4   Comparison of Gross Interest Expenses among Bank Classes

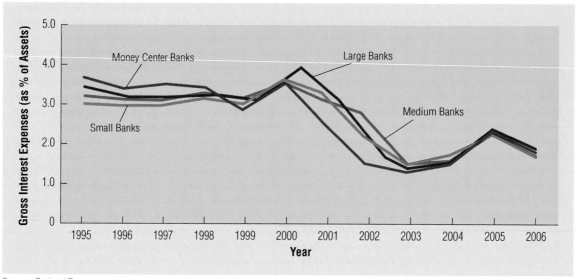

Source: Federal Reserve.

As shown earlier, small and medium banks tend to have higher gross interest income (as a proportion of assets), while their interest expenses (as a proportion of assets) are similar. Thus, as shown in Exhibit 20.5, the net interest margin for large banks and money center banks is typically lower than for smaller banks. As Exhibit 20.2 shows, gross interest income and gross interest expenses have been similarly affected by inter-

Exhibit 20.5   Comparison of Net Interest Margin among Bank Classes

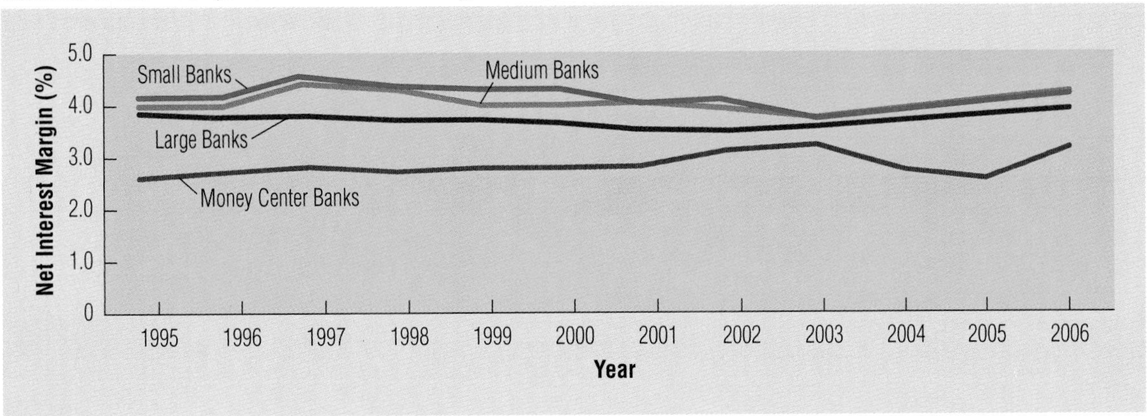

Source: Federal Reserve.

est rate movements; therefore, the net interest margin of all banks in aggregate has remained somewhat stable over time.

Banks that heavily emphasize credit card loans have a higher net interest margin because they earn high interest income. However, they tend to incur larger loan losses due to defaults by credit card holders.

Noninterest Income and Expenses

Noninterest income (in Row 4) results from fees charged on services provided, such as lockbox services, banker's acceptances, cashier's checks, and foreign exchange transactions. Until 2006, it had generally risen over time for all banks in aggregate, as banks are offering more fee-based services than in the past. As banks continue to offer new services (such as insurance or securities services), noninterest income will generally increase over time.

Exhibit 20.6 shows that noninterest income is usually higher for money center, large, and medium banks than for small banks. This difference occurs because the larger banks provide more services for which they can charge fees.

The **loan loss provision** (in Row 5) is a reserve account established by the bank in anticipation of loan losses in the future. It should increase during periods when loan losses are more likely, such as during a recessionary period. In many cases, there is a lagged impact because some borrowers survive the recessionary period but never fully recover from it and subsequently fail. The amount of loan losses is influenced by the volume of loans provided and economic conditions.

Noninterest expenses (in Row 6 of Exhibit 20.2) include salaries, office equipment, and other expenses not related to the payment of interest on deposits. Noninterest expenses are partially dependent on personnel costs associated with the credit assessment of loan applications, which in turn are affected by the bank's asset composition (proportion of funds allocated to loans). Noninterest expenses also depend on the liability composition because small deposits are more time-consuming to handle than large deposits. Banks offering more nontraditional services will incur higher noninterest expenses, although they expect to offset the higher costs with higher noninterest income.

Securities gains and losses (in Row 7 of Exhibit 20.2) result from the bank's sale of securities. They have been negligible, when all banks in aggregate are considered. An individual bank's gains and losses might be more significant.

Income before tax (in Row 8 of Exhibit 20.2) is obtained by summing net interest income, noninterest income, and securities gains and subtracting from this sum

Exhibit 20.6   Comparison of Noninterest Income among Bank Classes

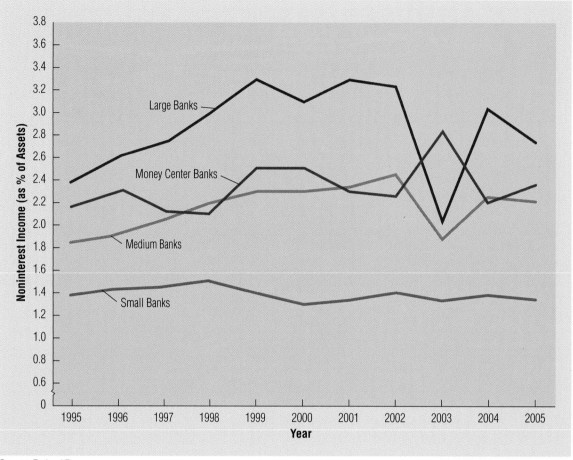

Source: Federal Reserve.

the provision for loan losses and noninterest expenses. Bank income has generally increased over the last several years.

Net Income

The key income statement item, according to many analysts, is **net income** (in Row 10 of Exhibit 20.2), which accounts for any taxes paid.

Return on Assets   The net income figure shown in Exhibit 20.2 is measured as a percentage of assets and therefore represents the **return on assets (ROA).** The ROA is influenced by all previously mentioned income statement items and therefore by all policies and other factors that affect those items. Fluctuations in the ROA for banks in aggregate can be explained by assessing changes in its components, as shown in Exhibit 20.7. Although the net interest margin has been somewhat stable, noninterest income has generally risen over time. In addition, noninterest expenses and loan loss provisions have decreased for some banks in recent years.

Exhibit 20.8 shows that the ROA for money center and large banks has been relatively high recently. This is primarily attributed to their lower loan loss provision and

Exhibit 20.7   Overview of the Key Components Affecting the ROA (for Banks in Aggregate)

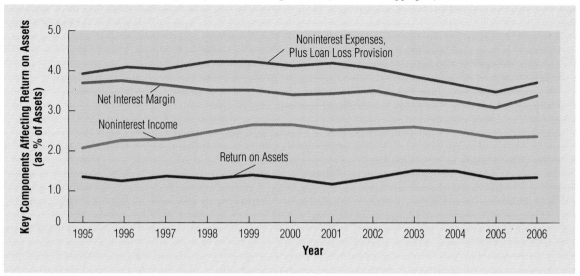

Source: Federal Reserve.

Exhibit 20.8   Comparison of Return on Assets (ROA) among Bank Classes

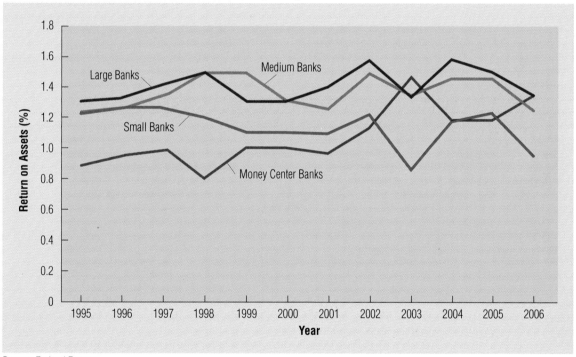

Source: Federal Reserve.

higher noninterest income. The increase in noninterest income is attributed to bank efforts to pursue nonbanking activities (such as brokerage and insurance).

Any individual bank's ROA depends on the bank's policy decisions as well as uncontrollable factors relating to the economy and government regulations, as shown in Exhibit 20.9. Gross interest income and expenses are affected by the sources and uses of bank funds and the movements in market interest rates.

Exhibit 20.9   Influence of Bank Policies and Other Factors on a Bank's Income Statement

Income Statement Item as a Percentage of Assets	Bank Policy Decisions Affecting the Income Statement Item	Uncontrollable Factors Affecting the Income Statement Item
(1) Gross interest income	• Composition of assets • Quality of assets • Maturity and rate sensitivity of assets • Loan pricing policy	• Economic conditions • Market interest rate movements
(2) Gross interest expenses	• Composition of liabilities • Maturities and rate sensitivity of liabilities	• Market interest rate movements
(3) Net interest income = (1) − (2)		
(4) Noninterest income	• Service charges • Nontraditional activities	• Regulatory provisions
(5) Noninterest expenses	• Composition of assets • Composition of liabilities • Nontraditional activities • Efficiency of personnel • Costs of office space and equipment • Marketing costs • Other costs	• Inflation
(6) Loan losses	• Composition of assets • Quality of assets • Collection department capabilities	• Economic conditions • Market interest rate movements
(7) Pretax return on assets = (3) + (4) − (5) − (6)		
(8) Taxes	• Tax planning	• Tax laws
(9) After-tax return on assets = (7) − (8)		
(10) Financial leverage, measured here as (assets/equity)	• Capital structure policies	• Capital structure regulations
(11) Return on equity = (9) × (10)		

Return on Equity An alternative measure of overall bank performance is **return on equity (ROE)**. A bank's ROE is affected by the same income statement items that affect ROA as well as by the bank's degree of financial leverage, as follows:

$$\text{ROE} = \text{ROA} \times \text{Leverage measure}$$

$$\frac{\text{Net income}}{\text{Equity capital}} = \frac{\text{Net income}}{\text{Total assets}} \times \frac{\text{Total assets}}{\text{Equity capital}}$$

The leverage measure is simply the inverse of the capital ratio (when only equity counts as capital). The higher the capital ratio, the lower the leverage measure and the lower the degree of financial leverage.

Exhibit 20.10 shows that in recent years small banks have experienced a lower ROE than other classes of banks. This is primarily attributed to the small banks' relatively low ROA and relatively high level of capital (a low degree of financial leverage) that they maintain.

How to Evaluate a Bank's Performance

Up to this point, the discussion has mostly focused on the performance of the overall industry and of banks of different sizes. Although this information can be beneficial, analysts often need to evaluate an individual bank's performance, in which case financial statements are used. The income and expenses shown earlier in Exhibit 20.2 can serve as an industry benchmark for evaluating a bank's performance.

Examination of Return on Assets (ROA)

The ROA will usually reveal when a bank's performance is not up to par, but it does not indicate the reason for poor performance. Its components must be evaluated separately. Exhibit 20.11 identifies the factors that affect bank performance as measured by the ROA and ROE. If a bank's ROA is less than desired, the bank is possibly incurring excessive interest expenses. Banks typically know what deposit rate is necessary to attract deposits and therefore are not likely to pay excessive interest. Yet, if all a bank's sources of funds require a market-determined rate, the bank will face relatively high interest expenses. A relatively low ROA could also be due to low interest received on

Exhibit 20.10   Comparison of Return on Equity (ROE) among Bank Classes

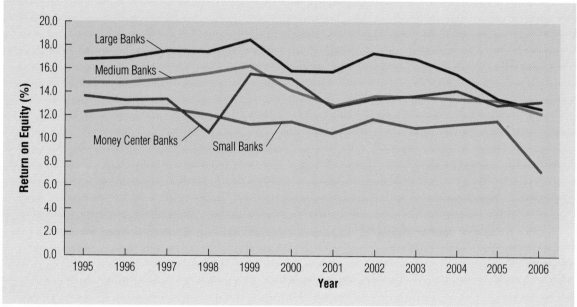

Source: Federal Reserve.

Exhibit 20.11   Breakdown of Performance Measures

Measures of Bank Performance	Financial Characteristics Influencing Performance	Bank Decisions Affecting Financial Characteristics
(1) Return on assets (ROA)	Net interest margin	Deposit rate decisions Loan rate decisions Loan losses
	Noninterest revenues Noninterest expenses	Bank services offered Overhead requirements Efficiency Advertising
	Loan losses	Risk level of loans provided
(2) Return on equity (ROE)	ROA Leverage measure	See above Capital structure decision

loans and securities because the bank has been overly conservative with its funds or was locked into fixed rates prior to an increase in market interest rates. High interest expenses and/or low interest revenues (on a relative basis) will reduce the net interest margin and therefore reduce the ROA.

A relatively low ROA may also result from insufficient noninterest income. Some banks have made a much greater effort than others to offer services that generate fee (noninterest) income. Because a bank's net interest margin is somewhat dictated by interest rate trends and balance sheet composition, many banks attempt to focus on noninterest income to boost their ROA.

A bank's ROA can also be damaged by heavy loan losses. Yet, if the bank is too conservative in attempting to avoid loan losses, its net interest margin will be low (because of the low interest rates received from very safe loans and investments). Because of the obvious tradeoff here, banks generally attempt to shift their risk-return preferences according to economic conditions. They may increase their concentration of relatively risky loans during periods of prosperity when they may improve their net interest margin without incurring excessive loan losses. Conversely, they may increase their concentration of relatively low-risk (and low-return) investments when economic conditions are less favorable.

A low ROA may also be attributed to excessive noninterest expenses, such as overhead and advertising expenses. Any waste of resources due to inefficiencies can lead to relatively high noninterest expenses.

Example

Consider the information shown in Exhibit 20.12 for Bank of America and the industry since 1995. Because of differences in accounting procedures, the information may not be perfectly comparable. The industry data are based on the class of money center banks. Bank of America's income before tax has typically exceeded the industry

Exhibit 20.12 Evaluation of Bank of America*

	1995		1998		2000		2001	
	BA	**Industry**	**BA**	**Industry**	**BA**	**Industry**	**BA**	**Industry**
Net interest margin	3.64%	2.68%	2.96%	2.73%	2.87%	2.78%	3.31%	2.87%
Noninterest income	1.96	2.16	1.97	2.15	2.25	2.51	2.24	2.23
Loan loss provision	.19	.11	.47	.31	.39	.35	.69	.59
Noninterest expenses	3.44	3.32	3.32	3.47	2.81	3.30	3.33	4.24
Income before tax	1.97	1.44	1.30	1.10	1.83	1.60	1.63	.97

	2002		2003		2005		2006	
	BA	**Industry**	**BA**	**Industry**	**BA**	**Industry**	**BA**	**Industry**
Net interest margin	3.26%	3.13%	2.80%	3.20%	2.37%	2.58%	2.34%	3.18%
Noninterest income	2.04	2.32	2.14	2.82	1.96	2.37	2.61	2.35
Loan loss provision	.56	.73	.37	.52	.31	.20	.34	.28
Noninterest expenses	2.79	4.14	2.63	3.41	2.22	2.99	2.42	3.25
Income before tax	1.95	1.12	2.07	2.18	1.80	1.76	2.19	2.00

*All variables are measured as a percentage of assets. The industry net income before tax also accounts for securities gains and losses.
Sources: Bank of America's Annual Reports; and *Federal Reserve Bulletin,* various issues.

norm since 1995. A comparison with the industry figures indicates that although Bank of America's net interest margin was recently lower than the norm, so were its noninterest expenses. Since 1995, Bank of America has performed relatively well, primarily because of its relatively low noninterest expenses. Exhibit 20.13 provides a separate comparison of each variable to the industry norm over time to confirm the conclusions drawn.

Any particular bank will perform a more thorough evaluation of itself than that shown here. For example, Bank of America's annual reports typically provided a comprehensive explanation for its performance in recent years, along with a discussion of how it plans to improve its performance over time.

Exhibit 20.13   Comparison of Bank of America Expenses and Income to the Industry

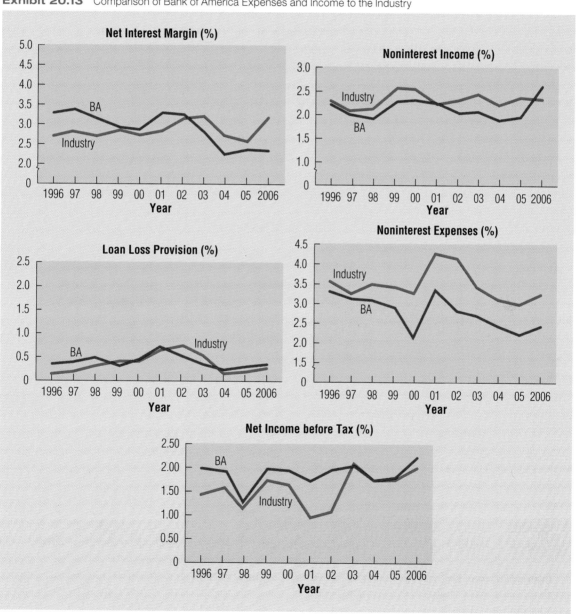

Summary

■ A bank's value is dependent on its expected future cash flows and the required rate of return by investors who invest in the bank. The bank's expected cash flows are influenced by economic growth, interest rate movements, regulatory constraints, and the abilities of the bank's managers. The required rate of return by investors who invest in the bank is influenced by the prevailing interest rate (which is affected by other economic conditions) and the risk premium (which is affected by economic growth, regulatory constraints, and the management abilities of the bank). In general, the value of commercial banks is favorably affected by strong economic growth, declining interest rates, and strong management abilities.

■ A bank's performance can be evaluated by comparing its income statement items (as a percentage of total assets) to a control group of other banks with a similar size classification. The return on assets (ROA) of the bank may be compared to the control group's mean ROA. Any difference in ROA between the bank and the control group is typically because of differences in net interest margin, loan loss reserves, noninterest income, or noninterest expenses.

If the bank's net interest margin is relatively low, it either is relying too heavily on deposits with higher interest rates or is not earning adequate interest on its loans. If the bank is forced to boost loan loss reserves, this suggests that its loan portfolio may be too risky. If its noninterest income is relatively low, the bank is not providing enough services that generate fee income. If the bank's noninterest expenses are relatively high, its cost of operations is excessive. There may be other specific details that make the assessment more complex, but the key problems of a bank can usually be detected with the approach described here.

■ A common measure of a bank's overall performance is its return on assets (ROA). The ROA of a bank is partially determined by movements in market interest rates, as many banks benefit from lower interest rates. In addition, the ROA is highly dependent on economic conditions, because banks can extend more loans to creditworthy customers and may also experience a higher demand for their services.

Another useful measure of a bank's overall performance is return on equity (ROE). A bank can increase its ROE by increasing its financial leverage, but its leverage is constrained by capital requirements.

Point Counter-Point

Does a Bank's Income Statement Clearly Indicate the Bank's Performance?

Point Yes. The bank's income statement can be partitioned to determine its performance and the underlying reasons for its performance.

Counter-Point No. The bank's income statement can be manipulated because the bank may not fully recognize loan losses (will not write off loans that are likely to default) until a future period.

Who Is Correct? Use the Internet to learn more about this issue. Offer your own opinion on this issue.

Questions and Applications

1. **Interest Income** How can gross interest income rise, while the net interest margin remains somewhat stable for a particular bank?

2. **Impact on Income** If a bank shifts its loan policy to pursue more credit card loans, how will its net interest margin be affected?

3. **Noninterest Income** What has been the trend in noninterest income in recent years? Explain.

4. **Net Interest Margin** How could a bank generate higher income before tax (as a percentage of assets) when its net interest margin has decreased?

5. **Net Interest Income** Suppose a bank generates net interest income as a percentage of assets of 1.50 percent. Based on past experience, would the bank experience a loss or a gain? Explain.

6. **Noninterest Income** Why have large money center banks' noninterest income levels typically been higher than those of smaller banks?

7. **Bank Leverage** What does the assets/equity ratio of a bank indicate?

8. **Analysis of a Bank's ROA** What are some of the more common reasons for a bank to experience a low ROA?

9. **Loan Loss Provisions** Explain why loan loss provisions of most banks could increase in a particular period.

10. **Evaluating a Bank's Performance** When evaluating a bank, what are some of the key aspects to review?

11. **Weak Performance** What are likely reasons for weak bank performance?

12. **Bank Income Statement** Assume that SUNY Bank plans to liquidate Treasury security holdings and use the proceeds for small business loans. Explain how this strategy will affect the different income statement items. Also identify any income statement items where the effects of this strategy are more difficult to estimate.

Interpreting Financial News

Interpret the following comments made by Wall Street analysts and portfolio managers:

a. "The three most important factors that determine a local bank's bad debt level are the bank's location, location, and location."

b. "The bank's profitability was enhanced by its limited use of capital."

c. "Low risk is not always desirable. Our bank's risk has been too low, given the market conditions. We will restructure operations in a manner to increase risk."

Managing in Financial Markets

Forecasting Bank Performance As a manager of Hawaii Bank, you anticipate the following:

■ Loan loss provision at end of year = 1 percent of assets

■ Gross interest income over the next year = 9 percent of assets

■ Noninterest expenses over the next year = 3 percent of assets

■ Noninterest income over the next year = 1 percent of assets

■ Gross interest expenses over the next year = 5 percent of assets

■ Tax rate on income = 30 percent

■ Capital ratio (capital/assets) at end of year = 5 percent

a. Forecast Hawaii Bank's net interest margin.

b. Forecast Hawaii Bank's earnings before taxes as a percentage of assets.

c. Forecast Hawaii Bank's earnings after taxes as a percentage of assets.

d. Forecast Hawaii Bank's return on equity.

e. Hawaii Bank is considering a shift in its asset structure to reduce its concentration of Treasury bonds and increase its volume of loans to small businesses. Identify each income statement item that would be affected by this strategy, and explain whether the forecast for that item would increase or decrease.

Problem

1. **Assessing Bank Performance** Select a bank whose income statement data are available. Using recent income statement information about the commercial bank, assess its performance. How does the performance of this bank compare to the performance of other banks? Is its return on equity higher or lower than the ROE of other banks as reported in this chapter? What is the main reason why its ROE is different from the norm? (Is it due to its interest expenses? Its noninterest income?)

Flow of Funds Exercise

How the Flow of Funds Affects Bank Performance

In recent years, Carson Company has requested the services listed below from Blazo Financial, a financial conglomerate. These transactions have created a flow of funds between Carson Company and Blazo.
a. Classify each service according to how Blazo benefits from the service.

- Advising on possible targets that Carson may acquire
- Futures contract transactions
- Options contract transactions
- Interest rate derivative transactions

- Loans
- Line of credit
- Purchase of short-term CDs
- Checking account

b. Explain why Blazo's performance from providing these services to Carson Company and other firms will decline if economic growth is reduced.
c. Given the potential impact of slow economic growth on a bank's performance, do you think that commercial banks would prefer that the Fed use a tight-money policy or a loose-money policy?

Internet/Excel Exercises

1. Go to http://www.suntrust.com. Click on "Investor Relations" and then on "Annual Reports." Use the income statement to determine SunTrust's performance. Describe SunTrust's performance in recent years.
2. Has SunTrust's ROA increased since the year before? Explain what caused its ROA to change over the last year. Has its net interest margin changed since last year? How has its noninterest income (as a percentage of assets) changed over the last year? How have its noninterest expenses changed over the last year? How have its loan loss reserves changed in the last year? Discuss how SunTrust's recent strategy and economic conditions might explain the changes in these components of its income statement.

WSJ Exercise

Assessing Bank Performance

Using a recent issue of *The Wall Street Journal*, summarize an article that discussed the recent performance of a particular commercial bank. Does the article suggest that the bank's performance was better or worse than the norm? What is the reason given for the performance?

Part 7: Nonbank Operations

The chapters in Part 7 cover the key nonbank operations. Each chapter is devoted to a particular type of operation, with a focus on sources of funds, uses of funds, regulations, management, and recent performance. Some of the institutions discussed are independent; others are units (subsidiaries) of financial conglomerates. Each financial institution's interactions with other institutions and its participation in financial markets are also emphasized in these chapters.

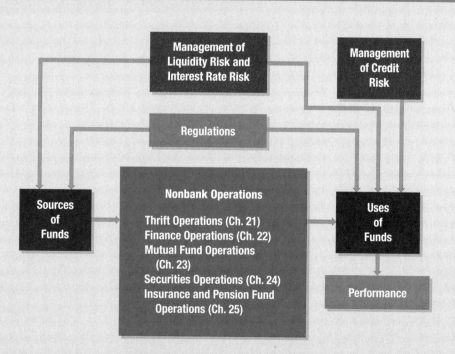

Chapter 23: Mutual Fund Operations

A **mutual fund** is an investment company that sells shares and uses the proceeds to manage a portfolio of securities. Mutual funds have grown substantially in recent years, and they serve as major suppliers of funds in financial markets.

The specific objectives of this chapter are to:

- explain how characteristics vary among mutual funds,
- describe the various types of stock and bond mutual funds, and
- describe the characteristics of money market funds.

Background on Mutual Funds

http://

http://www.bloomberg.com
Information on mutual fund performance.

Mutual funds serve as a key financial intermediary. They pool investments by individual investors and use the funds to accommodate financing needs of governments and corporations in the primary markets. They also frequently invest in securities in the secondary market.

Mutual funds provide an important service not only for corporations and governments that need funds, but also for individual investors who wish to invest funds. Small investors are unable to diversify their investments because of their limited funds. Mutual funds offer a way for these investors to diversify. Some mutual funds have holdings of 50 or more securities, and the minimum investment may be only $250 to $2,500. Small investors could not afford to create such a diversified portfolio on their own. Moreover, the mutual fund uses experienced portfolio managers, so investors do not have to manage the portfolio themselves. Some mutual funds also offer liquidity because they are willing to repurchase an investor's shares upon request. They also offer various services, such as 24-hour telephone or Internet access to account information, money transfers between different funds operated by the same firm, consolidated account statements, check-writing privileges on some types of funds, and tax information.

A mutual fund hires portfolio managers to invest in a portfolio of securities that satisfies the desires of investors. Like other portfolio managers, the managers of mutual funds analyze economic and industry trends and forecasts and assess the potential impact of various conditions on companies. They adjust the composition of their portfolio in response to changing economic conditions.

Because of their diversification, management expertise, and liquidity, mutual funds have grown at a rapid pace. The growth of mutual funds is illustrated in Exhibit 23.1. Today, there are more than 8,000 different mutual funds, with total assets exceeding $10 trillion. The value of mutual fund assets more than doubled from

Exhibit 23.1   Growth in Mutual Funds

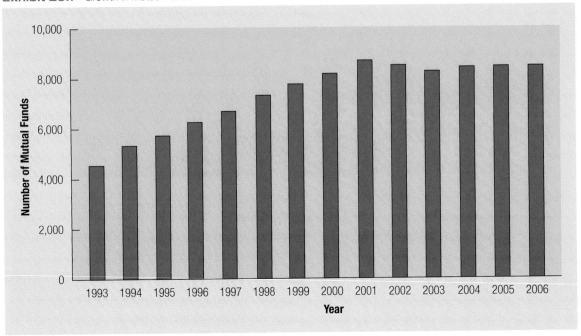

Note: The number shown here includes money market funds.
Source: *2007 Mutual Fund Fact Book.*

1993 to 2007. Over the last 25 years, total mutual fund assets have increased by more than 23 times. More than 88 million households now own shares of one or more mutual funds.

Types of Funds

Funds are classified as open-end, closed-end, exchange-traded, and hedge funds.

Open-End Funds   **Open-end funds** are open to investment from investors at any time. Investors can purchase shares directly from the open-end fund at any time. In addition, investors can sell (redeem) their shares back to the open-end fund at any time. Thus, the number of shares of an open-end fund is always changing. When the fund receives additional investment, it invests in additional securities. It maintains some cash on hand in case redemptions exceed investments on a given day. If there are substantial redemptions, the fund will have to sell some of its securities to obtain sufficient funds to accommodate the redemptions. There are many different categories of open-end mutual funds, allowing investors to invest in a fund that fits their particular investment objective. Investors can select from thousands of open-end mutual funds to meet their particular return and risk profile. When the term *mutual fund* is used, it normally refers to the open-end type just described.

Closed-End Funds   **Closed-end funds** do not repurchase (redeem) the shares they sell. Instead, investors must sell the shares on a stock exchange just like corporate stock. The number of outstanding shares sold by a closed-end investment company usually remains constant and is equal to the number of shares originally issued.

There are about 650 closed-end funds. Approximately 70 percent of the closed-end funds invest mainly in bonds or other debt securities, while the other 30 percent focus on stocks. The total market value of closed-end funds is less than $300 billion,

Price quotations for exchange-traded funds (ETFs) like those shown here are provided by *The Wall Street Journal.* The closing price, net change in price from the previous day, and year-to-date (from the beginning of the year to the present) return are provided for each ETF. Investors who own ETFs can monitor this table to assess the performance of their existing investments. In addition, they can monitor the performance of ETFs that they consider purchasing.

Source: Reprinted with permission of Dow Jones & Company, Inc., from *The Wall Street Journal,* April 6, 2007; permission conveyed through the Copyright Clearance Center, Inc.

ETF	Symbol	Closing price	Chg (%)	Ytd (%)
U.S. Pharm	IHE	55.29	1.10	4.2
U.S. Real Estate	IYR	86.50	0.08	3.8
U.S. Reg Banks	IAT	50.05	0.04	−3.6
U.S. Technology	IYW	55.13	0.49	1.3
U.S. Telecommun	IYZ	31.61	0.41	6.6
U.S. Total Market	IYY	70.53	0.28	2.7
U.S. Utilities	IDU	98.91	0.25	10.1
iShares: FTSE				
FTSE/Xinhua Chn 25	FXI	107.00	0.09	−4.0
iShares: Goldman Sachs				
GSCI Commdty	GSG	41.80	−0.17	4.3
Natural Resources	IGE	107.55	0.35	5.9
Networking	IGN	32.83	0.77	2.1
Semiconductor	IGW	61.63	0.80	1.0
Software	IGV	45.99	0.26	3.2
Technology	IGM	52.55	0.61	2.2
iShares: iBoxx				
Invest Gr Corp Bond	LQD	106.65	−0.21	...
iShares: KLD				
KLD 400	DSI	51.43	0.37	0.6
KLD Select Social Idx	KLD	59.41	0.44	0.6
iShares: Lehman Brothers				
10-20 Yr T-Bond	TLH	100.12	−0.28	−0.3
1-3 Year T-Bond	SHY	80.20	−0.04	0.3
1-3 Yr Credit Bond	CSJ	100.53	−0.02	0.4
20-plus Year T-Bond	TLT	87.75	−0.37	−0.8
3-7 Year T-Bond	IEI	100.62	−0.17	0.7
7-10 Year T-Bond	IEF	82.71	−0.25	0.3
Aggregate Bond	AGG	99.92	−0.09	0.2
Cr Bd	CFT	100.57	−0.31	...
Gov Cr Bnd	GBF	100.40	−0.10	0.2
Int Cr Bnd	CIU	100.54	−0.02	0.3
Intermediate Gov Cr	GVI	100.27	−0.16	0.3
MBS Fixed Rate	MBB	100.75	0.05	−0.1
Short Treasury	SHV	109.07	−0.01	0.3
TIPS Bond	TIP	100.57	−0.02	1.8

and, therefore, is much smaller than the total market value of open-end funds. In addition, the growth of closed-end funds has been smaller than that of open-end funds.

Exchange-Traded Funds **Exchange-traded funds (ETFs)** are designed to mimic particular stock indexes and are traded on a stock exchange just like stocks. They differ from open-end funds in that their shares are traded on an exchange, and their share price changes throughout the day. Also unlike an open-end fund, an ETF has a fixed number of shares. ETFs differ from most open-end and closed-end funds in that they are not actively managed. The management goal of an ETF is to mimic an index so that the share price of the ETF moves in line with that index. Because ETFs are not actively managed, they normally do not have capital gains and losses that must be distributed to shareholders. ETFs have become very popular in recent years because they are an efficient way for investors to invest in a particular stock index.

The first ETF was created in 1993. By 2006, the total value of ETF assets exceeded $350 billion. Today, there are more than 900 ETFs, and they are commonly classified as broad-based, sector, or global, depending on the specific index that they mimic. The broad-based funds are the most popular, but both sector and global ETFs have experienced substantial growth in recent years.

One disadvantage of ETFs is that each purchase of additional shares must be done through the exchange where they are traded. Investors incur a brokerage fee from purchasing the shares just as if they had purchased shares of a stock. This cost is especially important to investors who plan to frequently add to their investment in a particular ETF.

Unlike open-end mutual funds, ETFs can be shorted. Investors who expect that a specific country or sector index will decline over time commonly short ETFs. ETFs can also be purchased on margin.

A popular ETF is the so-called Cube (its trading symbol is QQQQ) created by the Bank of New York. Cubes are traded on the Amex and represent the Nasdaq 100 index, which consists of many technology firms. Thus, Cubes are ideal for investors who believe that technology stocks will perform well but do not want to select individual technology stocks. Cubes are also commonly sold short by investors who expect that technology stocks will decline in value.

Another example of an ETF is the Standard & Poor's Depository Receipt (also called Spider), which is a basket of stocks matched to the S&P 500 index. Spiders enable investors to take positions in the index by purchasing shares. Thus, investors who anticipate that the stock market as represented by the S&P 500 will perform well may purchase shares of Spiders, especially when their expectations reflect the composite as a whole rather than any individual stock within the composite. Spiders trade at one-tenth the S&P 500 value, so if the S&P 500 is valued at 1400, a Spider is valued at $140. Thus, the percentage change in the price of the shares over time is equivalent to the percentage change in the value of the S&P 500 index.

http://www.ishares.com
Information on the trading of iShares.

Diamond ETFs are shares of the Dow Jones Industrial Average (DJIA) and are measured as one one-hundredth of the DJIA value. Mid-cap Spiders are shares that represent the S&P 400 Midcap Index. There are also Sector Spiders, which are intended to match a specific sector index. For example, a Technology Spider is a fund representing 79 technology stocks from the S&P 500 composite. Another type of ETF is the world equity benchmark shares (WEBs), which are designed to track stock indexes of specific countries. Barclays Bank has created several different ETFs (which it calls iShares) that represent specific countries.

Hedge Funds   **Hedge funds** sell shares to wealthy individuals and financial institutions and use the proceeds to invest in securities. They differ from an open-end mutual fund in several ways. First, they require a much larger initial investment (such as $1 million), whereas mutual funds typically allow a minimum investment in the range of $250 to $2,500. Second, many hedge funds are not "open" in the sense that they may not always accept additional investments or accommodate redemption requests unless advance notice is provided. Third, hedge funds have been unregulated, although they are now subject to some regulation. They provide very limited information to prospective investors. Fourth, hedge funds invest in a wide variety of investments to achieve high returns. Consequently, they tend to take more risk than mutual funds.

Comparison to Depository Institutions

Mutual funds are like depository institutions in that they repackage the proceeds received from individuals to make various types of investments. Nevertheless, investing in mutual funds is distinctly different from depositing money in a depository institution in that it represents partial ownership, whereas deposits represent a form of credit. Thus, the investors share the gains or losses generated by the mutual fund, while depositors simply receive interest on their deposits. Individual investors view mutual funds as an alternative to depository institutions. In fact, much of the money invested in mutual funds in the 1990s came from depository institutions. When interest rates decline, many individuals withdraw their deposits and invest in mutual funds.

Regulation

Mutual funds must adhere to a variety of federal regulations. They must register with the Securities and Exchange Commission (SEC) and provide interested investors with a prospectus that discloses details about the components of the fund and the risks involved. Mutual funds are also regulated by state laws, many of which attempt to ensure that investors fully understand the fund.

Since July 1993, mutual funds have been required to disclose in the prospectus the names of their portfolio managers and the length of time that they have been employed by the fund in that position. Many investors regard this information as relevant because the performance of a mutual fund is highly dependent on its portfolio managers.

Mutual funds must also disclose their performance record over the past 10 years in comparison to a broad market index. They must also state in the prospectus how their performance was affected by market conditions.

If a mutual fund distributes at least 90 percent of its taxable income to shareholders, it is exempt from taxes on dividends, interest, and capital gains distributed to shareholders. The shareholders are, of course, subject to taxation on these forms of income.

Information Contained in a Prospectus

A mutual fund prospectus contains the following information:

1. The minimum amount of investment required.
2. The investment objective of the mutual fund.
3. The return on the fund over the past year, the past three years, and the past five years.
4. The exposure of the mutual fund to various types of risk.
5. The services (such as check writing, ability to transfer money by telephone, etc.) offered by the mutual fund.
6. The fees incurred by the mutual fund (such as management fees) that are passed on to the investors.

Estimating the Net Asset Value

The **net asset value (NAV)** of a mutual fund indicates the value per share. It is estimated each day by first determining the market value of all securities comprising the mutual fund (any cash is also accounted for). Any interest or dividends accrued from the mutual fund are added to the market value. Then any expenses are subtracted, and the amount is divided by the number of shares of the fund outstanding.

ILLUSTRATION Newark Mutual Fund has 20 million shares issued to its investors. It used the proceeds to buy stock of 55 different firms. A partial list of its stock holdings is shown below:

Name of Stock	Number of Shares	Prevailing Share Price	Market Value
Aztec Co.	10,000	$40	$ 400,000
Caldero, Inc.	20,000	30	600,000
⋮	⋮	⋮	⋮
Zurkin, Inc.	8,000	70	560,000
Total market value of shares today			$500,020,000
+ Interest and dividends received today			+10,000
− Expenses incurred today			−30,000
= Market value of fund			=$500,000,000

$$\text{Net asset value} = \text{Market value of fund/number of shares}$$
$$= \$500{,}000{,}000/20{,}000{,}000$$
$$= \$25 \text{ per share} \ \blacksquare$$

The SEC monitors the reporting of the NAV by mutual funds. When a mutual fund pays its shareholders dividends, its NAV declines by the per-share amount of the dividend payout.

Distributions to Shareholders

Mutual funds can generate returns to their shareholders in three ways. First, they can pass on any earned income (from dividends or coupon payments) as dividend payments to the shareholders. Second, they distribute the capital gains resulting from the sale of securities within the fund. A third type of return to shareholders is through mutual fund share price appreciation. As the market value of a fund's security holdings increases, the fund's NAV increases, and the shareholders benefit when they sell their mutual fund shares.

Although investors in a mutual fund directly benefit from any returns generated by the fund, they are also directly affected if the portfolio generates losses. Because they own the shares of the fund, there is no other group of shareholders to whom the fund must be accountable. This differs from commercial banks and stock-owned savings institutions, which obtain their deposits from one group of investors and sell shares of stock to another.

Mutual Fund Classifications

Mutual funds are commonly classified as stock (or equity) mutual funds, bond mutual funds, or money market mutual funds, depending on the types of securities in which they invest. The distribution of investments in these three classes of mutual funds is shown in Exhibit 23.2. Stock funds are dominant when measured by the market value of total assets among mutual funds. Many investment companies offer a family of many different mutual funds so that they can accommodate the diverse preferences of investors. With one phone call, an investor can normally transfer money from one mutual fund to another within the same family.

Exhibit 23.2
Distribution of
Investment in Mutual
Funds

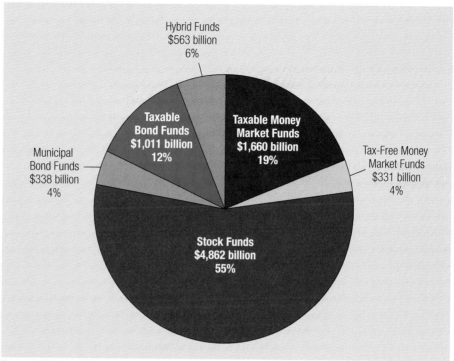

Source: *2007 Mutual Fund Fact Book.*

Management of Mutual Funds

Each mutual fund is managed by one or more portfolio managers, who must focus on the stated investment objective of that fund. These managers tend to purchase stocks in large blocks. They prefer liquid securities that can easily be sold in the secondary market at any time. Since open-end mutual funds allow shareholders to buy shares at any time, their managers continuously seek new investments. They may maintain a small amount of cash for liquidity purposes. If there are more redemptions than sales of shares at a given point in time, the managers can use the cash to cover the redemptions. If the cash is not sufficient to cover the redemptions, they sell some of their holdings of securities to obtain the cash they need.

Since closed-end funds are closed to new investment or redemptions by shareholders, their portfolio managers do not need to plan for new investment. In addition, they do not need to hold cash because the fund does not allow redemptions. Shareholders of closed-end funds sell their shares in the secondary market rather than redeem their shares with the fund.

Expenses Incurred by Shareholders

Mutual funds pass on their expenses to their shareholders. The expenses include compensation to the portfolio managers and other employees, research support and investment advice, record-keeping and clerical fees, and marketing fees. Some mutual funds have recently increased their focus on marketing, but marketing does not necessarily enable a mutual fund to achieve high performance relative to the market or other mutual funds. In fact, marketing expenses increase the expenses that are passed on to the mutual fund's shareholders.

Expenses can be compared among mutual funds by measuring the expense ratio, which is equal to the annual expenses per share divided by the fund's NAV. An expense ratio of 2 percent in a given year means that shareholders incur annual expenses reflecting 2 percent of the value of the fund. Many mutual funds have an expense ratio between 1 and 2 percent. A high expense ratio can have a major impact on the returns generated by a mutual fund for its shareholders over time.

ILLUSTRATION Consider two mutual funds, each of which generates a return on its portfolio of 9.2 percent per year, ignoring expenses. One mutual fund has an expense ratio of 3.2 percent, so its actual return to shareholders is 6 percent per year. The other mutual fund has an expense ratio of 0.2 percent per year (some mutual funds have expense ratios at this level), so its actual return to shareholders is 9 percent per year. Assume you have $10,000 to invest. Exhibit 23.3 compares the accumulated value of your shares over time between the two mutual funds. After five years, the value of the mutual fund with the low expense ratio is about 20 percent higher than the value of the mutual fund with the high expense ratio. After 10 years, its value is about 40 percent more than the value of the mutual fund with the high expense ratio. After 20 years, its value is about 87 percent more. Even though both mutual funds had the same return on investment when ignoring expenses, the returns to shareholders after expenses are very different because of the difference in expenses charged. ■

http://

http://www.sec.gov/answers/mffees.htm
Detailed information about fees charged by mutual funds to shareholders.

Thus, the higher the expense ratio, the lower the return for a given level of portfolio performance. Mutual funds with lower expense ratios tend to outperform others that have a similar investment objective. That is, funds with higher expenses are generally unable to generate higher returns that could offset those expenses. Since expenses can vary substantially among mutual funds, investors should review the annual expenses of any fund before making an investment.

Sales Load

Mutual funds can also be classified as either **load,** meaning that there is a sales charge, or **no-load,** meaning that the funds are promoted strictly by the mutual fund of concern. Load funds are promoted by registered representatives of brokerage firms, who earn a sales charge typically ranging between 3 percent and 8.5 percent. Investors in a load fund pay this charge through the difference between the bid and ask prices of the load fund. Loads, commissions, and bid-ask spreads are not included in the expense ratio of a mutual fund.

Exhibit 23.3
How the Accumulated Value Can Be Affected by Expenses (Assume Initial Investment of $10,000 and a Return before Expenses of 9.2%)

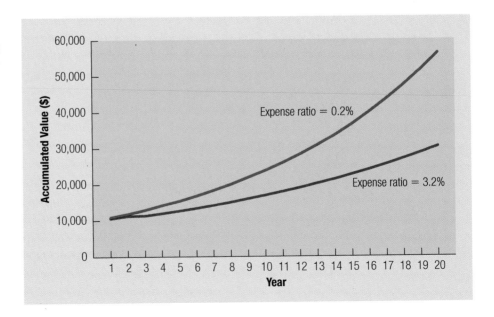

Some investors may feel that the sales charge is worthwhile, because the broker-age firm helps determine the type of fund that is appropriate for them. Other inves-tors who feel capable of making their own investment decisions often prefer to invest in no-load funds. Some no-load mutual funds can be purchased through a discount broker for a relatively low fee (such as 1 to 2 percent), although investors receive no advice from the discount broker.

ILLUSTRATION   As an example of the potential advantage of no-load funds, consider separate $10,000 investments in no-load and load funds. Assuming an 8.5 percent load fee, the actual investment in the load fund is $9,150. If the value of both funds grows by 10 percent per year, the investment in the no-load fund will be worth $2,204 more than the investment in the load fund after 10 years. ■

In recent years, some small no-load funds have become load funds because they could not attract investors without a large budget for national advertising. As a load fund, they will be recommended by various brokers and financial planners, who will earn a commission on any shares sold.

Types of Loads Mutual funds charge different types of loads: front-end loads and back-end loads.

A **front-end load** is paid only once, at the time you invest money in a mutual fund. The legal limit on front-end loads is 8.5 percent, but most funds charge 5.75 percent or less. Mutual funds with a front-end load often offer discounts like breakpoints, right of accumulation, letters of intent, or free transfers. Breakpoints are basically vol-ume discounts, which means that the percentage load becomes smaller as you invest more. Such discounts often start at $25,000. Many funds waive their loads entirely for investments of more than $1 million. A right of accumulation is a discount based on the total amount of money you invest in the fund family (as opposed to just the in-dividual fund). Letters of intent are often used for investors who invest only a small amount today but commit themselves to additional purchases over the next year. With this setup, the investor is entitled to the breakpoint discount today even though he or she has not yet invested enough money to actually qualify for it. Of course, if the in-vestor fails to invest the additional funds, the fund will retroactively collect the higher fee from the account. Free transfers allow investors to move money between funds with no additional load, provided the money stays in the same family.

A **back-end load** (also known as a rear load or reverse load) is a withdrawal fee as-sessed when you withdraw money from the mutual fund. Back-end loads are often be-tween 5 and 6 percent for the first year but decline by a certain percentage each sub-sequent year. Some mutual funds have features that can minimize the back-end load. For example, some funds permit investors to withdraw dividends and capital gains at any time without a charge. Other funds allow a certain percentage withdrawal of the investment each year without incurring a load. Also, many funds allow for free trans-fers within the fund family without incurring additional charges.

12b-1 Fees

In 1980, the SEC allowed mutual funds to charge shareholders a distribution fee, also called a 12b-1 fee in reference to SEC rule 12b-1. In some cases, funds have used the proceeds from 12b-1 fees to pay commissions to brokers whose clients invested in the fund. In essence, the fee substituted for the load (sales charge) that was directly charged to investors in load funds. A fund that states that it does not charge a sales load may charge shareholders 12b-1 fees and use the proceeds to pay commissions to brokers. Some shareholders who believe that they are not incurring a cost on a no-load fund do pay a commission indirectly through the 12b-1 fees. The fees are generally included in a fund's expense ratio as part of its marketing expenses. These fees are controversial because many mutual funds do not clarify how they use the money received from the fees.

Governance of Mutual Funds

A mutual fund is usually run by an investment company, whose owners are different from the shareholders in the mutual funds. In fact, some managers employed by mutual funds invest their money in the investment company rather than in the mutual funds that they manage. Thus, the investment company may have an incentive to charge high fees to the shareholders of the mutual fund. The expenses charged to the fund represent income generated by the investment company. Although valid expenses are incurred in running a mutual fund, the expenses charged by some investment companies may be excessive. Many mutual funds have grown substantially over time and should be able to capitalize on economies of scale. Nevertheless, their expense ratios have generally increased over time. Competition is expected to ensure that mutual funds will charge shareholders only reasonable expenses, but many investors are not aware of the expenses that they are charged.

Connection between Fees and Agency Problems The large fees at some mutual funds are due to agency problems. Managers of mutual funds are expected to serve their shareholders. However, they may focus on serving their own interests rather than those of shareholders. The managers provide very limited information about how they spend the money that they receive from fees. Since many mutual funds that charge high fees do not outperform funds with lower fees, the way they use the proceeds from the fees deserves to be questioned. Unfortunately, many shareholders do not recognize all the fees that they are charged by some mutual funds or how the fees affect the return on their investment. This may explain why some mutual funds that charge high fees continue to attract investments from shareholders.

Mutual funds, like corporations, are subject to some forms of governance that are intended to ensure that the managers are serving the shareholders. Each mutual fund has a board of directors who are supposed to represent the fund's shareholders. The effectiveness of the boards is questionable, however. The SEC requires that a majority of the directors of a mutual fund board be independent (not employed by the fund). However, an employee of the company can retire and qualify as an independent board member just two years later. In addition, the average annual compensation paid to the board members of large mutual funds exceeds $100,000. Thus, some board members may be willing to avoid confrontation with management if doing so enables them to keep their positions. This same criticism is also leveled at boards of publicly traded companies. Another problem is that board members of a mutual fund family commonly oversee all funds in the entire family. Consequently, they may concentrate on general issues that are not particular to any one fund and spend a relatively small amount of time on any individual fund within the family.

Mutual funds also have a compliance officer who is supposed to ensure that the fund's operations are in line with the fund's objective and guidelines for trading rules. Until recently, however, some compliance officers reported to the investment company instead of the mutual fund's board of directors. As a result of scandals, compliance officers are now reporting to the board.

Mutual Fund Scandals

BEHAVIORAL FINANCE In 2003, mutual funds received unfavorable publicity because some of the funds were allowing their large clients to buy or sell the fund's shares after the stock exchange's 4 P.M. closing but at the 4 P.M. prices. Thus, if favorable news about the market occurred after 4 P.M., the clients could buy fund shares at a price that was less than what was appropriate. This late trading, as it is called, is distinctly different from night trading (or after-hours trading) in the stock market where trades occur at prevailing market prices. Late trading of mutual funds involves engaging in a trade on prices that are "stale" or no longer appropriate. It is a clear violation of laws established by the SEC in 1968. Other shareholders of the mutual fund who were not able to trade on the inside information are adversely affected by these actions. The scandal was a major blow to mutual funds because they were commonly viewed as a safe way to diversify among firms and avoid exposure to possible scandals such as accounting irregularities that could affect a firm's stock price. Although many mutual funds were completely innocent, it was difficult for investors to identify the funds that had violated the rules.

As soon as this problem was publicized, the SEC began to investigate mutual funds and fined some of them heavily. The SEC was concerned that investors might come to mistrust all mutual funds (even those that were innocent) and withdraw their investments; massive redemptions could adversely affect the values of the securities that the funds invest in. Consequently, the SEC and other agencies of the federal government took steps to restore investor confidence in mutual funds including prosecuting managers of mutual funds who violated the rules. ∎

Corporate Control by Mutual Funds

http://www.fidelity.com
Links to information about mutual funds managed by Fidelity.

Regardless of whether mutual funds monitor their own management effectively, they have the power to monitor the management of the firms in which they invest. Since mutual funds invest large amounts of money in some stocks, they become major shareholders of firms. For example, Fidelity is the largest shareholder of more than 700 firms in which it owns stock. Portfolio managers of many mutual funds serve on the board of directors of various firms. Even when a fund's managers do not serve on a firm's board, the firm may still attempt to satisfy them so that they do not sell their holdings of the firm's stock. To illustrate the importance of mutual funds, Fidelity typically accounts for at least 5 percent of all the trading on the New York Stock Exchange on a given day. Fidelity is commonly one of the first institutional investors to be asked whether it wants to invest in a firm's new offerings of stock. Fidelity has more than 200 analysts who assess the financial condition of firms. Many firms discuss any major policy changes with analysts and portfolio managers of mutual funds to convince them that the changes should have a favorable effect on performance over time. In this way, a firm may discourage the funds from selling their holdings of the firm's stock and may even persuade them to purchase more.

Stock Mutual Fund Categories

Because investors have various objectives, no single portfolio can satisfy everyone. Consequently, a variety of stock mutual funds have been created. Investors select stock mutual funds with characteristics that fit their preferences. Some investors need mutual funds that can generate income, while others do not. Some investors want to earn a high return and are willing to tolerate a high level of risk, while others need a fund that is very conservative and offers more stable returns. The more popular categories include

- Growth funds
- Capital appreciation funds
- Growth and income funds
- International and global funds
- Specialty funds
- Index funds
- Multifund funds

Growth Funds

For investors who desire a high return and are willing to accept a moderate degree of risk, **growth funds** are appropriate. These funds are typically composed of stocks of companies that have not fully matured and are expected to grow at a higher than average rate in the future. The primary objective of a growth fund is to generate an increase in investment value, with less concern about the generation of steady income. Growth funds may entail different degrees of risk. Some concentrate on companies that have existed for several years but are still experiencing growth, while others concentrate on relatively young companies.

Capital Appreciation Funds

Also known as aggressive growth funds, **capital appreciation funds** are composed of stocks that have potential for very high growth but may also be unproven. These funds are suited to investors who are willing to risk a possible loss in value. As the economy changes, portfolio managers of capital appreciation funds constantly revise the portfolio composition to take full advantage of their expectations. They sometimes even use borrowed money to support their portfolios, thereby using leverage to increase their potential return and risk.

Growth and Income Funds

Some investors are looking for potential for capital appreciation along with some stability in income. For these investors, a **growth and income fund,** which contains a unique combination of growth stocks, high-dividend stocks, and fixed-income bonds, may be most appropriate.

International and Global Funds

GL🌐BALASPECTS In recent years, awareness of foreign securities has been increasing. Investors historically avoided foreign securities because of the high information and transaction costs associated with purchasing them and monitoring their performance. International mutual funds were created to enable investors to invest in foreign securities without incurring these excessive costs.

The returns on international stock mutual funds are affected not only by foreign companies' stock prices but also by the movements of the currencies that denominate these stocks. As a foreign currency's value strengthens against the U.S. dollar, the value of the foreign stock as measured in U.S. dollars increases. Thus, U.S. investors can benefit not only from higher stock prices but also from a strengthened foreign currency (against the dollar). Of course, they can also be adversely affected if the foreign currencies denominating the stocks depreciate.

An alternative to an international mutual fund is a global mutual fund, which includes some U.S. stocks in its portfolio. International and global mutual funds have historically included stocks from several different countries to limit the portfolio's exposure to economic conditions in any single foreign economy.

In recent years, some new international mutual funds have been designed to fully benefit from a particular emerging country or continent. Although the potential return from such a strategy is greater, so is the risk, because the entire portfolio value is sensitive to a single economy. For investors who prefer minimum transaction costs, mutual funds have begun to offer index funds. Each of these funds is intended to mirror a stock index of a particular country or group of countries. For example, Vanguard offers a fund representing a European stock index and a Pacific Basin stock index. Because these mutual funds simply attempt to mirror an existing stock index, they avoid the advisory and transaction costs that are common to other mutual funds. International funds are discussed further at the end of this chapter.

Mutual fund quotations like those shown here are provided by *The Wall Street Journal.* The sponsoring firms are identified in bold letters. The types of funds offered by the sponsor are listed below the sponsor name. The fund's net asset value (NAV) per share is disclosed for each mutual fund, along with the net change in NAV from the previous trading day, and the year-to-date (from the beginning of the year to the present) return. Investors use the information to monitor the performance of their existing investments or when they are considering investments in additional mutual funds.

Source: Reprinted with permission of Dow Jones & Company, Inc., from *The Wall Street Journal,* April 4, 2007; permission conveyed through the Copyright Clearance Center, Inc.

FUND	NAV	NET CHG	YTD %RET
TMMktwdVa	18.52	-0.01	3.6
TM USSmVa	26.14	-0.07	3.9
USLgCo	42.25	0.05	1.9
USLgVa	26.04	-0.01	3.3
US Micro	16.10	-0.02	2.6
US Small	22.07	-0.02	3.3
US SmCpVal	30.77	-0.08	4.2
Dodge & Cox			
Balanced	88.13	0.10	2.5
Income	12.60	...	1.4
Intl Stk	46.63	0.34	6.8
Stock	156.26	0.27	3.0
Dreyfus			
Aprec p	43.80	0.08	0.1
Dr500In t	40.74	0.05	1.9
Eaton Vance Class A			
LgCpVal	21.60	0.02	3.8
NatlMuni	11.88	...	0.6
Evergreen A			
AstAllA p	14.82	0.03	2.0
Evergreen C			
AstAllC t	14.37	0.04	1.9
Evergreen I			
CorBdl	10.46	0.01	1.6
Excelsior Funds			
ValRestr	55.24	0.14	5.1
Fairholme	29.98	0.10	3.4

Specialty Funds

Some mutual funds, called **specialty funds,** focus on a group of companies sharing a particular characteristic. For example, there are industry-specific funds such as energy, banking, and high-tech funds. Some funds include only stocks of firms that are likely takeover targets. Other mutual funds specialize in options or other commodities, such as precious metals. There are even mutual funds that invest only in socially conscious firms. The risk of specialty funds varies with the particular characteristics of each fund.

Some specialty funds focus their investment on Internet companies. Internet funds performed extremely well in the late 1990s when stock prices of Internet companies surged, but poorly in the 2000–2002 period. Investors who want to invest in technology but do not have any insight about specific companies commonly invest in these mutual funds.

Index Funds

Some mutual funds are designed to simply match the performance of an existing stock index. For example, Vanguard offers an **index fund** that is designed to match the S&P 500 index. Index funds are composed of stocks that, in aggregate, are expected to move in line with a specific index. They contain many of the same stocks contained in the corresponding index and tend to have very low expenses because they require little portfolio management and execute a relatively small number of transactions.

Index funds have become very popular over time as investors recognize that most mutual funds do not outperform indexes. Furthermore, investors benefit because the expenses of index funds are much lower than the expenses of actively managed mutual funds. Index funds are very similar to exchange-traded funds. The primary difference is that index funds are not traded throughout the day, whereas ETFs are.

Multifund Funds

In recent years, **multifund mutual funds** have been created. A multifund mutual fund's portfolio managers invest in a portfolio of different mutual funds. A multifund mutual fund achieves even more diversification than a typical mutual fund, because it contains several mutual funds. However, investors incur two types of management expenses: (1) the expenses of managing each individual mutual fund and (2) the expenses of managing the multifund mutual fund.

Bond Mutual Fund Categories

Investors in bonds are primarily concerned about interest rate risk, credit (default) risk, and tax implications. Thus, most bond funds can be classified according to either their maturities (which affect interest rate risk) or the type of bond issuers (which affects credit risk and taxes incurred).

Income Funds

For investors who are mainly concerned with stability of income rather than capital appreciation, **income funds** are appropriate. These funds are usually composed of bonds that offer periodic coupon payments and vary in exposure to risk. Income funds composed of only corporate bonds are susceptible to credit risk, while those composed of only Treasury bonds are not. A third type of income fund contains bonds backed by government agencies, such as the Government National Mortgage Association (GNMA, or Ginnie Mae). These funds are normally perceived to be less risky than a fund containing corporate bonds. Those income funds exhibiting more credit risk will offer a higher potential return, other things being equal.

The market values of even medium-term income funds are quite volatile over time because of their sensitivity to interest rate movements. Thus, income funds are best suited for investors who rely on the fund for periodic income and plan to maintain the fund over a long period of time.

Tax-Free Funds

Investors in high tax brackets have historically purchased municipal bonds as a way to avoid taxes. Because these bonds are susceptible to default, a diversified portfolio is desirable. Mutual funds containing municipal bonds allow investors in high tax brackets with even small amounts of money to avoid taxes while maintaining a low degree of credit risk.

High-Yield (Junk) Bond Funds

Investors desiring high returns and willing to incur high risk may wish to consider bond portfolios with at least two-thirds of the bonds rated below Baa by Moody's or BBB by Standard & Poor's. These portfolios are sometimes referred to as **high-yield (or junk bond) funds.** Typically, the bonds were issued by highly leveraged firms. The issuing firm's ability to repay the bonds is very sensitive to economic conditions.

International and Global Bond Funds

GL◯BALASPECTS International bond funds contain bonds issued by corporations or governments based in other countries. Global bond funds differ from international bond funds in that they contain U.S. as well as foreign bonds. Global funds may be more appropriate for investors who want a fund that includes U.S. bonds within a diversified portfolio, whereas investors in international bond funds may already have a sufficient investment in U.S. bonds and prefer a fund that focuses entirely on foreign bonds.

International and global bond funds provide U.S. investors with an easy way to invest in foreign bonds. However, these funds are subject to risk. Like bond funds containing U.S. bonds, these funds are subject to credit risk, based on the financial position of the corporations or governments that issued the bonds. They are also subject to interest rate risk, as the bond prices are inversely related to the interest rate movements in the currency denominating each bond. These funds are also subject to exchange rate risk, as the NAV of the funds is determined by translating the foreign bond holdings to dollars. Thus, when the foreign currency denominating the bonds weakens, the translated dollar value of those bonds will decrease.

Maturity Classifications

Since the interest rate sensitivity of bonds is dependent on the maturity, bond funds are commonly segmented according to the maturities of the bonds they contain. Intermediate-term bond funds invest in bonds with 5 to 10 years remaining until maturity. Long-term bond funds typically contain bonds with 15 to 30 years until maturity. The bonds in these funds normally have a higher yield to maturity and are more sensitive to interest rate movements than the bonds in intermediate-term funds. For a given type of bond fund classification (such as municipal or tax-free), various alternatives with different maturity characteristics are available, so investors can select a fund with the desired exposure to interest rate risk.

The variety of bond funds available can satisfy investors who desire combinations of the features described here. For example, investors who are concerned about interest rate risk and credit risk could invest in bond funds that focus on Treasury bonds with intermediate terms to maturity. Investors who expect interest rates to decline but are concerned about credit risk could invest in a long-term Treasury bond fund. Investors who expect interest rates to decline and are not concerned about credit risk may invest in high-yield bond funds. Investors who wish to avoid federal taxes on interest income and are concerned about interest rate risk may consider short-term municipal bond funds.

Asset Allocation Funds

Asset allocation funds contain a variety of investments (such as stocks, bonds, and money market securities). The portfolio managers adjust the compositions of these funds in response to expectations. For example, a given asset allocation fund will tend to concentrate more heavily on bonds if interest rates are expected to decline; it will focus on stocks if a strong stock market is expected. These funds may even concentrate on international securities if the portfolio managers forecast favorable economic conditions in foreign countries.

Growth and Size of Mutual Funds

Exhibit 23.4 shows how the number of mutual funds has grown over time. The number of stock and bond funds is substantially larger than it was during the 1980s. The popularity of stock funds is mainly due to the stock market boom periods that occurred during the 1990s, along with the relatively low returns offered by alternative short-term securities. The relative growth of investment in stock mutual funds versus bond mutual funds is illustrated in Exhibit 23.5, based on asset size. In the 1980s, investment in bond funds exceeded that of stock funds, but since the mid-1990s, investment in stock funds was higher, as investors substantially increased their investment in stock funds in response to unusually high returns in the stock market.

Growth funds, income funds, international and global funds, and long-term municipal bond funds are the most popular types of funds. Growth and income funds are

Exhibit 23.4   Growth in the Number of Stock Funds and Bond Funds

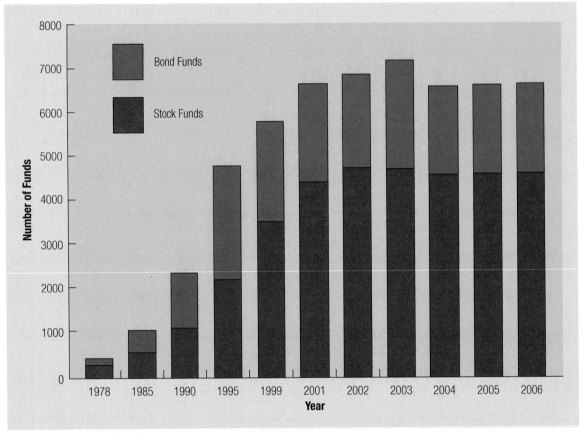

Source: *2007 Mutual Fund Fact Book.*

the most popular when measured according to total assets. Although mutual funds originally targeted more conservative investors, new kinds of funds have recently been created to accommodate all types of investors. Exhibit 23.6 shows the composition of all mutual fund assets in aggregate. Common stocks are clearly the dominant asset maintained by mutual funds.

Performance of Mutual Funds

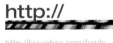

http://biz.yahoo.com/funds
Links to information about
mutual funds, including a list
of the top-performing funds.

Investors in mutual funds closely monitor the performance of these funds. They also monitor the performance of other mutual funds in which they may invest in the future. In addition, portfolio managers of a mutual fund closely monitor its performance, as their compensation is typically influenced by the performance level.

Performance of Stock Mutual Funds

The change in the performance (measured by risk-adjusted returns) of an open-end mutual fund focusing on stocks can be modeled as

$$\Delta\text{PERF} = f(\Delta\text{MKT}, \Delta\text{SECTOR}, \Delta\text{MANAB})$$

where MKT represents general stock market conditions, SECTOR represents conditions in the specific sector (if there is one) on which the mutual fund is focused, and MANAB represents the abilities of the mutual fund's management.

Exhibit 23.5
Investment in Bond and
Stock Mutual Funds

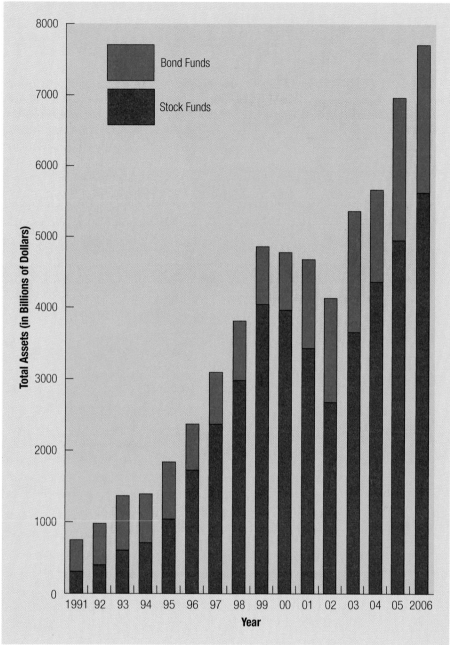

Source: *2007 Mutual Fund Fact Book.*

Change in Market Conditions A mutual fund's performance is usually closely related to market conditions. In fact, some mutual funds (index funds) attempt to resemble a particular stock market index. During the late 1990s, most mutual funds focusing on U.S. stocks experienced high performance because the U.S. market experienced high performance. Conversely, mutual funds focusing on Asian stocks experienced weak performance in the late 1990s because the Asian markets experienced weak performance. In the 2001–2002 period, weak economic conditions caused a major decline in stock prices, and most stock mutual funds performed poorly.

Exhibit 23.6
Distribution of
Aggregate Mutual
Fund Assets

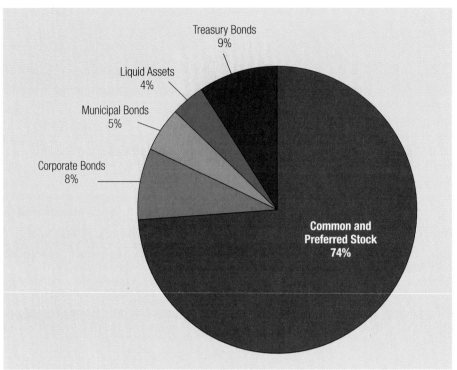

Source: *2007 Mutual Fund Fact Book.*

The attack on the United States on September 11, 2001, weakened economic conditions and caused stock prices to continue their decline. Stock valuations were weak because expected cash flows of firms had been reduced and were subject to much uncertainty. Since most stocks were adversely affected by the crisis, most mutual funds were adversely affected as well. Mutual funds that had a high concentration of travel services stocks or insurance stocks experienced larger declines in their prices. Even international mutual funds were adversely affected because stocks of most countries experienced a decline in price immediately after September 11.

However, in the 2003–2007 period, stock prices increased substantially in response to more favorable economic conditions. Consequently, stock mutual funds performed very well during this period.

To measure the sensitivity of a mutual fund's exposure to market conditions, investors estimate its beta. A mutual fund's beta is estimated in the same manner as a stock's beta. Mutual funds with high betas are more sensitive to market conditions and therefore have more potential to benefit from favorable market conditions. If unfavorable market conditions occur, however, they are subject to a more pronounced decline in NAV.

Change in Sector Conditions The performance of a stock mutual fund focused on a specific sector is influenced by market conditions in that sector. Mutual funds focusing on small stocks had higher returns in the early 1990s, while mutual funds focusing on large stocks had higher returns in the late 1990s. When economic conditions weakened in 2001, small stocks typically performed worse, which resulted in very poor performance of growth funds.

In the late 1990s, many mutual funds that focused on U.S. technology stocks experienced very high performance because most technology companies performed well

The Wall Street Journal summarizes the performance of various types of mutual funds. Lipper, Inc. classifies mutual funds by size, growth objective, and other characteristics. It has created an index for each classification in order to monitor the performance of each type of mutual fund. Some of its popular indexes include large-cap growth, large-cap value, equity income, science and technology, international, and balanced. It has also created indexes for bond mutual funds. For each stock or bond index created by Lipper, The Wall Street Journal provides the closing price and the return on the index since the previous day, the previous week, and the beginning of the calendar year. Market participants can use this table to compare the performances of different types of mutual funds. All types of mutual funds are generally driven by market conditions, as can be verified by the high correlation in returns among the types of funds. Nevertheless, the returns vary among the types of funds. Some investors commonly shift from one type of fund to another, attempting to speculate on the type of fund that will perform better in the future.

Source: Reprinted with permission of Dow Jones & Company, Inc., from The Wall Street Journal, April 4, 2007; permission conveyed through the Copyright Clearance Center, Inc.

Lipper Indexes

Stock-Fund Indexes	PRELIM CLOSE	PERCENT CHANGE FROM		
		PREV CLOSE	WK AGO	DEC. 31
Large-Cap Growth	3709.45	+0.49	+2.46	+2.92
Large-Cap Core	2895.14	+0.16	+1.60	+2.21
Large-Cap Value	13483.03	+0.09	+1.53	+1.95
Multi-Cap Growth	3490.27	+0.24	+1.85	+3.12
Multi-Cap Core	9704.38	+0.27	+2.03	+3.38
Multi-Cap Value	5858.15	+0.13	+1.54	+2.06
Mid-Cap Growth	919.00	+0.34	+2.10	+6.71
Mid-Cap Core	948.27	+0.12	+1.59	+6.15
Mid-Cap Value	1484.86	+0.07	+1.62	+6.07
Small-Cap Growth	702.74	−0.01	+1.52	+4.69
Small-Cap Core	564.71	+0.03	+1.69	+4.50
Small-Cap Value	944.86	−0.14	+1.59	+4.31
Equity Income Fd	5883.48	+0.07	+1.53	+2.49
Science and Tech Fd	767.85	+0.51	+1.70	+3.18
International Fund	1382.22	+0.62	+2.72	+5.47
Balanced Fund	6433.75	+0.11	+1.07	+2.44
Bond-Fund Indexes				
Short Inv Grade	277.37	+0.03	+0.01	+1.50
Intmdt Inv Grade	339.64	+0.06	−0.06	+1.55
US Government	440.88	+0.06	−0.03	+1.44
GNMA	482.87	+0.03	+0.02	+1.43
Corp A-Rated Debt	1206.46	+0.07	−0.04	+1.46

Indexes are based on the largest funds within the same investment objective and do not include multiple share classes of similar funds.

Source: Lipper Inc.

during this period. In 2001, these funds generally performed poorly because most stocks in the technology sector experienced weak performance during this year. During the 2003–2007 period, energy stock funds performed very well because their component oil company stock prices rose substantially.

Change in Management Abilities In addition to market and sector conditions, a mutual fund's performance may also be affected by the abilities of its managers. Mutual funds in the same sector can have different performance levels because of differences in management abilities. If the portfolio managers of one mutual fund in the sector can select stocks that generate higher returns, that fund should generate higher returns. Also important is a mutual fund's operating efficiency, which affects the expenses incurred by the fund and therefore affects its value. A fund that is managed efficiently such that its expenses are low may be able to achieve higher returns for its shareholders even if its portfolio performance is about the same as other mutual funds in the same sector.

Performance of Closed-End Stock Funds

The performance of closed-end stock funds is essentially driven by the same factors that influence open-end (mutual) stock funds. In addition, however, the performance of closed-end stock funds is affected by a change in their premium or discount.

When the demand for a particular closed-end mutual fund is strong, the market price may be higher than its NAV; the fund is thus priced at a premium. When a closed-end fund's market price per share is less than the NAV per share, the fund is priced at a discount.

Some closed-end funds, especially those focusing on securities of a foreign country, can have large premiums or discounts relative to their NAVs. If a fund's premium increases relative to its NAV (or if its discount is reduced), the return to the fund's shareholders is increased. The main reason for a change in the discount or premium is a shift in the demand for shares of the fund. For example, when large stock markets are priced relatively high, more investors from those markets seek investments in smaller, foreign markets where prices of securities are lower. Investing in individual stocks in those markets can be difficult, however, because the respective governments may impose restrictions. In that case, investing in a closed-end fund representing foreign markets is an easier approach than investing in those countries, and investors' demand for those funds increases. Given the fixed supply of closed-end fund shares, a strong demand for those shares by investors can push the market price of the shares high above the NAV.

Some research has documented high returns from investing in closed-end funds that are priced at a large discount from their NAV, which suggests that closed-end funds with large discounts in price are undervalued. Applying this strategy will not always generate high risk-adjusted returns, however, because the market price of some closed-end funds with large discounts continues to decline over time (their discount becomes larger).

Performance of Bond Mutual Funds

The change in the performance of an open-end mutual fund focusing on bonds can be modeled as

$$\Delta \text{PERF} = f(\Delta R_f, \Delta RP, \text{CLASS}, \Delta \text{MANAB})$$

where R_f represents the risk-free rate, RP represents the risk premium, CLASS represents the classification of the bond fund, and MANAB represents the abilities of the fund's managers.

Change in the Risk-Free Rate The prices of bonds tend to be inversely related to changes in the risk-free interest rate. In periods when the risk-free interest rate declines substantially, the required rate of return by bondholders declines, and most bond funds perform well. Those bond funds that are focused on bonds with longer maturities are more exposed to changes in the risk-free rate.

Change in the Risk Premium The prices of bonds tend to decline in response to an increase in the risk premiums required by investors who purchase bonds. When economic conditions deteriorate, the risk premium required by bondholders usually increases, which results in a higher required rate of return (assuming no change in the risk-free rate) and lower prices on risky bonds. In periods when risk premiums increase, prices of risky bonds tend to decrease, and bond mutual funds focusing on risky bonds perform poorly.

Change in Management Abilities The performance levels of bond mutual funds in a specific bond classification can vary due to differences in the abilities of the funds' managers. If the portfolio managers of one bond fund in that classification can select bonds that generate higher returns, that bond fund should generate higher returns. Also important is a bond fund's operating efficiency, which affects the expenses incurred by the fund and therefore affects the fund's value. A bond fund that is managed efficiently such that its expenses are low may be able to achieve higher returns for its shareholders even if its portfolio performance is about the same as other bond mutual funds in the same classification.

Performance of Closed-End Bond Funds

The performance levels of closed-end bond funds are driven by the same factors that influence open-end (mutual) bond funds. In addition, though, the performance of closed-end bond funds is affected by a change in their premium or discount. If demand for a closed-end fund's shares is abnormally high or low, its discount or premium relative to its NAV may adjust, thereby affecting the fund's performance. Closed-end bond funds that focus on bonds in a foreign country are most susceptible to an abrupt shift in the premium or discount. Thus, the performance levels of those closed-end bond funds are most likely to be affected by shifts in the premium or discount.

Performance from Diversifying among Mutual Funds

The performance of any given mutual fund may be primarily driven by a single economic factor. For example, the performance of growth stock funds may be highly dependent on the stock market's performance (market risk). The performance of any bond mutual fund is highly dependent on interest rate movements (interest rate risk). The performance of any international mutual fund is influenced by the dollar's value (exchange rate risk). When all securities in a given mutual fund are similarly influenced by an underlying economic factor, the fund does not achieve full diversification benefits. For this reason, some investors diversify among different types of mutual funds so that only a portion of their entire investment is susceptible to a particular type of risk.

Diversification among types of mutual funds can substantially reduce the volatility of returns on the overall investment. The proportion of the entire investment allocated to each type of mutual fund may be based on the forecasts for the underlying factors that affect each fund's value. To achieve full diversification benefits, constraints can be imposed on the maximum proportion allocated to any one type of mutual fund.

Research on Stock Mutual Fund Performance

A variety of studies have attempted to assess mutual fund performance over time. Measuring mutual fund performance solely by return is not a valid test, because the return will likely be highly dependent on the performance of the stock and bond markets during the period of concern. An alternative measure of performance is to compare the mutual fund return to the return of some market index (such as the Dow Jones Industrial Average or the S&P 500 index).

Most studies that assess mutual fund performance find that mutual funds do not outperform the market, especially when accounting for the type of securities that each fund invests in. A study by Malkiel[1] found that mutual funds tend to underperform the market, even when the expenses incurred from owning mutual funds are ignored.

To appropriately evaluate a mutual fund's performance, risk should also be considered. Even when returns are adjusted to account for risk, mutual funds have, on the average, failed to outperform the market. These results may seem surprising, because the funds are managed by experienced portfolio managers, but many individual stock purchase decisions are also ultimately derived from the so-called expert advice of

[1]Burton G. Malkiel, "Returns from Investing in Mutual Funds 1971 to 1991," *Journal of Finance* (June 1995): 549–572.

investment companies that instruct their brokers on what securities to recommend. In addition, advocates of market efficiency suggest that beyond insider information, market prices should already reflect any good or bad characteristics of each stock, making it difficult to construct a portfolio whose risk-adjusted returns will consistently outperform the market. Even if mutual funds do not outperform the market, they can still be attractive to investors who wish to diversify and who prefer that a portfolio manager make their investment decisions.

Research on Bond Mutual Fund Performance

A study by Blake, Elton, and Gruber[2] assessed the performance of bond mutual funds. One of the objectives was to determine whether mutual fund managers make better investment decisions than other investors in the bond market. The researchers found that, in general, bond mutual funds underperformed bond indexes. Their general results remain, regardless of the models used for comparing performance. They also determined that bond mutual funds with higher expense ratios generated lower returns. Thus, they recommended that investors select bond mutual funds that have lower expense ratios. Given their results, the authors suggest the creation of additional bond index funds, because these funds can provide bond diversification for small investors without requiring large management fees. Overall, bond mutual funds may still appeal to investors, but investors should recognize that the managers of these funds have not been able to outperform the market. This conclusion is only a generalization, as some bond mutual funds have experienced very high performance.

The authors also assessed whether past performance of bond mutual funds served as an accurate predictor of future performance. They found no conclusive evidence that the past performance of bond mutual funds can serve as a valuable predictor of future performance.

Money Market Funds

Money market mutual funds, sometimes called money market funds (MMFs), are portfolios of money market (short-term) instruments constructed and managed by investment companies. The portfolio is divided into shares that are sold to individual investors. Because investors can participate in some MMFs with as little as $1,000, they are able to invest in money market instruments that they could not afford on their own. Most MMFs allow check-writing privileges, although there may be restrictions on the number of checks written per month or on the minimum amount of the check.

MMFs send periodic account statements to their shareholders to update them on any changes in their balance. They also send shareholders periodic updates on any changes in the asset portfolio composition, providing a breakdown of the names of securities and amounts held in the MMF portfolio.

Because the sponsoring investment company is willing to purchase MMFs back at any time, investors can liquidate their investment whenever they desire. In most years, additional sales exceed redemptions, allowing the companies to build their MMF portfolios by purchasing more securities. When redemptions exceed sales, the company accommodates the amount of excessive redemptions by selling some of the assets contained in the MMF portfolios.

Exhibit 23.7 illustrates the growth in assets of MMFs over time. As investors increase their investment in MMFs, the asset level increases. When economic conditions are weak, the investment in MMFs tends to increase, as investors become more concerned about the risk of stocks and bonds.

http://
http://www.imoneynet.com/
Detailed information about money market funds.

[2]Christopher R. Blake, Edwin J. Elton, and Martin J. Gruber, "The Performance of Bond Funds," *Journal of Business* (July 1993): 371-403.

Exhibit 23.7 Growth in Money Market Fund Assets

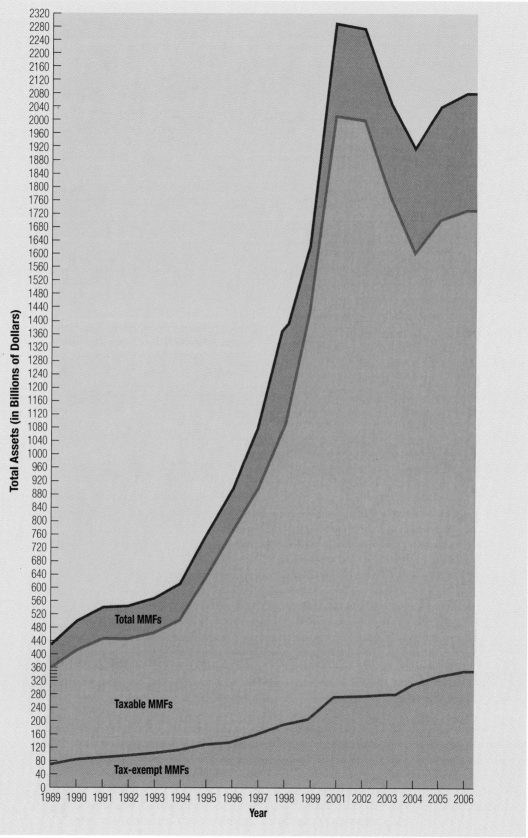

Source: *2007 Mutual Fund Fact Book.*

MMFs can be distinguished from one another and from other mutual funds by the composition, maturity, and risk of their assets. Each of these characteristics is described next.

Asset Composition of Money Market Funds

Exhibit 23.8 shows the composition of money market fund assets in aggregate. Commercial paper dominates, but repurchase agreements and Treasury securities are also popular. This composition reflects the importance of each type of asset for MMFs overall and does not represent the typical composition of any particular MMF. Each MMF is usually more concentrated in whatever assets reflect its objective. During recessionary periods, the proportion of Treasury bills in MMFs normally increases, and the proportion of the more risky money market securities decreases.

Maturity of Money Market Funds

Exhibit 23.9 shows the average maturity of MMFs over time. The average maturity is determined by individual asset maturities, weighted according to their relative value. In the mid-1970s, the average maturity was relatively long. As interest rates increased, yields of MMFs were slower to adjust, as the rates on existing assets were fixed. Those MMFs with shorter asset maturities were able to capitalize more quickly on higher interest rates. By the late 1970s, the average maturity on MMFs had declined to less than half of what it was during the mid-1970s. Thus, most MMFs were in a position to fully benefit from the very high short-term interest rates in 1981. During the 1980s, the average maturity of money market fund assets was about 40 days. The average maturity has generally increased since then.

Risk of Money Market Funds

From an investor's perspective, MMFs usually have a low level of credit risk. There may be some concern that an economic downturn could cause frequent defaults on commercial paper or that several banking failures could cause defaults on Eurodollar

Exhibit 23.8
Composition of Taxable Money Market Fund Assets in Aggregate

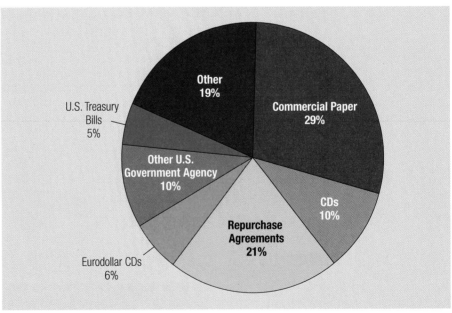

Source: *2007 Mutual Fund Fact Book.*

Exhibit 23.9 Weighted Average Maturity of Money Market Fund Assets

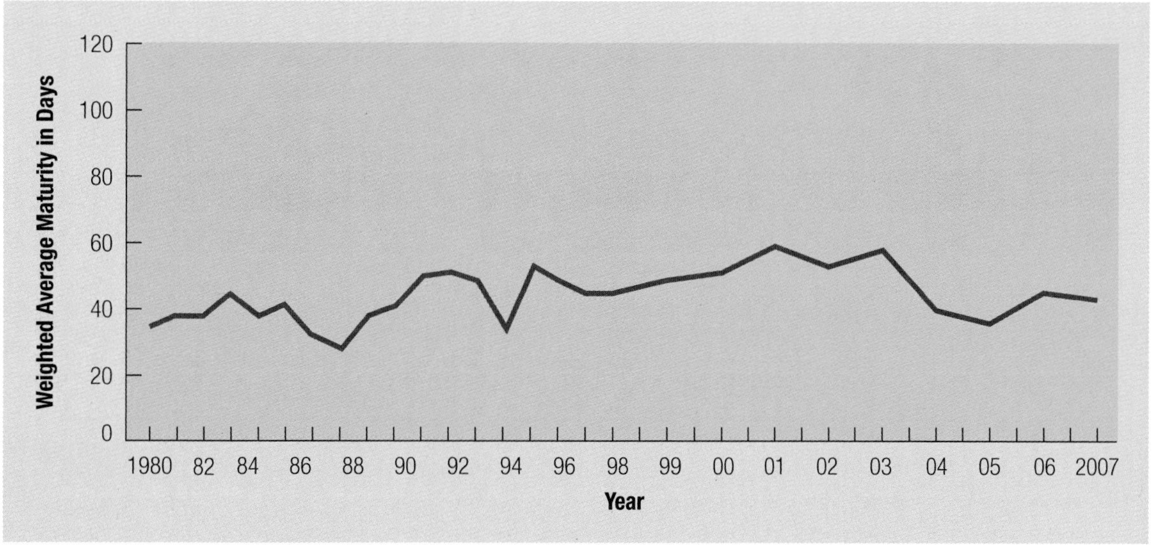

Source: *2007 Mutual Fund Fact Book.*

certificates of deposit and banker's acceptances. These instruments subject to credit risk have short-term maturities, however. Thus, MMFs can quickly shift away from securities issued by any particular corporations that may fail in the near future.

Because MMFs contain instruments with short-term maturities, their market values are not too sensitive to movements in market interest rates (as are mutual funds containing long-term bonds). Although the short-maturity characteristic is sometimes perceived as an advantage, it also causes the returns on MMFs to decline in response to decreasing market interest rates. For this reason, some investors choose to invest in an MMF offered by an investment company that also offers a bond mutual fund. During periods when interest rates are expected to decline, a portion of the investor's funds can be transferred from the MMF to the bond mutual fund upon the investor's request.

The expected returns on MMFs are low relative to bonds or stocks because of the following factors. First, the credit risk of MMFs is normally perceived to be lower than that of corporate bonds. Second, MMFs have less interest rate risk than bond funds. Third, they consistently generate positive returns over time, whereas bond and stock funds can experience negative returns. Because MMFs are normally characterized as having relatively low risk and low expected returns, they are popular among investors who need a conservative investment medium. Furthermore, they provide liquidity with their check-writing privileges.

Management of Money Market Funds

The role of MMF portfolio managers is to maintain an asset portfolio that satisfies the underlying objective of a fund. If the managers expect a stronger economy, they may replace maturing risk-free securities (Treasury bills) with more commercial paper or CDs. The return on these instruments will be higher but will not overexpose the fund to credit risk. For some MMFs there is very little flexibility in the composition. For example, some MMFs may as a rule maintain a high percentage of their investment in T-bills to assure investors that they will continue to refrain from risky securities.

Even if managers are unable to change the asset composition of MMFs, they can still influence performance by changing the maturities of the securities in which they invest. For example, if managers expect interest rates to increase in the future, they should use funds generated from maturing securities to purchase new securities with shorter maturities. The greater the degree to which a manager adjusts the average maturity of an MMF to capitalize on interest rate expectations, the greater the reward or penalty. If the expectation turns out to be correct, the MMF will yield relatively high returns, and vice versa.

Although individual investors and institutions do not manage the portfolio composition or maturity of an MMF, they have a variety of MMFs from which to choose. If they expect a strong economy, they may prefer an MMF that contains securities with some risk that offer higher returns than T-bills. If they expect interest rates to increase, they could invest in MMFs with a short average maturity. They are in a sense managing their investment by choosing an MMF with the characteristics they prefer. Some investment companies offer several MMFs, allowing investors to switch from one fund to another based on their expectations of economic conditions.

Regulation and Taxation of Money Market Funds

As a result of the Securities Act of 1933, sponsoring companies must provide full information on any MMFs they offer. In addition, they must provide potential investors with a current prospectus that describes the fund's investment policies and objectives. The Investment Company Act of 1940 contains numerous restrictions that prevent a conflict of interest by the fund's managers.

Earnings generated by an MMF are generally passed on to the fund's shareholders in the form of interest payments or converted into additional shares. If the fund distributes at least 90 percent of its income to its shareholders, the fund itself is exempt from federal taxation. This tax rule is designed to avoid double taxation. Although the fund can avoid federal taxes on its income, shareholders are subject to taxes on the income they receive, regardless of whether it is in the form of interest payments or additional shares.

Venture Capital and Private Equity Funds

Venture Capital (VC) funds and private equity funds use money that they receive from wealthy individuals and some institutional investors to invest in companies. They pool the money that is invested in the fund and use the proceeds to create a diversified equity portfolio. These funds typically require a large minimum investment (such as $100,000 or more) and therefore exclude small investors. Unlike mutual funds, VC and private equity funds typically invest in privately held firms rather than publicly traded firms, so their investments are not liquid. The investors in these funds recognize that their funds will be tied up for several years, because the funds cannot quickly sell the businesses that they buy.

The portfolio managers of these funds typically have some experience in running a business. A fund charges investors fees for managing the fund, such as 1 to 2 percent of the dollar value of its portfolio per year.

Venture Capital Funds

Venture capital funds invest in young, growing firms that need equity funding but are not ready or willing to go public. They may invest in businesses that are just being created, that have existed for only a few years, or that are in a later stage. More than half of all VC investing is in businesses that are being created.

Venture capital funds tend to focus on technology firms, which have the potential for high returns but also exhibit a high level of risk. Although many businesses want an equity investment from a VC fund, these funds invest in less than 1 percent of all the businesses that submit proposals. Sequoia Capital and Menlo Ventures are examples of popular VC funds.

When a VC fund provides equity funding, it becomes a partial owner and may expect to have some control (such as a seat on the board of directors) over the business. Thus, the portfolio managers who make investments for a VC fund may also be advisers to the business. Because VC funds invest in risky business ventures, a high percentage of their ventures fail. Even with a high failure rate, however, a fund can still perform well because some of its ventures may be major success stories. Many businesses that ultimately became famous, including Apple, Microsoft, and Oracle Corporation, were partially supported with venture capital in their earlier years.

A VC fund typically plans to exit from its original investment within about four to seven years. If the business goes public, the fund commonly can sell its stake (shares) in the secondary market between 6 and 24 months after the initial public offering (IPO). More than half of businesses that go public are partially backed by VC funds before the IPO. Many businesses backed by venture capital never become large enough to go public. They are typically acquired by other firms, and the VC funds receive payment for their stake in the business.

Private Equity Funds

Private equity funds pool money provided by individual and institutional investors and buy majority (or entire) stakes in businesses. Such a fund is usually created as a limited liability partnership, and the general partners develop a business plan for investing in businesses and managing the businesses that they acquire. They promote their business plan to attract funds from outside investors who become limited partners of the fund. Private equity funds appeal to institutional investors such as pension funds and insurance companies because they have the potential to earn very high returns. They also appeal to university endowments and individuals who can afford to invest $1 million or more. A private equity fund is typically closed to outside investors once it has reached its funding goal. The fund may be opened again to obtain more funding if it develops new plans for investing additional money. The fund managers commonly distribute 80 percent of the profits from their investments to their investors and retain 20 percent for themselves.

When a private equity fund purchases a business, it assumes control and is able to restructure the business in a manner that will improve its performance. These funds usually purchase private businesses, but sometimes they purchase public companies. They commonly purchase businesses that are struggling and have potential to improve. Thus, a private equity fund may purchase a business at a low price, restructure its operations to improve it, and sell the business for a much higher price than it paid. Examples of businesses purchased by private equity funds include Dunkin' Donuts, Hertz, La Quinta, and Neiman Marcus.

Among the most popular private equity funds are Blackstone, Permira, Apollo Investment, Providence Equity, Carlyle Partners, Kohlberg Kravis Roberts (KKR), and Texas Pacific Group. Each of these private equity funds has more than $10 billion in assets. At the other extreme, some private equity funds have less than $10 million in assets. Some major private equity funds are owned by commercial banks. Examples include Credit Suisse Private Equity and Barclays Private Equity. The United States has the largest market for private equity, followed by the United Kingdom, but private equity investments are increasing rapidly throughout Europe and Asia.

The Market for Private Equity Businesses The market for private businesses is not as efficient as the market for publicly traded stocks. Information about private businesses is very limited, so private equity fund managers may see opportunities to buy a business at a low price and improve it. The potential to capitalize on inefficiencies in this market has attracted much more investment in private equity and has led to the creation of many new private equity funds. In recent years, considerable money has flowed into private equity funds, as investors want to benefit from the high potential returns. Although private equity funds in aggregate raise more than $500 billion per year, these funds also commonly restructure the businesses they buy to rely on more debt financing. This enables them to use less equity per deal and to spread their investments across more deals. It also results in a higher degree of financial leverage for the businesses in which they invest. Thus, the funds can generate a higher rate of return on their equity investment from a given level of business profit, but the increased leverage increases the risk that the business will be unable to repay the debt.

A potential problem is that the large inflow of money into private equity funds could result in too much money chasing too few deals. The intense competition could cause some private equity funds to pay too much for some acquisitions in order to outbid competitors. This may result in a winner's curse, in which the winning bidders are cursed because they paid too much money for the target firms. It is more difficult for private equity firms to perform well in an environment in which there is intense competition with other bidders.

Vulture Funds A vulture fund is a type of private equity fund that purchases distressed assets of a firm that is in or near bankruptcy, or securities issued by such a firm. For example, a vulture fund may purchase the debt securities of a bankrupt firm at a steep discount. When a firm files for bankruptcy, its equity is commonly eliminated, and its creditors have claims on its assets. If the firm emerges from bankruptcy, the vulture fund will exchange some of its debt for equity in the firm and become the majority owner. The goal of the vulture fund will be to improve the firm's performance and thereby boost the value of its shares, so that the fund can ultimately sell its shares to other investors.

Views of Private Equity Funds

BEHAVIORAL FINANCE Private equity funds are viewed favorably because of their ability to improve weak businesses. Their investment in businesses is commonly intended to improve sales, increase profits, enhance efficiency, and increase value. Thus, private equity funds have the potential to generate high returns for their investors. Furthermore, some of the businesses they buy experience substantial growth and add new employees following private equity investment. Thus, private equity funds can stimulate economic growth and employment.

Some critics, however, suggest that private equity funds distribute too much of the return on their investment to their managers, and not enough to the investors. In addition, some private equity funds have performed poorly for their investors. Many of their investments might be viewed as excessively risky for pension funds, which manage money that will ultimately be allocated to support retirement for the people represented by the pension funds. Union lobbyists argue that private equity funds are too eager to fire employees after buying a company in order to achieve short-term efficiency, but at the expense of reducing the company's long-term performance. Social and environmental advocates are concerned that private equity funds may not consider the social and environmental consequences of the actions they take to enhance the value of businesses such as hospitals or casinos. ∎

Hedge Funds

As explained earlier in this chapter, hedge funds sell shares to wealthy individuals and financial institutions (such as pension funds) and use the proceeds to invest in securities. In recent years, some hedge funds have purchased businesses that they manage, similar to private equity funds. When hedge funds purchase securities, they are simply attempting to capitalize on a market inefficiency (improper market valuation of a security). When a hedge fund buys a business, it is attempting to capitalize on an inefficiency in the management of that firm. The fund either oversees or replaces the managers so that it can improve the performance of the business, with a goal of ultimately selling the business for a much higher price than it paid. In some cases, a hedge fund purchases distressed assets of a bankrupt firm, similar to a vulture fund.

Hedge funds have historically been unregulated, although they are not allowed to advertise. Most hedge funds are organized as limited partnerships. Many hedge funds allow investments only from individuals who have a net worth of $1 million or more. Some hedge funds permit investors to withdraw their investments, but require advance notice of 30 days or more. There are at least 9,000 hedge funds, with a combined market value of about $2 trillion. The investment strategies used by hedge funds include investing in derivative securities, selling stocks short, and using borrowed funds along with equity investments by investors to magnify returns on investment. Consequently, hedge funds strive for high returns, but also have a very high degree of risk. The performance of hedge funds is not publicized. Although some hedge funds have performed well, many have failed.

Hedge Fund Fees

Hedge funds charge a management fee of between 1 and 2 percent of the investment per year. In addition, they charge an incentive fee that is based on the return of the fund. The typical incentive fee is 20 percent of the return.

ILLUSTRATION

http://www.sec.gov/ answers/hedge.htm More information on hedge funds.

Consider a hedge fund that charges a management fee of 2 percent and an incentive fee of 20 percent of the annual return. In the most recent year, the fund earned a return of 15 percent. The investors in this fund would have paid an incentive fee of 3 percent (computed as 20 percent of the 15 percent return) along with a 2 percent management fee, or a total fee of 5 percent of their total investment. Considering that some index mutual funds have a very small management fee and no incentive fee, this hedge fund would have been a better investment only if its performance exceeded that of index funds by about 5 percent in that year. ■

Regulation

Hedge funds were not regulated until 2004, which allowed anyone who was capable of obtaining funds from investors to start one. In 2004, the SEC required that hedge funds register (starting in 2006). In fact, some individuals who have been charged with fraud when trading securities overseen by the SEC have become managers of hedge funds.

Financial Problems Experienced by Long-Term Capital Management

One of the best-known hedge funds was Long-Term Capital Management (LTCM), which was managed by a group of partners who had a very strong track record in the field of finance. In fact, two of its partners, Robert Merton and Myron Scholes (co-creator of the Black-Scholes pricing model for options), received the Nobel Prize in economics. LTCM was created in 1994 and earned relatively high returns in the mid-1990s, which caused more wealthy investors and financial institutions to invest in the fund.

LTCM relied heavily on quantitative models to identify pricing discrepancies in financial markets. For example, if the prices of two stocks that had historically moved together suddenly diverged, LTCM would consider purchasing the stock that had experienced the relatively weak price movement, while simultaneously selling short the stock that had experienced the relatively strong price movement. LTCM expected to benefit if the stock prices converged in the future. More commonly, LTCM applied this strategy to other securities by complementing an investment in one security with a short position in a derivatives contract representing the other security.

LTCM relied heavily on financial leverage to boost its returns. At times, it had about $30 in debt for every dollar of equity investment. By 1998, LTCM had about $5 billion in equity and $125 billion in debt to support its $130 billion portfolio, a ratio of $25 of debt for every dollar of equity. The overall leverage was actually higher than this because derivative positions magnify returns beyond the level of the underlying securities. From May to July of 1998, LTCM experienced losses of about 16 percent due to volatile market movements. In August 1998, Russia defaulted on some of its bonds, which aroused general concern about bond credit risk throughout the world. The prices of existing corporate bonds declined, as the risk premiums (reflected in the required rate of return of investors) on bonds increased. At the time, LTCM had investments in relatively risky bonds and short positions in AAA-rated bonds because it expected the spread between the yields to decline. The Russian bond default caused the risk premiums of the riskier bonds to increase much more than those of the AAA-rated bonds. Consequently, LTCM experienced a major loss. In August alone, it lost more than $2 billion or about 40 percent of its total capital; after accounting for the loss, its existing debt of $125 billion was about 50 times its remaining equity. On September 23, 1998, the Federal Reserve Bank of New York organized a rescue of LTCM by 14 large commercial banks and securities firms. These firms provided a capital infusion of $3.6 billion, which gave them a 90 percent stake in LTCM. The rescue plan was intended to prevent a default by LTCM on all of its positions, which could have caused the counterparties of those positions to lose billions of dollars. In addition, LTCM would have defaulted on some of its loans at a time when the debt markets had just recently been shaken by the Russian bond default; thus, a default by LTCM would have added to a potential international debt crisis. Asian countries were still suffering from the Asian crisis, and additional market paranoia would have resulted in more capital flows out of countries where funds were needed. Nevertheless, some critics suggest that LTCM was given preferential treatment because it was too big to fail.

As a result of the LTCM situation, regulators of several countries are considering ways to increase the regulation of hedge funds. For example, they may force commercial banks and other financial institutions that lend to hedge funds to retain a higher capital ratio on those loans.

Short Selling by Hedge Funds

BEHAVIORAL FINANCE One reason for the success of some hedge funds is that they can take a very large short position (selling stocks that they do not own) on overvalued stocks. Many institutional investors (including mutual funds) are commonly restricted from selling stocks short and therefore cannot attempt to capitalize when they believe specific stocks are overvalued. In addition, many individual investors do not sell stocks short because they do not fully understand the process. Given the limited number of investors who engage in short selling, there is much potential for hedge funds. In some cases, firms have issued misleading financial statements, causing their stock prices to be higher than their actual earnings justified. Hedge funds thoroughly investigate such firms, because a fund can earn very large returns by short-ing the stocks of these firms before other investors (and various regulators or credit agencies that attempt to detect financial fraud) recognize that the financial statements are misleading. For example, some hedge funds took large short positions in the stocks of Enron, Tyco, and Krispy Kreme. Once the media reported that the financial statements of these firms were questionable, the prices of these stocks declined, and the hedge funds closed out their positions.

Hedge funds are sometimes criticized for adversely affecting stocks prices by tak-ing large short positions. The hedge funds might counter that they are simply attempt-ing to capitalize on the market's excessive valuation of specific stocks. Furthermore, without their short selling, some stocks would be priced even higher until the market realized that the stocks were overvalued. In other words, the hedge funds would argue that the market is more efficient (or less inefficient) as a result of their short selling. ■

Hedge Funds of Funds

Since the minimum investment in some hedge funds may be $1 million or more, most small investors are unable to invest in them. However, some "hedge funds of funds" have been created to pool smaller investments by individuals and invest in hedge funds. For example, J.P. Morgan Multi-strategy Funds, which is sponsored by J.P. Morgan Alternative Investment Management, accepts minimum investments of $50,000 from individual investors. The fund pools their money so that it can invest in hedge funds that require much larger minimum investments. Thus, the investors who invest in this hedge fund of funds are essentially owners of a diversified set of hedge funds. The typical minimum investment to invest in a hedge fund of funds is between $25,000 and $100,000.

Performance The performance of hedge funds of funds is difficult to monitor because these funds do not have to report to the SEC. However, those that have re-ported to the SEC have generally experienced weaker performance than that of a ba-sic stock index fund. One reason for the weak performance is the high fees imposed on the investors. The sponsor of a fund of funds has a portfolio manager who decides how to allocate the money, and the costs incurred from that management are charged to investors. In addition, the money is invested in other hedge funds that also charge fees. Thus, investors in a hedge fund of funds essentially pay for two layers of fees re-sulting from the management of their money.

Real Estate Investment Trusts

A **real estate investment trust (REIT)** (pronounced "reet") is a closed-end mutual fund that invests in real estate or mortgages. Like other mutual funds, REITs allow small investors to participate with a low minimum investment. The funds are pooled to in-vest in mortgages and in commercial real estate. REITs generate income for share-holders by passing through rents on real estate or interest payments on mortgages. Most existing REITs can be sold on stock exchanges, which allow investors to sell them at any time. The composition of a REIT is determined by its portfolio manager, who is presumed to have expertise in real estate investments. In the early and mid-1970s, many of the mortgages held by REITs defaulted. Consequently, investors' in-terest in REITs declined. However, REITs have grown substantially since that time. Although the price of a REIT is somewhat influenced by its portfolio composition, it is basically determined by supply and demand. Even if the portfolio has performed well in the past, the REIT's share value may be low if investors are unwilling to invest in it.

REITs can be classified as **equity REITs,** which invest directly in properties, or **mortgage REITs,** which invest in mortgage and construction loans. A third type of REIT, called a hybrid, invests in both properties and mortgages.

Equity REITs are sometimes purchased to hedge against inflation, as rents tend to rise and property values rise with inflation. Their performance varies according to the perceived future value of the real estate held in each portfolio. REITs that have concentrated in potential high-growth properties are expected to generate a higher return than those with a more nationally diversified portfolio. However, they are also susceptible to more risk if the specific locations experience slow growth.

Because mortgage REITs essentially represent a fixed-income portfolio, their market value will be influenced by interest rate movements. As interest rates rise, the market value of mortgages declines, and therefore the demand for mortgage REITs declines. If interest rates are expected to decrease, mortgage REITs become more attractive.

Interaction with Other Financial Institutions

Mutual funds interact with various financial institutions, as described in Exhibit 23.10. They serve as an investment alternative for portfolio managers of financial institutions such as insurance companies and pension funds.

Some mutual funds are subsidiaries of commercial banks. At least 100 commercial banks such as Citigroup and Bank of America now offer mutual funds. This provides them with a means of retaining customer funds when customers wish to switch from bank deposits to stock or bond mutual funds. Since many customers periodically switch their savings between bank deposits and stocks (or bonds), commercial banks may be able to attract more funds in their mutual funds as they lose deposits, and vice versa. Their mutual funds also attract funds from investors who are not bank customers.

As interest rates declined in the 1990s and early 2000s, and investors withdrew deposits from commercial banks, they frequently invested the proceeds in mutual funds sold by subsidiaries of the banks. Some of these subsidiaries are conveniently located on the first floor of the bank, near the area where customers withdraw deposits.

Exhibit 23.10   Interaction between Mutual Funds and Other Financial Institutions

Type of Financial Institution	Interaction with Mutual Funds
Commercial banks and savings institutions (SIs)	• Money market mutual funds invest in certificates of deposit at banks and SIs and in commercial paper issued by bank holding companies. • Some commercial banks (such as Citigroup and J.P. Morgan Chase) have investment company subsidiaries that offer mutual funds. • Some stock and bond mutual funds invest in securities issued by banks and SIs.
Finance companies	• Some money market mutual funds invest in commercial paper issued by finance companies. • Some stock and bond mutual funds invest in stocks and bonds issued by finance companies.
Securities firms	• Mutual funds hire securities firms to execute security transactions for them. • Some mutual funds own a discount brokerage subsidiary that competes with other securities firms for brokerage services.
Insurance companies	• Some stock mutual funds invest in stocks issued by insurance companies. • Some insurance companies (such as Kemper) have investment company subsidiaries that offer mutual funds. • Some insurance companies invest in mutual funds.
Pension funds	• Pension fund portfolio managers invest in mutual funds.

Use of Financial Markets

Each type of mutual fund uses a particular financial market, as described in Exhibit 23.11. Because the main function of mutual funds is to invest, all securities markets are commonly used. The futures and options markets are also utilized to hedge against interest rate risk or market risk. Some specialized mutual funds sponsored by Morgan Stanley, Merrill Lynch, and other securities firms take speculative positions in futures contracts.

Many of the transactions by mutual funds in the financial markets finance economic growth, as illustrated in Exhibit 23.12. Mutual funds are major participants in stock and bond offerings and thereby finance corporate expansion. They are also major participants in bond offerings by the Treasury and municipalities and thereby finance government spending.

Exhibit 23.11   How Mutual Funds Utilize Financial Markets

Type of Market	How Mutual Funds Use That Market
Money markets	• Money market mutual funds invest in various money market instruments, such as Treasury bills, commercial paper, banker's acceptances, and certificates of deposit.
Bond markets	• Some bond mutual funds invest mostly in bonds issued by the U.S. Treasury or a government agency. Others invest in bonds issued by municipalities or firms. • Foreign bonds are sometimes included in a bond mutual fund portfolio.
Mortgage markets	• Some bond mutual funds invest in bonds issued by the Government National Mortgage Association (GNMA, or "Ginnie Mae"), which uses the proceeds to purchase mortgages that were originated by some financial institutions.
Stock markets	• Numerous stock mutual funds purchase stocks with various degrees of risk and potential return.
Futures markets	• Some bond mutual funds periodically attempt to hedge against interest rate risk by taking positions in interest rate futures contracts.
Options markets	• Some stock mutual funds periodically hedge specific stocks by taking positions in stock options. • Some mutual funds take positions in stock options for speculative purposes.
Swap markets	• Some bond mutual funds engage in interest rate swaps to hedge interest rate risk.

Exhibit 23.12   How Mutual Funds Finance Economic Growth

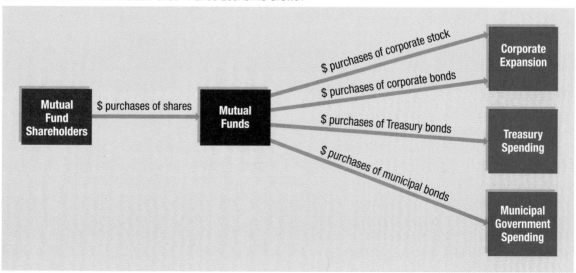

Globalization through Mutual Funds

GL🌐BALASPECTS International and global mutual funds have facilitated international capital flows and therefore have helped create a global securities market. They can reduce the excessive transaction costs that might be incurred by small investors who attempt to invest in foreign securities on their own. They also increase the degree of integration among stock markets. As international markets become more accessible, the volume of U.S. investment in foreign securities will become more sensitive to events and financial market conditions in those countries.

Mutual funds are popular not only in the United States but in other countries as well. The types of investment companies that sponsor mutual funds vary across countries. Insurance companies are the most common sponsor of mutual funds in the United Kingdom, while banks dominate in France, Germany, and Italy.

European countries have recently agreed to allow their respective mutual fund shares to be sold across their borders. The shares are under the supervision of their home country but are subject to marketing rules of the countries where they are being marketed. This deregulatory step in Europe may provide the momentum for other countries to do the same.

As a result of the North American Free Trade Agreement (NAFTA), qualified companies are allowed to sell mutual fund shares in Mexico. Consequently, many U.S. companies that commonly sponsor mutual funds, such as securities firms, commercial banks, and insurance companies, are generating new business in Mexico.

Summary

■ Mutual funds can be characterized as open-end funds (which are willing to repurchase their shares upon demand) or as closed-end funds (which do not repurchase the shares they sell). Mutual funds can also be characterized as load funds (which impose a sales charge) versus no-load funds (which do not impose a sales charge).

■ The more common types of mutual funds include capital appreciation funds, growth and income funds, income funds, tax-free funds, high-yield funds, international funds, global funds, asset allocation funds, and specialty funds.

■ Money market funds invest in short-term securities, such as commercial paper, repurchase agreements, CDs, and Treasury bills. The expected returns on MMFs are relatively low, but the risk levels are also low.

Point Counter-Point

Should Mutual Funds Be Subject to More Regulation?

Point No. Mutual funds can be monitored by their shareholders (just like many firms), and the shareholders can enforce governance.

Counter-Point Yes. Mutual funds need to be governed by regulators, because they are accountable for such a large amount of money. Without regulation, there could be massive withdrawals from mutual funds when unethical behavior by managers of mutual funds is publicized.

Who Is Correct? Use the Internet to learn more about this issue. Offer your own opinion on this issue.

Questions and Applications

1. **Mutual Fund Services** Explain why mutual funds are attractive to small investors. How can mutual funds generate returns to their shareholders?

2. **Open- versus Closed-End Funds** How do open-end mutual funds differ from closed-end mutual funds?

3. **Load versus No-Load Mutual Funds** Explain the difference between load and no-load mutual funds.

4. **Use of Funds** Like mutual funds, commercial banks and stock-owned savings institutions sell shares, but the proceeds received by mutual funds are used in a different way. Explain.

5. **Risk of Treasury Bond Funds** Support or refute the following statement: Investors can avoid all types of risk by purchasing a mutual fund that contains only Treasury bonds.

6. **Fund Selection** Describe the ideal mutual fund for investors who wish to generate tax-free income and also maintain a low degree of interest rate risk.

7. **Exposure to Exchange Rate Movements** Explain how changing foreign currency values can affect the performance of international mutual funds.

8. **Components of Mutual Funds** Considering all stock and bond mutual funds in aggregate, what type of security is dominant?

9. **Tax Effects on Mutual Funds** Explain how the income generated by a mutual fund is taxed when it distributes at least 90 percent of its taxable income to shareholders.

10. **Performance** According to research, have mutual funds outperformed the market? Explain. Would mutual funds be attractive to some investors even if they are not expected to outperform the market? Explain.

11. **Money Market Funds** How do money market funds differ from other types of mutual funds in terms of how they use the money invested by shareholders? Which security do money market funds invest in most often? How can a money market fund accommodate shareholders who wish to sell their shares when the amount of proceeds received from selling new shares is less than the amount needed?

12. **Risk of Money Market Funds** Explain the relative risk of the various types of securities in which a money market fund may invest.

13. **Risk of Mutual Funds** Is the value of a money market fund or a bond fund more susceptible to increasing interest rates? Explain.

14. **Diversification among Mutual Funds** Explain why diversification across different types of mutual funds is highly recommended.

15. **Tax Effects on Money Market Funds** Explain how the income generated by a money market fund is taxed if it distributes at least 90 percent of its income to shareholders.

16. **REITs** Explain the difference between equity REITs and mortgage REITs. Which type would likely be a better hedge against high inflation? Why?

Advanced Questions

17. **Comparing Management of Open- versus Closed-end Funds** Compare the management of a closed-end fund versus that of an open-end fund. Given the differences in the funds' characteristics, explain why the management of liquidity is different in the open-end fund as compared to the closed-end fund. Assume that the funds are the same size and have the same goal to invest in stocks and to earn a very high return. Which portfolio manager do you think will achieve a larger increase in the fund's net asset value? Explain.

18. **Selecting a Type of Mutual Fund** Consider the prevailing conditions that could affect the demand for stocks, including inflation, the economy, the budget deficit, the Fed's monetary policy, political conditions, and the general mood of investors. Based on current conditions, recommend a specific type of stock mutual fund that you think would perform well. Offer some logic to support your recommendation.

19. **Comparing Hedge Funds and Mutual Funds** Explain why hedge funds may be able to achieve higher returns for their investors than mutual funds. Explain why hedge funds and mutual funds may have different risks. When the market is overvalued, why might hedge funds be better able to capitalize on the excessive market optimism than mutual funds?

20. **How Private Equity Funds Can Improve Business Conditions** Describe private equity funds. How can they improve business conditions? Money that individual and institutional investors previously invested in stocks is now being invested in private

equity funds. Explain why this should result in improved business conditions.

21. **Source of Mutual Fund versus Private Equity Fund Returns** Equity mutual funds and private equity funds generate returns for their investors in different ways. Explain this difference. Which fund do you think would be better able to capitalize on a weak publicly traded firm that has ignored all forms of shareholder activism?

Interpreting Financial News

Interpret the following comments made by Wall Street analysts and portfolio managers:

a. "Just because a mutual fund earned a 20 percent return in one year, that does not mean that investors should rush into it. The fund's performance must be market adjusted."

b. "An international mutual fund's performance is subject to conditions beyond the fund manager's control."

c. "Small mutual funds will need to merge to compete with the major players in terms of efficiency."

Managing in Financial Markets

Investing in Mutual Funds As an individual investor, you are attempting to invest in a well-diversified portfolio of mutual funds so that you will be somewhat insulated from any type of economic shock that may occur.

a. An investment adviser recommends that you buy four different U.S. growth stock funds. Since these funds contain over 400 different U.S. stocks, the adviser says that you will be well insulated from any economic shocks. Do you agree? Explain.

b. A second investment adviser recommends that you invest in four different mutual funds that are focused on different countries in Europe. The adviser says that you will be completely insulated from U.S. economic conditions and that your portfolio will therefore have low risk. Do you agree? Explain.

c. A third investment adviser recommends that you avoid exposure to the stock markets by investing your money in four different U.S. bond funds. The adviser says that because bonds make fixed payments, these bond funds have very low risk. Do you agree? Explain.

Flow of Funds Exercise

How Mutual Funds Facilitate the Flow of Funds

Carson Company is considering a private placement of bonds with Venus Mutual Fund.

a. Explain the interaction between Carson and Venus. How would Venus serve Carson's needs, and how would Carson serve the needs of Venus?

b. Why does Carson interact with Venus Mutual Fund instead of trying to obtain the funds directly from individuals who invested in Venus Mutual Fund?

c. Would Venus Mutual Fund serve as a better monitor of Carson Company than the individuals who provided money to the mutual fund? Explain.

Internet/Excel Exercises

1. Assess today's mutual fund performance, using the website http://www.bloomberg.com/markets/. Click on "Mutual Funds." What is the best-performing mutual fund today in terms of the yield-to-date (YTD)? What is the net asset value (NAV) of this fund, and what is its YTD? What is the five-year return on this fund, and what is its YTD this year? Do you think mutual fund rankings change frequently? Why or why not?

2. Go to http://screen.yahoo.com/funds.html. Describe the constraints that you would impose when selecting funds. Impose those constraints on the

category, past performance, ratings, and other characteristics, and then allow the screener to screen the mutual funds for you. List one or more mutual funds that satisfied your criteria.

3. Go to http://finance.yahoo.com/, enter the symbol MVC Capital (for the closed-end fund MVC Capital that invests in U.S. stocks), and click on "Get Quotes." Click on "5y" just below the stock price trend to review the stock price movements over the last five years. Check the S&P box just above the graph and click on "Compare" in order to compare the trend of MVC's price with the movements

in the S&P stock index. Does it appear that MVC's performance is influenced by general stock market movements?

4. Go to http://finance.yahoo.com/, enter the symbol DNP (for the closed-end fund DNP Select Income Fund that invests in bonds), and click on "Get Quotes." Retrieve stock price data at the beginning of the last 20 quarters. Then go to http://research.stlouisfed.org/fred2/ and retrieve interest rate data at the beginning of the last 20 quarters for the three-month T-bill. Record the data on an Excel spreadsheet. Derive the quarterly return of DNP. Derive the quarterly change in the interest rate. Apply regression analysis in which the quarterly return of DNP is the dependent variable and the quarterly change in the interest rate is the independent variable (see Appendix B for more information about using regression analysis). Is there a positive or negative relationship between the interest rate movement and the stock return of DNP? Is the relationship significant? Offer an explanation for this relationship.

WSJ Exercise

Performance of Mutual Funds

Using an issue of *The Wall Street Journal*, summarize an article that discussed the recent performance of a specific mutual fund. Has this mutual fund's performance been better or worse than the norm? What reason is given for the particular level of performance?

Final Self-Exam

Final Review

Chapters 17 to 25 are focused on financial institutions. Here is a brief review of the chapters.

Chapter 17 explains how banks obtain most of their funds from deposits and allocate most of their funds toward loans or securities. Chapter 18 explains how banks are regulated according to the services they offer and the capital that they must maintain, and how regulators monitor their risk over time. Chapter 19 explains how banks manage their sources and uses of funds (within regulatory constraints) in a manner to achieve their return and risk preferences. Chapter 20 shows how a bank's performance is highly influenced by what it charges on loans versus what it pays on deposits (which affects its net interest margin), its income earned from services (noninterest income), and its level of noninterest expenses.

Chapter 21 explains that savings institutions are similar to banks in the manner by which they obtain funds, but use most of their funds to invest in mortgages or mortgage-related securities. This results in a higher exposure to interest rate risk, but savings institutions can hedge that risk. Chapter 22 explains that finance companies differ from banks and savings institutions in that they typically obtain their funds by issuing commercial paper and target their use of funds toward consumers or small businesses. In general, the credit risk of their assets is higher than that of commercial banks or savings institutions. Chapter 23 identifies the types of mutual funds and explains how the performance and risk vary across funds. In general, a mutual fund's asset portfolio is much more risky than other financial institutions. Chapter 24 describes how securities firms channel funds through financial markets. The investment banking portion of a securities firm places new securities with investors and thereby helps corporations obtain financing. The brokerage portion of a securities firm channels funds between investors in the secondary market. Chapter 25 explains how insurance companies obtain funds from the premiums they charge while pension funds rely on retirement contributions from employees or their respective employers. Insurance companies and pension funds are major investors in the bond and stock markets.

This self-exam allows you to test your understanding of some of the key concepts covered in the chapters on financial institutions. It does not replace the end-of-chapter questions nor does it cover all the concepts. It is simply intended to allow you to test yourself on a general overview of key concepts. Try to simulate taking an exam by answering the questions without using your book and your notes. The answers to this exam are provided at the end of the questions so that you can grade your exam. If you have any wrong answers, you should reread the related material and then redo any questions that you had wrong.

This exam may not necessarily match the level of rigor in your course. Your instructor may offer you specific information about how this Final Self-Exam relates to the coverage and rigor of the final exam in your course.

Final Self-Exam

1. Flagstaff Bank currently has assets heavily concentrated in secured loans and Treasury securities, while Mesa Bank has assets concentrated in consumer loans and credit card loans. The managerial capabilities of the two banks are similar. Mesa Bank's performance was much better than that of Flagstaff Bank last year, but Flagstaff Bank's performance is much better than that of Mesa Bank this year. Explain why the relative performance of the two banks is likely to change over time.

2. The Sarbanes-Oxley Act of 2002 requires publicly traded firms to be more transparent in their reporting. This may reduce the asymmetric information problem between firms (including banks) and their investors. Do you think Sarbanes-Oxley act will eliminate the need for CAMELS ratings?

3. Kentucky Bank has a new board of directors who believe that the bank has opportunities for major growth and want to ensure that the CEO makes good investment decisions to expand the bank's business. To give the CEO a strong incentive to perform well, the board set the CEO's quarterly compensation in line with the return on equity. The CEO immediately decided to repurchase as many shares as possible while barely meeting the bank's capital requirements. Why would the CEO take this action? Will the compensation structure remove agency problems?

4. Last year, Alabama Bank had a net interest margin of 3 percent, noninterest income was 1.5 percent of assets, noninterest expenses were 3 percent of assets, and loan loss reserves were .5 percent of assets. Alabama Bank wants to employ a strategy of using more of its resources to offer financial services. It expects that it can increase its noninterest income by .5 percent as a percentage of assets. What other components (or ratios) of the income statement may be affected by this strategy?

5. Maryland Savings Institution maintains most of its assets in fixed-rate mortgages of between 10 and 30 years. Most of its deposits have maturities of less than one year. Assume that the Fed implements a restrictive monetary policy.

   a. Explain how that monetary policy will affect interest rates.
   b. Assuming that interest rates change as expected, how will that affect the spread between interest revenue and interest expenses?
   c. Should Maryland hedge its asset portfolio, based on its expectations? If so, how should it hedge? If it should hedge, explain any limitations of the hedge.

6. How do financial institutions vary in terms of their main uses of funds?

7. Explain the role that insurance companies and pension funds play in financial markets.

8. Explain why a stock market benefits more when financial institutions are investors than when individual investors invest all their money directly into the stock market themselves.

9. Discuss the following: Money market funds attract money from investors who do not know what else to do with their money. Thus, money market funds are merely a last resort when there are no better alternatives for investment. Since

they invest only in short-term securities, they do not play a role in financing economic growth.

10. Closed-end funds tend to hold stocks that are less liquid than stocks held by open-end funds.

    a. Do you think this characteristic is an advantage for closed-end funds that want to achieve high returns?

    b. Why is it easier for closed-end funds to manage a portfolio of less liquid stocks than it would be for open-end funds?

11. Discuss the strategy of an investor who invests all of his money in four mutual funds that focus on growth companies. The investor believes he is fully insulated from market conditions because each fund contains 40 different stocks.

12. For a given type of mutual fund classification, what is a key characteristic that causes some mutual funds to outperform others?

13. When an investment bank serves as an underwriter for an initial public offering (IPO), is the bank working for the issuer or the institutional investors that may purchase shares? Explain the dilemma.

14. Do stock analysts reduce market inefficiencies?

15. Why might the value of an insurance company be affected by interest rate movements?

16. Should financial institutions be regulated in order to reduce their risk? Offer at least one argument for regulation and one argument against regulation.

17. Consider the typical sources and uses of funds at commercial banks, savings institutions, and securities firms. Explain the risk of each type of institution based on its typical sources and uses of funds.

Answers to Final Self-Exam

1. Under favorable economic conditions, Mesa Bank should perform better because it earns higher returns on its loans as long as the borrowers repay their loans (higher risk). Under unfavorable economic conditions, Flagstaff Bank should perform better because Mesa will likely experience many loan defaults, while Flagstaff will not.

2. Even if investors have more information, they may not be able to detect banks that have financial problems. In addition, CAMELS ratings are intended to detect financial problems of banks early so that there is time to correct the problems. This can prevent bank failures and therefore allow for a more stable banking system.

3. The stock repurchase will reduce equity so that the profits in the near future will result in a higher return on equity. This will enhance the CEO's compensation, but will not necessarily enhance the bank's value in the long run. In fact, the decreased equity will restrict the growth of the bank. Thus, this compensation structure will not remove agency problems.

4. Alabama Bank will incur more expenses when attempting to expand its financial services. This will increase the ratio of noninterest expenses to assets, and this increase could offset any increase in revenue.

5. a. Interest rates will rise.

    b. The spread will decrease because short-term deposit rates will increase, while long-term rates may not be affected as much or at all.

c. Maryland should hedge. It could sell interest rate futures. However, if it does sell interest rate futures and interest rates decline, it will incur a loss on its interest rate futures position, which may offset most of its gain from operations.

6. Commercial banks serve corporate borrowers, savings institutions serve homeowners, finance companies serve consumers and small businesses, while mutual funds, insurance companies, and pension funds serve corporate borrowers (investing in stocks and bonds and money market securities issued by corporations).

7. Insurance companies and pension funds are suppliers of funds and add much liquidity to the financial markets. They may also make the stock market more efficient because if a stock's price deviates from its fundamental value, they may take a position to capitalize on the discrepancy, and this should push the stock toward its fundamental value.

8. Institutional investors pool funds that come from many individuals and take much bigger stakes in a specific stock. Thus, the institutional investors have an incentive to make the correct investment choices (because of the large investment) and then to monitor the companies in which they invest. As a result, there is more governance over companies than if stocks were owned only by small investors.

9. Money market funds provide liquidity to investors, which is necessary even when investors have alternative investments that pay higher returns. In addition, money market funds play a major role in financing the budget deficit as they invest heavily in Treasury securities. They also channel funds to corporations in the form of commercial paper. Since the Treasury and corporations frequently reissue short-term securities, they are sometimes using the short-term securities to finance long-term investment.

10. a. The investment in illiquid stocks may be an advantage because it allows the closed-end funds to pursue stocks that are not followed by most investors. These stocks are more likely to be mispriced than other stocks.
    b. Closed-end funds do not have to accommodate redemptions whereas open-end funds do. Thus, closed-end funds do not need to worry about selling some of their stock holdings just for the purpose of satisfying redemptions.

11. These mutual funds will all be adversely affected during a weak economy because firms that have high growth potential will probably experience weak performance when economic conditions are weak. There is not sufficient demand under these conditions.

12. Mutual funds with a low expense ratio tend to perform better than those with higher expense ratios.

13. An investment bank attempts to satisfy the issuer of stock by ensuring that the price is sufficiently high, but it must also ensure that it can place all the shares. It also wants to satisfy investors who invest in the IPO. If the investors incur losses because they paid too much for the shares, they may not want to purchase any more stock from the underwriter in the future.

14. Some stock analysts may be able to detect when a specific stock is underpriced or overpriced in the market, and they can communicate their opinion through their stock ratings, which may cause investors to capitalize on the information. This could push stock prices closer to their fundamental values and reduce market inefficiencies. During the stock market bubble in the year 2000, however, analysts were overly optimistic about stocks and were not paying attention to fundamentals of the companies. Thus, they may have been a partial cause of the stock market bubble.

15. The value of an insurance company is partially influenced by the value of its asset portfolio. Its asset portfolio contains bonds. The market value of the bonds is inversely related to interest rate movements.

16. Regulation may be able to reduce failures of financial institutions, which may stabilize the financial system. The flow of funds into financial institutions will be larger if the people who provide the funds can trust that the financial institutions will not fail. However, regulation can also restrict competition. In some cases, it results in subsidies to financial institutions that are performing poorly. Thus, regulation can prevent firms from operating efficiently.

17. Commercial banks are exposed to default risk due to their commercial and consumer loans. They are exposed to interest rate risk because the maturities on some of their assets (especially bonds and some term loans) may be longer than the maturities on their liabilities. Savings institutions are exposed to default risk due to their mortgage loans (although these loans are normally backed by the home) and consumer loans. They are exposed to interest rate risk because the maturities on their fixed-rate mortgages are longer than the maturities on their liabilities. Securities firms are exposed to market risk from taking equity positions and to default risk when providing bridge loans. Their operations are especially sensitive to financial market activity. When financial transactions such as mergers and stock trades decline, their business declines because they serve as intermediaries for many types of financial transactions.

Comprehensive Project

One of the best ways to clearly understand the key concepts explained in this text is to apply them directly to actual situations. This comprehensive project enables you to apply numerous concepts regarding financial markets and institutions discussed throughout the text to actual situations. The tasks in this project can be categorized as follows:

Part I.   Applying "Financial Markets" concepts

Part II. Applying "Financial Institutions" concepts

Part III. Measuring Stock Performance

At the beginning of the school term, you should complete two tasks. First, compile the information on financial markets needed to fill in the blank spaces in steps (a) through (j) in Part I. This information will be needed when applying "Financial Markets" concepts in the questions that follow (Part I of the project). Second, obtain the information on financial institutions identified at the beginning of Part II below. This information will be needed when applying the "Financial Institutions" concepts in the questions that follow (Part II of the project).

Part I. Applying "Financial Markets" Concepts

The exercises on Financial Markets concepts require you to measure the change in the yields and values of securities over the school term and explain why the values changed. In doing so, you will apply the concepts in the chapters on financial markets to actual situations.

At the beginning of the school term and near the end of the term, use an issue of *The Wall Street Journal (WSJ)* or various financial websites to obtain the information requested here. Your professor will identify the dates to use as the beginning and end of the term. The dates will allow you sufficient time to assess the changes in the yields and values of securities so that you can answer the questions. Your professor will explain the specific format of the assignment, such as whether any parts are excluded or whether students should work in teams. Your professor will also indicate whether the answers will be handed in, presented to the class, or both. A commonly used format is to divide the project into parts and assign a team of students to present their answers to one specific part. Each student will be a member of one of the teams. All students may still be required to hand in answers to all parts of the project, even though their team's presentation focuses on only one part.

	Beginning of Term	End of Term

a. Lineup Stock Market Index Information:

S&P 500 (stock) index level: _____ _____

Nasdaq Composite (stock) index level: _____ _____

DJ World: _____ _____

b. Interest Rate Information:

Prime rate: _____ _____

Federal funds rate: _____ _____

Commercial paper rate (90 days): _____ _____

Certificate of deposit rate (3-month): _____ _____

Treasury bill rate (13 weeks): _____ _____

Treasury bill rate (26 weeks): _____ _____

c. Bond Yield Information:

Treasury long-term bond yield: _____ _____

DJ Corporate bond yield: _____ _____

Corporate (Master) bond yield: _____ _____

High-yield corporate bond yield: _____ _____

Tax-exempt (7–12 yr) bond yield: _____ _____

d. Use the Stock Exchange Quotations to record the stock price and dividend of one stock from each stock exchange in which you would like to invest:

New York Stock Exchange: Stock price: _____ _____

Name of firm _____ Dividend: _____ _____

American Stock Exchange: Stock price: _____ _____

Name of firm _____ Dividend: _____ _____

Nasdaq Market: Stock price: _____ _____

Name of firm _____ Dividend: _____ _____

e. Use the Futures Prices Quotations to record the recent ("settle") price of:

Treasury bond futures with the first settlement
   date beyond your school term: _____ _____

S&P 500 index futures with the first settlement
   date beyond your school term: _____ _____

British pound futures with the first settlement
   date beyond your school term: _____ _____

f.   Use an Options Quotations table to select a call option on a firm where you expect the stock price to increase (select the option with the first expiration month beyond the end of the school term):

Name of firm: _____

Expiration month: _____

Strike price: _____

Stock price: _____   _____

Option premium: _____   _____

g.   Use an Options Quotations table to select a put option on a firm where you expect the stock price to decrease (select the option with the first expiration month beyond the end of the school term):

Name of firm: _____

Expiration month: _____

Strike price: _____

Stock price: _____   _____

Option premium: _____   _____

h.   Use a Currency Exchange Rate table in the *WSJ* to record exchange rates:

Exchange rate of the British pound (in $):   _____   _____

Exchange rate of the Japanese yen (in $):   _____   _____

Exchange rate of the Mexican peso (in $):   _____   _____

i.   Use Currency Option data (if available) to select a call option on a foreign currency that you expect will strengthen against the dollar (select the option with the first expiration month beyond the end of the school term):

Currency: _____

Expiration month: _____

Strike price: _____

Currency's existing value: _____   _____

Option premium: _____   _____

j.   Use currency options data (if available) to select a put option on a foreign currency that you expect will weaken against the dollar (select the option with the first expiration month beyond the end of the school term):

Currency: _____

Expiration month: _____

Strike price: _____

Currency's existing value: _____   _____

Option premium: _____   _____

1. **Explaining changes in interest rates (from Chapter 2)**
   a. Compare the 13-week Treasury bill rate (which is a proxy for short-term interest rates) at the end of the school term to the rate that existed at the beginning of the school term.
   b. Recall that Chapter 2 offered reasons why interest rates change over time. Apply the concepts in that chapter to explain why you think that interest rates have changed over the school term.

2. **Comparing yields among securities (from Chapter 3)**
   a. What is the difference between the yield on corporate high-quality bonds and the yield on Treasury bonds as of the end of the school term?
   b. Apply the concepts discussed in Chapter 3 to explain why this premium exists.
   c. What is the difference between the yield on long-term Treasury bonds and the yield on long-term municipal bonds as of the end of the school term?
   d. Apply the concepts discussed in Chapter 3 to explain why this difference exists.

3. **Assessing the forecasting ability of the yield curve (from Chapter 3)**
   a. What was the difference between the 26-week T-bill yield and the 13-week T-bill yield at the beginning of the school term?
   b. Does this imply that the yield curve had an upward or downward slope at that time?
   c. Assuming that this slope can be primarily attributed to expectations theory, did the direction of the slope indicate that the market expected higher or lower interest rates in the future?
   d. Did interest rates move in that direction over the school term?

4. **Explaining shifts in the yield curve over time (from Chapter 3)**
   a. What was the difference between the long-term Treasury bond yield and the 13-week T-bill yield at the beginning of the school term?
   b. What is the difference between the long-term Treasury bond yield and the 13-week T-bill yield at the end of the school term?
   c. Given your answers to the two previous questions, describe how the yield curve changed over the school term. Explain the changes in expectations about future interest rates that are implied by the shift in the yield curve over the school term.

5. **The Fed's influence on interest rates (from Chapter 5)**
   a. Did the Fed change the federal funds rate over the school term?
   b. Do you think the movements in interest rates over the school term were caused by the Fed's monetary policy? Explain.

6. **Measuring and explaining premiums on money market securities (from Chapter 6)**
   a. What is the difference between the yield on 90-day commercial paper and the yield on 13-week T-bills as of the end of the school term? Apply the concepts discussed in Chapter 6 to explain why this premium exists.
   b. Compare the premium on the 90-day commercial paper yield (relative to the 13-week T-bill yield) that exists at the end of the school term to the premium that existed at the beginning of the term. Apply the concepts discussed in Chapter 6 to explain why the premium may have changed over the school term.

7. **Explaining bond premiums and price movements (from Chapter 8)**
   a. What is the difference between the yield on high-yield corporate bonds at the end of the school term versus the yield on high-quality corporate bonds as of

the beginning of the school term? Apply the concepts discussed in Chapter 8 to explain why this premium exists.

b. Compare the long-term Treasury bond yield at the end of the school term to the long-term Treasury bond yield that existed at the beginning of the school term. Given the direction of this change, did prices of long-term bonds rise or fall over the school term?

c. Compare the change in the yields of Treasury, municipal, and corporate bonds over the school term. Did the yields of all three types of securities move in the same direction and by about the same degree? Apply the concepts discussed in Chapter 8 to explain why yields of different types of bonds move together.

d. Compare the premium on high-yield corporate bonds (relative to Treasury bonds) at the beginning of the school term to the premium that existed at the end of the school term. Did the premium increase or decrease? Apply the concepts discussed in Chapter 8 to explain why this premium changed over the school term.

8. **Explaining mortgage rates (from Chapter 9)**

a. Compare the rate paid by a homeowner on a 30-year mortgage to the rate (yield) paid by the Treasury on long-term Treasury bonds as of the end of the school term. Explain the difference.

b. Compare the 30-year mortgage rate at the end of the school term to the 30-year mortgage rate that existed at the beginning of the school term. What do you think is the primary reason for the change in the 30-year mortgage rates over the school term?

9. **Explaining stock price movements (from Chapter 11)**

a. Determine the return on the stock market over your school term, based on the percentage change in the S&P 500 index level over the term. Annualize this return by multiplying the return times $(12/m)$, where m is the number of months in your school term. Apply concepts discussed in Chapter 11 to explain why the market return was high or low over your school term.

b. Repeat the previous question for smaller stocks by using the Nasdaq Composite instead of the S&P 500 index. What was the annualized return on the Nasdaq Composite over your school term?

c. Explain why the return on the Nasdaq Composite was high or low over your school term.

d. Determine the return over the school term on the stock in which you chose to invest. The return is $(P_t - P_{t-1} + D)/P_{t-1}$, where P_t is the stock price as of the end of the school term, P_{t-1} is the stock price at the beginning of the school term, and D is the dividend paid over the school term. In most cases, one quarterly dividend is paid over a school term, which is one-fourth of the annual dividend amount per share shown in stock quotation tables.

e. What was your return over the school term on the stock you selected from the New York Stock Exchange? What was your return over the school term on the stock you selected from the American Stock Exchange? What was your return over the school term on the stock you selected from the Nasdaq market? Apply the concepts discussed in Chapter 11 to explain why you think these three stocks experienced different returns over the school term.

10. **Measuring and explaining futures price movements (from Chapter 13)**

a. Assume that you purchased an S&P 500 futures contract at the beginning of the school term, with the first settlement date beyond the end of the school term. Also assume that you sold an S&P 500 futures contract with this same settlement date at the end of the school term. Given that this contract has a value of the futures price times $250, determine the difference between the dollar value of the contract you sold and the dollar amount of the contract that you purchased.

b. Assume that you invested an initial margin of 20 percent of the amount that you would owe to purchase the S&P 500 index at the settlement date. Measure your return from taking a position in the S&P 500 index futures as follows. Take the difference determined in the previous question (which represents the dollar amount of the gain on the futures position), and divide it by the amount you originally invested (the amount you originally invested is 20 percent of the dollar value of the futures contract that you purchased).

c. The return that you just derived in the previous question is not annualized. To annualize your return, multiply it by $(12/m)$, where m is the number of months in your school term.

d. Apply the concepts discussed in Chapter 13 to explain why your return on your S&P 500 index futures position was low or high over the school term.

e. Assume that you purchased a Treasury bond futures contract at the beginning of the school term with the first settlement date beyond the end of the school term. Also assume that you sold this same type of futures contract at the end of the school term. Recall that Treasury bond futures contracts are priced relative to a $100,000 face value, and the fractions are in thirty-seconds. What was the dollar value of the futures contract at the beginning of the school term when you purchased it?

f. What was the dollar value of the Treasury bond futures contract at the end of the school term when you sold it?

g. What was the difference between the dollar value of the Treasury bond futures contract when you sold it and the value when you purchased it?

h. Assume that you invested an initial margin of 20 percent of the amount that you would owe to purchase the Treasury bonds at settlement date. Your investment is equal to 20 percent of the dollar value of the Treasury bond futures contract as of the time you purchased the futures. Determine the return on your futures position, which is the difference you derived in the previous question as a percentage of your investment.

i. The return that you just derived in the previous question is not annualized. To annualize your return, multiply your return times $(12/m)$, where m is the number of months in your school term.

j. Apply the concepts discussed in Chapter 13 to explain why the return on your Treasury bond futures position was low or high.

11. Measuring and explaining option price movements (from Chapter 14)

a. Assume that you purchased a call option (representing 100 shares) on the specific stock that you identified in Part I (f) of this project. What was your return from purchasing this option? [Your return can be measured as $(\text{Prem}_t - \text{Prem}_{t-1})/\text{Prem}_{t-1}$, where Prem_{t-1} represents the premium paid at the beginning of the school term and Prem_t represents the premium at which the same option can be sold at the end of the school term.] If the premium for this option is not quoted at the end of the school term, measure the return as if you exercised the call option at the end of the school term (assuming that it is feasible to exercise the option at that time). That is, the return is based on purchasing the stock at the option's strike price and then selling the stock at its market price at the end of the school term.

b. Annualize the return on your option by multiplying the return you derived in the previous question by $(12/m)$, where m represents the number of months in your school term.

c. Compare the return on your call option to the return that you would have earned if you simply invested in the stock itself. Notice how the magnitude of the return on the call option is much larger than the magnitude of the return on the stock itself. That is, the gains are larger and the losses are larger when investing in call options on a stock instead of the stock itself.

d. Assume that you purchased a put option (representing 100 shares) on the specific stock that you identified in Part I (g) of this project. What was your return from purchasing this option? [Your return can be measured as $(\text{Prem}_t - \text{Prem}_{t-1})/\text{Prem}_{t-1}$, where Prem_{t-1} represents the premium paid at the beginning of the school term and Prem_t represents the premium at which the same option can be sold at the end of the school term.] If the premium for this option is not quoted at the end of the school term, measure the return as if you exercised the put option at the end of the school term (assuming that it is feasible to exercise the option at that time). That is, the return is based on purchasing the stock at its market price and then selling the stock at the option's strike price at the end of the school term.

12. **Determining swap payments (from Chapter 15)**
    a. Assume that at the beginning of the school term, you engaged in a fixed-for-floating rate swap in which you agreed to pay 6 percent in exchange for the prevailing 26-week T-bill rate that exists at the end of the school term. Assume that your swap agreement specifies the end of the school term as the only time at which a swap will occur, and that the notional amount is $10 million. Determine the amount that you owe on the swap, the amount you are owed on the swap, and the difference. Did you gain or lose as a result of the swap?

13. **Measuring and explaining exchange rate movements (from Chapter 16)**
    a. Determine the percentage change in the value of the British pound over the school term. Did the pound appreciate or depreciate against the dollar?
    b. Determine the percentage change in the value of the Japanese yen over the school term. Did the yen appreciate or depreciate against the dollar?
    c. Determine the percentage change in the value of the Mexican peso over the school term. Did the peso appreciate or depreciate against the dollar?
    d. Determine the per unit gain or loss if you had purchased British pound futures at the beginning of the term and sold British pound futures at the end of the term.
    e. Given that a single futures contract on British pounds represents 62,500 pounds, determine the dollar amount of your gain or loss.

Part II. Applying "Financial Institutions" Concepts

Obtain an annual report of (1) a commercial bank, (2) a savings and loan association, (3) an investment bank, and (4) an insurance company. The annual reports will allow you to relate the theory in specific related chapters to the particular financial institution of concern. The exercises in Part II of the Comprehensive Project require the use of these annual reports. The annual reports can be obtained by calling the Shareholder Services department for each financial institution, or they may be available online. Also, order a prospectus of a specific mutual fund in which you are interested. The prospectus can be obtained from the specific investment company that sponsors the mutual fund, or it may be available online.

1. **Commercial bank operations (from Chapter 17)**

   For the commercial bank that you selected at the beginning of the term, use its annual report or any other related information to answer the following questions:

   a. Identify the types of deposits that the commercial bank uses to obtain most of its funds.

   b. Identify the main uses of funds by the bank.

   c. Summarize any statements made by the commercial bank in its annual report about how recent or potential regulations will affect its performance.

   d. Does it appear that the bank is attempting to enter the securities industry by offering securities services? If so, explain how.

   e. Does it appear that the bank is attempting to enter the insurance industry by offering insurance services? If so, explain how.

2. **Commercial bank management (from Chapter 19)**

   For the commercial bank that you selected at the beginning of the term, use its annual report or any other related information to answer the following questions:

   a. Assess the bank's balance sheet as well as any comments in its annual report about the gap between its rate-sensitive assets and its rate-sensitive liabilities. Does it appear that the bank has a positive gap or a negative gap?

   b. Does the bank use any methods to reduce its gap and therefore reduce its exposure to interest rate risk?

   c. Summarize any statements made by the bank in its annual report about how it attempts to limit its exposure to credit risk on the loans it provides.

3. **Commercial bank performance (from Chapter 20)**

   For the commercial bank that you selected at the beginning of the term, use its annual report or any other related information to answer the following questions:

   a. Determine the bank's interest income as a percentage of its total assets.

   b. Determine the bank's interest expenses as a percentage of its total assets.

   c. Determine the bank's net interest margin.

   d. Determine the bank's noninterest income as a percentage of its total assets.

   e. Determine the bank's noninterest expenses (do not include the addition to loan loss reserves here) as a percentage of total assets.

   f. Determine the bank's addition to loan loss reserves as a percentage of its total assets.

   g. Determine the bank's return on assets.

   h. Determine the bank's return on equity.

   i. Identify the bank's income statement items described previously that would be affected if interest rates rise in the next year, and explain how they would be affected.

   j. Identify the bank's income statement items described previously that would be affected if U.S. economic conditions deteriorate, and explain how they would be affected.

4. **Savings institutions (from Chapter 21)**

   For the savings institution that you selected at the beginning of the term, use its annual report or any other related information to answer the following questions:

   a. Identify the types of deposits that the savings institution uses to obtain most of its funds.

   b. Identify the main uses of funds by the savings institution.

    c. Summarize any statements made by the savings institution in its annual report about how recent or potential regulations will affect its performance.

    d. Assess the savings institution's balance sheet as well as any comments in its annual report about the gap between its rate-sensitive assets and its rate-sensitive liabilities. Does it appear that the savings institution has a positive gap or a negative gap?

    e. Does the savings institution use any methods to reduce its gap and therefore reduce its exposure to interest rate risk?

    f. Summarize any statements made by the savings institution in its annual report about how it attempts to limit its exposure to credit risk on the loans it provides.

    g. Determine the savings institution's interest income as a percentage of its total assets.

    h. Determine the savings institution's interest expenses as a percentage of its total assets.

    i. Determine the savings institution's noninterest income as a percentage of its total assets.

    j. Determine the savings institution's noninterest expenses (do not include the addition to loan loss reserves here) as a percentage of total assets.

    k. Determine the savings institution's addition to loan loss reserves as a percentage of its total assets.

    l. Determine the savings institution's return on assets.

    m. Determine the savings institution's return on equity.

    n. Identify the savings institution's income statement items described previously that would be affected if interest rates rise in the next year, and explain how they would be affected.

    o. Identify the savings institution's income statement items described previously that would be affected if the U.S. economic conditions deteriorate, and explain how they would be affected.

5. Mutual funds (from Chapter 23)

For the mutual fund that you selected at the beginning of the term, use its prospectus or any other related information to answer the following questions:

    a. What is the investment objective of this mutual fund? Do you consider this mutual fund to have low risk, moderate risk, or high risk?

    b. What was the return on the mutual fund last year? What was the average annual return over the last three years?

    c. What is a key economic factor that influences the return on this mutual fund? (That is, are the fund's returns highly influenced by U.S. stock market conditions? By U.S. interest rates? By foreign stock market conditions? By foreign interest rates?)

    d. Must any fees be paid when buying or selling this mutual fund?

    e. What was the expense ratio for this mutual fund over the last year? Does this ratio seem high to you?

6. Investment banks (from Chapter 24)

For the investment bank that you selected at the beginning of the term, use its annual report or any other related information to answer the following questions:

    a. What are the main types of business conducted by the investment bank?

    b. Summarize any statements made by the investment bank in its annual report about how it may be affected by existing or potential regulations.

    c. Describe the recent performance of the investment bank, and explain why the performance has been favorable or unfavorable.

7. **Insurance companies (from Chapter 25)**

For the insurance company that you selected at the beginning of the term, use its annual report or any other related information to answer the following questions:

a. How does the insurance company allocate its funds? (That is, what is its asset composition?)

b. Is the insurance company exposed to interest rate risk? Explain.

c. Does the insurance company use any techniques to hedge its exposure to interest rate risk?

d. Summarize any statements made by the insurance company in its annual report about how it may be affected by existing or potential regulations.

e. Describe the recent performance of the insurance company (using any key financial ratios that measure its income). Explain why its recent performance was strong or weak.

Part III. Measuring Stock Performance

This part of the project enables you to analyze the risk and return characteristics of one particular stock that you own or would like to purchase. You should input your data on Excel or an alternative electronic spreadsheet. Perform the following tasks:

a. Obtain stock price data at the end of each of the last 16 quarters, and fill in that information in Column A of your electronic spreadsheet. Historical stock price data are available on the Yahoo! finance website and on other websites. Your professor may offer some suggestions on where to obtain this information.

b. Obtain the data on dividend per share for this firm for each of the last 16 quarters, and input that information in Column B of your electronic spreadsheet. When you obtain dividend data, recognize that it is often listed on an annual basis. In this case, divide the annual dividend by 4 to obtain the quarterly dividend.

c. Use "compute" statements to derive the quarterly return on your stock in Column C of your electronic spreadsheet. The return on the stock during any quarter is computed as follows. First, compute the stock price at the end of that quarter minus the stock price at the end of the previous quarter, then add the quarterly dividend, and then divide by the stock price at the end of the previous quarter.

d. Input the S&P 500 stock index level as of the end of each of the 16 quarters in Column D of your electronic spreadsheet.

e. Use "compute" statements to derive the quarterly stock market return in Column E, which is equal to the percentage change in the S&P 500 index level from the previous quarter.

f. Using the tools in an electronic package, run a regression analysis in which your quarterly stock return (Column C) represents the dependent variable, and the stock market return (Column E) represents the independent variable. This analysis can be easily run by Excel or Lotus.

g. Based on your regression results, what is the relationship between the market return and your stock's return? (The slope coefficient represents the estimate of your firm's beta, which is a measure of its systematic risk.)

h. Based on your regression results, does it appear that there is a significant relationship between the market return and your stock's return? (The t-statistic for the slope coefficient can be assessed to determine whether there is a significant relationship.)

i.   Based on your regression results, what proportion of the variation in the stock's returns can be explained by movements (returns) in the stock market overall? (The R-SQUARED statistic measures the proportion of variation in the dependent variable that is explained by the independent variable in a regression model like the one described previously.) Does it appear that the stock's return is driven mainly by stock market movements or by other factors that are not captured in the regression model?

j.   What is the standard deviation of your stock's quarterly returns over the 16-quarter period? (You can easily compute the standard deviation of your column of stock return data by using a compute statement.) What is the standard deviation of the quarterly stock market returns (as measured by quarterly returns on the S&P 500 index) over the 16-quarter period? Is your stock more volatile than the stock market in general? If so, why do you think it is more volatile than the market?

k.   Assume that the average risk-free rate per quarter over the 16-quarter period is 1.5 percent. Determine the Sharpe index for your stock. (The Sharpe index is equal to your stock's average quarterly return minus the average risk-free rate, divided by the standard deviation of your stock's returns.) Determine the Treynor index for your stock. (The Treynor index is equal to your stock's average quarterly return minus the average risk-free rate, divided by the estimated beta of your stock.)

APPENDIX B

Using Excel to Conduct Analyses

Excel spreadsheets are useful for organizing numerical data. In addition, they can execute computations for you. Excel not only allows you to compute general statistics such as average and standard deviations of cells, but also can be used to conduct regression analysis. This appendix begins by describing the use of Excel to compute general statistics. Then, a background of regression analysis is provided, followed by a discussion of how Excel can be used to run regression analysis.

General Statistics

Some of the more popular computations are discussed here.

Creating a Compute Statement

If you want to determine the percentage change in a value from one period to the next, type the compute statement in a cell where you want to see the result. For example, assume that you identify the month and year in Column A and record the stock price of Dell, Inc. at the beginning of that month in Column B. To assess the performance or risk characteristics of stocks, you should first convert the stock price data into "returns." This allows you to compare performance and risk among different stocks. Since Dell does not pay a dividend, the return from investing in Dell stock over a period is simply the percentage change in the price. Assume you want to compute the monthly percentage change in the stock price. In cell C2, you can create a compute statement to derive the percentage change in price from the beginning of the first month until the beginning of the second month. A compute statement begins with an = sign. The proper compute statement to compute a percentage change for cell B2 is =(B2-B1)/B1. Assume that in cell C3, you want to derive the percentage change in Dell's stock price as of the month in cell B3 from the previous month B2. Type the compute statement =(B3-B2)/B2 in cell C3.

Using the COPY Command

If you need to repeat a particular compute statement for several different cells, you can use the COPY command as follows:

1. Place the cursor in the cell with the compute statement that you want to copy to other cells.
2. Click "Edit" and then click "Copy" on your menu bar.
3. Highlight the cells where you want that compute statement copied.
4. Hit the Enter key.

For example, assume that you have 30 monthly prices of Dell stock in Column B and have already calculated the percentage change in the stock price in cell C2 as explained above. (You did not have a percentage change in cell C1 because you needed two dates [cells B1 and B2] to derive your first percentage change.) You can place the cursor on cell C2, click "Edit" and then click "Copy" on your menu bar, highlight cells C3 to C30, and then hit the Enter key.

Computing an Average

You can compute the average of a set of cells as follows. Assume that you want to determine the mean monthly return on Dell stock shown in cells C2 to C30. Go to any blank cell (such as cell C31), and type the compute statement =AVERAGE (C2:C30).

Computing a Standard Deviation

You can compute the standard deviation of a set of cells as follows. Assume that you want to determine the standard deviation of the returns on Dell stock. In cell C32 (or in any blank cell where you want to see the result), type the compute statement: =STDEV(C2:C30).

Regression Analysis

Various software packages are available to run regression analysis. The Excel package is recommended because of its simplicity. The following example illustrates the ease with which regression analysis can be run.

Assume that a financial institution wishes to measure the relationship between the change in the interest rate in a given period (Δi_t) and the change in the inflation rate in the previous period (ΔI_{t-1}); that is, the financial institution wishes to assess the lagged impact of inflation on interest rates. Assume that the data over the last 20 periods are as follows:

Column A Period	Column B Δi_t	Column C ΔINF_{t-1}
1	.50%	.90%
2	.65	.75
3	−.70	−1.20
4	.50	.30
5	.40	.60
6	−.30	−.20
7	.60	.85
8	.75	.45
9	.10	−.05
10	1.10	1.35
11	.90	1.10
12	−.65	−.80
13	−.20	−.35
14	.40	.55

Column A Period	Column B Δi_t	Column C $\Delta INF_{t\text{-}1}$
15	.30	.40
16	.60	.75
17	−.05	−.10
18	1.30	1.50
19	−.55	−.70
20	.15	.25

Assume the firm applies the following regression model to the data:

$$\Delta i_t = b_0 + b_1 \Delta INF_{t-1} + \mu$$

where Δi_t = change in the interest rate in period t

ΔINF_{t-1} = change in the inflation rate in period $t - 1$ (the previous period)

b_0 and b_1 = regression coefficients to be estimated by regression analysis

μ = error term

Regression Analysis Using Excel

In our example, Δi_t is the dependent variable, and ΔINF_{t-1} is the independent variable. The first step is to input the two columns of data that were provided earlier (Columns B and C) into a file using Excel. Then you can perform regression analysis as follows. Click the Tools menu and then click "Data Analysis." If "Data Analysis" does not appear on your Tools menu, select "Add Ins." Select "Analysis Toolpak" and click "OK." You should now be able to choose "Data Analysis" from your Tools menu. Once you click "Data Analysis," you are presented with a new menu in which you should select "Regression." For "Input Y Range," identify the range of the dependent variable ($B$1:$B$20 in our example). Then for "Input X Range," identify the range of the independent variable ($C$1:CC20 in our example). Click "OK," and within a few seconds, the regression analysis will be complete. For our example, the output is as follows:

Summary Output	
Multiple R	0.96884081
R-SQUARE	0.93865251
Adjusted R-SQUARE	0.93524431
Standard Error	0.1432744
Observations	20

ANOVA					
	df	SS	MS	F	Significance F
Regression	1	5.653504056	5.653504	275.4105	2.34847E-12
Residual	18	0.369495944	0.020528		
Total	19	6.023			

	Coefficients	Standard Error	t Stat	P-value	Lower 95%	Upper 95%
Intercept	0.0494173	0.035164424	1.405321	0.176951	−0.024460473	0.123295
X Variable 1	0.75774079	0.045659421	16.5955	2.35E-12	0.661813835	0.853668

The estimate of the so-called slope coefficient is about .76, which suggests that every 1 percent change in the inflation rate is associated with a .76 percent change (in the same direction) in the interest rate. The t-statistic is 16.6, which suggests that there is a significant relationship between Δi_t and ΔINF_{t-1}. The R-SQUARED statistic suggests that about 94 percent of the variation in Δi_t is explained by ΔINF_{t-1}. The correlation between Δi_t and ΔINF_{t-1} can also be measured by the correlation coefficient, which is the square root of the R-SQUARED statistic.

If you have more than one independent variable (multiple regression), you should place the independent variables next to each other in the file. Then, for the X-RANGE, identify this block of data. The output for the regression model will display the coefficient and standard error for each of the independent variables. The t-statistic can be estimated for each independent variable to test for significance. For multiple regression, the R-SQUARED statistic represents the percentage of variation in the dependent variable explained by the model as a whole.

Using Regression Analysis to Forecast

The regression results can be used to forecast future values of the dependent variable. In our example, the historical relationship between Δi_t and ΔINF_{t-1} can be expressed as

$$\Delta i_t = b_0 + b_1(\Delta INF_{t-1})$$

Assume that last period's change in inflation (ΔINF_{t-1}) was 1 percent. Given the estimated coefficients derived from regression analysis, the forecast for this period's Δi_t is

$$\Delta i_t = .0494\% + .7577(1\%)$$
$$= .8071\%.$$

There are some obvious limitations that should be recognized when using regression analysis to forecast. First, if other variables that influence the dependent variable are not included in the model, the coefficients derived from the model may be improperly estimated. This can cause inaccurate forecasts. Second, some relationships are contemporaneous rather than lagged, which means that last period's value for ΔINF could not be used. Instead, a forecast would have to be derived for ΔINF, to use as input for forecasting Δi_t. If the forecast for ΔINF is poor, the forecast for Δi_t will likely be poor even if the regression model is properly specified.

Glossary

A

adjustable-rate mortgage (ARM) Mortgage that requires payments that adjust periodically according to market interest rates.

adverse selection problem In an insurance context, the problem for the insurance industry stemming from the fact that those who are most likely to purchase insurance are also those who are most likely to need it.

American depository receipts (ADRs) Certificates representing ownership of foreign stocks.

amortization schedule Schedule developed from the maturity and interest rate on a mortgage to determine monthly payments broken down into principal and interest.

annuity Even stream of payments over a given period of time.

annuity plans Plans provided by insurance companies that offer a predetermined amount of retirement income to individuals.

appreciate Increase in the value of a foreign currency.

arbitrage activity In the securities industry, the purchasing of undervalued shares and the resale of these shares for a higher profit.

arbitrage firms (arbitrageurs) Securities firms that capitalize on discrepancies between prices of index futures and stocks.

arbitrage pricing theory (APT) Theory on the pricing of assets, which suggests that stock prices may be driven by a set of factors in addition to the market.

ask quote (ask price) Price at which a seller is willing to sell.

asset stripping A strategy of acquiring a firm, breaking it into divisions, segmenting the divisions, and then selling them separately.

at the money Refers to an option in which the prevailing price of the underlying security is equal to the exercise price.

automatic transfer service (ATS) Savings account that allows funds to be transferred to a checking account as checks are written.

B

back-end load A withdrawal fee assessed when money is withdrawn from a mutual fund.

balloon payment A required lump-sum payment of the principal of a loan.

balloon-payment mortgage Mortgage that requires payments for a three- to five-year period; at the end of the period, full payment of the principal is required.

banker's acceptance Agreement in which a commercial bank accepts responsibility for a future payment; it is commonly used for international trade transactions.

bank holding company (BHC) Company that owns a commercial bank.

Bank Insurance Fund Reserve fund used by the FDIC to close failing banks until 2006; the fund was supported with deposit insurance premiums paid by commercial banks.

basis Difference between the price movement of a futures contract and the price movement of the underlying security.

basis risk As applied to interest rate swaps, risk that the index used for an interest rate swap does not move perfectly in tandem with the floating-rate instrument specified in a swap arrangement. As applied to financial futures, risk that the futures prices do not move perfectly in tandem with the assets that are hedged.

bearer bonds Bonds that require the owner to clip coupons attached to the bonds and send them to the issuer to receive coupon payments.

bear-market certificates of deposit (CDs) CDs that reward depositors if the market performs poorly.

behavioral finance The application of psychology to make financial decisions.

Beige Book A consolidated report of economic conditions in each of the Federal Reserve districts; used by the FOMC in formulating monetary policy.

best-efforts agreement Arrangement in which the investment banking firm does not guarantee a price on securities to be issued by a corporation, but states only that it will give its best effort to sell the securities at a reasonable price.

beta Sensitivity of an asset's returns to market returns; measured as the covariance between asset returns and market returns divided by the variance of market returns.

bid quote (bid price) Price a purchaser is willing to pay for a specific security.

Big Bang Deregulatory event in London in 1986 that allowed investment firms trading in the United States and Japan to trade in London and eliminated the fixed commission structure on securities transactions.

Board of Governors Composed of seven individual members appointed by the President of the United States; also called the Federal Reserve Board. The board helps regulate commercial banks and control monetary policy.

Bond Buyer Index Index based on 40 actively traded general obligation and revenue bonds.

bond price elasticity Sensitivity of bond prices to changes in the required rate of return.

bonds Debt obligations with long-term maturities issued by governments or corporations.

Bretton Woods era Period from 1944 to 1971, when exchange rates were fixed (maintained within 1 percent of a specified rate).

bridge loans Funds provided as temporary financing until other sources of long-term funds can be obtained; commonly provided by securities firms to firms experiencing leveraged buyouts.

broker One who executes securities transactions between two parties.

bullet loan Loan structured so that interest payments and the loan principal are to be paid off in one lump sum at a specified future date.

bull-market certificates of deposit (CDs) CDs that reward depositors if the market performs well.

business finance companies Finance companies that concentrate on purchasing credit contracts from retailers and dealers.

C

call option Contract that grants the owner the right to purchase a specified financial instru-

ment for a specified price within a specified period of time.

call premium Difference between a bond's call price and its par value.

call provision (call feature) Provision that allows the initial issuer of bonds to buy back the bonds at a specified price.

callable certificates of deposit (CDs) CDs that can be called by the financial institution, forcing an earlier maturity.

callable swap (or swaption) Swap of fixed-rate payments for floating-rate payments, whereby the party making the fixed payments has the right to terminate the swap prior to maturity.

CAMELS ratings Characteristics used to rate bank risk.

capital As related to banks, capital is mainly composed of retained earnings and proceeds received from issuing stock.

capital appreciation funds Mutual funds composed of stocks of firms that have potential for very high growth, but may be unproven.

capital asset pricing model (CAPM) Theory that suggests the return of an asset is influenced by the risk-free rate, the market return, and the covariance between asset returns and market returns.

capital markets Financial markets that facilitate the flow of long-term funds.

capital market securities Long-term securities, such as bonds, whose maturities are more than one year.

capital ratio Ratio of capital to assets.

captive finance subsidiary (CFS) Wholly owned subsidiary of a finance company whose primary purpose is to finance sales

of the parent company's products and purchase receivables of the parent company.

cash flow underwriting Method by which insurance companies adapt insurance premiums to interest rates.

Central Liquidity Facility (CLF) Facility that acts as a lender for credit unions to accommodate seasonal funding and specialized needs or to boost liquidity.

certificate of deposit (CD) Deposit offered by depository institutions that specifies a maturity, a deposit amount, and an interest rate.

chattel mortgage bond Bond that is secured by personal property.

circuit breakers Used to temporarily halt the trading of some securities or contracts on an exchange.

closed-end funds Mutual funds that do not repurchase the shares they sell.

collateralized mortgage obligations (CMOs) Represent securities that are backed by mortgages; segmented into classes (or tranches) that dictate the timing of the payments.

commercial paper Short-term securities (usually unsecured) issued by well-known creditworthy firms.

commission brokers (floor brokers) Brokers who execute orders for their customers.

common stock Certificate representing partial ownership of a corporation.

Competitive Banking Equality Act Act passed in 1987 that prohibited commercial banks from creating nonbank banks and from offering new insurance, real estate, and securities underwriting services.

consumer finance companies Finance companies that concentrate on direct loans to consumers.

contagion effects Adverse effects of a single firm that become contagious throughout the industry.

convertible bonds Bonds that can be converted into a specified number of the firm's common stock.

corporate bonds Bonds issued by corporations in need of long-term funds.

covered call Sale of a call option to partially cover against the possible decline in the price of a stock that is being held.

covered interest arbitrage Act of capitalizing on higher foreign interest rates while covering the position with a simultaneous forward sale.

credit crunch A period during which banks are less willing to extend credit; normally results from an increased probability that some borrowers will default on loans.

credit risk The risk of loss that will occur when a counterparty defaults on a contract.

cross-hedging The use of a futures contract on one financial instrument to hedge a financial institution's position in a different financial instrument.

crowding-out effect Phenomenon that occurs when insufficient loanable funds are available for potential borrowers, such as corporations and individuals, as a result of excessive borrowing by the Treasury. Because limited loanable funds are available to satisfy all borrowers, interest rates rise in response to the increased demand for funds, thereby crowding some potential borrowers out of the market.

currency call option Contract that grants the owner the right to purchase a specified currency for a specified price, within a specified period of time.

currency futures contract Standardized contract that specifies an amount of a particular currency to be exchanged on a specified date and at a specified exchange rate.

currency put option Contract that grants the owner the right to sell a specified currency for a specified price, within a specified period of time.

currency swap An agreement that allows the periodic swap of one currency for another at specified exchange rates; it essentially represents a series of forward contracts.

D

day traders Traders of financial futures contracts who close out their contracts on the same day that they initiate them.

dealers Securities firms that make a market in specific securities by adjusting their inventories.

debentures Bonds that are backed only by the general credit of the issuing firm.

debt-equity swap An exchange of debt for an equity interest in the debtor's assets.

debt securities Securities that represent credit provided to the initial issuer by the purchaser.

default risk Credit risk; risk that loans provided or securities purchased will default, cutting off principal and/or interest payments.

defensive open market operations Implemented to offset the impact of other market conditions that affect the level of funds.

deficit units Individual, corporate, or government units that need to borrow funds.

defined-benefit plan Pension plan in which contributions are dictated by the benefits that will eventually be provided.

defined-contribution plan Pension plan in which benefits are determined by the accumulated contributions and on the fund's investment performance.

demand deposit account Deposit account that offers checking services.

demand-pull inflation Inflation caused by excess demand for goods.

Depository Institutions Deregulation and Monetary Control Act (DIDMCA) Act that deregulated some aspects of the depository institutions industry, such as removing the ceiling interest rates on deposits and allowing NOW accounts nationwide.

deposit transfer Procedure of handling failures of savings institutions; the deposits of a failing institution are transferred to a healthy depository institution for a fee.

depreciate Decrease in the value of a foreign currency.

derivative instruments Instruments created from a previously existing security.

derivative markets Markets that allow for the buying or selling of derivative securities.

derivative securities Financial contracts whose values are derived from the values of underlying assets.

direct access broker A trading platform for a computer website that allows investors to trade stocks without using a broker.

direct lease loan Occurs when a bank purchases assets and then leases the assets to a firm.

dirty float System whereby exchange rates are market determined without boundaries, but subject to government intervention.

discount bonds Bonds that sell below their par value.

discount brokerage firms Brokerage firms that focus on executing transactions.

discount rate Interest rate charged on loans provided by the Federal Reserve to depository institutions.

disintermediation Process in which savers transfer funds from intermediaries to alternative investments with market-determined rates.

Dow Jones Industrial Average Index of stocks representing 30 large firms.

dual banking system Regulatory framework of the banking system, composed of federal and state regulators.

duration Measurement of the life of a bond on a present value basis.

duration gap Difference between the average duration of a bank's assets versus its liabilities.

dynamic asset allocation Switching between risky and low-risk investment positions over time in response to changing expectations.

dynamic open market operations Implemented to increase or decrease the level of funds.

E

economies of scale Reduction in average cost per unit as the level of output increases.

Edge Act corporations Corporations established by banks to specialize in international banking and foreign financial transactions.

effective yield Yield on foreign money market securities adjusted for the exchange rate.

Employee Retirement Income Security Act (ERISA) Act that provided three vesting schedule options from which a pension fund could choose. It also stipulated that pension contributions be invested in a prudent manner and that employees can transfer any vested pension amounts to new employers as they switch employers.

employee stock ownership plans (ESOPs) Plans to offer periodic contributions of a corporation's stock to participating employees; ESOPs have been used as a means of preventing a takeover.

equity REIT REIT (real estate investment trust) that invests directly in properties.

equity securities Securities such as common stock and preferred stock that represent ownership in a business.

equity swap Swap arrangement involving the exchange of interest payments for payments linked to the degree of change in a stock index.

Euro-commercial paper (Euro-CP) Securities issued in Europe without the backing of a bank syndicate.

Eurodollar certificate of deposit Large U.S. dollar–denominated deposits in non-U.S. banks.

Eurodollar floating-rate CDs (FRCDs) Eurodollar CDs with floating interest rates that adjust periodically to the LIBOR.

Eurodollar loans Short-term loans denominated in dollars provided to corporations and governments by branches of U.S. banks located outside the United States and some foreign-owned banks.

Eurodollar market Market in Europe in which dollars are deposited and loaned for short time periods.

Eurodollars Large dollar-denominated deposits accepted by banks outside the United States.

Euronotes Notes issued in European markets in bearer form, with short-term maturities.

European Currency Unit (ECU) Multi-currency unit of account, composed of several European currencies, that was used to price some internationally traded goods and securities.

event risk An increase in the perceived risk of default on bonds resulting from the restructuring of debt or an acquisition.

exchange rate mechanism (ERM) Arrangement in which many European currency values were pegged to the European Currency Unit (within boundaries), which linked the exchange rates between these currencies.

exchange rate risk Risk that currency values will change in a manner that adversely affects future cash flows.

exchange-traded funds (ETFs) Mutual funds that are designed to mimic particular stock indexes and are traded on a stock exchange like stocks.

exercise price (or strike price) Price at which the instrument underlying an option contract can be purchased (in the case of a call option) or sold (in the case of a put option).

extendable swap Swap of fixed payments for floating payments that contains an extendable feature allowing the party making fixed payments to extend the swap period if desired.

F

factor Firm that purchases accounts receivable at a discount and is responsible for processing and collecting on the balances of these accounts; finance companies commonly have subsidiaries that serve as factors.

Federal Deposit Insurance Corporation (FDIC) Federal agency that insures the deposits of commercial banks.

Federal Deposit Insurance Corporation Improvement Act (FDICIA) Legislation enacted in 1991 to penalize banks that engage in high-risk activites and reduce the regulatory costs of closing troubled banks.

federal funds rate Interest rate charged on loans between depository institutions.

Federal National Mortgage Association (FNMA) Issues mortgage-backed securities and uses the funds to purchase mortgages.

Federal Open Market Committee (FOMC) Composed of the seven members of the Board of Governors plus the presidents of five Federal Reserve district banks. The main role of the FOMC is to control monetary policy.

Federal Reserve Central bank of the United States.

Federal Reserve district bank A regional government bank that facilitates operations within the banking system by clearing checks, replacing old currency, providing loans to banks, and conducting research; there are 12 Federal Reserve district banks.

financial futures contract Standardized agreement to deliver or receive a specified amount of a specified financial instrument at a specified price and date.

Financial Institutions Reform, Recovery, and Enforcement Act (FIRREA) Act intended to enhance the safety of savings institutions; prevented savings institutions from investing in junk bonds, increased capital requirements, and increased the penalties for fraud.

financial market Market in which financial assets (or securities) such as stocks and bonds are traded.

Financial Services Modernization Act (Gramm-Leach-Bliley Act) Legislation enacted in 1999 that allows affiliations between banks, securities firms, and insurance companies; repealed the Glass-Steagall Act.

first mortgage bond Bond that has first claim on specified assets as collateral.

Fisher effect Positive relationship between interest rates and expected inflation.

fixed-rate mortgage Mortgage that requires payments based on a fixed interest rate.

floor brokers Individuals who facilitate the trading of stocks on the New York and American Stock Exchanges by executing transactions for their clients.

floor traders (locals) Members of a futures exchange who trade futures contracts for their own account.

flotation costs Costs of placing securities.

flow-of-funds accounts Reports on the amount of funds channeled to and from various sectors.

foreign exchange derivatives Instruments created to lock in a foreign exchange transaction, such as forward contracts, futures contracts, currency swaps, and currency options contracts.

foreign exchange market The financial market that facilitates the exchange of currencies.

forward contract Contract typically negotiated with a commercial bank that allows a customer to purchase or sell a specified amount of a particular foreign currency at a specified exchange rate on a specified future date.

forward market Market that facilitates the trading of forward contracts; commercial banks serve as intermediaries in the market by matching up participants who wish to buy a currency forward with other participants who wish to sell the currency forward.

forward rate In the context of the term structure of interest rates, the market's forecast of the future interest rate. In the context of foreign exchange, the exchange rate at which a specified currency can be purchased or sold at a specified future point in time.

forward swap Involves an exchange of interest payments that does not begin until a specified future point in time.

freely floating system System whereby exchange rates are market determined, without any government intervention.

front-end load A fee paid when money is invested in a mutual fund.

full-service brokerage firms Brokerage firms that provide complete information and advice about securities, in addition to executing transactions.

fundamental forecasting Is based on fundamental relationships between economic variables and exchange rates.

futures contract Standardized contract allowing one to purchase or sell a specified amount of a specified instrument (such as a security or currency) for a specified price and at a specified future point in time.

G

gap Defined as rate-sensitive assets minus rate-sensitive liabilities.

gap ratio Measured as the value of rate-sensitive assets divided by the value of rate-sensitive liabilities.

Garn-St Germain Act Act passed in 1982 that allowed for the creation of money market deposit accounts (MMDAs), loosened lending guidelines for federally chartered savings institutions, and allowed failing depository institutions to be acquired by other depository institutions outside the state.

general obligation bonds Bonds that provide payments that are supported by the municipal government's ability to tax.

Glass-Steagall Act Act in 1933 that separated commercial banking and investment banking activities; largely repealed in 1999.

global crowding out Situation in which excessive government borrowing in one country can cause

higher interest rates in other countries.

global junk bonds Low-quality bonds issued globally by governments and corporations.

golden parachute Provisions that allow specific employees to receive specified compensation if they are terminated from their positions.

Government National Mortgage Association (Gnma) Agency that guarantees the timely payment of principal and interest to investors who purchase securities backed by mortgages.

graduated-payment mortgage (GPM) Mortgage that allows borrowers to initially make small payments on the mortgage; the payments are increased on a graduated basis.

greenmail The accumulation of shares of a target, followed by sale of the shares back to the target; the target purchases the shares back (at a premium) to remove the threat of a takeover.

gross interest expense Interest paid on deposits and on other borrowed funds.

gross interest income Interest income generated from all assets.

group life policy Policy provided to a group of policyholders with some common bond.

growing-equity mortgage Mortgage where the initial monthly payments are low and increase over time.

growth and income funds Mutual funds that contain a combination of growth stocks, high-dividend stocks, and fixed-income bonds.

growth funds Mutual funds containing stocks of firms that are expected to grow

at a higher than average rate; for investors who are willing to accept a moderate degree of risk.

H

health maintenance organizations (HMOs) Intermediaries between purchasers and providers of health care.

hedge funds Mutual funds that sell shares to wealthy individuals and financial institutions and use the proceeds to invest in securities; require a larger investment than open-end mutual funds, are subject to less regulation, and tend to be more risky.

hedgers Participants in financial futures markets who take positions in contracts to reduce their exposure to risk.

high-yield funds Mutual funds composed of bonds that offer high yields (junk bonds) and have a relatively high degree of credit risk.

highly leveraged transactions (HLTs) Credit provided that results in a debt-to-asset ratio of at least 75 percent.

I

immunize The act of insulating a security portfolio from interest rate movements.

impact lag Lag time between when a policy is implemented by the government and the time when the policy has an effect on the economy.

imperfect markets Markets in which buyers and sellers of securities do not have full access to information and cannot always break down securities to the precise size they desire.

implementation lag Lag time between when the

government recognizes a problem and the time when it implements a policy to resolve the problem.

income funds Mutual funds composed of bonds that offer periodic coupon payments.

indenture Legal document specifying the rights and obligations of both the issuing firm and the bondholders.

index arbitrage Act of capitalizing on discrepancies between prices of index futures and stocks.

index funds Mutual funds that are designed to match the performance of an existing stock index.

informal line of credit Financing arrangement that allows a business to borrow up to a specified amount within a specified period of time.

initial margin A margin deposit established by a customer with a brokerage firm before a margin transaction can be executed.

initial public offering (IPO) A first-time offering of shares by a specific firm to the public.

installment loans Loans to individuals to finance purchases of cars and household products.

insured plans Pension plans that are used to purchase annuity policies so that the life insurance companies can provide benefits to employees upon retirement.

interest-inelastic Insensitive to interest rates.

interest rate cap Arrangement that offers a party interest payments in periods when the interest rate on a specific money market instrument exceeds a specified ceiling rate; the payments are based on the amount by which the interest rate exceeds the ceiling as applied to the notional principal specified in the agreement.

interest rate collar The purchase of an interest rate cap and the simultaneous sale of an interest rate floor.

interest rate floor Agreement in which one party offers an interest rate payment in periods when the interest rate on a specified money market instrument is below a specified floor rate.

interest rate futures Financial futures contracts on debt securities such as Treasury bills, notes, or bonds.

interest rate parity Theory that suggests the forward discount (or premium) is dependent on the interest rate differential between the two countries of concern.

interest rate risk Risk that an asset will decline in value in response to interest rate movements.

interest rate swap Arrangement whereby one party exchanges one set of interest payments for another.

international mutual fund Portfolio of international stocks created and managed by a financial institution; individuals can invest in international stocks by purchasing shares of an international mutual fund.

in the money Describes a call option whose premium is above the exercise price or a put option whose premium is below the exercise price.

investment-grade bonds Bonds that are rated Baa or better by Moody's and BBB or better by Standard & Poor's.

investment-grade securities Securities that are rated as "medium" quality

or higher by rating agencies.

issue costs Cost of issuing stock, including printing, legal registration, and accounting expenses.

J

junk bonds Corporate bonds that are perceived to have a high degree of risk.

junk commercial paper Low-rated commercial paper.

L

letter of credit (L/C) Guarantee by a bank on the financial obligations of a firm that owes payment (usually an importer).

leveraged buyout (LBO) A buyout of a firm that is financed mostly with debt.

leverage measure Measure of financial leverage; defined as assets divided by equity.

limit orders Requests by customers to purchase or sell securities at a specified price or better.

liquidity Ability to sell assets easily without loss of value.

liquidity premium theory (liquidity preference theory) Theory that suggests the yield to maturity is higher for illiquid securities, other things being equal.

liquidity risk Potential price distortions due to a lack of liquidity.

load funds Mutual funds that have a sales charge imposed by brokerage firms that sell the funds.

loan commitment Obligation by a bank to provide a specified loan amount to a particular firm upon the firm's request.

loan loss provision A reserve account established by a bank in anticipation of loan losses in the future.

loan participation Arrangement in which several banks pool funds to provide a loan to a corporation.

loanable funds theory Theory that suggests the market interest rate is determined by the factors that control the supply and demand for loanable funds.

locational arbitrage Arbitrage intended to capitalize on a price (such as foreign exchange rate quote) discrepancy between two locations.

London Interbank Offer Rate (LIBOR) Interest rate charged on interbank loans.

long hedge The purchase of financial futures contracts to hedge against a possible decrease in interest rates.

long-term equity anticipations (LEAPs) Stock options with relatively long-term expiration dates.

low-coupon bonds Bonds that pay low coupon payments; most of the expected return to investors is attributed to the large discount in the bond's price.

M

M1 Definition of the money supply; composed of currency held by the public plus checking accounts.

M2 Definition of the money supply; composed of M1 plus savings accounts, small time deposits, MMDAs, and some other items.

M3 Definition of the money supply; composed of M2 plus large time deposits and other items.

maintenance margin A margin requirement that reduces the risk that participants will later default on their obligations.

margin account An account established with a broker that allows the investor to purchase stock on margin by putting up cash for part of the cost and borrowing the remainder from the broker.

margin call Call from a broker to participants in futures contracts (or other investments) informing them that they must increase their equity.

margin requirements The proportion of invested funds that must be paid in cash versus borrowed; set by the Federal Reserve.

market-based forecasting Process of developing forecasts from market indicators.

market-makers Individuals who facilitate the trading of stocks on the Nasdaq by standing ready to buy or sell specific stocks in response to customer orders made through a telecommunications network.

market microstructure Process by which securities are traded.

market orders Requests by customers to purchase or sell securities at the market price existing when the order reaches the exchange floor.

market risk Risk that the stock market experiences lower prices in response to adverse economic conditions or pessimistic expectations.

matched funding Strategy in which investment decisions are made with the objective of matching planned outflow payments.

McFadden Act of 1927 Act preventing all banks from establishing branches across state lines.

merger-conversion Procedure used in acquisitions whereby a mutual S&L

converts to a stock-owned S&L before either acquiring or being acquired by another firm.

mixed forecasting The use of a combination of forecasting techniques, resulting in a weighted average of the various forecasts developed.

monetizing the debt Action of the Fed to increase the money supply to offset any increased demand for funds resulting from a larger budget deficit.

money markets Financial markets that facilitate the flow of short-term funds.

money market deposit account (MMDA) Deposit account that pays interest and allows limited checking and does not specify a maturity.

money market mutual funds Mutual funds that concentrate their investment in money market securities.

money market securities Short-term securities, such as Treasury bills or certificates of deposit, whose maturities are one year or less.

moral hazard problem In a banking context, refers to the deposit insurance pricing system that existed until the early 1990s; insurance premiums per $100 of deposits were similar across all commercial banks. This system caused an indirect subsidy from safer banks to risky banks and encouraged banks to take excessive risk. In an insurance context, the problem for the insurance industry stemming from the fact that those who have insurance may take more risks because they are protected against losses.

mortgage-backed securities Securities backed by mortgages that are com-

monly sold and purchased by savings institutions.

mortgage pass-through securities Securities issued by a financial institution and backed by a group of mortgages. The mortgage interest and principal are sent to the financial institution, which then transfers the payments to the owners of the mortgage-backed securities after deducting a service fee.

mortgage REIT REIT (real estate investment trust) that invests in mortgage and construction loans.

multifund mutual fund A mutual fund composed of different mutual funds.

Municipal Bond Index (MBI) futures Futures contract allowing for the future purchase or sale of municipal bonds at a specified price.

municipal bonds Debt securities issued by state and local governments, which can usually be classified as either general obligation bonds or revenue bonds.

mutual fund An investment company that sells shares representing an interest in a portfolio of securities.

mutual S&Ls S&Ls that are owned by depositors.

mutual-to-stock conversion Procedure by savings institutions to shift the ownership structure from depositors to shareholders.

N

National Association of Insurance Commissioners (NAIC) Agency that facilitates cooperation among the various state agencies when an insurance issue is a concern.

National Association of Securities Dealers (NASD)

Regulator of the securities industry.

National Association of Securities Dealers Automatic Quotations (Nasdaq) A service for the over-the-counter market that reports immediate price quotations for many of the stocks.

National Credit Union Administration (NCUA) Regulator of credit unions; the NCUA participates in the creation of new CUs, examines the financial condition of CUs, and supervises any liquidations or mergers.

National Credit Union Share Insurance Fund (NCUSIF) Agency that insures deposits at credit unions.

negotiable certificate of deposit (NCD) Deposit account with a minimum deposit of $100,000 that requires a specified maturity; there is a secondary market for these deposits.

net asset value (NAV) Financial characteristic used to describe a mutual fund's value per share; estimated as the market value of the securities comprising the mutual fund, plus any accrued interest or dividends, minus any expenses. This value is divided by the number of shares outstanding.

net exposure In the context of futures markets, the difference between asset and liability positions.

net interest margin Estimated as interest revenues minus interest expenses, divided by assets.

noise traders Uninformed investors whose buy and sell positions push the stock price away from its fundamental value.

noise trading Theory used to explain that stock prices may deviate from their fundamental values as a result of the buy and sell

positions of uninformed investors (called "noise traders"); a market correction may not eliminate the discrepancy if the informed traders are unwilling to capitalize on the discrepancy (because of uncertainty surrounding the stock's fundamental value).

no-load funds Mutual funds that do not have a sales charge, meaning that they are not promoted by brokerage firms.

noninterest expenses Expenses, such as salaries and office equipment, that are unrelated to interest payments on deposits or borrowed funds.

noninterest income Income resulting from fees charged or services provided.

note issuance facility (NIF) Commitment in which a bank agrees to purchase the commercial paper of a firm if the firm cannot place its paper in the market at an acceptable interest rate.

notional principal Value to which interest rates from interest rate swaps are applied to determine the interest payments involved.

NOW (negotiable order of withdrawal) accounts Deposit accounts that allow unlimited checking and pay interest.

O

open-end funds Mutual funds that are willing to repurchase the shares they sell from investors at any time.

Open Market Desk Division of the New York Federal Reserve district bank that is responsible for conducting open market operations.

open market operations The Fed's buying and selling of government securities (through the Trading Desk).

operational risk The risk of losses as a result of inadequate management or controls.

option premium Price paid for an option contract.

organized exchange Visible marketplace for secondary market transactions.

origination Decisions by a firm (with the help of a securities firm) on how much stock or bonds to issue, the type of stock (or bonds) to be issued, and the price at which the stock (or bonds) should be sold.

out of the money Describes a call option whose premium is below the exercise price or a put option whose premium is above the exercise price.

over-the-counter (OTC) market Market used to facilitate transactions of securities not listed on organized exchanges.

P

participation certificates (PCs) Certificates sold by the Federal Home Loan Mortgage Association; the proceeds are used to purchase conventional mortgages from financial institutions.

Pension Benefit Guaranty Corporation (PBGC) Established as a result of the ERISA to provide insurance on pension plans.

perfect markets Markets in which all information about any securities for sale would be freely and continuously available to investors. Furthermore, all securities for sale could be broken down into any size desired by investors, and transaction costs would be nonexistent.

plain vanilla swap Involves the periodic exchange of fixed-rate payments for floating-rate payments.

policy directive Statement provided by the FOMC to the Trading Desk regarding the target money supply range.

portfolio insurance Program trading combined with the trading of stock index futures to hedge against market movements.

position traders Traders of financial futures contracts who maintain their futures positions for relatively long periods (such as weeks or months) before closing them out.

preemptive rights Priority given to a particular group of people to purchase newly issued stock, before other investors are given the opportunity to purchase the stock.

preferred habitat theory Theory that suggests that although investors and borrowers may normally concentrate on a particular natural maturity market, certain events may cause them to wander from it.

preferred stock Certificate representing partial ownership of a corporation, without significant voting rights; it provides owners dividends, but normally does not provide a share of the firm's profits.

prepayment risk The possibility that the assets to be hedged may be prepaid earlier than their designated maturity; also applies to mortgages.

primary market Market where securities are initially issued.

prime rate Interest rate charged on loans by banks to their most creditworthy customers.

private placement Process in which a corporation sells new securities directly without using underwriting services.

privatization Process of converting government ownership of businesses to private ownership.

program trading The simultaneous buying and selling of a portfolio of at least 15 different stocks valued at more than $1 million.

projective funding Strategy that offers pension fund managers some flexibility in constructing a pension portfolio that can benefit from expected market and interest rate movements.

prospectus A pamphlet that discloses relevant financial data on the firm and provisions applicable to the security.

protective covenants Restrictions enforced by a bond indenture (or a bank loan) that protect the bondholders (or the bank) from an increase in risk; such restrictions may include limits on the dividends paid, the salaries paid, and the additional debt the firm can issue.

purchasing power parity (PPP) Theory that suggests exchange rates adjust, on average, by a percentage that reflects the inflation differential between the two countries of concern.

pure expectations theory Theory suggesting that the shape of the yield curve is determined solely by interest rates.

put option Contract that grants the owner the right to sell a specified financial instrument for a specified price within a specified period of time.

putable swap Swap of fixed-rate payments for floating-rate payments whereby the party making floating-rate payments has the right to terminate the swap.

R

rate-capped swap Swap arrangement involving fixed-rate payments for floating-rate payments, whereby the floating payments are capped.

real estate investment trust (REIT) Closed-end mutual fund that invests in real estate or mortgages.

real estate mortgage conduit (REMIC) Allows financial institutions to sell mortgage assets and issue mortgage-backed securities.

real interest rate Nominal interest rate adjusted for inflation.

recognition lag Lag time between when a problem arises and when it is recognized by the government.

registered bonds Require the issuer to maintain records of who owns the bonds and automatically send coupon payments to the owners.

registration statement Statement of relevant financial information disclosed by a corporation issuing securities, which is intended to ensure that accurate information is disclosed by the issuing corporation.

Regulation Q Bank regulation that limited the interest rate banks could pay on deposits.

reinsurance Manner by which insurance companies can allocate a portion of their return and risk to other insurance companies, which share in insuring large policies.

repurchase agreement (repo) Agreement in which a bank (or some other firm) sells some of its government security holdings, with a commitment to purchase those securities back at a later date. This agreement essentially reflects a loan from the time the firm sold the securities until the securities are repurchased.

reserve requirement ratio Percentage of deposits that commercial banks must maintain as required reserves. This ratio is sometimes used by the Fed as a monetary policy tool.

Resolution Trust Corporation (RTC) Agency created in 1989 to help bail out failing savings institutions. The RTC liquidated an institution's assets and reimbursed depositors or sold the savings institution to another depository institution.

retail certificate of deposit (retail CD) Deposit requiring a specific minimum amount of funds to be deposited for a specified period of time.

return on assets (ROA) Defined as net income divided by assets.

return on equity (ROE) Defined as net income divided by equity.

revenue bonds Bonds that provide payments that are supported by the revenue generated by the project.

reverse leveraged buyout (reverse LBO) Process of issuing new stock after engaging in a leveraged buyout and improving the firm's performance.

reverse repo The purchase of securities by one party from another with an agreement to sell them in the future.

revolving credit loan Financing arrangement that obligates the bank to loan

some specified maximum amount of funds over a specified period of time.

S

S&P 500 Index Futures Futures contract allowing for the future purchase or sale of the S&P 500 index at a specified price.

Savings Association Insurance Fund (SAIF) Insuring agency for S&Ls from 1989 until 2006.

secondary market Market where securities are resold.

secondary stock offering A new stock offering by a firm that already has stock outstanding.

securities Certificates that represent a claim on the issuer.

Securities and Exchange Commission (SEC) Agency that regulates the issuance of securities disclosure rules for issuers, the exchanges, and participating brokerage firms.

Securities Exchange Act of 1933 Intended to ensure complete disclosure of relevant information on publicly offered securities and prevent fraudulent practices in selling these securities.

Securities Exchange Act of 1934 Intended to ensure complete disclosure of relevant information on securities traded in secondary markets.

securities gains and losses Bank accounting term that reflects the gains or losses generated from the sale of securities.

Securities Investor Protection Corporation (SIPC) Offers insurance on cash and securities deposited at brokerage firms.

securitization Pooling and repackaging of loans into

securities, which are sold to investors.

segmented markets theory Theory that suggests investors and borrowers choose securities with maturities that satisfy their forecasted cash needs.

semistrong-form efficiency Security prices reflect all public information, including announcements by firms, economic news or events, and political news or events.

shared-appreciation mortgage Mortgage that allows a home purchaser to pay a below-market interest rate; in return, the lender shares in the appreciation of the home price.

shareholder activism Actions taken by shareholders to correct a firm's deficiencies so that the stock price may improve.

Sharpe index Measure of risk-adjusted return; defined as the asset's excess mean return beyond the mean risk-free risk, divided by the standard deviation of returns of the asset of concern.

shelf-registration Registration with the SEC in advance of public placement of securities.

short hedge The sale of financial futures contracts to hedge against a possible increase in interest rates.

short selling The sale of securities that are borrowed, with the intent of buying those securities to repay what was borrowed.

Single European Act of 1987 Act that called for a reduction in barriers between European countries. This allowed for easier trade and capital flows throughout Europe.

sinking-fund provision Requirement that the firm retire a specific amount of the bond issue each year.

Smithsonian Agreement Agreement among major countries to devalue the dollar against some currencies and widen the boundaries around each exchange rate from 1 percent to 2.25 percent.

sovereign risk As applied to swaps, risk that a country's political conditions could prevent one party in the swap from receiving payments due.

specialists Individuals who facilitate the trading of stocks on the New York and American Stock Exchanges by taking positions in specific stocks; they stand ready to buy or sell these stocks on the trading floor.

specialty funds Mutual funds that focus on a group of companies sharing a particular characteristic.

speculators Those who take positions to benefit from future price movements.

spot exchange rate Present exchange rate.

spread Used to represent the difference between bid and ask quotes. This term is also sometimes used to reflect the difference between the average interest rate earned on assets and the average interest rate paid on liabilities.

Standard & Poor's 500 index Index of stocks of 500 large firms.

standby letter of credit Agreement that backs a customer's financial obligation.

stock index futures Financial futures contracts on stock indexes.

stock index option Provides the right to trade a specified stock index at a specified price by a specified expiration date.

stop-buy order Order to purchase a particular security when the price reaches a specified level above the current market price; often used in short sales.

stop-loss order Order of a sale of a specific security when the price reaches a specified minimum.

strike price (exercise price) Price at which an option can be exercised.

stripped securities Securities that are stripped of their coupon payments to create two separate types of securities: (1) a principal-only part that pays a future lump sum, and (2) an interest-only part that pays coupon payments, but no principal.

strips program Program created by the Treasury in which it exchanges stripped securities for Treasury securities.

strong-form efficiency Security prices fully reflect all information, including private (insider) information.

subordinated debentures Debentures that have claims against the firm's assets that are junior to the claims of both mortgage bonds and regular debentures.

surplus units Individual, business, or government units that have excess funds that can be invested.

swap options (swaptions) Options on interest rate swaps.

systematic risk Risk that is attributable to market movements and cannot be diversified away.

T

T-bill discount Percentage by which the price paid for a Treasury bill is less than the par value.

technical analysis Method of forecasting future stock prices with the use of historical stock price patterns.

technical forecasting Involves the use of historical exchange rate data to predict future values.

term insurance Temporary insurance over a specified term; the policy does not build a cash value.

term loan Business loan used to finance the purchase of fixed assets.

term structure of interest rates Relationship between the term remaining until maturity and the annualized yield of debt securities.

theory of rational expectations Suggests that the public will consider the historical effects of money supply growth when forecasting the effects of prevailing money supply growth.

time deposits Deposits that cannot be withdrawn until a specified maturity date.

time-series model Examines moving averages and allows forecasters to develop rules.

Trading Desk Located at the New York Federal Reserve district bank, it is used to carry out orders from the FOMC about open market operations.

Treasury bills Securities issued by the Treasury that have maturities of one year or less.

Treynor index Measure of risk-adjusted return;

defined as the asset's excess mean return beyond the mean risk-free rate, divided by the beta of the asset of concern.

triangular arbitrage Buying or selling a currency that is subject to a mispriced cross exchange rate.

trustee Appointed to represent the bondholders in all matters concerning the bond issue.

U

underwrite Act of guaranteeing a specific price to the initial issuer of securities.

underwriting spread Difference between the price at which an investment banking firm expects to sell securities and the price it is willing to pay the issuing firm.

underwriting syndicate Group of investment banking firms that are required to underwrite a portion of a corporation's newly issued securities.

universal life insurance Combines the features of term and whole life insurance. It specifies a period of time over which the policy will exist but also builds a cash value for policyholders over time.

usury laws Laws that enforce a maximum interest rate that can be imposed on loans to households.

V

variable life insurance Insurance in which benefits awarded by the life insurance company to a beneficiary vary with the assets backing the policy.

variable-rate bonds Bonds whose coupon rates

adjust to market interest rates over time.

W

weak-form efficiency Theory that suggests that security prices reflect all market-related data, such as historical security price movements and volume of securities traded.

whole life insurance Insurance that protects the insured policyholders until death or as long as premiums are promptly paid; the policy builds a cash value that the policyholder is entitled to even if the policy is canceled.

working capital loan Business loan designed to support ongoing operations, typically for a short-term period.

writer The seller of an option contract.

Y

yield curve Curve depicting the relationship between the term remaining until maturity and the annualized yield of Treasury securities.

yield to maturity Discount rate at which the present value of future payments would equal the security's current price.

Z

zero-coupon bonds Bonds that have no coupon payments.

zero-coupon-for-floating swap Swap arrangement calling for one party to swap a lump-sum payment at maturity in exchange for periodic floating-rate payments.

Index

52-week price range, 245

A

Abnormal returns, 56, 287–288, 293
ABS. *See* Automated Bond System
Accounts receivable, 25, 120, 604–605
Adjustable-rate mortgage, 202–204, 222, 583
Adjusted dividend discount model, 265–266, 299
ADR. *See* American depository receipt
Advisory committee, 74, 76–77
After-tax yield, 45–46, 49, 70
Agency cost, 254, 520
Agency problem, 248–249, 251, 254, 520, 622
Aggregate demand for loanable funds, 28, 30
Aggregate supply of loanable funds, 30
AICPA. *See* American Institute of Certified Public Accountants
Allstate Insurance Group, 14, 608
Amazon.com, 238
America Online, 238
American currency option, 465–466
American depository receipt, 255, 258
American Express, 13, 601
American Institute of Certified Public Accountants, 307
American Stock Exchange, 155, 241, 243–244, 248, 318, 321, 364, 616
American-style option, 394
Ameritrade, 311, 366

Amex. *See* American Stock Exchange
Amortization schedule, 206
Amsterdam stock exchange, 257
Analyst, 22, 39–40, 61, 67–68, 87, 110, 138, 165, 189–190, 217, 223, 236, 258, 261, 263, 275–277, 279, 287–288, 292–296, 306, 308, 323, 326, 534, 553, 560, 563, 623, 662–663
Analyst rating service, 277
Annuity, 264, 305, 504, 676–677, 693
Annuity plan, 676–677
Antitakeover amendment, 254
Apple Computer, 229, 243, 639
APT. *See* Arbitrage pricing model
Arbitrage, 267, 269, 348–349, 352–353, 360, 395–397, 426, 444–447, 449, 451, 463–466
Arbitrage firm, 654–657
Arbitrage pricing model, 267, 269
Arbitrage restriction, 463
Arbitrageur, 352, 397
Archipelago Exchange, 244, 321
ARM. *See* Adjustable-rate mortgage
Arthur Andersen, 305
Asian crisis, 293, 433, 453–461, 642
Asian Development Bank, 454
Ask quote, 14, 79, 309, 444
Asset allocation fund, 627, 646
Asset quality, 511–512, 580, 592, 596
Asset stripping, 654

Asymmetric information, 9–10, 154–155, 253, 656
At the money, 363, 390, 471
ATM. *See* Automated teller machine
ATS. *See* Automatic transfer service
Audit committee, 249–250, 302
Automated Bond System, 156
Automated teller machine, 478
Automatic transfer service, 479

B

B/A. *See* Banker's acceptance
Backdating options, 387, 390
Back-end load, 621
Balance-of-trade deficit, 432
Balloon-payment mortgage, 205, 484, 488
Bank failure, 479, 500, 506, 510, 514
Bank for International Settlements, 506
Bank holding company, 499
Bank Holding Company Act, 499, 505
Bank Insurance Fund, 500, 513–514, 574
Bank of America, 13, 306, 503, 564–565, 644
Bank of Canada, 86
Bank of England, 371
Bank of Japan, 86, 455
Bank of New York, 79–80, 84, 287, 616, 642
Banker's acceptance, 117, 125–128, 134, 137, 494, 559, 637, 645
Bankers Trust, 405, 536–537
Banking Act of 1933, 502–503, 518, 668
Banking Committee, 307
Banking syndicate, 135

Barbell strategy, 185
Barclays Bank, 616
Barings PLC, 371
Basel Accord, 506–509, 517
Basel Committee, 507–509
Basel II Accord, 507–509
Basis, 343
Basis risk, 355, 413, 421–422
Bearer bond, 141
Bear-market CD, 479
Before-tax yield, 45–46, 49, 65, 70
Beige Book, 78
BellSouth, 150
Beneficiary, 673, 675–676, 679
Best-efforts agreement, 651, 653
Beta, 267–269, 274, 278–286, 293, 630, 696
Bid quote, 309, 444
Bid-ask spread, 148, 319, 336, 365, 620
Big Bang, 669
Binomial pricing model, 394–396
BIS. *See* Bank for International Settlements
Black Monday, 323
Black-Scholes option-pricing model, 397–398, 400–401
Black-Scholes partial differential equation, 397–398
Bloody Thursday, 291, 456
BNP Paribus, 306
Board of directors, 10, 76, 229, 231, 249, 251–252, 254, 301, 304, 307, 387, 520, 542, 591, 622–623, 639, 694
Board of Governors, 74–78, 81, 84, 87, 494, 498, 661
Boeing, 150
Bond Buyer Index, 346
Bond convexity, 184–185

Bond dealer, 144–145, 148, 155–156
Bond index futures, 346
Bond market, 104, 115, 141–142, 155, 158–159, 161–163, 172–175, 177, 179, 189, 457, 546, 586, 609, 633–634, 645, 668, 686, 693, 697
Bond mutual fund, 103–104, 141, 151, 162–163, 357, 359, 386, 613, 618, 626–627, 632–634, 636
Bond price elasticity, 180–181
Bond rating, 44, 155, 164, 177–178, 457
Bookbuilding, 234
Boundary conditions, 463–464
Bretton Woods era, 429
Bridge loan, 654, 657, 664, 706
Broker, 14, 15, 124, 125, 127, 144–145, 148, 155–156, 239–240, 242–245, 259, 309–314, 316–317, 319, 321–322, 328, 335–336, 339, 354, 364–366, 371, 386, 388, 416–417, 481, 489, 582, 621, 634, 652, 658–659, 661, 668, 670, 685
Brokerage firm, 17, 144, 162, 209, 235, 242, 245, 258, 309–314, 316, 319, 335–336, 365–366, 388, 427, 532, 582, 586, 620–621, 652, 656, 659, 661, 667, 670, 684–685, 697
Brussels stock exchange, 257, 327
Budget deficit, 26–27, 34, 36, 39, 48, 86, 101, 105–108, 116, 143, 173–174, 211–212, 275, 416, 448, 454, 456, 555, 588, 608, 666, 688
Budget surplus, 149, 174, 212
Bullet loan, 483
Bullish stock market, 236, 254, 411, 664
Bull-market CD, 479
Business demand for loanable funds, 25, 30, 37
Business insurance, 673, 683
Business interruption insurance, 683
Bylaws, 231, 252

C

California Public Employees' Retirement System, 251, 694
Call feature, 145, 156, 177, 408
Call option, 284, 363, 366–370, 372–383, 385–389, 394–401, 437, 441–443, 465–466, 469, 486
Call premium, 152, 463
Callable CD, 478
Callable swap, 405, 408, 422
CALPERS. *See* California Public Employees' Retirement System
CAMELS rating, 510–512, 580–581
Cap, 203, 222, 410–411, 416–419, 422, 529, 532, 585
Capital adequacy, 510, 516, 580, 596
Capital appreciation fund, 623–624, 646
Capital asset pricing model, 267–269, 296
Capital budgeting, 167
Capital flight, 460
Capital gain, 6, 616–618, 621, 689
Capital market, 3–6, 13, 20, 21, 48–49, 107, 141, 229, 301, 650, 656, 685
Capital market securities, 3, 5–6, 13, 48–49, 141, 469
Capital ratio, 482, 507, 510, 539, 542, 562, 567, 592–593, 595–596, 642, 684
Capital requirements, 482, 504, 506–510, 517, 598, 661
Capital structure, 14, 158, 160–161, 177, 230, 233, 254, 521, 561, 563
CAPM. *See* Capital asset pricing model
Captive finance subsidiary, 602
Carve-out, 656, 660
Cash flow underwriting, 681
Cashier's check, 559
CBOE. *See* Chicago Board of Options Exchange
CBOT. *See* Chicago Board of Trade
CD. *See* Certificate of deposit
CD futures, 529
Central bank, 74, 84–87, 90, 92, 371, 429, 432–433,

447–449, 454–461, 480, 506, 516
Central Liquidity Facility, 595, 597
Certificate of deposit, 5, 97, 133–134, 334–335, 479–480, 491, 496, 501, 524, 529, 541, 544, 557, 576–577, 579–580, 583, 595, 638, 646
CFS. *See* Captive finance subsidiary
CFTC. *See* Commodity Futures Trading Commission
Charles Schwab, 311, 319, 322, 660
Chattel mortgage bond, 152
ChevronTexaco, 150
Chicago Board of Options Exchange, 335, 354, 364, 366
Chicago Board of Trade, 335–336, 346, 354, 358, 364
Chicago Mercantile Exchange, 335, 346, 352–353, 358, 364
Circuit breaker, 324, 352–353
Cisco, 387
Citicorp, 504, 592, 667, 685
Citigroup, 13, 144, 386, 494, 601, 644, 651, 667, 685
CLF. *See* Central Liquidity Facility
Closed-end fund, 614–615, 619, 632–633, 646
Closing cost, 202
CME. *See* Chicago Mercantile Exchange
CMO. *See* Collateralized mortgage obligation
CNA Insurance, 14
Coastal States Life Insurance Company, 221
Coca-Cola Company, 150, 246, 494
Coincident economic indicator, 99
Collar, 323, 416, 418–419, 422
Collateral, 44, 151–152, 160, 164, 166, 199, 218, 305, 311, 313, 355–356, 481, 484, 486–487, 508, 511, 535–536, 578, 591
Collateralized mortgage obligation, 210, 219–223
Commercial loan, 13, 19, 342, 362, 477, 486, 501, 505, 522, 529, 535, 541, 543–545, 577, 579, 586,

590, 604, 609, 652, 678, 697
Commercial mortgage, 207, 213, 223, 534, 679, 686
Commercial paper, 5, 15, 48, 50, 117, 120–123, 125, 127–132, 134–137, 493, 504, 587, 603, 605, 609–611, 636–637, 644–646, 668, 685, 686, 702
Commercial paper dealer, 121–122, 127, 603
Commercial paper yield curve, 122, 138
Commission broker, 242, 335
Commodity Futures Trading Commission, 334, 354
Community Reinvestment Act, 502
Compensating balance, 121
Competitive bid, 119, 143–144, 653
Comptroller of the Currency, 76, 499, 510
Conditional currency option, 441–442
Conference Board, 99–100, 301
Confidence level, 281–282, 509, 527, 537
Coniston Partners of New York, 252
Constant-growth dividend discount model, 265, 296
Consumer Advisory Council, 77
Consumer confidence survey, 99
Consumer finance, 19, 76, 586, 601, 606
Consumer finance operation, 19, 601
Consumer loan, 18, 19, 487–488, 491, 501, 503, 505, 522, 533, 535, 569, 579, 586–588, 597, 604, 607, 609, 610
Consumer price index, 100, 130, 146, 173, 212, 275, 338, 416
Contagion effect, 159
Continental Illinois Bank, 514–515
Contingency graph, 368
Conventional mortgage, 147, 200, 202, 216, 220, 222, 582, 592–593
Convertible bond, 153
Corporate bond, 47, 49–50, 66, 68, 141–142,

150–158, 160, 162, 163, 174–175, 177–178, 342, 344, 355, 357, 488, 502, 569, 578, 626, 637, 642, 656–657, 678, 682, 686, 692–693, 696
Corporate charter, 231, 254
Correlation coefficient, 278, 284
Cost of capital, 102, 109, 299, 306, 494
Cost of carry. *See* Net financing cost
Country risk, 535–536
Covariance, 267, 269
Covered call, 376–377
Covered interest arbitrage, 445–447, 449
CRA. *See* Community Reinvestment Act
Credit crunch, 92–93
Credit line insurance, 683
Credit rating, 44, 125, 152, 155–156, 163, 177, 302, 405, 493, 605, 655, 686
Credit risk. *See* Default risk
Credit risk premium, 44, 67, 166, 175
Credit union, 13, 15–17, 20–21, 77, 104, 207, 209, 574, 594–598, 609–610
Cross-exchange rate, 427, 445, 449
Cross-hedging, 343–344, 360
Crowding-out effect, 34, 106
Cube, 616
Curb. *See* Collar
Currency call option, 388, 441, 449, 451, 464
Currency futures contract, 336, 358–359, 420, 426, 439–440, 444, 448
Currency futures market, 358
Currency option, 104, 388, 426–427, 437, 439–442, 444, 448–449, 463–466
Currency option pricing, 437, 463–465
Currency options market, 442, 463
Currency put option, 388, 449, 465–466
Currency swap, 420–422, 439–440, 448, 493, 668
CyberTrader, 322

D

Davenport, Inc., 179
Day trader, 335
Dealer, 11, 14, 21, 79–80, 82, 106, 108, 121–125,

127, 135, 144–145, 148, 155–156, 158, 162, 243, 248, 321, 324, 326, 342, 344, 405, 416–417, 481, 591, 602–603, 661
Debenture, 152–153, 160
Debt-to-asset ratio, 485
Default premium. *See* Credit risk premium
Default risk, 44–45, 49–51, 65, 121, 125–126, 130, 132, 137, 147, 154, 156, 163, 174–175, 186–188, 210, 214, 216, 218, 355, 413–415, 419, 422–423, 485–488, 508, 529, 532–535, 541, 543, 545–546, 578–579, 582, 593, 597–599, 606, 610, 626–627, 636, 642, 664, 670, 678, 684–686, 699, 703
Defensive open market operations, 81
Deficit unit, 10–15, 20, 141, 230, 476
Defined-benefit plan, 690–693
Defined-contribution plan, 691, 697
Dell, 297
Demand deposit account, 82, 478, 557
Demand for loanable funds, 24–28, 30–32, 34–39, 61, 90, 94–95, 102, 106–107, 109, 112, 174, 212, 485
Demand-pull inflation, 91, 101
Depository Institutions Deregulation and Monetary Control Act of 1980, 76, 81, 498, 500, 518, 577, 579
Deregulation Act. *See* Depository Institutions Deregulation and Monetary Control Act of 1980
Derivative security, 6, 333, 536–537
Designated Order Turnaround system, 242, 322
Deutsche Bank, 537
Diamond, 616
DIDMCA. *See* Depository Institutions Deregulation and Monetary Control Act of 1980
Direct access broker, 322, 328

Direct exchange rate, 427–428
Direct foreign investment, 448
Direct intervention, 432, 455–456
Direct lease loan, 484
Dirty float, 429
Discount bonds, 170
Discount broker, 309, 621, 659, 670
Discount rate, 7, 83, 128, 142–143, 168–169, 180–181, 188, 194–196, 198, 264, 268
Discount window, 75, 481
Disintermediation, 577
Disposable income, 24, 35, 36, 554, 587
District bank. *See* Federal Reserve district bank
Diversification, 185, 187, 225, 255, 291, 499, 503, 536, 542, 613, 626, 633–634, 680, 688
Divestiture, 273, 654, 660
Dividend discount model, 263–266, 289, 293, 299
Dividend policy, 272, 274, 540
Dividend yield, 245–246, 261, 348
Division of Corporate Finance, 325
Division of Enforcement, 325
Division of Market Regulation, 325
DJIA. *See* Dow Jones Industrial Average
DOT system. *See* Designated Order Turnaround system
Douglas Amendment, 505, 518
Dow Chemical, 494
Dow Jones Industrial Average, 246–248, 288, 323–324, 353, 379, 616, 633
Dow Jones Utilities Average, 379
Downtick, 323
Downward-sloping yield curve, 61
Drexel Burnham Lambert, 121, 158
Dual banking system, 498
Duration, 181–184, 355, 525–528
Duration analysis, 522, 545, 583–584
Duration gap, 526, 528
Dutch auction, 238–239

Dynamic asset allocation, 351, 380
Dynegy, 306

E

E*Trade, 311, 366
Earnings per share, 238, 246, 266, 289, 297, 303–304, 482
Earnings surprise, 273, 294
ECB. *See* European Central Bank
ECNs. *See* Electronic communications networks
Economies of scale, 18, 20, 476, 495, 506, 542, 555, 594–595, 607, 622, 660
Economies of scope, 18, 498
ECU. *See* European Currency Unit
Edge Act corporation, 494
Effective yield, 135–137
Efficiency. *See* Market efficiency
Electronic communications networks, 244, 309, 319, 320–322, 327–328
Emerging market, 20, 161, 257–258, 291, 293, 327, 457, 461
Employee Retirement Income Security Act, 691–692
Energy and Commerce Committee, 307
Enron, 9, 44–45, 177, 249, 302–306, 388, 505, 643
Enron Online, 302
Equilibrium interest rate, 29–33, 35–36, 39, 90, 102
Equilibrium price, 7, 232, 239, 241, 258–259, 317
Equity REIT, 644, 647
Equity swap, 161, 405, 411, 422
Equity-for-debt swap, 161
Equivalent before-tax yield, 46
ERISA. *See* Employee Retirement Income Security Act
ERM. *See* Exchange rate mechanism
ETF. *See* Exchange-traded fund
Eurobank, 135, 481, 531
Eurobond, 163, 412
Euro-commercial paper, 135
Eurodollar, 84, 127, 132–134, 334, 478, 481, 483, 490
Eurodollar certificate of deposit, 133

Eurodollar deposit, 132–133, 481, 490
Eurodollar floating-rate CDs, 134–135
Eurodollar market, 133, 481
Eurolist, 327
Euronext, 257, 358
Euronotes, 132, 135
European Central Bank, 85–87, 432
European currency option, 465–466
European Currency Unit, 429
European Union, 85, 509
Exchange controls, 414, 430, 433
Exchange rate mechanism, 429
Exchange rate risk, 104, 137, 163, 186, 188, 328, 430, 438–440, 446–447, 538–539, 627, 633, 664
Exchange rate volatility, 436–437
Exchange-traded fund, 259, 329, 378–379, 615–616, 625
Exercise price, 284, 363, 366–370, 372–376, 378–393, 396, 398, 400–401, 437, 441–444, 463–466
Expectations theory. See Pure expectations theory
Expense ratio, 259, 619–622, 634
Expiration date, 236, 284, 363–364, 366–368, 370, 372–374, 376–378, 380–386, 437, 441–443, 465
Extendable swap, 405, 409–410, 422
Extended trading session, 244
ExxonMobil, 246

F

Fannie Mae. See Federal National Mortgage Association
Fannie Mae mortgage-backed securities, 219, 221
Farmers Insurance Group, 680
FASB. See Financial Accounting Standards Board
FDICIA. See Federal Deposit Insurance Corporation Improvement Act
Federal Advisory Council, 76
Federal agency bond, 141–143, 147, 163

Federal Deposit Insurance Corporation, 498–500, 513, 517, 521, 574
Federal Deposit Insurance Corporation Improvement Act, 498, 500, 513–514, 517
Federal funds, 79–81, 83, 89, 98, 100–102, 109–111, 117, 124–125, 127–128, 134–135, 137, 288, 345, 375, 478, 480–481, 483, 485, 489, 492, 495, 512, 521, 546
Federal funds broker, 124–125, 127, 481
Federal funds market, 79–80, 124–125, 127–128, 135, 480–481, 489, 495–496, 512, 521, 546, 557, 577, 579, 582
Federal funds rate, 79–81, 83, 98, 101–102, 109, 124, 134–135, 288, 375, 480–481, 485, 577
Federal funds target rate, 79, 98
Federal Home Loan Bank Board, 591
Federal Home Loan Mortgage Association, 147, 208, 220, 222, 488, 595
Federal Housing Administration, 147, 200, 219–220, 582
Federal National Mortgage Association, 147, 208–209, 219–222, 224, 488
Federal Open Market Committee, 34, 74, 76–80, 87, 97, 101–103, 109–111, 124
Federal Reserve Act, 74
Federal Reserve Board. See Board of Governors
Federal Reserve district bank, 74–79, 124, 480, 484
Federal Reserve float, 83–84
Federal Savings and Loan Insurance Corporation, 591
Federally insured mortgage, 200, 219
FHA. See Federal Housing Administration
Fidelity, 156, 623, 683
Finance company, 13, 15, 17, 601–608, 610
Financial Accounting Standards Board, 300, 302, 307
Financial conglomerate, 18–20, 477, 497, 503–504, 553, 568, 573–574, 586, 601, 606, 650,

661–662, 664, 667, 673, 685, 687, 701
Financial futures contract, 334–338, 341, 347, 358–359, 361, 529, 546, 668
Financial Institutions Reform, Recovery, and Enforcement Act, 159, 164, 499, 518, 590–593, 598–599
Financial leverage, 159–161, 254, 303, 306, 341, 486, 539, 562, 642, 655
Financial Performance Report, 596
Financial planner, 225, 621
Financial Services Modernization Act, 503–504, 518, 661, 667–668, 685
Fire Fly Trading, 322
FIRREA. See Financial Institutions Reform, Recovery, and Enforcement Act
First mortgage, 152, 204
First mortgage bond, 152
Fiscal policy, 36, 86, 88, 105–106, 108, 129, 179, 213, 274, 339, 375, 415, 447
Fisher effect, 33, 40
Fitch Investor Service, 121, 147
Fixed asset, 481–484, 490, 543, 569, 677
Fixed-for-floating swap. See Plain vanilla swap
Fixed-rate mortgage, 172, 189, 202–203, 205–206, 210–214, 216–217, 221–222, 356, 383, 389, 423, 467, 531, 582–585, 588, 598
Fixed-rate bond, 153, 189, 193, 412, 679, 694
Flight to quality, 132
Flipping, 237, 239
Floating-rate bond. See Variable-rate bond
Floating-rate loan, 41, 69, 403, 407, 423, 529, 532, 543, 545–546
Floating-rate mortgage, 542
Floor broker, 242, 316–317, 322, 328–329, 335–336, 365, 388
Floor trader, 241, 335, 661
Flotation cost, 652–653
FOMC. See Federal Open Market Committee
Ford, 13, 121, 601, 604
Forecasting error, 60
Foreign bond, 162, 187–188, 626–627, 645, 678

Foreign demand for loanable funds, 27, 30
Foreign exchange derivative, 333, 426–427, 429, 431, 433–435, 437–439, 441–443, 445, 447–449, 467, 508
Foreign exchange derivative market, 467
Foreign exchange market, 11, 85–86, 426–427, 429, 432, 434, 436–438, 444, 448–449, 453–456, 469
Foreign stock index futures, 358
Forward contract, 426–427, 439–441, 448–450, 492, 494, 537
Forward market, 439, 445, 447
Forward rate, 54–58, 60, 64, 66, 68, 70, 427, 435–436, 439–440, 445–449
Forward swap, 405, 407–408
Franchise, 486
Fraud, 9, 209, 257, 307, 371, 590, 598, 641, 643
FRCDs. See Eurodollar floating-rate CDs
Freddie Mac. See Federal Home Loan Mortgage Association
Free cash flow model, 267
Freely floating system, 429, 449
Front-end load, 621
Front-running, 318, 663
FSLIC. See Federal Savings and Loan Insurance Corporation
Full-service broker, 258, 309–310, 659, 670–671
Fundamental analysis, 263
Fundamental forecasting, 435
Futures contract, 322, 334–359, 362–363, 371, 381–386, 388, 392, 420, 426, 439, 440–444, 448–451, 469, 529, 546, 568, 584–585, 597, 609, 645, 668, 686, 694, 697
Futures market, 4, 334–335, 337–339, 343–345, 347, 349, 351–361, 448, 546, 586–587, 610, 686, 697
Futures options, 381, 383, 546, 587, 685

G

GAAP. See Generally accepted accounting principles

Gap, 523–529, 543–544, 546–547, 549, 583
Gap analysis, 523–524, 526, 528, 546
Gap ratio, 524, 544, 549
Garn-St Germain Act, 480, 501, 577, 579, 598
GDP. *See* Gross domestic product
GECC. *See* General Electric Credit Corporation
General Electric, 13, 162, 601–602
General Electric Credit Corporation, 602
General Motors, 13, 601, 604, 691
General Motors Acceptance Corporation, 604, 612
General obligation bond, 147, 502
Generally accepted accounting principles, 244, 258, 300
Gibson Greetings, Inc., 404
Ginnie Mae. *See* Government National Mortgage Association
Ginnie Mae mortgage-backed securities, 219–220
Glass-Steagall Act. *See* Banking Act of 1933
Global Crossing, 387
Global crowding out, 107–108
Global integration, 11, 414, 461
Global junk bond, 162
Global mutual fund, 624, 646
GLOBEX, 335, 358
GMAC. *See* General Motors Acceptance Corporation
Golden parachute, 254–255
Goldman Sachs, 14, 379, 651, 660, 669
Google, 3, 8, 238–239
Governance, 10, 188, 249, 300–302, 324, 387, 591, 622
Government agency, 488, 636, 645, 682, 692–693
Government agency securities, 488, 682
Government demand for loanable funds, 26–27, 30, 37, 39, 174
Government National Mortgage Association, 147, 208, 219–222, 626, 645
Government securities dealer, 79–80, 106, 124, 344, 481
GPM. *See* Graduated-payment mortgage

Graduated-payment mortgage, 202–204, 222
Gramm-Leach-Bliley Act. *See* Financial Services Modernization Act
Great Depression, 9, 500
Greenmail, 655, 671
Greenspan, Alan, 76
Gross domestic product, 78, 99, 112, 130, 174, 270, 338, 375, 416, 448
Gross interest expenses, 557–558, 562, 566–567
Gross interest income, 557–558, 561–562, 566–567
Group life policy, 674
Growing-equity mortgage, 202, 204, 222
Growth and income fund, 623–624, 627, 646
Growth fund, 623–624, 627, 630

H

Health insurance, 19, 673, 676–677, 689, 700
Health maintenance organization, 682–683
Hedge fund, 536, 614, 616, 641–643, 647
Hedge ratio, 395–396
Hedgers, 335, 358
Hewlett-Packard, 457
Highly leveraged transaction, 486, 496, 502
HLT. *See* Highly leveraged transaction
HMO. *See* Health maintenance organization
Holding period return, 143
Holiday effect, 288
Home Depot, 245
Hostile takeover, 256, 654
Household demand for loanable funds, 24–25, 30, 37, 39
Household International Inc., 609
Hybrid fund, 619

I

IBA. *See* Interstate Banking Act
IBF. *See* Investment bank
IBM, 162, 178, 242, 265, 268, 269, 493, 525, 697
ICE. *See* Intercontinental Exchange
IMF. *See* International Monetary Fund
Impact lag, 94
Imperfect market, 21
Implementation lag, 94, 109

Implied standard deviation, 283–284, 378, 437
Implied volatility, 380, 400
In the money, 363
Income fund, 623–624, 626, 627, 646, 649
Indenture, 151–152
Independent broker, 242
Index arbitrage, 352–353
Index mutual fund, 640
Index of Leading Economic Indicators, 99
Indirect exchange rate, 427–428
Indirect intervention, 432–433, 456–457
Individual retirement account, 14, 153, 692
Industrial loan, 477
Industrial production index, 99
Inflation rate, 33, 64, 71, 96–98, 100, 110, 146, 165, 294, 431, 448
Inflation-indexed bond, 146
Informal line of credit, 484–485
Information cost, 326–328, 426, 690
ING. *See* Internationale Nederlanden Groep
Initial margin, 311–312, 336, 341
Initial public offering, 228–229, 233–241, 276, 288, 603, 639, 651, 704
Inside board member, 249
Insider trading, 158–159, 258, 288, 292, 365, 502
Installment credit, 100, 602
Installment debt, 24
Installment loan, 487
Instinet, 244, 321
Institutional Shareholder Services Inc., 251–252
Insurance commissioner, 684
Insurance premium, 17, 202, 216, 380, 500, 514, 596, 673, 675, 677, 679–681, 683, 688, 700
Insurance Regulatory Information System, 683–684
Insured plan, 693–694
Intel, 243
Intercontinental Exchange, 336, 364
Interest rate cap, 416–419, 422, 424–425, 529, 532, 586
Interest rate collar, 416, 418–419, 422, 424
Interest rate derivative, 402, 416, 422, 425, 509, 568
Interest rate floor, 416–419, 422, 424

Interest rate futures contract, 334, 336, 343, 345, 359–360, 381, 383–384, 388, 467, 469, 529, 546, 584–585, 597, 645
Interest rate parity, 446–447, 449–451, 471, 473
Interest rate risk, 131, 134, 171–172, 182, 185, 191, 202–203, 205, 207–209, 213–214, 218, 342–344, 356–357, 381, 384, 386, 389, 392, 402–405, 407, 411, 413, 416, 418–419, 422–423, 468–469, 475, 520, 522–530, 532, 537–538, 541, 543, 546–548, 550, 573, 578–579, 582–586, 597–599, 606, 609, 610, 626–627, 633, 637, 645, 647, 664, 667, 670, 684, 686, 694, 699, 702
Interest rate strategy, 185
Interest rate swap, 209, 221, 402–405, 407–408, 410–417, 419–425, 467, 469, 493, 504, 529–531, 533, 546, 548, 584–586, 597–598, 609, 645, 668, 686, 697
Interest-inelastic, 26, 29
Interest-only CMO, 220
Internal ratings-based approach, 507
International arbitrage, 426, 444, 449
International debt crisis, 642
International Monetary Fund, 258–259, 261, 454–456, 459
International money market, 133, 135, 445
International mutual fund, 188, 258, 260–261, 361, 427, 467, 624, 630, 633, 647–648
International Securities Exchange, 364
International stock offering, 255, 669
International syndicate, 669
International trade, 78, 125, 133, 135, 421, 426
Internationale Nederlanden Groep, 371
Internet broker, 310
Internet fund, 625
Interstate Banking Act, 505–506, 516, 518
Inventory cost, 319–320
Inverted yield curve. *See* Downward-sloping yield curve

Investment bank, 22, 150, 151, 161, 163, 234–236, 238–240, 255–256, 260–261, 275–276, 295, 304, 335, 371, 650–656, 670–671, 704–705
Investment Company Act, 638
Investment-grade bonds, 44, 177, 691
Investor sentiment, 272, 294
Investor's Business Daily, 145, 277
IPO. *See* Initial public offering
IRB approach. *See* Internal ratings-based approach
IRIS. *See* Insurance Regulatory Information System
Irregular accounting method, 249
ISD. *See* Implied standard deviation
ishares, 259, 379, 616
Island, 321
ISS Inc. *See* Institutional Shareholder Services Inc.
Issue cost, 652

J

J.P. Morgan Chase, 13, 306, 386, 537, 644
January effect, 272, 288, 294
Joint venture, 354, 582, 669, 690
Junk bond, 156, 158–160, 162, 164–165, 221, 486, 578–579, 591–592, 598, 626, 654, 678, 683, 686, 691, 699
Junk bond fund, 626
Junk commercial paper, 121
Justice Department, 144

K

Key employee insurance, 683
Kohlberg Kravis Roberts, Inc., 160, 294, 639

L

L/C. *See* Letter of credit
Labor union, 594
Laddered strategy, 185
Laddering, 239, 261
Lagging economic indicator, 99
Late trading, 243–244, 622–623, 663
LBO. *See* Leveraged buyout
Lead underwriter, 233–235
Leading economic indicator, 99, 109

LEAPs. *See* Long-term equity anticipations
Leasing, 499, 516–517, 604–605, 609–611
Lender liability suit, 487
Letter of credit, 125–126, 493
Leverage. *See* Financial leverage
Leverage measure, 578, 603, 605
Leveraged buyout, 158–160, 254, 294, 486, 502, 604–605, 654–655, 667–670, 685
Liability insurance, 681, 683
Liberty Mutual, 14
LIBOR, 134–135, 153, 406–407, 412, 415–419, 424, 522, 531, 548, 678–679
License, 486, 683
Life insurance, 58, 158, 188, 207, 221, 251, 357, 381, 481, 595, 673, 675–681, 685, 687–688, 690, 693, 698–700
LIFFE. *See* London International Financial Futures and Options Exchange
Limit order, 156, 309–310, 317–318, 320–321, 336, 365, 656, 658, 670
Line of credit, 121, 140, 484–485, 568, 661
Liquidity premium, 49–50, 57–58, 60–61, 64–68, 70–71, 153
Liquidity premium theory, 51, 56–57, 60, 65–67
Liquidity ratio, 689
Liquidity risk, 50–51, 355, 529, 543, 573, 582, 597–599, 606, 610, 684–686
Lisbon stock exchange, 257
Listing requirements, 242–244, 364
Load fund, 620–621, 646
Loan commitment, 493, 495
Loan loss provision, 557, 559–561, 564–565, 588–589
Loan participation, 485
Loanable funds theory, 24, 33
Loan-to-value ratio, 202, 215
Locational arbitrage, 444–445, 449, 451
Lockbox, 559
Lockheed Martin, 694
Lockup provision, 235, 260
Lomas Financial, 121
London Interbank Offer Rate. *See* LIBOR

London International Financial Futures and Options Exchange, 354, 358
Long hedge, 344, 360
Long-Term Capital Management, 641–642
Long-term equity anticipations, 380
Loose money policy. *See* Stimulative monetary policy
Low-coupon bond, 181
LTCM. *See* Long-Term Capital Management

M

M1, 84
M2, 84
M3, 84
Maintenance margin, 311–313, 329
Making a market, 14, 317
Malpractice insurance, 683
Managed health care plan, 682
Management fee, 617, 634, 641, 659, 660
Managerial compensation, 299, 304
Margin account, 311, 336, 341
Margin call, 311, 313, 336, 353, 371
Margin requirement, 16, 311, 329, 336, 348, 661
Margin trade, 309
Marginal tax rate, 45
Marine insurance, 683
Market efficiency, 56, 130, 263, 287, 517, 634
Market for corporate control, 253–254, 259–260, 302, 306, 471
Market imperfections, 12, 404
Market microstructure, 227, 309
Market order, 156, 309–310, 316, 320, 329, 336, 365, 656–659, 670
Market risk, 349–350, 355, 469, 509, 536–538, 610, 633, 645, 664, 667, 670, 685–686, 697–698, 706
Market risk premium, 267–268, 274, 296, 375, 459–460
Market-based forecasting, 435
Market-maker, 316, 318–321, 325–326, 328, 365, 430, 661
MarketWatch.com, 236, 240
MasterCard, 487

Matched funding, 693, 698
Matching strategy, 185
Maturity matching, 529
Maximum Financial, 322
Mayer & Schweitzer, 319
MBI futures. *See* Municipal Bond Index futures
McDonald's, 366
McFadden Act, 505, 518
MCI, 300
Member bank, 74–77, 499
Merger, 14, 19–20, 243–244, 257, 275–276, 302, 324, 335–336, 504, 506, 517, 574–575, 655–656, 660, 667–670, 701, 706
Merger-conversion, 575
Merrill Lynch, 14, 20, 22, 146, 645, 651, 654, 668, 669, 672
Microsoft, 229, 238, 569, 639
Mid-cap spider, 616
Midwest Stock Exchange, 241
Mini Nasdaq 100, 347
Mini S&P 500, 346–347
Mini-crash, 291, 353
Mixed forecasting, 435–436
MMDA. *See* Money market deposit account
MMF. *See* Money market mutual fund
MNC. *See* Multinational corporation
Modified duration, 183–184
Monetary Control Act of 1980. *See* Depository Institutions Deregulation and Monetary Control Act of 1980
Monetary policy, 29, 34, 36, 40, 73–74, 76, 78–80, 82–88, 90–113, 129, 179, 190, 193, 213, 223, 274, 295, 339, 375, 390, 415, 447, 469–472, 647, 703
Monetizing the debt, 106, 109
Money center bank, 557–561, 563–564, 566–567
Money market deposit account, 84, 478, 480, 483, 496, 501, 524–525, 543–545, 549, 551, 557, 576–577, 580, 595, 598
Money market mutual fund, 13–14, 21, 84, 121, 127, 501, 586, 618, 634–638, 644–646, 668
Money market security, 128–131, 134–140
Money order, 595

Money supply growth, 38, 40, 77, 79–80, 83, 87, 89, 91, 94–95, 107, 109, 174, 189, 211, 555, 588, 608, 666, 688

Moody's Investor Service, 44, 121

Moral hazard problem, 500, 518, 673–675, 699

Morgan Stanley, 14, 379, 645, 651, 669

Morgan Stanley Biotechnology Index, 379

Morningstar, 277

Mortgage loan, 13, 200, 202–203, 205, 208, 216–217, 508, 521, 546, 556, 574, 578–583, 587–588, 590, 592, 593, 596, 601–602, 605, 706

Mortgage market, 104, 115, 199–200, 202–203, 205–213, 215, 217, 219–223, 546, 586–587, 609, 645, 668, 685–686, 697

Mortgage origination. *See* Origination

Mortgage pass-through security, 218–219

Mortgage rate, 102, 200, 202–205, 208, 210–211, 213, 216, 219, 222, 578

Mortgage REIT, 644, 647

Mortgage-backed securities, 200, 209, 217–221, 578–580, 586–587, 597, 686

Motorola, 245, 457

Multibank holding companies, 499

Multifund fund, 623, 626

Multinational corporation, 13, 436, 441, 494, 610, 690

Multinational finance companies, 610

Multinational insurance companies, 690

Multiplier effect, 82

Municipal bond, 26, 45, 49, 66, 68, 101, 141–142, 147–149, 153, 156–158, 162–163, 165–166, 175, 190–191, 346, 488, 619, 626–627, 630, 645, 656–657, 659, 668, 680–681, 696

Municipal Bond Index futures, 346

Municipal bond yield curve, 148–149

Municipal government, 18, 26, 28, 30, 147, 492, 581, 645, 657, 680, 696

Municipal security, 46, 149–150, 164, 488, 491–492, 544–545, 549, 551, 580–581, 682

Mutual fund, 13–22, 84, 103–104, 127, 141, 151, 158, 162–163, 188–189, 207, 209, 221, 230–232, 251, 258–262, 281, 322, 350, 357, 359, 361, 375, 386, 426–427, 467, 491, 501, 503, 517, 536, 542, 573, 586, 613–614, 616–649, 653–654, 657, 659, 663–664, 667–668, 684–685, 696–697, 701

Mutual life insurance company, 675–676

Mutual-to-stock conversion, 574

N

NADAL, 8–9

NAFTA. *See* North American Free Trade Agreement

NAIC. *See* National Association of Insurance Commissioners

Naked options, 366

NASD. *See* National Association of Securities Dealers

Nasdaq. *See* National Association of Securities Dealers Automatic Quotations

Nasdaq 100 index, 347, 379, 616

Nasdaq National Market, 243

Nasdaq Small Cap Market, 243

National Association of Insurance Commissioners, 684, 699

National Association of Securities Dealers, 155, 243, 321, 326, 661

National Association of Securities Dealers Automatic Quotations, 3, 243–244, 247–248, 297, 302, 311, 316, 318, 320–321, 324–326, 330, 347–348, 354, 364, 379, 616, 661

National Association of Securities Dealers' Trade Reporting and Compliance Engine, 155

National bank, 76, 499, 504

National Credit Union Administration, 596

National Credit Union Share Insurance Fund, 596

National income, 99, 454

Nationwide Insurance Enterprise, 680

NAV. *See* Net asset value

Navy Credit Union, 13

Navy Federal Credit Union, 594

NCD. *See* Negotiable certificate of deposit

NCUA. *See* National Credit Union Administration

NCUSIF. *See* National Credit Union Share Insurance Fund

Negotiable certificate of deposit, 122–123, 126–128, 133, 137–139, 479–480, 482, 569–571

Negotiable order of withdrawal account, 84, 318, 320, 476, 478–480, 492, 501, 543–545, 547, 549, 551, 557, 577, 580, 583–584, 595

Net asset value, 259, 617–619, 625, 627, 630–633, 648

Net demand for funds, 37

Net exposure, 345, 539

Net financing cost, 348–349

Net interest income, 557, 559, 562, 566–567, 588–590, 611

Net interest margin, 522–525, 529–530, 533–534, 543, 557–560, 564–568, 600, 702–703

Net present value, 25

Net underwriting margin, 689

Net worth, 182, 482, 575, 577, 591, 641, 689, 692

Netscape, 238

New York Stock Exchange, 3, 144, 155–156, 241–244, 248, 257, 302, 311, 313, 316–318, 320–324, 329, 352–354, 623, 663

New York Stock Exchange Composite Index, 248

NIF. *See* Note issuance facility

Nike, 5, 245, 457

Nikkei 225 Stock Average, 358

NobleTrading, 322

Noise trader, 319

No-load fund, 621, 646

Nominal interest rate, 33, 36, 40, 64, 100

Noncompetitive bid, 119, 137, 143, 144

Noninterest expenses, 541, 543, 545, 557, 559–571, 589–590, 594, 600, 611, 702–704

Noninterest income, 556–557, 559–562, 564–568, 588–590, 600, 608, 611, 702–703

Nonprofit organization, 594

North American Free Trade Agreement, 494, 646, 669, 690

Note issuance facility, 493

Notional principal, 402, 406–407, 411, 416–418, 424

NOW account. *See* Negotiable order of withdrawal account

NPV. *See* Net present value

NYSE. *See* New York Stock Exchange

O

OCC. *See* Options Clearing Corporation

Off-balance sheet activity, 476–477, 491, 493, 495, 518

Off-balance sheet transaction, 504

Offer price, 145, 234–237, 239, 240, 260–261, 651, 663, 671–672

Office of Thrift Supervision, 580, 591

Oil prices, 40, 78, 96–98, 101, 103–104, 110, 112, 173, 188–190, 223, 360, 450, 470, 590

One-bank holding company, 499

OneChicago, 354

Open interest, 345, 348

Open Market Desk. *See* Trading Desk

Open market operation, 77, 79–82, 85, 87, 91, 94, 106, 109, 144

Open-end fund, 614–615, 647

Operating risk, 538

Operational risk, 356, 508

Opportunity cost, 26, 205, 214, 320, 338

Option contract, 299, 363–367, 390, 441

Option market, 370, 374, 380

Option premium, 284, 363, 366, 372–374, 378, 381–383, 389–390, 392–395, 400, 437, 463–466

Options Clearing Corporation, 364–365

Oracle Corporation, 229, 297, 639
Orange County, California, 161, 404
Order cost, 319
Organizational structure, 18–19, 555, 587, 607, 665, 688
Organized exchange, 241–243, 260, 334, 402
Origination, 199, 202–203, 205, 207, 209, 215, 220, 578, 650, 652, 670
Origination fee, 199, 202
OTC bulletin board, 243–244
OTC market. *See* Over-the-counter market
OTS. *See* Office of Thrift Supervision
Out of the money, 363, 472, 474
Outside board member, 249
Overhead, 563–564, 674
Over-the-counter market, 155, 241, 243–244, 355–356, 386

P

Pacific Basin stock index, 624
Pacific stock exchange, 241, 321, 364
Paris Stock Exchange, 257
Participation certificate, 219–222
Passbook savings account. *See* Savings account
Patent, 317, 486
PBGC. *See* Pension Benefit Guaranty Corporation
PC. *See* Participation certificate
PC insurance. *See* Property and casualty insurance
PE method. *See* Price-earnings method
PE ratio. *See* Price-earnings ratio
Pegged exchange rate system, 429, 455
Penny stock, 243, 329
Penny-jumping. *See* Front-running
Pension Benefit Guaranty Corporation, 692, 699
Pension fund, 14–17, 20–21, 58, 103–104, 127–128, 141, 151, 153, 158, 161–162, 166, 185, 188, 190, 207, 228–232, 251, 259, 262, 281, 322, 342, 357, 359–360, 375–376, 379, 381, 386, 404–405, 411, 426–427, 439, 467,

481, 486, 503, 522, 536, 573, 600, 609, 639, 641, 644, 653, 657, 659, 667, 673, 685, 687, 689–700, 702–703, 705
Perpetuity, 264
Peso crisis, 432–433
Philadelphia Stock Exchange, 364–365
Pink sheet, 244
PIPs. *See* Publicly issued pass-through securities
Plain vanilla swap, 406–407, 409–410, 415–416, 423–424, 529
Poison pill, 254
Policy directive, 79–80, 84, 87
Policy loan, 678–679
Political risk, 293
Portfolio beta, 279
Portfolio insurance, 322, 352, 380
Position trader, 335
PPO. *See* Preferred provider organization
PPP. *See* Purchasing power parity
Precious metal, 624, 658
Preemptive right, 241
Preferred habitat theory, 59, 67
Preferred provider organization, 682–683
Preferred stock, 231, 482, 507, 630, 653
Premium. *See* Option premium
Prepayment risk, 213–214, 216–218, 355
Price index, 42, 100, 130, 146, 161, 165, 173, 212, 275, 338, 416
Price-earnings method, 264, 289, 294, 296, 299, 304
Price-earnings ratio, 246, 294, 330–331
Priceline.com, 238
Primary capital, 482
Primary credit, 83
Primary market, 3, 14, 20, 22, 106, 116, 141, 174, 229–230, 586, 613, 668
Prime rate, 100, 134, 485, 535
Principal-only CMO, 220, 223
Private equity, 228–229, 638, 640
Private equity funds, 229, 638–641, 648
Private placement, 150–151, 166, 648, 652–653, 668, 671, 700

Privatization, 10, 21, 255, 669
Procter & Gamble, 404
Producer price index, 42, 100, 130, 173, 212, 275, 338, 416
Product liability lawsuit, 97
Profit margin, 202–203, 218, 506, 538
Program trading, 322–323, 325
Projective funding, 693, 698
Property and casualty insurance, 19, 673, 678, 680–682, 689, 698
Prospectus, 150, 151, 233–235, 240, 259–260, 617, 638, 651–653
Protective covenant, 152, 484
Proxy contest, 251–252
Proxy statement, 325
Publicly issued pass-through securities, 219–220
Purchasing power parity, 431, 449, 453
Pure expectations theory, 51, 54–57, 59–62, 65, 95
Put option, 363, 366, 368, 370, 372–385, 387–393, 396, 401, 441–443, 449, 463–467, 469, 471, 587, 686
Putable swap, 405, 408–409, 422
Put-call parity, 396, 400, 465–466

Q

QX designation, 244

R

Raider, 302, 306
Rate-capped swap, 405, 410, 411, 422, 423
Rating agency, 67, 175, 307
Real estate investment trust, 643–644, 647
Real estate loan, 488, 490, 496, 514, 591, 604–605, 510
Real interest rate, 33, 40, 41, 64
Recession. *See* Recessionary period
Recessionary period, 24, 36, 61, 67–68, 70, 112, 121, 123, 138, 160, 173, 176–177, 200, 210–211, 344, 467, 511, 611, 701
Recognition lag, 94, 109
Reebok International Ltd., 253

Registered bond, 141
Registration statement, 241, 325, 651–653
Regression analysis, 42, 111, 268, 279, 523, 526–528, 550
Regression model. *See* Regression analysis
Regulation Fair Disclosure, 277, 326, 661
Regulation Q, 478–479, 501
Reigle-Neal Interstate Banking and Branching Efficiency Act. *See* Interstate Banking Act
Reinsurance, 681
REIT. *See* Real estate investment trust
Replicating portfolio, 395–396
Repo. *See* Repurchase agreement
Repo broker, 124
Repo rate, 124, 139
Repurchase agreement, 80, 84, 117, 123–124, 127–128, 137–139, 218, 478, 481, 483, 490, 492, 495, 496, 577, 579, 582, 636, 646, 682
Reserve requirement ratio, 81–83, 87
Reserve requirements, 74, 76–77, 81, 87, 133, 483, 499, 578, 602
Residential construction, 78, 102
Residential mortgage, 13, 147, 199–200, 202, 207, 209, 214, 222
Resolution Trust Corporation, 591–593, 598
Restrictive monetary policy, 92–93, 95–98, 108–109, 473, 568, 703
Retail CD. *See* Certificate of deposit
Retail sales index, 99
Return on assets, 330, 511, 527, 533, 539–540, 549, 560–563, 566, 570, 592
Return on equity, 330, 506, 527, 539, 546, 549, 562–563, 567, 571, 703–704
Return on net worth, 689
Revenue bond, 147, 346
Reverse LBO, 254
Reverse repo, 123
Revolving credit loan, 485
Reward-to-variability ratio. *See* Sharpe index
Riding the yield curve, 62
Risk aversion, 444, 680
Risk management, 6, 494

Risk-adjusted return, 286, 295, 628, 632, 634, 694
Riskless hedge, 397
RJR Nabisco, Inc., 160, 294
ROA. *See* Return on assets
Road show, 234, 259–261, 651
ROE. *See* Return on equity
RTC. *See* Resolution Trust Corporation
Rule 144A, 151, 652
Russell 1000, 379
Russell 2000, 347
Russian crisis, 433

S

S&L. *See* Savings and loan association
S&P 100 index, 379
S&P 400 Midcap Index, 616
S&P 500 index, 246–247, 268, 270–271, 297, 322, 346–347, 349–350, 362, 379–380, 384–385, 390, 411, 616, 625, 633
S&P 500 index futures, 346–347, 349–350, 384–385
S&P SmallCap 600, 379
SAIF. *See* Savings Association Insurance Fund
Salomon Brothers, 144
Salomon Smith Barney, 144, 651, 660, 667
Sarbanes-Oxley Act, 10, 240, 249–250, 261, 307, 471, 473, 518, 703
Savings account, 36, 81, 84, 478–479, 501, 557–558, 577, 595
Savings and loan association, 13, 21, 77, 123, 162, 356, 360, 383, 390, 392, 405, 499, 501, 513, 574, 578, 591, 599
Savings Association Insurance Fund, 574, 591
Savings bank, 13, 77, 220, 232, 405, 574, 577
Savings bond, 146–147
Savings deposit, 84, 477–479, 482–483, 495, 501, 579–580
Savings institution, 13, 15–18, 20, 59, 77, 127–128, 159, 172, 200, 207, 209, 218, 220, 223–224, 232, 342, 357, 359, 381, 386, 389, 403–404, 467, 499–500, 517–518, 526, 574–598, 601–602, 604, 606, 609–611, 618, 644, 647, 661, 666–667, 676, 685, 701–706

Savings institution crisis, 574, 579, 590, 599
SEC. *See* Securities and Exchange Commission
Second mortgage, 202, 228, 245, 646
Secondary capital, 514
Secondary credit, 89
Secondary markets, 3, 12, 116, 117, 207, 230
Secondary stock offering, 240, 253, 262–263, 285, 302
Sector Spider, 342
Securities Act of 1933, 9, 323, 350, 679
Securities and Exchange Commission, 9, 120, 144, 150–151, 233–234, 236, 240–241, 243–244, 255, 258–259, 276–277, 300, 302, 307, 318, 320, 323–326, 328–329, 354, 365, 503, 600, 612, 617, 621–623, 628, 641, 643, 651–653, 659–663, 670, 672
Securities Exchange Act of 1934, 9, 21, 323–324
Securities firm, 14–16, 18–21, 145–146, 232, 235, 237, 259, 306, 308, 322, 352, 357, 386, 404–405, 413, 416–417, 419, 423–424, 503, 642, 644–646, 650–651, 655, 659–672, 685, 697, 701
Securities gains, 557, 559, 564
Securities Investor Protection Corporation, 661
Securitization, 208, 521–522
Segmented markets theory, 51, 58–59, 60, 65–67, 109
Self-liquidating loan. *See* Working capital loan
Semistrong-form efficiency, 287–288
Sensitivity analysis, 131, 216–217, 583
September 11, 2001, 40, 86, 164, 313, 630, 660, 687
Series EE savings bond, 146
Settlement date, 334, 336–342, 345, 347–350, 354, 356, 359, 381, 385, 440, 443, 529
Settlement risk, 539
SFE. *See* Sydney Futures Exchange
Share draft, 595
Shared-appreciation mortgage, 202, 205, 222

Shareholder activism, 250–251, 648
Sharpe, William, 394
Sharpe index, 285–286, 295
Shelf-registration, 241
Short hedge, 342–343, 345, 357, 360, 362
Short interest ratio, 314–316, 320
Short sale, 309, 313–316, 658–659
SIMEX. *See* Singapore International Monetary Exchange
Singapore International Monetary Exchange, 358, 371
Single European Act, 516–518
Single stock futures, 354
Sinking-fund provision, 151, 164
SIPC. *See* Securities Investor Protection Corporation
SLC. *See* Standby letter of credit
Smithsonian Agreement, 429, 449
Social Security, 478, 690
Sony, 494
Sovereign risk, 413–415, 422–423
SOX Act. *See* Sarbanes-Oxley Act
SPE. *See* Special-purpose entity
Specialist, 242, 316–318, 320, 328–329, 658, 661, 663, 682
Special-purpose entity, 305, 307
Specialty fund, 623, 625, 646
Speculation, 6, 132, 311, 333, 337, 342, 359, 370, 381–382, 438, 450, 455, 685
Speculator, 333–335, 339, 341, 348, 357–360, 363, 366, 368, 370, 378–379, 381–383, 388–391, 435–436, 438, 442–444, 448–450, 456
Spider. *See* Standard & Poor's Depository Receipt
Spinning, 239, 261, 663
Spin-off, 656, 660
Spot exchange rate, 136, 420, 437, 444, 447, 463–464
Spot market, 441–443, 446, 463–465
Stale price, 623, 663
Standard & Poor's 500 index. *See* S&P 500 index
Standard & Poor's Corporation, 44, 121, 177

Standard & Poor's Depository Receipt, 616
Standby letter of credit, 493, 495
State bank, 499
State Employees Credit Union of North Carolina, 13
State Farm Insurance Group, 14, 680
State-chartered credit union, 596
State-chartered savings institution, 579–580
Stimulative monetary policy, 92–97, 107–109, 112–113, 577
Stock index, 161, 246–248, 259, 290–291, 312, 322–324, 334–335, 338, 346–353, 357–363, 371, 375, 379–391, 394, 412, 468, 470, 472, 474, 527, 551, 609, 615–616, 624–625, 643, 649, 672, 694–697, 700
Stock index futures contract, 334, 346–347, 351–353, 358–359, 384, 389, 467, 469
Stock index option, 363, 378–381, 386, 390, 474
Stock market efficiency. *See* Market efficiency
Stock mutual fund, 103–104, 230, 232, 259, 350, 357, 359, 386, 623–624, 627–630, 633, 644–645
Stock option, 284, 299, 301–302, 304, 335, 363–366, 371–372, 374–375, 378, 380, 386–390, 464, 645, 656, 697
Stock repurchase, 253, 260, 273, 477, 521, 704
Stock split, 288
Stock-owned institutions, 575
Stop-buy order, 310, 316, 658, 659
Stop-loss order, 310, 658
Strike price. *See* Exercise price
Stripped securities, 146
Stripped Treasury bonds, 145
STRIPS program. *See* Stripped securities
Strong-form efficiency, 287–288, 293–294
Structured notes, 161
Student loan, 2
Subordinated debenture, 153, 164
Subprime mortgages, 216, 593
Subscription period, 241

SunTrust Bank, 13
SuperDot system, 242, 318
Supply of loanable funds,
    28–31, 34, 37–41,
    90–92, 94, 102, 106,
    174, 193, 225, 469, 472
Surety bond insurance, 683
Surplus unit, 2–3, 5, 10–15,
    17, 20, 115, 141, 230,
    476
Swap contract, 403, 494–495
Swap market, 333, 402,
    404–405, 414, 416, 419,
    422–423, 467, 587, 609,
    645, 668, 685–686, 697
Swap option, 408, 423
Sydney Futures Exchange,
    358
Systematic risk, 267–268,
    274, 278–279, 284, 295

T

TAAPS-Link. *See* Treasury
    Automated Auction Pro-
    cessing System
Takeovers, 158, 252–253,
    255–256, 575, 654, 660
Tax advantage swap, 413
Tax bracket, 45–46, 49, 66,
    166, 191, 467, 626
Tax loss carryforward, 413
Tax-exempt security, 46
Tax-free fund, 626, 646
T-bill. *See* Treasury bill
T-bill futures contract, 337,
    339–340, 361
Technical analysis, 263, 272
Technical forecasting, 435
Technology Spider, 616
Term insurance, 676, 698
Term loan, 484, 496
Term structure of interest
    rates, 43, 46–47, 51, 54,
    59–61, 64–67, 109
Term to maturity, 43, 46–47,
    51–52, 57, 60, 63, 65–
    66, 70, 128, 150, 171,
    175, 182, 185, 366, 469,
    652
Theory of rational expecta-
    tions, 94
Thomson Financial, 275
Thrift institution. *See* Savings
    institution
Tight money policy. *See* Re-
    strictive monetary policy
TIGRs. *See* Treasury Invest-
    ment Growth Receipts
Time deposit, 83–84, 478–
    480, 482, 483, 495, 569
Time draft, 126
Time-series method,
    283–284

Time-series model, 284, 435,
    437
TIPS. *See* Treasury inflation-
    protected securities
Tokyo Stock Exchange, 669
Trace. *See* National Associa-
    tion of Securities Deal-
    ers' Trade Reporting and
    Compliance Engine
Trade-through rule, 318, 663
Trading booth, 242
Trading Desk, 79–80, 84
Trading halt, 324
Trading post, 242, 316, 322
Transaction deposit, 477–
    478, 483, 495
Traveler's checks, 595
Traveler's Insurance Group,
    504, 667
Treasury. *See* U.S. Treasury
Treasury Automated Auction
    Processing System, 118
Treasury bill, 5, 37, 41–42,
    48–50, 68–69, 80–81,
    111, 116–125, 127–130,
    132, 134, 137–140, 202,
    337, 339–340, 345, 361,
    394–396, 402, 416,
    425, 480–481, 485,
    569–571, 637–638,
    645–646, 649, 672,
    685–686, 700
Treasury bill auction,
    118–119
Treasury bill discount, 120
Treasury bond, 45, 49–50,
    66–67, 100, 138, 141–
    146, 148, 153–154, 156,
    158, 161–166, 172–174,
    176–177, 179, 189–190,
    197, 210–212, 214–216,
    224, 267, 275, 334–
    335, 337–339, 341–
    345, 355–357, 360–361,
    381–384, 392, 416, 468,
    470, 529, 567, 569, 578,
    585, 609, 626–627, 630,
    645, 647, 680–681, 693,
    696
Treasury bond auction, 143–
    144, 212, 275, 339, 416
Treasury bond futures con-
    tract, 338, 341, 343–
    345, 355–356, 360–
    361, 381–383, 529, 585
Treasury inflation-protected
    securities, 146
Treasury Investment Growth
    Receipts, 146
Treasury note, 79, 143, 162,
    177, 192, 334, 337, 345,
    381
Treasury note futures, 337,
    345, 381

Treasury strips, 146
Treynor index, 285–286
Triangular arbitrage, 445,
    449
Trigger, 441–442
Trustee, 151–152, 164, 217,
    521
Tyco, 249, 643

U

U.S. Department of Labor,
    692
U.S. Treasury, 3–4, 11, 71,
    116–117, 141–143, 162,
    165, 208, 225, 337, 430,
    596, 636, 645, 678
UAL. *See* United Airlines
Umbrella liability insurance,
    683
Underfunded pension,
    691–692
Underlying security, 338,
    344, 349, 363
Underwriting, 14, 19, 20,
    22, 235, 256, 288,
    346, 495, 503, 509, 516,
    518, 537, 542, 650–653,
    656, 659–660,
    662–663, 670–671,
    681, 689, 699
Underwriting risk, 163
Underwriting spread, 653
Underwriting syndicate, 151,
    163, 235, 651–652
Unemployment, 37–38,
    78, 85–87, 90, 94–100,
    109–110, 112,
    173, 454
Uniform capital adequacy
    guidelines, 517
Unit trust, 221
United Airlines, 252
United Technologies
    Corporation, 162
Universal life insurance, 676,
    698
Unsystematic risk, 267,
    278–279
Uptick, 323
Upward-sloping yield curve,
    58, 60–62, 66–67, 69,
    360, 569, 599
Usury law, 487

V

VA. *See* Veterans Adminis-
    tration
VA Linux, 236
Vail Company, 175
Value Line, 268, 277
Value-at-risk method, 281,
    294, 297, 509

Vanguard, 156, 624–625
Variable life insurance, 676
Variable-rate bond,
    153, 412
VC firm. *See* Venture capital-
    ist firm
VC fund. *See* Venture capi-
    tal funds
Venture capitalist firm, 236
Venture capital funds,
    228–229, 233,
    638–639
Veterans Administration,
    147, 200, 582
VISA, 487
Volcker, Paul, 76

W

Wachovia Corporation, 13,
    551–552
Walt Disney Company, 150
Wang Labs, 121
Weak-form efficiency,
    287–288, 293–294
WEBS. *See* World equity
    benchmark shares
Weekend effect, 288
Wells Fargo, 18, 592
William, John B., 264
Wilshire 5000 Total Market
    Index, 247
Working capital loan, 484
World Bank, 454, 456
World equity benchmark
    shares, 259
WorldCom, 9–10, 249, 300,
    505
Writer, 391

Y

Yahoo!, 238
Yield curve, 47, 51–55, 57–
    71, 122, 138, 148–150,
    153–154, 162, 164–165,
    190, 193, 223, 261, 297,
    330, 360, 362, 424–
    425, 450, 467, 472, 569,
    599
Yield to maturity, 49, 142–
    143, 145, 156, 181–182,
    185, 192–193, 195–196,
    526, 627

Z

Zero-coupon bond, 153,
    164–165, 170, 181–182,
    185, 189, 190–192, 410,
    525
Zero-coupon-for-floating
    swap, 405, 410